American Captivity Narratives

New Riverside Editions

General Editor for the American Volumes
Paul Lauter

STEPHEN CRANE, *The Red Badge of Courage, Maggie: A Girl of the Streets, and Other Selected Writings*
Edited by Phyllis Frus and Stanley Corkin

RALPH WALDO EMERSON, *Selected Writings* and MARGARET FULLER, *Woman in the Nineteenth Century*
Edited by John Carlos Rowe

OLAUDAH EQUIANO, MARY ROWLANDSON, AND OTHERS, *American Captivity Narratives*
Edited by Gordon M. Sayre

HENRY DAVID THOREAU, *Walden and Civil Disobedience*
Edited by Paul Lauter

MARK TWAIN, *Adventures of Huckleberry Finn*
Edited by Susan K. Harris

EDITH WHARTON, *The Age of Innocence*
Edited by Carol J. Singley

Other Riverside Literature Titles

Call and Response: The Riverside Anthology of the African American Literary Tradition
Edited by Patricia Liggins Hill et al.

The Riverside Anthology of Children's Literature, Sixth Edition
Edited by Judith Saltman

The Riverside Anthology of Literature, Third Edition
Edited by Douglas Hunt

The Riverside Anthology of Short Fiction: Convention and Innovation
Edited by Dean Baldwin

The Riverside Chaucer, Third Edition
Edited by Larry D. Benson

The Riverside Milton
Edited by Roy Flannagan

The Riverside Shakespeare, Second Edition
Edited by G. Blakemore Evans et al.

NEW RIVERSIDE EDITIONS

General Editor for the American Volumes
Paul Lauter, Trinity College

Olaudah Equiano, Mary Rowlandson, and Others

American Captivity Narratives

Selected Narratives with Introduction

edited by
Gordon M. Sayre
University of Oregon

HOUGHTON MIFFLIN COMPANY
Boston • New York

To a fellow anthologist, my father, Robert F. Sayre

Senior Sponsoring Editor: Suzanne Phelps Weir
Associate Editor: Jennifer Roderick
Senior Project Editor: Kathryn Dinovo
Senior Cover Design Coordinator: Deborah Azerrad Savona
Manufacturing Manager: Florence Cadran
Senior Marketing Manager: Nancy Lyman
Associate Marketing Manager: Carla Gray

Cover design: Steven Cooley
Cover image: © Corbis/Adam Woolfitt

Credits appear on page 453, which is a continuation of the copyright page.

Printed in the U.S.A.

Library of Congress Cataloging-in-Publication Data

American captivity narratives : selected narratives with introduction / Olaudah Equiano, Mary Rowlandson, and others ; edited by Gordon M. Sayre.
    p.   cm. — (New Riverside editions)
  Includes bibliographical references.
  ISBN 0-395-98073-9 (paper)
    1. Indian captivities—North America. I. Equiano, Olaudah, b. 1745.
II. Rowlandson, Mary White, ca. 1635–ca. 1678. III. Sayre, Gordon M. (Gordon Mitchell), 1964– IV. Series.

E85 A54 2000   99-56706
973--dc21

3456789-QF-03 02

Contents

Chapter Five: TWO PURITAN CAPTIVITIES AS TOLD BY COTTON MATHER 177

Chapter Six: TWO AFRICAN AMERICAN CAPTIVES 198

Chapter Seven: A PRISONER OF WAR ADOPTED BY THE IROQUOIS 258

Chapter Eight: A LEGEND OF THE AMERICAN REVOLUTION 347

Chapter Nine: TWO CAPTIVITY POEMS 377

Chapter Ten: TWO NINETEENTH-CENTURY POPULAR TALES 382

Chapter Eleven: A CAPTIVE INDIAN   419

About This Series

Paul Lauter

The Riverside name dates back well over a century. Readers of this book may have seen—indeed, may own—Riverside Editions of works by the best-known nineteenth-century American writers, such as Emerson, Thoreau, Lowell, Longfellow, and Hawthorne. Houghton Mifflin and its predecessor, Ticknor & Fields, were the primary publishers of the New England authors who constituted much of the undisputed canon of American literature until well into the twentieth century. The Riverside Editions of works by these writers, and of some later writers such as Amy Lowell, became benchmarks for distinguished and useful editions of standard American authors for home, library, and classroom.

In the 1950s and 1960s, the Riverside name was used for another series of texts, primarily for the college classroom, of well-known American and British literary works. These paperback volumes, edited by distinguished critics of that generation, were among the most widely used and appreciated of their day. They provided carefully edited texts in a handsome and readable format, with insightful critical introductions. They were books one kept beyond the exam, the class, or even the college experience.

In the last quarter century, however, ideas about the American literary canon have changed. Many scholars want to see a canon that reflects a broader American heritage, including significant literary works by previously marginalized writers, many of them women or men of color. These changes began to be institutionalized in curricula as well as in textbooks such as *The Heath Anthology of American Literature,* which Houghton Mifflin started publishing in 1998. The older Riverside series, excellent in its day, ran the risk of appearing outdated; the editors were long retired or deceased, and the authors were viewed by some as too exclusive.

Yet the name Riverside and the ideas behind it continued to have appeal. The name stood for distinction and worth in the publication of

America's literary heritage. Houghton Mifflin's New Riverside Series, initiated in the year 2000, is designed to uphold the Riverside reputation for excellence while offering a more inclusive range of authors. The Series also provides today's reader with books that contain, in addition to notable literary works, introductions by influential critics, as well as a variety of stimulating materials that bring alive the debates, the conversations, the social and cultural movements within which America's literary classics were formed.

Thus emerged the book you have in hand. Each volume of the New Riverside Editions will contain the basic elements that we think today's readers find interesting and useful: important literary works by significant authors, incisive introductions, and a variety of contextual materials to make the literary text fully engaging. These books will be useful in many kinds of classrooms, but they are also designed to offer the casual reader the enjoyment of a good read in a fresh and accessible format. Among the first group of New Riverside Editions are familiar titles, such as Henry David Thoreau's *Walden* and Mark Twain's *Adventures of Huckleberry Finn*. There are also works in fresh new combinations, such as the collection of early captivity narratives and the volume that pairs texts by Ralph Waldo Emerson and Margaret Fuller. And there are well-known works in distinctively interesting formats, such as the volume containing Edith Wharton's *The Age of Innocence* and the volume of writings by Stephen Crane. Future books will include classics as well as works drawing renewed attention.

The New Riverside Editions will provide discriminating readers with a wide range of important literary works, contextual materials that vividly illuminate those works, and the best of recent critical commentary and analysis. And because we have not confined our editors to a single monotonous format, we think our readers will find that each volume in this new series has a character appropriate to the literary work it presents.

We expect the New Riverside Editions to bring to the twenty-first century the same literary publishing distinction of its nineteenth- and twentieth-century predecessors.

Introduction

Gordon M. Sayre

The United States has a long history of concern for its citizens held captive by foreign peoples, which only begins with the Indian captivity narrative. During the Iran hostage crisis in 1980, the mass media kept a vigil, counting the days that Americans were held in the embassy in Tehran, and President Carter remained a voluntary captive in the White House, as if in solidarity with those whose freedom he could not secure. Even twenty years after the end of the Vietnam War, activists in POW/MIA organizations seized upon the most tenuous evidence that American soldiers were still being held prisoners there. During more recent wars against Iraq and Serbia, U.S. servicemen captured by the enemy immediately inspired intense media attention and diplomatic efforts for their release. Nonmilitary captives, such as hostages held in Lebanon, often became international celebrities and published best-selling narratives after their return. In a pluralist country with no ethnic national identity, captivity dramas have served to rally "us" around the figure of the innocent captive held in bondage by "them." And as with the wave of concern about abducted children in the 1980s, the captors need not be a foreign nation; they can be mysterious villains in our midst.

Beginning more than two centuries before the United States was formed, such internal foes were the Native American peoples who made captives of colonists as part of an effort to defend their homeland against European invaders. In December 1607 John Smith was captured in Virginia and taken to the Indian leader Powhatan, who treated him as a powerful enemy worthy of "thirtie or fortie tall fellowes" to guard him and "more bread and venison . . . then would have served twentie men" to feed him. Smith wrote that he was about to be executed when Powhatan's daughter Pocahontas suddenly "got her head in his armes, and laid her owne upon his to save him from death." In 1676 Mary Rowlandson was captured in an attack on her home in Lancaster, Massachusetts, by Indian warriors and refugees, whom she was forced to follow for eleven weeks through the New England winter. Rowlandson interpreted her suffering and survival as "the wonderful power and goodness of God." The two appear to have little in common beyond their experience of captivity, but the myriad contrasts between them and between their texts, as well as a few similarities in what they wrote about their Indian captors, suggest some of the diverse styles and purposes of the captivity genre and initiate patterns that persisted into the twentieth century. It is in these seventeenth-century narratives of Smith and Rowlandson that the American captivity narrative finds its dual origin.

Gender provides the most obvious contrast. Smith cuts a very masculine figure as a soldier of fortune and self-fashioned colonial leader adept at intimidation, whereas Rowlandson's Calvinist theology reinforces her position as a noncombatant mother and encourages her, as she quotes from Psalm 27, to "wait on the Lord; be of good courage, and he shall strengthen thy heart." There is also a regional contrast. Smith stands for the Virginia colony, his common birth blending with military prowess and a secular realpolitik to make a Virginia Cavalier both noble and democratic. Rowlandson represents Puritan New England, and her biblical interpretations of the war that wracked the region in 1675–76 fit the style of that colony's sermons and historical writing. The two captives conclude with quite different appeals to their readers. Rowlandson reminds us of her concern for her children and for others less fortunate than she, and her final paragraph, "Before I knew what affliction meant, I was ready sometimes to wish for it," warns others not to envy her heroic suffering. Smith, on the other hand, asks to be recognized as one "whose actions and valiant resolutions deserve a more worthy respect." The legend of Smith and Pocahontas, beginning with the captivity and culminating with the marriage of the "Indian princess" to the Englishman John Rolfe, suggests both English genteel superiority and an appropriation of American nativity. The Rowlandson text describes a tentative immersion in American Indian culture that prompts a resistant formation of religious, national, and bodily identity as utterly separate from the Native Americans.

The presentation of the two texts is also instructive. The episode of Smith and Pocahontas (told in just a few pages) appeared in Smith's grandiose chronicle, *The Generall Historie of Virginia, New England, and the Summer Isles,* which refers to him in the third person and overstates his role, given that he spent only two years in Virginia and briefly explored New England several years before its colonization. His tale has been continually contested and revised. Smith himself revised it from his two earlier books, and the romantic image of Pocahontas has inspired a small industry of paintings, plays, movies, and children's books, which have strayed far from the original version. Next to this pop culture montage,

Rowlandson's captivity is austerely literary. She presents herself as a modest and scrupulous eyewitness. Her text's publication history has been carefully documented, and archival work has gradually revealed more clues about the life of this pious woman who left us no other writings.

Although the captivity narrative genre in American literature has commonly identified Rowlandson as its founder, this collection includes her text, Smith's, and a range of others that reach back to the sixteenth century and outward toward other types of captivity. When examined in this larger context, a few common features emerge, connecting the genre's two Anglo-American originators with their successors. Rowlandson, like many captive women to come, faced suspicions that she had married one of her captors, which she denied categorically, if euphemistically: "not one of them ever offered the least abuse or unchastity to me in word or action." Smith, without ever expressing any overt desire toward Powhatan's eleven- or twelve-year-old daughter, capitalized on the suggestion of sexuality in Pocahontas. The hints of her exotic appeal and her humane pity touched off a legend that justifies colonial conquest through cross-cultural marriage.

Defying notions of captivity as the barbaric antithesis to civilized England, both captives continued to use their skills and roles from the colonial economy, and both seemed to desire to impress their captors. Rowlandson sewed shirts and sold them to her captors for food and, in one instance, for a knife that she brought to her "master," "not a little glad that I had anything that they would accept of." Powhatan spared Smith's life, we are told, so that "he should live to make him hatchets, and her [Pocahontas] bells, beads, and copper," listing several European technological[1] items sought after by Native Americans in early encounters. Just after his capture, Smith claims to have awed the Indians with his compass and knowledge of "the roundnesse of the earth," although how he communicated such concepts is not clear.

Captivity in Colonial America: A Historical Definition

Beginning with these two key texts from seventeenth-century Virginia and New England, the Indian captivity narrative became a popular genre of Anglo-American writing. Several were bestsellers in their day.[2] One leading

---

[1] John Smith actually coined this word.
[2] Mary Rowlandson's, John Williams's, Jonathan Dickinson's, and Mary Jemison's narratives; see Mott.

scholar of early American literature goes so far as to write that "the single narrative form indigenous to the New World is the victim's recounting of unwilling captivity" (Kolodny 6). Stories by women held captive by Indians in the Amazon were still surfacing in the 1980s (e.g., Biocca and Donner), and some critics see a continuity with media sensations such as Patty Hearst's kidnapping by the Symbionese Liberation Army (Castiglia 87–105). As realistic chronicle of frontier life, as ethnographic exploration of native cultures, or as pulp melodrama of ripped bodices and hairbreadth escapes, the captivity paradigm has endured and spread through both academic and popular American culture.

The genre's importance is unique to the English literature of America, however. It is not central to colonial New Spain, New France, or Portuguese Brazil, even though Native Americans certainly did take many colonials captive in those regions (see Frederick), and there are a handful of early captivity stories from these other regions and languages, some of which are represented in this anthology. To fully understand the captivity narrative, we must compare the enormous corpus of Anglo-American narratives with a smaller group of texts in other languages, and also examine the Indian captivity narrative alongside other versions of captivity. This collection aims to encourage such a broad, comparative conception of the American captivity genre.

Literary genres are never discrete and often defy simple definitions. With nonfiction genres, the problems thicken, for questions of fact and history are added to those of style and representation. Must Native Americans be the captors for a text to qualify? What if the protagonist willingly goes to live among the Indians or refuses to return once taken captive? To work toward definitions and answers, it helps to distinguish between the historical phenomenon of captivity and the literary traditions of the captivity narrative. The following definition attempts to clear away some of the unquestioned assumptions that have accumulated as a consequence of the very success and popularity of captivity narratives in the United States:

> The captivity phenomenon arises out of encounters between unfamiliar peoples, generally as a result of European imperialism in the Americas and Africa. The two cultures brought into conflict are so foreign to one another that an individual forced into the midst of the other community regards the new life as a kind of imprisonment, a deprivation of all the familiar patterns of his or her native surroundings. This "otherness" may be portrayed as racial, religious, or broadly cultural, but in any case it is profound enough that each side regards its own ways as superior to the other's, and captivity forces this prejudice to the surface, either to be defended or abandoned. Most captives

yearn to return home, and some die in the attempt, but a few embrace their new lives. Generally only those who survive and return are able to record their experiences in a published captivity narrative.

This somewhat abstract definition more accurately accounts for the range of texts in this collection than does the stereotyped plot of Indian captivity: an innocent woman and her children attacked at a frontier homestead, carried away by savages, and subjected to violence, privation, and humiliation, before finally being rescued or ransomed or escaping to the white community. This conventional version obscures others and casts Native American captors in an unfairly villainous role, given the larger historical circumstances of captivity.

Consider, for instance, the experience of an African, seized from his village by invaders who carry him far away and sell him as a bondsman to strangers who take him in a crowded ship across an ocean, only to sell him again. The speech, appearance, and customs of his captors mystify or even disgust the African, and their treatment of him is likewise cruel and incomprehensible. His survival depends on his courage and sound judgment of character. Yes, the African slave begins as a captive, and it should come as no surprise that the first published autobiographies by Africans in English include such scenes of capture, not only Olaudah Equiano's narrative of his childhood in Africa (in chap. 6), but also narratives by John Marrant (also in chap. 6) and Briton Hammon, who were born in America and were not slaves. And in the nineteenth century when the slave narrative became an important genre in American letters, it shared some devices and imagery with the earlier Indian captivity narratives (Slotkin 441; Zafar). In these early American texts, the colonies are not the home territory inside a hostile Indian frontier but a foreign land and place of confinement.

Or consider Squanto, remembered in popular myth as the Indian who befriended the Pilgrims upon their landing at Plymouth, bringing corn and celebrating the first Thanksgiving feast. What is less known is that he could welcome the Pilgrims in English only because he had previously been captured and taken to Europe. Squanto was a native of Patuxet, the Indian village on the site of Plymouth. John Smith himself had come to Patuxet in 1614 on a fishing and trading expedition led by Thomas Hunt. When Hunt sailed for Europe, he kidnapped Squanto and twenty other Patuxets and tried to sell them as slaves in Spain, an act Smith deplored (Barbour 2:401). Squanto avoided enslavement when Spanish priests took him in as a potential convert. Later, he somehow made his way to England and into the company of other colonial entrepreneurs, Thomas Dermer (who had also sailed with Smith) and Ferdinando Gorges. These men had made a habit of capturing Indians on the northeast coast of America, enslaving them or attempting to use them as interpreters and ambassadors on subsequent expeditions. Squanto seems to have understood that by playing along with this plan he might be able to return home. But when he got back to New England with Dermer in 1619, they were both taken captive by Pokanocket Indians, who had become justly fearful of European raiders and their guides. Squanto finally returned to his hometown only when he was ransomed by the newly arrived Plymouth colonists, who wanted his help as a go-between but likewise found they could not control him. Squanto's hometown was gone, as ninety percent of Indians in the area had died of diseases introduced by Europeans in the early 1600s. He may have fallen victim to one of these plagues himself when he died in 1622, "desiring the Governor to pray for him that he might go to the Englishmen's God in Heaven" (Bradford 126).

Although Squanto's story is known only by piecing together bits of writing by Gorges, Plymouth founder William Bradford, and others, if he had dictated his own narrative it would be a fascinating early captivity narrative.[3] Because they lacked literacy in English and access to the publishing establishment, no such Indian captives of whites told their stories in print until the nineteenth century. The autobiography of Geronimo, excerpted in the final chapter in this volume, is a later expression of what might be called the inverse captivity narrative. And such an inversion demands attention. After all, the typical captivity plot served ideologically to invert the true terms of the colonial invasion of America. The captives were typically an innocent woman and her children, yet they came from among the aggressors who were displacing Indians from their land. On the other side, the Indian captors in the typical plot take on a fearsome control that they rarely enjoyed in their ongoing resistance to the Europeans. The fate of Geronimo, Black Hawk, and other Indian leaders held as prisoners of war more accurately reflects the history of U.S. expansion than the captivity narrative does.

Yet the conventional plot is also susceptible to revisionary readings. Recent scholarship has described captivity as "culture-crossing," an experience that "destabilize[d] white culture's fiction of fixed and pure identity" (Castiglia 7) by taking women away from their husbands and fathers and into a larger world of adventure. As a historical phenomenon, this culture-crossing occurred in both directions, beginning with early colonization, and was not attributable to captivity alone, for some crossed over voluntarily. In French Canada, for instance, colonial literature did not

---

[3] The fragmentary sources have been masterfully assembled and analyzed by Salisbury.

represent life in Indian communities as a forced captivity. The French colonists depended on the fur trade and treated natives as suppliers and clients, not simply as inhabitants of land they desired. A few young French colonists, the *truchements* ("interpreters" or "spokesmen"), lived the reverse of Squanto's experience. Etienne Brulé volunteered in 1610 to live with Algonquin Indians along the Ottawa River. His assignment from colonial leader Samuel de Champlain was to learn the language and later serve as interpreter and messenger. Brulé traveled with Algonquin and Huron Indians from Lake Superior to Chesapeake Bay and was briefly taken captive by the Seneca. He was mysteriously killed by the Hurons in 1633, an event that Jean de Brébeuf (whose own death at the hands of the Iroquois is told in chap. 3) reported with consternation.

John Smith's Virginia had its own *truchements*. One, ironically named Thomas Savage, was exchanged by John Smith to Powhatan for an Indian named Namontacke (Barbour 1:216) and remained in Virginia for life. Another, Henry Spelman, was sold by Smith along with some copper to Little Powhatan in exchange for land. He later escaped to another chief, the king of Patowomeck, and spent a year with the Indians before being ransomed by Captain Samuel Argall. According to Smith, Spelman's life was also saved by the intervention of Pocahontas (Barbour 2:232). He served the colonists as a skilled interpreter until he was mysteriously killed in 1623 (Barbour 2:320–21). Unlike other *truchements*, Spelman was a literate gentleman and wrote a short narrative, "Relation of Virginia" (Arber c–cxiv).

The fate of these *truchements* suggests something of the complexity of culture-crossing, which might take the form of translation, adoption, or exile. Given the great contrasts between the two cultures, it is difficult even to settle on terms that make sense in both. For example, because most captives were taken in wars between colonists and Indians or between rival European colonies, it makes sense to think of them as prisoners of war, rather than as victims of some instinctual "savage" aggression. Native Americans could not hold captives in prisons, however, and did not share the Europeans' sense of rules for warfare distinct from rules of civil society (White 80). But the increasing involvement of northeastern native peoples in colonial wars in the eighteenth century meant that the Indians who captured Hannah Swarton and others may have had ransom money in mind from the start (see chap. 5). Thus some captives were essentially POWs, and the captivity genre does have something in common with the tradition of prison memoirs (H. B. Franklin 3–31). Swarton and other Puritan captives held in New France fit this definition, for they regarded living in Quebec or Montreal with all the horror of savage captivity, and their release was achieved through prisoner exchanges for Frenchmen held in New England.

According to Native American custom, however, taking captives in war was not done for ransom money, to punish or incarcerate the captives, or as acts of terrorism. Captives were valuable human lives who could add to the strength of a village; thus they were integrated into the tribe of their captors through a process so foreign to European notions of identity that captivity narrators often failed to understand it. James Smith's narrative in chapter 7 is one of the best accounts by a captive who did understand his adoption and the initiation rites that preceded it. Such initiations could be violent and extended in a few cases to gruesome torture and death. More often, however, these rites consisted of practices such as running the gauntlet, as Smith and Isaac Jogues (in chap. 3) both endured, or, according to many ethnohistorians, the mock execution, such as that of John Smith.

Adoption among the Iroquoian peoples (comprising the Iroquois and Huron confederacies) is the best documented, for many French missionaries besides Jogues and several captives and soldiers besides James Smith wrote detailed accounts of it. The process actually began when an Iroquoian individual died, leaving a gap in the social fabric. According to some accounts (e.g., Lahontan), female relatives of the deceased would encourage the male warriors to organize a party to attack an enemy tribe and take captives. If the war party returned successful, the captives would be presented to the families of the deceased for adoption. The captive then assumed the name and status of the person he or she replaced (Sayre 285–91). Some observers called it a "resurrection," and modern anthropologists term it requickening (Lafitau 2:155–57, 171–72; Dennis 106). If chosen to requicken a chief or person of importance, an adopted captive would acquire all the power and responsibility of that individual. European observers were particularly astonished that captives "when they grow up go to war against their own parents and the men of their nation as bravely as if they had been born enemies of their own country" (Sagard-Théodat 284), but the tribes took for granted that adoptees were transformed into their new identities. European dogmas of race, kinship, and nationality could not admit such transformations, but we can see in the captivity narratives of James Smith, John Tanner, John R. Jewitt, and Mary Jemison that it was possible. In other texts, such as Hannah Swarton's and Mary Rowlandson's, the captors aimed more for a ransom than for adoption. Many captivity narrators write of having a master, a mother, or a brother among the Indians, but do not absorb the identity of the person they have been adopted to replace. Of course, to publish a narrative, a captive generally had to abandon Indian identity and return to Anglo-America, and the few narratives by individuals who fully crossed between cultures twice can only remind us of others, like Etienne Brulé, who never returned.

American Indian Captivity Narrative:
The Literary History

This survey of captivity as a historical phenomenon, the result of violent conflicts along the frontiers of European imperialism, prepares us for understanding the American Indian captivity narrative as a literary tradition, one beginning with John Smith in Virginia and Mary Rowlandson in New England and continuing through the nineteenth century and into contemporary Westerns and hostage dramas. Rowlandson established many features that proved very influential. Her opening line, with the date and time of the attack thrusting the reader straight into the horror, and the subsequent image of a "sucking child" being "knock'd on the head," were both repeated in many accounts of Indian atrocities (in fact, there is an anthology of captivity narratives entitled *Indian Atrocity*). One might say that more than any other author since Thomas More and his *Utopia,* she created a genre. But her text and the Anglo-American tradition following upon it are better understood if one takes account of other literary versions of the captivity phenomenon and of other modes of writing that influenced her creation. Although Rowlandson probably did not know about John Smith and Pocahontas, she did draw on traditions of Puritan spiritual writing.

The New England Puritans had developed richly allegorical ways of interpreting the world according to the precedents of the Bible and Providential dispensations. Rowlandson's biblical glosses of her captivity resemble those in earlier Puritan writings—sermons, of course, but also histories of Indian wars and of the colonies generally. Foremost among these biblical tropes were the captivities of the Israelites in Egypt and in Babylon. Because the Puritan colonists imagined themselves as "visible saints," a people elect of God, the entire migration to America might be seen as an escape from persecution in England or, more pessimistically, as an entrance into captivity (Slotkin 93). But the captivity narratives need not be read so allegorically. James D. Hartman places Rowlandson's and other Puritan captivity narratives in the larger genre of the Providence tale: narratives of shipwrecks, witch apparitions, and other amazing happenings that "prove God exists by presenting undeniable evidence of inexplicable occurrences" (17). According to Hartman, the Providence tale genre was common in England and New England and connected science with faith and Protestant religious discourses with the emerging form of the novel. Yet captivity narratives, more often than Providential histories, were written in the first-person voice of the captive and claimed factuality both through eyewitness accounts of outward events and subjective representations of the captive's inward state. Thus many readers have noticed that

Puritan captives experience religious conversion as a result of their trauma, the kind of conversion required for full church membership at the time. Hannah Dustan, whose murderous revenge on her captors hardly seems spiritual, nonetheless wrote in 1724, twenty-seven years after her captivity: "I am thankful for my captivity, it was the Comfortablest time that I ever had; in my Affliction God made his Word Comfortable to me" (Ulrich 234; Derounian-Stodola and Levernier 136).

Because this collection looks beyond the New England origins of the captivity genre, we must also look afield for the sources and influences of some of the other texts. In European literature, the local equivalent of the American Indians was the Muslim nations of North Africa or Barbary. Many scholars have noted that 1492 saw both the beginning of the Spanish conquest of the New World and the expulsion of the Moors from the Iberian Peninsula. Captives, or prisoners of war, held in North Africa had written and published accounts in English of their experiences since the 1500s. Richard Hakluyt included several of these stories in his great compendium, *The Principall Navigations, Voiages and Discoveries of the English Nation*. Cervantes included in *Don Quixote* an episode based on his own experiences after the Battle of Lepanto (Book 1, chaps. 39–41). Several other narratives were published in seventeenth-century England.[4]

The genre became popular in the United States during the late 1700s when wartime blockades and piracy landed many Americans in captivity in North Africa. *A Journal of the Captivity and Sufferings of John Foss, Several Years a Prisoner in Algiers,* is one such text, and Royall Tyler's *The Algerine Captive,* is a novelization of the form. *An Authentic Narrative of the Loss of the American Brig* Commerce by James Riley is the most sensational such text, as he and his crew were shipwrecked, enslaved, and forced to march across the Sahara, their skin so sunburned it turned black with scabs. All three of these books not only told of captivity but devoted many chapters to descriptions of Arab life and customs. A new anthology incorporating these early American texts, edited by Paul Baepler, may revive their status in literary history. The genre is still active. Terry Anderson's *Den of Lions,* about being held hostage in Lebanon in the 1980s, and Betty Mahmoody's *Not without My Daughter,* about marrying into a Muslim family in Iran, then escaping, revise the captivity tradition by shifting the villain's role from the American Indian (the terrorist of the western frontier) to the Arab Muslims. This phenomenon shows that religious or national difference alone is enough to constitute the sensation of captivity. Another instance occurred in the 1830s when American readers flocked to buy two

---

[4]Three such narratives are Phelps's, Okeley's, and Knight's.

sensational exposés by women who claimed to have escaped from convents, books that catered to anti-Catholic prejudices (Franchot 135–61, Lewis).

Captivity narratives are thus a major vehicle for the representation of hostile, foreign peoples. For more than three hundred years, Anglo-Americans have seen American Indians through this genre, which presents racist and fear-mongering images of savages threatening white settlers on the frontier. A leading scholar of American frontier literature, Richard Slotkin, has written that "It almost seems as if the only experience of intimacy with the Indians that New England readers would accept was the experience of the captive" (95). Yet captivity narratives express both the popular fear of "savages" and a fascination with these Indian outsiders, whom the Anglo-American authorities refused to integrate into their settlements. Because the reading public was eager to read eyewitness accounts of Native American life, captives often wrote ethnographies, systematic descriptions of their captors' culture. Anthropologists studying Native American culture have often read early captivity narratives for this information, and Mary Louise Pratt has noted that "The experience of captivity resonates a lot with aspects of the experience of [anthropological] fieldwork—the sense of dependency, lack of control, the vulnerability to being either isolated completely or never left alone" (38). The example Pratt uses is Hans Staden, who included an ethnographic portrait of the Tupinamba in Part 2 of his *Warhaftige Historia* (which, unfortunately, there was not space to include in this volume). Henry Spelman devoted three-quarters of his brief text to ethnography. John Gyles's narrative, published in Boston in 1736, is the first Puritan captivity text to include separate ethnographic sections, including such titles as "Their Feasting" and "Their Mourning for the Dead" as well as natural history entries about the beaver, the tortoise, and the salmon (116–20). The ethnographic impulse is by no means unique to captives—most New World exploration narratives likewise included ethnographies of Native Americans—but a captive who had assimilated and lived with Indians for many years offered a special expertise that few explorers could match. Only a few missionaries and fur traders could boast of a greater familiarity with Native American life. Pierre-Esprit Radisson, who bargained his expertise about Indian trade and warfare back and forth between the rival French and English through much of the seventeenth century, begins his narrative with an account of a curiously benign captivity among the Iroquois (31). He even refused the offer to be released to the Dutch. Jean de Brébeuf wrote an extended ethnography of the Hurons in his *Relations* of 1634–36 (Thwaites, vols. 6–8) and several of his Jesuit brethren in New France also penned such texts.

By the nineteenth century in the United States, virtually any narrative by a person who had lived among American Indians had the word *captivity* in its title. The genre was enormously popular and could be characterized as split in two directions: melodramatic anti-Indian texts about captives who resisted assimilation and that offered no ethnography, and more sympathetic accounts by captives such as Jemison and Tanner who were proud to have assimilated their captors' culture. So popular was the genre that writers who had not been captured mimicked the authority of those who had. George Catlin, the famous painter of the life of the Plains Indians, began his narrative by claiming, "I have spent about eight years . . . immersed in Indian country . . . identifying myself with them as much as possible" (qtd. in Hartman 13). Melville's first novel, *Typee*, tells a semi-autobiographical story of deserting his whaling ship to live among South Pacific islanders whom he portrays as "children of nature" and describes in several ethnographic chapters (185–201, 238–58).

Thus there has always been a subtext of interest and sympathy for native peoples in the captivity genre. This sympathy has drawn more attention in the last thirty years, at the same time that literary and autobiographical writings of Native Americans have become popular in the United States. There has been some effort to recast the captivity tradition, and prominent Native American writers Louise Erdrich and Sherman Alexie have published poems on the captivity theme. Interest has grown in a few narratives by captives who embraced Indian life, remaining for years in native communities and living a life they portrayed quite favorably. Although they have been variously termed "transculturated" captives, "assimilated" captives, or "white Indians," they might more accurately be termed "adopted captives," so as to recognize the adoption process unique to Native American cultures. Their texts are intriguing, for they test the assumptions of cultural superiority that are typical of the captivity plot. The Puritans seemed secure in their religious and social identity, but beginning in the eighteenth century the prejudice of European Christians toward barbarous primitives was complicated by a concept of cultural evolution that imagined primitive instincts to be incompletely repressed by civilization. A widespread belief arose that one could slip backward into savagery, and frontier dwellers were often held up as proof. This was a version of the notion that ontogeny recapitulates phylogeny—that primitive life is the childhood of human evolution—it explained why captives taken as young children were most likely to adopt Indian ways and why a captive's desire for escape or release could no longer be taken for granted. When Crèvecoeur's Frontier Man character in *Letters from an American Farmer* considers taking his family to the Indians to escape the Revolutionary War, he fears "lest my children should be caught by that singular charm, so dangerous at their tender years . . . . By what power does it come to pass that children who have been adopted when young among these people can never be prevailed on to readopt European manners?" (213).[5] Colonists also found confirmation for this belief in Native Americans' resistance to giving up their traditions and their freedom and in captives' reluctance to leave their adopted families. One oft-cited scene occurred at an exchange of prisoners after the campaign led by Henri Bouquet against the native leader Pontiac's rebellion in 1764. William Smith described the reuniting of captives with their original families: "sisters and brothers unexpectedly meeting together after long separation, [were] scarce able to speak the same language, or for some time, to be sure that they were children of the same parents!" (76). These children, "having been accustomed to look upon Indians as the only connexions they had, having been tenderly treated by them, and speaking their language . . . considered their new state in the light of a captivity, and parted from the savages with tears" (80). As early as 1765 at least one writer had inverted the genre, applying the word *captivity* to Anglo-American colonial life.

The captive John Dunn Hunter later echoed Crèvecoeur's words: "It is a remarkable fact, that white people generally, when brought up among the Indians, become unalterably attached to their customs, and seldom afterward abandon them" (11). His own story defied this belief, however. First published in 1823, Hunter's book told how he was captured by Kickapoo Indians at an age so young that he could not remember his birth family. He was raised by various Plains tribes and learned all the skills of a hunter and warrior; he even journeyed overland to Oregon and back. But as a young adult he fled his tribe to warn a camp of white traders of an impending attack and stayed to rejoin the Euro-American world and pursue a modern education. Hunter was feted in London as a noble primitive whose culture-crossing affirmed the value of modern progress. In 1973 Richard Drinnon edited a new edition of Hunter's *Memoirs of a Captivity among the Indians of North America* for a major New York publisher and followed it with a biography of Hunter, but other scholars have labeled Hunter's story a hoax, as did some American reviewers in the 1820s.

Few other adopted captives enjoyed so easy a transition back to Anglo-American life as Hunter described. Females were often subjected to insinuations that they had had sexual relations with men among their captors, whether voluntary or not. Mary Rowlandson was at pains to assure readers that she had not been raped, and Neal Salisbury, who recently edited her narrative, has found other clues that she "wrote in order to clear her name with respect to a number of rumors and innuendoes" (43). Sarah Wakefield, captured during the Sioux uprising in Minnesota in 1862,

---

[5] Similar comments appear in Benjamin Franklin (4:481–82) and Colden (203–04).

credited a man named Chaska with saving her life during captivity, and, in the crackdown that followed the uprising, she unsuccessfully tried to intervene and save him from execution by the U.S. Army. Historian June Namias has concluded that Chaska was singled out for punishment because of his relationship with Wakefield (204–61). Male captives, too, were often objects of suspicion, because of the doctrine that savagery was much easier to slide into than climb out of. John Tanner, whose narrative is one of the most powerful accounts of Native American life, recalled how on his return he was not even recognized by his own brother and that white leaders had at first "taken me for one of those worthless white men who remain in the Indian country from indolence, and for the sake of marrying squaws" (277). As in the case of the *truchements*, there were many Europeans who found their way into Native American communities by means other than captivity, and even many who were captives did not return or did not publish narratives if they did return. Captivity was important because, as Slotkin observed, it offered an alibi for transculturation, an assurance against cultural regression and thereby credibility with mainstream readers (95, 125). James Smith, whose text has not been recently reissued by a major publisher as Hunter's, Tanner's, and Mary Jemison's have, writes in his preface that he waited nearly forty years to publish his story because he feared it would not be believed, then justified its publication through the utility of his "Observations on the Indian Mode of Warfare," a manual on using primitive methods for the defense of national civilization (see chap. 7).

The recent surge of interest in adopted captives has been strongest for one book, which appeared within a year after John Dunn Hunter's. *A Narrative of the Life of Mrs. Mary Jemison* has seen three new editions since 1975, to add to twenty-three from the period 1824 through 1929, and inspired a host of scholarly articles and book chapters. Like James Smith, Jemison was captured in Pennsylvania during the Seven Years' War. She passed from her Shawnee captors to the Seneca, married twice, and raised a family in western New York, weathering the Revolution and many subsequent conflicts with settlers and among her own children. Unlike Hunter and Tanner, her identity was not doubted, but her text is problematic because, unable to write in any language, she dictated her story to Dr. James Seaver, who added his own chapters, footnotes, and patronizing commentary before publishing it. Scholars have read the text closely to try to separate Jemison's own subjectivity from the interference of Seaver.

At a time when the word *captivity* was used to sell all kinds of narratives of violent western adventure, it was not included in Jemison's title. Her racial origin was emphasized with references to her blue eyes and pale complexion, but it seems that to admit a captive white woman would not

wish to return was to cede victory to savagery—an unthinkable conces-
sion. Jemison's unique case reveals how gender is as important as race in
captivity scholarship. Indeed, there are signs of a gender division among
scholars. Leslie Fiedler called Jemison "as irrelevant as those eccentric
males who resented rather than rejoiced in their captivity" (96). He assumed that Indian ways were attractive only to men and focused his interest on male adopted captives who formed close relationships with male
captors as James Smith does with Tecaughretenango and the Canadian
Alexander Henry does with Wawatam in his *Travels in Canada and the Indian Territories between the Years 1760 and 1776* (Fiedler 109–14). What
unites Fiedler, John Dunn Hunter, and the scholars of Jemison, however,
is a desire to show how a few extraordinary captives were able to succeed
at becoming Indian, a message that may not be as sympathetic to Native
Americans as it sounds. After all, assimilation is not necessarily a surrender of one's initial cultural values. It can be seen as an appropriation of the
Other's. Philip Deloria's recent *Playing Indian* argues that ever since the
Boston Tea Party, white Americans have used American Indian cultural
trappings to assert their own national authenticity, even as they excluded
Indians from that nation.

Captivity Narrative Scholarship

The issue of adopted captives also motivated the first scholarship on
Indian captivity. In the 1870s an amateur antiquarian named C. Alice
Baker began researching the fates of 1,606 New Englanders captured by
Indians. She was soon joined by Emma Lewis Coleman, who completed
the mammoth project in 1925 with the publication of *New England
Captives Carried to Canada between 1677 and 1760 during the French
and Indian Wars*. Their book drew little attention until it was digested
and summarized, with copious charts and graphs, by Alden T. Vaughan
and Daniel K. Richter in 1980. These two historians used the data to
dispel the idea that cultural backsliding was a common occurrence: "At
most 52 of the recorded New England captives, or 3.2 percent, under-
went completely the cultural transition from British American to American Indian" (60–62). They also confirmed that although younger captives
were more likely to stay with their captors, many more assimilated into a
life as a French Catholic than as an American Indian. Nonetheless, another
leading historian, James Axtell, found much evidence to support Crèvecoeur's comment that "thousands of Europeans are Indians" (Crèvecoeur
214) and examined why Native American society was so attractive to
colonial Americans, whether captives, traders, or renegades. A few other

researchers have analyzed, psychologically and sociologically, how Native Americans acculturated their adoptees so successfully (Heard; Swanton; Jacquin 181–90) drawing on many captives' narratives as well as other less direct sources.

A surge of scholarly interest in the captivity narrative genre came in the 1970s, fostered by myth-archetype literary theory. Influenced by the myth and folklore studies of Joseph Campbell and the psychology of Carl Jung, this theory held that American literature was built on a few archetypal myths residing in a collective unconscious and that the most powerful expressions of these myths were often the work of hack writers or ordinary folk, not the literary elite. The captivity narrative genre was an ideal proof of this theory, for it existed in hundreds of variations on an archetypal plot, it had absorbed all levels of colonial society, and it resembled the universal myth of the hero's descent into the underworld. Although rising doctrines of multicultural difference have displaced myth-archetype theory into the realm of New Age philosophy, Slotkin's and Fiedler's books still offer powerful interpretations of captivity narratives.

If myth study and a popular primitivism inspired the first wave of captivity narrative scholarship in the 1970s, attention to gender has transformed it since the 1980s. Rowlandson's and Jemison's have become the most studied narratives, and June Namias has added a new edition of Sarah Wakefield's narrative to her 1993 study, *White Captives: Gender and Ethnicity on the American Frontier.* Since 1996 one anthology and two additional scholarly books have been devoted exclusively to women captives (Derounian-Stodola; Castiglia; Burnham). This is not only because, since Rowlandson, the captivity genre has been one of the few avenues through which women of humble origins have published their experiences, but also because the sentimental and melodramatic devices of the captivity plot are common in other literature by and about women.

Michelle Burnham and other critics have examined the connections between captivity and the sentimental novel. *Clarissa,* Samuel Richardson's classic sentimental novel, is the story of a young woman lured away from her family and held captive by an aristocratic seducer, Mr. Lovelace. The most important American sentimental novel, Harriet Beecher Stowe's *Uncle Tom's Cabin,* implores readers' sympathy for slaves separated from their families and subjected to abuse by slave traders who are as vicious as any savage. Among the texts that most interest scholars of sentimental literature are *Miss McCrea* (in chap. 8 of this book) and Ann Eliza Bleecker's *History of Maria Kittle,* the first American novel based on Indian captivity. Sentimental language had entered captivity narratives as early as the 1728 narrative of a Quaker captive named Elizabeth Hanson. Some scholars, from Roy Harvey Pearce in his 1947 article, "The Significances of the Captivity Narrative," to Richard VanDerBeets in his 1973 anthology, regard this as symptomatic of a decline in the genre. Pearce identified three major stages in the history of the genre. The early Puritan narratives were "simple, direct religious documents" (2). This realism fell victim to a gradual stylization toward the motive of wartime propaganda against the French, such as in the Swarton narrative in chapter 5. And finally, stylization moved toward rank sensationalism and fictional appropriations in the nineteenth century. Burnham, Castiglia, and other recent literary scholars of the genre raise no such outcry against fraudulent or fictional captivity stories, for it is the common techniques that fiction and nonfiction literature employ toward readers that are of interest. Burnham aims at "determining the political implications of the production of sympathy around the scene of female captivity" (49), including how the reader's emotional sympathy for the captive metonymically renders the reader a passive victim of the Indians. Burnham's work changes the study of how American novelists used the captivity tradition, shifting attention from the plot elements in the works of Charles Brockden Brown and James Fenimore Cooper to a more theoretical consideration of domestic fiction and slave narratives, such as in Harriet Jacobs's *Incidents in the Life of a Slave Girl.*

The literary history of the American captivity narrative also includes numerous anthologies, a tradition that this collection continues and revises. The American Indian captivity genre has always been elastic and malleable, and many texts have been revised, plagiarized, reprinted, and adapted. Given this heritage, excerpted texts are included in this collection: Staden, the Ortiz captivity, Dustan, Swarton, Equiano, and Geronimo. Some, such as the Pocahontas legend, originated as episodes within much longer works that are rarely read in their entirety. Cotton Mather might be called the first captivity anthologist, and another collection, the so-called Manheim anthology, appeared in 1793 and many times thereafter.[6]

---

[6] An annotated list of previously published captivity anthologies precedes the Works Cited list at the end of this volume.

A Captive to Cannibals

HANS STADEN

One hundred twenty-five years before Mary Rowlandson's famous narrative was published, a captivity narrative appeared in Marburg, Germany, that anticipated many of the distinctive features of the genre as it would later develop in Anglo-America. Hans Staden wrote of his capture by fearsome, cannibalistic savages who threatened him with torture and death. He said he had survived through his faith in God and interpreted events that favored his preservation as marks of divine Providence. Staden hailed from a part of Germany where the Reformation had erupted just thirty years earlier, and although he never identified himself as a Lutheran, his spiritual response to captivity resembles that of the New England Puritans to come. Unlike Mary Rowlandson, but like other captives—from Alvar Nuñez Cabeza de Vaca to Gertrude Morgan—he built a reputation among his captors as a powerful healer, or shaman, by capitalizing on the awe with which indigenous people often regarded strange visitors.

Staden titled his book *Warhaftige Historia und Beschreibung eyner Landtschafft der Wilden, Nacketen, Grimmigen Menschfresser, Leuthen in der Neuwenvelt America gelegen,* or "True History and Description of a Country of Wild, Naked, Terrible Man-eaters Who Dwell in the New World Called America." Included herein is the core narrative of his captivity and escape in Part 1, but as the title suggests, the book also includes an ethnography of the Tuppin Imba. Part 2 comprises thirty-six short chapters with titles including "How They Make Fire" and "How They Give a Child Its First Name." It was common for colonial travelers during the sixteenth to eighteenth centuries to organize books they wrote in this way: a personal narrative of adventure, followed by a generalized description of the native peoples they encountered (Pratt 33; Sayre 79–123). Staden's de-

scriptions are enhanced by the dozens of woodcuts that illustrated the first
edition, two of which are reproduced in the excerpt that follows.

In the chapters preceding the selection, Staden recounted a voyage to
Brazil in 1547 and 1548, during which he sought prizes as a privateer
along the Barbary Coast of North Africa, then crossed the Atlantic to Per-
nambuco, where he helped defend a Portuguese fort against a siege by natives. An introduction by an esteemed German anatomist and professor,
Dr. Dryander, provides information about the author. Dr. Dryander declared of Hans Staden that "in Homberg in Hesse, where he now lives, he
is looked up to as an upright, pious, and worthy man and not unversed in
the arts" (21). Dryander attested to the veracity of the text and tried to
forestall the doubts and accusations that readers might have about this
amazing tale. These doubts included the then-proverbial unreliability of
travel narratives. As Dryander put it: "land travellers with their boundless
falsehoods and reports of vain and imagined things have so wrought that
honest and worthy people returning from foreign countries are now hardly
believed" (23). Staden himself admitted in his concluding chapter, "I can
well conceive that the contents of this book will seem strange to many"
(169). The Tuppin Imba (today, Tupinamba) with whom Staden lived were
indeed amazing, and America had been known in print for barely 60 years
when the book was published, so many readers may well have found the
story incredible. However, several contemporary sources provided ample
support for Staden's account. Jean de Léry, a Huguenot (French Protestant) colonist, visited the Tuppin Imba's territory in Rio de Janeiro from
1556 to 1558 and corroborated many of the ethnographic details Staden
reported, including cannibalism, in his *Histoire d'un Voyage faict en la
terre du Brésil*. As one learns from both the Staden and the Léry books,
Brazil was the scene of imperial competition among the French, the Dutch,
the Spanish, and the Portuguese. In this violent and contentious setting,
the natives were conscious not only of their own differences from the
Europeans but of the national differences among the colonists. Staden exploits these differences by claiming to be a Frenchman, since the French
were allied with the Tuppin Imba and opposed to the Tuppin Inka and
their Portuguese allies.

Although the captivity narrative genre never established itself in South
American literature as it did in the Anglophone North, Staden's text is an
important ethnographic source and a classic of Brazilian colonial literature.
There is a copiously annotated Portuguese translation of the text, and it
even inspired a movie, *Como Era Gostoso o Meu Francês* ("My Tasty Little
Frenchman") by Brazilian director Nelson Pereira dos Santos. It has not
been Staden's captivity but the practices of cannibalism that he represented

among the Tuppin Imba for which his text is remembered. Beginning with Michel de Montaigne's essay "Of Cannibals," many commentators have pointed out that sixteenth-century European practices of torture were no less barbaric than what the native Brazilians did to their prisoners of war. The martyrdom of Brébeuf and Lalemant in chapter 3 also depicts cannibalism as a ritual of honor and revenge toward the victim.

Source

Staden, Hans. *The True History of His Captivity.* Trans. and ed. Malcolm Letts. London: Routledge, 1928. [This edition reproduces all of the woodcuts from the original.]

Supplementary Readings

Léry, Jean de. *History of a Voyage to the Land of Brazil.* Trans. Janet Whatley. Berkeley: U of California P, 1990.

Lestringant, Frank. *Cannibals: The Discovery and Representation of the Cannibal from Columbus to Jules Verne.* Trans. Rosemary Morris. Berkeley: U of California P, 1997.

Montaigne, Michel de. "Of Cannibals." *Essays.* Trans. J. M. Cohen. Harmondsworth, UK: Penguin, 1958: 105–19.

Pratt, Mary Louise. "Fieldwork in Common Places." *Writing Culture: The Poetics and Politics of Ethnography.* Ed. James Clifford and George Marcus. Berkeley: U of California P, 1986. 27–50.

Staden, Hans. *Duos viagens ao Brasil.* Trans. Guiomar de Carvalho Franco. Belo Horizonte: Editora Itatiaia Limitada, 1974.

———. *Warhaftige Historia . . .* (1557). *Reisin in Südamerica 1529 bis 1555.* Ed. Karl Klüpfel. Amsterdam: Rodopi, 1969.

FROM *THE TRUE HISTORY OF HIS CAPTIVITY*

Hans Staden

The Situation of Sancte Vincente

Sancte Vincente is an island and lies close to the mainland. On it are two settlements: the one called in the Portuguese tongue Sancte Vincente, and in the savage tongue Orbioneme: the second settlement is situated some two miles away and is called Uwawa Supe. There are also certain houses on the island called Ingenio where sugar is made.

The Portuguese live on the island and are friendly with a Brazilian tribe called Tuppin Ikin. The country of the Tuppin Ikins reaches for eighty miles inland and for about forty miles along the coast.

This tribe is encompassed to the north and south by hostile tribes. Those to the south are called Carios; those to the north are named Tuppin Imba. They are also known by their foes as Tawaijar, which is to say enemy. The Portuguese have suffered much injury from these people, and even today they go in fear of them.

How the Place Is Named in which the Enemy Is Chiefly Gathered Together, and How It Is Situated

Five miles from Sancte Vincente is a place called Brikioka.[1] Here the people are in touch with the savages, their enemies, who sail thither between an island called Sancto Maro and the mainland. At this point a number of mameluke[2] brethren were stationed to protect the passage. Their father was a Portuguese and their mother was a Brazilian woman, and they were skilful and experienced both in Christian and savage speech and customs. The eldest among them was called Johan de Praga, the second Diego de

---

[1] Near the modern cities of Santos and São Paulo, Brazil. The islands of Sancte Vicente and Sancto Amaro are part of a river delta.
[2] A colonial term for the children of an Indian woman and a European man.

Praga, the third Domingus de Praga, the fourth Francisco de Praga, the fifth Andreas de Praga, and the father was known as Diego de Praga.

About two years before I arrived these five brethren had undertaken, in conjunction with the friendly savages, to build a fort in the native fashion as a bulwark against the enemy, and this they had accomplished. Certain Portuguese had joined them and dwelt there, as it was a fruitful country, but their enemies, the Tuppin Imba, had discovered this and had prepared themselves for war in their own country some twenty-five miles away. One night they arrived with seventy canoes and had attacked the settlement, as their custom was, an hour before daybreak, forcing the mamelukes and Portuguese into a hut which they had built of earth where they defended themselves. The other savages had also defended themselves stoutly in their huts, so that numbers of the enemy were killed. In the end, however, the enemy prevailed and burnt the settlement of Brikioka and captured all the savages, but the Christians, numbering about eight, and the mamelukes remained safe in their house, for God was their protector. As for the captives they were forthwith hacked in pieces and divided up, after which the attackers returned to their own country.

In What Manner the Portuguese Rebuilt Brikioka, and Later Constructed a Fort in the Island of Sancte Maro

It did not seem wise to the commanders and the community to leave the place, but they decided to rebuild it more strongly, since at this point the whole country could be defended. And they did so.

When the enemy observed that the settlement of Brikioka was too strong to be attacked, they passed at night close to the place by water and captured whomsoever they could in the neighbourhood around Sancte Vincente. For those who dwelt inland imagined that they were in no danger, since the settlement close by was so strongly fortified, and for this they paid the penalty. Then the dwellers there commenced to build a fort by the water in the Island of Sancte Maro, which lies immediately opposite Brikioka, and to furnish it with guns and men, with intent to prevent the passage of the savages. They began to set up the fort on the island, but it remained unfinished since, as I was told, no Portuguese gunner would stay there. I was then at that place looking about me, and when the people learnt that I was a German with some knowledge of guns, they desired me to take duty in the fort and prepare for the enemy, offering to find me companions and to pay me a good wage. They promised also if I would do this that I should receive favours from their King, who was always pleased to show his pleasure to those who offered help and counsel in the New World.

I then made an agreement with them to serve four months in the fort, by which time an officer was due to arrive from the King with ships and material for the building of a stone blockhouse which would be much stronger. And so it fell out. During most of the time I was in the blockhouse with three others and some guns, but we were in great danger from the savages, for the fort was not strong, and we had to keep perpetual watch lest the savages should slip past in the darkness, which they tried to do on several occasions; but God was with us and showed them to us in the night watches.

After some months the King's officer arrived, for the people had petitioned the King on account of the pride and insolence of the enemy thereabouts, and had reported how fine a country it was and that it ought not to be abandoned. Therefore the officer arrived, who was called Tome de Susse, with intent to improve matters and to survey the country and inspect those places which the inhabitants desired to strengthen.

Then the people made report to the officer concerning my services and told him how I had stationed myself in the fort where no Portuguese would remain, since it was so badly defended. The officer was much gratified and promised to report the matter to the King when God brought him safely home to Portugal, and that I should be rewarded.

My period of service, namely four months, being now finished, I desired my release, but the officer and the people begged me to remain for a further period in their service. I consented and agreed to serve for two years more on condition that when this time was at an end they would then without hindrance set me on the first ship for Portugal in order to obtain my reward. Then the officer gave me the commission, which it is customary to bestow on the King's gunners who demand it. The bulwark was constructed of stone and fortified with a number of cannon, and I was ordered to take charge of the place and keep a careful watch.

How and for What Reasons It Was Necessary to Keep Watch for the Enemy at One Season of the Year More Than at Other Times

It was necessary for us to keep particular watch at two seasons of the year, especially when the savages go forth to make war on their enemies. Of these two seasons the one occurred in the month of November, when certain fruit which they call in their language Abbati became ripe, from which fruit the savages made a drink called Kaa Wy.[3] At the same time they gather a root called mandioca which they mix with the fruit when it is ripe to make the drink. This drink is made ready against their return from war so that they can enjoy it when they eat their enemies, and they make merry for a whole year when the time of the Abbati arrives. We had also to look for attacks in the month of August when they go out to catch fish. The fish at this season ascend into the fresh water which flows into the sea, in order to deposit their spawn. The name of this fish in the savage tongue is Bratti, but the Spaniards call them Lysses. At this season the savages are accustomed to sally forth to make war, so that they may be well supplied with food. They catch the fish in small nets and shoot them also with arrows. Then they take them home and roast them, and make a meal from them which they call Pira Kui.

My Capture by the Savages and How It Occurred

I had a savage man for a slave of the tribe called Carios who caught game for me, and it was my custom to make expeditions with him into the forest.

It fell out after a time that a Spaniard from Sancte Vincente came to me to the island of Sancte Maro, a distance of about five miles, and was with me in the fort where I lived, and with him came also a German called Heliodorus Hessus,[4] son of the deceased Eobanus Hessus. He had been stationed in the island of Sancte Vincente in an Ingenio where they make sugar. This Ingenio belonged to a Genoese named Josepe Ornio, and Heliodorus was his clerk and manager. (Ingenio is used to designate the houses where sugar is made.) I had had dealings with this Heliodorus previously, for when I was shipwrecked with the Spaniards I found him in the Island of Sancte Vincente and he showed me much kindness. He came to see how I was situated, for he had heard perchance that I was sick.

The day previously I had sent my slave into the forest to hunt for game, intending to go on the following day to fetch it so that we might

---

[3] This word for the fermented beverage the Tupinamba made from manioc root is spelled *caouin* by the French author Léry, and "Kawawy" and "Kawi" by Staden later in the text. Staden's spellings are frequently inconsistent.

[4] The name signifies that he was from Hesse in Germany, as was Hans Staden.

have food, for in that country there is little to be had except what comes out of the wilderness.

As I was going through the forest I heard loud yells on either side of me, such as savages are accustomed to utter, and immediately a company of savages came running toward me, surrounding me on every side and shooting at me with their bows and arrows. Then I cried out: "Now may God preserve my soul." Scarcely had I uttered the words when they threw me to the ground and shot and stabbed at me. God be praised they only wounded me in the leg, but they tore my clothes from my body, one the jerkin, another the hat, a third the shirt, and so forth. Then they commenced to quarrel over me. One said he was the first to overtake me, another protested that it was he that caught me, while the rest smote me with their bows. At last two of them seized me and lifted me up, naked as I was, and taking me by the arms, some running in front and some behind, they carried me along with them through the forest at a great pace toward the sea where they had their canoes. As we approached the sea I saw the canoes about a stone's-throw away, which they had dragged out of the water and hidden behind the shrubs, and with the canoes were great multitudes of savages, all decked out with feathers according to their custom. When they saw me they rushed toward me, biting their arms and threatening me, and making gestures as if they would eat me. Then a king approached me carrying the club with which they kill their captives, who spoke saying that having captured me from the Perot, that is to say the Portuguese, they would now take vengeance on me for the death of their friends, and so carrying me to the canoes they beat me with their fists. Then they made haste to launch their canoes, for they feared that an alarm might be raised at Brikioka, as indeed was the case.

Before launching the canoes they bound my hands together, but since they were not all from the same place and no one wanted to go home empty-handed, they began to dispute with my two captors, saying that they had all been just as near to me when I was taken, and each one demanding a piece of me and clamouring to have me killed on the spot.

Then I stood and prayed, expecting every moment to be struck down. But at last the king, who desired to keep me, gave orders to carry me back alive so that their women might see me and make merry with me. For they intended to kill me *Kawewi Pepicke*: that is, to prepare a drink and gather together for a feast at which they would eat me. At these words they desisted, but they bound four ropes round my neck, and I was forced to climb into a canoe, while they made fast the ends of the ropes to the boats and then pushed off and commenced the homeward journey.

How My People Came Out When
the Savages Were Carrying Me Away,
Intending to Recapture Me,
and How They Fought with the Savages

There is another island close by the one where I was captured in which water-birds nest which are called Uwara,[5] and they have red feathers. The savages asked me whether their enemies the Tuppin Ikins had been there that year to take the birds during the nesting season. I told them that the Tuppin Ikins had been there, but they proposed to visit the island to see for themselves if this was so, for they value the feathers of these birds exceedingly since all their adornment depends on them. It is a peculiarity of these birds that when they are young the feathers are a whitish-grey. They then become dark grey and so they fly for about a year, after which the feathers turn red, as red as paint. The savages made for this island, hoping to take the birds, but when they were a distance of some two gun-shots from the place where they had left their canoes, they looked back and saw behind them a number of Tuppin Ikin savages with certain of the Portuguese who had set out to recapture me. For a slave who was with me had escaped when I was taken and had raised an alarm. They cried out to my captors that unless they were cowards they would turn and fight. My captors turned about and those on the land assailed us with blow-pipes and arrows while we replied. My captors then unbound my hands leaving the cord still fastened to my neck, and as the king had a gun and a little powder, which a Frenchman had given him in exchange for some Brazilian wood, I was forced to shoot with it towards the land.

After both parties had skirmished for a time my captors, fearing that those on shore might be reinforced with canoes and might give chase, made off with three casualties and passed about a gun-shot distance from the fort at Brikioka where I had been stationed, and as we passed I had to stand up in the canoe so that my companions might see me. They fired two large guns from the fort, but the shot fell short.

In the meantime some canoes had set out from Brikioka in pursuit, hoping to overtake us, but my captors rowed too fast, and when my friends saw that they could do nothing they returned to Brikioka.

---

[5]Flamingo.

In What Manner My Captors Returned
to Their Own Country

When we were about seven miles from Brikioka toward the country of the savages it was by the sun about four o'clock in the afternoon of the same day on which I was captured.

My captors passed by an island and ran the canoes ashore, intending to spend the night there, and they carried me from the canoe to the land. I could scarcely see, for I had been wounded in the face, nor could I walk on account of the wounds in my leg, but could only lie down on the sand. Then they stood round me and boasted that they would eat me.

So in mighty fear and terror I bethought me of matters which I had never dwelt upon before, and considered with myself how dark is the vale of sorrows in which we have our being. Then, weeping, I began in the bitterness of my heart to sing the Psalm: "Out of the depths have I cried unto thee." Whereupon the savages rejoiced and said: "See how he cries: now is he sorrowful indeed."

Then they considered and decided that the island was not a suitable place in which to spend the night, and they returned to the mainland where there were huts which they had erected previously, and it was night when we came there. The savages beached the canoes and lit a fire and afterward took me to it. There I had to sleep in a net which they call in their tongue Inni. These nets are their beds and they make them fast to two posts above the ground, or if they are in the forest they tie them to two trees. So I lay there with the cord which I had about my neck tied high up in a tree, and they lay round about me all night and mocked me saying in their speech: *Schere inbau ende,* which is to say: "You are my bound beast."

Before daybreak we were once more on our way and rowed all day, so that by Vespers we were some two miles from the place where they intended to spend the night. Then great black clouds arose behind me which were terrible to see, and the savages laboured at the oars, striving to reach land and to escape the wind and darkness. But when they saw that their efforts were in vain they said to me: *Ne mungitta dee Tuppan do Quabe, amanasu y an dee Imme Ranni me sisse,* which is to say: "Speak with your God that we may escape the wind and rain." I kept silence, but prayed in my heart as the savages required of me: "O almighty God, Lord of heaven and earth, who from the beginning hast succoured those that call upon thee, now among the heathen show thy mercy to me that I may know that thou art with me, and establish thee among these savages who know thee not, that they may see that thou hast heard my prayer."

I lay bound in the canoe and could not turn myself to regard the sky, but the savages looked steadfastly behind them and commenced to say: *Oqua moa amanasu,* which means: "The great storm is departing." Then I raised myself as best I could and looked back and saw that the clouds were passing, and I praised God.

When we came to land they did with me as before and bound me to a tree, and lay about me all night telling me that we were approaching their country where we should arrive on the morrow about evening, at which I rejoiced not at all.

How They Dealt with Me
on the Day on Which They Brought Me
to Their Dwellings

On the same day about Vesper time (reckoning by the sun) we came in sight of their dwellings after we had been journeying for three days. The place to which I had come was thirty miles distant from Brikioka where I had been captured.

When we were near the dwellings I saw that the place was a small village with seven huts, and it was called Uwattibi (Ubatúba). We landed on a beach close by the sea, and there were the womenfolk in a plantation of mandioca roots. They were going up and down gathering roots, and I was forced to call out to them and say: *A junesche been ermi vramme,* which means: "I your food have come."

As we landed, all the women, young and old, came running out of the huts, which were built on a hill, to stare at me. The men went into their huts with their bows and arrows, leaving me to the pleasure of the women who gathered round and went along with me, some in front and some behind, dancing and singing the songs they are wont to sing to their own people when they are about to eat them.

They then carried me to a kind of fort outside the huts called Ywara, which they defend against their enemies by means of great rails made like a garden fence. When I entered this enclosure the women fell upon me and beat me with their fists, plucking at my beard and crying out in their speech: *Sehe innamme pepikeae,* which is to say: "With this blow I avenge me of my friend, that one who was slain by your people."

After this they took me into the huts where I had to lie in a hammock while the women surrounded me and beat me and pulled at me on all sides, mocking me and offering to eat me. Meanwhile the men had assembled in a hut by themselves, drinking a drink which is known as Kawi, and having their gods, called Tammerka,[6] about them, to whom they sang praises, since these gods, they said, had foretold my capture. I could hear this singing, but for half an hour none of the men came near me, and I was left with the women and children.

How My Two Captors
Came to Me and Told Me That
They Had Presented Me to One of
Their Friends, Who Would Keep Me
and Slay Me When I Was
to Be Eaten

At this time I knew less of their customs than I knew later, and I thought to myself: now they are preparing to kill me. In a little time the two men who had captured me, namely Jeppipo Wasu and his brother, Alkindar Miri, came near and told me that they had presented me in friendship to their father's brother, Ipperu Wasu, who would keep me until I was ready to be eaten, when he would kill me and thus acquire a new name.

This Ipperu Wasu had captured a slave a year before, and had presented him in friendship to Alkindar Miri, who had slain him and gained a new name. This Alkindar Miri had then promised to present Ipperu Wasu with the first prisoner he caught. And I was that prisoner.

My two captors told me further that the women would lead me out Aprasse. This word I did not then understand, but it signifies a dance. Thus was I dragged from the huts by the rope which was still about my neck to the dancing place. All the women came running from the seven huts, and seized me while the men withdrew, some by the arms, some by the rope about my throat, which they pulled so tight that I could hardly breathe. So they carried me with them, for what purpose I knew not, and I could think only of our Saviour Jesus Christ, and of his innocent sufferings at the hands of the Jews, whereat I was comforted and grew more patient. They brought me to the hut of their king, who was called Vratinge Wasu, which

---

[6] In part 2 of his book, Staden explains that these Tammarakas (as he more commonly spells the word) are hollow gourds filed with stones and mounted on sticks, and that the Tuppin Imba pose questions to them, interpreting the sound as a spoken response. The word has entered English as *maraca*.

means the great white bird. In front of this hut was a heap of fresh earth, and they brought me to it and sat me there, holding me fast. I could not but think that they would slay me forthwith and began to look about me for the club Iwera Pemme which they use to kill their prisoners, and I asked whether I was now to die, but they told me "not yet." Upon this a woman approached carrying a piece of crystal fastened to a kind of ring and with it she scraped off my eyebrows and tried to scrape off my beard also, but I resisted, saying that I would die with my beard. Then they answered that they were not ready to kill me yet and left me my beard. But a few days later they cut it off with some scissors which the Frenchmen had given them.

How They Danced with Me
before the Huts in Which Their Idols
Tammerka Had Been Set Up

After this they carried me from the place where they had cut off my eyebrows to the huts where they kept their idols, Tammerka. Here they made a ring round me, I being with two women in the centre, and tied my leg with strings of objects which rattled. They bound me also with sheaves of feathers arranged in a square, which they fastened behind at my neck so that they stood up above my head. This ornament is called in their language Arasoya. Then the women commenced to sing all together, and I had to keep time with the rattles on my leg by stamping as they sang. But my wounded leg was so painful that I could hardly stand upright, for the wound had not been dressed.

How, After They Had Danced,
They Brought Me Home to Ipperu Wasu
Who Was to Kill Me

When the dance was ended I was handed over to Ipperu Wasu who guarded me closely. He told me that I had some time to live. And the people brought the idols from the huts and set them up around me, saying that these had prophesied that they would capture a Portuguese. Then I replied that the idols were powerless and could not speak, and that even so they lied, since I was no Portuguese, but a kinsman and friend to the

French, and that my native land was called Allemania.[7] They made answer
that it was I who lied, for if I was truly the Frenchmen's friend, how came
it that I was among the Portuguese? For they knew well that the French
were as much the enemies of the Portuguese as they were, and that they
came every year in their boats, bringing knives, axes, mirrors, combs and
scissors, and taking in exchange Brazilian wood, cotton, and other goods,
such as feathers and pepper. These men were their good friends which the
Portuguese were not. For the Portuguese, when they came to the country
and settled there, had made friends with their enemies. Moreover, the Portuguese had come to their country, desiring to trade with them, and when
they had gone down in all friendship and entered the ships, as they are to
this day accustomed to do with the Frenchmen, the Portuguese had waited
until sufficient numbers were on board, and had then seized and bound
them, carrying them away to their enemies who had killed and eaten them.
Others the Portuguese had slain with their guns, committing also many
further acts of aggression, and even joining with their enemies and waging
frequent war, with intent to capture them.

How My Captors Made
Angry Complaint That the Portuguese
Had Slain Their Father, Which Deed They
Desired to Avenge on Me

The savages said, moreover, that the Portuguese had wounded the father
of the two brothers, my captors, and had shot off one of his arms so that
he died of his wounds, and that they intended to take vengeance on me for
their father's death. To which I made answer that they should not visit this
upon me, since I was no Portuguese, but had arrived some time since with
the Castilians, and had been shipwrecked among the Portuguese, for
which reason I had remained with them.

Now there was a young man of their tribe who had been a slave
among the Portuguese, for the savages among whom the Portuguese dwell
had waged war on the Tuppin Imbas and had captured a whole village,
killing and eating the grown men. But the young ones had been carried off
and bartered to the Portuguese for goods, and among them was this young
man, who had passed into the hands of a master in the neighbourhood of

---

[7] The French word for "Germany," today spelled *Allemagne*.

Brikioka named Antonio Agudin of Galicia. My captors had taken this slave some three months before I fell into their hands, but as he belonged to their tribe they had not killed him. This young man knew me well and my captors enquired of him what manner of man I was. He told them that it was true that a ship had been cast away, and that the people in it were called Castilians, and that they were friends of the Portuguese. He said also that I was among them, but knew nothing more of me.

When I heard this and understood that there were Frenchmen among them who came there in their ships, I persisted in my story that I was a kinsman and friend to the French, and that they should leave me alive until the Frenchmen arrived and recognized me. And they kept me in close confinement, for there were certain Frenchmen in the district who had been left there to collect pepper.

How a Frenchman Who Had Been Left among the Savages Came to See Me and Bade Them Eat Me, Saying That I Was Truly a Portuguese

There was a Frenchman four miles distant from the village in which I was, and when he heard news of me he came and entered one of the huts opposite to the one in which I was kept. Then the savages came running to me and said: "Here is a Frenchman. Now we shall see whether you are in truth a Frenchman or not." At this I rejoiced greatly, for I told myself that he was at least a Christian and would do his best for me.

Then they took me to him, naked as I was, and I found him to be a youth known to the savages by the name Karwattuware. He commenced to speak to me in French, which I could not well understand, and the savages stood round about and listened. Then, when I was unable to reply to him, he spoke to the savages in their own tongue and said: "Kill him and eat him, the good-for-nothing, for he is indeed a Portuguese, your enemy and mine." This I understood, and I begged him for the love of God to tell them not to eat me, but he replied only: "They will certainly eat you." Whereupon I bethought me of the words of the Prophet Jeremy (chapter 17) when he said: "Cursed be the man that trusteth in man," [8] and I departed from them with a heavy heart. I had on my shoulders a linen cloth which the savages had given me, although I know not where they can have obtained it. This I tore off and flung it at the Frenchman's feet, saying to myself (for the sun

---

[8] The line is from Jer. 17.5. Significantly, the previous verse includes the warning, "I will cause thee to serve thine enemies in a land which thou knowest not."

had burnt me severely) that it was useless to preserve my flesh for others if I was to die. And they carried me back to the hut which was my prison where I stretched myself in my hammock. God alone knows the misery that I endured, and weeping I commenced to sing the verse: "Let us now beseech the Holy Ghost to save and guard us when death approaches and we pass from sorrows into peace. Kyrioleys." But the savages said only: "He is indeed a true Portuguese. Now he cries. Truly he is afraid to die."

The Frenchman remained for two days in the huts, and on the third day he departed. The savages had resolved to make their preparations and to kill me on the day when everything should be ready. In the meantime they kept me very closely and mocked me continuously, both young and old.

How I Suffered Greatly from Toothache

It fell out during my misery, just as men say, that troubles never come singly, for one of my teeth commenced to ache so violently that by reason of the pain I could not eat and lost flesh. Whereat my master enquired of me why I ate so little, and I replied that I had toothache. Then he came with an instrument made of wood, and wanted to pull out the tooth. I told him that it had ceased to trouble me, but nevertheless he tried to pull it out with force, and I resisted so vigorously that he gave up the attempt. Then he threatened that if I did not eat and grow fat again they would kill me before the appointed day. God knows how earnestly, from my heart, I desired, if it was his will, to die in peace without the savages perceiving it and before they could work their will on me.

In What Manner They
Brought Me to Their Chief Ruler,
King Konyan Bebe, and How They
Dealt with Me There

A few days later they took me to another village called Arirab, the dwelling place of their chief king who was called Konyan Bebe. Here a great company had assembled, with much rejoicing in the native manner, for the people desired to see me, and he had ordered me to be brought there on that day.

As I arrived at the huts I heard a great noise, with singing and blowing of trumpets, and in front of the huts some fifteen heads had been set up on posts. These were the heads of their enemies, called Markayas, whom they had eaten, and as they took me past them they told me what they were. Then I was afraid, for I could not but consider that they might treat me in the same way. When we entered the huts one of my keepers went forward and spoke, with cruel words, so that all might hear, saying: "Behold I bring you a Portuguese slave," as if it were a fine thing for him to have his adversary in his power, and speaking much else besides according to their custom. He then took me to the place where the king sat, and he and his companions drank together of the drink called Kawawy until they were drunken, and they all regarded me with evil looks, saying: "Is not our enemy now come to us?" And I replied: "I am indeed come to you, but I am not your enemy." Then they gave me to drink.

Now I had heard much of this king who was called Konyan Bebe, how that he was a mighty king and a great tyrant and eater of men's flesh, and when I saw the one among them who looked like a king I went forward and spoke to him, as if I had been of his people. And I said: "Are you king Konyan Bebe, do you still live?" He made answer: "Yes, I am still alive," and I said: "I have heard much of you, how that you are a very mighty man." Upon this he rose up and began to strut about before me with great pomp. He had a round green stone thrust through his lips (as their custom is). These people make also a kind of pater noster of sea-shells, which they use for ornament. This king wore six ropes of them hanging at his neck whereby I saw that he was a great personage.

The king then sat down again and began to question me as to what his enemies the Tuppin Ikins and the Portuguese were about to do; and why I had tried to shoot his people at Brikioka (for he had learnt that I was employed as a gunner against them). I made answer that the Portuguese had placed me there and I had to obey orders. But he said that I was also a Portuguese, for the Frenchman who had seen me, whom he called his son, had told him that I could not speak with him, and that I was a true Portuguese. Whereupon I told him that I had been so long absent from my country that I had forgotten my native tongue. Then said he: "I have already helped to catch and eat five Portuguese who said they were Frenchmen, but they all lied."

Then, indeed, I abandoned all hope of life and commended myself to God, for I saw clearly that I must die. But he still questioned me and enquired what the Portuguese reported of him, for they must surely go in fear of him. And I replied that they spoke much of him, and of the mighty wars which he waged against them, but that now they had greatly strengthened Brikioka. Nevertheless he boasted that he would catch them all in time in the forest, as he had caught me. To which I answered that his true enemies the Tuppin Ikins were preparing twenty-five canoes to attack his country, and this indeed fell out as I had said.

While the king was speaking with me the others stood by and listened, for he asked me much and told me much, bragging how many of his enemies, both Portuguese and savages, he had killed. In the meantime, while he spoke thus, the drink in the huts had been consumed, and the people were moving to another hut where more drink had been prepared. And with this the king made an end of speaking.

There in the other huts they began to mock me, and the king's son bound my legs in three places, and I was forced to hop thus through the huts on both feet, at which they made merry, saying: "Here comes our food hopping toward us." Then I asked my master whether he had brought me there to be killed, and he said "No," but that it was the people's custom to treat enemy slaves so. They now unbound my legs and began to walk round

Figure One: This woodcut illustrated the scene in the narrative where Konyan Bebe spoke to Staden of how many enemies he had killed and Staden was forced to hop through the huts.

me, tearing at my flesh, one saying that the skin on my head was his, another claiming the fat on my legs. After this I had to sing to them, and I sang holy songs, and when they asked me what I sang I told them that I was singing of my God. But they replied that my God was no better than dirt, calling him in their tongue Teuire. These words caused me much anguish, and I prayed and said: "O God, thou art long-suffering indeed." When all in the village had seen me and abused me, the king, Konyan Bebe, gave orders on the following day that I was to be closely guarded. Then they carried me away from the huts towards Uwattibi where they were to kill me, and the people mocked me, crying out after me that they would not fail to come to my master's hut to drink to me while they ate me; but my master comforted me, saying that they would not kill me yet.

How the Tuppin Ikins Came with Twenty-Five Canoes, as I Had Predicted to the King, Intending to Attack the Huts Where I Was Kept

In the meantime the twenty-five canoes of the savages who were friendly to the Portuguese, of whom I spoke before I was captured, came out in warlike array, and one morning they attacked the village.

Now when these Tuppin Ikins commenced to attack and were shooting at us, there was consternation in the huts and the women prepared to flee. But I said: "You take me for a Portuguese, your enemy, now give me a bow and arrows and free me, and I will help you to defend the huts." This they did, and I called out and shot my arrows, doing as they did, and encouraging them to be of good heart and no evil would befall them. My intention was to break through the stockade surrounding the huts and run toward the attackers, for they knew me well and were apprised that I was in the village, but my captors guarded me too well. And when the Tuppin Ikins saw that they could do nothing they returned to their canoes and departed, and as for me I was watched all the more closely.

In What Manner the Chiefs Assembled in the Moonlight

On the day on which the others departed, toward evening, when it was moonlight, the people assembled in the space between the huts and took counsel and deliberated when to kill me, placing me in their midst, and

mocking and threatening me. I was much cast down and as I regarded the
moon I thought within myself and said: "O Lord God, rescue me from this
danger and bring it to a peaceful end." Then they asked me why I looked
so intently at the moon, and I replied: "I perceive that the moon is wrath,"
for the face in the moon seemed to me to have (God forgive me) so terrible
an aspect that I imagined God and all creatures must be angry with me.
Then the king who desired to kill me, by name Jeppipo Wasu, one of the
chiefs of the huts, enquired of me with whom the moon was angry, and I
replied: "She is looking toward your huts," whereupon he began to rage
and dispute with me, and to appease him I added: "Perchance it is not you
with whom she is wrath, but the Carios slaves" (these being a savage tribe
so called). "Yes," said he, "upon them let the misfortune fall," and thus
the matter remained, and it passed from my mind.

How the Tuppin Ikins Burnt Another
Village Called Mambukabe

News came the next day from a village called Mambukabe that the Tuppin
Ikins, after they had departed leaving me a captive, had descended upon
the village and burnt it, but the inhabitants had escaped except a small boy
who had been captured. Upon this Jeppipo Wasu, who had charge of me
and who did me many injuries, hurried off, since the people of the village
were his friends, to help them to rebuild their huts. And with him went all
his companions from the huts. His intention was to bring back clay and
root meal in order to prepare the feast at which I was to be eaten, and as
he departed he gave orders to Ipperu Wasu, to whom he had presented me,
that I was to be closely guarded. They were absent for more than a fortnight making their preparations.

How a Ship Came from Brikioka Enquiring
for Me, and of the Brief Report
Which Was Given

In the meantime a Portuguese ship arrived from Brikioka and anchored not
far from the place where I was, and shot off a gun so that the savages might
come and parley with them. As soon as the savages heard this they said:
"Here are your friends, the Portuguese. Doubtless they wish to hear
whether you are still alive and to buy you." And I replied: "This will certainly be my brother," for I was sure that the Portuguese ship which was

there would enquire for me, and lest the savages should take me for Portuguese, I told them that I had a brother, a Frenchman, among them. As soon as the ship drew near I told them that my brother had come, but the savages continued to maintain that I was a Portuguese, and they approached within speaking distance of the ship. When the Portuguese enquired after me the savages replied only that they might cease their enquiries. Whereupon the ship sailed away, the Portuguese thinking doubtless that I was dead. God alone knows what my thoughts were when I saw the ship depart, but the savages said amongst themselves: "We have the right man. They are already sending ships after him."

How the Brother of King Jeppipo Wasu Returned from Mambukabe with the News That His Brother and Mother, and All the Company Had Fallen Sick, and Entreated Me to Procure My God to Make Them Well Again

When I was daily expecting the return of the others who, as I have reported, were preparing for my death, I heard one day the sound of howling in the huts of the king who was absent. I was much afraid, for I thought that they had now returned, since it is the custom of the savages, when one of them has been absent for not longer than four days, to cry over him with joy when he returns. Presently one of the savages came to me and reported that the brother of him who owned a share in me had returned with the news that the others were all sick, whereat I greatly rejoiced, for I told myself that now God would show his might. Not long afterward this brother himself came to the hut where I was, and sitting down by me he commenced to cry aloud, saying that his brother, his mother, and his brother's children had all fallen sick, and that his brother had sent him to me with the message that I was to make my God restore them to health; and he added that his brother was persuaded that my God was wrath with them. To which I replied: "My God is indeed angry with you for threatening to eat me, and for going to Mambukabe to prepare the feast, and for falsely accusing me of being a Portuguese." I told him, further, to return to his brother and bid him come back to the huts, and I would intercede with my God to make him well again. He replied that his brother was too ill to come, but that he knew and had observed that if I desired it he would recover. Whereupon I made answer that he must wait until he was strong enough to come home to his huts, and that then he would be restored to health. With this answer he returned to Mambukabe, which is situated four miles from Uwattibi, where I was.

In What Manner the Sick King
Jeppipo Wasu Returned Home

After some days the sick persons all came back. Then was I taken to the king's huts, and he told me how the sickness had come upon them, and that I must have known of it, for he well remembered my saying that the moon was wrath with them. When I heard this I told myself that it was indeed God's doing that I had spoken of the moon on that evening, and I rejoiced greatly and said: "This day is God with me."

I told the king that this misfortune had befallen him because he had threatened to eat me, although I was no enemy of his, and he promised that if he recovered his health no evil should happen to me. But I was at a loss what to ask of God, for it seemed to me that if the savages recovered they would kill me at once, and if they died the others would say: "Let us kill him lest greater misfortunes befall us," as indeed they had already begun to say, and I could only submit the whole matter to God, the king beseeching me anew to make them well again. I went to and fro laying my hands on their heads as they desired me to do, but God did not suffer it and they began to die. A child died first, and then the king's mother, an old woman, whose business it was to prepare the pots for the drink with which I was to be eaten. Some days later a brother died, and then again a child, and then another brother, that one who had first brought me news of their illness.

When the king saw that his children and his mother and brother were dead he began to fear that he and his wives would die also, and he begged me to tell my God to make an end of his wrath so that he might live. I comforted him mightily, telling him not to despair, and that when he recovered his health he must give up all thought of killing me, which he promised, giving orders to those in his huts to cease from mocking me and threatening to eat me. He remained sick for a time, but finally he recovered, as did one of his wives who had been stricken, but there died of his family some eight persons, besides others, all of whom had treated me with great cruelty.

There were two kings in two other huts, one called Vratinge Wasu, the other Kenrimakui. Vratinge Wasu dreamed a dream, and in his dream I appeared before him and told him that he would die, and the next morning early he came to me and made complaint to me, but I comforted him, saying that he would live, but that he also must not think of killing me, nor give counsel to others to kill me. He replied that he would not do so, and that so long as those who had captured me did not kill me, so long he would do me no harm, and that even if they killed me he would not eat of me.

The second king, Kenrimakui, also dreamed a dream about me which greatly terrified him, and he called me into his hut and gave me to eat, and then he spoke to me of it and told me how, in one of his expeditions, he had captured a Portuguese whom he had killed with his own hands, after which he had eaten so much of him that his stomach had been afflicted ever afterward, and that he would never eat another Portuguese. But now he had dreamed about me, and his dream was so terrible that he thought he was about to die. I comforted him also, and told him he would recover, but that he must eat no more human flesh.

The old women about the huts who had done me much injury, beating me and threatening to eat me, now called me *Scheraeire,* which signifies: "Son, do not let me die," saying that when they ill-treated me they thought I was one of the Portuguese whom they hated. Further that they had eaten many Portuguese whose God had never been as angry as mine, and that it was clear that I was not a Portuguese at all.

After this they left me alone for a time, for they did not know what to do with me, nor whether I was in truth a Portuguese or a Frenchman. They remarked that I had a red beard like the Frenchmen, whereas the Portuguese, although they had seen some with red beards, had in general black beards.

When the terror was abated, and one of my masters had recovered, there was no more talk of eating me, but they guarded me closely and would not suffer me to go about unattended.

How the Frenchman Returned Who Had Told the Savages to Eat Me, and How I Begged Him to Take Me Away, but My Masters Would Not Suffer Me to Go

The Frenchman, called Karwattuware, of whom I have reported that he had abandoned me, had remained with the savages, his friends, trading with them and collecting pepper and feathers, and when he was travelling to those parts called Mungu Wappe and Iterroenne, where the ships arrive, he passed by the place where I was. Now when he left me he thought that the savages would certainly eat me, as he had recommended them to do, and having been absent for some time he expected to find me dead.

When, therefore, he entered the huts and saw me he addressed me in the savage tongue, and at that time I was not bound as previously. He asked me how it came about that I was still alive, and I told him that God in his goodness had protected me until then. It occurred to me that he might have heard from the savages how matters had fallen out, and I drew him aside privately, so that the savages might not hear us, and told him again that God had spared my life, and that I was no Portuguese, but a German who had suffered shipwreck with certain Spaniards and had afterward fallen among the Portuguese. I urged him to tell the savages this, and to make clear to them that I was his kinsman and friend, and to take me away with him when the ships arrived. For I was fearful that if he did not do this the savages would consider all that I had told them to be lies, and that sooner or later in their anger they would kill me. And I reproached him in the savage tongue, and asked whether he had a Christian heart in his bosom when he enjoined the savages to kill me, or had considered the life that was to come, whereupon he began to be ashamed and excused himself, saying that he had thought that I was indeed a Portuguese, who were such scoundrels that if the French could catch them anywhere in the province of Brazil they would hang them forthwith, which was indeed the truth. He said also that his people had to submit to the savages and be content with their treatment of their enemies, since the Portuguese were their hereditary foes.

Accordingly the Frenchman informed the savages that at our first meeting he had not properly recognized me, that I was from Germany, and was a friend of his nation, and that he proposed to take me to the place where the ships came. But the savages refused to deliver me up, stating that if my own father or brother came with a shipload of axes, mirrors, knives, combs and scissors and gave them these goods, they would not let me go, for they had captured me in the enemy's country and I belonged to them. When the Frenchman heard this he told me that, as I could see, the savages would not part with me. Then I begged him, for the love of God, to send for me and take me back in the first ship sailing for France, and this he promised to do, bidding the savages to care for me and on no account to kill me, for my friends were at hand and would certainly come for me. And with this he departed.

When the Frenchman had gone, one of my masters named Alkindar Miri (not the one who was sick) asked me what Karwattuware (which was the savages' name for the Frenchman) had given me. He enquired also whether he was indeed my countryman, and I replied that he was. Then said he: "Why did he not give you a knife which you could have given to me?" and he was angry; and later, when they had been restored to health, the savages began to murmur against me, saying that after all a Frenchman was not worth more than a Portuguese, and I commenced to be afraid again.

Of the Manner in Which the Savages
Ate a Prisoner and Carried Me to the Feast

Some days later the savages made preparations to eat one of their captives. These preparations took place in a village called Teckquarippe, about six miles away, and a company of people set out for the village, taking me with them. The slave who was to be eaten belonged to a nation called Marcaya, and we travelled thither in a canoe.

Now it is their custom when they are about to kill a man for the people to brew a drink from roots called Kawi, and after they had drunk this they kill their victim. I went to the prisoner on the eve of the day on which they were to drink in preparation for his death, and said: "All is ready for your death," and he laughed and said: "Yes." Now the rope with which they bind their victims is called Mussurana, and it is made of cotton, being thicker than a man's finger, and the man agreed that all was in order, only the rope was too short, for it wanted some six fathoms in length, and he added that with his people the matter would have been better arranged. And he spoke and acted as if he were going to a merrymaking.

I had with me a book in the Portuguese tongue, which the savages had taken from a ship they had captured with the help of the French, and they had given it to me. I departed from the prisoner and read in the book, and was consumed with pity for him. I therefore returned to him, for the Portuguese are friendly with the Marcaya tribe, and told him that I also was a prisoner as he was, and had not come to eat him, but had been brought there by my masters. He replied that he knew well that we did not eat human flesh. I then told him to be comforted for they would eat his body only, but his soul would be gathered to another place with the people of our nation where all was happiness and joy, but he doubted whether this was true, for he said he had never seen God. I told him that he would indeed see him in another life, and so left him.

That night a great storm of wind arose and blew so furiously that pieces of the roofs of the huts were carried away. Then the savages began to murmur against me, saying in their speech: *Apo Meiren geuppawy wittu wasu Immou:* "This evil fellow, the magician, has brought this wind upon us, for he looked by day into his book of thunder," meaning the book which I had, and they insisted that I had done this because the prisoner was a friend of the Portuguese, saying that I intended, perchance, to hinder the feast with bad weather. Then I prayed to God and said: "Lord, thou hast protected me until now, protect me still further," for they murmured much against me.

When day broke it was fine weather and the savages drank and were merry, but I went to the victim and told him that the great wind was my God, and that he had come to claim him. And on the following day he was eaten. The manner of this is related hereafter.[9]

What Happened on the Homeward Journey After the Man Had Been Eaten

When the feast was over we returned to our dwellings, my masters bringing some of the roast meat with them. The journey, which usually occupies one day, took three days to accomplish owing to the wind and rain, and the first evening, as we were setting up huts of wood to protect us, the savages asked me to make the rain cease. Now there was a boy with us who had a piece of the leg-bone of the dead slave with some flesh upon it, which he was eating. I told the boy to throw it away, but he grew angry, as did also the others, saying that it was their proper food. So I left the matter.

When we arrived within a quarter of a mile of our dwellings we could proceed no further, since the waves were too much for us. We beached the canoe and waited for the next day, when we looked for better weather, and hoped to be able to take the canoe home, but it remained stormy. Then they resolved to proceed by land and come back for the canoe when the weather improved. As we were about to go, the savages finished their meal, and the boy continued gnawing the flesh off the bone, after which he threw it away, and as soon as we set out the weather improved. "Now see," said I, "you doubted when I said that my God was angry because the boy ate the flesh from the bone," and they all agreed, saying that he should have eaten it out of my sight, and that the weather would then have continued fine, and so the matter rested.

After we had at last reached the huts, one of the men who owned a part of me, named Alkindar, inquired whether I had seen what they did with their enemies, and I replied that I had seen it indeed, but that the eating was more terrible to me than the killing. Whereupon he answered: "Such is our custom, and so we do also with the Portuguese."

---

[9]In part 2, chapter 28, Staden describes the cannibal rite in great detail, with eleven illustrations.

This Alkindar was very incensed against me and would have rejoiced if the man to whom he had presented me had killed me, for, as you will have read above, Ipperu Wasu had presented him with a slave for him to kill in order to obtain a fresh name for himself, and Alkindar in return had vowed to present him with the first slave he caught. Since he had not killed me, however, Alkindar would gladly have done so himself, but his brother prevented this, fearing that fresh misfortunes might befall him.

Before the others had taken me to the place where they ate the man, this same Alkindar had renewed his threats to kill me, but when I returned I found that during my absence he had been attacked by pains in the eyes, and was forced to lie still. He was quite blind for a time, and begged me continually to speak with my God so that he might be cured. I consented upon condition that he should cease to ill-treat me, which he promised, and in a few days he was restored to health.

How Once More a Ship Was Sent After Me by the Portuguese

After I had been five months among the savages, another ship came from the island of Sancto Vincente, for it is the custom of the Portuguese from time to time to send ships which are well armed into the country of their enemies to trade with them, giving them knives and sickles in exchange for mandioca meal, which the savages have in great quantities. The Portuguese have many slaves employed in the sugar plantations and require the meal for their food. When the ships come to trade, the savages row out, one or two in a canoe, and keeping as far away as possible, they hand out their goods, and name what they require in exchange which the Portuguese then give them. All the time that the two men are close to the ship, their companions keep a look out some distance off in their canoes, and when the trading is at an end, the savages often draw near and skirmish with the Portuguese and shoot their arrows at them, after which they return.

The crew of the ship fired a gun so that the savages might know that a ship had arrived, and when the savages rowed out, they inquired of them concerning me, whether I was still alive, and the savages answered "Yes." Then the Portuguese desired to see me, stating that they had a box full of things for me from my brother, also a Frenchman, who was in the ship with them.

Now there was a Frenchman called Claudio Mirando with the Portuguese in the ship who had been my companion. This man I called my brother, and I thought that he might be in the ship inquiring for me, as he had made the voyage before. The savages returned from the ship, and told me that my brother had come back, bringing me a box of goods, and that he desired to see me. Then I said, "Carry me to a place near at hand so that I can speak with my brother. The Portuguese will not understand what we say, and I will tell him to ask my father, when he returns home, to send a ship full of goods and take me away." To this they agreed, but they were much concerned lest the Portuguese should understand what we said, for the savages intended to make war during the month of August in the neighbourhood of Brikioka where I was captured, and I knew all their plans, and they were afraid I might disclose them. But I assured the savages that the Portuguese could not understand our speech. Then they carried me to within a stone's throw of the ship, naked as I was and had been all the time of my captivity, and I spoke to those in the ship and said: "The Lord God be with you, my brothers. Let one speak to me alone and do not allow it to be seen that I am otherwise than a Frenchman." Then one spoke who was called Johann Senches, a Biscayan,[10] whom I knew well, and he said: "My dear brother, on your account have we come in the ship, not knowing whether you were dead or alive, for the first ship brought no news of you. Captain Brascupas at Sanctus has ordered us to find out whether you were still alive, and if so to endeavour to buy you back, and if that failed to try and capture some of the savages to exchange for you."

Then I said: "Now may God reward you in eternity, for I am here in great fear and peril, and know not what may befall me. But for God's merciful intervention I should have been eaten." I said further: "They will not sell me to you: they would not even think of it, but do not you in the ship let the savages think of me otherwise than as a Frenchman, and give me, for the love of God, knives and fish-hooks." This they did at once, and a man returned to the ship and fetched them.

When I saw that the savages would not suffer me to parley any longer, I said to the Portuguese: "Look well to it, they are going to attack Brikioka." They replied that the savages, their allies, were also preparing for war, and would attack the village where I was, and that I was to be of good cheer, since God would do what was best, but, as I could see, they were powerless to help me. I agreed, saying: "All this has befallen me on account of my sins. It is better that God should punish me now, rather than in the world to come, but pray you to God for my deliverance": and I commended them to God. The Portuguese desired to speak further with me, but the savages would not permit it and carried me back again to the huts.

---

[10] From the shores of the Bay of Biscay, between northern Spain and southwestern France.

Then I took the knives and fish-hooks and gave them to the savages saying: "All these my brother, the Frenchman, gave me." And they inquired what he had spoken about with me. I replied that I had told my brother to escape from the Portuguese and return to our home, and bring a ship well stocked with goods to fetch me: "For," said I, "you are good people and treat me well and I am anxious to reward you when the ship comes." Thus at all times I had to conciliate them and they were well pleased.

Afterward they spoke among themselves and said: "He must surely be a Frenchman, let us in future treat him more kindly." So matters continued for a while, I telling them that a ship would shortly come to fetch me and that they were to treat me well. Then they carried me about with them in the forest and forced me to labour for them.

How a Slave, Who Had Perpetually Defamed Me and Desired to Have Me Killed, Was Himself Killed and Eaten in My Presence

There was a slave among the savages belonging to the nation called Carios, who were enemies of the savages and allies of the Portuguese. This man had been a slave among the Portuguese, but had escaped from them. The savages do not kill those who escape in this wise unless they commit some crime, but keep them as slaves to serve them. This slave had been three years among the Tuppin Imba people, and had declared that he had seen me among the Portuguese, shooting with the Tuppin Imba when they made war upon them.

Now some years previously the Portuguese had slain one of their kings, and this man maintained that the king had been shot by me, and he urged the savages constantly to kill me, saying that I was their real enemy as he himself had seen, but this was all lies, for he had been three years there and only a year had passed since I had reached Sancto Vincente, from which place he had escaped. And I prayed God to save me from his lies.

It happened about the year 1554, in the sixth month of my captivity, that this Cario fell ill, and his master besought me to help him and make him well again, so that he might catch game for us to eat, especially since, as I knew well, the food that was brought in was shared with me. But if I was of opinion that the man could not recover, then he would give him to one of his friends, so that he might kill him and take a fresh name for himself. And the man had been ill for nine or ten days.

Now the savages are accustomed to use for several purposes the teeth of a wild beast called Backe, which they sharpen, and when the blood is sluggish they cut the skin with one of these teeth so that the blood flows freely. This is equivalent with us to letting blood. I took one of these teeth, intending to open the median vein, but I could not cut it as the tooth was too blunt, and the savages stood round about. As I left him I saw that it was useless, but the savages continued to inquire whether he would recover, to which I replied that I could do nothing and that, as they saw, the blood would not flow. Then they said: "He will surely die. Let us kill him before he is dead." I answered: "No, do not kill him, for possibly he may recover," but I could not restrain them. They dragged him in front of the hut of the king Vratinge, while two men held him, although he was so ill

Figure Two: In this scene, the captive from the Cario nation whom Staden failed to cure is cut up and roasted. He remarks to his captors that the man had always spoken ill of him.

that he did not know what they were doing. Then the man came up, to whom the Cario had been given, and beat out his brains, after which they left him lying before the huts ready to be eaten. But I warned them that he was a sick man, and that they might also fall sick if they ate him, and they knew not what to do. Nevertheless, one came from the huts where I was and called the womenfolk to make a fire beside the body. Then he cut off the head, for the man had lost an eye from his disease and his appearance was horrible, and throwing away the head, he singed the body at the fire. After this he cut him up and divided the flesh equally, as is their custom, and they devoured everything except the head and intestines, which they did not fancy, on account of the man's sickness.

As I went to and fro in the huts I saw them roasting here the feet, there the hands, and elsewhere a piece of the trunk, and I told the savages that this Cario whom they were roasting and eating had always spoken ill of me, saying that while I was among the Portuguese I had shot several of their friends, and that he lied, for he had never seen me before. "Now see," said I, "he had been several years with you and had never been sick, but on account of his lying stories about me, my God was angry with him and smote him with sickness and put it into your minds to kill and eat him. So will my God do to all evil persons who seek or have sought to injure me." And they were greatly terrified at my words, but I thanked God that he had in this wise shown his might and power through me. Note reader, and mark well my writing, for I do this not in order to tell you strange things, but only to make known the wonderful works of God.

The time now approached when the savages proposed to make war, having prepared themselves during three months. I hoped that when they departed they would leave me with the women, so that I might escape in their absence.

How a French Ship Arrived to Trade with the Savages for Cotton and Brazil-Wood, to Which Ship I Tried to Escape, but God Did Not Intend It

Some eight days before the savages intended to set out for war, a French ship arrived in a harbour called by the Portuguese Rio de Janeiro, and by the savages Iteronne, which was about eight miles away. There the French are accustomed to load wood,[11] and they came now with their boat to the

---

[11] Brazil took its name from brazilwood, a tree that yielded a red dye valued in Europe.

village where I was, and traded with the savages for pepper, apes and parrots. One of the crew came from the boat on shore, who was called Jacob and knew the savage speech, and as he traded with the people, I begged him to take me back to his ship, but my master declined to let me go, saying that they would require much goods for me. Then I told the savages to take me themselves to the ship, and my friends would give them all that they required, but they would not, saying: "These are not your true friends, or they would have given you a shirt when they saw that you were naked. It is clear that they take no account of you" (which was indeed true). I replied that they would clothe me when I reached the great ship, but they answered that the ship would not depart at present and they had first to set off to war, but when they returned they would take me to it. So the boat prepared to go back to the ship, having anchored for a night at the village.

Now when I saw that the boat was preparing to depart, I prayed and said: "O merciful God, if the ship sails without me I shall certainly perish, for this is a people in whom no man can trust." With this I left the huts and ran toward the water, but the savages saw me and came after me. I ran as fast as I could, while they tried to seize me. The first that came up with me I struck down, and soon the whole village was at my heels, but I escaped and swam out beside the boat. When I tried to climb into the boat the Frenchmen thrust me away, for they thought that if they took me thus the savages would rise against them and become their enemies. So, very sadly, I swam back to the shore, for I saw it was God's will that I should remain there still longer in misery. But if I had not tried to escape then I should have blamed myself afterward.

When the savages saw me return they rejoiced and said: "Now he comes back to us." But I was wrath with them and said: "Do you think that I would leave you thus? I went to the boat to tell my people that they must send again for me after your return from the wars, so that when you bring me to them they will have much to give you in exchange." This pleased them greatly and they were once more contented.

How the Savages Went Forth to War Taking Me with Them and What Befell Me on the Way

Four days later the canoes began to assemble in the village in readiness for the expedition, and the chief king Konyan Bebe came also with his boats. My master announced that he would take me with him, but I asked to be left behind, and this would have happened if the king, Konyan Bebe, had not ordered otherwise. I let them see that I went unwillingly, lest they should think that I intended to escape when they reached the enemy country, and that they might guard me less closely. But it had been my intention, if they left me at home, to run away to the French ship.

However, they took me with them. There were thirty-eight canoes, each canoe carrying eighteen men more or less. Certain of them had inquired of their idols by dreams and had committed other follies concerning the expedition, as is their custom, and they were all much puffed up. Their intention was to make for the neighbourhood of Brikioka, where they had captured me, and to conceal themselves in the forest close by, and take back those who fell into their hands.

It was now about the 14th day of August in the year 1554. At this time, as I have stated before, it is the custom for the fish which is called in Portuguese *Doynges,* in Spanish *Liesses,* and in the savage tongue *Bratti,* to leave the sea for the fresh waters in order to spawn there, and this season of the year the savages call *Pirakaen.* At this time the savages go forth to war, both they and their enemies, catching and eating the fish by the way, and on the journey out they travel slowly, but on the journey back they travel as speedily as they can.

I hoped that the savages who were friendly to the Portuguese would also then be going to war, for those in the ship had told me that the savages, their allies, intended to attack at this time. My companions inquired of me continually during the voyage whether they would capture any prisoners, and in order not to anger them I said "Yes." I also told them that the enemy would engage them. One night we lay at the place called Uwattibi, where we caught many of the fish called Bratti, which are as large as a good-sized pike. That night the wind blew mightily, and the savages talked much to me and asked me many questions, whereupon I said that the wind was blowing over the bodies of dead men. Now it happened that another party of savages had set out by water to a river called Paraibe, and my companions concluded that this party must have reached the enemy country, and that some of the men were dead. This, as I heard later, had in fact happened.

When we were a day's journey further on, and were preparing for the attack, we hid ourselves in a wood close to an island which is called by the Portuguese S. Sebastian, and by the savages Meyenbipe. At night the king, Konyan Bebe, went to and fro in the camp and harangued and said that we had now arrived close to the enemy country, and that each one was to take note of his dreams that night, and that all were to see to it that their dreams were good. When he had finished speaking, the men danced with their idols until far into the night, after which they slept, and as my master laid himself down he told me to be sure to dream well, but I replied that

I took no account of dreams which are delusions. He then bade me speak to my God so that they might take many prisoners.

At daybreak the chiefs gathered round a cauldron of stewed fish, and while they ate they recounted their dreams, insofar as they were propitious; others danced with their idols, and that day they elected to set out for a place called Boywassu Kange, which was close to the enemy's country, where they would rest until evening. When we left the place called Meyenbipe, where we spent the night, the savages inquired of me what was in my mind, and I said at a venture that the enemy would meet us close to Boywassu Kange, but that we had nothing to fear; and it was my intention at Boywassu Kange to make my escape, for it was only six miles from the place where I had been captured.

As we were coasting along we saw a number of canoes approaching us from behind an island, and the savages called out: "Here come our enemies the Tuppin Ikins," and we hid ourselves behind a rock so that the others might pass without observing us, but they became aware of us and commenced to row in the direction of their home. We rowed after them as swiftly as we could, and gave chase for four whole hours until we came up with them. There were five canoes full of men, and they all came from Brikioka. I knew them all. In one of the canoes were six mamelukes who had been baptized, and among them were two brothers, one called Diego de Praga, the other Domingus de Praga, who defended themselves stoutly, one with a gun, the other with a bow and arrows. These two alone kept our thirty canoes at bay for two whole hours. But when their arrows were exhausted the Tuppin Imba fell upon them and captured them, and some were knocked on the head at once or shot. The two brothers were unhurt, but two of the six mamelukes were badly wounded, as were also several of the Tuppin Ikin, among whom was one woman.

How the Prisoners Were Disposed of on the Return Voyage

The capture had taken place at sea, two full miles from land, and we hurried back as quickly as we could in order to encamp in the place where we had spent the previous night. When we reached the land called Meyenbipe it was evening and the sun was setting, and each man took his prisoner to his hut. Those that had been badly wounded they carried to the land, where they were killed at once and cut up and roasted. Among those who were roasted that night were two of the mamelukes who were Christians; one was a Portuguese named George Ferrero, the son of a captain by a native woman. The other was called Hieronymus. He had been captured by a native belonging to my hut, whose name was Parwaa, and this man spent the whole night roasting Hieronymus, scarcely a step from the spot where I lay. This same Hieronymus (God have his soul) was blood relation to Diego de Praga.

That night, when we were encamped, I went into the hut where the two brothers were to talk with them, for they had been my good friends at Brikioka where I was captured. They inquired of me whether they would also be eaten, but I told them that they must trust in our Heavenly Father and in his Son Jesus Christ, who was crucified for our sins, and in whose name we were baptized. I said also: "This is my belief. God has watched over me so long here among the savages, and what God decrees must satisfy us."

The two brothers enquired also concerning their cousin Hieronymus, and I told them that he lay by the fire roasting, and that I had seen a piece of Ferrero's son being eaten. Then they commenced to weep, and I comforted them, telling them that I had been eight months or thereabouts among the savages, and that God had been my protector. "So also," I said, "will he protect you, if you trust in him." I told them also that it was harder for me than for them, for I had come from foreign countries, knowing nothing of the dreadful practices of the savages, but, as for them, they had been born in the country and bred there. They replied, however, that I had been hardened by misery and should therefore take less account of it.

As I was discoursing with them, the savages came and ordered me to depart, and they wanted to know what matters I had discussed with them at such length. I was sad at leaving them, and told them to put their whole trust in God, and to remember what sufferings were ours in this vale of sorrows, and they replied that never until then had they realized this, that they owed their lives to God, and that they would die more happily since I was with them. With that I left them and went through the whole camp visiting the prisoners. I went alone and none heeded me, and I could have escaped then, for the island Meyenbipe was only some ten miles from Brikioka, but I refrained on account of the Christian prisoners, of whom four were still alive. I thought that if I escaped, the savages would kill them at once in their anger. It might well be that God would still preserve us all, and I resolved to remain with them and comfort them, and this I did. The savages were now very favourably disposed towards me, since I had predicted, by chance, that the enemy would encounter us, as indeed it fell out. They said also that I was a better prophet than their prophet Miraka.[12]

---

[12] Another spelling of "Tammaraka."

How They Danced in the Camp
on the Following Day with Their Enemies

On the day following we reached a place not far from the country of my captors, called Occarasu, a great mountain. There we camped for the night, and I went to the hut of Konyan Bebe, the chief king, and asked what he intended to do with the two mamelukes. He replied that they would be eaten, and forbade me to speak with them, for he was very wrath, saying that they should have stayed at home instead of going to fight with his enemies. I begged him to spare their lives and sell them back again to their friends, but he was resolved that they should be eaten.

This same Konyan Bebe had then a great vessel full of human flesh in front of him and was eating a leg which he held to my mouth, asking me to taste it. I replied that even beasts which were without understanding did not eat their own species, and should a man devour his fellow creatures? But he took a bite saying *Jau ware sehe:* "I am a tiger; it tastes well," and with that I left him.

In the evening he gave orders that each man should bring his prisoner to an open space by the water, and this was done, and the savages gathered together into a circle with the prisoners in the centre, and they forced them to sing and rattle the idols which are called Tammaraka. When the prisoners had finished singing, they commenced to talk wantonly among themselves, saying: "We set forth like brave men intending to capture you, our enemies, and to eat you. Now you have the mastery, and have taken us, but we do not crave for mercy, for brave men are willing to die in an enemy country. But our land is wide and there are many waiting to take vengeance for our deaths." [13] And the others made answer: "You have slain many of our fellows. Now will we be the avengers." When this speech was ended the prisoners were taken back to the huts.

Three days later we reached our country and each man took his prisoner to his dwelling. In the village of Uwattibi, where I was, there were eight live savages who were prisoners and three Christian mamelukes, namely Diego and his brother, and another Christian called Antonio, the latter having been captured by my master's son. The two other mamelukes they carried home roasted, ready to be eaten. The journey out and home again had lasted eleven days.

---

[13] As with the Iroquois who tortured Brébeuf and Lalemant (chap. 3), the Tuppin Imba expected their victims to make a speech or sing a song of defiance toward their captors.

How the French Ship, to Which the Savages Had Promised to Bring Me, Was Still There When They Returned from the War

When we returned home I asked to be taken to the French ship, telling my captors that I had been with them upon their expedition, and had assisted them to capture their enemies, and from this alone they must have seen that I was no Portuguese. They replied that they would carry me to the ship, but that they must first rest and eat the Mokaen, that is the flesh of the two Christians.

How They Ate George Ferrero, the Portuguese Captain's Son, and the First of the Two Roasted Christians

There was a king over certain huts which were close to my hut, named Tatamiri, and he had charge of the roasted flesh. He caused drink to be prepared, according to their custom, and all the savages gathered together, drinking, singing, and making very merry. The day following they cooked the flesh again and ate it. But the flesh of Hieronymus remained in the hut where I was, hanging in the smoke, in a pot over the fire for three weeks, until it was as dry as wood. This was due to the fact that one of the savages named Parwaa had gone to collect roots with which to prepare drink to be served when Hieronymus was eaten, and so the time passed. The savages would not take me to the ship until they had celebrated their feast and eaten the remains of Hieronymus, and in the meantime the ship had departed, for it lay about eight miles from the place where I was.

When I heard the news of this I was much cast down, but the savages assured me that the ship came every year, and with this I had to be content.

How Almighty God Worked a Wonder

I had made a cross of reeds and set it up in front of my hut, and it was my custom to say my prayers there. I had told the savages not to remove it, lest some misfortune should befall them. But they gave no heed to my words, and once when I was away fishing, a woman tore up the cross and gave it to her husband to use for rubbing down the charms which they make from the shells of sea-snails, since it was round. At this I was very sad, and some days later it began to rain heavily. The rain endured for several days, and the savages came to my hut and asked me to tell my God to stop the rain, for if it continued it would spoil their planting, the time for which had then arrived. I replied that it was their own fault, for they had angered my God by pulling up the wooden stick in front of which I used to speak with him. When they heard that this was the cause of the rain, my master's son helped me to set up another cross, and it was then about an hour after midday, reckoning by the sun. As soon as the cross was set up the weather, which before noon had been very stormy, began at once to improve. And they all marvelled, saying that my God, in truth, did as I told him.

How I Went Fishing One Evening with Two Savages, and God Worked Another Wonder with Rain and Storm

One day I went fishing with the chief named Parwaa, the man who had roasted Hieronymus, and as I stood fishing with him and another at the close of day, there arose a great storm of rain and thunder not far from where we stood, and the wind blew the rain in our direction. Then the two men begged me to ask my God to see to it that the rain did not hinder us, so that we might catch more fish since, as I knew, there was nothing to eat in the hut. Thus moved, I prayed to God from the depths of my heart, that he might show his power in me and make plain to the heathen that he was with me at all times. As I finished my supplication the wind, blowing mightily, carried the rain toward us, so that it was raining heavily some six feet away from us, but on the place where we stood we felt nothing. Then the savage Parwaa spoke saying: "Now I see that you have indeed prayed to your God," and we caught a number of fish.

When we returned to the huts the two men told the others what had happened when I spoke to my God, and they were all amazed.

How the Savages Ate the Second Roasted Christian, Called Hieronymus

When all was made ready, as I have already related, the savage Parwaa caused drink to be prepared which was to be served when Hieronymus was eaten. When they had finished drinking they brought out the two brothers and another named Anthonius who had been captured by my master's son, and we four Christians were there together. We were forced to drink with the savages, but before doing so we prayed to God to have mercy on the dead man's soul, and to us also when our time came. And the savages spoke with us and were merry, but we were full of sorrow. The next day, early in the morning, they cooked the flesh again and ate it very quickly.

They now took me to be given away, and as I parted from the two brothers they begged me to pray to God for them, and I advised them, in case they should escape, what direction they should take in the mountains, and how best to cover their tracks, for I knew the mountains well. They were able to take advantage of my counsel, for I heard later that they had escaped, but whether they were recaptured I know not.

How They Carried Me to be Given Away

The savages now carried me to a place called Tackwara Sutibi, where they intended to give me away. When we were a short distance from the shore I looked behind me toward the huts and saw a black cloud hovering over them. I pointed this out to my companions, and told them that my God was wrath with the whole village for having eaten Christian flesh. When we arrived at the end of our journey I was presented to a king called Abbati Bossange, and the savages warned him that he was not to injure me or suffer me to be injured, since my God was very mighty against those that did me evil, which thing they had seen while I was with them. And I added my own warning, saying that my brother and friends would shortly arrive with a ship full of goods, and if they took care of me I would make them large gifts; for I knew full well that my God would send my brother with the ship right speedily. This pleased the savages greatly, and the king called me his son and I went with his sons hunting.

How the Savages of This Place Reported to Me that the French Ship had Sailed Away Again

The savages now told me that the French ship called *Maria Bellete* from Dieppe, which I had wished to join, had departed, having taken in a cargo of Brazil-wood, pepper, cotton, feathers, monkeys, parrots and the like. Also that the crew had captured a Portuguese ship in the harbour of Rio de Janeiro, and had given a Portuguese sailor to a king called Ita Wu who had eaten him. I learnt, further, that the Frenchman who saw me when I was captured, and told the savages to eat me, was returning home in this ship. It was this ship's boat which I had tried to reach when I made my escape and the crew refused to take me in. She was, however, lost on the voyage home, for when I reached France in another ship, as I shall relate hereafter, no one could tell me what had become of her.

How Shortly After I Had Been Given Away, Another Ship Arrived from France, the *Catherine of Vattavilla,* Which through God's Providence Was Able to Buy Me, and of the Manner in Which This Fell Out

I remained some fourteen days in the place Tackwara Sutibi with king Abbati Bossange, and one day it happened that certain of the savages came to me and reported that they had heard the sound of shooting, which must have come from the harbour of Iteronne, or Rio de Janeiro. As I was sure that a ship must have arrived there, I told them to carry me to it, for this was doubtless my brother's ship. They agreed to do this, but detained me for a few days more.

In the meantime it happened that the Frenchmen who had arrived there heard that I was a prisoner among the savages, and the captain sent two of his men, together with certain native kings, their friends, to the place where I was, and they came to a hut, the chief king of which was called Sowarasu. My hut was close at hand, and news was brought to me that the two men had arrived from the ship. At this I rejoiced greatly, and went to them and bade them welcome in the native tongue, and when they saw my misery and nakedness they were full of pity and shared their clothes with me. I asked them why they had come and they said that it was on my account, and that their orders were to take me to the ship and to use force if necessary. Then my heart overflowed with gratitude to God, and I told one of the men, who was called Perot and knew the savage tongue, that he must make believe he was my brother, and that he was to say that he had brought me certain chests full of merchandise and must take me with him to the ship to fetch them. He was to tell the savages also that I would then return to collect pepper and other things and wait until the ship came again next year. Then they took me to the ship, my master going with us, where they received me in all pity and showed me great kindness. After we had been some five days in the ship, the king Abbati Bossange, to whom I had been given, asked me for the chests which they had brought me, so that we might now return home. I reported this to the ship's captain who told me to put him off until the ship had taken in the full cargo, in case the savages should become angry when they saw that I was kept in the ship and work some mischief, since they were a people in whom no trust could be placed. My master still thought that he would take me back with him, but I held him with empty words, telling him not to hurry, for he knew that when good friends came together they could not part at once, and that when the ship left we would return to the huts. And so I satisfied him.

At last the ship was ready and the Frenchmen were all mustered together and I with them, the king, my master, with his people, being also there. Then the ship's captain spoke to the savages through his interpreter, and said that he was well pleased that they had not killed me when they captured me from among their enemies. He said also, in order to make it easier for him to take me away, that he had ordered me to be brought to the ship so that he might reward them for their care of me. Further, that it was his intention to give me goods and wares, and as I was known to them, to leave me there to collect pepper and other useful commodities until he came again. Meanwhile we had arranged between us that some ten of the crew, who were not unlike me, should gather round and say that they were my brothers and wanted to take me home. And so it fell out. My brothers would not suffer me to land, saying that I must return with them, as my father longed to see me once more before he died. Upon this the captain told the savages that he was captain in the ship and would have preferred that I should return with them, but that he was only one against many and could do nothing. All this was ordained so that we might part from the savages on friendly terms. I told the king, my master, that I should greatly like to return with him, but that, as he could see, my brothers would not allow me to do so. Thereupon he began to howl and cry in the ship, saying that if they took me away I must return with the first boat, for he looked upon me as his son, and was wrath with those of Uwattibi for threatening to eat me. And one of his wives who was in the ship began to cry over me, according to their custom, and I cried also. Then the captain gave them goods, some five ducats' worth in knives, axes, looking-glasses, and combs, and the savages returned with them to their dwellings.

Thus Almighty God, the God of Abraham, Isaac and Jacob, saved me from the hands of these evil men. To him be praise and glory through Jesus Christ, his Son, our Redeemer. Amen.[14]

---

[14]Staden reached Honfleur, in Normandy, France, on February 20, 1555, and soon after returned to Hesse, where he wrote and published his book.

Saved by the Chief's Daughter

JUAN ORTIZ AND JOHN SMITH

Shortly after Columbus's voyages, the Spanish began to refer to the land north of the Gulf of Mexico as Florida. In the 1520s Hernán Cortés completed the conquest of Mexico, and there was great hope that Florida might contain similar riches to those seized in the attack on Moctezuma at Tenochtitlán. An expedition was organized under the command of Pánfilo de Narváez, who landed with many ships at what is now Tampa Bay. These conquistadors planned to march westward around the gulf to the frontier of New Spain at Panuco, but the distance was far greater than they imagined, and attacks by the natives quickly reduced the army to starvation and dissention. The account of this disastrous expedition was recorded by Alvar Nuñez Cabeza de Vaca, one of only four men who survived, in his concise and dramatic *Naufragios* (literally "castaways" or "shipwrecks," but published in English translations under various titles). Cabeza de Vaca was a captive for a time, and he escaped to other areas where he gained a reputation as a healer far more powerful than anything Hans Staden achieved, but his account is less a captivity narrative than a broader-ranging history of the expedition as a whole.

The story of Juan Ortiz more closely fits the genre of the captivity narrative as it later developed. Ortiz did not write his own text, and his historical importance fades beside that of his commanders and his chronicler, but he played a key role in the ill-fated Spanish exploration of North America in the sixteenth century, and his immersion in native culture was as complete as that of any subsequent captive.

Juan Ortiz must have known Cabeza de Vaca, as they went to Florida together on Narváez's expedition, but Ortiz sailed from Tampa Bay back

to Cuba, where Narváez's expedition had originated from. He returned to
Tampa Bay at the request of Narváez's wife to look for signs of the commander. It was then that he and three others were captured by Native
Americans who had been provoked by the Spaniards' earlier attacks. For
ten years he remained in local villages and might well have joined the unknown ranks of Europeans who assimilated into native America had not
another Spanish expedition stumbled upon him. Hernando de Soto landed
in Florida in 1539 with an army of 600 men, 223 horses, and 700 hogs
(the origin of the wild razorbacks in the southeast). They had riches and
glory in mind but were no more successful at finding wealth or establish-
ing settlements than Narváez had been; they better survived the attacks of
the natives, however. De Soto's men resorted to extremely brutal tactics in
victimizing the Indians, and they left a devastating path of death and destruction across the Southeast. After four years de Soto was dead, and the
surviving stragglers, who numbered only a third of the original army, made
their retreat on rafts down the Mississippi River. That even this many survived was thanks in part to Juan Ortiz. After the selection included in this
chapter, the history tells how Ortiz joined de Soto's troops to serve as
interpreter and how by the time they reached the Chicaça (Chickasaw)
Nation on the Mississippi-Alabama border a chain of ten to twelve interpreters was used to communicate with the local tribes, with Ortiz serving
as the terminal translator to and from the Spanish tongue.

The story of Juan Ortiz's captivity appeared in several accounts of the
de Soto expedition. The first of these, "The True Relation of the Gentleman
of Elvas" by another member of de Soto's army, was published in 1557.
But the version reprinted here is from *La Florida* by the Inca Garcilaso de
la Vega, one of the most fascinating figures in colonial American literature.
Garcilaso was born Gómez Suárez de Figueroa in Cuzco, the Inca capital,
in 1539. His mother, Isabel Chimpu Occllo, was the granddaughter of the
emperor Tupac Inca Yupanqui, and his father, Garcilaso de la Vega, was
a Spanish nobleman who had participated in the conquest of Peru a few
years before.[1] Because this crossblood union was not recognized, when his
father soon after married a Spanish woman, he was considered illegiti-
mate, though of noble blood through both his parents. The young man
traveled to Spain in 1563, but was rebuffed in his efforts to claim his father's legacy. He adopted his father's name nonetheless, then turned to a

---

[1] Because "Garcilaso de la Vega" is also the name of another Spanish writer of the
Renaissance, this one is generally called "the Inca Garcilaso." The Spanish title of the
book from which Juan Ortiz's story is taken was *La Florida del Inca*, "The Florida of
the Inca."

career in letters, writing under the name of "the Inca Garcilaso de la Vega." The younger de la Vega sought to elevate the reputation of his mother's people to the level of courtly culture and historical grandeur for which Golden Age Spain prized itself. His masterpiece, *Royal Commentaries of the Inca and General History of Peru*, recounts the rise of the Inca Empire, portraying it as a worthy counterpart to the Spanish Empire and its religion as similar to Christianity. Similarly, in *La Florida*, which was first published in 1605 but completed at least ten years earlier, the Inca Garcilaso represents the American Indian victims of de Soto more favorably than did other accounts.

Although the Inca Garcilaso had never been to North America, when writing *La Florida* he worked with a survivor of the expedition, Gonzalo Silvestre, and from many documentary sources. According to the customs of history writing at the time, he also composed eloquent speeches for Indian chiefs, which often criticize the Spaniards' brutality and lack of honor. Writing in an age when the values of the chivalric romances satirized in *Don Quixote* still carried immense weight, the Inca Garcilaso imbued the senseless violence of the de Soto expedition with some of the dignity of knight errantry. The influence of this literary tradition can be seen in the quest given to Ortiz to kill the lion and the devotion from Hirrihigua's daughter that his success earns him.

Compare the chivalric gratitude of Ortiz, throwing himself at his savior's feet, with John Smith's less gracious treatment of Pocahontas in the next selection. Smith's rugged practicality and the prosaic style of his writing are a world apart from the elegance and courtly pretensions of the Inca Garcilaso even though the plot of the rescues is much the same.

The son of a yeoman farmer from Lincolnshire, England, John Smith became a soldier at age sixteen and fought in several wars in Europe, including battles against the Ottoman Turks. His nonaristocratic origins and his military prowess provide the essence of the image he presented in his writings. When he sailed for Virginia in 1607, he was just one of seven "councillors" charged with guiding the interests of the Virginia Company investors who had financed the expedition. The following year, he was elected president of the settlement at Jamestown and attempted to impose a regimen of labor upon the gentlemen who formed the majority of the colonists. In his own and in many historians' accounts, he appears as a practical man of action who singlehandedly supported the struggling English outpost. He returned to England in 1609 after sustaining a severe injury in a gunpowder explosion. He made a later voyage to New England and wrote a short book, *A Description of New England*, which promoted that region as a land of opportunity for English colonists. Right up until his death in 1631, Smith hoped to be called upon to lead another expedition to America and put his ideas into practice, but the opportunity never materialized.

During this short stay in Virginia, Smith explored much of the Chesapeake Bay region and skirmished several times with American Indians of a confederacy united under Powhatan, a powerful leader who controlled most of what is now eastern Virginia. Smith's captivity took place in December 1607 and January 1608 as he and a small party of Englishmen were exploring the Pamunkey River, north of Jamestown. His narrative was published in 1624 in his own *The Generall Historie of Virginia, New England, and the Summer Isles.* In the selection in this chapter Smith refers to himself in the third person, as he does elsewhere in the *Historie.* The end of the chapter shows four men as authors, one of whom is J. S.—Smith himself. It is unlikely that these coauthors really wrote the parts attributed to them—Smith seems to have used this technique as a means of corroborating his heroic exploits through the words of others.

This brief captivity episode is the origin of one of the most powerful and enduring legends in United States history: the story of Pocahontas rescuing Smith from execution by her father, Powhatan. The legend has been elaborated and embellished many times, from John Davis's romantic version of 1803 to the Disney movies of the 1990s, and these retellings have raised both Smith and Pocahontas to a quasi-mythical status in the national imagination. Several nineteenth-century novels, such as *Hope Leslie,* and a few captivity accounts, such as those by Jonas Groves and Josiah Mooso, have followed the pattern of a young Indian maiden saving the life of a male captive.

The veracity of the story of Pocahontas's rescue of Smith has long been disputed among historians. The primary reason is that in Smith's two earlier published accounts of his Virginia exploits, *A True Relation of Such Occurrences and Accidents of Noate as Hath Hapned in Virginia . . . ,* dispatched from the colony and published in 1608, and *A Map of Virginia,* published in 1612, the narrative of his capture by Powhatan makes no mention of Pocahontas. Skeptics suggest that by including the rescue scene in the 1624 version, Smith was seeking to capitalize on popular fascination with Pocahontas following her visit to England with her husband, colonist John Rolfe, and her death there in 1618. Other evidence that Smith may have fabricated the story includes a parallel to his experience in Turkey, where he had been captured and enslaved by the enemy then spared through the intervention of a Lady Tragabigzanda. Finally, as the readings in this chapter show, the Pocahontas rescue legend resembles the narrative of Juan Ortiz, a version of which had been published in English by Richard Hukluyt in *Virginia Richly Valued* (1609).

On the other hand, many historians have pointed out that the mock execution may have been part of an initiation rite designed to incorporate Smith into the tribal kinship system, with Pocahontas becoming his sister or daughter. After all, the natives' initial reception of their captive—listening to his discourse about the compass and the earth's antipodes, which Smith must have delivered in English, and offering him enough venison for "twentie men"—suggests a respectful welcome, not a prelude to execution. Considered in this ethnohistorical context, Smith's narrative may be as credible as the Ortiz story. Elements of European heroic romances and aspects of Native American customs appear in both accounts. The interest lies not in accepting or rejecting the facts of these events but in examining the ways in which European ideas of love, gender roles, loyalty, and heroism affected both the confrontation with Native Americans and the nascent captivity genre that grew out of these encounters.

Sources

Smith, John. *Generall Historie of Virginia*. Ed. Philip Barbour. *The Complete Works of Captain John Smith (1580–1631)*. 3 vols. Chapel Hill: Inst. for Early American History and Culture/U of North Carolina P, 1986. 2:146–153. [Barbour's definitive edition includes a wealth of useful annotations.]

Vega, Garcilaso de la. *La Florida*. Trans. Charmion Shelby. *The DeSoto Chronicles: The Expedition of Hernando de Soto to North America, 1539–1543*. Ed. Lawrence A. Clayton, Vernon James Knight, Jr., and Edward C. Moore. Vol. 2. Tuscaloosa: U of Alabama P, 1993. 99–118.

Supplementary Readings

"Account by a Gentleman from Elvas." 1557. *The De Soto Chronicles*. Vol. 1.

Barbour, Philip. *The Three Worlds of Captain John Smith*. Boston: Lippincott, 1964.

Brading, David A. *The First America: The Spanish Monarchy, Creole Patriots, and the Liberal State, 1492–1867*. Cambridge: Cambridge UP, 1991: 255–72.

Cabeza de Vaca, Alvar Nuñez. *Castaways*. 1542. Trans. Frances M. López-Morillas. Berkeley: U of California P, 1993.

Cervantes, Miguel de. *Don Quixote*. 1605, 1615. Trans. J. M. Cohen. Harmondsworth, UK: Penguin, 1950.

Crowley, Frances G. "Biographical Introduction to *La Florida.*" Ed. Lawrence A. Clayton, Vernon James Knight, Jr., and Edward C. Moore. *The De Soto Chronicles:* 2:1–24.

Davis, John. *Travels of Four Years and a Half in the United States of America in 1798, 1799, 1800, 1801, and 1802.* London: 1803.

Fieldler, Leslie. *The Return of the Vanishing American.* New York: Stein, 1968.

Fritz, Jean. *The Double Life of Pocahontas.* New York: Putnam, 1983.

Groves, Jonas. "A Tale of Other Times . . ." *Western Herald and Steubenville Gazette* 13:33–34 (1820). Vol. 37. *Garland Library of Narratives of North American Indian Captivities.* New York: Garland, 1977.

Hakluyt, Richard. *Virginia Richly Valued.* London: 1609.

Lemay, J. A. Leo. *Did Pocahontas Save Captain John Smith?* Athens: U of Georgia P, 1992.

Mooso, Josiah. *The Life and Travels of Josiah Mooso.* Winfield: 1888. Vol. 97. *Garland Library of Narratives of North American Indian Captivities.* New York: Garland, 1977.

Sedgwick, Catherine Maria. *Hope Leslie, or, Early Times in the Massachusetts.* New York: 1827.

Vega, Garcilaso de la. *La Florida del Inca: Historia del adelantado Hernando de Soto, gobernador y capitan general del reino de la Florida, y de otros heroicos caballeros espanoles e indios.* 1605. Mexico City: Fondo de Cultura Economica, 1956.

———. *Royal Commentaries of the Incas.* 1609. Trans. Harold V. Livermore. Austin: U of Texas P, 1966.

Young, Philip. "The Mother of us All: Pocahontas Reconsidered." *Kenyon Review* 94(1962): 391–415.

FROM *LA FLORIDA*

Garcilaso de la Vega
[The Inca]

The Governor Arrives in La Florida, and Finds Traces of Pánphilo de Narváez

The governor Hernando de Soto, who as we said was sailing toward La Florida, sighted its shores on the last day of May, having spent nineteen days at sea because of encountering unfavorable weather. The vessels anchored in a deep and good bay, which they named El Espíritu Santo, and because it was late, no one disembarked that day. On the first of June the small boats went to the shore and returned laden with grass for the horses, and they brought also many green grapes from the vines they found growing wild in the woods. The Indians of all this great kingdom of La Florida do not cultivate this plant or regard it as highly as do other nations, though they eat its fruit when it is well ripened or made into raisins. Our people were much pleased with these good specimens they brought from the land, for they were similar to the grapes of Spain, and they had not found them in the lands of México nor in the whole of El Perú. On the second day of June the governor ordered that three hundred infantry go ashore for the act and ceremony of taking possession of the land for the Emperor Charles V, king of Spain. Following the ceremony, the men marched all day along the coast without seeing a single Indian, and they remained that night and slept on land. Toward dawn the Indians fell upon them with such impetuosity and boldness that they retreated to the water's edge, and as they sounded the alarm both infantry and cavalry came out from the ships to their assistance as rapidly as if they had been on land.

The lieutenant general Vasco de Porcallo was in command of the relief party, and he found the infantry who were on the shore as confused and perturbed as raw recruits, getting in one another's way in fighting, and some of them already wounded with arrows. Having brought up the relief and followed the enemy for some distance, they returned to their quarters and had scarcely reached them when the lieutenant general's horse fell dead from an arrow wound near the saddle, which they gave him during the skirmish; the arrow passed through the trappings, saddletree and pads, and penetrated the ribs more than a third, up to the notch. Vasco Porcallo was much gratified that the first horse employed in the conquest and the first lance thrown against the enemy should have been his.

On this day and the next they continued to disembark the horses, and all the people went ashore. Having rested for eight or nine days and left orders with regard to the ships, they marched inland a little more than two leagues to the pueblo of a cacique named Hirrihigua, with whom Pánphilo de Narváez had fought when he went to conquer that province. Although afterward the Indian had been induced to become a friend, during that time, it is not known for what reason, Pánphilo de Narváez, angered, had committed certain offenses against him, which as they are so detestable are not recounted.

Because of these injustices and offenses the cacique Hirrihigua was left with such fear and hatred of the Spaniards that when he learned of the coming of Hernando de Soto to his country he went to the forest, abandoning his house and pueblo, and despite the friendly messages, gifts and promises the governor sent him by his Indian subjects whom he seized, he was never willing to come back peaceably nor to hear any of the messages he sent him. On the other hand he was incensed against those who brought them, saying that since they knew how offended and aggrieved he was with that nation they should have known better than to bring him their messages; that if it were their heads, he would receive them with pleasure, but their words and names he had no desire to hear. All this and more can infamy bring about, especially if it was done without blame on the part of the injured. So that the extent of this Indian's fury against the Spaniards may be better seen, it is fitting to tell here some of the cruelties and martyrdoms he imposed upon four Spaniards who must have been of Pánphilo de Narváez's party, which though it will prolong our *History* somewhat is not beside the point, but rather will be very useful for it.

Some days, then, after Pánphilo de Narváez left the country of this cacique, having done what we have told, there came to that bay one of his ships that had remained behind, in search of him. Inasmuch as the cacique suspected that it was one of Narváez's ships and that it was searching for him, he wished to capture all who were in it and burn them alive. In order to secure them, he feigned friendship for Pánphilo de Narváez and sent word to them saying that their captain had been there and had left orders as to what that ship was to do if it should make that port; and to persuade them to believe him, he showed from land two or three sheets of white paper and some old letters he had obtained from past friendship with the Spaniards or in some other manner, and had kept carefully.

In spite of all this, those on the ship were cautious and did not wish to go ashore. Then the cacique sent four of his principal Indians to the ship in a canoe, saying that since they did not trust him he was sending those four men, nobles and *caballeros* (this term *caballero* does not seem applicable to the Indians, because they had no horses, from which word the name is derived, but since in Spain they are regarded as nobles, and since among the Indians there are nobles of highest rank, they may also be called so), as hostages and security so that the Spaniards who desired word of their captain Pánphilo de Narváez might leave the ship, and if they still were not reassured, he offered to send them further pledges. Seeing this, four Spaniards came out and entered the canoe with the Indians who had brought the hostages. The cacique, who desired all of them, seeing that only four were coming, did not insist further upon asking for more Castilians, in order that these few who were going to him might not be alarmed and return to the ship.

As soon as the Spaniards set foot on the shore, the four Indians who had remained in the ship as hostages, seeing that the Christians were now in the power of their people, threw themselves into the water, and, diving deeply and swimming like fish, they went ashore, thus carrying out the order that their chief had given them. Those on the ship, seeing themselves victims of a hoax, left the bay before something worse should befall them, very sad at having lost their companions through such an indiscretion.

Concerning the Tortures that a Cacique Inflicted upon a Spaniard, His Slave

The cacique Hirrihigua ordered the four Spaniards to be guarded securely so that on the occasion of their deaths he might hold a solemn festival, which according to his heathen custom he expected to celebrate within a few days. When the time came he ordered them to be brought forth naked to the plaza and to be shot with arrows one at a time like wild beasts, running them from one side to the other; and that too many arrows were not to be shot at the same time, in order that they should die more slowly, and their torment be greater, and the Indians' celebration and enjoyment longer and more festive. Thus they dealt with three of the Spaniards, the cacique deriving great satisfaction and pleasure from seeing them run in all directions, seeking help and nowhere finding succor, but only death. When they wished to bring out the fourth, who was a youth scarcely eighteen years of age, a native of Sevilla named Juan Ortiz, the cacique's wife came out accompanied by her three young daughters. Facing her husband, she said to him that she begged him to be content with the three Spaniards killed and pardon that youth, because neither he nor his companions had been to blame for the evil their predecessors had done, for they had not come with Pánphilo de Narváez; and that the boy especially deserved to be pardoned, for his youth absolved him of blame and called for mercy; and that it would be enough for him to remain as a slave and not be killed so cruelly without his having committed any crime.

In order to satisfy his wife and daughters, the cacique granted Juan Ortiz his life for the time, though afterward it was so sad and bitter that often he envied his three dead companions, because the continuous and unceasing labor of carrying wood and water was so great and his food and sleep so scanty, the daily cuffings, buffetings and lashes so cruel, besides the other torments that they inflicted upon him at the time of their special festivals, that often, if he had not been a Christian, he would have taken death by his own hands as a remedy. Thus it was that, aside from the daily torment, for his own pastime the cacique ordered on many festival days that Juan Ortiz run all day without stopping (from dawn to dark) in a large plaza that was in the pueblo, where they had shot his companions to death with arrows. The cacique himself would come out to see him run, and with him would come his nobles armed with their bows and arrows in order to shoot him if he ceased running. Juan Ortiz would begin his race at sunrise and would not pause on one side or the other of the plaza until sunset, which was the time that they set for him. And when the cacique would go to eat he would leave his nobles to watch him, so that, if he should cease running, they might kill him. At the end of the day he was left in the sad state that may be imagined, stretched on the ground, more dead than alive. The pity of the wife and daughters of the cacique succored him on these days, because they took him immediately, clothed him, and did him other kindnesses whereby they saved his life. It would have been better to take it away, in order to free him from those excessive hardships. Seeing that so many and such continuous tortures were not sufficient to kill Juan Ortiz, and the hatred that he bore him increasing hourly, the cacique, in order to put an end to him, commanded on one of his feast days that a great fire be built in the middle of the plaza, and when he saw a large bed of coals formed, he ordered it tended and a wooden framework[1] be placed over it in the form of a gridiron, one vara[2] above the ground, and they put Juan Ortiz upon it in order to roast him alive.

---

[1] The Spanish word in the original version is *barbacoa,* adopted from the Taino language of native Hispaniola and the source of the English "barbecue."
[2] A Spanish unit of measure, slightly less than a yard.

This was done, and here the poor Spaniard remained for some time stretched on one side, fastened to the frame. At the cries that the poor unfortunate gave in the midst of the fire, the wife and daughters of the cacique came, and begging the husband and even reproaching his cruelty, they took him from the fire, already half roasted, having blisters on that side as large as half-oranges, some of them broken and bleeding freely, so that it was pitiful to see him. The cacique allowed it because they were women for whom he cared so much, and perhaps he did it also in order to have someone upon whom to visit his wrath in the future and to show his desire for vengeance, because he would have someone to excite it, and though very little in proportion to his desires, still he could amuse himself with that little. Thus he said many times that he regretted having killed the three Spaniards so quickly. The women carried Juan Ortiz to their house, and moved by pity at seeing him in that state, they treated him with juices of herbs (the Indians, both men and women, since they have no physicians, are great herbalists). Time and again they repented having saved him from death on the first occasion, because of seeing how slowly and with what cruel tortures they were killing him day by day. After many days Juan Ortiz was cured, though large scars from the burns still remained.

In order not to see him thus, and to free himself from the bother that his wife and daughters gave him with their entreaties, and so that he might not become lazy, the cacique directed that he be exercised in another punishment, less severe than the past ones. This was that he guard day and night the dead bodies of the inhabitants of that pueblo, which were deposited in the country in a forest at a distance from the settlements, at a place set apart for them. They were placed above ground in wooden chests that served as sepulchers, without hinges or any other security for the cover than some boards placed over them, with stones or timbers on top. Because of the poor protection these chests afforded for the bodies of the dead, they were carried away by the lions,[3] of which there are many in that country, much to the grief and anger of the Indians. The cacique ordered Juan Ortiz to guard this place carefully so that the lions should not carry off any body or part of it, protesting and vowing that, if they did so, he would infallibly be roasted to death. For guarding them he gave him four darts to throw at the lions or at other wild beasts that might approach the chests. Juan Ortiz, giving thanks to God for having rid him of the continued presence of the cacique Hirrihigua, his master, went to guard the dead,

---

[3] This animal must have been a Florida panther, a regional subspecies of the cougar of the western United States.

hoping to have a better life with them than with the living. He guarded them with all care, chiefly at night, because then there was greater danger. It happened that, on one of the nights when he was thus watching, he fell asleep toward dawn, unable to resist his drowsiness, for at this hour it usually attacks most strongly those who are watching. Just at this time a lion came and, knocking off the covers of one of the chests, dragged out the body of a child, which had been thrown into it two days before, and carried it off. Juan Ortiz heard the noise that the covers made in falling, and as he hurried to the chest and failed to find the child's body therein, he considered himself lost; but with all his anxiety and dismay he did not cease hunting for the lion, so that, if he should find him, he might recover the body or die in the attempt. On the other hand he trusted to our Lord to give him strength to die on the following day, confessing and calling upon His name, for he knew that as soon as daylight came the Indians must visit the chests, and not finding the child's body, they would burn him alive. Walking through the forest from one side to another, in fear of death, he came to a wide path that passed through the center of it, and following it for a time with the intention of fleeing, though it was impossible to escape, he heard in the woods not far from where he was walking a noise as of a dog that is gnawing bones. Listening carefully, he made sure of it, and suspecting that it might be the lion that was eating the child, he felt his way very carefully through the underbrush, approaching the place where he heard the noise. By the light of the moon, which was shining, though not very brightly, he saw near him the lion, which was eating the child at its pleasure. Calling upon God and taking courage, Juan Ortiz threw a dart at it, and though he could not then see the shot that he had made, because of the underbrush, yet he felt that it had not been bad because his hand was left "salty," as the hunters say when they feel that they have made a good shot against wild beasts at night. With this very slender hope, and also because he had not heard the lion leave the place where he had shot at him, he waited for morning, commending himself to our Lord, that he might succor him in that necessity.

The Hard Life of the Captive Christian Continues, and How He Fled from His Master

With the light of day Juan Ortiz verified the good shot that he had made by guess that night, for he saw the lion dead, the entrails and the center of the heart transfixed (as was found later when they opened it), a thing that he himself, though he saw it, could not believe. With a satisfaction and joy that may be better imagined than told, he dragged it by one foot, not pulling out the dart, so that his master might see it just as he had found it, having first gathered up and taken back to the chest the fragments of the child's body that he found uneaten. The cacique and all those in his pueblo wondered greatly at this deed, for in that land it is held generally to be a miraculous thing for a man to kill a lion, and thus they treat him who succeeds in killing one with great veneration and respect. And because this is such a fierce animal, he who kills it ought to be esteemed everywhere, especially if he does so without a shot from a crossbow or harquebus, as Juan Ortiz did. Although it is true that the lions of La Florida, México, and El Perú are not so large or so fierce as those of Africa, still they are lions, and the name is enough; and even if the popular proverb may say that they are not as fierce as they are painted, those who have been near them say that they are as much fiercer than their descriptions, as there is difference between the real and the imagined.

With this good fortune on the part of Juan Ortiz, the wife and daughters of the cacique took more spirit and courage to intercede for him, that he might be pardoned entirely and made use of in honorable employments worthy of his strength and valor. For a few days thereafter Hirrihigua treated his slave better, both in the esteem and favor he accorded him in his pueblo and house, and in referring to the heroic deed that they in their vain religion so esteem and honor that they regard it as sacred and more than human. However (and this was the injury that he could not pardon), every time he remembered that they had thrown his mother to the dogs and left her to be eaten by them, and when he went to blow his nose and could not find his nostrils, the devil possessed him to avenge himself on Juan Ortiz, as if he had cut them off; and inasmuch as he always carried the offense before his eyes, with the memory of it his ire, rancor, and desire to take revenge increased from day to day. Though he restrained these passions for some time, being able to resist them no longer, he said one day to his wife and daughters that it was impossible for him to allow that Christian to remain alive because his life was very odious and abominable to him; that every time he saw him past injuries were revived and he was offended anew. Therefore he commanded them that they were in no manner to intercede for him further unless they desired to participate in the same rage and anger, and that in order to finish finally with that Spaniard he had determined that on a certain feast day (which was soon to be celebrated) he was to be shot to death with arrows as his companions had been, notwithstanding his bravery, for as an enemy he should be rather abhorred than esteemed. The wife and daughters of the cacique, because they saw him enraged and understood that no intercession would be effective, and also because it seemed to them that it was too much to importune and so displease the master for the sake of the slave, did not

dare say a word in opposition to him. Rather with feminine astuteness they
came to tell him that this would be a good thing to do because it was his
pleasure. But the eldest of the daughters, in order to further her plan and
make it succeed, a few days before the celebration secretly notified Juan
Ortiz of her father's determination against him, and that neither she nor
her sisters nor her mother would avail or could do anything with the father, he having imposed silence upon them and threatened them if they
should break it.

Desiring to encourage the Spaniard, she added to this sad notice others contrary to it and said to him: "So that you may not distrust me, nor
despair of your life, nor fear that I will not do all that I can to save it, if
you are a man and have courage to flee, I will favor and help you so that
you may escape and reach safety. Tonight at a certain hour and in a certain place you will find an Indian to whom I entrust your safety and my
own. He will guide you to a bridge that is two leagues from here; upon
reaching it, you will order him not to pass beyond but to return to the
pueblo before dawn so that they may not miss him, and my own daring
and his may not become known, so that evil may not befall him and me
for having done you a good turn. Six leagues beyond the bridge is a pueblo
whose lord wishes me well and desires to marry me; his name is Mucoço.
Tell him on my behalf that I send you to him so that he may succor and
favor you, as he ought to do. I know that he will do all he can for you, as
you will see. Commend yourself to your God, for I can do no more for
you." Juan Ortiz threw himself at her feet in acknowledgment of the
mercy and favor that she was conferring and had always conferred upon
him, and he at once made ready to travel on the following night. At the
hour appointed, after the members of the cacique's household were asleep,
he set out in search of the promised guide and left the pueblo with him
without anyone hearing them. Upon reaching the bridge, he told the Indian to return at once very cautiously to his house, having first learned
from him that there was no chance of his losing the road as far as the
pueblo of Mucoço.

Of the Magnanimity of the Curaca
or Cacique Mucoço, to Whom the Captive
Commended Himself

Juan Ortiz, as a man who was fleeing, reached the place before dawn but,
for fear of causing a disturbance, did not dare enter it. When it was day he
saw two Indians come out from the pueblo along the same road that he

was taking. They attempted to shoot him with their bows and arrows, as they always go armed with these weapons. Juan Ortiz, who also had them, put an arrow in his bow to defend himself from them and also to attack them. How potent is a little favor, especially if it be from a lady! For we see that shortly before he did not know where to hide himself, being in fear of death; now he dared give it to others with his own hand, simply because of having been favored by a pretty, discreet and generous girl, whose favor exceeds all other human gifts. With which, having recovered spirit and strength and even pride, he told them that he was not an enemy but that he was coming with a message from a lady for the lord of that place.

Hearing this, the Indians did not shoot him but returned with him to the pueblo and notified the cacique that the slave of Hirrihigua was there with a message for him. Mucoço or Mococo—for it is the same—informed of this, went out to the plaza to receive the message Juan Ortiz was bringing to him. After having saluted him as best he could after the manner of the Indians themselves, Juan Ortiz told him briefly of the martyrdom his master had imposed upon him, as evidence of which he showed on his body the scars of the burns, blows and wounds they had given him, and how now finally his lord was determined to kill him in order to celebrate and solemnize with his death such-and-such a feast day, which he expected to hold soon. He told how the wife and daughters of the cacique, his master, though they had often saved his life, did not now dare to speak in his favor because of the lord's having forbidden it under penalty of his anger; and how the eldest daughter of his lord, desiring that he should not die, as the last and best remedy had ordered and encouraged him to flee and, giving him a guide, had set him on his way to his pueblo and house. In her name he presented himself before him, whom he supplicated by the love that he had for her to receive him under his protection, and as a thing commended by her to favor him, as he ought to do. Mucoço received him affably and heard him with pity at learning of the abuses and torments that he had experienced, which were plainly shown by the scars on his body, for, dressed after the manner of the Indians of the country, he wore only some trousers.

Alonso de Carmona tells at this point, in addition to what we have said, that he embraced him and kissed him on the face as a sign of peace.

He replied that he was welcome and told him to try to forget the fears of his past life; that in his company and house he would have a very different and opposite existence; that for the sake of serving the person who had sent him, and for him who had come to his person and house for succor, he would do all he could, as he would see by future actions; and that he might be certain that while he lived no one would be allowed to molest him.

All that this good cacique said in favor of Juan Ortiz he performed, and indeed much more than he promised, for he immediately made him his steward and kept him constantly with him, day and night, doing him much honor, more particularly after he learned that he had killed the lion with the dart. In short, he treated him like a well-beloved brother (for there are brothers who love one another like water and fire), and although Hirrihigua, suspecting that he had gone to Mocoço for protection, asked for him many times, Mucoço always made an excuse for not giving him up, saying finally, among other things, that since he had come to his house to let him be, and that he was so odious that he had lost very little in losing such a slave. He made the same reply to another cacique, his brother-in-law, named Urribarracuxi, through whom Hirrihigua made the request. Seeing that his messages were of no effect, he went personally to ask him, and in his presence Mocoço replied the same as in his absence, adding other angry words, and told him that since he was his brother-in-law it was unjust to order him to do a thing against his reputation and honor; that he would not be doing his duty if he should turn over to his own enemy an unfortunate who had come to him for refuge, so that the Hirrihigua might sacrifice and kill him like a wild beast for his own entertainment and pastime.

Mocoço defended Juan Ortiz from these two caciques, who asked for him so urgently and insistently, with such generosity that he was willing to forgo (as he did) the marriage he affectionately desired to make with the daughter of Hirrihigua, and the relationship and friendship of the father-in-law, rather than return the slave to him who asked for him in order to kill him. He kept the latter constantly with him, much esteemed and well treated, until Governor Hernando de Soto entered La Florida.

Juan Ortiz was among those Indians for ten years, one and a half in the power of Hirrihigua and the rest with the good Mocoço. Though a barbarian, he dealt with this Christian in quite another manner than those most famous men of the Triumvirate who at Layno, a place near Bologna, made that never sufficiently condemned proscription and agreement to give and exchange their relatives, friends, and defenders for enemies and adversaries. And he did much better than other Christian princes who later have committed here other acts as abominable and worse than that one, considering the innocence of those given up, the rank of some of them, and the faith that their betrayers should have had and kept with them; considering also that the former were heathen and the latter prided themselves on the Christian name and religion. These latter, breaking the laws and statutes of their kingdoms and not respecting their own position and rank, they being kings and great princes, and disregarding their sworn and promised word (a thing unworthy of such names), simply for the purpose of avenging their own anger, delivered up those who had not offended them in order to obtain the offenders, exchanging the innocent for the guilty, as both ancient and modern historians will testify. But we shall leave them, so as not to offend powerful ears and distress the pious.

It suffices to describe the magnanimity of a heathen so that faithful princes may be forced to imitate and excel him if they can, not in his heathenism, as do some who are unworthy of that name, but in virtue and similar noble qualities, to which they are more obligated because of their higher estate. Certainly, considering well the circumstances of the courageous action of this Indian, and seeing by whom and against whom it was performed, and the amount that he was willing to put aside and lose, going even against his own affection and desires in refusing the succor and favor demanded and promised by him, it will be seen that it arose from a most generous and heroic mind, which did not deserve to have been born and to live amidst the barbarous heathendom of that country. But God and human nature often produce such spirits in such uncultivated and sterile deserts for the greater humiliation and shame of those who are born and reared in lands that are fertile and abound in all good doctrine, sciences, and the Christian religion.

The Governor Sends for Juan Ortiz

The governor heard this account, which we have given, of the life of Juan Ortiz, although in a confused form, in the pueblo of the cacique Hirrihigua, where we have left him at present; and he had heard it before, more briefly, in La Havana from one of the four Indians whom we said that the accountant, Juan de Añasco, had seized when he was sent to explore the coast of La Florida, and who happened to be a subject of this cacique.[4] When this Indian mentioned Juan Ortiz in the account that he gave in La Havana, leaving off the name Juan, because he did not know it, he said Ortiz, and as to the poor speech of the Indian was added the worse understanding of the good interpreters who stated what he was trying to say, and as all the listeners had for their chief purpose going to seek gold, on hearing the Indian say "Orotiz," without waiting for further statements on his part they thought that he was plainly saying that in his country there was much gold,[5] and they congratulated themselves and

---

[4] In the first book of *La Florida,* the Inca Garcilaso had told how Añasco was sent on two reconnaissance missions to explore the west coast of Florida and find the best ports. He had captured two Indians on each of the two trips.

[5] The Spanish word for gold is *oro.*

rejoiced merely at hearing it mentioned, although with such a different significance and sense.

But when the governor ascertained that Juan Ortiz was in the power of the cacique Mucoço, he thought it would be well to send for him, alike in order to deliver him from the power of the Indians and because he was in need of a speaker and interpreter upon whom he could depend. He therefore chose a gentleman from Sevilla named Baltasar de Gallegos, who was serving as *alguacil mayor* of the fleet and the army—who because of his great virtue, strength and valor deserved to be general of a greater army than that one—and told him to take sixty lancers with him and go to Mucoço, and tell him on his behalf how gratified were he and all the Spaniards who accompanied him by the honor and favors he had shown to Juan Ortiz, and how much he desired that he might have an opportunity of requiting them. At present he begged that he give him to him, for he needed him for very important matters, and he asked when it would be convenient for him to make him a visit, as it would give him great pleasure to know and have him for a friend. In accordance with the orders given him, Baltasar de Gallegos left the camp with the sixty lancers and an Indian guide.

The cacique Mucoço, on the other hand, having learned of the coming of the governor Hernando de Soto with such a force of men and horses, and that he had landed so near his own country, and fearing that he might do him some harm there, desired very prudently and advisedly to avert the evil that might come to him. In order to do so, he summoned Juan Ortiz and said to him: "You must know, brother, that in the pueblo of your good friend Hirrihigua there is a Spanish captain with a thousand fighting men and many horses, who are coming to conquer this country. You well know what I have done for you, and how in order to save your life and not deliver you to him who held you as a slave and desired to kill you, I chose rather to fall into disgrace with all my relatives and neighbors than to do what they asked me against you. Now a time and occasion has come in which you can repay me for the good reception, entertainment and friendship I have accorded you, though I never did it with the expectation of any reward, but since events have happened thus it will be wise not to lose what is offered us.

"Go to the Spanish general and on your behalf and my own beg him that, in return for the service that I have done him and his whole nation through you (since I would do the same for any of them), he be pleased not to do me harm in this small land that I have, and that he deign to receive me into his friendship and service; that from this time forth I offer him my person, house and estate to be placed under his guardianship and protection; and so that you may be escorted as becomes both you and me, I send with you fifty nobles of my household, and you will protect them and me as our friendship obligates you to do."

Juan Ortiz, rejoicing at the good news and inwardly giving thanks to God for it, replied to Mucoço that he was much pleased that a time and occasion had arisen in which to repay the kindness and benefits that he had done him, not only in saving his life, but also in the many favors, and the esteem and honor he had received from his great virtue and courtesy. He would give a very full account and report of all this to the Spanish captain and all his people, so that he might concede to and reward him with that which he asked of them now in his name, and in what might come up in the future. He was very confident that the general on his part would do what he asked, for the Spanish nation prided itself upon being a people grateful for favors received, and thus certainly he could confidently hope to obtain that which he sent to ask of the governor. The fifty Indians whom the cacique had ordered to prepare came at once, and with Juan Ortiz they took the public road that goes from one pueblo to the other; and they set out on the same day that Baltasar de Gallegos left the camp to find him.

It happened that, after the Spaniards had marched more than three leagues along the wide and straight highway that went to the pueblo of Mucoço, the Indian who guided them, thinking that it was not a good thing to behave so loyally toward people who were going to subjugate them and take away their lands and freedom, and who long before had shown themselves to be declared enemies—though up to the present they had not received injuries of which they could complain from that army—changed his plan in guiding them and took the first footpath he saw that led into the highway. After following it a short distance, he left it, as it was not straight, and thus he led them most of the day without a road and lost, drawing them always in an arc toward the seacoast with the design of coming upon some swamp, creek, or bay in which to drown them, if possible. The Castilians did not discover the deception of the Indian, since they were not acquainted with the country, until one of them saw, through the trees of an open forest through which they were marching, the topsails of the ships they had left and saw that they were very near the coast, of which fact he advised Captain Baltasar de Gallegos. The latter, seeing the guide's iniquity, threatened him with death, making a gesture of throwing a lance at him. Fearing that they would kill him, the Indian indicated with signs and such words as he could that they should return to the highway, but that it was necessary to retrace all their route that lay off the road, and thus they returned by the same way to seek it.

What Happened between Juan Ortiz and the
Spaniards Who Were Coming for Him

Proceeding along the highway, Juan Ortiz came to the footpath by which
the Indian led Baltasar de Gallegos and his Castilians off the road. Suspecting what had happened and fearing that the Castilians would go by
another route and inflict some damage on the pueblo of Mucoço, he consulted with the Indians as to what they should do. They all agreed that it
would be well to follow the trail of the horses as rapidly as possible until
overtaking them, and that they would not take another road for fear of
missing them.

Since the Indians followed the trail of the Spaniards, and the latter
were returning by the same route that they had gone, they sighted one another on a large plain on a part of which was a dense growth of thick underbrush. The Indians, seeing the Castilians, said to Juan Ortiz that it
would be prudent to safeguard their persons and lives by entering that
thicket until the Christians should recognize them as friends, so that they
should not fall upon them in the open field, believing them to be enemies.
Juan Ortiz was unwilling to accept the good advice of the Indians, confid-
ing in the fact that he was a Spaniard and that his people must recognize
him as soon as they should see him, as if he were dressed in the Spanish
fashion or were in any way different from the Indians, so that he might be
known as a Spaniard. He, like the rest, wore only some trousers for clothing, carried a bow and arrows in his hands, and wore a plume half a
fathom high upon his head for display and ornament.

The Castilians—being inexperienced and anxious to fight—on seeing
the Indians, fell upon them violently, and as much as their captain shouted
at them he could not stop them. Who can stop undisciplined troops when
they get out of hand?

When they saw how boldly and recklessly the Castilians were coming
at them, all the Indians threw themselves into the thicket, there remaining
in the field only Juan Ortiz and an Indian who was not so quick as the others in placing himself in safety. He was wounded by a Spaniard from
Sevilla who had been a soldier in Italy, named Francisco de Morales, by a
lance-thrust in the loins, he overtaking him at the edge of the woods. Juan
Ortiz was assailed by another Spaniard, named Alvaro Nieto, a native of
the villa of Albuquerque, one of the stoutest and strongest Spaniards in the
whole army, who, engaging Juan Ortiz, vigorously thrust a lance at him.
Juan Ortiz had good luck and dexterity, so that, warding off the lance with
his bow and jumping sideways, he avoided at the same time the blow of

the lance and an encounter with the horse. Seeing that Alvaro Nieto was coming at him again, he shouted in a loud voice, saying "Xivilla, Xivilla" for "Sevilla, Sevilla."

Juan Coles adds at this point that Juan Ortiz, being unable to speak in Spanish, made the sign of the cross with his hand and the bow so that the Spaniard might see that he was a Christian. For with the little or no use that he had for the Spanish language among the Indians, he had even forgotten how to pronounce the name of his own country, as I can also say for myself. Because of not having had anyone in Spain with whom to speak my native and maternal tongue, which is the one generally spoken throughout El Perú (although the Incas have another special one that they speak among themselves, one to another), I have forgotten it to such an extent that—having once known how to speak it as well or better, and with more elegance, than the Indians themselves who are not Incas, because I am a son of *palla* and the nephew of Incas, who are the ones who speak it best and most correctly, because of its having been the language of the court of its princes and they having been the chief courtiers—now I am unable to put six or seven words together in a sentence in order to make clear what I wish to say, and, moreover, many terms have escaped my memory and I do not know what is the word for this or that thing in the Indian tongue. Although it is true that, if I should hear an Inca speak, I would understand all that he said, and, if I should hear the forgotten words, I could tell what they mean, I myself, however I try, cannot say what they are. This I have learned from experience in the use and neglect of languages, which foreigners learn by using them and natives forget in not using them.

Returning to Juan Ortiz, whom we left in great danger of being killed by those who most desired to see him alive, as Alvaro Nieto heard him say "Xivilla," he asked whether he were Juan Ortiz, and as he replied that he was, he grasped him by one arm and lifted him behind his horse as if he were a child, for this good soldier was stout and strong.

Much elated at having found the one he was seeking, and giving thanks to God for not having killed him, though it seemed to him that he was still in that danger, he took him to Captain Baltasar de Gallegos. The latter received Juan Ortiz with great joy and at once ordered them to recall the other horsemen who were scouring the woods, anxious to kill Indians, as if they were deer, so that all of them might assemble to enjoy the good fortune that had befallen them, and before they should do some injury to their friends because of not recognizing them. Juan Ortiz entered the woods to call the Indians, shouting to them to come out and not be afraid. Many of them did not stop until they reached their pueblo, to advise their cacique of what had happened. Others who had not gone so far returned in groups of three and four as they happened to be found, and together and singly they very angrily and bitterly reproached Juan Ortiz for his rashness and lack of caution. When they saw the Indian, their companion, wounded because of him they became so enraged that they scarcely could refrain from laying hands on him and would have done so had the Spaniards not been present. But they vented their wrath with a thousand insults they heaped upon him, calling him dolt, fool, meddler, and no Spaniard or soldier, and saying that he had learned little or nothing from his past sufferings and misadventures; that they had been inflicted upon him to no purpose, and he deserved much worse. In short, no Indian came out of the woods who was not quarreling with him; all of them spoke almost the same words and he himself stated them to the other Spaniards, the more to reproach them. Juan Ortiz was well reprimanded for having been too confident, but it was worth it all provided he found himself among Christians. The latter treated the wounded Indian and, putting him on a horse, went with him and Juan Ortiz and the rest of the Indians to the camp, desirous of seeing the governor, in order to bring within so short a time such a good report of what he had ordered them to do. Before they left that place Juan Ortiz sent an Indian to Mucoço with the report of all that had happened, so that he would not be alarmed by what the Indians who fled might have told him.

All that we have said concerning Juan Ortiz, Juan Coles and Alonso de Carmona also tell in their accounts, and one of them says that he had worms in the sores made by the fire when they burned him. The other, who is Juan Coles, says that the governor gave him at once a black velvet suit, and that, because he was accustomed to go about unclothed, he could not tolerate it; that he wore only a shirt and linen trousers, a cap, and shoes, and that he went about thus for more than twenty days until, a little at a time, he was able to wear clothing. These two eyewitnesses say further that, among other benefits and favors that the cacique Mucoço conferred upon Juan Ortiz, one was to make him his captain-general on sea and land.

The Celebration That the Whole Army Held for Juan Ortiz, and How Mucoço Came to Visit the Governor

A good part of the night had passed when Baltasar de Gallegos and his companions entered the camp. The governor, who heard them, was alarmed, fearing that since they were returning so quickly, some accident had befallen them, because he had not expected them until the third day. But upon learning of the good report they brought, all his dismay was changed to rejoicing and pleasure. He thanked the captain and his soldiers, who had done so well, and received Juan Ortiz as his own son, with pity and grief at hearing of so many hardships and martyrdoms as he told of and as his own body showed that he had experienced—for the scars of the burns from the time that they had roasted him were so large that one whole side was nothing but a burn, or a scar of it—from which hardships he thanked God for having delivered him, and also from the peril of that day, which had not been the least of those through which he had passed. He treated kindly the Indians who came with him and ordered that the one who was wounded be treated with great care and attention. At the same hour he dispatched two Indians to the cacique Mucoço with acknowledgments for the kindnesses that he had done Juan Ortiz and for having sent him freely, and for the offer of his person and friendship, which he said he accepted in the name of the emperor and king of Spain, his lord, who was the chief and greatest of all Christendom, in the name of all those captains and gentlemen who were with him, and in his own, in order to acknowledge and repay what he had done for all of them in having rescued Juan Ortiz from death; he said also that all of them begged him to visit them, as they desired to see and know him.

The captains and officials, both of the army and of the real hacienda, and the gentlemen and all the other soldiers in general, entertained Juan Ortiz royally; they refused to accept as comrade anyone who did not come to embrace him and congratulate him on his arrival. So passed the night, in which they did not sleep for general rejoicing.

Then on the following day the general summoned Juan Ortiz so that he might inform him concerning what he knew about the country and might tell him in detail what had happened to him while he was in the power of those two caciques. He replied that he knew little or nothing about the country, although he had been there so long; because while he was in the power of Hirrihigua, his master, when he was not tormenting him with new martyrdoms, did not allow him to go a step beyond the ordinary service that he performed in carrying water and wood for all the households; and while he was in the hands of Mucoço, though he had freedom to go where he liked, he did not make use of it because the vassals of his master, seeing him apart from Mucoço, might kill him, as they had his order and command to do. For these reasons he could not give much information about the nature of the country, but he heard that it was good, and that the farther inland one went, the better and more fertile it became. The life he had led with the two caciques had been of the two extremes of good and evil that could be found in this world; because Mucoço had shown himself as compassionate and humane toward him as the other had been cruel and revengeful, without his being able to extol sufficiently the virtue of the one or the passion of the other, as his lordship had already been informed, as a proof of which he showed the scars on his body, uncovering those that could be seen and amplifying the account of his life, which we have given; and he related anew many other torments through which he had passed, which aroused the compassion of the listeners and which we shall omit, to avoid prolixity.

FROM *GENERALL HISTORIE OF VIRGINIA*

John Smith

The next voyage hee proceeded so farre that with much labour by cutting of trees in sunder he made his passage, but when his Barge could passe no farther, he left her in a broad bay out of danger of shot, commanding none should goe a shore till his returne: himselfe with two English and two Salvages went up higher in a Canowe, but hee was not long absent, but his men went a shore, whose want of government, gave both occasion and opportunity to the Salvages to surprise one George Cassen, whom they slew, and much failed not to have cut of[1] the boat and all the rest. Smith little dreaming of that accident, being got to the marshes at the rivers head, twentie myles in the desert,[2] had his two men slaine (as is supposed) sleeping by the Canowe, whilst himselfe by fowling sought them victuall, who finding he was beset with 200 Salvages, two of them hee slew, still defending himselfe with the ayd of a Salvage his guid, whom he bound to his arme with his garters, and used him as a buckler, yet he was shot in his thigh a little, and had many arrowes that stucke in his cloathes but no great hurt, till at last they tooke him prisoner. When this newes came to James towne, much was their sorrow for his losse, fewe expecting what ensued. Sixe or seven weekes those Barbarians kept him prisoner, many strange triumphes and conjurations they made of him, yet hee so demeaned himselfe amongst them, as he not onely diverted them from surprising the Fort, but procured his owne libertie, and got himselfe and his company such estimation amongst them, that those Salvages admired him more then their owne *Quiyouckosucks.*[3] The manner how they used and delivered him, is as followeth.

---

[1] Off.

[2] The word meant "uninhabited lands," not "arid land," at the time.

[3] Smith elsewhere used this word to refer to the Indians' minor or "pettie" deities.

The Salvages having drawne from George Cassen whether Captaine Smith was gone, prosecuting that opportunity they followed him with 300 bowmen, conducted by the King of Pamaunkee, who in divisions searching the turnings of the river, found Robinson and Emry by the fire side, those they shot full of arrowes and slew. Then finding the Captaine, as is said, that used the Salvage that was his guide as his sheld (three of them being slaine and divers other so gauld[4]) all the rest would not come neere him. Thinking thus to have returned to his boat, regarding them, as he marched, more then his way, slipped up to the middle in an oasie[5] creeke and his Salvage with him, yet durst they not come to him till being neere dead with cold, he threw away his armes. Then according to their composition they drew him forth and led him to the fire, where his men were slaine. Diligently they chafed his be-nummed limbs. He demanding for their Captaine, they shewed him Opechankanough, King of Pamaunkee, to whom he gave a round Ivory double compass Dyall. Much they marvailed at the playing of the Fly and Needle, which they could see so plainely, and yet not touch it, because of the glasse that covered them. But when he demonstrated by that Globe-like Jewell, the roundnesse of the earth, and skies, the spheare of the Sunne, Moone, and Starres, and how the Sunne did chase the night round about the world continually; the greatnesse of the Land and Sea, the diversitie of Nations, varietie of complexions, and how we were to them Antipodes, and many other such like matters, they all stood as amazed with admiration. Notwithstanding, within an houre after they tyed him to a tree, and as many as could stand about him prepared to shoot him, but the King holding up the Compass in his hand, they all laid downe their Bowes and Arrowes, and in a triumphant manner led him to Orapaks, where he was after their manner kindly feasted, and well used.

Their order in conducting him was thus; Drawing themselves all in fyle, the King in the middest had all their Peeces and Swords borne before him. Captaine Smith was led after him by three great Salvages, holding him fast by each arme: and on each side six went in fyle with their Arrowes nocked. But arriving at the Towne (which was but onely thirtie or fortie hunting houses made of Mats, which they removed as they please, as we our tents) all the women and children staring to behold him, the souldiers first all in fyle performed the forme of a Bissone so well as could be; and on each flanke, officers as Serjeants to see them keepe their order. A good time they continued this exercise, and then cast themselves in a ring,

[4] Galled, or wounded by shot.
[5] Oozy.

daucing in such severall Postures, and singing and yelling out such hellish notes and screeches; being strangely painted, every one his quiver of
Arrowes, and at his backe a club; on his arme a Fox or an Otters skinne,
or some such matter for his vambrace; their heads and shoulders painted
red, with Oyle and *Pocones*[6] mingled together, which Scarlet-like colour
made an exceeding handsome shew; his Bow in his hand, and the skinne
of a Bird with her wings abroad dryed, tyed on his head, a peece of copper,
a white shell, a long feather, with a small rattle growing at the tayles of
their snakes tyed to it, or some such like toy. All this while Smith and the
King stood in the middest guarded, as before is said, and after three dances
they all departed. Smith they conducted to a long house, where thirtie or
fortie tall fellowes did guard him, and ere long more bread and venison
was brought him then would have served twentie men, I thinke his stom-
acke at that time was not very good; what he left they put in baskets and
tyed over his head. About midnight they set the meate againe before him,
all this time not one of them would eate a bit with him, till the next morning they brought him as much more, and then did they eate all the old, and
reserved the new as they had done the other, which made him thinke they
would fat him to eat him. Yet in this desperate estate to defend him from
the cold, one Maocassater brought him his gowne, in requitall of some
beads and toyes Smith had given him at his first arrivall in Virginia.

Two dayes after a man would have slaine him (but that the guard prevented it) for the death of his sonne, to whom they conducted him to recover the poore man then breathing his last. Smith told them that at James
towne he had a water would doe it, if they would let him fetch it, but they
would not permit that; but made all the preparations they could to assault
James towne, craving his advice, and for recompence he should have life,
libertie, land, and women. In part of a Table booke he writ his minde to
them at the Fort, what was intended, how they should follow that direction to affright the messengers, and without fayle send him such things as
he writ for. And an Inventory with them. The difficultie and danger, he told
the Salvages, of the Mines, great gunnes, and other Engins exceedingly affrighted them, yet according to his request they went to James towne, in as
bitter weather as could be of frost and snow, and within three dayes returned with an answer.

But when they came to James towne, seeing men sally out as he had
told them they would, they fled; yet in the night they came againe to the
same place where he had told them they should receive an answer, and
such things as he had promised them, which they found accordingly, and

---

[6] A red vegetable dye.

with which they returned with no small expedition, to the wonder of them all that heard it, that he could either divine, or the paper could speake: then they led him to the Youghtanunds, the Mattapanients, the Payanka-tanks, the Nantaughtacunds, and Onawmanients upon the rivers of Rapa-hanock, and Patawomek, over all those rivers, and backe againe by divers other severall Nations, to the Kings habitation at Pamaunkee, where they entertained him with most strange and fearefull Conjurations;

> As if neare led to hell,
> Amongst the Devils to dwell.[7]

Not long after, early in a morning a great fire was made in a long house, and a mat spread on the one side, as on the other, on the one they caused him to sit, and all the guard went out of the house, and presently came skipping in a great grim fellow, all painted over with coale, mingled with oyle; and many Snakes and Wesels skins stuffed with mosse, and all their tayles tyed together, so as they met on the crowne of his head in a tas-sell; and round about the tassell was as a Coronet of feathers, the skins hanging round about his head, backe, and shoulders, and in a manner covered his face; with a hellish voyce and a rattle in his hand. With most strange gestures and passions he began his invocation, and environed the fire with a circle of meale; which done, three more such like devils came rushing in with the like antique tricks, painted halfe blacke, halfe red: but all their eyes were painted white, and some red stroakes like Mutchato's,[8] along their cheekes: round about him those fiends daunced a pretty while, and then came in three more as ugly as the rest; with red eyes, and white stroakes over their blacke faces, at last they all sat downe right against him; three of them on the one hand of the chiefe Priest, and three on the other. Then all with their rattles began a song, which ended, the chiefe Priest layd downe five wheat cornes: then strayning his armes and hands with such violence that he sweat, and his veynes swelled, he began a short Oration: at the conclusion they all gave a short groane; and then layd down three graines more. After that, began their song againe, and then an-other Oration, ever laying downe so many cornes as before, till they had twice incirculed the fire; that done, they tooke a bunch of little stickes pre-

---

[7] This and the four other verse quotations in the selection are from the *Atheomastix; Clearing Four Truths, against Atheists* . . . (1622) by Martin Fotherby, Bishop of Sarum. Although Fotherby is not today considered a major figure in English literature, he was a favorite of John Smith's, for he quoted his work many times in the *Generall Historie.* Most are verse translations of classical Greek and Roman texts.
[8] Moustaches.

pared for that purpose, continuing still their devotion, and at the end of every song and Oration, they layd downe a sticke betwixt the divisions of Corne. Till night, neither he nor they did either eate or drinke, and then they feasted merrily, with the best provisions they could make. Three dayes they used this Ceremony; the meaning whereof they told him, was to know if he intended them well or no. The circle of meale signified their Country, the circles of corne the bounds of the Sea, and the stickes his country. They imagined the world to be flat and round, like a trencher,[9] and they in the middest. After this they brought him a bagge of gunpowder, which they carefully preserved till the next spring, to plant as they did their corne; because they would be acquainted with the nature of that seede. Opitchapam the Kings brother invited him to his house, where, with as many platters of bread, foule, and wild beasts, as did environ him, he bid him wellcome; but not any of them would eate a bit with him, but put up all the remainder in Baskets. At his returne to Opechancanoughs, all the Kings women, and their children, flocked about him for their parts, as a due by Custome, to be merry with such fragments.

> But his waking mind in hydeous dreames did oft see wondrous
>   shapes,
> Of bodies strange, and huge in growth, and of stupendious makes.

At last they brought him to Meronocomoco, where was Powhatan their Emperor. Here more then two hundred of those grim Courtiers stood wondering at him, as he had beene a monster; till Powhatan and his trayne had put themselves in their greatest braveries. Before a fire upon a seat like a bedsted, he sat covered with a great robe, made of Rarowcun[10] skinnes, and all the tayles hanging by. On either hand did sit a young wench of 16 or 18 yeares, and along on each side the house, two rowes of men, and behind them as many women, with all their heads and shoulders painted red; many of their heads bedecked with the white downe of Birds; but every one with something: and a great chayne of white beads about their necks. At his entrance before the King, all the people gave a great shout. The Queene of Appamatuck was appointed to bring him water to wash his hands, and another brought him a bunch of feathers, in stead of a Towell to dry them: having feasted him after their best barbarous manner they could, a long consultation was held, but the conclusion was, two great stones were brought before Powhatan: then as many as could layd hands on him,

---

[9] A wooden cutting board.
[10] Raccoon.

dragged him to them, and thereon laid his head, and being ready with their clubs, to beate out his braines, Pocahontas the Kings dearest daughter, when no intreaty could prevaile, got his head in her armes, and laid her owne upon his to save him from death: whereat the Emperour was contented he should live to make him hatchets, and her bells, beads, and copper; for they thought him as well of all occupations as themselves. For the King himselfe will make his owne robes, shooes, bowes, arrowes, pots; plant, hunt, or doe any thing so well as the rest.

> They say he bore a pleasant shew,
> But sure his heart was sad.
> For who can pleasant be, and rest,
> That lives in feare and dread:
> 5   And having life suspected, doth
> It still suspected lead.

Two dayes after, Powhatan having disguised himselfe in the most feare-fullest manner he could, caused Captaine Smith to be brought forth to a great house in the woods, and there upon a mat by the fire to be left alone. Not long after from behinde a mat that divided the house, was made the most dolefullest noyse he ever heard; then Powhatan more like a devill then a man with some two hundred more as blacke as himselfe, came unto him and told him now they were friends, and presently he should goe to James towne, to send him two great gunnes, and a gryndstone, for which he would give him the Country of Capahowosick, and for ever esteeme him as his sonne Nantaquoud. So to James towne with 12 guides Powhatan sent him. That night they quarterd in the woods, he still expecting (as he had done all this long time of his imprisonment) every houre to be put to one death or other: for all their feasting. But almightie God (by his divine providence) had mollified the hearts of those sterne Barbarians with compassion. The next morning betimes they came to the Fort, where Smith having used the Salvages with what kindnesse he could, he shewed Rawhunt, Powhatans trusty servant two demi-Culverings and a millstone to carry Powhatan: they found them somewhat too heavie; but when they did see him discharge them, being loaded with stones, among the boughs of a great tree loaded with Isickles, the yce and branches came so tumbling downe, that the poore Salvages ran away halfe dead with feare. But at last we regained some conference with them, and gave them such toyes, and sent to Powhatan, his women, and children such presents, as gave them in generall full content. Now in James towne they were all in combustion, the strongest preparing once more to run away with the Pinnace; which with the hazzard of his life, with Sakre falcon and musket shot, Smith forced now the third time to stay or sinke. Some no better then they should be, had plotted with the President, the next day to have put him to death by the Leviticall law, for the lives of Robinson and Emry, pretending the fault was his that had led them to their ends:[11] but he quickly tooke such order with such Lawyers, that he layd them by the heeles till he sent some of them prisoners for England. Now ever once in foure or five dayes, Pocahontas with her attendants, brought him so much provision, that saved many of their lives, that els for all this had starved with hunger.

> Thus from numbe death our good God sent reliefe,
> The sweete asswager of all other griefe.

His relation of the plenty he had seene, especially at Werawocomoco, and of the state and bountie of Powhatan, (which till that time was un-knowne) so revived their dead spirits (especially the love of Pocahontas) as all mens feare was abandoned. Thus you may see what difficulties still crossed any good indevour: and the good successe of the businesse being thus oft brought to the very period of destruction; yet you see by what strange means God hath still delivered it. As for the insufficiency of them admitted in Commission, that error could not be prevented by the Electors; there being no other choise, and all strangers to each others education, qualities, or disposition. And if any deeme it a shame to our Nation to have any mention made of those inormities, let them peruse the Histories of the Spanyards Discoveries and Plantations, where they may see how many mutinies, disorders, and dissentions have accompanied them, and crossed their attempts: which being knowne to be particular mens offences; doth take away the generall scorne and contempt, which malice, presumption, covetousnesse, or ignorance might produce; to the scandall and reproach of those, whose actions and valiant resolutions deserve a more worthy respect.

Now whether it had beene better for Captaine Smith, to have concluded with any of those severall projects, to have abandoned the Countrey, with some ten or twelve of them, who were called the better sort, and have left Master Hunt our Preacher, Master Anthony Gosnoll, a most honest, worthy, and industrious Gentleman, Master Thomas Wotton, and some 27 others of his Countrymen to the fury of the Salvages, famine, and all manner of mischiefes, and inconveniences, (for they were but fortie in all to keepe possession of this large Country;) or starve himselfe with them

---

[11] Smith alludes to the book of Leviticus in the Bible as his foes' justification for wishing to execute him in revenge for the deaths of the two men at the time he was captured.

for company, for want of lodging: or but adventuring abroad to make them
provision, or by his opposition to preserve the action, and save all their
lives; I leave to the censure of all honest men to consider. But

> We men imagine in our Jolitie,
> That 'tis all one, or good or bad to be.
> But then anone wee alter this againe,
> If happily wee feele the sence of paine;
> 5   For then we're turn'd into a mourning vaine.

Written by Thomas Studley, the first Cape Merchant in Virginia,
Robert Fenton, Edward Harrington, and J. S.

Jesuit Missionary Martyrs

ISAAC JOGUES, JEAN DE BRÉBEUF, AND GABRIEL LALEMANT

The captivity narratives of missionaries form a distinct group within the genre. Their presence among the Indians was voluntary, and they became captives only when they abused the natives' hospitality, or, as in the two narratives in this chapter, when their hosts were attacked by enemies. But even when missionaries sought to understand the culture of those they were proselytizing, the contest of belief systems prevented the kind of assimilation that Juan Ortiz (chap. 2) and James Smith (chap. 8) accepted as a means of self-preservation.

Isaac Jogues, Jean de Brébeuf, and Gabriel Lalemant were missionaries of the Society of Jesus, or Jesuits, sent to the fledgling colony of New France with the support of the French king and his powerful minister, Cardinal Richelieu. Since 1608, when the settlement at Quebec was founded by Samuel de Champlain, a few missionaries had tested the faith of local Indian tribes. Beginning in 1632, however, the Jesuits were given an exclusive mandate, and they chose as their primary target the Huron Nation, a populous agricultural people living on the southern shores of the lake that bears their name. Brébeuf was among the first to journey there in the early 1630s, utilizing trade routes and alliances established by Champlain when he first visited Huronia in 1615 and fought for that nation against their enemies, the Iroquois. The captivity and martyrdom of these three missionaries arose from this same war. The conflict between the Hurons and the Iroquois, two confederacies with similar languages, mythology, and subsistence practices, had begun before European contact. By 1649 Iroquois attacks had penetrated to the heart of Huronia, and thus Brébeuf was captured and martyred by Iroquois warriors near the village the missionaries had named St. Ignace, after the founder of their order, Ignatius Loyola. By the 1650s, however, the Hurons, their numbers reduced by diseases introduced by the Europeans, were defeated and dispersed from their homeland.

Isaac Jogues was born in Orléans, France, in 1607. At age ten he was enrolled in a Jesuit school, and upon his ordination in 1636 he went to Canada. His narrative, known as "Novum Belgium" after a Latin name for the colony of New Netherland where he wrote it, opens with his departure from the Huron missions in the spring of 1642 on a long canoe journey to Quebec to obtain badly needed supplies. He traveled with a large group, which included several Huron converts and two donnés, volunteer laymen who served the priests in the field. Christophe Regnaut, the narrator of Brébeuf's and Lalemant's captivity, was also a donné. On his return trip, Jogues paddled up the St. Lawrence River, along the northern edge of Iroquois territory, and the group was attacked in Lake St. Pierre in August 1642.

The most astonishing aspect of Jogues's narrative is his acceptance of, even zealous desire for, the pain and humiliation the Iroquois inflicted on his body. In running the gauntlet, the customary reception for new captives at an Iroquois village, he recalled that "it is delightful and glorious to suffer," even to the point of death. This spirit of martyrdom, common among the Jesuits in New France but which readers today might see as a bizarre masochism, was grounded in a belief that suffering demonstrated the power of one's faith, even to torturers who were enemies of that faith. Jogues passed up opportunities to escape because he felt an obligation to remain with the Huron converts, who were the first to be tortured, and to baptize others who had not yet converted. The graphic depiction of such tortures was likely less shocking to seventeenth-century readers than it is today, for torture was an accepted practice in judicial interrogations in Europe, and accounts of martyrdom, both Catholic and Protestant, were part of popular literature.

Although not motivated by the same religious zeal, the Iroquois' customs of torture created an ironic mimicry between the behavior of each side in the violent scenes of martyrdom. If a native victim of torture displayed fortitude and did not cry out in pain, his heart would be ritually consumed, his strength symbolically passing into the bodies of his conquerors. When Brébeuf's torturers drank his blood, they unwittingly repeated an act of communion, raising their victim to the status of Christ. Brébeuf's torture also revealed the Iroquois' knowledge of the beliefs of the missionaries and their desire to ridicule these beliefs in the mock baptism. For his part, Brébeuf was likely aware that a brave torture victim was supposed to sing his chanson de mort, or death song, a litany of boasts and insults aimed at his torturers. As a version of this death song, his preaching at once fulfilled and subverted the Indians' traditional practices, just as the mock baptism fulfilled the ideal of martyrdom even in its blasphemy. This convergence of the motives of captive and captor contrasts with the resistance of the Protestant Mary Rowlandson. While both she and Jogues relied on biblical citations to sustain their courage and interpreted their experiences within a doctrine of Divine Providence, and both recalled petty cruelties and the challenge of eating their captors' food, the two captives' sense of the meaning and outcome of their suffering could not be more different.

Jogues's letter was first published in 1655 by Philip Alegambe in *Mortes Illustres,* a Catholic book of martyrs, and first translated into English by Catholic historian John Gilmary Shea two centuries later. The text of Brébeuf's martyrdom is taken from the *Jesuit Relations,* a series of dispatches from the Jesuit missions of New France published in Paris from 1632 to 1673. These were translated as part of a huge set titled *The Jesuit Relations and Allied Documents,* edited by Reuben Gold Thwaites and published from 1896 to 1901. The *Relation of 1647,* in volume 31 of the series, includes a different version of Jogues's story, one that intersperses passages from his letter with commentary by Jerome Lalemant (an uncle of the martyred Gabriel) and adds Jogues's account of a prophetic dream he had while captive. That version also includes Lalemant's accounts of subsequent events. Jogues was released from his Mohawk captors by the Dutch Reformed minister Johannes Megapolensis at Renssalaerswyck, a settlement near today's Albany, New York. Jogues stayed there and in Manhattan for some weeks in conditions he describes as being little better than conditions among the Mohawks, until he finally returned on a ship to France. Even after being treated to a hero's welcome by Jesuits in France and being given an audience with the queen, he desired to return to the colony in Canada. In 1644 he traveled to the new settlement of Montreal, and in September 1646 he returned to missionary work among the Mohawks. A month later he was killed, his destiny of martyrdom finally fulfilled.

For Jogues and Brébeuf, martyrdom, rather than escape or ransom, led to redemption. The adulation of Brébeuf's remains, which the narrator Regnaut began with his repetition of "I saw and touched . . . ," in an allusion to the story of doubting Thomas in the Gospels, seems designed to promote the canonization of the martyrs. In the late nineteenth century, a campaign was mounted, and on June 29, 1930, Jogues, Brébeuf, Gabriel Lalemant, and René Goupil, along with four other Jesuit martyrs of New France, were beatified as saints by Pope Pius XI. Although little known in American literature, these martyred captives are still heroes in Quebec and to many Catholics in the United States.

Sources

Jogues, Isaac. "Novum Belgium." *Perils of the Ocean and Wilderness*. Ed. and trans. John Gilmary Shea. Boston: 1857. 16–62. [Jogues's chapter and verse citations are often inexact. I have corrected a few of these.]

Regnaut, Christophe. "A Veritable Account of the Martyrdom and Blessed Death of Father Jean de Brébeuf and of Father Gabriel Lalemant." *The Jesuit Relations and Allied Documents*. Ed. Reuben Gold Thwaites. Vol. 34. Cleveland: Burrows, 1896–1900. 24–37. [Some spelling and punctuation have been modernized.]

Supplementary Readings

Donnelly, Joseph Peter. *Jean de Brébeuf: 1593–1649*. Chicago: Loyola UP, 1975.

Franchot, Jenny. *Roads to Rome: The Antebellum Protestant Encounter with Catholicism*. Berkeley: U of California P, 1994.

Greer, Alan, ed. *The Jesuit Relations: Natives and Missionaries in Seventeenth-Century North America*. Boston: Bedford, 2000.

Lestringant, Frank. *Cannibals: The Discovery and Representation of the Cannibal from Columbus to Jules Verne*. Trans. Rosemary Morris. Berkeley: U of California P, 1997: 131–35.

Sayre, Gordon. "Communion in Captivity: Torture, Martyrdom, and Gender in New France and New England." *Finding Colonial Americas: Essays Honoring J. A. Leo Lemay*. Ed. Carla Mulford and David Shields. Newark: U of Delaware P, 2000.

Viau, Roland. *Enfants du néant et mangeurs d'âmes: Guerre, culture et société en Iroquoisie ancienne*. Montreal: Boréal, 1997.

NOVUM BELGIUM

Isaac Jogues

Reverend Father in Christ—The Peace of Christ—

Wishing, as I do, to write to your reverence, I hesitate first in which language to address you, for, after such long disuse, almost equally forgetful of both, I find equal difficulty in each.[1] Two reasons, however, induce me to employ the less common idiom. I shall be better able to use the words of Holy Scripture, which have been, at all times, my greatest consolation: "Amid the tribulations which have found us exceedingly." (Ps. 45.2.) I also wished this letter to be less open to all. The exceeding charity of your reverence, which, in other days, overlooked my manifold transgressions, will excuse, in a man for eight years a companion and associate of savages, nay, a savage now himself in form and dress, whatever may be wanting in decorum or correctness. I fear more that, wanting in language, I may be still more so in knowledge, "nor know the time of my visitation," nor remember what character I here bear imposed on me by God as a preacher of his gospel, a Jesuit and a priest. This induced me to write to your reverence that, if this letter should ever reach your hands, I may, though lying here in this hard land, amid Iroquois and Maaquas, be helped by your masses, and the prayers of your whole province. This, I am in hopes, will be more earnestly given, when, from the perusal of this letter, you shall see, both how much I am indebted to the Almighty, and in what need I am of the prayers of the pious, in which, I am aware, I have a powerful shield.

We sailed from the Huron territory on the 13th of June, 1642, in four small boats, here called canoes; we were twenty-three souls in all, five of us being French. This line of travel is, in itself, most difficult for many reasons, and especially because, in no less than forty places, both canoes and baggage had to be carried by land on the shoulders. It was now too full of danger from fear of the enemy, who, every year, by lying in wait on the roads to the French settlements, carry off many as prisoners; and, indeed,

---

[1] Joques hesitated between writing in Latin or French and chose Latin. Translator Shea anglicized some of the names, e. g., Guillaume Couture (p. 97) becomes "William."

Father John Brébeuf was all but taken the year before. Besides this, not long before they carried off two Frenchmen, but afterward brought them back to their countrymen unharmed, demanding peace on most unjust terms, and then conducted themselves in a very hostile manner, so that they were driven off by the cannons of the fort. On this, they declared that, if they took another Frenchman prisoner, they would torture him cruelly, like their other captives, and burn him alive by a slow fire. The Superior, conscious of the dangers I was exposed to on this journey, which was, however, absolutely necessary for God's glory, so assigned the task to me, that I might decline it if I chose; "I did not, however, resist; I did not go back;" (Isa. 1.5) but willingly and cheerfully accepted this mission imposed upon me by obedience and charity. Had I declined it, it would have fallen to another, far more worthy than myself.

Having, therefore, loosed from St. Mary's of the Hurons, amid ever-varying fears of the enemy, dangers of every kind, losses by land and water, we at last, on the thirtieth day after our departure, reached in safety the Conception of the Blessed Virgin. This is a French settlement or colony, called Three Rivers,[2] from a most charming stream near it, which discharges itself into the great river St. Lawrence, by three mouths. We returned hearty thanks to God, and remained here and at Quebec about two weeks.

The business which had brought us, having been concluded, we celebrated the feast of our holy Father Ignatius,[3] and, on the second of August, were once more on our way for Huronia. The second day after our departure had just dawned, when, by the early light, some of our party discovered fresh foot-prints on the shore. While some were maintaining that they were the trail of the enemy, others, that of a friendly party, Eustace Ahatsistari, to whom, for his gallant feats of arms, all yielded the first rank, exclaimed: "Brothers! be they the bravest of the foe, for such I judge them by their trail, they are no more than three canoes, and we number enough not to dread such a handful of the enemy." We were, in fact, forty, for some others had joined us.

We consequently urged on our way, but had scarcely advanced a mile, when we fell into an ambush of the enemy, who lay in two divisions on the opposite banks of the river, to the number of seventy in twelve canoes.

As soon as we reached the spot where they lay in ambush, they poured in a volley of musketry from the reeds and tall grass, where they lurked.

---

[2] The modern Trois Rivières, Quebec.
[3] Ignatius Loyola, the founder of the Jesuit Order. Jogues frequently referred to dates by the saint's day in the calendar.

Our canoes were riddled, but, though well supplied with fire-arms, they killed none, one Huron only being shot through the hand. At the first report of the fire-arms, the Hurons, almost to a man, abandoned the canoes, which, to avoid the more rapid current of the centre of the river, were advancing close by the bank, and in headlong flight, plunged into the thickest of the woods. We, four Frenchmen, left with a few, either already Christians, or at least Catechumens, offering up a prayer to Christ, faced the enemy. We were, however, outnumbered, being scarcely twelve or fourteen against thirty; yet we fought on, till our comrades, seeing fresh canoes shoot out from the opposite bank of the river, lost heart and fled. Then a Frenchman named René Goupil, who was fighting with the bravest, was taken with some of the Hurons. When I saw this, I neither could, nor cared to fly. Where, indeed, could I escape, barefooted as I was? Conceal myself amid the reeds and tall grass, I could indeed, and thus escape; but could I leave a countryman, and the unchristened Hurons already taken or soon to be? As the enemy, in hot pursuit of the fugitives, had passed on, leaving me standing on the battle-field, I called out to one of those who remained to guard the prisoners, and bade him make me a fellow captive to his French captive, that, as I had been his companion on the way, so would I be in his dangers and death. Scarce giving credit to what he heard, and fearful for himself, he advanced and led me to the other prisoners.

Dearest brother, I then exclaimed, wonderfully hath God dealt with us! "but he is the Lord, let him do what is good in his sight;" (1 Kings 3.18). "As it hath pleased him, so hath it come to pass, blessed be his name;" then, hearing his confession, I gave him absolution. I now turned to the Huron prisoners, and, instructing them one by one, baptized them; as new prisoners were constantly taken in their flight, my labor was constantly renewed. At length Eustace Ahatsistari, that famous Christian chief, was brought in; when he saw me, he exclaimed, "Solemnly did I swear, brother, that I would live or die by thee." What I answered, I know not, so had grief overcome me. Last of all, William Couture was dragged in; he too, had set out from Huronia with me. When he saw all in confusion, he had, with the rest, taken to the woods, and, being a young man endowed with great gifts in body as well as in mind, had, by his great agility, left the enemy far behind. When he looked around and could see nothing of me, "Shall I," he said to himself, "abandon my dear Father, a prisoner in the hands of savages, and fly without him? Not I." Then returning by the path which he had taken in flight, he gave himself up to the enemy. Would that he had fled, nor swelled our mournful band! for, in such a case, it is no comfort to have companions, especially those whom you love as yourself. Yet such are the souls, who, though but laymen, (with no views of earthly reward), serve God and the Society among the Hurons.

It is painful to think, even, of all his terrible sufferings. Their hate was enkindled against all the French, but especially against him, as they knew that one of their bravest had fallen by his hand in the fight. He was accordingly first stripped naked, all his nails torn out, his very fingers gnawed, and a broad-sword driven through his right hand. Mindful of the wounds of our Lord Jesus Christ, he bore, as he afterward told me, this pain, though most acute, with great joy.

When I beheld him, thus bound and naked, I could not contain myself, but, leaving my keepers, I rushed through the midst of the savages who had brought him, embraced him most tenderly, exhorted him to offer all this to God for himself, and those at whose hands he suffered. They at first looked on in wonder at my proceedings; then, as if recollecting themselves, and gathering all their rage, they fell upon me, and, with their fists, thongs, and a club, beat me till I fell senseless. Two of them then dragged me back to where I had been before, and scarcely had I begun to breathe, when some others, attacking me, tore out, by biting, almost all my nails, and crunched my two fore-fingers with their teeth, giving me intense pain. The same was done to René Goupil, the Huron captives being left untouched.

When all had come in from the pursuit, in which two Hurons were killed, they carried us across the river, and there shared the plunder of the twelve canoes, (for eight had joined us). This was very great, for, independent of what each Frenchman had with him, we had twenty packages containing church plate and vestments, books and other articles of the kind; a rich cargo indeed, considering the poverty of our Huron mission. While they were dividing the plunder, I completed the instruction of such as were unchristened, and baptized them. Among the rest was one sere, octogenarian chief, who, when ordered to enter the canoe to be borne off with the rest, exclaimed, "How shall I, a hoary old man, go to a strange and foreign land? Never! here will I die." As he absolutely refused to go, they slew him on the very spot where he had just been baptized.

Raising then a joyful shout which made the forest ring, "as conquerors who rejoice after taking a prey," (Isa. 9.3), they bore us off, twenty-two captives, toward their own land; three had been killed. By the favor of God our sufferings on that march, which lasted thirteen days, were indeed great—hunger, and heat, and menaces, the savage fury of the Indians, the intense pain of our untended and now putrefying wounds, swarming even with worms; but no trial came harder upon me than when, five or six days after, they would come up to us, weary with the march, and in cold blood, with minds in no wise aroused by passion, pluck out our hair and beard, and drive their nails, which are always very sharp, deep into parts most tender and sensitive to the slightest impression. But this was outward; my internal sufferings affected me still more when I beheld that

funeral procession of doomed Christians pass before my eyes, among them
five old converts, the main pillars of the infant Huron church.

Indeed, I ingenuously admit, that I was again and again unable to
withold my tears, mourning over their lot and that of my other companions, and full of anxious solicitude for the future. For I beheld the way to
the Christian faith closed by these Iroquois, on the Hurons, and countless
other nations, unless they were checked by some seasonable dispensation
of Divine Providence.

On the eighth day we fell in with a troop of two hundred Indians going out to fight. And as it is the custom for the savages, when out on war
parties, to initiate themselves as it were by cruelty, under the belief that
their success will be greater as they shall have been more cruel, they thus
received us. First rendering thanks to the sun, which they imagine presides
over war, they congratulated their countrymen by a joyful volley of musketry. Each then cut off some stout clubs in the neighboring wood in order
to receive us. When, therefore, we landed from the canoes, they fell upon
us from both sides with their clubs, with such fury, that I, who was the last,
and therefore most exposed to their blows, sank, overcome by their number and severity, before I had accomplished half the rocky way that led to
the hill on which a stage had been erected for us. I thought I should soon
die there; and so, partly because I could not, partly because I cared not, I
did not arise. How long they spent their fury on me, he knows for whose
love and sake I suffered all, and for whom it is delightful and glorious to
suffer. Moved at length by a cruel mercy, and wishing to carry me into
their country alive, they refrained from beating me. And, thus half dead,
and drenched in blood, they bore me to the stage. I had scarce begun to
breathe, when they ordered me to come down, to load me with scoffs and
insults, and countless blows on my head and shoulders, and indeed on my
whole body. I should be tedious were I to attempt to tell all that the French
prisoners suffered. They burnt one of my fingers, and crunched another
with their teeth; others already thus mangled, they so wrenched by the tat-
tered nerve, that, even now, though healed, they are frightfully deformed.
Nor indeed was the lot of my fellow-sufferers much better.

But one thing showed that God watched over us, and was trying us
rather than casting us off. One of these savages, breathing nought but
blood and cruelty, came up to me, scarce able to stand on my feet, and,
seizing my nose with one hand, prepared to cut if off with a large knife
which he held in the other. What could I do? Believing that I was soon to
be burnt at the stake, unmoved, I awaited the stroke, groaning to my God
in heart; when stayed, as if by a supernatural power, he drew back his
hand in the very act of cutting. About a quarter of an hour after, he returned, and as if condemning his cowardice and faint-heartedness, again

prepared to do it; when again held back by some unseen hand, he departed. Had he carried out his design, my fate was sealed, for it is not their custom to grant life to captives thus mutilated. At length, late at night, and last of all, I was taken to my captors, without receiving a morsel of food, which I had scarcely touched for several days. The rest of the night I spent in great pain.

My sufferings, great in themselves, were heightened by the sight of what a like cruelty had wreaked on the Christian Hurons, fiercer than all in the case of Eustace; for they had cut off both his thumbs, and, through the stump of his left, with savage cruelty, they drove a sharp stake to his very elbow. This frightful pain he bore most nobly and piously.

The following day we fell in with some other war-canoes, who cut off some of our companions' fingers, amid our great dread.

At last, on the tenth day, about noon, we left our canoes, and performed on foot, the rest of the journey, which lasted four days. Besides the usual hardships of the march, now came that of carrying the baggage. Although my share of this was done quite remissly, both because I was unable, and because I disdained to do it, for my spirit was haughty, even in fetters and death; so that only a small package was given me to bear. We were now racked by hunger, from the ever-increasing want of food. Thus, three days in succession, (and when, on the fourth, we were met by a party from the village), we tasted nothing but some berries, once gathered on the way. For my part, I had, in the beginning of the march, neglected to avail myself of the food which our canoes had supplied abundantly, that I might not offer to their fire and torture, a strong and vigorous frame, for I ingenuously confess my weakness; and when my body worn down by fasting called for food, it found nothing but water; for, on the second day, when we halted, weary with our march, they set a large kettle on the fire as if to prepare food; but it was merely to enable us to drink as much as each chose of the water thus slightly warmed.

At last, on the eve of the Assumption of the Blessed Virgin, we reached the first village of the Iroquois. I thank our Lord Jesus Christ, that, on the day when the whole Christian world exults in the glory of his Mother's Assumption into heaven, he called us to some small share and fellowship of his sufferings and cross. Indeed, we had during the journey always foreseen that it would be a sad and bitter day for us. It would have been easy for René and myself to escape that day and the flames, for, being unbound and often at a distance from our guards, we might, in the darkness of night, have struck off from the road, and even though we should never reach our countrymen, we would at least meet a less cruel death in the woods. He constantly refused to do this, and I was resolved to suffer all that could befall me, rather than forsake, in death, Frenchmen and Christian Hurons, depriving them of the consolation which a priest can afford.

On the Eve of the Assumption then about 3 o'clock we reached a river which flows by their village. Both banks were filled with Iroquois and Hurons formerly captured, now coming forth to meet us, the latter to salute us by a warning that we were to be burnt alive; the former received us with clubs, fists and stones.

And as baldness or thin hair, a shaved, or lightly covered head is an object of their aversion, this tempest burst in its fury on my bare head. Two of my nails had hitherto escaped; these they tore out with their teeth, and with their keen nails stripped off the flesh beneath to the very bones. When satisfied with the cruelties and mockeries which we thus received by the river side, they led us to their village on the top of the hill.

At its entrance we met the youth of all that district awaiting us with clubs, in a line on each side of the road.

Conscious that, if we withdrew ourselves from the ranks of those chastised, we no less withdrew ourselves from that of the children, we cheerfully offered ourselves to our God, thus like a father chastising us, that in us he might be well pleased. Our order was as follows: in the front of the line they placed a Frenchman, alas, entirely naked, not having even his drawers. René Goupil was in the centre, and I last of all closed the line, (we were more fortunate as they had left us our shirts and drawers). The Iroquois scattered themselves through our lines between us and the Hurons, both to check our speed, and to afford more time and ease to our torturers, to strike us thus separately as we passed. Long and cruelly indeed did the "wicked work upon my back," (Ps. 128.3), not with clubs merely, but even with iron rods, which they have in abundance from their proximity to the Europeans; one of the first, armed with a ball of iron of the size of a fist, slung to a thong, dealt me so violent a blow that I should have fallen senseless, had not fear of a second given me strength and courage. Running then our long race amid this fearful hail of blows, we with difficulty reached the stage erected in the centre of the village.

If each here presented a face to excite compassion, that of René was certainly the most pitiable. Being by no means quick or active, he had received so many blows all over his body, but especially on his face, that nothing could be distinguished there but the white of his eyes; more beautiful truly as he more resembled him, whom we have beheld "as a leper, and smitten by God for us," "in whom there was no comeliness or beauty." (Isa. 53.2).

We had but just time to gain breath on this stage, when one with a huge club gave us Frenchmen three terrible blows on the bare back; the savages now took out their knives and began to mount the stage and cut off the fingers of many of the prisoners; and, as a captive undergoes their cruelty in proportion to his dignity, they began with me, seeing, by my conduct, as well as by their words, that I was in authority among the French and Hurons. Accordingly, an old man and a woman approached the spot where I stood; he commanded his companion to cut off my thumb; she at first drew back, but at last, when ordered to do so three or four times by the old wretch, as if by compulsion she cut off my left thumb where it joins the hand. She was an Algonquin, that is, one of that nation which dwells near the French, in New France; she had been captured a few months before, and was a Christian. Her name was Jane. Surely it is pleasing to suffer at the hands of those for whom you would die, and for whom you chose to suffer the greatest torment rather than leave them exposed to the cruelty of visible and invisible enemies.

Then, taking in my other hand the amputated thumb, I offered it to thee, my true and living God, calling to mind the sacrifice which I had for seven years constantly offered thee in thy Church. At last, warned by one of my comrades to desist, since they might otherwise force it into my mouth and compel me to eat it as it was, I flung it from me on the scaffold and left it I know not where.

René had his right thumb cut off at the first joint. I must thank the Almighty that it was his will that my right should be untouched, thus enabling me to write this letter to beg my dear fathers and brothers to offer up their masses, prayers, supplications and entreaties in the holy church of God, to which we know that we are now entitled by a new claim, for she often prays for the afflicted and the captive.

On the following day, the Assumption of the Blessed Virgin, after spending the morning on the stage, we were taken about mid-day to another village, some two miles distant from the first. As I was on the point of marching, the Indian who had brought me, loth to lose my shirt, sent me off naked, except an old and wretched pair of drawers. When I beheld myself thus stripped, "Surely, brother," said I, "thou wilt not send me off thus naked, thou hast taken enough of our property to enrich thee." This touched him, and he gave me enough of the hempen bagging in which our packages had been put up, to cover my shoulders and part of my body. But my shoulders, mangled by their blows and stripes, could not bear this rough and coarse cloth. On the way, while scarcely and at last not at all covered by it, the heat of the sun was so intense, that my skin was dried as though in an oven, and peeled off from my back and arms.

As we entered the second village, blows were not spared, though this is contrary to their usual custom, which is to be content with once bastinadoing the prisoners. The Almighty surely wished us to be somewhat likened in this point to his apostle, who glories that he was thrice beaten with rods; and although they received us with fewer blows than the last, their blows were the more cruel, since, being less embarrassed by the crowd, they were better aimed; some striking constantly on the shins to our exquisite pain.

The rest of the day we spent on the stage, and the night in a hut tied down half naked to the bare ground, at the mercy of all ages and sexes. For we had been handed over to the sport of the children and youth who threw hot coals on our naked bodies, which, bound as we were, it was no easy matter to throw off. In this manner they make their apprenticeship in cruelty, and from less, grow accustomed to greater. We spent there two days and nights with scarcely any food or sleep, in great anguish of mind as far as I was concerned. For, from time to time, they mounted the stage, cutting off the fingers of my Huron companions, binding hard cords around their fists with such violence, that they fainted, and, while each of them suffered but his own pain, I suffered that of all; I was afflicted with as intense grief as you can imagine a father's heart to feel at the sight of his children's misery; for, with the exception of a few old Christians, I had begotten them all recently in Christ by baptism.

Yet amid all this the Lord gave me such strength that, suffering myself, I was able to console the suffering Hurons and French. So that, both on the road and on the stage, when the tormenting crowd of "saluters," (for so they call those who wreak their cruelty on the captives as they arrive,) had dropped away, I exhorted them, at one time generally, at another individually, to preserve their patience, nor lose confidence which would have a great reward; to remember "that, by many tribulations it behooves us to enter the kingdom of heaven;" that the time was come indeed, foretold to us by God, when he said: "Ye shall lament and weep, but the world shall rejoice, but your sorrow shall be turned into joy;" that we were like to "a woman in travail, who, when she brings forth, hath sorrow, because her hour is come; but, when she has brought forth, no longer remembers her anguish for joy that a man is born into the world;" (John 26.21); so should they feel assured that, in a few days, these momentary pains would give place to never-ending joys. And surely I had reason to rejoice when I beheld them so well disposed, especially the older Christians, Joseph, Eustace, and the other two; for, on the very day that we reached the first village, Theodore had freed himself from his bonds; but, as during the battle he had had his shoulder blade broken by the butt-end of a musket, he died on his way to the French.

Never till now had the Indian scaffold beheld French or other Christians captives. So that, contrary to usual custom, we were led around through all their villages to gratify the general curiosity. The third, indeed, we entered scathless, but on the scaffold a scene met my eyes more heart-rending than any torment; it was a group of four Hurons, taken elsewhere by some other party, and dragged here to swell our wretched company. Among other cruelties every one of these had lost some fingers, and the eldest of the band his two thumbs. Joining these, I at once began to instruct them, separately, on the articles of faith; then, on the very stage itself, I baptized two, with rain-drops gathered from the leaves of a stalk of Indian corn, given us to chew; the other two, I christened as we were led by a stream on our way to another village. At this place, cold setting in after the rain, we suffered extremely from it, as we were entirely uncovered. Often shivering with cold on the stage, I would without orders come down and enter some hut, but I had scarcely begun to warm myself when I was commanded to return to the scaffold.

William Couture had thus far lost none of his fingers; this, exciting the displeasure of an Indian in this village, he sawed off the fore-finger of his right hand in the middle; the pain was most excruciating as for this amputation he employed not a knife, but in its stead a kind of shell, there very abundant. As it could not cut the sinews which were hard and slippery, he wrenched the finger so violently, that, when the sinews gave way, the poor fellow's arm swelled fearfully up to the very elbow. An Indian, touched by mercy, took him to his hut and kept him there two days which we spent in that village; leaving me in ignorance and great anxiety as to his fate.

At nightfall, we were taken to a hut where the youth awaited us. They ordered us to sing as other captives are wont to do; we at last complied, for alas, what else could we do? but we sang the "Canticles of the Lord in a strange land." Torture followed the chanting, and its fury burst especially on René and myself, for the good savage still kept William in his hut. Accordingly, on me, and especially on René, they threw hot ashes and live coals, burning him terribly in the breast.

They next hung me up between two poles in the hut, tied by the arms above the elbow with coarse rope woven of the bark of trees. Then I thought I was to be burnt, for this is one of their usual preliminaries. And that I might know that, if I had thus far borne anything with fortitude or even with patience, these came not from myself, but from him who gives strength to the weary; now, as though left to myself in this torture, I groaned aloud, for "I will glory in my infirmities that the power of Christ may dwell in me," (2 Cor. 12.9), and from my intense pain, I begged my torturers to ease me some little from those hard, rough ropes. But God justly ordained that the more I pleaded, the more tightly they drew my chains. At last when I had been hanging thus about a quarter of an hour, they unloosed me as I was on the point of fainting. I render thee thanks, O Lord Jesus, that I have been allowed to learn, by some slight experience, how much thou didst deign to suffer on the cross for me, when the whole weight of thy most sacred body hung not by ropes, but by thy hands and feet pierced by hardest nails! Other chains followed these, for we were tied to the ground to pass the rest of the night. What did they not then do to my poor Huron companions thus tied hand and foot? What did they not attempt on me? But once more I thank thee, Lord, that thou didst save me, thy priest, ever unsullied from the impure hands of the savages. When we had thus spent two days in that village, we were led back to the second which we had entered, that our fate might be finally determined.

We had now been for seven days led from village to village, from scaffold to scaffold, become a spectacle to God and to his angels, as we may hope from his divine goodness; a scoff and jeer to the vilest savages, when we were at last told that that day should end our lives amid the flames. Though, in sooth, this last act was not without its horrors, yet the good pleasure of God and the hope of a better life subject to no sin rendered it more one of joy. Then, addressing my French and Huron companions as it were for the last time, I bid them be of good heart, amid their mental and bodily sufferings to think "diligently upon him that had endured such opposition of sinners against himself not to be weary, fainting in their minds" (Heb. 12.3), but to hope that the morrow would unite us to our God to rein forever.

Fearing lest we might be torn from one another, I especially advised Eustace to look toward me when we could not be together, and by placing his hands on his breast and raising his eyes to heaven to show his contrition for his sins, so that I could absolve him, as I had already frequently done after hearing his confession on the way, and after our arrival. As advised, he several times made the signal.

The sachems, however, on further deliberation, resolved, that no precipitate step was to be taken with regard to the French, and, when they had summoned us before the council, they declared that our lives were spared. To almost all the Hurons likewise they granted their lives: three were excepted, Paul, Eustace, and Stephen, who were put to death in the three villages which make up the tribe; Stephen in the village where we were, known as Andagoron, Paul in Ossernenon, and Eustace in Teonontogen. The last was burned in almost every part of his body and then beheaded; he bore all most piously, and while it is usual for dying captives to cry out:

Exoriatur nostris ex ossibus ultor,
May an avenger arise from our ashes,

he, on the contrary, in the Christian spirit which he had so deeply imbibed in baptism, implored his countrymen standing around, not to let any

feeling for his fate prevent the concluding of a peace with the Iroquois.[4]
Paul Ononhoratoon, who, after going through the usual fiery ordeal was
tomahawked in the village of Ossernenon, was a young man of about
twenty-five, full of life and courage; for such they generally put to death,
to sap as it were the life-blood of the hostile tribe. With a noble contempt
of death arising, as he openly professed on the way, from his hope of a better life, this generous man had repeatedly, when the Iroquois came up to
me to tear out my nails, or inflict some other injury, offered himself to
them, begging them to leave me and turn their rage on him. May the Lord
return him a hundred fold with usury for that heroic charity, which led
him to give his life for his friends, and for those who had begotten him in
Christ in bondage!

Toward evening of that day they carried off William Couture, whom
they regarded as a young man of unparalleled courage, to Teonontogen,
the farthest village of their territory, and gave him to an Indian family. It
is the custom of these savages, when they spare a prisoner's life, to adopt
him into some family to supply the place of a deceased member, to whose
rights he in a manner succeeds; he is subject thenceforward to no man's orders except those of the head of that family, who, to acquire this right, offers some presents. But seeing that René and I were less vigorous, they led
us to the first village, the residence of the party that had captured us, and
left us there till some new resolution should be taken.

After so many a long day spent fasting, after so many sleepless nights,
after so many wounds and stripes, and especially after such heart-rending
anguish of mind, when at last time was, so to speak, given us to feel our
sufferings, we sank into a state of helplessness, scarce able to walk, or even
stand erect: neither night nor day brought a moment of repose; this resulted from many causes, but chiefly from our still untended wounds; this
state was rendered more trying by the myriads of lice, fleas, and bedbugs,
of which the maimed and mutilated state of our fingers did not permit us
to clear our persons. Besides this, we suffered from hunger; more truly here
than elsewhere is the saying,

Cibus non utilis ægro.
Food is hurtful to the sick.

So that, with nothing to add to their American corn, (which in Europe we
call Turkish), carelessly bruised between two stones, but unripe squashes,

---

[4] Jogues referred to the custom of the victim's death song, as in Staden's and Regnaut's
texts. He was reminding readers that it is more Christian to forgive one's torturers than
to taunt them.

we were brought to the brink of the grave; and René, especially, whose stomach refused this food, and who, from his many wounds, had almost lost his sight.

The Indians then, seeing us fail day by day, hunted up in the village some small fishes and some bits of meat dried by the fire and sun, and, pounding these, mixed them with our sagamity.

After three weeks, we were just recovering from our illness when they sought to put us to death.

The two hundred Indians who had maltreated us so on the way, advanced into New France, to the point where the River Iroquois, so called from them, empties into the great river St. Lawrence; here, seeing a party of the French engaged in laying the foundations of Fort Richelieu,[5] they thought they could easily kill some and carry off the rest as prisoners. Accordingly, to the number of two hundred, in a single column and almost all armed with muskets, they rushed almost unexpected upon the whites engaged in the various works. At the first onset of the foe, the French, though but a handful compared to the number of the savages, flew to arms, and so bravely and successfully repulsed their fierce assailants, that, after killing two, and wounding many more, they put the rest to flight. The war party returned furious, and, as though they had been greatly wronged who had gone forth to do wrong, demanded the death of those of us who were yet alive. They asserted it to be a shame that three Frenchmen should live quietly among them when they had so lately slain three Iroquois. By these complaints, René's safety, especially, and my own, were in great jeopardy. He alone, who, as he gave, protecteth life, warded off the blow.

On the eve of the Nativity of the Blessed Virgin, one of the principal Hollanders,[6] who have a settlement not more than twenty leagues from these Indians, came with two others, to endeavor to effect our liberation. He remained there several days, offered much, promised more, obtained nothing. But, as they are a wily and cunning race of savages, in order not to appear to refuse all that a friend asked, but to concede something to his desires, they lyingly asserted that they would, in a few days, restore us to our countrymen. This was, perhaps, the wish of some of them, but, in the latter part of September (for constant rain had put the matter off till that time), a final council was held on our fate, although provisions had been prepared and men appointed to take us back. Here the opinion of the few well inclined was rejected. Confusion carried the day, and some clamorous chiefs declared that they would never suffer a Frenchman to be taken back

---

[5] At Sorel, Quebec, fifty miles northeast of Montreal.
[6] Arendt Van Corlaer, a leader of the Dutch colony near today's Albany, New York.

alive. The council broke up in alarm, and each, as if in flight, returned home, even those who came from other villages. Left thus to the cruelty of bloodthirsty men, attempts were constantly made on our lives. Some, tomahawk in hand, prowled around the cabins to find and dispatch us. However, toward the close of the council, God had inspired me with some thought that induced me to draw my companions together without the village in a field belonging to the house where I was; here, ignorant of what had transpired, we lay hid as it were in safety, until the storm, beneath which we should all have fallen, had we remained in the village, was somewhat calmed.

William was, after this, taken back by his master, to his own village; René and I, perceiving that there was now no hope of our return, withdrew to a neighboring hill, which commands the village, in order to pray. Here, remote from every witness, and from all officious intrusion, we resigned ourselves entirely to God and to his holy will; on our road back to the village, we were reciting our beads, and had already completed four decades of the rosary, when we met two young men who commanded us to return to the village. "Dear brother," said I, "we know not what may be, in this period of general excitement, the design of these men. Let us commend ourselves earnestly to God, and to the most Blessed Virgin, our good Mother." We had reached the village in prayer, when, at its very entrance, one of the two whom we had met, plucking forth his tomahawk which was concealed in his dress, dealt René so deadly a blow on the head, that he fell lifeless, invoking the most holy name of Jesus as he fell. We had happily, mindful of the indulgence thereby gained, often reminded each other to close our life by uttering, with our dying voice, that most holy name.

At the sight of the reeking hatchet, I knelt down on the spot, and, uncovering my head, awaited a like blow. But, when I had been there a moment or two, they bade me rise, as they had no right to kill me, for I was the slave of another family. Rising then in haste, I ran to my still breathing companion, and conferred absolution, which I was in the habit of giving him after his confession every other day; then two other blows, dealt before my very face, added him to the number of the blessed. He was thirty-five years of age, eminent for his simplicity of manners, his innocence of life, his patience in adversity, entirely submissive to God, whom he, in all things, regarded as present before his eyes, and resigned to his most holy will in love. Most worthy is he, Reverend Father, to be counted among thy children, not only because he had spent several months in one of the novitiates of the Society, in a most edifying manner, and had afterward, by the command of superiors, to whom he gave the entire disposal of his life, proceeded to Huronia, to aid the Christian population by his medical knowledge, but especially does he merit it from the fact, that, a few days before his death, impelled by a desire of uniting himself more closely to God, he pronounced the usual vows of the Society to subject himself to it as far as in him lay. And certain it is that, in life as in death, where his last word was the most holy name of Jesus, he had proved himself no unworthy son of the Society. Nay, I not only love him as a brother, but revere him as a martyr—martyr to obedience, and still more, a martyr to the faith and to the cross. As he was very pious, and accustomed to be with the Christians, or such as were most intimate with our Christians, he daily spent a long time in prayer, to the wonder and even suspicion of the savages, so novel did it seem to them. These suspicions were confirmed in their minds when one day, taking off the cap of a child in the hut where he lived, he made him make a sign of the cross on his breast and forehead; for a superstitious old Indian, the grandfather of the boy, seeing this, ordered him to be killed. This I afterward learned from the boy's mother, who told me that he had been killed by the old man for that reason.

But to resume my narrative: after I had been seated a little while in our hut, where my life had been pretty quiet, I was taken to another, the hut of him who had cut off my thumb, a most bitter enemy of the Algonquins, and consequently of the French. Here, not I alone, but the other Iroquois, every moment expected to see me tomahawked. Accordingly, some who had given me articles of clothing, that I might, in part at least, cover my person, now asked them back, for fear of losing them by my death.

The next day, I was filled with the greatest anxiety to know what had become of my dear companion, that I resolved to look for his body at all hazards, and commit it, if possible, to the earth. After stripping it entirely, they had contemptuously tied a rope around the neck, and dragging it through the village, had flung it into a ravine at a considerable distance. As I was going out of the village, I met the old man in whose hut I had formerly been; he advised me to stay at home. "Whither art thou hurrying?" he exclaimed, "thou art scarce alive; they seek thee everywhere to slay thee, and yet thou goest to find an already putrefying corpse; dost thou not see those fierce young braves, who are about to kill thee?" Some, in fact, went out of the village armed, just before me; but I fearlessly pursued my way; for, in my bitter anguish, it was a pain to live, a gain to die in such a work of charity. When the old man saw me so resolute, he asked another Indian to go with me. By his assistance, I found the body, which the dogs had begun to gnaw about the hips, and, sinking it in the deepest part of the torrent, covered it with a heap of stones, intending to return the next day with a spade, and bury it secretly and alone, for I was afraid they would disinter it.

As I re-entered our hut, two young men were waiting to take me to their village to put me to death. Aware of their design, I told them that I was in the hands of those with whom I lived, that if they gave the slightest consent, I would accompany them, and would in fact have done so. Seeing that they gained nothing in this way, the next day one of them who, at the time of our capture, had been wounded with his brother, seeing me in the field whither I had gone to execute some order of my owners, seized a hatchet and was rushing on me to kill me, when he was stopped by an old man of our family, and prevented from accomplishing his design. Thus did the Almighty teach me "to cast all my solicitude on him," knowing that he hath care of me, and that I should not fear the face of a man when the Almighty was the protector of my life, without whose permission not a hair could fall from my head.

As I could not that day accomplish my design, early the next morning I proceeded to the spot with a spade or hoe to inter the body, but alas, they had carried off my brother. I returned to the spot; I descended the mount at the foot of which the torrent ran; I descended again; I searched the wood on the opposite side—all, all in vain. The torrent ran swollen by the night rains, but, unrestrained by either its depth or the cold, for it was the first of October, I tried the bottom with my stick and feet, as I thought that the stream might have borne it to another spot; I asked all whom I met, whether they knew anything of him; but as they are a most lying race, and always give an affirmative answer without regard to truth, they falsely told me that he had been dragged to a quite distant river. What groans did I not utter then! What tears did I not shed, mingling them with the waters of that mountain stream, chanting to thee, my God, the psalms thy holy Church employs in the service of the dead!

When, however, the snows had melted away, I heard from the young men that they had seen the scattered bones of the Frenchman. Hurrying to the spot, I gathered up the half-gnawed bones, the remnants left by the dogs, the foxes and the crows, and especially the skull fractured in many places; these reverently kissing, I committed to the earth, that I might, one day, if such were God's will, bear with me as a great treasure to a conse-crated Christian land.

From many other dangers, which I knew and knew not, did the Lord rescue me, in spite of all the ill will and hate of the Iroquois, unwilling and furious as the Iroquois were. But the following I should not omit. There was in our cabin an idiot who asked me to let him cut off two hands' breadth from a wretched bit of cloth not seven palms long, yet all that I had to cover me. Brother! said I, you see me shivering every night under this short thin covering; yet do as thou wilt. My modest excuse offended him, and when soon after I went to the huts of the baptized Hurons, whom I daily instructed and bore again till Christ should be formed in them (Gal. 4.19), he came in search of me, and fiercely bade me return. When I had entered our cabin, René's murderer was sent for, that the same hand might end both our lives; they looked for him in vain, he could not be found. I was accordingly sent the next day into a field of my master's with two women, under the pretext of bringing back some article or other, but in fact to expose me to death; for, two days before, the only son of one of their noble women had died in our cabin, and I was to be sacrificed to his *manes*.[7]

These women had with them the squashes, corn and other articles of the kind which were to be the fee of my executioner. "But I, like a deaf man, heard not" the vain things they devised, "and like a dumb man opened not my mouth, and I became like a man that heareth not, nor hath a reply in his mouth," (Ps. 37.14), "because in thee, O Lord, have I hoped;" but, mindful of his meekness "who was led like a lamb to the slaughter," (Acts 8.32), I went to my death, begging the Lord with David "to turn away evil from my enemies and scatter them in his truth." (Ps. 53.7). About midway we met the looked-for murderer; seeing him coming at a distance, I commended myself for the last time to God, begging him to receive my life spent with care and anguish; but my sins still rendered me unworthy. He passed quietly by us, and meeting his mother, she addressed some words, of what import I know not, to those who conducted me; on this, trembling and fleeing as it were, they left me in the road, for they saw that I was aware of their design.

Amid this frequent fear and death, while every day I die, or rather drag on a life more bitter than any death, two months glided away. During this time I made no effort to learn their language, for why should I, who every moment expected to die? The village was a prison for me. I avoided being seen. I loved the wild wood, where I begged the Lord not to disdain to speak to his servant, to give me strength in such fearful trials, in which, indeed, if I have become a prodigy to many, God was my stout Helper, and often by his unfailing goodness roused my drooping spirits. I had recourse to the Holy Scriptures, my only refuge in the tribulations, which had found me exceedingly: these did I venerate; with these I wished to die. Of all the books which we were carrying to Huronia for the use of the Frenchmen living there, none had fallen into my hands but the Epistle of St. Paul to the Hebrews, with the paraphrase of the Rt. Rev. Anthony Godeau, Bishop of Gratz. This little book, with a picture of St. Bruno, the illustrious founder of the Carthusian Order, to which some indulgences were attached, and a rude wooden cross which I had made, I always carried about me, so that, whenever death, which I had ever present before my eyes, should strike me

---

[7]The spirit or memory of a dead person. The term is of Roman origin, but Jogues applied it to the Iroquois practice of "covering" for the death of an individual by adopting, or occasionally killing, a captive.

down, I could most cheerfully die with the Holy Scriptures which had ever been my greatest consolation, with the graces and indulgences of my most holy Mother the Church, whom I had always greatly, but now most tenderly, loved, and with the cross of my Lord and Savior.

And now the middle of October was come when the Indians leave their villages to go and hunt deer, which they take by traps, or kill with their guns, in the use of which they are very skilful. This season, to the Indians one of relaxation and enjoyment, brought its new burden of sorrows for me; for I was given to a party, who were first amazed at me, then ridiculed, and at last began to hate me.

Mindful of the character imposed upon me by God, I began with modesty to discourse with them of the adoration of one only God, of the observance of his commandments, of heaven, hell, and the other mysteries of our Faith, as fully as I was able. At first, indeed, they listened, but when they saw me constantly recur to these things, and especially when the chase did not meet with the desired success, then they declared that I was an Otkon,[8] who caused them to take so little game. But what turned their ill-will into perfect rage and fury, so to speak, was this: It is a custom with all these nations to have recourse, in their hunting, fishing, war, sickness, and the like, to a certain demon whom they call Aireskoi.[9] Whoever desires his fishing, hunting, or other expeditions to be successful, takes meat, and other of the better articles of food, and begs the oldest of the house or village to *bless* them for him, if I may use the term; and there are some to whose blessings they attach more value than to others. The old man, standing opposite the one that holds the meat, in a loud and distinct voice, speaks thus: "O, demon Aireskoi, behold, we offer this meat to thee, and from it we prepare thee a banquet, that thou mayest eat thereof, and show us where the deer are lurking, mayest lead them into our traps"—(if not during the chase)—"that by thee we may again behold the spring, taste the new harvest, and again engage in the chase in the fall"—(if in illness)— "that by these we may recover health."

The very first time I heard a formula couched in such words, I was filled with a deep detestation of this savage superstition, and firmly resolved to abstain forever from meats thus offered. They interpreted this abstinence on my part, and this contempt of their demon, as the cause of their taking so little game; "the wicked have hated me without cause." (John 15.25). As, under the influence of this hate, they would neither listen to my in-

---

[8] A demon or evil spirit.

[9] This was the Iroquois and Huron war deity, not a "Great Spirit" or monotheistic God. Thus although Jogues's captors would have made offerings to Aireskoi in preparation for a war, he was misplaced in his accusation that they were in thrall to a demon of this name.

structions, nor help me to acquire their language, in which I refuted their fables, I resolved to devote my time entirely to spiritual exercises. Accordingly, I went forth every morning from the midst of this Babylon, that is, our hut where constant worship was paid to the devil and to dreams, and "saved myself in the mountain" (Gen. 19.17), a neighboring hill. Here I had formed a large cross on a majestic tree by stripping off the bark, and, at its foot, I spent the whole day with my God, whom, almost alone in those vast regions, I worshipped and loved; sometimes in meditation or in prayer, at other times reading an "Imitation of Christ," [10] which I had just before recovered. This for sometime was unperceived; but, on one occasion, finding me, as was my wont, in prayer before my cross, they attacked me most violently, saying that they hated the cross; that it was a sign that they and their friends the neighbors, (Europeans), knew not, alluding to the Dutch Protestants.[11]

Upon this, I changed my conduct, and whereas I had before carefully avoided praying or kneeling in their hut, that I might not give them the slightest reason to complain, (for we should, especially among savages, but little accustomed to such things, act in all prudence), I now conceived that I should no longer refrain from those pious exercises which make up a spiritual life, a life I far preferred to my temporal one. This I believed would be serviceable to them when the moment of their conversion should come, "which the Father hath put in his own power." (Acts 1.7).

While thus an object of their enmity, I certainly suffered much from hunger and cold, the contempt of the lowest of the men, the bitter hatred of their women.

The latter, who are the greatest gainers by the hunting season, regarded me as the cause of their want and poverty. I suffered most from hunger; for, as almost all the venison on which they chiefly lived had been offered to the devil in these oblations, I spent many days fasting; and, almost every night, when I came in fasting, I would see our Egyptians sitting over their fleshpots, which my severe, though self-imposed law, prevented my touching. And, although reasons occurred to me, at times dissuading me from this course, yet, by God's grace, I never suffered myself to break my resolution, but in hunger said to my God: "We shall be filled with the good things of thy house." (Ps. 65.5). "I shall be satisfied when thy glory shall appear." (Ps. 16.15). "When thou wilt truly fill the desire of thy hungry

---

[10] *De Imitatione Christi* (1417–1421), a religious work attributed to Thomas à Kempis. The term is also applied to reenactments of or comparisons to Christ, such as Jogues did in his tortures.

[11] As the Jesuits were leaders of the Counter-Reformation, Jogues did not hesitate to denounce Protestantism as impious.

servants in thy holy city, Jerusalem, which thou wilt fill forever with the fat of corn." (Ps. 147.14).

I suffered also greatly from cold, amid the deep snows under my scanty, worn-out cloak, especially at night, when ordered to sleep uncovered on the bare ground on some rough bark; for, though they had plenty of deer-skins, perfectly useless to them, not one was given to me; nay, when some-times on a very bitter night, I would, overcome by the cold, secretly take one, they rose at once and pulled it from me; so great was their enmity against me. My skin was now in such a state that I could with David say: "It had withered with the filth of dust." (Job 7.5). It burst with cold, and gave me great pain all over my body. But when inward afflictions came crowding on these outward cares, then indeed my grief became intolerable. I remembered that I had been recently covered with the life's blood of my dearest companion; and those who came from William's village told me he had already been put to death with exquisite tortures, and that I myself, on my return, was to meet the same fate. With this came up the remem-brance of my past life, stained with so many sins, and so unfaithful to God, and I grieved that I was thus to be torn away unaided by any of the sacra-ments in the very midst of my course, rejected as it were by God, with no good works sent on to plead my cause. In this state, loathing life, yet shrink-ing from death, I uttered many a mournful cry, and said unto my God: "When shall sorrows and miseries have an end? How long wilt thou for-get our want and our tribulation? When, after this tempest, wilt thou give us calm, and, after weeping, joy and exultation? And, had not those days been shortened, my flesh had not been saved."(Mark 13.20).

I had recourse to my wonted refuge of the Scriptures, my usual retreat, and passages which my memory had retained taught me how I should think of God in goodness, even though not upheld by sensible devotion; that I should know that the just man lives by faith. I searched them; I fol-lowed their stream, and sought, as it were, to quench my daily thirst. "I meditated on the law of God night and day." (Ps. 1.2); and, "had not the law of God been my meditation, I had then, perhaps, perished in my ab-jection." (Ps. 109.92). "And my soul had passed through a water unsup-portable." (Ps. 124.5). "But, blessed be God, who did not give us a prey to the teeth of our enemies." (Ps. 124.6). "Whose hour had come and the power of darkness." (Luke 22.53). In which we "were overmuch op-pressed." (2 Cor. 1.8). So that I was weary of life, and could say with Job, though in a different meaning, "Although he should kill me, I will trust in him." (Job 13.15).

Thus passed two months away in this retreat, where, like St. Bernard, the disciple of the trees of the forest, I thought of naught but God, until be-come an object too hateful to all to be any longer borne with, I was sent back to the village before the usual time. During the way, which took us eight days, "I was become like a beast of burden before God," (Ps. 73.23), under the heavy load of venison which I carried; and, being ignorant what fate might await me at the village, endeavored to be ever united with him, for a party that had gone before had spread many reports about me. My sufferings in this journey, from the intense cold, were extreme; for I was nearly naked, and we generally passed the night in the open air.

My unhealed fingers were another source of misery; for the wounds were hardly closed by the middle of January. In the village, however, a thin skin was added to my worn out cloak; in this wretched guise I traversed the streets of our village, begging that the Lord would one day join me with his saints who formerly served him in "sheepskins and goatskins, distressed, afflicted, of whom the world was not worthy." (Heb. 11.37). And I daily saw the Indians well dressed in the cloth and garments which our baggage had plentifully supplied, while I was shivering night and day with cold; but this was little; more was I moved to see these heathen men unworthily profane things dedicated to the service of God. One of them had made himself leggings of two of the veils used at mass: "*Non hos servatum munus in usus.*" [12]

I can in truth say, before God, of all that period up to mid-January, "Even unto this hour, we both hunger and thirst, and are naked and are buffeted, and have no fixed abode. And we labor, working with our hands; we are reviled, and we bless; we are persecuted, and we suffer it; we are ill-spoken of and we entreat; we are made as the refuse of this world, the off-scouring of all even until now."(1 Cor. 4.11).

When, in the middle of January, my owners returned from the chase, they, in a manner, dressed me in skins, until a Lorrainese who lived among our Dutch neighbors, hearing that I suffered greatly from cold, sent me from his house, a dress, such as they usually sell to the Indians. This brought some slight alleviation to my pains, but I found still greater in the care of an old woman, whose only son had died not long before. She was of very noble rank in the nation, for barbarism, too, has its nobles; she took care of me, and the Lord gave me grace in her eyes, yet all this was but a slight solace in such woe.

When I saw that my life was at last in some sort spared, I applied myself to the study of the language, and, as our cabin was the council hall, not only of the village, but of almost all that country, I began to instruct the oldest on the articles of our faith. They, too, put me many questions, as to the sun, and moon, the face, which seemed to appear on his disk, of

---

[12] An object not destined to such a use." From the *Aeneid* 4.64 [Shea's note].

the circumference of the earth, of the size of the ocean, its tides, whether, as they had heard, the heavens and the earth anywhere met each other; adapting my philosophy to their reach, I satisfied them on all these; then, indeed, they began to wonder, and say, "Indeed, we should have lost a great treasure, had we put this man to death, as we have been so often on the point of doing." Then I endeavored to raise their minds from creatures, to a knowledge of the Creator; I confuted their old wives' tales of the creation of the world, which their fable makes out to have been created by a tortoise;[13] the sun was, I showed them, not only without an intellect, but even a lifeless mass, much less a God; "that if, delighted by its appearance, they believed it to be a God, they should now that the Lord was much more beautiful than it;" that Aireskoi, whom they falsely asserted to be the Author and Preserver of life, and the Giver of all the good things which they enjoyed, was not a God but a demon. Were they as easy in belief as they are easy to be convinced, the matter would soon be settled. But the prince of the world expelled from almost every quarter of the globe, by the power of the cross, seems to have retreated into these regions, as his last stronghold; so that the kingdom which this strong man armed has possessed here for so many thousand years, can be overthrown only in lapse of time, and by unconquerable constancy on the part of the soldiers of Christ. From time to time, however, Christ, their true Lord and Lord of all, chooses some for himself, not only among the infants, many of whom are now in heaven, but even among adults, some of whom I baptized in sickness or in bondage.

Many other native adults I instructed, but some refused to listen to me, others rejected me, others assented with their lips, merely from a kind of politeness which makes them consider it rude to contradict you; and without attention to which, many would be deceived. I sometimes even made excursions to the neighboring villages, to console and instruct the Christian Hurons, "who had not bent their knee before Baal," and to absolve them after hearing their confessions; to announce God everywhere as far as I was able, to succor the dying, but especially to save infants in danger of death. This was my only solace in my bitterest mental pangs; and once, with this view, I visited a neighboring village, and there baptized five children; I learnt, soon after, in another excursion, that all had been called to heaven.

In these and like exercises, therefore, and attempts to study their language, (for what study can there be without writing?) two months

---

[13] The Iroquois creation myth involves a woman who falls out of the sky onto the back of a tortoise, then obtains soil from the bottom of the watery world from which to make land.

glided by. About the middle of March, when the snow had melted away, they took me with them to their fishing ground. We accordingly started; the party consisted of the old man and woman, a little boy and myself; four days' travel brought us to a lake where we caught nothing but a few little fishes.

The intestines of these generally served as a seasoning for our sagamity, the fish being laid by to carry back to the village.

Such food as this, with the intestines of deer full of blood, and half putrefied excrement, and mushrooms boiled, and rotten oysters, and frogs, which they eat whole, head and feet, not even skinned or cleaned; such food, had hunger, custom, and want of better, made, I will not say tolerable, but even pleasing. How often, in those journeys, and in that quiet wilderness, "did we sit by the rivers of Babylon, and weep, while we remembered thee, Sion," not only exulting in heaven, but even praising thy God on earth! "How often, though in a strange land, did we sing the canticle of the Lord;" and mountain and wildwood resound with the praises of their Maker, which from their creation they had never heard! How often, on the stately trees of the forest, did I carve the most sacred name of Jesus, that, seeing it, the demons might fly, who tremble when they hear it! How often on them too, did I not strip off the bark, to form the most holy Cross of the Lord, that the foe might fly before it, and that by it, thou, O Lord, my king, "mightst reign in the midst of thy enemies," the enemies of thy cross, the misbelievers and the pagans who dwell in that land, and the demons who rule so powerfully there! I rejoice, too, that I had been led by the Lord into the wilderness, at the very time when the church recalls the story of his Passion, so that I might more uninterruptedly remember the course of its bitterness and gall, and my soul might pine away at the remembrance.

Accordingly, after performing the services which I owed as a slave to my masters, the slave of savages, (my occupation being to cut and bring in wood for the hut), I spent almost all my time before a large cross which I had formed on a huge tree at a considerable distance from the hut. But I was not long allowed to enjoy this holy repose; indeed, too many days had I passed, unharmed by my wonted terrors. On Monday, in Holy Week, an Indian came to us from our village; the reason of his coming was this. Ten Iroquois, among whom was the son of the man who had cut off my thumb, and in whose hut I now dwelt, had gone out on a war-party about midsummer. (Summer, fall, and even the whole winter, passed without their being heard of), they were consequently given up, especially as neighboring nations said that they had fallen victims to the cruelty of the enemy. But when, early in the spring, a captive was brought in during our absence, who, being also questioned as to them, gave the same answer, and said that they had been killed; then, indeed, deeming beyond a doubt, what they already believed to be true, they sacrificed that very captive to the *manes* of the young brave, the son of my master.

But the soul of this captive seemed too vile to atone for the life of the noble youth. I was accordingly sent for, from the lake where we were, that, together with him, I might compensate for the death of the chief. Such, at least, was the conclusion to which one or two old women and a decrepit old man had come. We consequently set out the next day, as if in flight, and, as a pretext, they said that parties of the enemy were around us. We reached the village toward evening, on Maundy Thursday. The morrow, which had closed the Savior's life, was now to close mine also! when it pleased him, who, by dying on that day, had given life to my spirit, to give it also to my body. Accordingly, on that day when I was to have been put to death, a rumor was first spread without any good authority, that those supposed to be dead were still alive; then it came that they had joined another war party, and were now bringing in twenty-two captives.

Thus did God scatter the malignant designs of the savages, instructing and showing me that he took care of me, that I should cast myself wholly on him, conscious that he would not recoil and let me fall.

Although I naturally rejoiced to be rescued from these and other dangers, yet I sighed to see myself again given over to new sorrows and heartbreaking torments, compelled me to drag on a life more painful than the most cruel death. For the success, as well as the reverses of these men, fell heavily on me alone; if any one was slain in battle, I was at once demanded as a victim to be offered to his shade. But if, as was generally the case, they brought in prisoners after having killed more, my heart was always rent with grief, for they were either Frenchmen or allies of the French.

Naturally, therefore, did I prefer retirement and solitude, where, far from the villages, I as no longer dismayed at the wonted cruelty of these savages, and where I could better and more freely hold converse with God. Yet knowing, that, though Leah was blear-eyed, she was more fruitful than Rachel, and bore more children; mindful, too, of the Institute of our Society,[14] which prefers our neighbor's salvation to our private spiritual delights, I reluctantly remained at home; for the village enabled me to make greater progress in the language, and to secure the salvation of infants and adults by baptism; for I was greatly grieved whenever, during my absence, an adult died without instruction or a child without baptism.

To return to our war party: they came in bringing twenty-two prisoners, but belonging to a nation with whom they had as yet never been at war;

---

[14] Rules of the Society of Jesus, or Jesuits.

still, in violation of all right and justice, they were beaten with clubs and stripes, and mutilated by the usual cutting off of fingers. Five of them were to be put to death, for all the rest, being boys and girls, or women, were kept as slaves. Their instruction was now an object of my solicitude, for I was ignorant of their language; yet by God's grace I was able, by a few words that I picked up, but chiefly by the kindness of one who knew both languages, to instruct and baptize them. This happened at Easter. At Whitsuntide, they brought in new prisoners, three women with their little children, the men having been killed near the French settlements. They were led into the village entirely naked, not even with any kind of petticoat on; and, after being severely beaten on the way, had their thumbs cut off. One of them, a thing not hitherto done, was burnt all over her body, and afterwards thrown into a huge pyre. And worthy of note is a strange rite I then beheld, when this woman was burnt; at each wound which they inflicted, by holding lighted torches to her body, an old man in a loud voice exclaimed, "Demon Aireskoi, we offer thee this victim, whom we burn for thee, that thou mayst be filled with her flesh, and render us ever anew victorious over our enemies." Her body was cut up, sent to the various villages and devoured; for about mid-winter, grieving as it were, that they had refrained from eating the flesh of some prisoners, they had in a solemn sacrifice of two bears, which they offered to their demon, uttered the words, "Justly dost thou punish us, oh, Demon Aireskoi; lo! this long time we have taken no captives; during the summer and fall, we have taken none of the Algonquins.[15] (These they consider properly their enemies.) We have sinned against thee, in that we ate not the last captives thrown into our hands; but, if we shall ever again capture any, we promise thee to devour them as we now consume these two bears"; and they kept their word. This poor woman I baptized in the midst of the flames, unable to do so before, and then only while raising a drink to her parched lips.

On the eve of St. John the Baptist, of whom it is written "that many shall rejoice at his birth," a new weight was added to my usual sorrows; eleven Hurons and a Frenchman were brought in; three Frenchmen and ten Hurons, among them some of the most celebrated Christians, had been killed, treacherously circumvented by a show of friendship. Of these, they bore the scalps or hair, which they tear off with the skin, from their fallen enemies. I certainly felt, in my own person, this punishment deserved by my sins, and pronounced of old by God to his

---

[15] This nation lived north of the St. Lawrence River and were long-standing enemies of the Iroquois. Although the name is sometimes applied to all the natives of eastern North America speaking Algonquian languages, it is properly used only for this tribe.

people, when he said "that their new moons, their festivals, and solemnities should be turned into grief and sorrow," as Easter and Whitsuntide, and the nativity of St. John the Baptist, each brought sorrows on me, to be afterward increased to agony by the slaughter of a hundred Hurons, most of whom, racked by fearful torments, were burnt to death in the neighboring cantons. "Wo is me, wherefore was I born to see the ruin of my people." (1 Macc. 2.7).

Verily, in these, and like heart-rending cares, "my life is wasted with grief, and my years with sighs;" (Ps. 30.2), "for the Lord hath corrected me for mine iniquity, and hath made my soul waste away as a spider."— 38.12. "He hath filled me with my bitterness, he hath inebriated me with wormwood, (Lam. 3.15), because the comforter, the relief of my soul, is far from me," (1.16.) "but, in all these things, we overcome," and by the favor of God will overcome, "because of him that hath loved us," (Rom. 8.37), until "he come that is to come and will not delay (Heb. 10.37), until my day like that of a hireling come, (Job 7.1), or my change be made." (14.14). Although I could, in all probability, escape either through the Europeans or the savage nations around us, did I wish to fly, yet on this cross, to which our Lord has nailed me beside himself, am I resolved by his grace to live and die. For who in my absence would console the French captives? who absolve the penitent? who remind the christened Huron of his duties? who instruct the prisoners to be brought in from time to time? who baptize the dying, encourage them in their torments? who cleanse the infants with the saving waters? who provide for the safety of the dying adults, the instruction of those in health? And indeed I cannot but think it a peculiar interposition of divine goodness, that while on one side a nation fallen from the true Catholic religion barred the entrance of the faith to these regions, and on the other a fierce war between savage nations, and on their account with the French did the same, I should have fallen into the hands of these Indians, who, by the will of God, reluctantly, and, I may say, against their will, have, thus far, spared my life, that through me, though unworthy, those might be instructed, believe and be baptized, who are predestined to eternal life. Since the time when I was taken, I have baptized seventy, children, young and old, of five different nations and languages, that of every tribe, and people, and tongue, they might stand in the sight of the Lamb.

Therefore do I daily bow my knees to the Lord and to the Father of my Lord, that, if it be for his glory, he may confound all the designs of the Europeans and savages, for ransoming me or sending me back to the whites. For many of the Indians speak of my being restored, and the Dutch, among whom I write this, have frequently offered, and now again offer, to rescue me and my companions. I have twice visited them and been most kindly welcomed; they leave no stone unturned to effect our deliverance; and have made many presents to the Indians with whom I am, to induce them to treat me humanely.

But I am now weary of so long and so prolix a letter; I therefore earnestly beg your reverence, ever to recognize me, though unworthy, as one of yours; for, though a savage in dress and manner, and almost without God in so tossed a life, yet, as I have ever lived a son of the most holy Church of Rome, and of the Society, so do I wish to die. Obtain for me from God, Reverend Father, by your holy sacrifices, that although I have hitherto but ill employed the means he gave me to attain the highest sanctity, I may at least employ well this last occasion which he offers me. Your bounty owes this surely to your son who has recourse to you, for I lead a truly wretched life, where every virtue is in danger. Faith in the dense darkness of paganism; hope in so long and hard trials; charity amid so much corruption, deprived of all the Sacraments. Purity is not indeed here endangered by delights, yet it is amid this promiscuous and intimate intercourse of both sexes; in the perfect liberty of each to hear and do what he pleases, and most of all in their constant nakedness. For here, willing or not, you must often see what elsewhere is shut out, not only from wandering, but even from curious eyes. Hence I daily groan to my God, begging him not to leave me without help amid the dead; begging him, I say, that amid so much impurity and such superstitious worship of the devil to which he has exposed me, naked as it were, and unarmed, "my heart may be undefiled in his justifications," (Ps. 119.80), so that, when that good Shepherd shall come, "who will gather together the dispersed of Israel," (Ps. 147.2), he may gather us from among the nations to bless his holy name. Amen! Amen! (Ps. 106.47).

> *Your Reverence's*
> *Most humble servant*
> *and son in Christ,*
> *Isaac Jogues*

Permit me, through your Reverence, to salute all my dear Fathers and Brothers, whom I tenderly love and cherish in Christ, and to commend myself to their Holy Sacrifices and Prayers.

> *Your most humble*
> *servant and*
> *son in Christ,*
> *Isaac Jogues*
>
> *Renssalaerswyck in*
> *New Netherland,*
> *August 5, 1643*

A VERITABLE ACCOUNT OF THE MARTYRDOM AND BLESSED DEATH OF FATHER JEAN DE BRÉBEUF AND OF FATHER GABRIEL LALEMANT, IN NEW FRANCE, IN THE COUNTRY OF THE HURONS, BY THE IROQUOIS, ENEMIES OF THE FAITH

Christophe Regnaut

Father Jean de Brébeuf and Father Gabriel Lalemant had set out from our cabin, to go to a small Village, called St. Ignace, distant from our cabin about a short quarter of a League, to instruct the Savages and the new Christians of that Village. It was on the 16th Day of March, in the morning, that we perceived a great fire at the place to which these two good Fathers had gone. This fire made us very uneasy; we did not know whether it were enemies, or if the fire had caught in some of the huts of the village. The Reverend Father Paul Raguenau, our Superior, immediately Resolved to send some one to learn what might be the cause. But no sooner had we formed the design of going there to see, than we perceived several savages on the road, coming straight toward us. We all thought it was the Iroquois who were coming to attack us; but, having considered them more closely, we perceived that they were Hurons who were fleeing from the fight, and who had escaped from the combat. These poor savages caused great pity in us. They were all covered with wounds. One had his head fractured; an-

other his arm broken; another had an arrow in his eye; another had his
hand cut off by a blow from a hatchet. In fine, the day was passed in receiving into our cabins all these poor wounded people, and in looking with
compassion toward the fire, and the place where were those two good
Fathers. We saw the fire and the barbarians, but we could not see anything
of the two Fathers.

This is what these Savages told us of the taking of the Village of
St. Ignace, and about Fathers Jean de Brébeuf and Gabriel Lalemant:

"The Iroquois came, to the number of twelve hundred men; took our
village, and seized Father Brébeuf and his companion; and set fire to all the
huts. They proceeded to vent their rage on those two Fathers; for they took
them both and stripped them entirely naked, and fastened each to a post.
They tied both of their hands together. They tore the nails from their
fingers. They beat them with a shower of blows from cudgels, on the shoulders, the loins, the belly, the legs, and the face—there being no part of their
body which did not endure this torment." The savages told us further,
that, although Father de Brébeuf was overwhelmed under the weight of
these blows, he did not cease continually to speak of God, and to encourage all the new Christians who were captives like himself to suffer well, that
they might die well, in order to go in company with him to Paradise. While
the good Father was thus encouraging these good people, a wretched Huron
renegade [1]—who had remained a captive with the Iroquois, and whom Father de Brébeuf had formerly instructed and baptized—hearing him speak
of Paradise and Holy Baptism, was irritated, and said to him, "Echon,"
that is Father de Brébeuf's name in Huron, "thou sayest that Baptism and
the sufferings of this life lead straight to Paradise; thou wilt go soon, for I
am going to baptize thee, and to make thee suffer well, in order to go the
sooner to thy Paradise." The barbarian, having said that, took a kettle full
of boiling water, which he poured over his body three different times, in
derision of Holy baptism. And, each time that he baptized him in this manner, the barbarian said to him, with bitter sarcasm, "Go to Heaven, for
thou art well baptized." After that, they made him suffer several other torments. The first was to make hatchets red-hot, and to apply them to the
loins and under the armpits. They made a collar of these red-hot hatchets,
and put it on the neck of this good Father. This is the fashion in which I
have seen the collar made for other prisoners: They make six hatchets red-

---

[1] This man had presumably been taken captive in an earlier raid and adopted by the
Iroquois. In calling him a *renégat* or "renegade," Regnaut used the word applied to
captives of the Moors who converted to Islam.

hot, take a large withe of green wood, pass the six hatchets over the large end of the withe, take the two ends together, and then put it over the neck of the sufferer. I have seen no torment which more moved me to compassion than that. For you see a man, bound naked to a post, who, having this collar on his neck, cannot tell what posture to take. For, if he lean forward, those above his shoulders weigh the more on him; if he lean back, those on his stomach make him suffer the same torment; if he keep erect, without leaning to one side or other, the burning hatchets, applied equally on both sides, give him a double torture.

After that they put on him a belt of bark, full of pitch and resin, and set fire to it, which roasted his whole body. During all these torments, Father de Brébeuf endured like a rock, insensible to fire and flames, which astonished all the bloodthirsty wretches who tormented him. His zeal was so great that he preached continually to these infidels, to try to convert them. His executioners were enraged against him for constantly speaking to them of God and of their conversion. To prevent him from speaking more, they cut off his tongue, and both his upper and lower lips. After that, they set themselves to strip the flesh from his legs, thighs, and arms, to the very bone; and then put it to roast before his eyes, in order to eat it.

While they tormented him in this manner, those wretches derided him, saying: "Thou seest plainly that we treat thee as a friend, since we shall be the cause of thy Eternal happiness; thank us, then, for these good offices which we render thee, for, the more thou shalt suffer, the more will thy God reward thee."

Those butchers, seeing that the good Father began to grow weak, made him sit down on the ground; and, one of them, taking a knife, cut off the skin covering his skull. Another one of those barbarians, seeing that the good Father would soon die, made an opening in the upper part of his chest, and tore out his heart, which he roasted and ate. Others came to drink his blood, still warm, which they drank with both hands, saying that Father de Brébeuf had been very courageous to endure so much pain as they had given him, and that, by drinking his blood, they would become courageous like him.

This is what we learned of the Martyrdom and blessed death of Father Jean de Brébeuf, by several Christian savages worthy of belief, who had been constantly present from the time the good Father was taken until his death. These good Christians were prisoners to the Iroquois, who were taking them into their country to be put to death. But our good God granted them the favor of enabling them to escape by the way; and they came to us to recount all that I have set down in writing.

Father de Brébeuf was captured on the 16th day of March, in the morning, with Father Lalemant, in the year 1649. Father de Brébeuf died

the same day as his capture, about 4 o'clock in the afternoon. Those barbarians threw the remains of his body into the fire; but the fat which still
remained on his body extinguished the fire, and he was not consumed.

I do not doubt that all which I have just related is true, and I would
seal it with my blood; for I have seen the same treatment given to Iroquois
prisoners whom the Huron savages had taken in war, with the exception
of the boiling water, which I have not seen poured on any one.

I am about to describe to you truly what I saw of the Martyrdom and
of the Blessed deaths of Father Jean de Brébeuf and of Father Gabriel Lalemant. On the next morning, when we had assurance of the departure of
the enemy, we went to the spot to seek for the remains of their bodies, to
the place where their lives had been taken. We found them both, but a little
apart from each other. They were brought to our cabin, and laid uncovered upon the bark of trees, where I examined them at leisure, for more
than two hours, to see if what the savages had told us of their martyrdom
and death were true. I examined first the Body of Father de Brébeuf, which
was pitiful to see, as well as that of Father Lalemant. Father de Brébeuf had
his legs, thighs, and arms stripped of flesh to the very bone; I saw and
touched[2] a large number of great blisters, which he had on several places
on his body, from the boiling water which these barbarians had poured
over him in mockery of Holy Baptism. I saw and touched the wound from
a belt of bark, full of pitch and resin, which roasted his whole body. I saw
and touched the marks of burns from the Collar of hatchets placed on his
shoulders and stomach. I saw and touched his two lips, which they had cut
off because he constantly spoke of God while they made him suffer.

I saw and touched all parts of his body, which had received more than
two hundred blows from a stick. I saw and touched the top of his scalped
head; I saw and touched the opening which these barbarians had made to
tear out his heart.

In fine, I saw and touched all the wounds of his body, as the savages
had told and declared to us; we buried these precious Relics on Sunday, the
21st day of March, 1649, with much Consolation.

I had the happiness of carrying them to the grave, and of burying them
with those of Father Gabriel Lalemant. When we left the country of the

---

[2] Regnaut alluded to the biblical story of "doubting Thomas" in John 20.24–29. After
Christ's resurrection, the disciple Thomas had not seen yet seen him as others had,
and said, "Except I shall see in his hands the print of the nails . . . and thrust my hand
into his side, I will not believe." Jesus then came again, Thomas did these things, and
Jesus said, "Blessed are they that have not seen, and yet have believed." Regnaut used
the allusion to persuade those who did not witness the martyrdom to believe in its miraculous truth.

Hurons, we raised both bodies out of the ground, and set them to boil in strong lye. All the bones were well scraped, and the care of drying them was given to me. I put them every day into a little oven which we had, made of clay, after having heated it slightly; and, when in a state to be packed, they were separately enveloped in silk stuff. Then they were put into two small chests, and we brought them to Quebec, where they are held in great veneration.

It is not a Doctor of the Sorbonne who has composed this, as you may easily see; it is a relic from the Iroquois, and a person who has lived more than thought—who is, and shall ever be,

Sir,
Your Very Humble and
very obedient servant,
Christophe Regnaut

The Foundational Narrative of Mary Rowlandson

The narrative of Mary Rowlandson is the classic of the captivity genre. In most anthologies of captivity literature, including the 112-volume series *Garland Library of Narratives of North American Indian Captivities*, it is placed first, and in many literary histories it has been granted the status of the original—a model that later texts imitated and the foundation of a myth that transcends literature, reaching deep into Anglo-America's history and psyche. It appears in the fourth chapter in this anthology because one of this collection's goals is to show that the primacy of the Rowlandson text applies only within the English colonies and that captivity among Indians was written and thought about quite differently in New France, in New Spain, and even in Virginia in the case of John Smith. This should not diminish the importance of Rowlandson, however, because it was out of New England and her narrative that Indian captivity literature came to play such a large role in American culture.

Rowlandson's text appeared in 1682, printed both in London and in Cambridge, Massachusetts. The English edition bore the title *A True History of the Captivity and Restoration of Mrs. Mary Rowlandson, A Minister's Wife in New England*, while that published in New England carried a different title, reflecting the Puritans' religious interpretation of her experience: *The Soveraignty and Goodness of God, Together, With the Faithfulness of His Promises Displayed; Being a Narrative Of the Captivity and Restauration of Mrs. Mary Rowlandson*. It was immediately popular—twenty-three separate editions had been published by 1828. Seven of these reeditions came out in the 1770s, suggesting that the Revolutionary War prompted readers to return to this founding text of the captivity myth even as it spawned new narratives in which the British enemy often assumed the role of captors.

Rowlandson was taken captive in the midst of King Philip's War, a cataclysmic conflict between natives and colonists in 1675 and 1676, which by its end claimed the lives of one-third of the American Indian population in southern New England and one-tenth of the colonists. Jogues and Brébeuf were caught up in a war between the Hurons and the Iroquois; Staden, Ortiz and Smith were fighting men venturing into little-known Indian territory; later, captives like Hannah Swarton and Jane McCrea were captured in wars between rival colonial powers; but Rowlandson was a civilian taken prisoner in a war between colonists and Indians. Her story therefore set the melodramatic paradigm of an innocent frontier mother torn from her family by "heathen savages." Although this was the ideological purpose to which it and other captivity narratives were often applied in the following two centuries, the initial conception of the text among the New England Puritans was somewhat different.

In describing the scene of the initial attack, Rowlandson compared the Indians to "Wolves" and "ravenous Bears" and in the next paragraph called them "Barbarous Creatures" and "black creatures of the night." Though one might dismiss these as racist epithets, they form an image of captivity as a hell on earth, a supernatural setting in which her captors were hardly human, barely even real. Later passages, however, humanized her captors, when she expressed gratitude for gifts of food and satisfaction at pleasing her master, Quanopen, from whom she earned a knife by sewing a shirt for him. The text operates on both literal and theological planes, as both a personal narrative of conversion and an allegory for the larger war, according to a figural logic common in Puritan New England writing.

Since the 1660s, New England had been wracked by moral and spiritual anxiety as a second generation of settlers outgrew the communal and patriarchal utopias of the initial Plymouth and Massachusetts Bay settlements. Church membership declined, and sectarian and economic divisions arose. When King Philip's War came, many ministers and leaders of public discourse, such as Increase Mather (who almost certainly was the author of the preface to Rowlandson's text), interpreted it as God's punishment for the manifold sins of New England. "God hath let us see that he could easily have destroyed us, by such a contemptible enemy as the Indians have been in our eyes, yea he hath convinced us that we our selves could not subdue them" (143), Mather wrote in a history of the war. Therefore, although Mather respected the real terror that Rowlandson experienced, he saw her trial, and that of all the soldiers and victims in the war, as part of a divine plan. God afflicts and punishes his chosen people for their sins, and if they hold fast to their faith, he will redeem them, just as Rowlandson herself is ransomed or "redeemed." Rowlandson followed this allegorical or typological reading, but did not concur with Mather's interpretation. At several points she referred to "the strange providence of God in preserving the Heathen," suggesting that although the Indians may be inspired by the devil, it was God who allowed them to successfully attack the English. Rowlandson may have used this formula to veil her criticism of the English soldiers, who often showed their ignorance of the wilderness terrain and of the Indians' tactics.

The Soveraignty and Goodness of God was the first published narrative by an Anglo-American woman. Although as a woman Rowlandson could enter literature only with the sponsorship of Mather, she was nonetheless a gentlewoman with certain perquisites. She had been born in Somerset in England around 1637, the sixth of ten children. Her parents, John and Joan White, soon emigrated to Salem, Massachusetts, then moved to Lancaster at the time it was founded in 1653. Three years later Mary wed Joseph Rowlandson, a match that paired the daughter of a wealthy and prominent man with the small town's minister. Their lives were apparently uneventful for the next twenty years, but Mary's captivity made her famous. As a minister's wife, she was among the colony's elite, and great efforts were made to ransom her. She returned to Boston a hero, although her final paragraphs suggest she found it difficult to return to the life she'd lived before the war. Her husband took a post as minister in Wethersfield, Connecticut, in 1677, but died the following year. Most early editions of her narrative include as an appendix his final sermon, which bore the significant title "The Possibility of God's Forsaking a People." Although scholars long believed that she died shortly after the publication of her narrative, recent research by David Greene revealed that after being widowed she married Samuel Talcott, a merchant in Wethersfield, and lived until 1711.

Compared to other captives in this book, Mary's role among the Indians is somewhat ambiguous. She was not tortured, of course, nor enslaved, yet neither was she fully adopted into a family, as many other captives were. Her status seems most like that of a household servant within an extended family. In Lancaster, she had been mistress of her own household, which coincidently included as a servant an Indian man who twenty-two years later would be Hannah Dustan's "master," or captor. The servant most certainly called her "mistress"; likewise others in the town would have used that word, in distinction from the common form "goodwife." Captivity inverted these relationships, as she called Quinnapin "master" and Weetamoo "mistress." Her high status may explain why she was placed in the family of Weetamoo, a powerful Pocasset leader and sister-in-law to Metacom, and why she met twice with Metacom or "King Philip," the enemy leader. The mixed band of Pocasset, Wampanoag, and

Nipmuc Indians who attacked Lancaster, then fled from colonial troops, must have recognized her importance and expected to gain a large ransom price for her.

Due to its presence in many anthologies, in recent years Rowlandson's narrative has probably been the most-read text of colonial Anglo-American literature, and it has generated a large body of criticism; an entire book has been devoted to it. Perhaps the most salient critical debate over the text concerns the degree to which Rowlandson's writing may have been influenced, coerced, or edited by the powerful Puritan ministers who managed and interpreted the war effort. Several scholars have written of two competing voices in the text, one more personal or independent and one that articulates the collective or consensus view of her experience. Some see the dense web of biblical quotations and allusions in the text as part of her creative and learned mind, while others find that the religious discourse inhibits the representation of her direct experience. Some contend that she develops some understanding and sympathy for her native captors, while others maintain that her ethnocentric outlook does not change even after her release. The text continues to challenge new readers and inspire competing interpretations, for it is dense with meaning on many levels, from religious to ethnographic to psychological to sentimental.

Source

Rowlandson, Mary. "The Soveraignty [sic] and Goodness of God, Together with the Faithfulness of His Promises Displayed; Being a Narrative of the Captivity and Restauration of Mrs. Mary Rowlandson." 2nd ed. Cambridge: 1682. *So Dreadfull a Judgment: Puritan Responses to King Philip's War, 1676–1676.* Ed. Richard Slotkin and James K. Folsom. Middletown: Wesleyan UP, 1978. 317–66. [Slotkin and Folsom modernized some spelling and corrected some errors from the original. I am indebted to these editors and to Neal Salisbury for much of the information in the footnotes.]

Supplementary Readings

Breitwieser, Mitchell. *American Puritanism and the Defense of Mourning: Religion, Grief, and Ethnology in Mary White Rowlandson's Captivity Narrative.* Madison: U of Wisconsin P, 1990.

Burnham, Michelle. *Captivity and Sentiment: Cultural Exchange in American Literature, 1682–1861.* Hanover: UP of New England, 1997.

Ebersole, Gary. *Captured by Texts: Puritan to Postmodern Images of Indian Captivity.* Charlottesville: U of Virginia P, 1995.

Fitzpatrick, Tara. "The Figure of Captivity: The Cultural Work of the Puritan Captivity Narrative." *American Literary History* 3:1 (1991): 1–26.

Greene, David L. "New Light on Mary Rowlandson." *Early American Literature* 20:1 (1985): 24–38.

Henwood, Dawn. "Mary Rowlandson and the Psalms: The Textuality of Survival." *Early American Literature* 32:2 (1997): 169–86.

Logan, Lisa. "Mary Rowlandson's Captivity and the 'Place' of the Woman Subject." *Early American Literature* 28:3 (1993): 255–77.

Mather, Increase. *A Brief History of the Warr with the Indians in New-England.* 1676. Slotkin and Folsom 79–163.

Salisbury, Neal. Introduction. *The Sovereignty and Goodness of God, . . . and Related Documents.* Boston: Bedford, 1997: 1–60.

THE SOVEREIGNTY
AND GOODNESS OF GOD

Together with the Faithfulness of His Promises Displayed; Being a Narrative of the Captivity and Restoration of Mrs. Mary Rowlandson. Commended by her to all that Desire to Know the Lord's Doings to, and Dealings with Her. Especially to Her Dear Children and Relations.

Written by Her Own Hand for Her Private Use, and Now Made Public at the Earnest Desire of Some Friends, and for the Benefit of the Afflicted.

Deut. 32.29. See Now that I, Even I am He, and There Is No God with Me; I Kill and I Make Alive, I Wound and I Heal, Neither Is There Any Can Deliver Out of My Hand.[1]

The Preface to the Reader

It was on Tuesday, Feb. 1, 1675,[2] in the afternoon, when the Narragansetts' quarters (in or toward the Nipmuck country, whither they are now retired for fear of the English army lying in their own country) were the second time beaten up, by the forces of the united colonies, who thereupon soon betook themselves to flight, and were all the next day pursued by the English, some overtaken and destroyed. But on Thursday, Feb. 3rd, the English having now been six days on their march, from their headquarters, at Wickford, in the Narragansett country, toward, and after the enemy, and provision grown exceeding short, insomuch that they were fain to kill some horses for the supply, especially of their Indian friends, they were necessitated to consider what was best to be done. And about noon (having

---

[1] The citation from Deuteronomy is actually in 32.39.
[2] Because the old Julian calendar began the new year on March 25, dates in January and February are, by today's reckoning, assigned to the following year. These events would be in February 1676.

hitherto followed the chase as hard as they might) a council was called, and though some few were of another mind, yet it was concluded by far the greater part of the council of war, that the army should desist the pursuit, and retire: the forces of Plymouth and the Bay to the next town of the Bay, and Connecticut forces to their own next towns; which determination was immediately put in execution. The consequence whereof, as it was not difficult to be foreseen by those that knew the causeless enmity of these barbarians, against the English, and the malicious and revengeful spirit of these heathen: so it soon proved dismal.

The Narragansetts were now driven quite from their own country, and all their provisions there hoarded up, to which they durst not at present return, and being so numerous as they were, soon devoured those to whom they went, whereby both the one and other were now reduced to extreme straits, and so necessitated to take the first and best opportunity for supply, and very glad, no doubt, of such an opportunity as this, to provide for themselves, and make spoil of the English at once; and seeing themselves thus discharged of their pursuers, and a little refreshed after their flight, the very next week upon Thursday, Feb. 10th, they fell with mighty force and fury upon Lancaster: which small town, remote from aid of others, and not being garrisoned as it might, the army being now come in,[3] and as the time indeed required (the design of the Indians against that place being known to the English some time before) was not able to make effectual resistance: but notwithstanding utmost endeavor of the inhabitants, most of the buildings were turned into ashes; many people (men, women and children) slain, and others captivated. The most solemn and remarkable part of this tragedy, may that justly be reputed, which fell upon the family of that reverend servant of God, Mr. Joseph Rowlandson, the faithful pastor of Christ in that place, who being gone down to the council of the Massachusetts to seek aid for the defense of the place, at his return found the town in flames, or smoke, his own house being set on fire by the enemy, through the disadvantage of a defective fortification, and all in it consumed: his precious yokefellow, and dear children, wounded and captivated (as the issue evidenced, and following narrative declares) by these cruel and barbarous savages. A sad catastrophe! Thus all things come alike to all: none knows either love or hatred by all that is before him. It is no new thing for God's precious ones to drink as deep as others, of the cup

---

[3] This line appears to refer to the retreat described in the previous paragraph. The author of the Preface recognized that Lancaster might have been better defended (the town had requested reinforcements) but was reluctant to admit any mistake.

of common calamity: take just Lot (yet captivated)[4] for instance beside others. But it is not my business to dilate on these things, but only in few words introductively to preface to the following script, which is a narrative of the wonderfully awful, wise, holy, powerful, and gracious providence of God, toward that worthy and precious gentlewoman, the dear consort of the said Reverend Mr. Rowlandson, and her children with her, as in casting of her into such a waterless pit, so in preserving, supporting, and carrying through so many such extreme hazards, unspeakable difficulties and disconsolateness, and at last delivering her out of them all, and her surviving children also. It was a strange and amazing dispensation, that the Lord should so afflict His precious servant, and handmaid. It was as strange, if not more, that He should so bear up the spirits of His servant under such bereavements and of His handmaid under such captivity, travels and hardships (much too hard for flesh and blood) as he did, and at length deliver and restore. But He was their saviour, who hath said, *When thou passest through the waters, I will be with thee, and through the rivers, they shall not overflow thee: When thou walkest through the fire thou shalt not be burnt, nor shall the flame kindle upon thee,* (Isa. 43.2), and again, *He woundeth and his hands make whole. He shall deliver three in six troubles, yea in seven there shall no evil touch thee. In famine he shall redeem thee from death, and in war from the power of the sword.* (Job 5.18–20). Methinks this dispensation doth bear some resemblance to those of Joseph, David and Daniel;[5] yea, and of the three children too, the stories whereof do represent us with the excellent textures of divine providence, curious pieces of divine work: and truly so doth this, and therefore not to be forgotten, but worthy to be exhibited to, and viewed, and pondered by all, that disdain not to consider the operation of His hands.

The works of the Lord (not only of creation, but of providence also, especially those that do more peculiarly concern His dear ones, that are as the apple of His eye, as the signet upon His hand, the delight of His eyes, and the object of His tenderest care) are great, sought out of all those that have pleasure therein. And of these verily this is none of the least.

This narrative was penned by the gentlewoman herself, to be to her a memorandum of God's dealing with her, that she might never forget, but remember the same, and the several circumstances thereof, all the days of her life. A pious scope which deserves both commendation and imitation.

---

[4] See Genesis 14.

[5] As Rowlandson herself did, the author of the Preface alluded to stories of captivity from the Bible.

Some friends having obtained a sight of it, could not but be so much affected with the many passages of working providence discovered therein, as to judge it worthy of public view, and altogether unmeet that such works of God should be hid from present and future generations: and therefore though this gentlewoman's modesty would not thrust it into the press, yet her gratitude unto God made her not hardly persuadable to let it pass, that God might have his due glory, and others benefit by it as well as herself. I hope by this time none will cast any reflection upon this gentlewoman, on the score of this publication of her affliction and deliverance. If any should, doubtless they may be reckoned with the nine lepers, of whom it is said, *Were there not ten cleansed, where are the nine?*[6] but one returning to give God thanks. Let such further know that this was a dispensation of public note, and of universal concernment, and so much the more, by how much the nearer this gentlewoman stood related to that faithful servant of God, whose capacity and employment was public in the house of God, and his name on that account of a very sweet savor in the churches of Christ. Who is there of a true Christian spirit, that did not look upon himself much concerned in this bereavement, this captivity in the time therefore, and in this deliverance when it came, yea more than in many others; and how many are there, to whom so concerned, it will doubtless be a very acceptable thing to see the way of God with this gentlewoman in the aforesaid dispensation, thus laid out and portrayed before their eyes.

To conclude: whatever any coy fantasies may deem, yet it highly concerns those that have so deeply tasted, how good the Lord is, to inquire with David, *What shall I render to the Lord for all his benefits to me?* (Ps. 116.12). He thinks nothing too great; yea, being sensible of his own disproportion to the due praises of God he calls in help. *Oh, magnify the Lord with me, let us exalt his name together* (Ps. 34.3). And it is but reason, that our praises should hold proportion with our prayers: and that as many hath helped together by prayer for the obtaining of His mercy, so praises should be returned by many on this behalf; and forasmuch as not the general but particular knowledge of things make deepest impression upon the affections, this narrative particularizing the several passages of this providence will not a little conduce thereunto. And therefore holy David in order to the attainment of that end, accounts himself concerned to declare what God has done for his soul (Ps. 66.16). *Come and hear, all ye that fear God, and I will declare what God hath done for my soul, i.e.*

---

[6] Christ healed ten lepers in Luke 12–18, but only one gave thanks, which elicited this question from Jesus.

for his life (see verses 9, 10). *He holdeth our soul in life, and suffers not our feet to be moved, for thou our God hast proved us, thou hast tried us, as silver is tried.* Life mercies, are heart-affecting mercies, of great impression and force, to enlarge pious hearts, in the praises of God, so that such know not how but to talk of God's acts, and to speak of and publish His wonderful works. Deep troubles, when the waters come in unto thy soul, are wont to produce vows: vows must be paid. It is better not vow, than vow and not to pay. I may say, that as none knows what it is to fight and pursue such an enemy as this, but they that have fought and pursued them: so none can imagine what it is to be captivated, and enslaved to such atheistical, proud, wild, cruel, barbarous, brutish (in one word) diabolical creatures as these, the worst of the heathen; nor what difficulties, hardships, hazards, sorrows, anxieties and perplexities do unavoidably wait upon such a condition, but those that have tried it. No serious spirit then (especially knowing anything of this gentlewoman's piety) can imagine but that the vows of God are upon her. Excuse her then if she come thus into public, to pay those vows, come and hear what she hath to say.

I am confident that no friend of divine providence will ever repent his time and pains spent in reading over these sheets, but will judge them worth perusing again and again.

Here reader, you may see an instance of the sovereignty of God, who doth what He will with His own as well as others; and who may say to Him, What dost Thou? Here you may see an instance of the faith and patience of the saints, under the most heart-sinking trials; here you may see, the promises are breasts full of consolation, when all the world besides is empty, and gives nothing but sorrow. That God is indeed the supreme Lord of the world, ruling the most unruly, weakening the most cruel and savage, granting His people mercy in the sight of the unmerciful, curbing the lusts of the most filthy, holding the hands of the violent, delivering the prey from the mighty, and gathering together the outcasts of Israel. Once and again you have heard, but here you may see, that power belongeth unto God; that our God is the God of salvation, and to Him belong the issues from death. That our God is in the heavens, and doth whatever pleases Him. Here you have Samson's riddle exemplified, and that great promise, Romans 8.28, verified, *Out of the eater comes forth meat, and sweetness out of the strong;* [7] The worst of evils working together for the best good. How evident is it that the Lord hath made this gentlewoman a gainer by all this affliction, that she can say, 'tis good for her yea better that she hath been, than that she should not have been thus afflicted.

---

[7] This riddle of Samson is in Judges 14.14, not in Romans, as the text suggests.

Oh how doth God shine forth in such things as these!

Reader, if thou gettest no good by such a declaration as this, the fault must needs be thine own. Read therefore, peruse, ponder, and from hence lay by something from the experience of another against thine own turn comes, that so thou also through patience and consolation of the scripture mayest have hope.

Ter Amicam[8]

[Increase Mather]

A Narrative of the Captivity
and Restoration of Mrs. Mary Rowlandson

On the tenth of February 1675, came the Indians with great numbers upon Lancaster: Their first coming was about sun-rising; hearing the noise of some guns, we looked out; several houses were burning, and the smoke ascending to heaven. There were five persons taken in one house, the father, and the mother and a sucking child, they knocked on the head; the other two they took and carried away alive. There were two others, who being out of their garrison upon some occasion were set upon; one was knocked on the head, the other escaped: another there was who running along was shot and wounded, and fell down; he begged of them his life, promising them money (as they told me) but they would not hearken to him but knocked him in the head, and stripped him naked, and split open his bowels. Another seeing many of the Indians about his barn, ventured and went out, but was quickly shot down. There were three others belonging to the same garrison who were killed; the Indians getting up upon the roof of the barn, had advantage to shoot down upon them over their fortification. Thus these murderous wretches went on, burning, and destroying before them.

At length they came and beset our own house, and quickly it was the dolefullest day that ever mine eyes saw. The house stood upon the edge of a hill; some of the Indians got behind the hill, others into the barn, and others behind any thing that could shelter them; from all which places they shot against the house, so that the bullets seemed to fly like hail; and quickly they wounded one man among us, then another, and then a third. About two hours (according to my observation, in that amazing time) they had been about the house before they prevailed to fire it (which they did

---

[8] Latin for "thy three-fold friend." It is probably a printer's error, however. The London edition of 1682 reads "Per Amicam" or "by a friend."

with flax and hemp, which they brought out of the barn, and there being no defense about the house, only two flankers[9] at two opposite corners and one of them not finished) they fired it once and one ventured out and quenched it, but they quickly fired again, and that took. Now is the dreadful hour come, that I have often heard of (in time of war, as it was the case of others) but now mine eyes see it. Some in our house were fighting for their lives, others wallowing in their blood, the house on fire over our heads, and the bloody heathen ready to knock us on the head, if we stirred out. Now might we hear mothers and children crying out for themselves, and one another, Lord, What shall we do? Then I took my children (and one of my sisters, hers) to go forth and leave the house: but as soon as we came to the door and appeared, the Indians shot so thick that the bullets rattled against the house, as if one had taken a handful of stones and threw them, so that we were fain to give back. We had six stout dogs belonging to our garrison, but none of them would stir, though another time, if any Indian had come to the door, they were ready to fly upon him and tear him down. The Lord hereby would make us the more to acknowledge his hand, and to see that our help is always in him. But out we must go, the fire increasing, and coming along behind us, roaring, and the Indians gaping before us with their guns, spears and hatchets to devour us. No sooner were we out of the house, but my brother-in-law (being before wounded, in defending the house, in or near the throat) fell down dead whereat the Indians scornfully shouted, and holloed, and were presently upon him, stripping off his clothes, the bullets flying thick, one went through my side, and the same (as would seem) through the bowels and hand of my dear child in my arms.[10] One of my elder sister's children, named William, had then his leg broken, which the Indians perceiving, they knocked him on the head. Thus were we butchered by those merciless heathen, standing amazed, with the blood running down to our heels. My eldest sister[11] being yet in the house, and seeing those woeful sights, the infidels haling mothers one way, and children another, and some wallowing in their blood: and her elder son telling her that her son William was dead, and myself was wounded, she said, And, Lord, let me die with them; which was no sooner said, but she was struck with a bullet, and fell down dead over the threshold. I hope she is reaping the fruit of her good labors, being faithful to the service of God in her place. In her younger years she lay under much trouble upon

---

[9] In military architecture, flankers are towers at the corner of a fort which enable defenders to shoot at attackers scaling the walls.
[10] Her daughter Sarah.
[11] Elizabeth Kerley.

spiritual accounts, till it pleased God to make that precious scripture take hold of her heart, 2 Corinthians 12.9, *And he said unto me, my grace is sufficient for thee.* More than twenty years after I have heard her tell how sweet and comfortable that place was to her. But to return: the Indians laid hold of us, pulling me one way, and the Children another, and said, Come go along with us; I told them they would kill me: they answered, If I were willing to go along with them, they would not hurt me.

Oh the doleful sight that now was to behold at this house! *Come, behold the works of the Lord, what desolations he has made in the earth.*[12] Of thirty-seven persons who were in this one house, none escaped either present death, or a bitter captivity, save only one, who might say as he, Job 1.15, *And I only am escaped alone to tell the news.* There were twelve killed, some shot, some stabbed with their spears, some knocked down with their hatchets. When we are in prosperity, oh the little that we think of such dreadful sights, and to see our dear friends, and relations lie bleeding out their heart's blood upon the ground. There was one who was chopped into the head with a hatchet, and stripped naked, and yet was crawling up and down. It is a solemn sight to see so many Christians lying in their blood, some here, and some there, like a company of sheep torn by wolves. All of them stripped naked by a company of hell-hounds, roaring, singing, ranting and insulting, as if they would have torn our very hearts out; yet the Lord by his almighty power preserved a number of us from death, for there were twenty-four of us taken alive and carried captive.

I had often before this said, that if the Indians should come, I should choose rather to be killed by them than be taken alive but when it came to the trial my mind changed; their glittering weapons so daunted my spirit, that I chose rather to go along with those (as I may say) ravenous beasts, than that moment to end my days; and that I may the better declare what happened to me during that grievous captivity, I shall particularly speak of the several removes we had up and down the wilderness.

The First Remove[13]

Now away we must go with those barbarous creatures, with our bodies wounded and bleeding, and our hearts no less than our bodies. About a mile we went that night, up upon a hill within sight of the town, where they intended to lodge. There was hard by a vacant house (deserted by the

---

[12] Ps. 46.8.

[13] In Rowlandson's usage, as in the British Isles today, "remove" could mean to move one's home. One might hire a "removing company" with a large truck, for example.

English before, for fear of the Indians). I asked them whether I might not lodge in the house that night to which they answered, What will you love English men still? This was the dolefullest night that ever my eyes saw. Oh the roaring, and singing and dancing, and yelling of those black creatures in the night, which made the place a lively resemblance of hell. And as miserable was the waste that was there made, of horses, cattle, sheep, swine, calves, lambs, roasting pigs, and fowl (which they had plundered in the town) some roasting, some lying and burning, and some boiling to feed our merciless enemies; who were joyful enough though we were disconsolate. To add to the dolefulness of the former day, and the dismalness of the present night: my thoughts ran upon my losses and sad bereaved condition. All was gone, my husband gone (at least separated from me, he being in the Bay;[14] and to add to my grief, the Indians told me they would kill him as he came homeward) my children gone, my relations and friends gone, our house and home and all our comforts within doors, and without, all was gone (except my life) and I knew not but the next moment that might go too. There remained nothing to me but one poor wounded babe, and it seemed at present worse than death that it was in such a pitiful condition, bespeaking compassion, and I had no refreshing for it, nor suitable things to revive it. Little do many think what is the savageness and brutishness of this barbarous enemy, aye even those that seem to profess[15] more than others among them, when the English have fallen into their hands.

Those seven that were killed at Lancaster the summer before upon a Sabbath day, and the one that was afterward killed upon a week day, were slain and mangled in a barbarous manner, by One-eyed John, and Marlborough's praying Indians, which Captain Mosely brought to Boston, as the Indians told me.[16]

The Second Remove

But now, the next morning, I must turn my back upon the town, and travel with them into the vast and desolate wilderness, I knew not whither. It is not my tongue, or pen can express the sorrows of my heart, and bitterness

---

[14] The Massachusetts Bay colony, centered at Boston, where Joseph Rowlandson was going on the day of the attack.
[15] To profess Christianity. This is the first of several derogatory comments Rowlandson made about the "praying Indians" of New England.
[16] Rowlandson referred to another attack on Lancaster the previous August which was led by "one-eyed" John Monoco, and which Capt. Samuel Moseley had charged fifteen praying Indians of the town of Marlborough with participating in.

of my spirit, that I had at this departure: but God was with me, in a wonderful manner, carrying me along, and bearing up my spirit, that it did not quite fail. One of the Indians carried my poor wounded babe upon a horse, it went moaning all along, I shall die, I shall die. I went on foot after it, with sorrow that cannot be expressed. At length I took it off the horse, and carried it in my arms till my strength failed, and I fell down with it: Then they set me upon a horse with my wounded child in my lap, and there being no furniture[17] upon the horse's back, as we were going down a steep hill, we both fell over the horse's head, at which they like inhuman creatures laughed, and rejoiced to see it, though I thought we should there have ended our days, as overcome with so many difficulties. But the Lord renewed my strength still, and carried me along, that I might see more of his power; yea, so much that I could never have thought of, had I not experienced it.

After this it quickly began to snow, and when night came on, they stopped: and now down I must sit in the snow, by a little fire, and a few boughs behind me, with my sick child in my lap; and calling much for water, being now (through the wound) fallen into a violent fever. My own wound also growing so stiff, that I could scarce sit down or rise up; yet so it must be, that I must sit all this cold winter night upon the cold snowy ground, with my sick child in my arms, looking that every hour would be the last of its life; and having no Christian friend near me, either to comfort or help me. Oh, I may see the wonderful power of God, that my spirit did not utterly sink under my affliction: still the Lord upheld me with his gracious and merciful spirit, and we were both alive to see the light of the next morning.

The Third Remove

The morning being come, they prepared to go on their way. One of the Indians got up upon a horse, and they set me up behind him, with my poor sick babe in my lap. A very wearisome and tedious day I had of it; what with my own wound, and my child's being so exceeding sick, and in a lamentable condition with her wound. It may be easily judged what a poor feeble condition we were in, there being not the least crumb of refreshing that came within either of our mouths, from Wednesday night to Saturday night, except only a little cold water. This day in the afternoon, about an hour by sun, we came to the place where they intended, *viz.* an

---

[17] No saddle.

Indian town called Wenimesset, northward of Quabaug. When we were come, Oh the number of pagans (now merciless enemies) that there came about me, that I may say as David, Psalms 27.13, *I had fainted, unless I had believed,* etc. The next day was the Sabbath: I then remembered how careless I had been of God's holy time, how many Sabbaths I had lost and misspent, and how evilly I had walked in God's sight; which lay so close unto my spirit, that it was easy for me to see how righteous it was with God to cut off the thread of my life, and cast me out of his presence forever. Yet the Lord still showed mercy to me, and upheld me; and as he wounded me with one hand, so he healed me with the other. This day there came to me one Robert Pepper (a man belonging to Roxbury) who was taken in Captain Beers his fight,[18] and had been now a considerable time with the Indians; and up with them almost as far as Albany, to see King Philip, as he told me, and was now very lately come into these parts. Hearing, I say, that I was in this Indian town, he obtained leave to come and see me. He told me, he himself was wounded in the leg at Captain Beers his fight; and was not able some time to go, but as they carried him, and as he took oaken leaves and laid to his wound, and through the blessing of God he was able to travel again. Then I took oaken leaves and laid to my side, and with the blessing of God it cured me also; yet before the cure was wrought, I may say, as it is in Psalms 38.5–6, *My wounds stink and are corrupt, I am bowed down greatly, I go mourning all the day long.* I sat much alone with a poor wounded child in my lap, which moaned night and day, having nothing to revive the body, or cheer the spirits of her, but instead of that, sometimes one Indian would come and tell me in one hour, that your master will knock your child in the head, and then a second, and then a third, your master will quickly knock your child in the head.

This was the comfort I had from them, miserable comforters are ye all, as he said.[19] Thus nine days I sat upon my knees, with my babe in my lap, till my flesh was raw again; my child being even ready to depart this sorrowful world, they bade me carry it out to another wigwam (I suppose because they would not be troubled with such spectacles) whither I went with a very heavy heart, and down I sat with the picture of death in my lap. About two hours in the night, my sweet babe like a lamb departed this life, on Feb. 18, 1675, it being about six years, and five months old. It was nine days from the first wounding, in this miserable condition, without any re-

---

[18] Captain Beers's fight. Beers and his troops had been attacked near Northfield, Massachusetts, in September 1675. Robert Pepper was taken captive, while Beers and nineteen others were killed.

[19] Job said, in Job 16.2.

freshing of one nature or other, except a little cold water. I cannot, but take notice, how at another time I could not bear to be in the room where any dead person was, but now the case is changed; I must and could lie down by my dead babe, side by side all the night after. I have thought since of the wonderful goodness of God to me, in preserving me in the use of my reason and senses, in that distressed time, that I did not use wicked and violent means to end my own miserable life. In the morning, when they understood that my child was dead they sent for me home to my master's wigwam: (by my master in this writing, must be understood Quinnapin, who was a sagamore,[20] and married King Philip's wife's sister; not that he first took me, but I was sold to him by another Narragansett Indian, who took me when first I came out of the garrison). I went to take up my dead child in my arms to carry it with me, but they bid me let it alone: there was no resisting, but go I must and leave it. When I had been at my master's wigwam, I took the first opportunity I could get, to go look after my dead child: when I came I asked them what they had done with it? Then they told me it was upon the hill: then they went and showed me where it was, where I saw the ground was newly digged, and there they told me they had buried it: there I left that child in the wilderness, and must commit it, and myself also in this wilderness condition, to Him who is above all. God having taken away this dear child, I went to see my daughter Mary, who was at this same Indian town, at a wigwam not very far off, though we had little liberty or opportunity to see one another. She was about ten years old, and taken from the door at first by a Praying Indian and afterward sold for a gun. When I came in sight, she would fall a-weeping; at which they were provoked, and would not let me come near her, but bade me begone; which was a heart-cutting word to me. I had one child dead, another in the wilderness, I knew not where, the third they would not let me come near to: *Me* (as he said) *have ye bereaved of my children, Joseph is not, and Simeon is not, and ye will take Benjamin also, all these things are against me.*[21] I could not sit still in this condition, but kept walking from place to another. And as I was going along, my heart was even overwhelmed with the thoughts of my condition, and that I should have children, and a nation which I knew not ruled over them. Whereupon I earnestly entreated the Lord, that He would consider my low estate, and show me a token for good, and if it were His blessed will, some sign and hope of some relief. And indeed quickly the Lord answered, in some measure, my poor prayers:

---

[20] An Indian leader, synonymous with "sachem."
[21] Gen. 42.36.

for as I was going up and down mourning and lamenting my condition, my son came to me, and asked me how I did; I had not seen him before, since the destruction of the town, and I knew not where he was, till I was informed by himself, that he was amongst a smaller parcel of Indians, whose place was about six miles off; with tears in his eyes, he asked me whether his sister Sarah was dead; and told me he had seen his sister Mary; and prayed me, that I would not be troubled in reference to himself. The occasion of his coming to see me at this time, was this: there was, as I said, about six miles from us, a small plantation of Indians, where it seems he had been during his captivity: and at this time, there were some forces of the Indians gathered out of our company, and some also from them (among whom was my son's master) to go to assault and burn Medfield: In this time of the absence of his master, his dame brought him to see me. I took this to be some gracious answer to my earnest and unfeigned desire. The next day, *viz.* to this, the Indians returned from Medfield, all the company, for those that belonged to the other small company, came through the town that now we were at. But before they came to us, Oh! the outrageous roaring and whooping that there was: They began their din about a mile before they came to us. By their noise and whooping they signified how many they had destroyed (which was at that time twenty-three). Those that were with us at home, were gathered together as soon as they heard the whooping, and every time that the other went over their number, these at home gave a shout, that the very earth rung again: and thus they continued till those that had been upon the expedition were come up to the Sagamore's wigwam; and then, Oh, the hideous insulting and triumphing that there was over some Englishmen's scalps that they had taken (as their manner is) and brought with them. I cannot but take notice of the wonderful mercy of God to me in those afflictions, in sending me a Bible. One of the Indians that came from Medfield fight, had brought some plunder, came to me, and asked me, if I would have a Bible, he had got one in his basket. I was glad of it, and asked him, whether he thought the Indians would let me read? He answered, Yes: So I took the Bible, and in that melancholy time, it came into my mind to read first the 28th Chapter of Deuteronomy, which I did, and when I had read it, my dark heart wrought on this manner, That there was no mercy for me, that the blessings were gone, and the curses come in their room, and that I had lost my opportunity. But the Lord helped me still to go on reading till I came to Chapter 30 the seven first verses, where I found, there was mercy promised again, if we would return to him by repentance; and though we were scattered from one end of the earth to the other, yet the Lord would gather us together, and turn all those curses upon our enemies. I do not desire to live to forget this scripture, and what comfort it was to me.

Now the Indians began to talk of removing from this place, some one way, and some another. There were now besides myself nine English captives in this place (all of them children, except one woman). I got an opportunity to go and take my leave of them; they being to go one way, and I another, I asked them whether they were earnest with God for deliverance, they told me, they did as they were able, and it was some comfort to me, that the Lord stirred up children to look to Him. The woman *viz.* Goodwife Joslin told me, she should never see me again, and that she could find in her heart to run away; I wished her not to run away by any means, for we were near thirty miles from any English town, and she very big with child, and had but one week to reckon; and another child in her arms, two years old, and bad rivers there were to go over, and we were feeble, with our poor and coarse entertainment. I had my Bible with me, I pulled it out, and asked her whether she would read; we opened the Bible and lighted on Psalm 27, in which Psalm we especially took notice of that, *ver. ult.,*[22] *Wait on the Lord, Be of good courage, and he shall strengthen thine heart, wait I say on the Lord.*

The Fourth Remove

And now I must part with that little company I had. Here I parted from my daughter Mary (whom I never saw again till I saw her in Dorchester, returned from captivity), and from four little cousins and neighbors, some of which I never saw afterward: the Lord only knows the end of them. Amongst them also was that poor woman before mentioned, who came to a sad end, as some of the company told me in my travel: she having much grief upon her spirit, about her miserable condition, being so near her time, she would be often asking the Indians to let her go home; they not being willing to that, and yet vexed with her importunity, gathered a great company together about her, and stripped her naked, and set her in the midst of them; and when they had sung and danced about her (in their hellish manner) as long as they pleased, they knocked her on head, and the child in her arms with her: when they had done that, they made a fire and put them both into it, and told the other children that were with them, that if they attempted to go home, they would serve them in like manner: the children said, she did not shed one tear, but prayed all the while. But to return to my own journey; we travelled about half a day or little more, and came to a desolate place in the wilderness, where there were no wigwams

---

[22] The "ultimate" or last verse.

or inhabitants before; we came about the middle of the afternoon to this place, cold and wet, and snowy, and hungry, and weary, and no refreshing, for man, but the cold ground to sit on, and our poor Indian cheer.

Heart-aching thoughts here I had about my poor children, who were scattered up and down among the wild beasts of the forest: my head was light and dizzy (either through hunger or hard lodging, or trouble or all together) my knees feeble, my body raw by sitting double night and day, that I cannot express to man the affliction that lay upon my spirit, but the Lord helped me at that time to express it to himself. I opened my Bible to read, and the Lord brought that precious scripture to me, Jeremiah 31.16. *Thus saith the Lord, refrain thy voice from weeping, and thine eyes from tears, for thy work shall be rewarded, and they shall come again from the land of the enemy.* This was a sweet cordial to me, when I was ready to faint, many and many a time have I sat down, and wept sweetly over this scripture. At this place we continued about four days.

The Fifth Remove

The occasion (as I thought) of their moving at this time, was, the English army, it being near and following them: for they went, as if they had gone for their lives, for some considerable way, and then they made a stop, and chose some of their stoutest men, and sent them back to hold the English army in play whilst the rest escaped: and then, like Jehu, they marched on furiously,[23] with their old, and with their young: some carried their old decrepit mothers, some carried one, and some another. Four of them carried a great Indian upon a bier; but going through a thick wood with him, they were hindered, and could make no haste; whereupon they took him upon their backs, and carried him, one at a time, till they came to Baquag River. Upon a Friday, a little after noon we came to this river. When all the company was come up, and were gathered together, I thought to count the number of them, but they were so many, and being somewhat in motion, it was beyond my skill. In this travel, because of my wound, I was somewhat favored in my load; I carried only my knitting work and two quarts of parched meal: being very faint I asked my mistress to give me one spoonful of the meal, but she would not give me a taste. They quickly fell to cutting dry trees, to make rafts to carry them over the river: and soon my turn came to go over: by the advantage of some brush which they had laid upon the raft to sit upon, I did not wet my foot (which many of themselves at

---

[23] See 2 Kings 9.20.

the other end were mid-leg deep) which cannot but be acknowledged as a favor of God to my weakened body, it being a very cold time. I was not before acquainted with such kind of doings or dangers. *When thou passeth through the waters I will be with thee, and through the rivers they shall not overflow thee,* Isaiah 43.2. A certain number of us got over the river that night, but it was the night after the Sabbath before all the company was got over. On the Saturday they boiled an old horse's leg which they had got, and so we drank of the broth, as soon as they thought it was ready, and when it was almost all gone, they filled it up again.

The first week of my being among them, I hardly ate anything; the second week, I found my stomach grow very faint for want of something; and yet it was very hard to get down their filthy trash: but the third week, though I could think how formerly my stomach would turn against this or that, and I could starve and die before I could eat such things, yet they were sweet and savory to my taste. I was at this time knitting a pair of white cotton stockings for my mistress; and had not yet wrought upon a Sabbath day; when the Sabbath came they bade me go to work; I told them it was the Sabbath day, and desired them to let me rest, and told them I would do as much more tomorrow; to which they answered me, they would break my face. And here I cannot but take notice of the strange providence of God in preserving the heathen: they were many hundreds, old and young, some sick, and some lame, many had papooses at their backs, the greatest number at this time with us, were squaws, and they travelled with all they had, bag and baggage, and yet they got over this river aforesaid; and on Monday they set their wigwams on fire, and away they went: on that very day came the English army after them to this river, and saw the smoke of their wigwams, and yet this river put a stop to them. God did not give them courage or activity to go over after us; we were not ready for so great a mercy as victory and deliverance; if we had been, God would have found out a way for the English to have passed this river, as well as for the Indians with their squaws and children, and all their luggage. *Oh, that my people had hearkened to me, and Israel had walked in my ways, I should soon have subdued their enemies, and turned my hand against their adversaries,* Psalms 81.13–14.

The Sixth Remove

On Monday (as I said) they set their wigwams on fire, and went away. It was a cold morning, and before us there was a great brook with ice on it; some waded through it, up to the knees and higher, but others went till they came to a beaver dam, and I amongst them, where through the good providence of God, I did not wet my foot. I went along that day mourning and lamenting, leaving farther my own country, and travelling into the vast and howling wilderness, and I understood something of Lot's wife's temptation, when she looked back:[24] we came that day to a great swamp, by the side of which we took up our lodging that night. When I came to the brow of the hill, that looked toward the swamp, I thought we had been come to a great Indian town (though there were none but our own company). The Indians were as thick as the trees: it seemed as if there had been a thousand hatchets going at once: if one looked before one, there was nothing but Indians, and behind one, nothing but Indians, and so on either hand, I myself in the midst, and no Christian soul near me, and yet how hath the Lord preserved me in safety! Oh the experience that I have had of the goodness of God, to me and mine!

The Seventh Remove

After a restless and hungry night there, we had a wearisome time of it the next day. The swamp by which we lay, was, as it were, a deep dungeon, and an exceeding high and steep hill before it. Before I got to the top of the hill, I thought my heart and legs, and all would have broken, and failed me. What through faintness, and soreness of body, it was a grievous day of travel to me. As we went along, I saw a place where English cattle had been: that was comfort to me, such as it was: quickly after that we came to an English path, which so took with me, that I thought I could have freely lain down and died. That day, a little after noon, we came to Squakeag, where the Indians quickly spread themselves over the deserted English fields, gleaning what they could find; some picked up ears of wheat that were crickled[25] down, some found ears of Indian corn, some found ground nuts, and others sheaves of wheat that were frozen together in the shock, and went to threshing of them out. Myself got two ears of Indian corn, and whilst I did but turn my back, one of them was stolen from me, which much troubled me. There came an Indian to them at that time, with a basket of horse liver. I asked him to give me a piece: What, says he, can you eat horse liver? I told him, I would try, if he would give a piece, which he did, and I laid it on the coals to roast; but before it was half ready they got half of it away from me, so that I was fain to take the rest and eat it as it was, with the blood about my mouth, and yet a savory bit it was to me: *for to the*

---

[24] When God destroyed the city of Sodom, Lot's wife looked back at it as she fled, and was turned into a pillar of salt (Gen. 19.26).
[25] Trampled.

hungry soul, every bitter thing is sweet.[26] A solemn sight methought it was, to see fields of wheat and Indian corn forsaken and spoiled: and the remainders of them to be food for our merciless enemies. That night we had a mess of wheat for our supper.

The Eighth Remove

On the morrow morning we must go over the river, *i.e.* Connecticut, to meet with King Philip; two canoes full, they had carried over, the next turn I myself was to go; but as my foot was upon the canoe to step in, there was a sudden outcry among them, and I must step back; and instead of going over the river, I must go four or five miles up the river farther northward. Some of the Indians ran one way, and some another. The cause of this rout was, as I thought, their espying some English scouts, who were thereabout. In this travel up the river, about noon the company made a stop, and sat down; some to eat, and others to rest them. As I sat amongst them, musing of things past, my son Joseph unexpectedly came to me: we asked of each other's welfare, bemoaning our doleful condition, and the change that had come upon us. We had husband and father, and children, and sisters, and friends, and relations, and house, and home, and many comforts of this life: but now we may say, as Job, *Naked came I out of my mother's womb, and naked shall I return: the Lord gave, and the Lord hath taken away, blessed be the name of the Lord.*[27] I asked him whether he would read; he told me, he earnestly desired it. I gave him my Bible, and he lighted upon that comfortable scripture, Psalms 118.17–18, *I shall not die but live, and declare the works of the Lord: the Lord hath chastened me sore, yet he hath not given me over to death.* Look here, mother (says he), did you read this? And here I may take occasion to mention one principal ground of my setting forth these lines: even as the psalmist says, To declare the works of the Lord, and His wonderful power in carrying us along, preserving us in the wilderness, while under the enemy's hand, and returning of us in safety again, and His goodness in bringing to my hand so many comfortable and suitable scriptures in my distress. But to return, we travelled on till night; and in the morning, we must go over the river to Philip's crew. When I was in the canoe, I could not but be amazed at the numerous crew of pagans that were on the bank on the other side. When I came ashore, they gathered all about me, I sitting alone in the midst: I observed they asked one another questions, and laughed, and rejoiced over their

---

[26] Proverbs 27.7
[27] Job 1.21.

gains and victories. Then my heart began to fail: and I fell a-weeping which was the first time to my remembrance, that I wept before them. Although I had met with so much affliction, and my heart was many times ready to break, yet could I not shed one tear in their sight: but rather had been all this while in a maze, and like one astonished: but now I may say as, Psalms 137.1, *By the rivers of Babylon, there we sat down: yea, we wept when we remembered Zion.* There one of them asked me, why I wept, I could hardly tell what to say: yet I answered, they would kill me: No, said he, none will hurt you. Then came one of them and gave me two spoonfuls of meal to comfort me, and another gave me half a pint of peas; which was more worth than many bushels at another time. Then I went to see King Philip, he bade me come in and sit down, and asked me whether I would smoke[28] (a usual compliment nowadays amongst saints and sinners) but this no way suited me. For though I had formerly used tobacco, yet I had left it ever since I was first taken. It seems to be a bait, the devil lays to make men lose their precious time: I remember with shame, how formerly, when I had taken two or three pipes, I was presently ready for another, such a bewitching thing it is: but I thank God, he has now given me power over it; surely there are many who may be better employed than to lie sucking a stinking tobacco pipe.

Now the Indians gather their forces to go against Northampton: overnight one went about yelling and hooting to give notice of the design. Whereupon they fell to boiling of ground nuts, and parching of corn (as many as had it) for their provision: and in the morning away they went. During my abode in this place, Philip spake to me to make a shirt for his boy, which I did, for which he gave me a shilling: I offered the money to my master, but he bade me keep it: and with it I bought a piece of horse flesh. Afterwards he asked me to make a cap for his boy, for which he invited me to dinner. I went, and he gave me a pancake, about as big as two fingers; it was made of parched wheat, beaten, and fried in bear's grease, but I thought I never tasted pleasanter meat in my life. There was a squaw who spake to me to make a shirt for her sannup,[29] for which she gave me a piece of bear. Another asked me to knit a pair of stockings, for which she gave me a quart of peas: I boiled my peas and bear together, and invited my master and mistress to dinner, but the proud gossip, because I served them both in one dish, would eat nothing, except one bit that he gave her upon the point of his knife. Hearing that my son was come to this place, I

---

[28] It was customary among many Native American groups to begin trading and diplomatic meetings with the sharing of a pipe.

[29] An Algonquian word for "married man," in this case her husband.

went to see him, and found him lying flat upon the ground: I asked him how he could sleep so? He answered me, that he was not asleep, but at prayer; and lay so, that they might not observe what he was doing. I pray God he may remember these things now he is returned in safety. At this place (the sun now getting higher) what with the beams and heat of the sun, and the smoke of the wigwams, I thought I should have been blind. I could scarce discern one wigwam from another. There was here one Mary Thurston of Medfield, who seeing how it was with me, lent me a hat to wear: but as soon as I was gone, the squaw (who owned that Mary Thurston) came running after me, and got it away again. Here was the squaw that gave me one spoonful of meal. I put it in my pocket to keep it safe: yet notwithstanding somebody stole it, but put five Indian corns in the room of it: which corns were the greatest provisions I had in my travel for one day.

The Indians returning from Northampton, brought with them some horses, and sheep, and other things which they had taken: I desired them, that they would carry me to Albany, upon one of those horses, and sell me for powder: for so they had sometimes discoursed. I was utterly hopeless of getting home on foot, the way that I came. I could hardly bear to think of the many weary steps I had taken, to come to this place.

The Ninth Remove

But instead of going either to Albany or homeward, we must go five miles up the river, and then go over it. Here we abode a while. Here lived a sorry Indian, who spoke to me to make him a shirt. When I had done it, he would pay me nothing. But he living by the riverside, where I often went to fetch water, I would often be putting of him in mind, and calling for my pay: at last he told me if I would make another shirt, for a papoose not yet born, he would give me a knife, which he did when I had done it. I carried the knife in, and my master asked me to give it him, and I was not a little glad that I had anything that they would accept of, and be pleased with. When we were at this place, my master's maid came home, she had been gone three weeks into the Narragansett country, to fetch corn, where they had stored up some in the ground: she brought home about a peck and a half of corn. This was about the time that their great captain, Naananto,[30] was killed in the Narragansett country. My son being now about a mile from me, I asked liberty to go and see him, they bade me go, and away I went: but quickly lost myself, travelling over hills and through swamps,

---

[30] Better known as Canonchet, the chief of the Narragansetts, he was captured by the English on April 2.

and could not find the way to him. And I cannot but admire at the wonderful power and goodness of God to me, in that, though I was gone from home, and met with all sorts of Indians, and those I had no knowledge of, and there being no Christian soul near me; yet not one of them offered the least imaginable miscarriage to me. I turned homeward again, and met with my master, he showed me the way to my son: when I came to him I found him not well: and withall he had a boil on his side, which much troubled him: we bemoaned one another a while, as the Lord helped us, and then I returned again. When I was returned, I found myself as unsatisfied as I was before. I went up and down mourning and lamenting: and my spirit was ready to sink, with the thoughts of my poor children: my son was ill, and I could not but think of his mournful looks, and no Christian friend was near him, to do any office of love for him, either for soul or body. And my poor girl, I knew not where she was, nor whether she was sick, or well, or alive, or dead. I repaired under these thoughts to my Bible (my great comfort in that time) and that scripture came to my hand, *Cast thy burden upon the Lord, and He shall sustain thee* (Ps. 55.22).

But I was fain to go and look after something to satisfy my hunger, and going among the wigwams, I went into one, and there found a squaw who showed herself very kind to me, and gave me a piece of bear. I put it into my pocket, and came home, but could not find an opportunity to broil it, for fear they would get it from me, and there it lay all that day and night in my stinking pocket. In the morning I went to the same squaw, who had a kettle of ground nuts boiling: I asked her to let me boil my piece of bear in her kettle, which she did, and gave me some ground nuts to eat with it: and I cannot but think how pleasant it was to me. I have sometimes seen bear baked very handsomely among the English, and some like it, but the thought that it was bear, made me tremble: but now that was savory to me that one would think was enough to turn the stomach of a brute creature.

One bitter cold day, I could find no room to sit down before the fire: I went out, and could not tell what to do, but I went into another wigwam, where they were also sitting around the fire, but the squaw laid a skin for me, and bade me sit down, and gave me some ground nuts, and bade me come again: and told me they would buy me, if they were able, and yet these were strangers to me that I never saw before.

The Tenth Remove

That day a small part of the company removed about three-quarters of a mile, intending further the next day. When they came to the place where they intended to lodge, and had pitched their wigwams, being hungry I went again back to the place we were before at, to get something to eat: being encouraged by the squaw's kindness, who bade me come again; when I was there, there came an Indian to look after me, who when he had found me, kicked me all along: I went home and found venison roasting that night, but they would not give me one bit of it. Sometimes I met with favor, and sometimes with nothing but frowns.

The Eleventh Remove

The next day in the morning they took their travel, intending a day's journey up the river. I took my load at my back, and quickly we came to wade over the river: and passed over tiresome and wearisome hills. One hill was so steep that I was fain to creep up upon my knees, and to hold by the twigs and bushes to keep myself from falling backward. My head also was so light, that I usually reeled as I went; but I hope all these wearisome steps that I have taken, are but a forewarning to me of the heavenly rest. *I known, O Lord, that thy judgments are right, and that thou in faithfulness hast afflicted me* (Ps. 119.75).

The Twelfth Remove

It was upon a Sabbath day morning, that they prepared for their travel. This morning I asked my master whether he would sell me to my husband; he answered me Nux,[31] which did much rejoice my spirit. My mistress, before we went, was gone to the burial of a papoose, and returning, she found me sitting and reading in my Bible; she snatched it hastily out of my hand, and threw it out of doors; I ran out and caught it up, and put it into my pocket, and never let her see it afterward. Then they packed up their things to be gone, and gave me my load: I complained it was too heavy, whereupon she gave me a slap in the face, and bade me go; I lifted up my heart to God, hoping the redemption was not far off: and the rather because their insolence grew worse and worse.

But the thoughts of my going homeward (for so we bent our course) much cheered my spirit, and made my burden seem light, and almost nothing at all. But (to my amazement and great perplexity) the scale was soon turned: for when we had gone a little way, on a sudden my mistress gives out, she would go no further, but turn back again, and said, I must go back again with her, and she called her sannup, and would have had him gone

---

[31] Yes.

back also, but he would not, but said, he would go on, and come to us again in three days. My spirit was upon this, I confess, very impatient, and almost outrageous. I thought I could as well have died as went back: I cannot declare the trouble that I was in about it; but yet back again I must go. As soon as I had an opportunity, I took my Bible to read, and that quieting scripture came to my hand, Psalms 46.10, *Be still, and know that I am God.* Which stilled my spirit for the present: but a sore time of trial, I concluded, I had to go through. My master being gone, who seemed to me the best friend that I had of an Indian, both in cold and hunger, and quickly so it proved. Down I sat, with my heart as full as it could hold, and yet so hungry that I could not sit neither: but going out to see what I could find, and walking among the trees, I found six acorns, and two chestnuts, which were some refreshment to me. Toward night I gathered me some sticks for my own comfort, that I might not lie a-cold: but when we came to lie down they bade me go out, and lie somewhere else, for they had company (they said) come in more than their own: I told them, I could not tell where to go, they bade me go look; I told them, if I went to another wigwam they would be angry, and send me home again. Then one of the company drew his sword, and told me he would run me through if I did not go presently. Then was I fain to stoop to this rude fellow, and to go out in the night, I knew not whither. Mine eyes have seen that fellow afterward walking up and down Boston, under the appearance of a friendly Indian, and several others of the like cut. I went to one wigwam, and they told me they had no room. Then I went to another, and they said the same; at last an old Indian bade me come to him, and his squaw gave me some ground nuts; she gave me also something to lay under my head, and a good fire we had: and through the good providence of God, I had a comfortable lodging that night. In the morning, another Indian bade me come at night, and he would give me six ground nuts, which I did. We were at this place and time about two miles from Connecticut River. We went in the morning to gather ground nuts, to the river, and went back again that night. I went with a good load at my back (for they when they went, though but a little way, would carry all their trumpery with them). I told them the skin was off my back, but I had no other comforting answer from them than this, That it would be no matter if my head were off too.

The Thirteenth Remove

Instead of going toward the Bay, which was that I desired, I must go with them five or six miles down the river into a mighty thicket of brush: where we abode almost a fortnight. Here one asked me to make a shirt for her papoose, for which she gave me a mess of broth, which was thickened with meal made of the bark of a tree, and to make it the better, she had put into it about a handful of peas, and a few roasted ground nuts. I had not seen my son a pretty while, and here was an Indian of whom I made inquiry after him, and asked him when he saw him: he answered me, that such a time his master roasted him, and that himself did eat a piece of him, as big as his two fingers, and that he was very good meat: but the Lord upheld my spirit, under this discouragement; and I considered their horrible addictedness to lying, and that there is not one of them that makes the least conscience of speaking of truth. In this place, on a cold night, as I lay by the fire, I removed a stick that kept the heat from me, a squaw moved it down again, at which I looked up, and she threw a handful of ashes in my eyes: I thought I should have been quite blinded, and have never seen more: but lying down, the water run out of my eyes, and carried the dirt with it, that by the morning, I recovered my sight again. Yet upon this, and the like occasions, I hope it is not too much to say with Job, *Have pity upon me, have pity upon me, O ye my friends, for the hand of the Lord has touched me.*[32] And here I cannot but remember how many times sitting in their wigwams, and musing on things past, I should suddenly leap up and run out, as if I had been at home, forgetting where I was, and what my condition was: but when I was without, and saw nothing but wilderness, and woods, and a company of barbarous heathens, my mind quickly returned to me, which made me think of that, spoken concerning Samson, who said, *I will go out and shake myself as at other times, but he wist not that the Lord was departed from him.*[33] About this time I began to think that all my hopes of restoration would come to nothing. I thought of the English army, and hoped for their coming, and being taken by them, but that failed. I hoped to be carried to Albany, as the Indians had discoursed before, but that failed also. I thought of being sold to my husband, as my master spake, but instead of that, my master himself was gone, and I left behind, so that my spirit was now quite ready to sink. I asked them to let me go out and pick up some sticks, that I might get alone, and pour out my heart unto the Lord. Then also I took my Bible to read, but I found no comfort here neither, which many times I was wont to find: so easy a thing it is with God to dry up the streams of scripture comfort from us. Yet I can say, that in all my sorrows and afflictions, God did not leave me to have my impatience work toward himself, as if his ways were unrighteous. But I knew that he

---

[32] Job 19.21.
[33] Judg. 16.20.

laid upon me less than I deserved. Afterward, before this doleful time ended with me, I was turning the leaves of my Bible, and the Lord brought to me some scriptures, which did a little revive me, as that Isaiah 55.8, *For my thoughts are not your thoughts, neither are your ways my ways, saith the Lord.* And also that, Psalms 37.5, *Commit thy way unto the Lord, trust also in him, and he shall bring it to pass.* About this time they came yelping from Hadley, where they had killed three Englishmen, and brought one captive with them, *viz.* Thomas Read. They all gathered about the poor man, asking him many questions. I desired also to go and see him; and when I came, he was crying bitterly, supposing they would quickly kill him. Whereupon I asked one of them, whether they intended to kill him; he answered me, they would not: he being a little cheered with that, I asked him about the welfare of my husband, he told me he saw him such a time in the Bay, and he was well, but very melancholy. By which I certainly understood (though I suspected it before) that whatsoever the Indians told me respecting him was vanity and lies. Some of them told me, he was dead, and they had killed him: some said he was married again, and that the governor wished him to marry; and told him he should have his choice, and that all persuaded I was dead. So like were these barbarous creatures to him who was a liar from the beginning.

As I was sitting once in the wigwam here, Philip's maid came in with the child in her arms, and asked me to give her a piece of my apron, to make a flap for it. I told her I would not: then my mistress bade me give it, but still I said no: the maid told me if I would not give her a piece, she would tear a piece off it: I told her I would tear her coat then, with that my mistress rises up, and takes up a stick big enough to have killed me, and struck at me with it, but I stepped out, and she struck the stick into the mat of the wigwam. But while she was pulling of it out, I ran to the maid and gave her all my apron, and so that storm went over.

Hearing that my son was come to this place, I went to see him, and told him his father was well, but very melancholy: he told me he was as much grieved for his father as for himself; I wondered at his speech, for I thought I had enough upon my spirit in reference to myself, to make me mindless of my husband and everyone else: they being safe among their friends. He told me also, that a while before, his master (together with other Indians) were going to the French for powder; but by the way the Mohawks met with them, and killed four of their company which made the rest turn back again, for which I desired that myself and he may bless the Lord; for it might have been worse with him, had he been sold to the French, than it proved to be in his remaining with the Indians.

I went to see an English youth in this place, one John Gilbert of Springfield. I found him lying without doors, upon the ground; I asked him how he did? He told me he was very sick of a flux, with eating so much blood: they had turned him out of the wigwam, and with him an Indian papoose, almost dead (whose parents had been killed), in a bitter cold day, without fire or clothes: the young man himself had nothing on, but his shirt and waistcoat. This sight was enough to melt a heart of flint. There they lay quivering in the cold, the youth round like a dog; the papoose stretched out, with his eyes and nose and mouth full of dirt, and yet alive, and groaning. I advised John to go and get to some fire: he told me he could not stand, but I persuaded him still, lest he should lie there and die: and with much ado I got him to a fire, and went myself home. As soon as I was got home, his master's daughter came after me, to know what I had done with the Englishman, I told her I had got him to a fire in such a place. Now had I need to pray Paul's prayer, 2 Thessalonians 3.2, *That we may be delivered from unreasonable and wicked men.* For her satisfaction I went along with her, and brought her to him; but before I got home again, it was noised about, that I was running away and getting the English youth, along with me; that as soon as I came in, they began to rant and domineer: asking me where I had been, and what I had been doing? and saying they would knock him on the head: I told them, I had been seeing the English youth, and that I would not run away, they told me I lied, and taking up a hatchet, they came to me, and said they would knock me down if I stirred out again; and so confined me to the wigwam. Now may I say with David, 2 Samuel 24.14, *I am in a great strait.* If I keep in, I must die with hunger, and if I go out, I must be knocked in head. This distressed condition held that day, and half the next; and then the Lord remembered me, whose mercies are great. Then came an Indian to me with a pair of stockings that were too big for him, and he would have me ravel them out, and knit them fit for him. I showed myself willing, and bade him ask my mistress if I might go along with him a little way; she said yes, I might, but I was not a little refreshed with that news, that I had my liberty again. Then I went along with him, and he gave me some roasted ground nuts, which did again revive my feeble stomach.

Being got out of her sight, I had time and liberty again to look into my Bible: which was my guide by day, and my pillow by night. Now that comfortable scripture presented itself to me, Isaiah 54.7, *For a small moment have I forsaken thee, but with great mercies will I gather thee.* Thus the Lord carried me along from one time to another, and made good to me this precious promise, and many others. Then my son came to see me, and I asked his master to let him stay a while with me, that I might comb his head, and look over him, for he was almost overcome with lice. He told me, when I had done, that he was very hungry, but I had nothing to relieve him; but bid him go into the wigwams as he went along, and see if he could get anything among them. Which he did, and it seems tarried a little too long; for his master was angry with him, and beat him, and then sold him. Then he came running to tell me he had a new master, and that he had given him some ground nuts already. Then I went along with him to his new master who told me he loved him: and he should not want. So his master carried him away, and I never saw him afterward, till I saw him at Pascataqua in Portsmouth.

That night they bade me go out of the wigwam again: my mistress's papoose was sick, and it died that night, and there was one benefit in it, that there was more room. I went to a wigwam, and they bade me come in, and gave me a skin to lie upon, and a mess of venison and ground nuts, which was a choice dish among them. On the morrow they buried the papoose, and afterward, both morning and evening, there came a company to mourn and howl with her: though I confess, I could not much condole with them. Many sorrowful days I had in this place: often getting alone; *like a crane, or a swallow, so did I chatter: I did mourn as a dove, mine eyes ail with looking upward. Oh, Lord, I am oppressed; undertake for me* (Isa. 38.14). I could tell the Lord as Hezekiah, verse 3. *Remember now O Lord, I beseech thee, how I have walked before thee in truth.* Now had I time to examine all my ways: my conscience did not accuse me of unrighteousness toward one or other: yet I saw how in my walk with God I had been a careless creature. As David said, *Against thee, thee only have I sinned:* and I might say with the poor publican, *God be merciful unto me a sinner.*[34] On the Sabbath days, I could look upon the sun and think how people were going to the house of God, to have their souls refreshed; and then home, and their bodies also: but I was destitute of both; and might say as the poor prodigal, *he would fain have filled his belly with the husks that the swine did eat, and no man gave unto him* (Luke 15.16). For I must say with him, *Father I have sinned against heaven, and in thy sight,* verse 21.[35] I remembered how on the night before and after the Sabbath, when my family was about me, and relations and neighbors with us, we could pray and sing, and then refresh our bodies with the good creatures of God; and then have a comfortable bed to lie down on: but instead of all this, I had only a little swill for the body, and then like a swine, must lie down on the ground. I cannot express to man the sorrow that lay upon my spirit, the Lord knows it. Yet that comfortable scripture would often

---

[34] These two lines are from Psalms 51.4 and Luke 18.13.

[35] Rowlandson here compared herself to the Prodigal Son, showing how thoroughly she saw her captivity as her sinfulness. See also the reference to the "fatted calf" at the end of the text.

come to my mind, *For a small moment have I forsaken thee, but with great mercies will I gather thee.*

The Fourteenth Remove

Now must we pack up and be gone from this thicket, bending our course toward the Bay towns, I having nothing to eat by the way this day, but a few crumbs of cake, that an Indian gave my girl the same day we were taken. She gave it me, and I put it in my pocket; there it lay, till it was so moldy (for want of good baking) that one could not tell what it was made of; it fell all to crumbs, and grew so dry and hard, that it was like little flints; and this refreshed me many times, when I was ready to faint. It was in my thoughts when I put it into my mouth, that if ever I returned, I would tell the world what a blessing the Lord gave to such mean food. As we went along, they killed a deer, with a young one in her, they gave me a piece of the fawn, and it was so young and tender, that one might eat the bones as well as the flesh, and yet I thought it very good. When night came on we sat down; it rained, but they quickly got up a bark wigwam, where I lay dry that night. I looked out in the morning, and many of them had lain in the rain all night, I saw by their reeking. Thus the Lord dealt mercifully with me many times, and I fared better than many of them. In the morning they took the blood of the deer, and put it into the paunch, and so boiled it; I could eat nothing of that, though they ate it sweetly. And yet they were so nice[36] in other things, that when I had fetched water, and had put the dish I dipped the water with, into the kettle of water which I brought, they would say, they would knock me down: for they said, it was a sluttish trick.

The Fifteenth Remove

We went on our travel. I having got one handful of ground nuts, for my support that day, they gave me my load, and I went on cheerfully (with the thoughts of going homeward) having my burden more on my back than my spirit: we came to Baquag River again that day, near which we abode a few days. Sometimes one of them would give me a pipe, another a little

---

[36] Fastidious, neat. Rowlandson didn't understand certain food taboos of the Indians, as in "The Eighth Remove" when her mistress refused to eat the dish she had prepared.

tobacco, another a little salt: which I would change for a little victuals. I cannot but think what a wolfish appetite persons have in a starving condition: for many times when they gave me that which was hot, I was so greedy, that I should burn my mouth, that it would trouble me hours after, and yet I should quickly do the same again. And after I was thoroughly hungry, I was never again satisfied. For though sometimes it fell out, that I got enough, and did eat till I could eat no more, yet I was as unsatisfied as I was when I began. And now could I see that scripture verified (there being many scriptures which we do not take notice of, or understand till we are afflicted), Micah 6.14, *Thou shalt eat and not be satisfied.* Now I might see more than ever before, the miseries that sin hath brought upon us: many times I should be ready to run out against the heathen, but the scripture would quiet me again, Amos 3.6, *Shall there be evil in the city, and the Lord hath not done it?* The Lord help me to make a right improvement of His word, and that I might learn that great lesson, Micah 6.8–9, *He hath showed thee (O Man) what is good, and what doth the Lord require of thee, but to do justly, and love mercy, and walk humbly with thy God? Hear ye the rod, and who hath appointed it.*

The Sixteenth Remove

We began this remove with wading over Baquag River: the water was up to the knees, and the stream very swift, and so cold that I thought it would have cut me in sunder. I was so weak and feeble, that I reeled as I went along, and thought there I must end my days at last, after my bearing and getting through so many difficulties; the Indians stood laughing to see me staggering along: but in my distress the Lord gave me experience of the truth, and goodness of that promise, Isaiah 43.2, *When thou passest through the waters, I will be with thee, and through the rivers, they shall not overflow thee.* Then I sat down to put on my stockings and shoes, with the tears running down mine eyes, and many sorrowful thoughts in my heart, but I got up to go along with them. Quickly there came up to us an Indian, who informed them, that I must go to Wachusett to my master, for there was a letter come from the Council to the Sagamores,[37] about redeeming the captives, and that there would be another in fourteen days, and that I must be there ready. My heart was so heavy before that I could

---

[37] This letter was part of negotiations between the Massachusetts Council and the Indian leaders that led to Rowlandson's release. For the text, see Salisbury, 132–33.

scarce speak or go in the path; and yet now so light, that I could run. My strength seemed to come again, and recruit my feeble knees, and aching heart: yet it pleased them to go but one mile that night, and there we stayed two days. In that time came a company of Indians to us, near thirty, all on horseback. My heart skipped within me, thinking they had been Englishmen at the first sight of them, for they were dressed in English apparel, with hats, white neckcloths, and sashes about their waists, and ribbons upon their shoulders: but when they came near, there was a vast difference between the lovely faces of Christians, and the foul looks of these heathens, which much damped my spirit again.

The Seventeenth Remove

A comfortable remove it was to me, because of my hopes. They gave me a pack, and along we went cheerfully; but quickly my will proved more than my strength; having little or no refreshing my strength failed me, and my spirits were almost quite gone. Now may I say with David, Psalms 109.22– 24, *I am poor and needy, and my heart is wounded within me. I am gone like the shadow when it declineth: I am tossed up and down like the locust; my knees are weak through fasting, and my flesh faileth of fatness.* At night we came to an Indian town, and the Indians sat down by a wigwam discoursing, but I was almost spent, and could scarce speak. I laid down my load, and went into the wigwam, and there sat an Indian boiling of horse's feet (they being wont to eat the flesh first, and when the feet were old and dried, and they had nothing else, they would cut off the feet and use them). I asked him to give me a little of his broth, or water they were boiling in; he took a dish, and gave me one spoonful of samp, and bid me take as much of the broth as I would. Then I put some of the hot water to the samp, and drank it up, and my spirit came again. He gave me also a piece of the ruff or ridding of the small guts,[38] and I broiled it on the coals; and now may I say with Jonathan, *See, I pray you, how mine eyes have been enlightened, because I tasted a little of this honey,* 1 Samuel 14.29, Now is my spirit revived again; though means be never so inconsiderable, yet if the Lord bestow his blessing upon them, they shall refresh both soul and body.

---

[38] Rowlandson made her meal from samp, or corn meal porridge, and horse intestines, which by her custom would have been considered too rough to eat, and would have been gotten "rid" of.

The Eighteenth Remove

We took up our packs and along we went, but a wearisome day I had of it. As we went along I saw an Englishman stripped naked, and lying dead upon the ground, but knew not who it was. Then we came to another Indian town, where we stayed all night. In this town there were four English children, captives; and one of them my own sister's. I went to see how she did, and she was well, considering her captive condition. I would have tarried that night with her, but they that owned her would not suffer it. Then I went into another wigwam, where they were boiling corn and beans, which was a lovely sight to see, but I could not get a taste thereof. Then I went to another wigwam, where there were two of the English children; the squaw was boiling horse's feet, then she cut me off a little piece, and gave one of the English children a piece also. Being very hungry I had quickly eaten up mine, but the child could not bite it, it was so tough and sinewy, but lay sucking, gnawing, chewing and slobbering of it in the mouth and hand, then I took it of the child, and ate it myself, and savory it was to my taste. Then I may say as Job 6.7, *The things that my soul refused to touch, are as my sorrowful meat.* Thus the Lord made that pleasant refreshing, which another time would have been an abomination. Then I went home to my mistress's wigwam; and they told me I disgraced my master with begging, and if I did so any more, they would knock me in the head: I told them, they had as good knock me in the head as starve me to death.

The Nineteenth Remove

They said, when we went out, that we must travel to Wachusett this day. But a bitter weary day I had of it, travelling now three days together, without resting any day between. At last, after many weary steps, I saw Wachusett hills, but many miles off. Then we came to a great swamp, through which we travelled, up to the knees in mud and water, which was heavy going to one tired before. Being almost spent, I thought I should have sunk down at last, and never gotten out; but I may say, as in Psalms 94.18, *When my foot slipped, thy mercy, O Lord, held me up.* Going along, having indeed my life, but little spirit, Philip, who was in the company, came up and took me by the hand, and said, Two weeks more and you shall be mistress again. I asked him, if he spake true? He answered, Yes, and quickly you shall come to your master again; who had been gone from us three weeks. After many weary steps we came to Wachusett, where he was: and glad I was to see him. He asked me, When I washed me? I told him not this month, then he fetched me some water himself, and bid me wash, and gave me the glass to see how I looked; and bid his squaw give me something to eat: so she gave me a mess of beans and meat, and a little ground nut cake. I was wonderfully revived with this favor showed me, Psalms 106.46, *He made them also to be pitied, of all those that carried them captives.*

My master had three squaws, living sometimes with one, and sometimes with another one, this old squaw, at whose wigwam I was, and with whom my master had been those three weeks. Another was Weetamoo, with whom I had lived and served all this while: a severe and proud dame she was, bestowing every day in dressing herself neat as much time as any of the gentry of the land: powdering her hair, and painting her face, going with necklaces, with jewels in her ears, and bracelets upon her hands: when she had dressed herself, her work was to make girdles of wampum and beads.[39] The third squaw was a younger one, by whom he had two papooses. By that time I was refreshed by the old squaw, with whom my master was, Weetamoo's maid came to call me home, at which I fell a-weeping. Then the old squaw told me, to encourage me, that if I wanted victuals, I should come to her, and that I should lie there in her wigwam. Then I went with the maid, and quickly came again and lodged there. The squaw laid a mat under me, and a good rug over me; the first time I had any such kindness showed me. I understood that Weetamoo thought, that if she should let me go and serve with the old squaw, she would be in danger to lose, not only my service, but the redemption pay also. And I was not a little glad to hear this; being by it raised in my hopes, that in God's due time there would be an end of this sorrowful hour. Then in came an Indian, and asked me to knit him three pair of stockings, for which I had a hat, and a silk handkerchief. Then another asked me to make her a shift, for which she gave me an apron.

Then came Tom and Peter,[40] with the second letter from the Council, about the captives. Though they were Indians, I got them by the hand, and burst out into tears; my heart was so full that I could not speak to them; but recovering myself, I asked them how my husband did, and all my friends and acquaintance: They said, They are all very well, but melancholy. They brought me two biscuits, and a pound of tobacco. The tobacco I quickly gave away; when it was all gone, one asked me to give him a pipe

---

[39] Wampum was made from clamshells, usually ground down and drilled to make beads. It was a common trade currency among natives in the northeast.
[40] Two Nipmuc Christian Indians who engaged in shuttle diplomacy for the release of captives.

of tobacco, I told him it was all gone; then began he to rant and threaten. I told him when my husband came I would give him some: Hang him rogue (says he) I will knock out his brains, if he comes here. And then again, in the same breath they would say, That if there should come an hundred without guns, they would do them no hurt. So unstable and like madmen they were. So that fearing the worst, I durst not send to my husband, though there were some thoughts of his coming to redeem and fetch me, not knowing what might follow. For there was little more trust to them than to the master they served.[41] When the letter was come, the sagamores met to consult about the captives, and called me to them to inquire how much my husband would give to redeem me. When I came I sat down among them, as I was wont to do, as their manner is: then they bade me stand up, and said, they were the General Court.[42] They bid me speak what I thought he would give. Now knowing that all we had was destroyed by the Indians, I was in a great strait: I thought if I should speak of but a little, it would be slighted, and hinder the matter; if of a great sum, I knew not where it would be procured: yet at a venture, I said twenty pounds, yet desired them to take less; but they would not hear of that, but sent that message to Boston, that for twenty pounds I should be redeemed. It was a Praying Indian that wrote their letter for them.[43] There was another Praying Indian, who told me, that he had a brother, that would not eat horse; his conscience was so tender and scrupulous (though as large as hell, for the destruction of poor Christians). Then he said, he read that scripture to him, 2 Kings, 6.25, *There was a famine in Samaria, and behold they besieged it, until an ass's head was sold for fourscore pieces of silver, and the fourth part of a kab*[44] *of dove's dung, for five pieces of silver.* He expounded this place to his brother, and showed him that it was lawful to eat that in a famine which is not at another time. And now, says he, he will eat horse with any Indian of them all. There was another Praying Indian, who when he had done all the mischief that he could, betrayed his own father into the English hands, thereby to purchase his own life. Another Praying Indian was at Sudbury fight, though, as he deserved, he was afterward hanged for it. There was another Praying Indian, so wicked and cruel, as to wear a string about his neck, strung with Christians' fingers. Another

---

[41] The devil.

[42] Her captors were asking her to name the price her husband would pay in ransom, as if she were addressing the General Court, the Massachusetts colonial legislature.

[43] This was James Printer, who ironically would later set the type for Rowlandson's narrative while employed by Samuel Green in Cambridge. See Salisbury, 48–49, for more on Printer; 133–37 for texts of letters in these negotiations.

[44] An ancient Hebrew unit of volume.

Praying Indian, when they went to Sudbury fight, went with them, and his squaw also with him, with her papoose at her back: before they went to that fight, they got a company together to powwow; the manner was as followeth. There was one that kneeled upon a deerskin, with the company round him in a ring who kneeled, and striking upon the ground with their hands, and with sticks, and muttering or humming with their mouths; beside him who kneeled in the ring, there also stood one with a gun in his hand: then he on the deerskin made a speech, and all manifested assent to it: and so they did many times together. Then they bade him with the gun go out of the ring, which he did, but when he was out, they called him in again; but he seemed to make a stand, then they called the more earnestly, till he returned again: then they all sang. Then they gave him two guns, in either hand one: and so he on the deerskin began again; and at the end of every sentence in his speaking, they all assented, humming or muttering with their mouths, and striking upon the ground with their hands. Then they bade him with the two guns go out of the ring again; which he did, a little way. Then they called him in again, but he made a stand; so they called him with greater earnestness; but he stood reeling and wavering as if he knew not whither he should stand or fall, or which way to go. Then they called him with exceeding great vehemency, all of them, one and another: after a little while he turned in, staggering as he went, with his arms stretched out, in either hand a gun. As soon as he came in, they all sang and rejoiced exceedingly a while. And then he upon the deerskin, made another speech unto which they all assented in a rejoicing manner: and so they ended their business, and forthwith went to Sudbury fight. To my thinking they went without any scruple, but that they should prosper, and gain the victory. And they went out not so rejoicing, but they came home with as great a victory. For they said they had killed two captains, and almost a hundred men. One Englishman they brought along with them: and he said, it was too true, for they had made sad work at Sudbury, as indeed it proved. Yet they came home without that rejoicing and triumphing over their victory, which they were wont to show at other times, but rather like dogs (as they say) which have lost their ears. Yet I could not perceive that it was for their own loss of men: they said, they had not lost above five or six: and I missed none, except in one wigwam. When they went, they acted as if the devil had told them that they should gain the victory: and now they acted, as if the devil had told them they should have a fall.[45] Whether

---

[45] The fight at Sudbury, on April 18, 1676, resulted in the death of about thirty English, not "almost a hundred" as Rowlandson reports. In spite of losing only five or six, the Indians did not regard it as a victory, for their tactics of warfare emphasized surprise strikes that guarded the life of every warrior.

it were so or no, I cannot tell, but so it proved, for quickly they began to fall, and so held on that summer, till they came to utter ruin. They came home on a Sabbath day, and the powwow that kneeled upon the deerskin came home (I may say, without abuse) as black as the devil. When my master came home, he came to me and bid me make a shirt for his papoose, of a holland-laced pillowbeer.[46] About that time there came an Indian to me and bid me come to his wigwam, at night, and he would give me some pork and ground nuts. Which I did, and as I was eating, another Indian said to me, he seems to be your good friend, but he killed two Englishmen at Sudbury, and there lie their clothes behind you: I looked behind me, and there I saw bloody clothes, with bullet holes in them; yet the Lord suffered not this wretch to do me any hurt; yea, instead of that, he many times refreshed me: five or six times did he and his squaw refresh my feeble carcass. If I went to their wigwam at any time, they would always give me something, and yet they were strangers that I never saw before. Another squaw gave me a piece of fresh pork, and a little salt with it, and lent me her pan to fry it in; and I cannot but remember what a sweet, pleasant and delightful relish that bit had to me, to this day. So little do we prize common mercies when we have them to the full.

The Twentieth Remove

It was their usual manner to remove, when they had done any mischief, lest they should be found out: and so they did at this time. We went about three or four miles, and there they built a great wigwam, big enough to hold a hundred Indians, which they did in preparation to a great day of dancing. They would say now amongst themselves, that the governor would be so angry for his loss at Sudbury, that he would send no more about the captives, which made me grieve and tremble. My sister being not far from the place where we now were, and hearing that I was here, desired her master to let her come and see me, and he was willing to it, and would go with her: but she being ready before him, told him she would go before, and was come within a mile or two of the place; then he overtook her, and began to rant as if he had been mad; and made her go back again in the rain; so that I never saw her till I saw her in Charlestown. But the Lord requited many of their ill doings, for this Indian her master, was hanged after at Boston. The Indians now began to come from all quarters, against their merry dancing day. Among some of them came one Goodwife Kettle: I

---

[46] A pillowcase made of Dutch linen.

told her my heart was so heavy that it was ready to break: so is mine too, said she, but yet said, I hope we shall hear some good news shortly. I could hear how earnestly my sister desired to see me, and I as earnestly desired to see her: and yet neither of us could get an opportunity. My daughter was also now about a mile off, and I had not seen her in nine or ten weeks, as I had not seen my sister since our first taking. I earnestly desired them to let me go and see them: yea, I entreated, begged, and persuaded them, but to let me see my daughter; and yet so hard-hearted were they, that they would not suffer it. They made use of their tyrannical power whilst they had it: but through the Lord's wonderful mercy, their time was now but short.

On a Sabbath day, the sun being about an hour high in the afternoon, came Mr. John Hoar (the Council permitting him, and his own forward spirit inclining him) together with the two forementioned Indians, Tom and Peter, with their third letter from the Council. When they came near, I was abroad: though I saw them not, they presently called me in, and bade me sit down and not stir. Then they caught up their guns, and away they ran, as if an enemy had been at hand; and the guns went off apace. I manifested some great trouble, and they asked me what was the matter? I told them, I thought they had killed the Englishman (for they had in the meantime informed me that an Englishman was come), they said, No; they shot over his horse, and under, and before his horse; and they pushed him this way and that way, at their pleasure, showing what they could do: then they let them come to their wigwams. I begged of them to let me see the Englishman, but they would not. But there was I fain to sit their pleasure. When they had talked their fill with him, they suffered me to go to him. We asked each other of our welfare, and how my husband did, and all my friends? He told me they were all well, and would be glad to see me. Amongst other things which my husband sent me, there came a pound of tobacco: which I sold for nine shillings in money: for many of the Indians for want of tobacco, smoked hemlock, and ground ivy. It was a great mistake in any, who thought I sent for tobacco: for through the favor of God, that desire was overcome. I now asked them, whether I should go home with Mr. Hoar? They answered No, one and another of them: and it being night, we lay down with that answer; in the morning, Mr. Hoar invited the sagamores to dinner; but when we went to get it ready, we found that they had stolen the greatest part of the provision Mr. Hoar had brought, out of his bags, in the night. And we may see the wonderful power of God, in that one passage, in that when there was such a great number of the Indians together, and so greedy of a little good food; and no English there, but Mr. Hoar and myself: that there they did not knock us in the head, and take what we had: there being not only some provision, but also trading cloth, a part of the twenty pounds agreed upon: but instead of doing us any mischief, they seemed to be ashamed of the fact, and said, it were some matchit[47] Indian that did it. Oh that we could believe that there is nothing too hard for God! God showed his power over the heathen in this, as he did over the hungry lions when Daniel was cast into the den. Mr. Hoar called them betime to dinner, but they ate very little, they being so busy in dressing themselves, and getting ready for their dance: which was carried on by eight of them, four men and four squaws; my master and mistress being two. He was dressed in his holland shirt, with great laces sewed at the tail of it, he had his silver buttons, his white stockings, his garters were hung round with shillings, and he had girdles of wampum upon his head and shoulders. She had a kersey coat, and covered with girdles of wampum from the loins upward: her arms from her elbows to her hands were covered with bracelets; there were handfuls of necklaces about her neck, and several sorts of jewels in her ears. She had fine red stockings, and white shoes, her hair powdered and face painted red, that was always before black. And all the dancers were after the same manner. There were two other singing and knocking on a kettle for their music. They kept hopping up and down one after another, with a kettle of water in the midst, standing warm upon some embers, to drink of when they were dry. They held on till it was almost night, throwing out wampum to the standers-by. At night I asked them again, if I should go home? They all as one said No, except my husband would come for me. When we were lain down, my master went out of the wigwam, and by and by sent in an Indian called James the Printer, who told Mr. Hoar, that my master would let me go home tomorrow, if he would [let] him have one pint of liquors. Then Mr. Hoar called his own Indians, Tom and Peter, and bid them go and see whether he would promise before them three: and if he would, he should have it; which he did, and he had it. Then Philip smelling the business called me to him, and asked me what I would give him, to tell me some good news, and speak a good word for me. I told him, I could not tell what to give him, I would [give] anything I had, and asked him what he would have? He said, two coats and twenty shillings in money, and half a bushel of seed corn, and some tobacco. I thanked him for his love: but I knew the good news as well as the crafty fox. My master after he had had his drink, quickly came ranting into the wigwam again, and called for Mr. Hoar, drinking to him, and saying, He was a good man: and then again he would say, Hang him, rogue: being almost drunk, he would drink to him, and yet presently say he should be hanged. Then he called for me. I trembled to hear him,

---

[47] Algonquian word for "bad."

yet I was fain to go to him, and he drank to me, showing no incivility. He was the first Indian I saw drunk all the while that I was amongst them. At last his squaw ran out, and he after her, around the wigwam, with his money jingling at his knees: but she escaped him: but having an old squaw he ran to her: and so through the Lord's mercy, we were no more troubled that night. Yet I had not a comfortable night's rest: for I think I can say, I did not sleep for three nights together. The night before the letter came from the council, I could not rest, I was so full of fears and troubles, God many times leaving us most in the dark, when deliverance is nearest: yea, at this time I could not rest night nor day. The next night I was overjoyed, Mr. Hoar being come, and that with such good tidings. The third night I was even swallowed up with the thoughts of things, *viz.* that ever I should go home again; and that I must go, leaving my children behind me in the wilderness; so that sleep was now almost departed from my eyes.

On Tuesday morning they called their General Court (as they call it) to consult and determine, whether I should go home or no: and they all as one man did seemingly consent to it, that I should go home; except Philip, who would not come among them.

But before I go any further, I would take leave to mention a few re-markable passages of providence, which I took special notice of in my afflicted time.

1. Of the fair opportunity lost in the long march, a little after the fort fight,[48] when our English army was so numerous, and in pursuit of the enemy, and so near as to take several and destroy them: and the enemy in such distress for food, that our men might track them by their rooting in the earth for ground nuts, whilst they were flying for their lives. I say, that then our army should want provision, and be forced to leave their pursuit and return homeward: and the very next week the enemy came upon our town, like bears bereft of their whelps, or so many ravenous wolves, rend-ing us and our lambs to death. But what shall I say? God seemed to leave His people to themselves, and order all things for His own holy ends. *Shall there be evil in the city and the Lord hath not done it? They are not grieved for the affliction of Joseph, therefore shall they go captive, with the first that go captive.*[49] It is the Lord's doing, and it should be marvelous in our eyes.

2. I cannot but remember how the Indians derided the slowness, and dullness of the English army, in its setting out. For after the desolations at Lancaster and Medfield, as I went along with them, they asked me when I

---

[48] The "fort-fight" was an attack on the Narragansetts in their stronghold in coastal Rhode Island in December 1675, a major early victory for the English.

[49] Amos 3.6; 6.6–7.

thought the English army would come after them? I told them I could not tell: It may be they will come in May, said they. Thus did they scoff at us, as if the English would be a quarter of a year getting ready.

3. Which also I have hinted before, when the English army with new supplies were sent forth to pursue after the enemy, and they understanding it, fled before them till they came to Baquag River, where they forthwith went over safely: that that river should be impassible to the English. I can but admire to see the wonderful providence of God in preserving the heathen for further affliction to our poor country. They could go in great numbers over, but the English must stop: God had an overruling hand in all those things.

4. It was thought, if their corn were cut down, they would starve and die with hunger: and all their corn that could be found, was destroyed, and they driven from that little they had in store, into the woods in the midst of winter; and yet how to admiration did the Lord preserve them for his Holy ends, and the destruction of many still amongst the English! Strangely did the Lord provide for them; that I did not see (all the time I was among them) one man, woman, or child, die with hunger.

Though many times they would eat that, that a hog or a dog would hardly touch; yet by that God strengthened them to be a scourge to His people.

The chief and commonest food was ground nuts: they ate also nuts and acorns, artichokes, lily roots, ground beans, and several other weeds and roots, that I know not.

They would pick up old bones, and cut them to pieces at the joints, and if they were full of worms and maggots, they would scald them over the fire to make the vermin come out, and then boil them, and drink up the liquor, and then beat the great ends of them in a mortar, and so eat them. They would eat horse's guts, and ears, and all sorts of wild birds which they could catch: also bear, venison, beaver, tortoise, frogs, squirrels, dogs, skunks, rattlesnakes; yea, the very bark of trees; besides all sorts of creatures, and provision which they plundered from the English. I can but stand in admiration to see the wonderful power of God, in providing for such a vast number of our enemies in the wilderness, where there was nothing to be seen, but from hand to mouth. Many times in a morning, the generality of them would eat up all they had, and yet have some further supply against what they wanted. It is said, Psalms 81.13–14, *Oh, that my people had hearkened to me, and Israel had walked in my ways, I should soon have subdued their enemies, and turned my hand against their adversaries.* But now our perverse and evil carriages in the sight of the Lord, have so offended Him, that instead of turning His hand against them, the Lord feeds and nourishes them up to be a scourge to the whole land.

5. Another thing that I would observe is, the strange providence of God, in turning things about when the Indians were at the highest, and the English at the lowest. I was with the enemy eleven weeks and five days, and not one week passed without the fury of the enemy, and some desolation by fire and sword upon one place or other. They mourned (with their black faces) for their own losses, yet triumphed and rejoiced in their inhuman, and many times devilish cruelty to the English. They would boast much of their victories; saying, that in two hours time they had destroyed such a captain, and his company at such a place; and such a captain and his company, in such a place; and such a captain and his company in such a place: and boast how many towns they had destroyed, and then scoff, and say, They had done them a good turn, to send them to heaven so soon. Again, they would say, This summer that they would knock all the rogues in the head, or drive them into the sea, or make them fly the country: thinking surely, Agag-like, *The bitterness of death is past.*[50] Now the heathen begin to think all is their own, and the poor Christians' hopes to fail (as to man) and now their eyes are more to God, and their hearts sigh heavenward: and to say in good earnest, *Help Lord, or we perish:* When the Lord had brought His people to this, that they saw no help in anything but Himself: then He takes the quarrel into His own hand: and though they had made a pit, in their own imaginations, as deep as hell for the Christians that summer, yet the Lord hurled themselves into it. And the Lord had not so many ways before to preserve them, but now He hath as many to destroy them.

But to return again to my going home, where we may see a remarkable change of providence: at first they were all against it, except my husband would come for me; but afterward they assented to it, and seemed much to rejoice in it; some asked me to send them some bread, others some tobacco, others shaking me by the hand, offering me a hood and scarf to ride in; not one moving hand or tongue against it. Thus hath the Lord answered my poor desire, and the many earnest requests of others put up unto God for me. In my travels an Indian came to me, and told me, if I were willing, he and his squaw would run away, and go home along with me: I told him No: I was not willing to run away, but desired to wait God's time, that I might go home quietly, and without fear. And now God hath granted me my desire. O the wonderful power of God that I have seen, and the experience that I have had: I have been in the midst of those roaring lions, and savage bears, that feared neither God, nor man, nor the devil, by night and day, alone and in company: sleeping all sorts together, and yet

---

[50] I Sam. 15.32. Rowlandson's point was that in spite of the Indians' confidence of victory, Samuel soon after killed Agag, the leader of the enemy Amalekites.

not one of them ever offered me the least abuse of unchastity to me, in word
or action. Though some are ready to say, I speak it for my own credit; but
I speak it in the presence of God, and to His glory. God's power is as great
now, and as sufficient to save, as when he preserved Daniel in the lions'
den; or the three children in the fiery furnace. I may well say as his Psalms
136.1, *Oh give thanks unto the Lord for He is good, for His mercy en-
dureth forever.* Let the redeemed of the Lord say so, whom He hath redeemed from the hand of the enemy, especially that I should come away in
the midst of so many hundreds of enemies quietly and peaceably, and not
a dog moving his tongue. So I took my leave of them, and in coming along
my heart melted into tears, more than all the while I was with them, and I
was almost swallowed up with the thoughts that ever I should go home
again. About the sun going down, Mr. Hoar, and myself, and the two Indians came to Lancaster, and a solemn sight it was to me. There had I lived
many comfortable years amongst my relations and neighbors, and now
not one Christian to be seen, nor one house left standing. We went on to
a farm house that was yet standing, where we lay all night: and a comfortable lodging we had, though nothing but straw to lie on. The Lord preserved us in safety that night, and raised us up again in the morning, and
carried us along, that before noon, we came to Concord. Now was I full
of joy, and yet not without sorrow: joy to see such a lovely sight, so many
Christians together, and some of them my neighbors: there I met with my
brother, and my brother-in-law, who asked me, if I knew where his wife
was? Poor heart! He had helped to bury her, and knew it not; she being
shot down by the house was partly burnt: so that those who were at Boston at the desolation of the town, and came back afterward, and buried the
dead, did not know her. Yet I was not without sorrow, to think how many
were looking and longing, and my own children amongst the rest, to enjoy that deliverance that I had now received, and I did not know whether
ever I should see them again. Being recruited with food and raiment we
went to Boston that day, where I met with my dear husband, but the
thoughts of our dear children, one being dead, and the other we could not
tell where, abated our comfort each to other. I was not before so much
hemmed in with the merciless and cruel heathen, but now as much with
pitiful, tender-hearted and compassionate Christians. In that poor, and
distressed, and beggarly condition I was received in, I was kindly entertained in several houses: so much love I received from several (some of
whom I knew, and others I knew not) that I am not capable to declare it.
But the Lord knows them all by name: the Lord reward them sevenfold
into their bosoms of His spirituals, for their temporals! The twenty pounds
the price of my redemption was raised by some Boston gentlemen, and
Mrs. Usher, whose bounty and religious charity, I would not forget to

make mention of. Then Mr. Thomas Shepard of Charlestown received us into his house, where we continued eleven weeks; and a father and mother they were to us. And many more tender-hearted friends we met with in that place. We were now in the midst of love, yet not without much and frequent heaviness of heart for our poor children, and other relations, who were still in affliction. The week following, after my coming in, the governor and Council sent forth to the Indians again; and that not without success; for they brought in my sister, and goodwife Kettle: their not knowing where our children were, was a sore trial to us still, and yet we were not without secret hopes that we should see them again. That which was dead lay heavier upon my spirit, than those which were alive and amongst the heathen; thinking how it suffered with its wounds, and I was in no way able to relieve it; and how it was buried by the heathen in the wilderness from among all Christians. We were hurried up and down in our thoughts, sometimes we should hear a report that they were gone this way, and sometimes that; and that they were come in, in this place or that: we kept inquiring and listening to hear concerning them, but no certain news as yet. About this time the Council had ordered a day of public thanksgiving: though I thought I had still cause of mourning, and being unsettled in our minds, we thought we would ride toward the eastward, to see if we could hear anything concerning our children. And as we were riding along (God is the wise disposer of all things) between Ipswich and Rowley we met with Mr. William Hubbard, who told us that our son Joseph was come in to Major Waldron's, and another with him, which was my sister's son. I asked him how he knew it? He said, the Major himself told him so. So along we went till we came to Newbury; and their minister being absent, they desired my husband to preach the thanksgiving for them. But he was not willing to stay there that night, but would go over to Salisbury, to hear further, and come again in the morning; which he did, and preached there that day. At night, when he had done, one came and told him that his daughter was come in at Providence: here was mercy on both hands: now hath God fulfilled that precious scripture which was such a comfort to me in my distressed condition. When my heart was ready to sink into the earth (my children being gone I could not tell whither) and my knees trembled under me, and I was walking through the valley of the shadow of death: then the Lord brought, and now has fulfilled that reviving word unto me: *Thus saith the Lord, Refrain thy voice from weeping, and thine eyes from tears, for thy work shall be rewarded, saith the Lord, and they shall come again from the land of the enemy.*[51] Now we were between them, the one on

---

[51] Jer. 31.16.

the east, and the other on the west: our son being nearest, we went to him first, to Portsmouth, where we met with him, and with the major also: who told us he had done what he could, but could not redeem him under seven pounds; which the good people thereabouts were pleased to pay. The Lord reward the major, and all the rest, though unknown to me, for their labor of love. My sister's son was redeemed for four pounds, which the Council gave order for the payment of. Having now received one of our children, we hastened toward the other; going back through Newbury, my husband preached there on the Sabbath day: for which they rewarded him many-fold.

On Monday we came to Charlestown, where we heard that the governor of Rhode Island had sent over for our daughter, to take care of her, being now within his jurisdiction: which should not pass without our acknowledgments. But she being nearer Rehoboth than Rhode Island, Mr. Newman went over, and took care of her, and brought her to his own house. And the goodness of God was admirable to us in our low estate, in that he raised up passionate friends on every side to us, when we had nothing to recompense any for their love. The Indians were now gone that way, that it was apprehended dangerous to go to her: but the carts which carried provision to the English army, being guarded, brought her with them to Dorchester, where we received her safe: blessed be the Lord for it, for great is His power, and He can do whatsoever seemeth Him good. Her coming in was after this manner: she was travelling one day with the Indians, with her basket at her back; the company of Indians were got before her, and gone out of sight, all except one squaw; she followed the squaw till night, and then both of them lay down, having nothing over them but the heavens, and under them but the earth. Thus she travelled three days together, not knowing whither she was going: having nothing to eat or drink but water, and green hurtleberries. At last they came into Providence, where she was kindly entertained by several of that town. The Indians often said, that I should never have her under twenty pounds: but now the Lord hath brought her in upon free-cost,[52] and given her to me the second time. The Lord make us a blessing indeed, each to others. Now have I seen that scripture also fulfilled, Deuteronomy 30.4, 7, *If any of thine be driven out to the outmost parts of heaven, from thence will the Lord thy God gather thee, and from thence will he fetch thee. And the Lord thy God will put all these curses upon thine enemies, and on them which hate thee, which persecuted thee.* Thus hath the Lord brought me and mine out of that horrible pit, and hath set us in the midst of tender-

---

[52] Without paying any ransom.

hearted and compassionate Christians. It is the desire of my soul, that we may walk worthy of the mercies received, and which we are receiving.

Our family being now gathered together (those of us that were living) the South Church in Boston hired a house for us: then we removed from Mr. Shepard's, those cordial friends, and went to Boston, where we continued about three-quarters of a year: still the Lord went along with us, and provided graciously for us. I thought it somewhat strange to set up housekeeping with bare walls; but as Solomon says, *Money answers all things;*[53] and that we had through the benevolence of Christian friends, some in this town, and some in that, and others: and some from England, that in a little time we might look, and see the house furnished with love. The Lord hath been exceeding good to us in our low estate, in that when we had neither house nor home, nor other necessaries, the Lord so moved the hearts of these and those toward us, that we wanted neither food, nor raiment for ourselves or ours, Proverbs 18.24, *There is a friend which sticketh closer than a brother.* And how many such friends have we found, and are now living amongst? And truly such a friend have we found him to be unto us, in whose house we lived, *viz.* Mr. James Whitecomb, a friend unto us near hand, and afar off.

I can remember the time, when I used to sleep quietly without workings in my thoughts, whole nights together, but now it is other ways with me. When all are fast about me, and no eye open, but His who ever waketh, my thoughts are upon things past, upon the awful dispensation of the Lord toward us; upon His wonderful power and might, in carrying of us through so many difficulties, in returning us in safety, and suffering none to hurt us. I remember in the night season, how the other day I was in the midst of thousands of enemies, and nothing but death before me: it is then hard work to persuade myself, that ever I should be satisfied with bread again. But now we are fed with the finest of the wheat, and, as I may say, with honey out of the rock:[54] instead of the husk, we have the fatted calf: the thoughts of these things in the particulars of them, and of the love and goodness of God toward us, make it true of me, what David said of himself, Psalms 6.6. *I watered my couch with my tears.* Oh! the wonderful power of God that mine eyes have seen, affording matter enough for my thoughts to run in, that when others are sleeping mine are weeping.

I have seen the extreme vanity of this world: one hour I have been in health, and wealth, wanting nothing: but the next hour in sickness and wounds, and death, having nothing but sorrow and affliction.

---

[53] Eccles. 10.19.
[54] Ps. 81.16.

Before I knew what affliction meant, I was ready sometimes to wish for it. When I lived in prosperity, having the comforts of the world about me, my relations by me, my heart cheerful, and taking little care for anything; and yet seeing many, whom I preferred before myself, under many trials and afflictions, in sickness, weakness, poverty, losses, crosses, and cares of the world, I should be sometimes jealous lest I should not have my portion in this life, and that scripture would come to my mind, Hebrews 12.6, *For whom the Lord loveth he chasteneth, and scourgeth every son whom he receiveth.* But now I see the Lord had his time to scourge and chasten me. The portion of some is to have their afflictions by drops, now one drop and then another; but the dregs of the cup, the wine of astonishment, like a sweeping rain that leaveth no food, did the Lord prepare to be my portion. Affliction I wanted, and affliction I had, full measure (I thought) pressed down and running over; yet I see, when God calls a person to anything, and through never so many difficulties, yet He is fully able to carry them through and make them see, and say they have been gainers thereby. And I hope I can say in some measure, as David did, *It is good for me that I have been afflicted.*[55] The Lord hath showed me the vanity of these outward things. That they are the vanity of vanities, and vexation of spirit; that they are but a shadow, a blast, a bubble, and our whole dependence must be upon Him. If trouble from smaller matters begin to arise in me, I have something at hand to check myself with, and say, why am I troubled? It was but the other day that if I had had the world, I would have given it for my freedom, or to have been a servant to a Christian. I have learned to look beyond present and smaller troubles, and to be quieted under them, as Moses said, Exodus 14.13, *Stand still and see the salvation of the Lord.*

FINIS

---

[55] Ps. 119.71.

Two Puritan Captivities as told by Cotton Mather

HANNAH DUSTAN
AND HANNAH SWARTON

During the two decades after Mary Rowlandson's narrative was published to such success, captivity stories became part of popular discourse in Puritan New England. The number of captives increased, and although not every returned captive wrote his or her own narrative, their stories passed into conversations, histories, and especially sermons. Hannah Swarton's 1690 captivity was an early example of a pattern common through much of the eighteenth century—she was captured by Indians on the frontier of New England, then taken north to Canada and sold to French colonists. This pattern developed during an almost continuous series of wars between the French and English colonies and their Indian allies, wars often motivated by conflicts in Europe. The first of these colonial wars, King William's War, was so called because the French objected to England's Glorious Revolution of 1689, which replaced the Catholic-leaning King James II with the strongly Protestant William of Orange. This conflict was followed by Queen Anne's War (1702–13), which was connected to the War of the Spanish Succession in Europe and which ended with the English claiming Nova Scotia and Newfoundland from the French. Violence erupted again in the 1740s and finally climaxed in 1754–60 with what U.S. history usually calls the French and Indian War but is more properly known as the Seven Years' War, since it was connected to the war of the same name in Europe. Captivities in New France ended in 1760 when the French were defeated at Quebec and Canada became an English colony. Soon after, the captivity genre turned to portraying the British in the Revolutionary War as the savage captors.

In many Puritan narratives of captivity from these wars with New France, the threat of Indian savagery is blended with the threat of Catholicism. Swarton "dreaded going to Canada for fear lest I should be overcome by them to yield to their religion which I had vowed unto God that I would not do." In the narrative of John Williams, a prominent minister captured at Deerfield, Massachusetts, in 1704, "Popish captivity" is the primary horror of the tale, as when his Indian masters try to force him to attend mass (Vaughn and Clark 184). On the other hand, Jemima Howe recounts how her daughter, like Swarton's, lodged in a nunnery at Montreal, refused to return to New England, "so extremely bigoted was she to the customs and religion of the place" (Calloway 96). Many narratives waver ambivalently between denunciations of "papists" as being worse than the "savages" and admissions that the French were kind and generous toward the English prisoners.

So in spite of what Puritan wartime propaganda such as Mather's sermon on Swarton (the second selection in this chapter) might suggest about the "savages," these captives were prisoners of war. As a form of terrorism against the small towns of New England, native warriors were encouraged by their colonial allies to take captives—men, women, and children. Abenaki Indians taking captives in northern New England could look forward to collecting a bounty by redeeming their captives with the French, who would then exchange them for French captives taken by the English. Once this process became regularized, there was little effort at adoption and acculturation such as Juan Ortiz or James Smith experienced. In some instances, however, such as in the celebrated case of Eunice Williams or the less celebrated one of Hannah Swarton's daughter, English and French efforts to redeem a captive were unsuccessful because the captive had willingly joined a family that refused to sell her back. Laurel Thatcher Ulrich has determined that "a third of all adult female captives made at least some capitulation to the French" (212).

The narratives of Swarton and Dustan come to us from the writings of Cotton Mather, the son of Increase Mather, sponsor of Mary Rowlandson's narrative. Cotton followed his father's path to Harvard (where he enrolled at age twelve) and into the ministry, serving for forty years as his father's assistant at Boston's North Church. He read Hebrew, Greek, and Latin and frequently quoted classical authors as well as the Bible. His prolific writings—more than four hundred published titles—engaged topics from history to theology to science; he is also infamous for his efforts to promote prosecution of the accused witches at Salem in 1692. Three of his works included short accounts of Indian captivity. A sermon,

Humiliations Followed with Deliverances, contained the first versions of
the Swarton and Dustan narratives. Its title describes the essential plot
structure of Puritan captivity narratives. *Decennium Luctuosum: An History of Remarkable Occurrences in the Long War, Which New-England
Has Had with the Indian Salvages, from the Year 1688, to . . . 1698*
records the decade-long King William's War, although the true enemy,
the French, is not mentioned in the title. The versions of the Swarton and
Dustan narratives printed in this chapter are taken from the seven-volume
Magnalia Christi Americana: Or, the Ecclesiastical History of New England, which contained a revised version of the *Decennium Luctuosum* and
the Swarton sermon.

By incorporating them into larger works, Mather subordinated the
captives' stories to his own purposes. Dustan's heroics are recorded entirely in the third person. Swarton's narrative speaks from her own experience, but the didactic interpretation of it suggests Mather's influence.
When Swarton recalls moving from Beverley, Massachusetts, to Casco
Bay, Maine, "where there was no church," it implies that her captivity was
her own fault since she exposed her family to danger by moving to the
frontier. A later passage emphasizes her desire to repent "of that sin which
had been especially a burden to me, namely, that I left the public worship
and ordinances of God to go live in a remote place without the public ministry." Since the expansion in the 1640s of the Plymouth colony, Puritan
patriarchs had been concerned that growth would lead to a breakdown in
their theocratic authority. There was also a widespread feeling during the
last third of the seventeenth century in New England that standards of piety
and morality were declining from the rigid self-discipline of the founders'
generation. Elite ministers like the Mathers reacted with Jeremiads, harsh
warnings of God's coming wrath against the backsliders and sinners, so
called after the prophet Jeremiah in the Old Testament. The Swarton narrative, like Rowlandson's, bears the influence of these cultural elements in
that it is not only accusatory but confessional, as when Swarton paraphrases her Indian mistress's comment that the Puritan missionary efforts
had not "been as careful to instruct her in our religion as the French were
to instruct her in theirs." A similar comment appears in the Dustan story
about the piety of her captors.

The capture and violent revenge of Hannah Dustan were initially
recorded only in Mather's terse, three-page account printed here and in
brief journal entries by a few other New Englanders, including the famous diarist Samuel Sewell (W. Franklin 115–16). Her own direct narrative was never set to paper. Yet her actions created a sensation when they
first came to light, and the significance of her story far exceeds these brief
written sources. Rather than following the common pattern that Swarton's

experience did, Dustan's actions were extraordinary. And like the story of
John Smith's rescue by Pocahontas, the captivity of Hannah Dustan as-
sumes the status of a legend—it is a story that has grown and changed
across time, through retellings by prominent writers and historians and
through local oral traditions reflected in many published sources: the retelling by Henry David Thoreau (included in this chapter) and the writings
about Dustan by historian Thomas Hutchinson, poet Timothy Dwight,
Nathaniel Hawthorne, and others. Today she continues to be a touchstone
for scholars of early American culture. The site of her capture in Haverhill,
Massachusetts, and the site of the murder of the captors in Boscowen,
Maine, were memorialized in the 1870s with the erection at each site of a
large statue of her, and she remains a local hero in Haverhill. From the
fifty-pound reward she shared with her two cocaptives (a sum they collected despite the fact that the official bounty on Indian scalps had just
been rescinded by the Massachusetts authorities) to the two bronze memo-
rials, Dustan's revenge was met with applause—but it also aroused dis-
comfort.

Thoreau's account of Dustan comes from his philosophical travel
book, *A Week on the Concord and Merrimack Rivers.* It is occasioned by
his paddling with his brother down the same stretch of the Merrimack in
1839 that he imagined Dustan paddled down in a stolen birch bark canoe
in 1697. Thoreau's reference to the apple tree was inspired by local legend
about a tree in Haverhill. This led him to the seemingly unlikely equation
of Hannah Dustan with Eve. The first line of the paragraph following the
excerpt reads, "This seems a long while ago, and yet it happened since
Milton wrote his *Paradise Lost.*" For Thoreau, the lost paradise is the connection with Nature that Dustan's victims enjoyed and that was violated
by her act of vengeance.

For modern scholars of the captivity narrative, Hannah Dustan offers a radical antithesis to Mary Rowlandson, an alternative archetype
of the female captive and her place within Puritan society. Rowlandson
was a highly literate upper-class woman, wife of a minister who capitalized
on her story in his sermons, and mother of three children who shared the
trial of captivity. In contrast, Dustan's family was, to use a modern term,
dysfunctional. Her father was abusive. Her husband was a farmer and
bricklayer who is not known to have written anything and was publicly re-
buked by ministers for rebellious and abusive behavior. Worst of all, her
sister, Elizabeth Emerson, was executed for killing a child she had borne
out of wedlock (Ulrich 184–85). Rowlandson piously trusted in God to
deliver her from the trials of captivity—Dustan took matters into her own
hands with a tomahawk. Her violent action remains sensational and has

been variously interpreted. June Namias regards her as the origin of the "Amazon" archetype of female captives, the opposite of the more sentimental "frail flower" type, who was more likely to faint than attempt escape (29–48). That Dustan could give birth less than a week before she was captured, endure a long forced march, then plot a bloody murder infuses femininity with a violent heroism that might threaten masculine roles. Ulrich points out that many colonial women had to be "deputy husbands" while their spouses were absent (35–50), as Thomas Dustan was at the moment of attack. Leslie Fiedler regards Hannah Dustan from a somewhat resentful masculine perspective, calling her a "Great WASP Mother of Us All" and her tomahawk the weapon of the castrating "termagant wife" akin to Mrs. Rip Van Winkle in Washington Irving's story (95). It is this folkloric and critical heritage, beginning in the 1700s, that has made Dustan so significant.

Sources

Mather, Cotton. *Magnalia Christi Americana: Or, The Ecclesiastical History of New England.* 1702. Vol. 2. New York: Russell, 1967. 357–61 (Swarton); 634–36 (Dustan).

Thoreau, Henry David. *A Week on the Concord and Merrimack Rivers.* New York: Library of America, 1985.

Vaughan, Alden T., and Edward W. Clark, eds. *Puritans among the Indians: Accounts of Captivity and Redemption, 1676–1724.* Cambridge: Belknap–Harvard UP, 1981. 145–64. [Reprints the Swarton and Dustan captivity narratives with excellent notes and annotations.]

Supplementary Readings

Calloway, Colin G., ed. *North Country Captives: Selected Narratives of Indian Captivity from Vermont and New Hampshire.* Hanover: UP of New England, 1992.

Demos, John. *The Unredeemed Captive: A Family Story from Early America.* New York: Vintage, 1994. [Reconstructs the story of Eunice Williams, John's daughter, who lived out her life among the Iroquois.]

Fiedler, Leslie. *The Return of the Vanishing American.* New York: Stein, 1968.

Franklin, Wayne, ed. *American Voices, American Lives.* New York: Norton, 1997. [Includes several retellings of the Dustan legend.]

Namias, June. *White Captives: Gender and Ethnicity on the American Frontier.* Chapel Hill: U of North Carolina P, 1993.

Ulrich, Laurel Thatcher. *Good Wives: Image and Reality in the Lives of Women in Northern New England, 1650–1750.* New York: Oxford UP, 1980.

Williams, John. "The Redeemed Captive Returning to Zion." Vaughan and Clark 165–226.

A NOTABLE EXPLOIT; WHEREIN, DUX FAEMINA FACTI

On March 15, 1697, the Salvages made a Descent upon the Skirts of Haverhil, Murdering and Captiving about Thirty-nine Persons, and Burning about half a Dozen Houses. In this Broil, one Hannah Dustan having lain-in about a Week, attended with her Nurse, Mary Neff,[1] a Widow, a Body of terrible Indians drew near unto the House where she lay, with Designs to carry on their Bloody Devastations. Her Husband hastened from his Employments abroad unto the relief of his Distressed Family; and first bidding Seven of his Eight Children (which were from Two to Seventeen Years of Age) to get away as fast as they could unto some Garrison in the Town, he went in to inform his Wife of the horrible Distress come upon them. E'er she could get up, the fierce Indians were got so near, that utterly despairing to do her any Service, he ran out after his Children; resolving that on the Horse which he had with him, he would Ride away with *That* which he should in this Extremity find his Affections to pitch most upon, and leave the rest unto the Care of the Divine Providence. He overtook his Children about Forty Rod from his Door; but then such was the Agony of his Parental Affections, that he found it impossible for him to distinguish any one of them from the rest; wherefore he took up a Courageous Resolution to Live and Die with them all. A Party of Indians came up with him; and now though they Fired at him, and he Fired at them, yet he Manfully kept at the Reer of his Little Army of Unarmed Children, while they Marched off with the Pace of a Child of Five Years Old; until, by the Singular Providence of God, he arrived safe with them all unto a Place of Safety about a Mile or two from his House. But his House must in the mean time have more dismal Tragedies acted at it. The Nurse trying to escape with the New-born Infant, fell into the Hands of the Formidable Salvages; and those furious Tawnies coming into the House, bid poor Dustan

---

[1] Mary Neff was a midwife, who had attended at the birth of Dustan's infant just a week before.

to rise immediately. Full of Astonishment she did so; and sitting down in
the Chimney with an Heart full of most fearful Expectation, she saw the
raging Dragons rifle all that they could carry away, and set the House on
Fire. About Nineteen or Twenty Indians now led these away, with about
half a Score other English Captives; but e'er they had gone many Steps,
they dash'd out the Brains of the Infant against a Tree; and several of the
other Captives, as they began to Tire in their sad Journey, were soon sent
unto their Long Home; the Salvages would presently Bury their Hatchets
into their Brains, and leave their Carcasses on the Ground for Birds and
Beasts to Feed upon. However, Dustan (with her Nurse) notwithstanding
her present Condition, Travelled that Night about a Dozen Miles, and then
kept up with their New Masters in a long Travel of an Hundred and Fifty
Miles, more or less, within a few Days Ensuing, without any sensible Damage in their Health, from the Hardships of their Travel, their Lodging, their
Diet, and their many other Difficulties. These Two poor Women were now
in the Hands of those whose Tender Mercies are Cruelties; but the good
God, who hath all Hearts in his own Hands, heard the Sighs of these Prisoners, and gave them to find unexpected Favour from the Master who laid
claim unto them. That Indian Family consisted of Twelve Persons; Two
Stout Men, Three Women, and Seven Children; and for the Shame of many
an English Family, that was the Character of Prayerless upon it, I must now
Publish what these poor Women assure me: 'Tis this, in Obedience to the
Instructions which the French have given them, they would have Prayers
in their Family no less than Thrice every Day; in the Morning, at Noon,
and in the Evening; nor would they ordinarily let their Children Eat or
Sleep without first saying their Prayers. Indeed these *Idolaters* were like the
rest of their whiter Brethren *Persecutors,* and would not endure that these
poor Women should retire to their English Prayers, if they could hinder
them. Nevertheless, the poor Women had nothing but Fervent Prayers to
make their Lives Comfortable or Tolerable; and by being daily sent out
upon Business, they had Opportunities together and asunder to do like another *Hannah,* in *Pouring out their Souls before the Lord:* Nor did their
praying Friends among our selves forbear to Pour out Supplications for
them. Now they could not observe it without some Wonder, that their Indian Master sometimes when he saw them dejected would say unto them,
*What need you Trouble your self? If your God will have you delivered,
you shall be so!* And it seems our God would have it so to be. This Indian
Family was now Travelling with these Two Captive Women, (and an English Youth taken from Worcester a Year and half before,)[2] unto a Ren-

---

[2] The youth's name was Samuel Lennardson.

dezvous of Salvages, which they call a Town somewhere beyond Penacook; and they still told these poor Women, that when they came to this Town they must be Stript, and Scourg'd, and Run the Gantlet through the whole Army of Indians. They said this was the Fashion when the Captives first came to a Town; and they derided some of the Faint-hearted English, which they said, fainted and swoon'd away under the Torments of this Discipline. But on April 30, while they were yet, it may be, about an Hundred and Fifty Miles from the Indian Town, a little before break of Day, when the whole Crew was in a Dead Sleep, (Reader, see if it prove not so!) one of these Women took up a Resolution to intimate the Action of Jael upon Sisera;[3] and being where she had not her own Life secured by any Law unto her, she thought she was not forbidden by any Law to take away the Life of the Murderers, by whom her Child had been Butchered. She heartened the Nurse and the Youth to assist her in this Enterprize; and all furnishing themselves with Hatchets for the purpose, they struck such home Blows upon the Heads of their sleeping Oppressors, that e'er they could any of them struggle into any effectual resistance, at the Feet of those poor Prisoners, *they bow'd, they fell, they lay down; at their Feet they bowed, they fell; where they bowed, there they fell down Dead.* Only one Squaw escaped sorely Wounded from them in the Dark; and one Boy, whom they reserved asleep, intending to bring him away with them, suddenly wak'd and Scuttled away from this Desolation. But cutting off the Scalps of the Ten Wretches, they came off, and received Fifty Pounds from the General Assembly of the Province, as a Recompence of their Action; besides which, they received many Presents of Congratulation from their more private Friends; but none gave 'em a greater Taste of Bounty than Colonel Nicholson, the Governor of Maryland, who hearing of their Action, sent 'em a very generous Token of his Favour.

---

[3] The story is from Judges 4 and 5. Jael welcomed Sisera, the enemy Canaanite general, into her tent, giving him milk and butter. Then she took a tent stake and drove it into his head.

A NARRATIVE
OF HANNAH SWARTON,
CONTAINING WONDERFUL
PASSAGES, RELATING
TO HER CAPTIVITY
AND HER DELIVERANCE

I was taken by the Indians when Casco Fort was taken (May 1690), my husband being slain and four children taken with me. The eldest of my sons they killed about two months after I was taken, and the rest scattered from me. I was now left a widow and as bereaved of my children though I had them alive, yet it was very seldom that I could see them, and I had not liberty to discourse with them without danger either of my own life or theirs; for our consoling each other's condition and showing natural affection was so displeasing to our Indian rulers unto whose share we fell, that they would threaten to kill us if we cried each to other or discoursed much together. So that my condition was like what the Lord threatened the Jews in Ezekiel 24:22, 23. We durst not mourn or weep in the sight of our enemies, lest we lost our own lives. For the first times, while the enemy feasted on our English provisions, I might have had some with them, but then I was so filled with sorrow and tears that I had little stomach to eat. And when my stomach was come, our English food was spent. The Indians wanted themselves and we more, so that then I was pined with want. We had no corn or bread but sometimes groundnuts, acorns, purslain, hogweed, weeds, roots, and sometimes dogs' flesh but not sufficient to satisfy hunger with these, having but little at a time. We had no success at hunting save that one bear was killed, which I had part of, and a very small part of a turtle I had another time. And once an Indian gave me a piece of moose's liver, which was a sweet morsel to me, and fish if we could catch it.

Thus I continued with them, hurried up and down the wilderness from May 20 till the middle of February, carrying continually a great burden in our travels, and I must go their pace or else be killed presently. And yet [I] was pinched with cold for want of clothing, being put by them into an Indian dress with a slight blanket, no stockings, and but one pair of Indian shoes, and of their leather stockings for the winter. My feet were pricked with sharp stones and prickly bushes sometimes and other times pinched with snow, cold, and ice that I traveled upon, ready to be frozen and faint for want of food, so that many times I thought I could go no further but must lie down and, if they would kill me, let them kill me. Yet then the Lord did so renew my strength that I went on still further as my master would have me and held out with them. Though many English were taken and I was brought to some of them at times while we were about Casco Bay and Kennebeck River, yet at Norridgewock[1] we were separated and no English were in our company but one John York and myself who were both almost starved for want and yet told that if we could not hold up to travel with them they would kill us. And accordingly, John York growing weak by his wants, they killed him and threatened me with the like.

One time my Indian mistress and I were left alone while the rest went to look for eels, and they left us no food from Sabbath-day morning till the next Saturday, save that we had a bladder (of moose I think) which was well filled with maggots; and we boiled it and drank the broth, but the bladder was so tough we could not eat it. On the Saturday I was sent by my mistress to that part of the island most likely to see some canoe and there to make fire and smoke to invite some Indians, if I could spy any, to come to relieve us, and I espied a canoe and by signs invited them to come to shore. It proved to be some squaws who, understanding our wants, one of them gave me a roasted eel which I ate and it seemed unto me the most savory food I ever tasted before. Sometimes we lived on wortle berries, sometimes on a kind of wild cherry which grew on bushes, which I was sent to gather once in so bitter a cold season that I was not able to bring my fingers together to hold them fast. Yet under all these hardships the Lord kept me from any sickness or such weakness as to disenable me from traveling when they put us upon it.

My Indian mistress was one that had been bred by the English at Black Point[2] and now married to a Canada Indian and turned papist. And she would say that had the English been as careful to instruct her in our religion as the French were to instruct her in theirs, she might have been of our religion. And she would say that God delivered us into their hands to punish us for our sins. And this I knew was true as to myself. And as I desired

---

[1] Swarton was captured at Casco Fort, near Falmouth, Maine, and taken up the Kennebeck River toward Quebec. Norridgewalk was at the site of the town of Madison.
[2] Near Scarborough, Maine.

to consider of all my sins for which the Lord did punish me, so this lay very
heavy upon my spirit many a time that I had left the public worship and
ordinances of God where I formerly lived (*viz.* at Beverley) to remove to
the north part of Casco Bay where there was no church or minister of the
Gospel. And this we did for large accommodations in the world, thereby
exposing our children to be bred ignorantly like Indians and ourselves to
forget what we had been formerly instructed in, and so we turned our
backs upon God's ordinances to get this world's goods. But now God hath
stripped me of these things also so that I must justify the Lord in all that
has befallen me and acknowledged that He hath punished me less than my
iniquities deserved. I was now bereaved of husband, children, friends,
neighbors, house, estate, bread, clothes, or lodging suitable, and my very
life did hang daily in doubt, being continually in danger of being killed by
the Indians, or pined to death with famine, or tired to death with hard
traveling, or pinched with cold till I died in the winter season. I was so
amazed with many troubles and hurried in my spirit from one exercise to
another how to preserve myself in danger and supply myself in the want
that was present that I had not time or leisure so composedly to consider
of the great concernments of my soul as I should have done, neither had I
any Bible, or good book to look into, or Christian friend to be my coun-
selor in these distresses. But I may say the words of God which I had formerly heard or read, many of them came oft into my mind and kept me
from perishing in my afflictions. As when they threatened to kill me many
times, I often thought of the words of our savior to Pilate, John 19.11,
"Thou couldest have no power at all against me except it were given thee
from above."

I knew they had no power to kill me but what the Lord gave them, and
I had many times hope that the Lord would not suffer them to slay me but
deliver me out of their hands and in His time I hoped return me to my
country again. When they told me that my eldest son was killed by the
Indians, I thought of that in Jeremiah 33.8, "I will cleanse them from all
their iniquities whereby they have sinned against me, and I will pardon all
their iniquities." I hoped, though the enemy had barbarously killed his
body, yet that the Lord had pardoned his sins and that his soul was safe.
When I thought upon my many troubles, I thought of Job's complaint,
chapter 14.16, 17, "Thou numberest my steps and watchest over my sin;
my transgression is sealed up into a bag, and thou sewest up mine iniquity." This was for my humiliation and put me upon prayer to God for His
pardoning mercy in Christ. And I thought upon David's complaint, Psalms
13.1, 2, and used it in my prayers to the Lord: "How long wilt Thou forget me, O Lord, forever? How long wilt Thou hide Thy face from me?
How long shall I take counsel in my soul, having sorrow in my heart? How

long shall my enemy be exalted over me?" I sometimes bemoaned myself as Job, chapter 19.9, 10, "He hath stripped me of my glory and taken my crown from my head; He hath destroyed me on every side, and I am gone, and my hope hath He removed like a tree." Yet sometimes encouraged from Job 22.27, "Thou shalt make thy prayer to Him, and He shall hear thee, and thou shalt pay thy vows." I made vows to the Lord that I would give up myself to Him if He would accept me in Jesus Christ and pardon my sins, and I desired and endeavored to pay my vows unto the Lord. I prayed to Him, "Remember not against me the sins of my youth," and I besought Him, "Judge me, O God, and plead my cause against an ungodly nation; deliver me from the deceitful and unjust man. Why go I mourning because of the oppression of the enemy?" And by many other scriptures that were brought to my remembrance was I instructed, directed, and comforted.

I traveled over steep and hideous mountains one while, and another while over swamps and thickets of fallen trees lying one, two, three foot from the ground which I have stepped on from one to another, nigh a thousand in a day, carrying a great burden on my back. Yet I dreaded going to Canada for fear lest I should be overcome by them to yield to their religion which I had vowed unto God that I would not do. But the extremity of my sufferings were such that at length I was willing to go to preserve my life. And after many weary journeys through frost and snow, we came to Canada about the middle of February 1690. And traveling over the river, my master pitched his wigwam in sight of some French houses westward of us and then sent me to those houses to beg victuals for them, which I did and found the French very kind to me, giving me beef and pork and bread which I had been without near nine months before so that now I found a great change as to diet. But the snow being knee-deep and my legs and hams very sore, I found it very tedious to travel, and my sores bled so that as I traveled I might be tracked by my blood that I left behind me on the snow. I asked leave to stay all night with the French when I went to beg again, which my master consented unto, and sent me eastward to houses which were toward Quebec (though then I knew it not). So, having begged provisions at a French house, and it being near night after I was refreshed myself and had food to carry to the Indians, I signified as well as I could to make the French woman understand that I desired to stay by her fire that night. Whereupon she laid a good bed on the floor and good coverings for me, and there I lodged comfortably.

And the next morning when I had breakfasted with the family and the menkind were gone abroad, as I was about to go to my Indian master the French woman stepped out and left me alone in her house, and I then stayed her return to give her thanks for her kindness. And while I waited, came in two men, and one of them spake to me in English, "I am glad to see you, country-woman!" This was exceedingly reviving to hear the voice of an Englishman, and, upon inquiry, I found he was taken at the North-west Passage and the other was a French ordinary keeper.[3] After some discourse he asked me to go with him to Quebec, which he told me was about four miles off. I answered my Indian master might kill me for it when I went back. Then, after some discourse in French with his fellow-traveler, he said this Frenchman engaged that if I would go with them he would keep me from returning to the Indians, and I should be ransomed. And my French hostess, being now returned indoors, persuaded me to go with them to Quebec, which I did, and was conveyed unto the house of the Lord Intendant, Monsieur Le Tonant,[4] who was the chief judge and second to the governor. And I was kindly entertained by the lady and had French clothes given me with good diet and lodging and was carried thence unto the hospital where I was physicked and blooded[5] and very courteously provided for. And sometime after my Indian master and mistress coming for me, the Lady Intendant paid a ransom for me, and I became her servant. And I must speak it to the honor of the French, they were exceeding kind to me at first, even as kind as I could expect to find the English so that I wanted nothing for my bodily comfort which they could help me unto.

Here was a great and comfortable change as to my outward man in my freedom from my former hardships and hardhearted oppressors. But here began a greater snare and trouble to my soul and danger to my inward man. For the Lady, my mistress, the nuns, the priests, the friars, and the rest set upon me with all the strength of argument they could from scripture, as they interpreted it, to persuade me to turn papist, which they pressed with very much zeal, love, entreaties, and promises if I would turn to them, and with many threatenings and sometimes hard usages because I did not turn to their religion. Yea, sometimes the papists, because I would not turn to them, threatened to send me to France, and there I should be burned because I would not turn to them.

Then was I comforted from that in 2 Corinthians 1.8, 9, 10: "We were pressed out of measure above strength insomuch that we despaired even of life, but we had the sentence of death in ourselves that we should not trust in ourselves but in God who raises the dead, who delivered us from so great a death and doth deliver; in whom we trust that He will yet deliver us." I knew God was able to deliver me as He did Paul and as He did the three

---

[3] Tavern keeper.
[4] The Intendant of New France at the time was Jean Bochart de Champigny. Swarton and/or Mather seems to have mistaken his title for his name.
[5] Given medicine and bled as treatment.

children out of the fiery furnace. And I believed He would either deliver me from them or fit me for what He called me to suffer for His sake and name. For their praying to angels they brought the history of the angel that was sent to the Virgin Mary in the first of Luke. I answered them from Revelations 19.10 and 22.9. They brought Exodus 17.11 of Israel's prevailing while Moses held up his hands. I told them we must come to God only by Christ, John 6.37, 44. For purgatory they brought Matthew 5.25. I told them to agree with God while here on earth was to agree with our adversary in the way, and if we did not, we should be cast into hell and should not come out until we paid the utmost farthing, which could never be paid. But it's bootless for me, a poor woman, to acquaint the world with what arguments I used if I could now remember them, and many of them are slipped out of my memory.[6]

I shall proceed to relate what trials I met with in these things. I was put upon it either to stand to the religion I was brought up in and believed in my conscience to be true or to turn to another which I believed was not right. And I was kept from turning by that scripture, Matthew 10.32, 33: "Whosoever shall confess me before men, him will I confess before my Father which is in heaven, and whosoever denies me before men, him also will I deny before my Father which is in heaven." I thought that if I should deny the truth and own their religion, I should deny Christ. Yet upon their persuasions I went to see and be present at their worship sometimes but never to receive their sacrament. And once when I was at their worship that scripture, 2 Corinthians 6.14 to the end, came into my mind: "What communion hath light with darkness, what concord hath Christ with Belial, what part hath he that believeth with an infidel, and what agreement hath the temple of God with idols? Wherefore come out from among them and be ye separate and touch not the unclean thing, and I will receive you, and I will be a Father unto you, and ye shall be my sons and daughters, saith the Lord Almighty." This scripture was so strong upon my spirit that I thought I was out of my way to be present at the idolatrous worship, and I resolved never to come unto it again. But when the time drew nigh that I was to go again, I was so restless that night that I could not sleep, thinking what I would say to them when they urged me to go again, and what I should do. And so it was in the morning that a Frenchwoman of my acquaintance told me if I would not be of their religion I did but mock at it to go to their worship and bid me that if I would not be of their religion I

---

[6] Swarton summarized the arguments she carried on with her Catholic hosts over Christian doctrine. The Puritans held that it was improper to pray to saints, as distinct from God, and did not believe in Purgatory.

should go no more. I answered her that I would not be of their religion, and I would go no more to their worship. And accordingly I never went more, and they did not force me to it.

I have had many conflicts in my own spirit, fearing that I was not truly converted unto God in Christ and that I had no saving interest in Christ. I could not be of a false religion to please men, for it was against my conscience. And I was not fit to suffer for the true religion and for Christ. For I then feared I had no interest in Him. I was neither fit to live nor fit to die and brought once to the very pit of despair about what would become of my soul. In this time I had gotten an English Bible and other good books by the help of my fellow captives. I looked over the scripture and settled on the prayer of Jonah and those words, "I said I am cast out of Thy sight, yet will I look again towards Thy holy temple." I resolved I would do as Jonah did. And in the meditation upon this scripture the Lord was pleased by His Spirit to come into my soul and so fill me with ravishing comfort that I cannot express it.

Then came to mind the history of the transfiguring of Christ and Peter's saying, Matthew 17.4, "Lord, it is good for us to be here!" I thought it was good for me to be here, and I was so full of comfort and joy I even wished I could be so always and never sleep or else die in that rapture of joy and never live to sin any more against the Lord. Now I thought God was my God, and my sins were pardoned in Christ, and now I could suffer for Christ, yea, die for Christ, or do anything for Him. My sins had been a burden to me. I desired to see all my sins and to repent of them all with all my heart and of that sin which had been especially a burden to me, namely, that I left the public worship and ordinances of God to go live in a remote place without the public ministry, depriving ourselves and our children of so great a benefit for our souls, and all this for worldly advantages. I found a heart to repent of them all and to lay hold of the blood of Christ to cleanse me from them all.

I found much comfort while I was among the French by the opportunities I had sometimes to read the scriptures and other good books and pray to the Lord in secret and the conference that some of us captives had together about things of God and prayer together sometimes, especially with one that was in the same house with me, Margaret Stilson. Then was the word of God precious to us, and they that feared the Lord spake one to another of it as we had opportunity. And Col. Tyng and Mr. Alden,[7] as they were permitted, did speak to us to confirm and strengthen us in the

---

[7]Edward Tyng and John Alden had been captured by a French Ship during King William's War in 1691. Margaret Stilson was from Marblehead, Massachusetts.

ways of the Lord. At length the French debarred our coming together for religious conference or other duties. And word was sent us by Mr. Alden that this was one kind of persecution that we must suffer for Christ.

These are some of the scriptures which have been my support and comfort in the affliction of my captivity among the papists. That of Ezekiel 16.6–8 I applied unto myself, and I desired to enter into covenant with God and to be His, and I prayed to the Lord and hoped the Lord would return me to my country again that I might enter into covenant with Him among His people and enjoy communion with Him in His churches and public ordinances. Which prayers the Lord hath now heard and graciously answered, praised be His name! The Lord enable me to live suitably to His mercy and to those public and precious privileges which I now enjoy. So, that in Ezekiel 11.16, 17 was a great comfort unto me in my captivity, "Although I have cast them far off among the heathen, yet will I be a little sanctuary to them. I will gather you from the people where you have been scattered." I found that God was a little sanctuary to me there and hoped that the Lord would bring me unto the country from whence I had been scattered. And the Lord hath heard the prayer of the destitute and not despised my prayer but granted me the desire of my soul in bringing me to His house and my relations again. I often thought on the history of the man born blind of whom Christ, when His disciples asked whether this man had sinned or his parents, answered neither this man nor his parents, but this was that the works of God might be made manifest in him. So, though I had deserved all this, yet I knew not but one reason of God's bringing all these afflictions and miseries upon me and then enabling me to bear them was that the works of God might be made manifest. And in my great distress I was revived by that in Psalms 118.17, 18, "I shall not die but live and declare the works of the Lord. The Lord hath chastened me sore, but He hath not given me over to death."

I had very often a secret persuasion that I should live to declare the works of the Lord. And 2 Chronicles 6.36, 37, 38, 39 was a precious scripture to me in the day of evil. We have read over and prayed over this scripture together and talked together of this scripture, Margaret and I, how the Lord had promised though they were scattered for their sins, yet there should be a return if they did bethink themselves and turn and pray. So we did bethink ourselves in the land where we were carried captive, did turn, did pray, and endeavor to return to God with all our hearts. And, as they were to pray towards the temple, I took it that I should pray towards Christ and accordingly did so and hoped the Lord would hear, and He hath heard from heaven, His dwelling-place, my prayer and supplication and maintained my cause and not rejected me but returned me. And oh, how affectionate was my reading of the 84th Psalm in this condition!

The means of my deliverance were by reason of letters that had passed between the governments of New England and of Canada. Mr. Cary was sent with a vessel to fetch captives from Quebec, and when he came, I, among others with my youngest son, had our liberty to come away. And by God's blessing upon us we arrived in safety at Boston in November 1695, our desired haven. And I desire to praise the Lord for His goodness and for His wonderful works to me. Yet still I have left behind two children, a daughter of twenty years old at Montreal whom I had not seen in two years before I came away and a son of nineteen years old whom I never saw since we parted the next morning after we were taken.[8] I earnestly request the prayers of my Christian friends that the Lord will deliver them.

What shall I render to the Lord for all His benefits?

---

[8] Hannah's daughter Mary converted to Catholicism, married a Canadian man, and never returned to New England. Her son John's fate is not known.

FROM *A WEEK ON THE CONCORD AND MERRIMACK RIVERS*

Henry David Thoreau

On the thirty-first day of March, one hundred and forty-two years before this, probably about this time in the afternoon, there were hurriedly paddling down this part of the river, between the pine woods which then fringed these banks, two white women and a boy, who had left an island at the mouth of the Contoocook before daybreak. They were slightly clad for the season, in the English fashion, and handled their paddles unskillfully, but with nervous energy and determination, and at the bottom of their canoe lay the still bleeding scalps of ten of the aborigines. They were Hannah Dustan, and her nurse, Mary Neff, both of Haverhill, eighteen miles from the mouth of this river, and an English boy, named Samuel Lennardson, escaping from captivity among the Indians. On the fifteenth of March previous, Hannah Dustan had been compelled to rise from childbed, and half dressed, with one foot bare, accompanied by her nurse, commence an uncertain march, in still inclement weather, through the snow and the wilderness. She had seen her seven elder children flee with their father, but knew not of their fate. She had seen her infant's brains dashed out against an apple-tree, and had left her own and her neighbors' dwellings in ashes. When she reached the wigwam of her captor, situated on an island in the Merrimack, more than twenty miles above where we now are, she had been told that she and her nurse were soon to be taken to a distant Indian settlement, and there made to run the gauntlet naked. The family of this Indian consisted of two men, three women, and seven children, beside an English boy, whom she found a prisoner among them. Having determined to attempt her escape, she instructed the boy to inquire of one of the men, how he should dispatch an enemy in the quickest manner, and take his scalp. "Strike 'em there," said he, placing his finger on his temple, and he also showed him how to take off the scalp. On the morning of the thirty-first she arose before daybreak, and awoke her nurse and the boy, and taking the Indians' tomahawks, they killed them all in their sleep, excepting one favorite boy, and one squaw who fled wounded with him to the woods. The English boy struck the Indian who had given him the information, on the temple, as he had been directed. They then collected all the provision they could find, and took their master's tomahawk and gun, and scuttling all the canoes but one, commenced their flight to Haverhill, distant about sixty miles by the river. But after having proceeded a short distance, fearing that her story would not be believed if she should escape to tell it, they returned to the silent wigwam, and taking off the scalps of the dead, put them into a bag as proofs of what they had done, and then retracing their steps to the shore in the twilight, recommenced their voyage.

Early this morning this deed was performed, and now, perchance, these tired women and this boy, their clothes stained with blood, and their minds racked with alternate resolution and fear, are making a hasty meal of parched corn and moosemeat, while their canoe glides under these pine roots whose stumps are still standing on the bank. They are thinking of the dead whom they have left behind on that solitary isle far up the stream, and of the relentless living warriors who are in pursuit. Every withered leaf which the winter has left seems to know their story, and in its rustling to repeat it and betray them. An Indian lurks behind every rock and pine, and their nerves cannot bear the tapping of a woodpecker. Or they forget their own dangers and their deeds in conjecturing the fate of their kindred, and whether, if they escape the Indians, they shall find the former still alive. They do not stop to cook their meals upon the bank, nor land, except to carry their canoe about the falls. The stolen birch forgets its master and does them good service, and the swollen current bears them swiftly along with little need of the paddle, except to steer and keep them warm by exercise. For ice is floating in the river; the spring is opening; the muskrat and the beaver are driven out of their holes by the flood; deer gaze at them from the bank; a few faint-singing forest birds, perchance, fly across the river to the northernmost shore; the fish-hawk sails and screams overhead, and geese fly over with a startling clangor; but they do not observe these things, or they speedily forget them. They do not smile or chat all day. Sometimes they pass an Indian grave surrounded by its paling on the bank, or the frame of a wigwam, with a few coals left behind, or the withered stalks still rustling in the Indian's solitary cornfield on the interval. The birch stripped of its bark, or the charred stump where a tree has been burned down to be made into a canoe, these are the only traces of man— a fabulous wild man to us. On either side, the primeval forest stretches away uninterrupted to Canada, or to the "South Sea";[1] to the white man a drear and howling wilderness, but to the Indian a home, adapted to his nature, and cheerful as the smile of the Great Spirit.

While we loiter here this autumn evening, looking for a spot retired enough, where we shall quietly rest tonight, they thus, in that chilly March evening, one hundred and forty-two years before us, with wind and current favoring, have already glided out of sight, not to camp, as we shall, at night, but while two sleep one will manage the canoe, and the swift stream bear them onward to the settlements, it may be, even to old John Lovewell's house[2] on Salmon Brook tonight.

According to the historian, they escaped as by a miracle all roving bands of Indians, and reached their homes in safety, with their trophies, for which the General Court paid them fifty pounds. The family of Hannah Dustan all assembled alive once more, except the infant whose brains were dashed out against the apple-tree, and there have been many who in later times have lived to say that they had eaten of the fruit of that apple-tree.

---

[1] The Pacific Ocean.
[2] Captain Lovewell led attacks on the Indians in 1725.

Two African American Captives

JOHN MARRANT
AND OLAUDAH EQUIANO

If the captivity narrative is a story told by a person abducted from his or her community in an attack by a foreign nation, taken to a distant place, exposed to suffering, and pressured to conform to a different culture, then the stories of African slaves are among the most harrowing of captivity narratives. Slavery began with kidnapping and captivity in Africa, and the slave narrative as it developed in nineteenth-century America often drew on the styles of captivity narratives still so popular at that time, notably the sentimental representations of families torn apart by slavery/captivity. Yet in the two eighteenth-century texts by Africans reprinted in this chapter, the strongest connection to the captivity tradition is their common use of a third genre, the Protestant conversion narrative.

John Marrant and Olaudah Equiano both became Methodists, a Protestant denomination begun in the 1740s by John Wesley. Like other evangelical movements, it appealed to ethnic minorities who were denied access to the more established churches of America and England. Methodism's success also owed much to the efforts of George Whitefield, who was probably the most popular preacher of his day and regularly spoke to audiences of thousands, as Benjamin Franklin memorably describes in his *Autobiography*. Whitefield made several trips to America, and even organized a Methodist colony in Georgia. It was on one of these visits that Marrant heard him in Charleston, South Carolina, and experienced his dramatic conversion, characterized by intense physical effects that many Methodists regarded as evidence of divine power (but which the sect's critics assailed

as false or histrionic). Equiano's conversion to Methodism was also inspired by seeing Whitefield, but it occurs many pages after the selection
that is reprinted here. By the time he published his book, Equiano was a
famous exemplar for the movement. Wesley cited the *Interesting Narrative*
as one of his favorite books, reportedly asking to be read to from it on his
deathbed in 1791. Both Marrant and Equiano as well as other eighteenth-
century African American writers such as Phyllis Wheatley and James Albert Ukawsaw Gronniosaw sought patronage from the countess of Huntingdon, a wealthy Methodist who wished to promote missionary work
and the abolition of slavery. Equiano was employed in 1786 in a project
for an economic and missionary colony in Sierra Leone in Africa, while
Marrant went to Nova Scotia the same year his narrative was published.

Marrant's story may surprise readers familiar with slave narratives and
captivity narratives. He was never a slave, but born of free black parents in
New York City in 1755. He makes almost no mention of slavery or of his
racial identity, and in fact the episode toward the end in which he instructs
slaves on "a plantation belonging to Mr. Jenkins" was omitted from the
first three editions of the narrative. Moreover, Marrant was not captured by
Indians; he refuses an offer from the Indian he meets to be guided back to
his home in Charleston. Although these details may appear to defy the traditions of two genres, Marrant was following other textual models. The
story of escaping execution and converting his executioner and the Cherokee king follows the biblical story of Daniel and the lions' den. To drive the
point home, he told the Cherokees this story. The subsequent scene when
the king's daughter took Marrant's Bible and said "the book would not
speak to her" is not only a distant echo of Pocahontas and John Smith, but
also an instance of "The Trope of the Talking Book," which Henry Louis
Gates Jr. has traced through many early texts by black authors, including
Equiano and Gronniosaw. But whereas in Equiano's text the talking book
scene shows the illiterate young slave's amazement at the magical powers
of his master, Marrant used it to show the power of his own literacy and of
God's Scripture over the illiterate Indians. It made a fine demonstration of
his promise as a missionary, the task he would soon take on in Nova Scotia.

Vincent Carretta, who has edited and researched both these texts,
points out that because the United States did not offer Africans the in-
alienable rights it had promised, "Britain and not the new United States
continued to serve as the promised land of freedom for present and former
slaves" (*Unchained Voices*, 7). Many times more slaves sided with the British than with the Rebels. After the Revolutionary War, the defeated British
faced the problem of how to resettle thousands of "Black Loyalists," African Americans who had fought on their side, often as a means of gaining
freedom from Rebel masters. They could not remain in the United States

without fear of reprisals or reenslavement, yet they were not very welcome in England either. Many were sent to Nova Scotia, which had recently been won from the French. Marrant went there too, with plans to preach to the native Micmac Indians as well as to these black settlers. The support he expected from the countess of Huntingdon was not provided to him, however, and he soon went on to Boston, where he preached antislavery sermons for Prince Hall in his lodge of African Masons. He then returned to England and died there in 1791.

At the time when Marrant was publishing his narrative and preparing to depart for Nova Scotia, Equiano was in London, where he had become involved in the movement to abolish the slave trade, in part by writing letters to periodicals. To support his planned book, Equiano sought out influential persons to pay for copies before publication and included this list of subscribers (which eventually numbered more than eight hundred) at the beginning of the book, making it in effect a petition to the English Parliament to pass abolitionist legislation. As the last chapter of his *Narrative* explains, Equiano also joined in a scheme of African colonization, a project that formed part of the Abolitionists' policy. The plan was to reestablish freed slaves in Sierra Leone in West Africa, where they would Christianize the Africans and modernize the economy so as to provide a market for English goods and a source of commodities that would be an alternative to those produced by the slave industries of the British West Indian colonies. As he put it near the end of his book, "If the blacks were permitted to remain in their own country, they would double themselves every fifteen years. In proportion to such increase will be the demand for manufactures" (235). The plan was wildly optimistic and quickly ran into difficulties. Equiano himself was accused of mismanaging funds in his position as commissary to the colony. On a happier note, he also wrote of his marriage to Susanna Cullen, an Englishwoman of a wealthy family, with whom he fathered two daughters. Equiano died in 1797.

The Equiano selection in this chapter draws from the first three chapters of a narrative that runs to more than 200 pages in modern editions. Whereas other captives often described the curious ways of their Native American captors, Equiano was himself from another culture, one that English readers were curious about. In the first chapter of his book, he supplied an ethnography of his native African culture that showed it to be the product of an industrious, chaste, artistic, and courageous people, a portrayal at odds with popular stereotypes of the time but consistent with John Wesley's *Thoughts on Slavery*. Chapter 2 most closely matches the form of the Indian captivity narratives; it depicts the raid on Equiano's village by African slave traders, his sentimental bond for his sister, the new bonds created by implicit adoption into the household of his "master," and the trauma of being resold and removed to a foreign land. Because he had known slavery in the culture of his birth, the horror of being kidnapped was not slavery, but captivity and removal into a hostile people. Equiano employs many tropes of the representation of cultural otherness, but does so from a position opposed to that of most colonial writing. "[T]he white people looked and acted . . . in so savage a manner" that he feared they were cannibals, and he was puzzled and shocked by their technologies of navigation and of torture. Yet as his first sight of the quadrant foreshadowed, Equiano quickly learned to master some of these tools and turned these skills into valuable assets. Later in the *Narrative,* he recounted how when he was put to work as a sailor in the West Indies by his master, Mr. King, he earned much money through entrepreneurial trade in the ports. This fair-minded master eventually made good on his promise to Equiano that he might buy his freedom.

Equiano's sea voyages took him all over the world, and he witnessed many significant events of eighteenth-century history. He fought naval battles in the Mediterranean and at the seige of Louisburg, Nova Scotia, during the Seven Years' War. He even participated in a voyage of exploration to the Arctic. As a merchant captain employed by his former master, he was shipwrecked in the Bahamas, where his courageous leadership preserved the lives of the entire crew.

If Marrant played the unusual role of the captive Daniel, persuading and converting his captors, Equiano fit the more common type of the transculturated captive, for he assimilated the religious and mercantile beliefs of his captors. He even accepted employment as an overseer of slaves in a project to set up a plantation on the Mosquito Coast in today's Nicaragua, where he encountered and described the native Indians of that region. After he abandoned that project, he was nearly ensnared and forced into slavery once more, but reached England safely in 1777, when he left his seafaring life and began his literary and political activities.

Sources

Marrant, John. "A Narrative of the Lord's Wonderful Dealings with John Marrant, a Black. (Now Going to Preach the Gospel in Nova-Scotia). Born in New York, in North-America. Taken Down from His Own Relation, Arranged, Corrected, and Published by the Rev. Mr. Aldridge.)" *Unchained Voices: An Anthology of Black Authors of the English-Speaking World of the Eighteenth Century.* Ed. Vincent Carretta. Lexington: UP of Kentucky, 1996. 110–28.

Equiano, Olaudah. *The Life of Olaudah Equiano or Gustavus Vassa, the African.* 1789. Rpt. London: Dawsons, 1969.

I am indebted to Vincent Carretta for his annotations and editorial work on both texts.

Supplementary Readings

Benezet, Anthony. *Some Historical Account of Guinea, Its Situation, Produce, and the General Disposition of Its Inhabitants. With an Inquiry into the Rise and Progress of the Slave Trade, Its Nature, and Lamentable Effects.* London: 1788.

Carretta, Vincent, ed. *Unchained Voices: An Anthology of Black Authors in the English-Speaking World of the Eighteenth Century.* Lexington: U of Kentucky P, 1996.

Franklin, Benjamin. *The Autobiography and Other Writings.* New York: Penguin, 1986.

Gates, Henry Louis, Jr. *The Signifying Monkey: A Theory of Afro-American Literary Criticism.* New York: Oxford UP, 1980.

Montgomery, Benilde. "Recapturing John Marrant." *A Mixed Race: Ethnicity in Early America.* Ed. Frank Shuffleton. New York: Oxford UP, 1993. 105–15.

Saillant, John. "Explaining Syncretism in African-American Views of Death: An Eighteenth Century Example." *Culture and Tradition* 17 (1995): 25–41.

Wesley, John. *Thoughts on Slavery.* London: 1774.

Zafar, Rafia. "Capturing the Captivity: African Americans among the Puritans." *MELUS* 17:2 (1991–92): 19–35.

A NARRATIVE OF THE LORD'S WONDERFUL DEALINGS WITH JOHN MARRANT

Thy people shall be willing in the day of thy power, Ps. 110.3.

Declare his wonders among all the people, Ps. 96.3.

Preface

Reader,

The following Narrative is as plain and artless, as it is surprising and extraordinary. Plausible reasonings may amuse and delight, but facts, and facts like these, strike, are felt, and go home to the heart. Were the power, grace and providence of God ever more eminently displayed, than in the conversion, success, and deliverances of John Marrant? *He and his companion enter the meeting at* Charles-Town *together; but the one is taken, and the other is left. He is struck to the ground, shaken over the mouth of hell, snatched as a brand from the burning; he is pardoned and justified; he is washed in the atoning blood, and made happy in his God. You soon have another view of him, drinking into [sic] his master's cup; he is tried and perplext, opposed and despised; the neighbours hoot at him as he goes along; his mother, sisters, and brother, hate and persecute him; he is friendless and forsaken of all. These uneasy circumstances call forth the corruptions of his nature, and create a momentary debate, whether the pursuit of ease and pleasure was not to be preferred to the practice of religion, which he now found so sharp and severe? The stripling is supported and strengthened. He is persuaded to forsake his family and kindred altogether. He crosses the fence, which marked the boundary between the wilderness and the cultivated country; and prefers the habitations of brutal residence, to the less hospitable dwellings of enmity to God and godliness. He wanders, but Christ is his guide and protector. Who can view him among the* Indian *tribes without wonder? He arrives among the* Cherokees, *where gross ignorance wore its rudest forms, and savage despotism exercised its most terrifying empire. Here the child just turned fourteen, without sling or stone, engages, and with the arrow of prayer pointed with faith, wounded* Goliah, *and conquers the King.*

The untutor'd monarch feels the truth, and worships the God of the Christians; the seeds of the Gospel are disseminated among the Indians *by a youthful hand, and Jesus is received and obeyed.*

The subsequent incidents related in this Narrative are great and affecting; but I must not anticipate the reader's pleasure and profit.

The novelty or magnitude of the facts contained in the following pages, may dispose some readers to question the truth of them. My answer to such is, 1. I believe it is clear to great numbers, and to some competent judges, that God is with the subject of them; but if he knowingly permitted an untruth to go abroad in the name of God, whilst it is confessed the Lord is with him, would it not follow, that the Almighty gave his sanction to a falsehood? 2. I have observed him to pay a conscientious regard to his word. 3. He appeared to me to feel most sensibly, when he related those parts of his Narrative, which describe his happiest moments with God, or the most remarkable interpositions of Divine Providence for him; and I have no reason to believe it was counterfeited.

I have always preserved Mr. Marrant's *ideas, tho' I could not his language; no more alterations, however, have been made, than were thought necessary.*

I now commit the whole to God—That he may make it generally useful is the prayer of thy ready servant, for Christ's sake,

> W. Aldridge[1]
> *London,*
> *July 19th, 1785*

---

[1] William Aldridge was a Methodist minister who was also associated for a time with the countess of Huntingdon. It was common for slave narratives, Native American autobiographies, and even captivity narratives such as Mary Jemison's, to be presented by an editor who transcribed the text and attested to its authenticity as in this preface. Usually it was because the narrator was illiterate, although this was not the case with Marrant.

A Narrative

I, John Marrant, born June 15th, 1755, in New-York, in North-America, wish these gracious dealings of the Lord with me to be published, in hopes they may be useful to others, to encourage the fearful, to confirm the wavering, and to refresh the hearts of true believers. My father died when I was little more than four years of age, and before I was five my mother removed from New-York to St. Augustine, about seven hundred miles from that city. Here I was sent to school, and taught to read and spell; after we had resided here about eighteen months, it was found necessary to remove to Georgia, where we remained; and I was kept to school until I had attained my eleventh year. The Lord spoke to me in my early days, by these removes, if I could have understood him, and said, "Here we have no continuing city." We left Georgia, and went to Charles-Town, where it was intended I should be put apprentice to some trade. Some time after I had been in Charles-Town, as I was walking one day, I passed by a school, and heard music and dancing, which took my fancy very much, and I felt a strong inclination to learn the music. I went home, and informed my sister, that I had rather learn to play upon music than go to a trade. She told me she could do nothing in it, until she had acquainted my mother with my desire. Accordingly she wrote a letter concerning it to my mother, which, when she read, the contents were disapproved of by her, and she came to Charles-Town to prevent it. She persuaded me much against it, but her persuasions were fruitless. Disobedience either to God or man, being one of the fruits of sin, grew out from me in early buds. Finding I was set upon it, and resolved to learn nothing else, she agreed to it, and went with me to speak to the man, and to settle upon the best terms with him she could. He insisted upon twenty pounds currency, which was paid, and I was engaged to stay with him eighteen months, and my mother to find me every thing during that term. The first day I went to him he put the violin into my hand, which pleased me much, and, applying close, I learned very fast, not only to play, but to dance also; so that in six months I was able to play for the whole school. In the evenings after the scholars were dismissed, I used to resort to the bottom of our garden, where it was customary for some musicians to assemble to blow the French-horn. Here my improvement was so rapid, that in a twelve-month's time I became master both of the violin and of the French-horn, and was much respected by the Gentlemen and Ladies whose children attended the school, as also by my master. This opened to me a large door of vanity and vice, for I was invited to all the balls and assemblies that were held in the town, and met with the general applause of the inhabitants. I was a stranger to want, being supplied with as much money as I had any occasion for; which my sister observing, said, "You have now no need of a trade." I was now in my thirteenth year, devoted to pleasure, and drinking in iniquity like water; a slave to every vice suited to my nature and to my years. The time I had engaged to serve my master being expired, he persuaded me to stay with him, and offered me anything, or any money, not to leave him. His intreaties proving ineffectual, I quitted his service, and visited my mother in the country; with her I staid two months, living without God or hope in the world, fishing and hunting on the sabbath-day. Unstable as water, I returned to town, and wished to go to some trade. My sister's husband being informed of my inclination, provided me with a master, who was a carpenter in that town, on condition that I should serve him one year and a half on trial, and afterwards be bound, if he approved of me.[1] Accordingly I went, but every evening I was sent for to play on music, somewhere or another; and I often continued out very late, sometimes all night, so as to render me incapable of attending my master's business the next day, yet in this manner I served him a year and four months, and was much approved of by him. He wrote a letter to my mother to come and have me bound, and whilst my mother was weighing the matter in her own mind, the gracious purposes of God, respecting a perishing sinner, were now to be disclosed. One evening I was sent for in a very particular manner to go and play for some Gentlemen, which I agreed to do, and was on my way to fulfill my promise; and passing by a large meeting house I saw many lights in it, and crowds of people going in. I enquired what it meant, and was answered by my companion, that a crazy man was hallooing there; this raised my curiosity to go in, that I might hear what he was hallooing about. He persuaded me not to go in, but in vain. He then said, "If you will do one thing I will go in with you." I asked him what that was? He replied, "Blow the French horn among them." I liked the proposal well enough, but expressed my fears of being beaten for disturbing them; but upon his promising to stand by and defend me, I agreed. So we went, and with much difficulty got within the doors. I was pushing the people to make room, to get the horn off my shoulder to blow it, just as Mr. Whitefield was naming his text, and looking round, and, as I thought, directly upon me, and pointing with his finger, he uttered these words, "PREPARE TO MEET THY GOD, O ISRAEL." The Lord accompanied the word with such power, that I was struck to the ground, and lay both speechless and sense-

---

[1] Young apprentices were "bound" for a number of years to a master from whom they might learn a trade.

less near half an hour. When I was come a little too, I found two men attending me, and a woman throwing water in my face, and holding a
smelling-bottle to my nose; and when something more recovered, every
word I heard from the minister was like a parcel of swords thrust into me,
and what added to my distress, I thought I saw the devil on every side of
me. I was constrained in the bitterness of my spirit to halloo out in the
midst of the congregation, which disturbing them, they took me away; but
finding I could neither walk or stand, they carried me as far as the vestry,
and there I remained till the service was over. When the people were dismissed Mr. Whitefield came into the vestry, and being told of my condition he came immediately, and the first word he said to me was, "JESUS
CHRIST HAS GOT THEE AT LAST." He asked where I lived, intending
to come and see me the next day; but recollecting he was to leave the town
the next morning, he said he could not come himself, but would send another minister; he desired them to get me home, and then taking his leave
of me, I saw him no more. When I reached my sister's house, being carried
by two men, she was very uneasy to see me in so distressed a condition.
She got me to bed, and sent for a doctor, who came immediately, and after looking at me, he went home, and sent me a bottle of mixture, and desired her to give me a spoonful every two hours; but I could not take anything the doctor sent, nor indeed keep in bed; this distressed my sister very
much, and she cried out, "The lad will surely die." She sent for two other
doctors, but no medicine they prescribed could I take. No, no; it may be
asked, a wounded spirit who can cure? as well as who can bear? In this
distress of soul I continued for three days without any food, only a little
water now and then. On the fourth day, the minister Mr. Whitefield had
desired to visit me came to see me, and being directed upstairs, when he
entered the room, I thought he made my distress much worse. He wanted
to take hold of my hand, but I durst not give it to him. He insisted upon
taking hold of it, and I then got away from him on the other side of the
bed; but being very weak I fell down, and before I could recover he came
to me and took me by the hand, and lifted me up, and after a few words
desired to go to prayer. So he fell upon his knees, and pulled me down also;
after he had spent some time in prayer he rose up, and asked me how I did
now; I answered much worse; he then said, "Come, we will have the old
thing over again," and so we kneeled down a second time, and after he had
prayed earnestly we got up, and he said again, "How do you do now?" I
replied worse and worse, and asked him if he intended to kill me? "No,
no," said he, "you are worth a thousand dead men, let us try the old thing
over again," and so falling upon our knees, he continued in prayer a considerable time, and near the close of his prayer, the Lord was pleased to set
my soul at perfect liberty, and being filled with joy I began to praise the

Lord immediately; my sorrows were turned into peace, and joy, and love. The minister said, "How is it now?" I answered, all is well, all happy. He then took his leave of me; but called every day for several days afterwards, and the last time he said, "Hold fast that thou hast already obtained, 'till Jesus Christ come." I now read the Scriptures very much. My master sent often to know how I did, and at last came himself, and finding me well, asked me if I would not come to work again? I answered no. He asked me the reason, but receiving no answer he went away. I continued with my sister about three weeks, during which time she often asked me to play upon the violin for her, which I refused; then she said I was crazy and mad, and so reported it among the neighbours, which opened the mouths of all around against me. I then resolved to go to my mother, which was eighty-four miles from Charles-Town. I was two days on my journey home, and enjoyed much communion with God on the road, and had occasion to mark the gracious interpositions of his kind Providence as I passed along. The third day I arrived at my mother's house, and was well received. At supper they sat down to eat without asking the Lord's blessing, which caused me to burst out into tears. My mother asked me what was the matter? I answered, I wept because they sat down to supper without asking the Lord's blessing. She bid me, with much surprise, to ask a blessing. I remained with her fourteen days without interruption; the Lord pitied me, being a young soldier.[2] Soon, however, Satan began to stir up my two sisters and brother, who were then at home with my mother; they called me every name but that which was good. The more they persecuted me, the stronger I grew in grace. At length my mother turned against me also, and the neighbours joined her, and there was not a friend to assist me, or that I could speak to; this made me earnest with God. In these circumstances, being the youngest but one of our family, and young in Christian experience, I was tempted so far as to threaten my life; but reading my Bible one day, and finding that if I did destroy myself I could not come where God was, I betook myself to the fields, and some days staid out from morning to night to avoid the persecutors. I staid one time two days without any food, but seemed to have clearer views into the spiritual things of God.

Not long after this I was sharply tried, and reasoned the matter within myself, whether I should turn to my old courses of sin and vice, or serve and cleave to the Lord; after prayer to God, I was fully persuaded in my mind, that if I turned to my old ways I should perish eternally. Upon this I went home, and finding them all as hardened, or worse than before, and every body saying I was crazy; but a little sister I had, about nine years of

---

[2] That is, a soldier for Christ.

age, used to cry when she saw them persecute me, and continuing so about five weeks and three days, I thought it was better for me to die than to live among such people. I rose one morning very early, to get a little quietness and retirement, I went into the woods, and staid till eight o'clock in the morning; upon my return I found them all at breakfast; I passed by them, and went up-stairs without any interruption; I went upon my knees to the Lord, and returned him thanks; then I took up a small pocket Bible and one of Dr. Watts's hymnbooks,[3] and passing by them went out without one word spoken by any of us. After spending some time in the fields, I was persuaded to go from home altogether. Accordingly I went over the fence, about half a mile from our house, which divided the inhabited and culti-vated parts of the country from the wilderness. I continued travelling in the desert all day without the least inclination of returning back. About eve-ning I began to be surrounded with wolves; I took refuge from them on a tree, and remained there all night. About eight o'clock next morning I de-scended from the tree, and returned God thanks for the mercies of the night. I went on all this day without anything to eat or drink.

The third day, taking my Bible out of my pocket, I read and walked for some time, and then being wearied and almost spent, I sat down, and after resting awhile I rose to go forward; but had not gone above a hun-dred yards when something tripped me up, and I fell down; I prayed to the Lord upon the ground that he would command the wild beasts to devour me, that I might be with him in glory. I made this request to God the third and part of the fourth day.

The fourth day in the morning, descending from my usual lodging, a tree, and having nothing all this time to eat, and but a little water to drink, I was so feeble that I tumbled half way down the tree, not being able to support myself, and lay upon my back on the ground about an hour and a half, praying and crying; after which, getting a little strength, and trying to stand upright to walk, I found myself not able; then I went upon my hands and knees, and so crawled till I reached a tree that was tumbled down, in order to get across it, and there I prayed with my body leaning upon it above an hour, that the Lord would take me to himself. Such near-ness to God I then enjoyed, that I willingly resigned myself into his hands. After some time I thought I was strengthened, so I got across the tree with-out my feet or hands touching the ground; but struggling I fell over on the other side, and then thought the Lord will now answer my prayer, and take me home. But the time was not come. After laying there a little, I rose, and

---

[3] Isaac Watts's hymnbooks were among the most popular publications in English in the eighteenth century.

looking about, saw at some distance bunches of grass, called deer-grass; I felt a strong desire to get at it; though I rose, yet it was only on my hands and knees, being so feeble, and in this manner I reached the grass. I was about three-quarters of an hour going in this form twenty yards. When I reached it I was unable to pull it up, so I bit it off like a horse, and prayed the Lord to bless it to me, and I thought it the best meal I ever had in my life, and I think so still, it was so sweet. I returned my God hearty thanks for it, and then lay down about an hour. Feeling myself very thirsty, I prayed the Lord to provide me with some water. Finding I was something strengthened, I got up, and stood on my feet, and staggered from one tree to another, if they were near each other, otherwise the journey was too long for me. I continued moving so for some time, and at length passing between two trees, I happened to fall upon some bushes, among which were a few large hollow leaves, which had caught and contained the dews of the night, and lying low among the bushes, were not exhaled by the solar rays; this water in the leaves fell upon me as I tumbled down and was lost, I was now tempted to think the Lord had given me water from Heaven, and I had wasted it, I then prayed the Lord to forgive me. What poor unbelieving creatures we are! though we are assured the Lord will supply all our needs. I was presently directed to a puddle of water very muddy, which some wild pigs had just left; I kneeled down, and asked the Lord to bless it to me, so I drank both mud and water mixed together, and being satisfied I returned the Lord thanks, and went on my way rejoicing. This day was much chequered with wants and supplies, with dangers and deliverances. I continued travelling on for nine days, feeding upon grass, and not knowing whither I was going; but the Lord Jesus Christ was very present, and that comforted me through the whole.

The next morning, having quitted my customary lodging, and returned thanks to the Lord for my preservation through the night, reading and travelling on, I passed between two bears, about twenty yards distance from each other. Both sat and looked at me, but I felt very little fear; and after I had passed them, they both went the same way from me without growling, or the least apparent uneasiness. I went and returned God thanks for my escape, who had tamed the wild beasts of the forest, and made them friendly to me: I rose from my knees and walked on, singing hymns of praise to God, about five o'clock in the afternoon, and about fifty-five miles from home, right through the wilderness. As I was going on, and musing upon the goodness of the Lord, an Indian hunter, who stood at some distance, saw me; he hid himself behind a tree; but as I passed along he bolted out, and put his hands on my breast, which surprized me a few moments. He then asked me where I was going? I answered I did not know, but where the Lord was pleased to guide me. Having heard me

praising God before I came up to him, he enquired who I was talking to?
I told him I was talking to my Lord Jesus; he seemed surprized, and asked
me where he was? for he did not see him there. I told him he could not be
seen with bodily eyes. After a little more talk, he insisted upon taking me
home; but I refused, and added, that I would die rather than return home.
He then asked me if I knew how far I was from home? I answered, I did
not know; you are fifty-five miles and a half, says he, from home. He farther asked me how I did to live? I said I was supported by the Lord. He
asked me how I slept? I answered, the Lord provided me with a bed every
night; he further enquired what preserved me from being devoured by the
wild beasts? I replied, the Lord Jesus Christ kept me from them. He stood
astonished, and said, you say the Lord Jesus Christ do this, and do that,
and do every thing for you, he must be a very fine man, where is he? I replied, he is here present. To this he made me no answer, only said, I know
you, and your mother and sister; and upon a little further conversation I
found he did know them, having been used in winter to sell skins in our
Town. This alarmed me, and I wept for fear he should take me home by
force; but when he saw me so affected, he said he would not take me home
if I would go with him. I objected against that, for fear he would rob me
of my comfort and communion with God: But at last, being much pressed,
I consented to go. Our employment for ten weeks and three days was
killing deer,[4] and taking off their skins by day, which we afterwards hung
on the trees to dry till they were sent for; the means of defence and security against our nocturnal enemies always took up the evenings: We collected a number of large bushes, and placed them nearly in a circular form,
which uniting at the extremity, afforded us both a verdant covering, and a
sufficient shelter from the night dews. What moss we could gather was
strewed upon the ground, and this composed our bed. A fire was kindled
in the front of our temporary lodging-room, and fed with fresh fuel all
night, as we slept and watched by turns; and this was our defense from the
dreadful animals, whose shining eyes and tremendous roar we often saw
and heard during the night.

   By constant conversation with the hunter, I acquired a fuller knowledge of the Indian tongue: This, together with the sweet communion I enjoyed with God, I have considered as a preparation for the great trial I was
soon after to pass through.

   The hunting season being now at an end, we left the woods, and directed our course toward a large Indian town, belonging to the Cherokee

---

[4]The trade in buckskins dominated colonial commerce with Indians in the Southeast.
The colloquial term "buck" for dollar comes from this origin.

nation; and having reached it, I said to the hunter, they will not suffer me to enter in. He replied, as I was with him, nobody would interrupt me.

There was an Indian fortification all round the town, and a guard placed at each entrance. The hunter passed one of these without molestation, but I was stopped by the guard and examined. They asked me where I came from, and what was my business there? My companion of the woods attempted to speak for me, but was not permitted; he was taken away, and I saw him no more. I was now surrounded by about fifty men, and carried to one of their principal chiefs and Judge to be examined by him. When I came before him, he asked me what was my business there? I told him I came there with a hunter, whom I met with in the woods. He replied, "Did I not know that whoever came there without giving a better account of themselves than I did, was to be put to death?" I said I did not know it. Observing that I answered him so readily in his own language, he asked me where I learnt it? To this I returned no answer, but burst out into a flood of tears, and calling upon my Lord Jesus. At this he stood astonished, and expressed a concern for me, and said I was young. He asked me who my Lord Jesus was? To this I gave him no answer, but continued praying and weeping. Addressing himself to the officer who stood by him, he said he was sorry; but it was the law, and it must not be broken. I was then ordered to be taken away, and put into a place of confinement. They led me from their court into a low dark place, and thrust me into it, very dreary and dismal; they made fast the door, and set a watch. The judge sent for the executioner, and gave him his warrant for my execution in the afternoon of the next day. The executioner came, and gave me notice of it, which made me very happy, as the near prospect of death made me hope for a speedy deliverance from the body: And truly this dungeon became my chapel, for the Lord Jesus did not leave me in this great trouble, but was very present, so that I continued blessing him, and singing his praises all night without ceasing. The watch hearing the noise, informed the executioner that somebody had been in the dungeon with me all night; upon which he came in to see and to examine, with a great torch lighted in his hand, who it was I had with me; but finding nobody, he turned round, and asked me who it was? I told him it was the Lord Jesus Christ; but he made no answer, turned away, went out, and fastened the door. At the hour appointed for my execution I was taken out, and led to the destined spot, amidst a vast number of people. I praised the Lord all the way we went, and when we arrived at the place I understood the kind of death I was to suffer, yet, blessed be God, none of those things moved me.

When the executioner shewed me a basket of turpentine wood, stuck full of small pieces, like skewers; he told me I was to be stripped naked, and laid down on one side by the basket, and these sharp pegs were to be stuck into me, and then set on fire, and when they had burnt to my body, I was to be turned on the other side, and served in the same manner, and then to be taken by four men and thrown into the flame, which was to finish the execution; I burst into tears, and asked what I had done to deserve so cruel a death? To this he gave me no answer. I cried out, Lord, if it be thy will that it should be so, thy will be done: I then asked the executioner to let me go to prayer; he asked me to whom? I answered, to the Lord my God; he seemed surprized, and asked me where he was? I told him he was present; upon which he gave me leave. I desired them all to do as I did, so I fell down upon my knees, and mentioned to the Lord his delivering of the three children in the fiery furnace, and of Daniel in the lion's den,[5] and had close communion with God. I prayed in English a considerable time, and about the middle of my prayer, the Lord impressed a strong desire upon my mind to turn into their language, and pray in their tongue. I did so, and with remarkable liberty, which wonderfully affected the people. One circumstance was very singular, and strikingly displays the power and grace of God. I believe the executioner was savingly converted to God. He rose from his knees, and embracing me round the middle was unable to speak for about five minutes; the first words he expressed, when he had utterance, were, "No man shall hurt thee till thou hast been to the king."

I was taken away immediately, and as we passed along, and I was reflecting upon the deliverance which the Lord had wrought out for me, and hearing the praises which the executioner was singing to the Lord, I must own I was utterly at a loss to find words to praise him. I broke out in these words, what can't the Lord Jesus do! and what power is like unto his! I will thank thee for what is passed, and trust thee for what is to come. I will sing thy praise with my feeble tongue whilst life and breath shall last, and when I fail to sound thy praises here, I hope to sing them round thy throne above: And thus, with unspeakable joy, I sung two verses of Dr. Watts's hymns:

> My God, the spring of all my joys,
>   The life of my delights;
> The glory of my brightest days,
>   And comfort of my nights.
> 5   In darkest shades, if thou appear,
>   My dawning is begun;
> Thou art my soul's bright morning star,
>   And thou my rising sun.

---

[5] These are two stories in Daniel 3 and 6.

Passing by the judge's door, he stopped us, and asked the executioner why he brought me back? The man fell upon his knees, and begged he would permit me to be carried before the king, which being granted, I went on, guarded by two hundred men with bows and arrows. After many windings I entered the king's outward chamber, and after waiting some time he came to the door, and his first question was, how came I there? I answered, I came with a hunter whom I met with in the woods, and who persuaded me to come there. He then asked me how old I was? I told him not fifteen. He asked me how I was supported before I met with this man? I answered, by the Lord Jesus Christ, which seemed to confound him. He turned round, and asked me if he lived where I came from? I answered, yes, and here also. He looked about the room, and said he did not see him; but I told him I felt him. The executioner fell upon his knees, and intreated the king in my behalf, and told him what he had felt of the same Lord. At this instant the king's eldest daughter came into the chamber, a person about nineteen years of age, and stood at my right hand. I had a Bible in my hand, which she took out of it, and having opened it, she kissed it, and seemed much delighted with it. When she had put it into my hand again, the king asked me what it was? And I told him the name of my God was recorded there; and after several questions, he bid me read it, which I did, particularly the fifty-third chapter of Isaiah, in the most solemn manner I was able; and also the twenty-sixth chapter of Matthew's Gospel; and when I pronounced the name of Jesus, the particular effect it had upon me was observed by the king. When I had finished reading, he asked me why I read those names with so much reverence? I told him, because the Being to whom those names belonged made heaven and earth, and I and he; this he denied. I then pointed to the sun, and asked him who made the sun, and moon, and stars, and preserved them in their regular order; He said there was a man in their town that did it. I laboured as much as I could to convince him to the contrary. His daughter took the book out of my hand a second time; she opened it, and kissed it again; her father bid her give it to me, which she did; but said, with much sorrow, the book would not speak to her. The executioner then fell upon his knees again, and begged the king to let me go to prayer, which being granted, we all went upon our knees, and now the Lord displayed his glorious power. In the midst of the prayer some of them cried out, particularly the king's daughter, and the man who ordered me to be executed, and several others seemed under deep conviction of sin: This made the king very angry; he called me a witch, and commanded me to be thrust into the prison, and to be executed the next morning. This was enough to make me think, as old Jacob once did, "All these things are against me;" for I was dragged away, and thrust into the dungeon with much indignation; but God, who never forsakes his people, was with me. Though I was weak in body, yet was I strong in the spirit: The executioner went to the king, and assured him, that if he put me to death, his daughter would never be well. They used the skill of all their doctors that afternoon and night; but physical prescriptions were useless. In the morning the executioner came to me, and, without opening the prison door, called to me, and hearing me answer, said, "Fear not, thy God who delivered thee yesterday, will deliver thee to-day." This comforted me very much, especially to find he could trust the Lord. Soon after I was fetched out; I thought it was to be executed; but they led me away to the king's chamber with much bodily weakness, having been without food two days. When I came into the king's presence, he said to me, with much anger, if I did not make his daughter and that man well, I should be laid down and chopped into pieces before him. I was not afraid, but the Lord tried my faith sharply. The king's daughter and the other person were brought out into the outer chamber, and we went to prayer; but the heavens were locked up to my petitions. I besought the Lord again, but received no answer: I cried again, and he was intreated. He said, "Be it to thee as thou wilt;" the Lord appeared most lovely and glorious; the king himself was awakened, and the others set at liberty. A great change took place among the people; the king's house became God's house; the soldiers were ordered away, and the poor condemned prisoner had perfect liberty, and was treated like a prince. Now the Lord made all my enemies to become my great friends. I remained nine weeks in the king's palace, praising God day and night: I was never out but three days all the time. I had assumed the habit of the country, and was dressed much like the king, and nothing was too good for me. The king would take off his golden ornaments, his chain and bracelets, like a child, if I objected to them, and lay them aside. Here I learnt to speak their tongue in the highest stile.

I began now to feel an inclination growing upon me to go farther on, but none to return home. The king being acquainted with this, expressed his fears of my being used ill by the next Indian nation, and to prevent it, sent fifty men, and a recommendation to the king, with me. The next nation was called the Creek Indians, at sixty miles distance. Here I was received with kindness, owing to the king's influence, from whom I had parted; here I staid five weeks. I next visited the Catawar Indians, at about fifty-five miles distance from the others: Lastly, I went among the Housaw[6] Indians, eighty miles distant from the last mentioned; here I staid seven weeks. These nations were then at peace with each other, and I passed among them without danger, being recommended from one to the other.

---

[6] The "Catawar" are the Choctaw Indians and the "Housaw" are the Chickasaw.

When they recollect, that the white people drove them from the American shores, they are full of resentment. These nations have often united, and murdered all the white people in the back settlements which they could lay hold of, men, women, and children. I had not much reason to believe any of these three nations were savingly wrought upon, and therefore I returned to the Cherokee nation, which took me up eight weeks. I continued with my old friends seven weeks and two days.

I now and then found, that my affections to my family and country were not dead; they were sometimes very sensibly felt, and at last strengthened into an invincible desire of returning home. The king was much against it; but feeling the same strong bias towards my country, after we had asked Divine direction, the king consented, and accompanied me sixty miles with one hundred and forty men. I went to prayer three times before we could part, and then he sent forty men with me a hundred miles farther; I went to prayer, and then took my leave of them, and passed on my way. I had seventy miles now to go to the back settlements of the white people. I was surrounded very soon with wolves again, which made my old lodging both necessary and welcome. However it was not long, for in two days I reached the settlements, and on the third I found a house: It was about dinner-time, and as I was coming to the door the family saw me, were frightened, and ran away. I sat down to dinner alone, and eat very heartily, and, after returning God thanks, I went to see what was become of the family. I found means to lay hold of a girl that stood peeping at me from behind a barn. She fainted away, and it was upwards of an hour before she recovered; it was nine o'clock before I could get them all to venture in, they were so terrified.

My dress was purely in the Indian stile; the skins of wild beasts composed my garments; my head was set out in the savage manner, with a long pendant down my back, a sash round my middle, without breeches, and a tomohawk by my side. In about two days they became sociable. Having visited three or four other families, at the distance of sixteen or twenty miles, I got them altogether to prayer on the Sabbath days, to the number of seventeen persons. I staid with them six weeks, and they expressed much sorrow when I left them. I was now one hundred and twelve miles from home. On the road I sometimes met with a house, then I was hospitably entertained; and when I met with none, a tree lent me the use of its friendly shelter and protection from the prowling beasts of the woods during the night. The God of mercy and grace supported me thus for eight days, and on the ninth I reached my uncle's house.

The following particulars, relating to the manner in which I was made known to my family, are less interesting; and yet, perhaps, some readers would not forgive their omission: I shall, however, be as brief as I can. I asked my uncle for a lodging, which he refused. I enquired how far the town was off; three quarters of a mile, said he. Do you know Mrs. Marrant and family, and how the children do? was my next question. He said he did, they were all well, but one was lately lost; at this I turned my head and wept. He did not know me, and upon refusing again to lodge me, I departed. When I reached the town it was dark, and passing by a house where one of my old school-fellows lived, I knocked at the door; he came out, and asked me what I wanted? I desired a lodging, which was granted: I went in, but was not known. I asked him if he knew Mrs. Marrant, and how the family were? He said, he had just left them, they were all well; but a young lad, with whom he went to school, who after he had quitted school, went to Charles-Town to learn some trade; but came home crazy, rambled in the woods, and was torn in pieces by the wild beasts. How do you know, said I, that he was killed by wild beasts? I, and his brother, and uncle, and others, said he, went three days into the woods in search of him, and found his carcase torn, and brought it home and buried it. This affected me very much, and I wept; observing it, he said what is the matter? I made no answer. At supper they sat down without craving a blessing, for which I reproved them; this so affected the man, that I believe it ended in a sound conversion. Here is a wild man, says he, come out of the woods to be a witness for God, and to reprove our ingratitude and stupefaction! After supper I went to prayer, and then to bed. Rising a little before daylight, and praising the Lord, as my custom was, the family were surprised, and got up: I staid with them till nine o'clock, and then went to my mother's house in the next street. The singularity of my dress drew everybody's eyes upon me, yet none knew me. I knocked at my mother's door, my sister opened it, and was startled at my appearance. Having expressed a desire to see Mrs. Marrant, I was answered, she was not very well, and that my business with her could be done by the person at the door, who also attempted to shut me out, which I prevented. My mother being called, I went in, and sat down, a mob of people being round the door. My mother asked, "what is your business;" only to see you, said I. She said she was much obliged to me, but did not know me. I asked, how are your children? how are your two sons? She replied, her daughters were in good health, of her two sons, one was well, and with her, but the other—unable to contain, she burst into a flood of tears, and retired. I was overcome, and wept much; but nobody knew me. This was an affecting scene! Presently my brother came in: He enquired, who I was, and what I was? My sister did not know; but being uneasy at my presence, they contrived to get me out of the house, which, being over-heard by me, I resolved not to stir. My youngest sister, eleven years of age, came in from school, with a book under her arm. I was then sitting in the parlour, and as she passed by the parlour door, she peep'd in and seeing a strange person there, she recollected me; she goes into the kitchen, and tells the servants, her brother was come; but her report finding no credit, she came and peep'd again, that she might be certain it was me; and then passing into the next room, through the parlour where I was sitting, she made a running curtsy, and says to my eldest sister, who was there, it is my brother John! She called her a foolish girl, and threatened to beat her: Then she came again and peep'd at me, and being certain she was not mistaken, she went back, and insisted that it was me: Being then beat by my sister she went crying up-stairs to my mother, and told her; but neither would my mother believe her. At last they said to her, if it be your brother, go and kiss him, and ask him how he does? She ran and clasped me round the neck, and, looking me in the face, said, "Are not you my brother John?" I answered yes, and wept. I was then made known to all the family, to my friends, and acquaintances, who received me, and were glad, and rejoiced: Thus the dead was brought to life again; thus the lost was found. I shall now close the Narrative, with only remarking a few incidents in my life, until my connection with my Right Honourable Patroness, the Countess of HUNTINGDON.

I remained with my relations till the commencement of the American troubles.[7] I used to go and hear the Word of God, if any Gospel ministers came into the country, though at a considerable distance, and thereby got acquainted with a few poor people, who feared God in Wills' Town, and Borough Town, Dorchester Town, and other places thereabouts; and in those places we used to meet and associate together for Christian Conversation, and at their request I frequently went to prayer with them, and at times enjoyed much of the Lord's presence among them.

About this time I went with my brother, who was a house-carpenter, to repair a plantation belonging to Mr. Jenkins, of Cumbee, about seventy miles from Charles-Town, where after I had done work in the evening, I used to spend my time in reading God's Word, singing Watts's hymns and in Prayer, the little Negro children would often come round the door with their pretty wishful looks, and finding my heart much drawn out in Love to their souls, I one evening called several of them in, and asked them if they could say the Lord's Prayer, etc. finding they were very ignorant, I told them, if they would come every evening I would teach them, which they did, and learned very fast, some of them in about four weeks could say the Lord's Prayer, and [a] good part of the Catechism, after teaching, I used to go to prayer with them before we parted; this continued without interruption for three or four months, in which time, by the children acquainting

---

[7] The American Revolution.

their parents with it, I soon had my society increased to about thirty persons; and the Lord was pleased often to refresh us with a sense of his love and presence amongst us; one of the Negro boys made a very great proficiency in that time, and could exercise in extemporary prayer much to my satisfaction. We are well advised in Ecclesiasticus 2.1, *My Son, if thou come to serve the Lord, prepare thy heart for temptation:* Nor was it long before they were made to pledge our dear Lord in the bitter cup of suffering; for now the old Lion began to roar, their mistress became acquainted with our proceedings, and was full of rage at it, and determined to put a stop to it. She had two of the children brought before her to examine, and made them say the Lord's prayer to her, she then asked who taught them? and they told her the free Carpenter. She also enquired, how many he had instructed, and at what time he taught them; and they told her, it was in the Evening after they had done work. She then stirred up her husband against us, who before had several times come in while I was instructing the children, and did not appear displeased with it: she told him it was the ready way to have all his Negroes ruin'd, and made him promise to examine further into the matter, and break up our meeting; which he then very soon did, for a short space; for he, together with his overseer and Negro-driver, and some of his neighbours, beset the place wherein we met, while we were at prayers; and as the poor creatures came out they caught them, and tied them together with cords, till the next morning, when all they caught, men, women, and children were strip'd naked and tied, their feet to a stake, their hands to the arm of a tree, and so savagely flogg'd that the blood ran from their backs and sides to the floor, to make them promise they would leave off praying, etc. though several of them fainted away with the pain and loss of blood, and lay upon the ground as dead for a considerable time after they were untied. I did not hear that she obtained her end of any of them. She endeavoured to perswade her husband to flog me also, but he told her he did not dare to do it because I was free, and would take the law of him, and make him pay for it; which she told him, she had rather he should run the hazard of, than let me go without the benefit of a good flogging, and was afterwards very angry with him because he was afraid to gratify her. He told me afterwards that I had spoiled all his Negroes, but could not help acknowledging, that they did their tasks sooner than the others who were not instructed, and thereby had time after their tasks were done, to keep their own fields in better order than the others, who used to employ the Sabbath for that purpose, as is the common practice among the Negroes. He then said, I should make them so wise that he should not be able to keep them in subjection. I asked him whether he did not think they had Souls to be saved? He answered, yes. I asked him whether he thought they were in the way to save their Souls whilst they were ignorant of that

God who made and preserved them. He made me no answer to that. I then told him that the blood of those poor Negroes which he had spilt that morning would be required by God at his hands. He then left me. Soon after, meeting with his wife, I told her the same; but she laught at it, and was only sorry that she had not been able to get me flog'd with them. Finding I could not any longer live peaceably there, I encouraged the poor creatures to call upon God as well as they could, and returned home; where I afterwards heard that their Mistress continued to persecute them for meeting together as often as she discover'd them, and her husband for not being more severe against them; they were then obliged to meet at midnight in different corners of the woods that were about the plantation, and were sure to be flog'd if ever she caught them, they nevertheless continued their meetings though in such imminent danger, and by what I have since heard, I believe it continues to this day, by which it appears that the work was of God; therefore neither the devil nor his servants could overthrow it; and to our faithful Covenant God be all the Glory.

In about two months after I left them, it pleased God to lay his hand upon their Mistress, and she was seized with a very violent fever, which no medicine that they could procure would remove, and in a very few days after she was taken ill, she died in a very dreadful manner, in great anger with her husband, for not preventing their meetings, which she had heard they continued, notwithstanding all her endeavours to stop it. After she was dead, her husband gave them liberty to meet together as before, and used sometimes to attend with them; and I have since heard that it was made very useful to him.

About this time I was an eye-witness of the remarkable conversion of a child seven and a half years old, named Mary Scott, which I shall here mention, in hopes the Lord may make it useful and profitable to my young readers. Her parents lived in the house adjoining to my sister's. One day as I was returning from my work, and passing by the school where she was instructed, I saw the children coming out, and stop'd and looked among them for her, to take her home in my hand; but not seeing her among those that were coming out, I supposed she was gone before, and went on towards home; when passing by the church-yard, which was in my way, I saw her very busy walking from one tomb to another, and went to her, and asked her what she was doing there? She told me, that in the lesson she had set herself at school that morning, in the Twentieth of the Revelations, she read, "I saw the Dead, small and great, stand before God," etc. and she had been measuring the graves, with a tape she then held in her hand, to see if there were any so small as herself among them, and that she had found six that were shorter. I then said, and what of that? She answered, "I will die, Sir." I told her I knew she would, but hoped she would live till she was grown a woman; but she continued to express her desire to depart, and be with Christ, rather than to live till she was grown up. I then took her by the hand and brought her home with me. After this, she was observed to be always very solid and thoughtful, and that passage appeared always to be fresh upon her mind. I used frequently to be with her when in town, and at her request we often read and prayed together, and she appeared much affected. She never afterward was seen out at play with other children; but spent her leisure time in reading God's word and prayer. In about four months after this she was taken ill, and kept her room about three weeks; when first taken, she told me, she should never come down stairs alive. I frequently visited her during her illness, and made light of what she said about her dying so soon; but in the last week of her illness she said to me in a very solemn manner, "Sir, I shall die before Saturday-night." The Physicians attended her, but she took very few if any medicines, and appeared quite calm and resigned to God's will. On Friday morning, which was the day she died, I visited her, and told her that I hoped she would not die so soon as she said, but she told me that she should certainly die before six o'clock that Evening. About five o'clock I visited her again. She was then sitting in a chair, and reading in her Bible, to all appearance pretty well recovered. After setting with her about a quarter of an hour, she got up, and desired me to go down, and send her mother up with a clean shift for her, which I did; and after a little time, when I went up again, I found her lying on the bed, with her eyes fixed up to heaven; when turning herself and seeing me, she said, "Mr. Marrant, don't you see that pretty town, and those fine people, how they shine like gold? O how I long to be with my Lord and his redeemed Children in Glory!" and then turning to her parents and two sisters, (who were all present, having by her desire been called to her) she shook hands with them, and bade them farewell; desiring them not to lament for her when she was dead, for she was going to that fine place where God would wipe away all tears from her eyes, and she should sing Hallelujahs to God and the Lamb for ever and ever, and where she hoped afterwards to meet them; and then turning again to me, she said, "Farewell, and God bless you," and then fell asleep in the arms of Jesus. This afterward proved the conversion of her mother.

In those troublesome times, I was pressed on board the *Scorpion*,[8] sloop of war, as their musician, as they were told I could play on music. I continued in his majesty's service six years and eleven months; and with

[8] The Royal Navy was empowered to "press" or force the service of young men on other ships or on shore. Equiano also wrote of the practice. However, Vincent Carretta reports that British Naval records do not confirm Marrant's service on the *Scorpion* or the *Princess Amelia*.

shame confess, that a lamentable stupor crept over all my spiritual vivacity, life and vigour; I got cold and dead. What need, reader, have we to be continually mindful of our Lord's exhortation, "*What I say unto you, I say unto all, Watch.*" My gracious God, my dear Father in his dear Son, roused me every now and then by dangers and deliverances. I was at the siege of Charles-Town,[9] and passed through many dangers. When the town was taken, my old royal benefactor and convert, the king of the Cherokee Indians, riding into the town with General Clinton, saw me, and knew me: He alighted off his horse, and came to me; said he was glad to see me; that his daughter was very happy, and sometimes longed to get out of the body.

Some time after this I was cruising about in the American seas, and cannot help mentioning a singular deliverance I had from the most imminent danger, and the use the Lord made of it to me. We were overtaken by a violent storm; I was washed overboard, and thrown on again; dashed into the sea a second time, and tossed upon deck again. I now fastened a rope round my middle, as a security against being thrown into the sea again; but, alas! forget to fasten it to any part of the ship; being carried away the third time by the fury of the waves, when in the sea, I found the rope both useless and an encumbrance. I was in the sea the third time about eight minutes, and several sharks came round me; one of an enormous size, that could easily have taken me into his mouth at once, passed and rubbed against my side. I then cried more earnestly to the Lord than I had done for some time, and he who heard Jonah's prayer, did not shut out mine, for I was thrown aboard again; these were the means the Lord used to revive me, and I began now to set out afresh.

I was in the engagement with the Dutch off the Dogger Bank, on board the *Princess Amelia,* of eighty-four guns. We had a great number killed and wounded; the deck was running with blood; six men were killed, and three wounded, stationed at the same gun with me; my head and face were covered with the blood and brains of the slain: I was wounded, but did not fall, till a quarter of an hour before the engagement ended, and was happy in my soul during the whole of it. After being in the hospital three months and 16 days, I was sent to the West-Indies, on board a ship of war, and, after cruising in those seas we returned home as a convoy. Being taken ill of my old wounds I was put into the hospital at Plymouth, and had not been there long when the physician gave it as his opinion, that I should not be capable of serving the king again; I was therefore discharged, and came to London, where I lived with a respectable and pious merchant near three years, who was unwilling to part with me. During this time I saw my call

---

[9] Charleston, South Carolina, was beseiged by the British from February to May 1780.

to the ministry fuller and clearer; had a feeling concern for the salvation of my countrymen: I carried them constantly in the arms of prayer and faith to the throne of grace, and had continual sorrow in my heart for my brethren, for my kinsmen, according to the flesh. I wrote a letter to my brother, who returned me an answer, in which he prayed some ministers would come and preach to them, and desired me to show it to the minister whom I attended. I used to exercise my gifts on a Monday evening in prayer and exhortation, in Spa-fields chapel, and was approved of, and sent down to Bath; where I was ordained,[10] in Lady Huntingdon's Chapel. Her Ladyship having seen the letter from my brother in Nova Scotia, thought Providence called me there: To which place I am now bound, and expect to sail in a few days.

I have now only to intreat the earnest prayers of all my kind Christian friends, that I may be carried safe there; kept humble, made faithful, and successful; that strangers may hear of and run to Christ; that Indian tribes may stretch out their hands to God; that the black nations may be made white in the blood of the Lamb; that vast multitudes, of hard tongues, and of a strange speech, may learn the language of Canaan, and sing the song of Moses, and of the Lamb; and, anticipating the glorious prospect, may we all with fervent hearts, and willing tongues, sing Hallelujah; the kingdoms of the world are become the kingdoms of our God, and of his Christ. Amen and Amen.

Nor can I take my leave of my very dear London Friends without intreating GOD to bless them with every blessing of the upper and nether Springs: May the good will of Him that dwelt in the bush ever preserve and lead them! is the fervent prayer of their affectionate and grateful Servant in the Gospel,

> J. Marrant
> London, No. 69,
> Mile-End Road
> Aug. 18, 1785

PS. 107
Dr. WATTS

GIVE Thanks to God; He reigns above;
Kind are his Thoughts, his Name is Love;
His Mercy Ages past have known,
And Ages long to come shall own.

---

[10] Marrant was ordained as a Methodist preacher on May 15, 1785.

5   Let the Redeemed of the LORD
The Wonders of his Grace record;
Isr'el, the Nation whom he chose,
And rescu'd from their mighty Foes.

When GOD's Almighty Arm had broke
10 Their Fetters and th' Egyptian Yoke,
They trac'd the Desert, wand'ring round
A wild and solitary Ground!

There they could find no leading Road,
Nor City with a fix'd Abode;
15 Nor Food, nor Fountain to assuage
Their burning Thirst, or Hunger's Rage.

In their Distress to GOD they cry'd;
GOD was their Saviour and their Guide;
He led their March, far wand'ring round,
20 'Twas the right Path to Canaan's Ground.

Thus when our first Release we gain
From Sin's old Yoke, and Satan's Chain,
We have this desert World to pass,
A dang'rous and a tiresome Place.

25 He feeds and clothes us all the Way,
He guides our Footsteps lest we stray;
He guards us with a pow'rful Hand,
And brings us to the heav'nly Land.

O let the Saints with Joy record
30 The Truth and Goodness of the LORD!
How great his Works! how kind his Ways!
Let ev'ry Tongue pronounce his Praise.

FINIS

FROM *THE INTERESTING NARRATIVE OF THE LIFE OF OLAUDAH EQUIANO, OR GUSTAVUS VASSA, THE AFRICAN*

I

I believe it is difficult for those who publish their own memoirs to escape the imputation of vanity; nor is this the only disadvantage under which they labour: it is also their misfortune, that what is uncommon is rarely, if ever, believed, and what is obvious we are apt to turn from with disgust, and to charge the writer with impertinence. People generally think those memoirs only worthy to be read or remembered which abound in great or striking events, those, in short, which in a high degree excite either admiration or pity: all others they consign to contempt and oblivion. It is therefore, I confess, not a little hazardous in a private and obscure individual, and a stranger too, thus to solicit the indulgent attention of the public; especially when I own I offer here the history of neither a saint, a hero, nor a tyrant. I believe there are few events in my life, which have not happened to many: it is true the incidents of it are numerous; and, did I consider myself an European, I might say my sufferings were great: but when I compare my lot with that of most of my countrymen, I regard myself as a *particular favourite of Heaven,* and acknowledge the mercies of Providence in every occurrence of my life. If then the following narrative does not appear sufficiently interesting to engage general attention, let my motive be some excuse for its publication. I am not so foolishly vain as to expect from it either immortality or literary reputation. If it affords any satisfaction to my numerous friends, at whose request it has been written, or in the smallest degree promotes the interests of humanity, the ends for which it was undertaken will be fully attained, and every wish of my heart gratified. Let it therefore be remembered, that, in wishing to avoid censure, I do not aspire to praise.

That part of Africa, known by the name of Guinea, to which the trade for slaves is carried on, extends along the coast above 3,400 miles, from the Senegal to Angola, and includes a variety of kingdoms. Of these the most considerable is the kingdom of Benen, both as to extent and wealth, the richness and cultivation of the soil, the power of its king, and the number and warlike disposition of the inhabitants. It is situated nearly under the line,[1] and extends along the coast about 170 miles, but runs back into the interior part of Africa to a distance hitherto I believe unexplored by any traveller; and seems only terminated at length by the empire of Abyssinia, near 1,500 miles from its beginning. This kingdom is divided into many provinces or districts: in one of the most remote and fertile of which, called Eboe, I was born, in the year 1745, in a charming fruitful vale, named Essaka.[2] The distance of this province from the capital of Benin and the sea coast must be very considerable; for I had never heard of white men or Europeans, nor of the sea: and our subjection to the king of Benin was little more than nominal; for every transaction of the government, as far as my slender observation extended, was conducted by the chiefs or elders of the place. The manners and government of a people who have little commerce with other countries are generally very simple; and the history of what passes in one family or village may serve as a specimen of a nation. My father was one of those elders or chiefs I have spoken of, and was styled Embrenche; a term, as I remember, importing the highest distinction, and signifying in our language a mark of grandeur. This mark is conferred on the person entitled to it, by cutting the skin across at the top of the forehead, and drawing it down to the eye-brows; and while it is in this situation applying a warm hand, and rubbing it until it shrinks up into a thick weal across the lower part of the forehead. Most of the judges and senators were thus marked; my father had long born it: I had seen it conferred on one of my brothers, and I was also destined to receive it by my parents. Those Embrence, or chief men, decided disputes and punished crimes; for which purpose they always assembled together. The proceedings were generally short; and in most cases the law of retaliation prevailed. I remember a man was brought before my father, and the other judges, for kidnapping a boy; and, although he was the son of a chief or senator, he was condemned to make recompense by a man or woman slave. Adultery, however, was sometimes punished with slavery or death; a punishment which I believe is inflicted on it throughout most of the nations of Africa[3]: so sacred among them is the honour of the marriage bed, and so jealous

---

[1] The equator. Equiano's homeland is close to the equator, though north of it.
[2] This locale has not been identified, but Equiano's references to the "Eboe" or Ibo people nearby situates it in modern Nigeria.
[3] See Benezet's "Account of Guinea" throughout [Equiano's note]. Anthony Benezet was a prominent abolitionist and the author of Some Historical Account of Guinea.

are they of the fidelity of their wives. Of this I recollect an instance: a woman was convicted before the judges of adultery, and delivered over, as the custom was, to her husband to be punished. Accordingly he determined to put her to death: but it being found, just before her execution, that she had an infant at her breast; and no woman being prevailed on to perform the part of nurse, she was spared on account of the child. The men, however, do not preserve the same constancy to their wives, which they expect from them; for they indulge in a plurality, though seldom in more than two. Their mode of marriage is thus: both parties are usually betrothed when young by their parents, (though I have known the males to betroth themselves). On this occasion a feast is prepared, and the bride and bridegroom stand up in the midst of all their friends, who are assembled for the purpose, while he declares she is thenceforth to be looked upon as his wife, and that no other person is to pay any addresses to her. This is also immediately proclaimed in the vicinity, on which the bride retires from the assembly. Some time after she is brought home to her husband, and then another feast is made, to which the relations of both parties are invited: her parents then deliver her to the bridegroom, accompanied with a number of blessings, and at the same time they tie round her waist a cotton string of the thickness of a goose-quill, which none but married women are permitted to wear: she is now considered as completely his wife; and at this time the dowry is given to the new married pair, which generally consists of portions of land, slaves, and cattle, household goods, and implements of husbandry. These are offered by the friends of both parties; besides which the parents of the bridegroom present gifts to those of the bride, whose property she is looked upon before marriage; but after it she is esteemed the sole property of her husband. The ceremony being now ended the festival begins, which is celebrated with bonefires, and loud acclamations of joy, accompanied with music and dancing.

We are almost a nation of dancers, musicians, and poets. Thus every great event, such as a triumphant return from battle, or other cause of public rejoicing is celebrated in public dances, which are accompanied with songs and music suited to the occasion. The assembly is separated into four divisions, which dance either apart or in succession, and each with a character peculiar to itself. The first division contains the married men, who in their dances frequently exhibit feats of arms, and the representation of a battle. To these succeed the married women, who dance in the second division. The young men occupy the third; and the maidens the fourth. Each represents some interesting scene of real life, such as a great achievement, domestic employment, a pathetic story, or some rural sport; and as the subject is generally founded on some recent event, it is therefore ever new. This gives our dances a spirit and variety which I have scarcely seen elsewhere. We have many musical instruments, particularly drums of different kinds, a piece of music which resembles a guitar, and another much like a stickado.[4] These last are chiefly used by betrothed virgins, who play on them on all grand festivals.

As our manners are simple, our luxuries are few. The dress of both sexes is nearly the same. It generally consists of a long piece of calico, or muslin, wrapped loosely round the body, somewhat in the form of a highland plaid. This is usually dyed blue, which is our favourite colour. It is extracted from a berry, and is brighter and richer than any I have seen in Europe. Besides this, our women of distinction wear golden ornaments; which they dispose with some profusion on their arms and legs. When our women are not employed with the men in tillage, their usual occupation is spinning and weaving cotton, which they afterward dye, and make it into garments. They also manufacture earthen vessels, of which we have many kinds. Among the rest tobacco pipes, made after the same fashion, and used in the same manner, as those in Turkey.

Our manner of living is entirely plain; for as yet the natives are unacquainted with those refinements in cookery which debauch the taste: bullocks, goats, and poultry, supply the greatest part of their food. These constitute likewise the principal wealth of the country, and the chief articles of its commerce. The flesh is usually stewed in a pan; to make it savoury we sometimes use also pepper, and other spices, and we have salt made of wood ashes. Our vegetables are mostly plantains, eadas,[5] yams, beans, and Indian corn. The head of the family usually eats alone; his wives and slaves have also their separate tables. Before we taste food we always wash our hands: indeed our cleanliness on all occasions is extreme; but on this it is an indispensable ceremony. After washing, libation is made, by pouring out a small portion of the food, in a certain place, for the spirits of departed relations, which the natives suppose to preside over their conduct, and guard them from evil. They are totally unacquainted with strong or spirituous liquours; and their principal beverage is palm wine. This is gotten from a tree of that name by tapping it at the top, and fastening a large gourd to it; and sometimes one tree will yield three or four gallons in a night. When just drawn it is of a most delicious sweetness; but in a few days it acquires a tartish and more spirituous flavour: though I never saw any one intoxicated by it. The same tree also produces nuts and oil. Our principal luxury is in perfumes; one sort of these is an odoriferous wood of delicious fragrance: the other a kind of earth; a small portion of which

---

[4] A xylophone.
[5] Like yams, an edible tuber.

thrown into the fire diffuses a most powerful odour. We beat this wood into powder, and mix it with palm oil; with which both men and women perfume themselves.

In our buildings we study convenience rather than ornament. Each master of a family has a large square piece of ground, surrounded with a moat or fence, or enclosed with a wall made of red earth tempered; which, when dry, is as hard as brick. Within this are his houses to accommodate his family and slaves; which, if numerous, frequently present the appearance of a village. In the middle stands the principal building, appropriated to the sole use of the master, and consisting of two apartments; in one of which he sits in the day with his family, the other is left apart for the reception of his friends. He has besides these a distinct apartment in which he sleeps, together with his male children. On each side are the apartments of his wives, who have also their separate day and night houses. The habitations of the slaves and their families are distributed throughout the rest of the enclosure. These houses never exceed one story in height: they are always built of wood, or stakes driven into the ground, crossed with wattles, and neatly plastered within, and without. The roof is thatched with reeds. Our dayhouses are left open at the sides; but those in which we sleep are always covered, and plastered in the inside, with a composition mixed with cow-dung, to keep off the different insects, which annoy us during the night. The walls and floors also of these are generally covered with mats. Our beds consist of a platform, raised three or four feet from the ground, on which are laid skins, and different parts of a spungy tree called plaintain. Our covering is calico or muslin, the same as our dress. The usual seats are a few logs of wood; but we have benches, which are generally perfumed, to accommodate strangers: these compose the greater part of our household furniture. Houses so constructed and furnished require but little skill to erect them. Every man is a sufficient architect for the purpose. The whole neighbourhood afford their unanimous assistance in building them and in return receive, and expect no other recompense than a feast.

As we live in a country where nature is prodigal of her favours, our wants are few and easily supplied; of course we have few manufactures. They consist for the most part of calicoes, earthern ware, ornaments, and instruments of war and husbandry. But these make no part of our commerce, the principal articles of which, as I have observed, are provisions. In such a state money is of little use; however we have some small pieces of coin, if I may call them such. They are made something like an anchor; but I do not remember either their value or denomination. We have also markets, at which I have been frequently with my mother. These are sometimes visited by stout mahogany-coloured men from the south west of us:

we call them Oye-Eboe, which term signifies red men living at a distance.
They generally bring us fire-arms, gunpowder, hats, beads, and dried fish.
The last we esteemed a great rarity, as our waters were only brooks and
springs. These articles they barter with us for odoriferous woods and
earth, and our salt of wood ashes. They always carry slaves through our
land; but the strictest account is exacted of their manner of procuring them
before they are suffered to pass. Sometimes indeed we sold slaves to them,
but they were only prisoners of war, or such among us as had been convicted of kidnapping, or adultery, and some other crimes, which we esteemed heinous. This practice of kidnapping induces me to think, that,
notwithstanding all our strictness, their principal business among us was
to trepan[6] our people. I remember too they carried great sacks along with
them, which not long after I had an opportunity of fatally seeing applied
to that infamous purpose.

Our land is uncommonly rich and fruitful, and produces all kinds of
vegetables in great abundance. We have plenty of Indian corn, and vast
quantities of cotton and tobacco. Our pine apples grow without culture;
they are about the size of the largest sugar-loaf, and finely flavoured. We
have also spices of different kinds, particularly pepper; and a variety of delicious fruits which I have never seen in Europe; together with gums of various kinds, and honey in abundance. All our industry is exerted to improve
those blessings of nature. Agriculture is our chief employment; and every
one, even the children and women, are engaged in it. Thus we are all habituated to labour from our earliest years. Every one contributes something to the common stock; and as we are unacquainted with idleness, we
have no beggars. The benefits of such a mode of living are obvious. The
West India planters prefer the slaves of Benin or Eboe to those of any other
part of Guinea, for their hardiness, intelligence, integrity, and zeal. Those
benefits are felt by us in the general healthiness of the people, and in their
vigour and activity; I might have added too in their comeliness. Deformity
is indeed unknown amongst us, I mean that of shape. Numbers of the natives of Eboe now in London might be brought in support of this assertion:
for, in regard to complexion, ideas of beauty are wholly relative. I remember while in Africa to have seen three negro children, who were tawny, and
another quite white, who were universally regarded by myself, and the natives in general, as far as related to their complexions, as deformed. Our
women too were in my eyes at least uncommonly graceful, alert, and modest to a degree of bashfulness; nor do I remember to have ever heard of an

---

[6] To trap or cheat, often used with reference to kidnappers or press-gangs, as when Marrant is "pressed on board" a Navy ship.

instance of incontinence amongst them before marriage. They are also remarkably cheerful. Indeed cheerfulness and affability are two of the leading characteristics of our nation.

Our tillage is exercised in a large plain or common, some hours walk from our dwellings, and all the neighbours resort thither in a body. They use no beasts of husbandry; and their only instruments are hoes, axes, shovels, and beaks, or pointed iron to dig with. Sometimes we are visited by locusts, which come in large clouds, so as to darken the air, and destroy our harvest. This however happens rarely, but when it does, a famine is produced by it. I remember an instance or two wherein this happened. This common is often the theatre of war; and therefore when our people go out to till their land, they not only go in a body, but generally take their arms with them for fear of a surprise; and when they apprehend an invasion they guard the avenues to their dwellings, by driving sticks into the ground, which are so sharp at one end as to pierce the foot, and are generally dipt in poison. From what I can recollect of these battles, they appear to have been irruptions of one little state or district on the other, to obtain prisoners or booty. Perhaps they were incited to this by those traders who brought the European goods I mentioned amongst us. Such a mode of obtaining slaves in Africa is common; and I believe more are procured this way, and by kidnapping, than any other. When a trader wants slaves, he applies to a chief for them, and tempts him with his wares. It is not extraordinary, if on this occasion he yields to the temptation with as little firmness, and accepts the price of his fellow creatures liberty with as little reluctance as the enlightened merchant. Accordingly he falls on his neighbours, and a desperate battle ensues. If he prevails and takes prisoners, he gratifies his avarice by selling them; but, if his party be vanquished, and he falls into the hands of the enemy, he is put to death: for, as he has been known to foment their quarrels, it is thought dangerous to let him survive, and no ransom can save him, though all other prisoners may be redeemed. We have firearms, bows and arrows, broad two-edged swords and javelins: we have shields also which cover a man from head to foot. All are taught the use of these weapons; even our women are warriors, and march boldly out to fight along with the men. Our whole district is a kind of militia: on a certain signal given, such as the firing of a gun at night, they all rise in arms and rush upon their enemy. It is perhaps something remarkable, that when our people march to the field a red flag or banner is borne before them. I was once a witness to a battle in our common. We had been all at work in it one day as usual, when our people were suddenly attacked. I climbed a tree at some distance, from which I beheld the fight. There were many women as well as men on both sides; among others my mother was there, and armed with a broad sword. After fighting for a

considerable time with great fury, and after many had been killed our
people obtained the victory, and took their enemy's Chief prisoner. He was
carried off in great triumph, and, though he offered a large ransom for his
life, he was put to death. A virgin of note among our enemies had been
slain in the battle, and her arm was exposed in our market-place, where
our trophies were always exhibited. The spoils were divided according to
the merit of the warriors. Those prisoners which were not sold or redeemed we kept as slaves: but how different was their condition from that
of the slaves in the West Indies! With us they do no more work than other
members of the community, even their masters; their food, clothing and
lodging were nearly the same as theirs, (except that they were not permitted to eat with those who were free-born); and there was scarce any other
difference between them, than a superior degree of importance which the
head of a family possesses in our state, and that authority which, as such,
he exercises over every part of his household. Some of these slaves have
even slaves under them as their own property, and for their own use.

As to religion, the natives believe that there is one Creator of all things,
and that he lives in the sun, and is girted round with a belt that he may
never eat or drink; but, according to some, he smokes a pipe, which is our
own favourite luxury. They believe he governs events, especially our deaths
or captivity; but, as for the doctrine of eternity, I do not remember to have
ever heard of it: some however believe in the transmigration of souls in a
certain degree. Those spirits, which are not transmigrated, such as our dear
friends or relations, they believe always attend them, and guard them from
the bad spirits or their foes. For this reason they always before eating, as I
have observed, put some small portion of the meat, and pour some of their
drink, on the ground for them; and they often make oblations of the blood
of beasts or fowls at their graves. I was very fond of my mother, and almost constantly with her. When she went to make these oblations at her
mother's tomb, which was a kind of small solitary thatched house, I sometimes attended her. There she made her libations, and spent most of the
night in cries and lamentations. I have been often extremely terrified on
these occasions. The loneliness of the place, the darkness of the night, and
the ceremony of libation, naturally awful and gloomy, were heightened by
my mother's lamentations; and these, concuring with the cries of doleful
birds, by which these places were frequented, gave an inexpressible terror
to the scene.

We compute the year from the day on which the sun crosses the line,
and on its setting that evening there is a general shout throughout the land;
at least I can speak from my own knowledge throughout our vicinity. The
people at the same time make a great noise with rattles, not unlike the basket rattles used by children here, though much larger, and hold up their

hands to heaven for a blessing. It is then the greatest offerings are made; and those children whom our wise men foretel will be fortunate are then presented to different people. I remember many used to come to see me, and I was carried about to others for that purpose. They have many offerings, particularly at full moons; generally two at harvest before the fruits are taken out of the ground: and when any young animals are killed, sometimes they offer up part of them as a sacrifice. These offerings, when made by one of the heads of a family, serve for the whole. I remember we often had them at my father's and my uncle's, and their families have been present. Some of our offerings are eaten with bitter herbs. We had a saying among us to any one of a cross temper, "That if they were to be eaten, they should be eaten with bitter herbs."

We practised circumcision like the Jews, and made offerings and feasts on that occasion in the same manner as they did. Like them also, our children were named from some event, some circumstance, or fancied foreboding at the time of their birth. I was named *Olaudah*, which, in our language, signifies vicissitude or fortune also, one favoured, and having a loud voice and well spoken. I remember we never polluted the name of the object of our adoration; on the contrary, it was always mentioned with the greatest reverence; and we were totally unacquainted with swearing, and all those terms of abuse and reproach which find their way so readily and copiously into the languages of more civilized people. The only expressions of that kind I remember were "May you rot, or may you swell, or may a beast take you."

I have before remarked that the natives of this part of Africa are extremely cleanly. This necessary habit of decency was with us a part of religion, and therefore we had many purifications and washings; indeed almost as many, and used on the same occasions, if my recollection does not fail me, as the Jews. Those that touched the dead at any time were obliged to wash and purify themselves before they could enter a dwelling-house. Every woman too, at certain times, was forbidden to come into a dwelling-house, or touch any person, or any thing we ate. I was so fond of my mother I could not keep from her, or avoid touching her at some of those periods, in consequence of which I was obliged to be kept out with her, in a little house made for that purpose, till offering was made, and then we were purified.

Though we had no places of public worship, we had priests and magicians, or wise men. I do not remember whether they had different offices, or whether they were united in the same persons, but they were held in great reverence by the people. They calculated our time, and foretold events, as their name imported, for we called them Ah-affoe-way-cah, which signifies calculators or yearly men, our year being called Ah-affoe.

They wore their beards, and when they died they were succeeded by their
sons. Most of their implements and things of value were interred along
with them. Pipes and tobacco were also put into the grave with the corpse,
which was always perfumed and ornamented, and animals were offered in
sacrifice to them. None accompanied their funerals but those of the same
profession or tribe. These buried them after sunset, and always returned
from the grave by a different way from that which they went.

The magicians were also our doctors or physicians. They practiced
bleeding by cupping; and were very successful in healing wounds and ex-
pelling poisons. They had likewise some extraordinary method of discovering jealousy, theft, and poisoning; the success of which no doubt they derived from their unbounded influence over the credulity and superstition
of the people. I do not remember what those methods were, except that as
to poisoning: I recollect an instance or two, which I hope it will not be
deemed impertinent here to insert, as it may serve as a kind of specimen of
the rest, and is still used by the Negroes in the West Indies. A virgin had
been poisoned, but it was not known by whom: the doctors ordered the
corpse to be taken up by some persons, and carried to the grave. As soon as
the bearers had raised it on their shoulders, they seemed seized with some
sudden impulse, and ran to and fro unable to stop themselves. At last, after having passed through a number of thorns and prickly bushes unhurt,
the corpse fell from them close to a house, and defaced it in the fall; and,
the owner being taken up, he immediately confessed the poisoning.[7]

The natives are extremely cautious about poison. When they buy any
eatable the seller kisses it all round before the buyer, to shew him it is not
poisoned; and the same is done when any meat or drink is presented, particularly to a stranger. We have serpents of different kinds, some of which
are esteemed ominous when they appear in our houses, and these we never
molest. I remember two of those ominous snakes, each of which was as

---

[7] An instance of this kind happened at Montserrat in the West Indies in the year 1763. I
then belonged to the *Charming Sally*, Capt. Doran. The chief mate, Mr. Mansfield, and
some of the crew being one day on shore, were present at the burying of a poisoned negro girl. Though they had often heard of the circumstance of the running in such cases,
and had even seen it, they imagined it to be a trick of the corpse-bearers. The mate therefore desired two of the sailors to take up the coffin, and carry it to the grave. The sailors,
who were all of the same opinion, readily obeyed; but they had scarcely raised it to their
shoulders, before they began to run furiously about, quite unable to direct themselves,
till, at last, without intention, they came to the hut of him who had poisoned the girl.
The coffin then immediately fell from their shoulders against the hut, and damaged part
of the wall. The owner of the hut was taken into custody on this, and confessed the poisoning. I give this story as it was related by the mate and crew on their return to the ship.
The credit which is due to it I leave with the reader [Equiano's note].

thick as the calf of a man's leg, and in colour resembling a dolphin in the water, crept at different times into my mother's night-house, where I always lay with her, and coiled themselves into folds, and each time they crowed like a cock. I was desired by some of our wise men to touch these, that I might be interested in the good omens, which I did, for they were quite harmless, and would tamely suffer themselves to be handled; and then they were put into a large open earthen pan, and set on one side of the highway. Some of our snakes, however, were poisonous: one of them crossed the road one day when I was standing on it, and passed between my feet without offering to touch me, to the great surprise of many who saw it; and these incidents were accounted by the wise men, and therefore by my mother and the rest of the people, as remarkable omens in my favour.

Such is the imperfect sketch my memory has furnished me with of the manners and customs of a people among whom I first drew my breath. And here I cannot forbear suggesting what has long struck me very forcibly, namely, the strong analogy which even by this sketch, imperfect as it is, appears to prevail in the manners and customs of my countrymen and those of the Jews, before they reached the Land of Promise, and particularly the patriarchs while they were yet in that pastoral state which is described in Genesis—an analogy, which alone would induce me to think that the one people had sprung from the other. Indeed this is the opinion of Dr. Gill,[8] who, in his commentary on Genesis, very ably deduces the pedigree of the Africans from Afer and Afra, the descendants of Abraham by Keturah his wife and concubine (for both these titles are applied to her). It is also conformable to the sentiments of Dr. John Clarke, formerly Dean of Sarum, in his Truth of the Christian Religion: both these authors concur in ascribing to us this original. The reasonings of these gentlemen are still further confirmed by the scripture chronology; and if any further corroboration were required, this resemblance in so many respects is a strong evidence in support of the opinion. Like the Israelites in their primitive state, our government was conducted by our chiefs or judges, our wise men and elders; and the head of a family with us enjoyed a similar authority over his household with that which is ascribed to Abraham and the other patriarchs. The law of retaliation obtained almost universally with us as with them: and even their religion appeared to have shed upon us a ray of its glory, though broken and spent in its passage, or eclipsed by the

---

[8] In this paragraph and the next, Equiano referred to several English authors of his day. John Gill, John Clarke, and Arthur Belford wrote works on the Bible and religion, while Thomas Clarkson and John Mitchel wrote treatises asserting the common origin of all humans regardless of racial differences.

cloud with which time, tradition, and ignorance might have enveloped it; for we had our circumcision (a rule I believe peculiar to that people:) we had also our sacrifices and burnt-offerings, our washings and purifications, on the same occasions as they had.

As to the difference of colour between the Eboan Africans and the modern Jews, I shall not presume to account for it. It is a subject which has engaged the pens of men of both genius and learning, and is far above my strength. The most able and Reverend Mr. T. Clarkson, however, in his much admired Essay on the Slavery and Commerce of the Human Species, has ascertained the cause, in a manner that at once solves every objection on that account, and, on my mind at least, has produced the fullest conviction. I shall therefore refer to that performance for the theory, contenting myself with extracting a fact as related by Dr. Mitchel. "The Spaniards, who have inhabited America, under the torrid zone, for any time, are become as dark coloured as our native Indians of Virginia; of which I *myself have been a witness.*" There is also another instance of a Portuguese settlement at Mitomba, a river in Sierra Leona; where the inhabitants are bred from a mixture of the first Portuguese discoverers with the natives, and are now become in their complexion, and in the woolly quality of their hair, *perfect Negroes,* retaining however a smattering of the Portuguese language.

These instances, and a great many more which might be adduced, while they shew how the complexions of the same persons vary in different climates, it is hoped may tend also to remove the prejudice that some conceive against the natives of Africa on account of their colour. Surely the minds of the Spaniards did not change with their complexions! Are there not causes enough to which the apparent inferiority of an African may be ascribed, without limiting the goodness of God, and supposing he forbore to stamp understanding on certainly his own image, because "carved in ebony." Might it not naturally be ascribed to their situation? When they come among Europeans, they are ignorant of their language, religion, manners, and customs. Are any pains taken to teach them these? Are they treated as men? Does not slavery itself depress the mind, and extinguish all its fire and every noble sentiment? But, above all, what advantages do not a refined people possess over those who are rude and uncultivated. Let the polished and haughty European recollect that his ancestors were once, like the Africans, uncivilized, and even barbarous. Did Nature make *them* inferior to their sons? and should *they too* have been made slaves? Every rational mind answers, No. Let such reflections as these melt the pride of their superiority into sympathy for the wants and miseries of their sable brethren, and compel them to acknowledge, that understanding is not confined to feature or colour. If, when they look round the world, they feel exultation, let it be tempered with benevolence to others, and gratitude to God, "who hath made of one blood all nations of men for to dwell on all the face of the earth;[9] and whose wisdom is not our wisdom, neither are our ways his ways."

II

I hope the reader will not think I have trespassed on his patience in introducing myself to him with some account of the manners and customs of my country. They had been implanted in me with great care, and made an impression on my mind, which time could not erase, and which all the adversity and variety of fortune I have since experienced served only to rivet and record; for, whether the love of one's country be real or imaginary, or a lesson of reason, or an instinct of nature, I still look back with pleasure on the first scenes of my life, though that pleasure has been for the most part mingled with sorrow.

I have already acquainted the reader with the time and place of my birth. My father, besides many slaves, had a numerous family, of which seven lived to grow up, including myself and a sister, who was the only daughter. As I was the youngest of the sons, I became, of course, the greatest favourite with my mother, and was always with her; and she used to take particular pains to form my mind. I was trained up from my earliest years in the art of war; my daily exercise was shooting and throwing javelins; and my mother adorned me with emblems, after the manner of our greatest warriors. In this way I grew up till I was turned the age of eleven, when an end was put to my happiness in the following manner: Generally when the grown people in the neighbourhood were gone far in the fields to labour, the children assembled together in some of the neighbours' premises to play; and commonly some of us used to get up a tree to look out for any assailant, or kidnapper, that might come upon us; for they sometimes took those opportunities of our parents' absence to attack and carry off as many as they could seize. One day, as I was watching at the top of a tree in our yard, I saw one of those people come into the yard of our next neighbour but one, to kidnap, there being many stout young people in it. Immediately on this I gave the alarm of the rogue, and he was surrounded by the stoutest of them, who entangled him with cords, so that he could not escape till some of the grown people came and secured him. But

---

[9]From Acts 17.26. Equiano mounted this evidence against the doctrine of polygenesis, which held that Africans or other races were the result of a separate creation, or a separate species of humankind.

alas! ere long it was my fate to be thus attacked, and to be carried off, when none of the grown people were nigh. One day, when all our people were gone out to their works as usual, and only I and my dear sister were left to mind the house, two men and a woman got over our walls, and in a moment seized us both, and, without giving us time to cry out, or make resistance, they stopped our mouths, and ran off with us into the nearest wood. Here they tied our hands, and continued to carry us as far as they could, till night came on, when we reached a small house, where the robbers halted for refreshment, and spent the night. We were then unbound, but were unable to take any food; and, being quite overpowered by fatigue and grief, our only relief was some sleep, which allayed our misfortune for a short time. The next morning we left the house, and continued travelling all the day. For a long time we had kept the woods, but at last we came into a road which I believed I knew. I had now some hopes of being delivered; for we had advanced but a little way before I discovered some people at a distance, on which I began to cry out for their assistance: but my cries had no other effect than to make them tie me faster and stop my mouth, and then they put me into a large sack. They also stopped my sister's mouth, and tied her hands; and in this manner we proceeded till we were out of the sight of these people. When we went to rest the following night they offered us some victuals; but we refused it; and the only comfort we had was in being in one another's arms all that night, and bathing each other with our tears. But alas! we were soon deprived of even the small comfort of weeping together. The next day proved a day of greater sorrow than I had yet experienced; for my sister and I were then separated, while we lay clasped in each other's arms. It was in vain that we besought them not to part us; she was torn from me, and immediately carried away, while I was left in a state of distraction not to be described. I cried and grieved continually; and for several days I did not eat any thing but what they forced into my mouth. At length, after many days travelling, during which I had often changed masters, I got into the hands of a chieftain, in a very pleasant country. This man had two wives and some children, and they all used me extremely well, and did all they could to comfort me; particularly the first wife, who was something like my mother. Although I was a great many days journey from my father's house, yet these people spoke exactly the same language with us. This first master of mine, as I may call him, was a smith,[10] and my principal employment was working his bellows, which were the same kind as I had seen in my vicinity. They were in some respects

---

[10] A goldsmith, as Equiano suggested below, whose bellows pumped air to heat fires for melting the metal.

not unlike the stoves here in gentlemen's kitchens; and were covered over with leather, and in the middle of that leather a stick was fixed, and a person stood up, and worked it, in the same manner as is done to pump water out of a cask with a hand pump. I believe it was gold he worked, for it was of a lovely bright yellow colour, and was worn by the women on their wrists and ancles. I was there I suppose about a month, and they at last used to trust me some little distance from the house. This liberty I used in embracing every opportunity to inquire the way to my own home: and I also sometimes, for the same purpose, went with the maidens, in the cool of the evenings, to bring pitchers of water from the springs for the use of the house. I had also remarked where the sun rose in the morning, and set in the evening, as I had travelled along; and I had observed that my father's house was towards the rising of the sun. I therefore determined to seize the first opportunity of making my escape, and to shape my course for that quarter; for I was quite oppressed and weighed down by grief after my mother and friends; and my love of liberty, ever great, was strengthened by the mortifying circumstance of not daring to eat with the free-born children, although I was mostly their companion. While I was projecting my escape, one day an unlucky event happened, which quite disconcerted my plan, and put an end to my hopes. I used to be sometimes employed in assisting an elderly woman slave to cook and take care of the poultry; and one morning, while I was feeding some chickens, I happened to toss a small pebble at one of them, which hit it on the middle and directly killed it. The old slave, having soon after missed the chicken, inquired after it; and on my relating the accident (for I told her the truth, because my mother would never suffer me to tell a lie) she few into a violent passion, threatened that I should suffer for it; and, my master being out, she immediately went and told her mistress what I had done. This alarmed me very much, and I expected an instant flogging, which to me was uncommonly dreadful; for I had seldom been beaten at home. I therefore resolved to fly; and accordingly I ran into a thicket that was hard by, and hid myself in the bushes. Soon afterwards my mistress and the slave returned, and, not seeing me, they searched all the house, but not finding me, and I not making answer when they called to me, they thought I had run away, and the whole neighbourhood was raised in the pursuit of me. In that part of the country (as in ours) the houses and villages were skirted with woods, or shrubberies, and the bushes were so thick that a man could readily conceal himself in them, so as to elude the strictest search. The neighbours continued the whole day looking for me, and several times many of them came within a few yards of the place where I lay hid. I then gave myself up for lost entirely, and expected every moment, when I heard a rustling among the trees, to be found out, and punished by my master: but they never discovered me, though they were often so near that I even heard their conjectures as they were looking about for me; and I now learned from them, that any attempt to return home would be hopeless. Most of them supposed I had fled towards home; but the distance was so great, and the way so intricate, that they thought I could never reach it, and that I should be lost in the woods. When I heard this I was seized with a violent panic, and abandoned myself to despair. Night too began to approach, and aggravated all my fears. I had before entertained hopes of getting home, and I had determined when it should be dark to make the attempt; but I was now convinced it was fruitless, and I began to consider that, if possibly I could escape all other animals, I could not those of the human kind; and that, not knowing the way, I must perish in the woods. Thus was I like the hunted deer:

> Ev'ry leaf and ev'ry whisp'ring breath
> Convey'd a foe, and ev'ry foe a death.[11]

I heard frequent rustlings among the leaves; and being pretty sure they were snakes I expected every instant to be stung by them. This increased my anguish, and the horror of my situation became now quite insupportable. I at length quitted the thicket, very faint and hungry, for I had not eaten or drank any thing all the day; and crept to my master's kitchen, from whence I set out at first, and which was an open shed, and laid myself down in the ashes with an anxious wish for death to relieve me from all my pains. I was scarcely awake in the morning when the old woman slave, who was the first up, came to light the fire, and saw me in the fire place. She was very much surprised to see me, and could scarcely believe her own eyes. She now promised to intercede for me, and went for her master, who soon after came, and, having slightly reprimanded me, ordered me to be taken care of, and not to be ill-treated.

Soon after this my master's only daughter, and child by his first wife, sickened and died, which affected him so much that for some time he was almost frantic, and really would have killed himself, had he not been watched and prevented. However, in a small time afterwards he recovered, and I was again sold. I was now carried to the left of the sun's rising, through many different countries, and a number of large woods. The people I was sold to used to carry me very often, when I was tired, either on their shoulders or on their backs. I saw many convenient well-built sheds along the roads, at proper distances, to accommodate the merchants

---

[11] Carretta has traced these lines to "Cooper's Hill" by John Denham (1642).

and travellers, who lay in those buildings along with their wives, who often accompany them; and they always go well armed.

From the time I left my own nation I always found somebody that understood me till I came to the sea coast. The languages of different nations did not totally differ, nor were they so copious as those of the Europeans, particularly the English. They were therefore easily learned; and, while I was journeying thus through Africa, I acquired two or three different tongues. In this manner I had been travelling for a considerable time, when one evening, to my great surprise, whom should I see brought to the house where I was but my dear sister! As soon as she saw me she gave a loud shriek, and ran into my arms—I was quite overpowered: neither of us could speak; but, for a considerable time, clung to each other in mutual embraces, unable to do any thing but weep. Our meeting affected all who saw us; and indeed I must acknowledge, in honour of those sable destroyers of human rights, that I never met with any ill treatment, or saw any offered to their slaves, except tying them, when necessary, to keep them from running away. When these people knew we were brother and sister they indulged us together; and the man, to whom I supposed we belonged, lay with us, he in the middle, while she and I held one another by the hands across his breast all night; and thus for a while we forgot our misfortunes in the joy of being together: but even this small comfort was soon to have an end; for scarcely had the fatal morning appeared, when she was again torn from me for ever! I was now more miserable, if possible, than before. The small relief which her presence gave me from pain was gone, and the wretchedness of my situation was redoubled by my anxiety after her fate, and my apprehensions lest her sufferings should be greater than mine, when I could not be with her to alleviate them. Yes, thou dear partner of all my childish sports! thou sharer of my joys and sorrows! happy should I have ever esteemed myself to encounter every misery for you, and to procure your freedom by the sacrifice of my own. Though you were early forced from my arms, your image has been always rivetted in my heart, from which neither time nor fortune have been able to remove it; so that, while the thoughts of your sufferings have damped my prosperity, they have mingled with adversity and increased its bitterness. To that Heaven which protects the weak from the strong, I commit the care of your innocence and virtues, if they have not already received their full reward, and if your youth and delicacy have not long since fallen victims to the violence of the African trader, the pestilential stench of a Guinea ship, the seasoning in the European colonies, or the lash and lust of a brutal and unrelenting overseer.

I did not long remain after my sister. I was again sold, and carried through a number of places, till, after travelling a considerable time, I came

to a town called Tinmah, in the most beautiful country I had yet seen in
Africa. It was extremely rich, and there were many rivulets which flowed
through it, and supplied a large pond in the centre of the town, where the
people washed. Here I first saw and tasted cocoa-nuts, which I thought superior to any nuts I had ever tasted before; and the trees, which were
loaded, were also interspersed amongst the houses, which had commodi-
ous shades adjoining, and were in the same manner as ours, the insides being neatly plastered and whitewashed. Here I also saw and tasted for the
first time sugar-cane. Their money consisted of little white shells, the size
of the finger nail. I was sold here for one hundred and seventy-two of them
by a merchant who lived and brought me there. I had been about two or
three days at his house, when a wealthy widow, a neighbour of his, came
there one evening, and brought with her an only son, a young gentleman
about my own age and size. Here they saw me; and, having taken a fancy
to me, I was bought of the merchant, and went home with them. Her house
and premises were situated close to one of those rivulets I have mentioned,
and were the finest I ever saw in Africa: they were very extensive, and she
had a number of slaves to attend her. The next day I was washed and perfumed, and when meal-time came I was led into the presence of my mistress, and ate and drank before her with her son. This filled me with astonishment; and I could scarce help expressing my surprise that the young
gentleman should suffer me, who was bound, to eat with him who was
free;[12] and not only so, but that he would not at any time either eat or
drink till I had taken first, because I was the eldest, which was agreeable
to our custom. Indeed every thing here, and all their treatment of me, made
me forget that I was a slave. The language of these people resembled ours
so nearly, that we understood each other perfectly. They had also the very
same customs as we. There were likewise slaves daily to attend us, while
my young master and I with other boys sported with our darts and bows
and arrows, as I had been used to do at home. In this resemblance to my
former happy state I passed about two months; and I now began to think
I was to be adopted into the family, and was beginning to be reconciled to
my situation, and to forget by degrees my misfortunes, when all at once the
delusion vanished; for, without the least previous knowledge, one morning early, while my dear master and companion was still asleep, I was wak-
ened out of my reverie to fresh sorrow, and hurried away even amongst the
uncircumcised.

---

[12] Equiano expressed surprise that as a slave or servant "bound" to the young boy, his
master, he should be allowed to eat with him.

Thus, at the very moment I dreamed of the greatest happiness, I found myself most miserable; and it seemed as if fortune wished to give me this taste of joy, only to render the reverse more poignant. The change I now experienced was as painful as it was sudden and unexpected. It was a change indeed from a state of bliss to a scene which is inexpressible by me, as it discovered to me an element I had never before beheld, and till then had no idea of, and wherein such instances of hardship and cruelty continually occurred as I can never reflect on but with horror.

All the nations and people I had hitherto passed through resembled our own in their manners, customs, and language: but I came at length to a country, the inhabitants of which differed from us in all those particulars. I was very much struck with this difference, especially when I came among a people who did not circumcise, and ate without washing their hands.[13] They cooked also in iron pots, and had European cutlasses and cross bows, which were unknown to us, and fought with their fists amongst themselves. Their women were not so modest as ours, for they ate, and drank, and slept, with their men. But, above all, I was amazed to see no sacrifices or offerings among them. In some of those places the people ornamented themselves with scars, and likewise filed their teeth very sharp. They wanted sometimes to ornament me in the same manner, but I would not suffer them; hoping that I might some time be among a people who did not thus disfigure themselves, as I thought they did. At last I came to the banks of a large river, which was covered with canoes, in which the people appeared to live with their household utensils and provisions of all kinds. I was beyond measure astonished at this, as I had never before seen any water larger than a pond or a rivulet: and my surprise was mingled with no small fear when I was put into one of these canoes, and we began to paddle and move along the river. We continued going on thus till night; and when we came to land, and made fires on the banks, each family by themselves, some dragged their canoes on shore, others stayed and cooked in theirs, and laid in them all night. Those on the land had mats, of which they made tents, some in the shape of little houses: in these we slept; and after the morning meal we embarked again and proceeded as before. I was often very much astonished to see some of the women, as well as the men, jump into the water, dive to the bottom, come up again, and swim about. Thus I continued to travel, sometimes by land, sometimes by water,

---

[13] This may be a comment on the change from the Muslim area where Equiano was raised, and where, as with the Jews, circumcision would have been practiced, to this coastal region inhabited by followers of native African religions.

through different countries and various nations, till, at the end of six or
seven months after I had been kidnapped, I arrived at the sea coast. It
would be tedious and uninteresting to relate all the incidents which befell
me during this journey, and which I have not yet forgotten; of the various
hands I passed through, and the manners and customs of all the different
people among whom I lived: I shall therefore only observe, that in all the
places where I was the soil was exceedingly rich; the pomkins, eadas, plantains, yams, etc. etc. were in great abundance, and of incredible size. There
were also vast quantities of different gums, though not used for any purpose; and every where a great deal of tobacco. The cotton even grew quite
wild; and there was plenty of red-wood. I saw no mechanics [14] whatever in
all the way, except such as I have mentioned. The chief employment in all
these countries was agriculture, and both the males and females, as with
us, were brought up to it, and trained in the arts of war.

The first object which saluted my eyes when I arrived on the coast was
the sea, and a slave ship, which was then riding at anchor, and waiting for
its cargo. These filled me with astonishment, which was soon converted
into terror when I was carried on board. I was immediately handled and
tossed up to see if I were sound by some of the crew; and I was now persuaded that I had gotten into a world of bad spirits, and that they were going to kill me. Their complexions too differing so much from ours, their
long hair, and the language they spoke (which was very different from any
I had ever heard) united to confirm me in this belief. Indeed such were the
horrors of my views and fears at the moment, that, if ten thousand worlds
had been my own, I would have freely parted with them all to have exchanged my condition with that of the meanest slave in my own country.
When I looked round the ship too and saw a large furnace or copper boiling, and a multitude of black people of every description chained together,
every one of their countenances expressing dejection and sorrow, I no
longer doubted of my fate; and, quite overpowered with horror and anguish, I fell motionless on the deck and fainted. When I recovered a little I
found some black people about me, who I believed were some of those
who brought me on board, and had been receiving their pay; they talked
to me in order to cheer me, but all in vain. I asked them if we were not to
be eaten by those white men with horrible looks, red faces, and loose hair.
They told me I was not; and one of the crew brought me a small portion
of spirituous liquor in a wine glass; but, being afraid of him, I would not
take it out of his hand. One of the blacks therefore took it from him and

---

[14] Workers in skilled trades, as opposed to peasant farmers.

gave it to me, and I took a little down my palate, which, instead of reviving me, as they thought it would, threw me into the greatest consternation at the strange feeling it produced, having never tasted any such liquor before. Soon after this the blacks who brought me on board went off, and left me abandoned to despair. I now saw myself deprived of all chance of returning to my native country, or even the least glimpse of hope of gaining the shore, which I now considered as friendly; and I even wished for my former slavery in preference to my present situation, which was filled with horrors of every kind, still heightened by my ignorance of what I was to undergo. I was not long suffered to indulge my grief; I was soon put down under the decks, and there I received such a salutation in my nostrils as I had never experienced in my life: so that, with the loathsomeness of the stench, and crying together, I became so sick and low that I was not able to eat, nor had I the least desire to taste any thing. I now wished for the last friend, death, to relieve me; but soon, to my grief, two of the white men offered me eatables; and, on my refusing to eat, one of them held me fast by the hands, and laid me across I think the windlass,[15] and tied my feet, while the other flogged me severely. I had never experienced any thing of this kind before; and although, not being used to the water, I naturally feared that element the first time I saw it, yet nevertheless, could I have got over the nettings,[16] I would have jumped over the side, but I could not; and, besides, the crew used to watch us very closely who were not chained down to the decks, lest we should leap into the water: and I have seen some of these poor African prisoners most severely cut for attempting to do so, and hourly whipped for not eating. This indeed was often the case with myself. In a little time after, amongst the poor chained men, I found some of my own nation, which in a small degree gave ease to my mind. I inquired of these what was to be done with us; they gave me to understand we were to be carried to these white people's country to work for them. I then was a little revived, and thought, if it were no worse than working, my situation was not so desperate: but still I feared I should be put to death, the white people looked and acted, as I thought, in so savage a manner; for I had never seen among any people such instances of brutal cruelty; and this not only shewn towards us blacks, but also to some of the whites themselves. One white man in particular I saw, when we were permitted to be on deck, flogged so unmercifully with a large rope near the foremast, that he died in consequence of it; and they tossed him over the side as they

---

[15] A large human-powered winch that sailors used to raise an anchor or sails.
[16] The ship's deck was ringed with nets to catch those who tried to jump overboard.

would have done a brute. This made me fear these people the more; and I
expected nothing less than to be treated in the same manner. I could not
help expressing my fears and apprehensions to some of my countrymen: I
asked them if these people had no country, but lived in this hollow place
(the ship): they told me they did not, but came from a distant one. "Then,"
said I, "how comes it in all our country we never heard of them?" They
told me because they lived so very far off. I then asked where were their
women? had they any like themselves? I was told they had: "and why,"
said I, "do we not see them?" they answered, because they were left behind. I asked how the vessel could go? they told me they could not tell; but
that there were cloths put upon the masts by the help of the ropes I saw,
and then the vessel went on; and the white men had some spell or magic
they put in the water when they liked in order to stop the vessel. I was exceedingly amazed at this account, and really thought they were spirits. I
therefore wished much to be from amongst them, for I expected they
would sacrifice me: but my wishes were vain; for we were so quartered that
it was impossible for any of us to make our escape. While we stayed on the
coast I was mostly on deck; and one day, to my great astonishment, I saw
one of these vessels coming in with the sails up. As soon as the whites saw
it, they gave a great shout, at which we were amazed; and the more so as
the vessel appeared larger by approaching nearer. At last she came to an
anchor in my sight, and when the anchor was let go I and my countrymen
who saw it were lost in astonishment to observe the vessel stop; and were
now convinced it was done by magic. Soon after this the other ship got her
boats out,[17] and they came on board of us, and the people of both ships
seemed very glad to see each other. Several of the strangers also shook
hands with us black people, and made motions with their hands, signifying I suppose we were to go to their country; but we did not understand
them. At last, when the ship we were in had got in all her cargo, they made
ready with many fearful noises, and we were all put under deck, so that we
could not see how they managed the vessel. But this disappointment was
the least of my sorrow. The stench of the hold while we were on the coast
was so intolerably loathsome, that it was dangerous to remain there for
any time, and some of us had been permitted to stay on the deck for the
fresh air; but now that the whole ship's cargo were confined together, it became absolutely pestilential. The closeness of the place, and the heat of the
climate, added to the number in the ship, which was so crowded that each
had scarcely room to turn himself, almost suffocated us. This produced copious perspirations, so that the air soon became unfit for respiration, from

---

[17]Launches or lifeboats carried on larger ships.

a variety of loathsome smells, and brought on a sickness among the slaves, of which many died, thus falling victims to the improvident avarice, as I may call it, of their purchasers. This wretched situation was again aggravated by the galling of the chains, now become insupportable; and the filth of the necessary tubs, into which the children often fell, and were almost suffocated. The shrieks of the women, and the groans of the dying, rendered the whole a scene of horror almost inconceivable. Happily perhaps for myself I was soon reduced so low here that it was thought necessary to keep me almost always on deck; and from my extreme youth I was not put in fetters. In this situation I expected every hour to share the fate of my companions, some of whom were almost daily brought upon deck at the point of death, which I began to hope would soon put an end to my miseries. Often did I think many of the inhabitants of the deep much more happy than myself. I envied them the freedom they enjoyed, and as often wished I could change my condition for theirs. Every circumstance I met with served only to render my state more painful, and heighten my apprehensions, and my opinion of the cruelty of the whites. One day they had taken a number of fishes; and when they had killed and satisfied themselves with as many as they thought fit, to our astonishment who were on the deck, rather than give any of them to us to eat as we expected, they tossed the remaining fish into the sea again, although we begged and prayed for some as well as we could, but in vain; and some of my countrymen, being pressed by hunger, took an opportunity, when they thought no one saw them, of trying to get a little privately; but they were discovered, and the attempt procured them some very severe floggings. One day, when we had a smooth sea and moderate wind, two of my wearied countrymen who were chained together (I was near them at the time), preferring death to such a life of misery, somehow made through the nettings and jumped into the sea: immediately another quite dejected fellow, who, on account of his illness, was suffered to be out of irons, also followed their example; and I believe many more would very soon have done the same if they had not been prevented by the ship's crew, who were instantly alarmed. Those of us that were the most active were in a moment put down under the deck, and there was such a noise and confusion amongst the people of the ship as I never heard before, to stop her, and get the boat out to go after the slaves. However two of the wretches were drowned, but they got the other, and afterward flogged him unmercifully for thus attempting to prefer death to slavery. In this manner we continued to undergo more hardships than I can now relate, hardships which are inseparable from this accursed trade. Many a time we were near suffocation from the want of fresh air, which we were often without for whole days together. This, and the stench of the necessary tubs, carried off many. During our passage I first saw flying fishes, which surprised me very much: they used frequently to fly across the ship, and many of them fell on the deck. I also now first saw the use of the quadrant;[18] I had often with astonishment seen the mariners make observations with it, and I could not think what it meant. They at last took notice of my surprise; and one of them, willing to increase it, as well as to gratify my curiosity, made me one day look through it. The clouds appeared to me to be land, which disappeared as they passed along. This heightened my wonder; and I was now more persuaded than ever that I was in another world, and that every thing about me was magic. At last we came in sight of the island of Barbadoes, at which the whites on board gave a great shout, and made many signs of joy to us. We did not know what to think of this; but as the vessel drew nearer we plainly saw the harbour, and other ships of different kinds and sizes; and we soon anchored amongst them off Bridge Town. Many merchants and planters now came on board, though it was in the evening. They put us in separate parcels, and examined us attentively. They also made us jump, and pointed to the land, signifying we were to go there. We thought by this we should be eaten by these ugly men, as they appeared to us; and, when soon after we were all put down under the deck again, there was much dread and trembling among us, and nothing but bitter cries to be heard all the night from these apprehensions, insomuch that at last the white people got some old slaves from the land to pacify us. They told us we were not to be eaten, but to work, and were soon to go on land, where we should see many of our country people. This report eased us much; and sure enough, soon after we were landed, there came to us Africans of all languages. We were conducted immediately to the merchant's yard, where we were all pent up together like so many sheep in a fold, without regard to sex or age. As every object was new to me every thing I saw filled me with surprise. What struck me first was that the houses were built with stories, and in every other respect different from those in Africa: but I was still more astonished on seeing people on horseback. I did not know what this could mean; and indeed I thought these people were full of nothing but magical arts. While I was in this astonishment one of my fellow prisoners spoke to a countryman of his about the horses, who said they were the same kind they had in their country. I understood them, though they were from a distant part of Africa, and I thought it odd I had not seen any horses there; but afterwards, when I came to converse with different Africans, I found they had many horses amongst them, and much larger than those I then saw. We were not many

---

[18] Like a sextant, a navigational instrument used for measuring the sun's or a star's height above the horizon.

days in the merchant's custody before we were sold after their usual manner, which is this: On a signal given, (as the beat of a drum) the buyers rush at once into the yard where the slaves are confined, and make choice of that parcel they like best. The noise and clamour with which this is attended, and the eagerness visible in the countenances of the buyers, serve not a little to increase the apprehensions of the terrified Africans, who may well be supposed to consider them as the ministers of that destruction to which they think themselves devoted. In this manner, without scruple, are relations and friends separated, most of them never to see each other again. I remember in the vessel in which I was brought over, in the men's apartment, there were several brothers, who, in the sale, were sold in different lots; and it was very moving on this occasion to see and hear their cries at parting. O, ye nominal Christians! might not an African ask you, learned you this from your God, who says unto you, Do unto all men as you would men should do unto you? Is it not enough that we are torn from our country and friends to toil for your luxury and lust of gain? Must every tender feeling be likewise sacrificed to your avarice? Are the dearest friends and relations, now rendered more dear by their separation from their kindred, still to be parted from each other, and thus prevented from cheering the gloom of slavery with the small comfort of being together and mingling their sufferings and sorrows? Why are parents to lose their children, brothers their sisters, or husbands their wives? Surely this is a new refinement in cruelty, which, while it has no advantage to atone for it, thus aggravates distress, and adds fresh horrors even to the wretchedness of slavery.

III

I now totally lost the small remains of comfort I had enjoyed in conversing with my countrymen; the women too, who used to wash and take care of me, were all gone different ways, and I never saw one of them afterwards.

I stayed in this island for a few days; I believe it could not be above a fortnight; when I and some few more slaves, that were not saleable amongst the rest, from very much fretting, were shipped off in a sloop for North America. On the passage we were better treated than when we were coming from Africa, and we had plenty of rice and fat pork. We were landed up a river a good way from the sea, about Virginia county, where we saw few or none of our native Africans, and not one soul who could talk to me. I was a few weeks weeding grass, and gathering stones in a plantation; and at last all my companions were distributed different ways, and only myself was left. I was now exceedingly miserable, and thought myself worse off than any of the rest of my companions; for they could talk to each other, but I had no person to speak to that I could understand. In this state I was constantly grieving and pining, and wishing for death rather than any thing else. While I was in this plantation the gentleman, to whom I suppose the estate belonged, being unwell, I was one day sent for to his dwelling house to fan him; when I came into the room where he was I was very much affrighted at some things I saw, and the more so as I had seen a black woman slave as I came through the house, who was cooking the dinner, and the poor creature was cruelly loaded with various kinds of iron machines; she had one particularly on her head, which locked her mouth so fast that she could scarcely speak; and could not eat nor drink. I was much astonished and shocked at this contrivance, which I afterwards learned was called the iron muzzle. Soon after I had a fan put into my hand, to fan the gentleman while he slept; and so I did indeed with great fear. While he was fast asleep I indulged myself a great deal in looking about the room, which to me appeared very fine and curious. The first object that engaged my attention was a watch which hung on the chimney, and was going. I was quite surprised at the noise it made, and was afraid it would tell the gentleman any thing I might do amiss: and when I immediately after observed a picture hanging in the room, which appeared constantly to look at me, I was still more affrighted, having never seen such things as these before. At one time I thought it was something relative to magic; and not seeing it move I thought it might be some way the whites had to keep their great men when they died, and offer them libation as we used to do to our friendly spirits. In this state of anxiety I remained till my master awoke, when I was dismissed out of the room, to my no small satisfaction and relief; for I thought that these people were all made up of wonders. In this place I was called Jacob; but on board the African snow[19] I was called Michael. I had been some time in this miserable, forlorn, and much dejected state, without having any one to talk to, which made my life a burden, when the kind and unknown hand of the Creator (who in very deed leads the blind in a way they know not) now began to appear, to my comfort; for one day the captain of a merchant ship, called the *Industrious Bee,* came on some business to my master's house. This gentleman, whose name was Michael Henry Pascal, was a lieutenant in the royal navy, but now commanded this trading ship, which was somewhere in the confines of the county many miles off. While he was at my master's house it happened that he saw me, and liked me so well that he made a purchase of me. I think I have often heard him say he gave thirty or forty pounds

---

[19] A small sailing vessel with one mast.

sterling for me; but I do not now remember which. However, he meant me for a present to some of his friends in England: and I was sent accordingly from the house of my then master, one Mr. Campbell, to the place where the ship lay; I was conducted on horseback by an elderly black man, (a mode of travelling which appeared very odd to me). When I arrived I was carried on board a fine large ship, loaded with tobacco, etc. and just ready to sail for England. I now thought my condition much mended; I had sails to lie on, and plenty of good victuals to eat; and every body on board used me very kindly, quite contrary to what I had seen of any white people before; I therefore began to think that they were not all of the same disposition. A few days after I was on board we sailed for England. I was still at a loss to conjecture my destiny. By this time, however, I could smatter a little imperfect English; and I wanted to know as well as I could where we were going. Some of the people of the ship used to tell me they were going to carry me back to my own country, and this made me very happy. I was quite rejoiced at the sound of going back; and thought if I should get home what wonders I should have to tell. But I was reserved for another fate, and was soon undeceived when we came within sight of the English coast. While I was on board this ship, my captain and master named me *Gustavus Vassa.*[20] I at that time began to understand him a little, and refused to be called so, and told him as well as I could that I would be called Jacob; but he said I should not, and still called me Gustavus; and when I refused to answer to my new name, which at first I did, it gained me many a cuff; so at length I submitted, and was obliged to bear the present name, by which I had been known ever since.

The ship had a very long passage; and on that account we had very short allowance of provisions. Toward the last we had only one pound and a half of bread per week, and about the same quantity of meat, and one quart of water a-day. We spoke with only one vessel the whole time we were at sea, and but once we caught a few fishes. In our extremities the captain and people told me in jest they would kill and eat me; but I thought them in earnest, and was depressed beyond measure, expecting every moment to be my last. While I was in this situation one evening they caught, with a good deal of trouble, a large shark, and got it on board. This glad-

---

[20] The name was taken from the Swedish king who in 1521 to 1523 liberated his people from Danish rule. Slaves were frequently given the names of historical rulers, such as Caesar or Scipio, as an ironic way to call attention to their subjugated status. Although the title of his book gives both the African and the slave name, Gustavus Vassa was the one the author used in his daily life.

dened my poor heart exceedingly, as I thought it would serve the people to eat instead of their eating me; but very soon, to my astonishment, they cut off a small part of the tail, and tossed the rest over the side. This renewed my consternation; and I did not know what to think of these white people, though I very much feared they would kill and eat me. There was on board the ship a young lad who had never been at sea before, about four or five years older than myself: his name was Richard Baker. He was a native of America, had received an excellent education, and was of a most amiable temper. Soon after I went on board he shewed me a great deal of partiality and attention, and in return I grew extremely fond of him. We at length became inseparable; and, for the space of two years, he was of very great use to me, and was my constant companion and instructor. Although this dear youth had many slaves of his own, yet he and I have gone through many sufferings together on shipboard; and we have many nights laid in each other's bosoms when we were in great distress. Thus such a friendship was cemented between us as we cherished till his death, which, to my very great sorrow, happened in the year 1759, when he was up the Archipelago,[21] on board his majesty's ship the *Preston:* an event which I have never ceased to regret, as I lost at once a kind interpreter, an agreeable companion, and a faithful friend; who, at the age of fifteen, discovered a mind superior to prejudice; and who was not ashamed to notice, to associate with, and to be the friend and instructor of one who was ignorant, a stranger, of a different complexion, and a slave! My master had lodged in his mother's house in America: he respected him very much, and made him always eat with him in the cabin. He used often to tell him jocularly that he would kill me to eat. Sometimes he would say to me—the black people were not good to eat, and would ask me if we did not eat people in my country. I said, No: then he said he would kill Dick (as he always called him) first, and afterward me. Though this hearing relieved my mind a little as to myself, I was alarmed for Dick and whenever he was called I used to be very much afraid he was to be killed; and I would peep and watch to see if they were going to kill him: nor was I free from this consternation till we made the land. One night we lost a man overboard; and the cries and noise were so great and confused, in stopping the ship, that I, who did not know what was the matter, began, as usual, to be very much afraid, and to think they were going to make an offering with me, and perform some magic; which I still believed they dealt in. As the waves were very high I thought the Ruler of the seas was angry, and I expected to be offered up to

[21] The Greek islands, where Baker died, as confirmed by British Naval records.

appease him. This filled my mind with agony, and I could not any more that night close my eyes again to rest. However, when daylight appeared I was a little eased in my mind; but still every time I was called I used to think it was to be killed. Some time after this we saw some very large fish, which I afterward found were called grampusses.[22] They looked to me extremely terrible, and made their appearance just at dusk; and were so near as to blow the water on the ship's deck. I believed them to be the rulers of the sea; and, as the white people did not make any offerings at any time, I thought they were angry with them: and, at last, what confirmed my belief was, the wind just then died away, and a calm ensued, and in consequence of it the ship stopped going. I supposed that the fish had performed this, and I hid myself in the fore part of the ship, through fear of being offered up to appease them, every minute peeping and quaking: but my good friend Dick came shortly towards me, and I took an opportunity to ask him, as well as I could, what these fish were. Not being able to talk much English, I could but just make him understand my question; and not at all, when I asked him if any offerings were to be made to them: however, he told me these fish would swallow any body; which sufficiently alarmed me. Here he was called away by the captain, who was leaning over the quarter-deck railing and looking at the fish; and most of the people were busied in getting a barrel of pitch to light, for them to play with. The captain now called me to him, having learned some of my apprehensions from Dick; and having diverted himself and others for some time with my fears, which appeared ludicrous enough in my crying and trembling, he dismissed me. The barrel of pitch was now lighted and put over the side into the water: by this time it was just dark, and the fish went after it; and, to my great joy, I saw them no more.

However, all my alarms began to subside when we got sight of land; and at last the ship arrived at Falmouth, after a passage of thirteen weeks. Every heart on board seemed gladdened on our reaching the shore, and none more than mine. The captain immediately went on shore, and sent on board some fresh provisions, which we wanted very much: we made good use of them, and our famine was soon turned into feasting, almost without ending. It was about the beginning of the spring 1757 when I arrived in England, and I was near twelve years of age at that time. I was very much struck with the buildings and the pavement of the streets in Falmouth; and, indeed, any object I saw filled me with new surprise. One morning, when I got upon deck, I saw it covered all over with the snow

----

[22] Whales.

that fell over-night: as I had never seen any thing of the kind before, I thought it was salt; so I immediately ran down to the mate and desired him, as well as I could, to come and see how somebody in the night had thrown salt all over the deck. He, knowing what it was, desired me to bring some of it down to him: accordingly I took up a handful of it, which I found very cold indeed; and when I brought it to him he desired me to taste it. I did so, and I was surprised beyond measure. I then asked him what it was; he told me it was snow: but I could not in anywise understand him. He asked me if we had no such thing in my country; and I told him, No. I then asked him the use of it, and who made it; he told me a great man in the heavens, called God: but here again I was to all intents and purposes at a loss to understand him; and the more so, when a little after I saw the air filled with it, in a heavy shower, which fell down on the same day. After this I went to church; and having never been at such a place before, I was again amazed at seeing and hearing the service. I asked all I could about it; and they gave me to understand it was worshipping God, who made us and all things. I was still at a great loss, and soon got into an endless field of inquiries, as well as I was able to speak and ask about things. However, my little friend Dick used to be my best interpreter; for I could make free with him, and he always instructed me with pleasure: and from what I could understand by him of this God, and in seeing these white people did not sell one another, as we did, I was much pleased; and in this I thought they were much happier than we Africans. I was astonished at the wisdom of the white people in all things I saw; but was amazed at their not sacrificing, or making any offerings, and eating with unwashed hands, and touching the dead. I likewise could not help remarking the particular slenderness of their women, which I did not at first like; and I thought they were not so modest and shamefaced as the African women.

I had often seen my master and Dick employed in reading; and I had a great curiosity to talk to the books, as I thought they did; and so to learn how all things had a beginning: for that purpose I have often taken up a book, and have talked to it, and then put my ears to it, when alone, in hopes it would answer me; and I have been very much concerned when I found it remained silent.

My master lodged at the house of a gentleman in Falmouth, who had a fine little daughter about six or seven years of age, and she grew prodigiously fond of me; insomuch that we used to eat together, and had servants to wait on us. I was so much caressed by this family that it often reminded me of the treatment I had received from my little noble African master. After I had been here a few days, I was sent on board of the ship; but the child cried so much after me that nothing could pacify her till I was sent for again. It is ludicrous enough, that I began to fear I should be betrothed to this young lady; and when my master asked me if I would stay there with her behind him, as he was going away with the ship, which had taken in the tobacco again, I cried immediately, and said I would not leave her. At last, by stealth, one night I was sent on board the ship again; and in a little time we sailed for Guernsey,[23] where she was in part owned by a merchant, one Nicholas Doberry. As I was now amongst a people who had not their faces scarred, like some of the African nations where I had been, I was very glad I did not let them ornament me in that manner when I was with them. When we arrived at Guernsey, my master placed me to board and lodge with one of his mates, who had a wife and family there; and some months afterwards he went to England, and left me in care of this mate, together with my friend Dick: This mate had a little daughter, aged about five or six years, with whom I used to be much delighted. I had often observed that when her mother washed her face it looked very rosy; but when she washed mine it did not look so: I therefore tried oftentimes myself if I could not by washing make my face of the same colour as my little play-mate (Mary), but it was all in vain; and I now began to be mortified at the difference in our complexions. This woman behaved to me with great kindness and attention; and taught me every thing in the same manner as she did her own child, and indeed in every respect treated me as such. I remained here till the summer of the year 1757; when my master, being appointed first lieutenant of his majesty's ship the Roebuck, sent for Dick and me, and his old mate: on this we all left Guernsey, and set out for England in a sloop bound for London. As we were coming up towards the Nore,[24] where the *Roebuck* lay, a man of war's boat came alongside to press our people;[25] on which each man ran to hide himself. I was very much frightened at this, though I did not know what it meant, or what to think or do. However I went and hid myself also under a hencoop. Immediately afterwards the press-gang came on board with their swords drawn, and searched all about, pulled the people out by force, and put them into the boat. At last I was found out also: the man that found me held me up by the heels while they all made their sport of me, I roaring and crying out all the time most lustily: but at last the mate, who was my conductor, seeing this, came to my assistance, and did all he could to pacify me; but all to very little purpose, till I had seen the boat go off. Soon afterward we

---

[23] One of the Channel Islands, between England and France.

[24] The Nore was a place outside the mouth of the Thames River where naval fleets assembled. The name was also given to a famous naval mutiny case.

[25] The navy was often in need to sailors during wartime, and press-gangs would board merchant ships or go on shore, even in foreign ports, to "press" or kidnap men and force them to serve.

came to the Nore, where the *Roebuck* lay; and, to our great joy, my master came on board to us, and brought us to the ship. When I went on board this large ship, I was amazed indeed to see the quantity of men and the guns. However my surprise began to diminish as my knowledge increased; and I ceased to feel those apprehensions and alarms which had taken such strong possession of me when I first came among the Europeans, and for some time after. I began now to pass to an opposite extreme: I was so far from being afraid of any thing new which I saw, that, after I had been some time in this ship, I even began to long for a battle. My griefs too, which in young minds are not perpetual, were now wearing away; and I soon enjoyed myself pretty well, and felt tolerably easy in my present situation. There was a number of boys on board, which still made it more agreeable; for we were always together, and a great part of our time was spent in play. I remained in this ship a considerable time, during which we made several cruises, and visited a variety of places: among others we were twice in Holland, and brought over several persons of distinction from it, whose names I do not now remember. On the passage, one day, for the diversion of those gentlemen, all the boys were called on the quarter-deck, and were paired proportionably, and then made to fight; after which the gentleman gave the combatants from five to nine shillings each. This was the first time I ever fought with a white boy; and I never knew what it was to have a bloody nose before. This made me fight most desperately; I suppose considerably more than an hour: and at last, both of us being weary, we were parted. I had a great deal of this kind of sport afterward, in which the captain and the ship's company used very much to encourage me. Sometime afterward the ship went to Leith in Scotland, and from thence to the Orkneys, where I was surprised in seeing scarcely any night: and from thence we sailed with a great fleet, full of soldiers, for England. All this time we had never come to an engagement, though we were frequently cruising off the coast of France: during which we chased many vessels, and took in all seventeen prizes.[26] I had been learning many of the manoeuvres of the ship during our cruise; and I was several times made to fire the guns. One evening, off Havre de Grace, just as it was growing dark, we were standing off shore, and met with a fine large French-built frigate. We got all things immediately ready for fighting; and I now expected I should be gratified in seeing an engagement, which I had so long wished for in vain. But the very mo-

---

[26] As England and France were on opposing sides in the Seven Years' War, it was common for each side to capture merchant ships flying the enemy flag and claim the cargo as a prize. The ship encountered on the next page was flying a French flag in an effort to decoy actual French ships into approaching.

ment the word of command was given to fire we heard those on board the other ship cry 'Haul down the jib;' and in that instant she hoisted English colours. There was instantly with us an amazing cry of—Avast! or stop firing; and I think one or two guns had been let off, but happily they did no mischief. We had hailed them several times; but they not hearing, we received no answer, which was the cause of our firing. The boat was then sent on board of her, and she proved to be the Ambuscade man of war, to my no small disappointment. We returned to Portsmouth, without having been in any action, just at the trial of Admiral Byng (whom I saw several times during it): and my master having left the ship, and gone to London for promotion, Dick and I were put on board the *Savage* sloop of war, and we went in her to assist in bringing off the *St. George* man of war, that had ran ashore somewhere on the coast. After staying a few weeks on board the *Savage*, Dick and I were sent on shore at Deal, where we remained some short time, till my master sent for us to London, the place I had long desired exceedingly to see. We therefore both with great pleasure got into a waggon, and came to London, where we were received by a Mr. Guerin, a relation of my master. This gentleman had two sisters, very amiable ladies, who took much notice and great care of me. Though I had desired so much to see London, when I arrived in it I was unfortunately unable to gratify my curiosity; for I had at this time the chilblains to such a degree that I could not stand for several months, and I was obliged to be sent to St. George's Hospital. There I grew so ill, that the doctors wanted to cut my left leg off at different times, apprehending a mortification; but I always said I would rather die than suffer it; and happily (I thank God) I recovered without the operation. After being there several weeks, and just as I had recovered, the small-pox broke out on me, so that I was again confined; and I thought myself now particularly unfortunate. However I soon recovered again; and by this time my master having been promoted to be first lieutenant of the Preston man of war of fifty guns, then new at Deptford, Dick and I were sent on board her, and soon after we went to Holland to bring over the late Duke of ——— to England. While I was in this ship an incident happened, which, though trifling, I beg leave to relate, as I could not help taking particular notice of it, and considering it then as a judgment of God. One morning a young man was looking up to the fore-top,[27] and in a wicked tone, common on shipboard, d—d his eyes about something. Just at the moment some small particles of dirt fell into his left eye, and by the evening it was very much inflamed. The next day it grew worse; and within six or seven days he lost it. . . .

---

[27] The top of the forward mast.

A Prisoner of War
Adopted by the Iroquois

JAMES SMITH

Francis Parkman, the esteemed nineteenth-century historian of the French and English colonies in America, called James Smith's narrative "perhaps the best of all the numerous narratives of captives among the Indians" (989). Although Smith's book was first published in 1799, his captivity took place in the 1750s during the Seven Years' War, the climactic battle between the French and English for colonial dominance in northeastern North America. The war's first major battle was at Fort Duquesne, today's Pittsburgh, a strategic site for control of the Ohio River. Fearing that the French colonists' stronger efforts at exploration and trade in the West would connect the colony of Canada to that in Louisiana and thus secure control of the entire region, England dispatched General Edward Braddock and a force of 1,400 soldiers to attack Fort Duquesne. But the challenge of transporting troops and their supplies across the mountainous terrain from Virginia so delayed and weakened the army that they were easily defeated through a campaign of ambushes by Indian allies of the French. James Smith was part of this ill-fated expedition. A young man at the time, he was employed in building a road when he was captured near the town of Bedford in July 1755. He identified the band that captured him as the Caughnewagas, a name taken from their settlement on the south bank of the St. Lawrence River near Montreal, which had grown up around a French Jesuit mission early in the eighteenth century. (The name was also written as "Kahnawake," among many other spellings.) The inhabitants were mostly Mohawks, the easternmost of the six Iroquois nations, but also included converts and refugees from other tribes, such as the Hurons, or Wiandots, whom the Iroquois had defeated a century before. At the very end of his four years' captivity Smith reached Caughnewaga. There he escaped from the Indians, only to be imprisoned by the French at the time of their defeat by General Wolfe in the war's last major battle. After the surrender, he was exchanged for French prisoners held by the English, as Hannah Swarton and many other captives had been. For most of Smith's narrative he was in today's Ohio or at forts in Detroit and elsewhere around Lake Erie with native bands buffeted by the colonial wars that destroyed traditional tribal frontiers and mixed native peoples together.

Smith's narrative carefully negotiated a balance between the loyalty that a captive was supposed to retain for white society and the assimilation of and education in the ways of the Indians that would ensure his survival. He described in detail the rituals of his adoption shortly after his capture: the running of the gauntlet, his hair being cut, his nose and ears being pierced, and undergoing a native version of baptism, all of which assured his captors that "every drop of white blood was washed out of your veins." Early French ethnographers of the Iroquois were astonished that adopted prisoners of war frequently fought against their former tribesmen and that their new Iroquois compatriots did not fear that adoptees would cross enemy lines and rejoin the people of their birth. Smith's narrative voice, however, was careful to assure readers that although he had learned the ways of the Indians and admired their virtues—notably hospitality and sharing of food—he retained a sense of his white identity. When new captives were brought in and Smith found himself forming the gauntlet rather than running it, he played his expected role, but struck a soft blow "with a piece of a pumpkin." Although he wrote of participating in the preparations of the warriors and of the results of their success, he did not write of actually fighting against Anglo-Americans. There is a sense that when he joined the Indians he had to learn basic skills as a child would. He wrote that he was at first considered unqualified even to hunt and was instead sent out to cultivate corn, traditionally women's work for the Iroquois. But his Indian education was a sound one. In a key scene later in the narrative, he set out to hunt alone and suggested that his captors did indeed suspect him of a plot to "run off to Pennsylvania, my native country," but that he was restrained by a sense of obligation to share the produce of his hunt with the tribe.

Richard Slotkin, in his landmark book *Regeneration through Violence,* made the captivity narrative genre a key part of his argument that early Americans sanctioned the temporary immersion of frontier individuals into "savage" society as a means of acquiring quasi-spiritual powers for the reform of their own culture. The violence of captivity or Indian warfare could regenerate the colonies. James Smith's narrative strongly supports

Slotkin's thesis, for the latter part of his narrative suggests that he learned from the Indians how to align his loyalties in the subsequent conflicts that reshaped his world, including the American Revolution, and how to lead his side to victory. When Indian hostilities continued after the end of the war with the French, Smith quickly entered battles against his former tribesmen, and in his narrative he called upon other former Indian captives to form an elite corps of rangers. Even when threatened with imprisonment, he insisted that frontier traders be prohibited from selling arms to the Indians, who had become the perceived military and racial enemy. The traders appealed to the British troops for protection; thus Smith's resentment of the English foreshadowed the lines drawn during the Revolution. In the final pages of his narrative Smith offered a brief ethnography of Indian customs, as Hans Staden and many others had, and he advocated training American soldiers in Indian methods of warfare, the better to defeat European armies.

Although past sixty and living in the Kentucky backcountry when his narrative was first published, Colonel Smith clearly believed he still had something to contribute to American military strategy. In 1812, as another war against the British began, Smith revised the advice appended to his captivity narrative and republished it in Paris, Kentucky, as *A Treatise on the Mode and Manner of Indian War*. He had also published there, in 1810, two pamphlets denouncing the Shaker sect, which his son James Jr. had joined, much to the annoyance of James Sr., a Presbyterian.

The text in this chapter is taken from an early anthology of captivity narratives published by Archibald Loudon in 1808, but it is basically unchanged from the 1799 first edition. Smith's narrative has received surprisingly little attention from scholars of the captivity genre and historians of the Seven Years' War.

Source

Smith, James. "An Account of the Remarkable Occurrences in the Life and Travels of Col. James Smith (Now a Citizen of Bourbon County, Kentucky,) During his Captivity with the Indians, in the Years 1755, '56, '57, '58, and '59." *A Selection of Some of the Most Interesting Narratives of Outrages Committed by the Indians in Their Wars with the White People*. Ed. Archibald Loudon. 1808. New York: Arno, 1971. 119–251.

Supplementary Readings

Parkman, Francis. *Montcalm and Wolfe: France and England in North America*. Vol. 2. New York: Library of America, 1983.

Slotkin, Richard. *Regeneration through Violence: The Mythology of the American Frontier, 1600–1860.* Middletown: Wesleyan UP, 1973.

Smith, James. *Scoouwa: James Smith's Indian Captivity Narrative.* Ed. William M. Darlington and John J. Barsotti. 1870. Rpt. Columbus: Ohio Historical Soc., 1978. [The annotations by Darlington and Barsotti in *Scoouwa* have been invaluable for my footnotes.]

———. *A Treatise on the Mode and Manner of Indian Warfare.* Paris, KY: Lyle, 1812.

Smith, William, and Thomas Hutchins. *Historical Account of Bouquet's Expedition against the Ohio Indians, in 1764.* 1765. Rpt. Cincinnati: Clarke, 1868.

AN ACCOUNT OF THE REMARKABLE OCCURRENCES IN THE LIFE AND TRAVELS OF COL. JAMES SMITH

(Now a Citizen of Bourbon County, Kentucky,)
DURING HIS CAPTIVITY WITH THE INDIANS,
IN THE YEARS 1755, '56, '57, '58, & '59,
In which the Customs, Manners, Traditions, Theological Sentiments, Mode of Warfare, Military Tactics, Discipline and Encampments, Treatment of prisoners, &c. are better explained, and more minutely related, than has been heretofore done, by any author on that subject. Together with a Description of the Soil, Timber and Waters, where he travelled with the Indians, during his captivity.

TO WHICH IS ADDED,
A Brief Account of some very Uncommon Occurrences, which transpired after his return from captivity; as well as of the Different Campaigns carried on against the Indians to the westward of Fort Pitt, since the year 1755, to the present date.

WRITTEN BY HIMSELF

Preface

I was strongly urged to publish the following work, immediately after my return from captivity, which was nearly forty years ago—but, as at that time the Americans were so little acquainted with Indian affairs, I apprehended a great part of it would be viewed as fable or romance.

As the Indians never attempted to prevent me either from reading or writing, I kept a Journal, which I revised shortly after my return from captivity, and which I have kept ever since: and as I have had but a moderate English education, have been advised to employ some person of liberal education to transcribe and embellish it—but believing that nature always outshines art, have thought, that occurrences truly and plainly stated, as they happened, would make the best history, be better understood, and most entertaining.

In the different Indian speeches copied into this work, I have not only imitated their own style, or mode of speaking, but have also preserved the ideas meant to be communicated in those speeches—In common conversation, I have used my own style, but preserved their ideas. The principal advantage that I expect will result to the public, from the publication of the following sheets, is the OBSERVATIONS ON THE INDIAN MODE OF WARFARE. Experience has taught the Americans the necessity of adopting their mode, and the more perfect we are in that mode, the better we shall be able to defend ourselves against them, when defence is necessary.

James Smith
Bourbon County,
June 1st, 1799

Remarkable Occurrences

In May, 1755, the province of Pennsylvania agreed to send out three hundred men, in order to cut a waggon road from Fort Loudon, to join Braddock's road, near the Turkey Foot, or three forks of Youghiogeny.[1] My brother-in-law, William Smith, Esq. of Conococheague, was appointed commissioner, to have the oversight of these road-cutters.

Though I was at the time only eighteen years of age, I had fallen violently in love with a young lady, whom I apprehended was possessed of a large share of both beauty and virtue; but being born between Venus and Mars, I concluded I must also leave my dear fair one, and go out with this company of road-cutters, to see the event of this campaign; but still expecting that sometime in the course of this summer, I should again return to the arms of my beloved.

---

[1] The route that Smith called "Braddock's Road" ran across southwestern Pennsylvania from the Potomac River to the Monongahela, and another, which Smith was working on, roughly followed the route of the Pennsylvania turnpike west from Fort Loudon, which is north of modern Hagerstown, Maryland. The forks of the Youghiogeny River (a name Smith spells variously in his narrative) is south of Uniontown, Pennsylvania.

We went on with the road, without interruption, untill near the Allegheny Mountain; when I was sent back, in order to hurry up some provision waggons that were on the way after us. I proceeded down the road as far as the crossings of Juniata,[2] where, finding the waggons were coming on as fast as possible, I returned up the road again toward the Allegheny Mountain, in company with one Arnold Vigoras. About four or five miles above Bedford, three Indians had made a blind of bushes, stuck in the ground, as though they grew naturally, where they concealed themselves, about fifteen yards from the road. When we came opposite to them, they fired upon us, at this short distance, and killed my fellow traveller, yet their bullets did not touch me; but my horse making a violent start, threw me, and the Indians immediately ran up, and took me prisoner. The one that laid hold on me was Canasataugua, the other two were Delawares. One of them could speak English, and asked me if there were any more white men coming after? I told them not any near, that I knew of. Two of these Indians stood by me, whilst the other scalped my comrade: they then set off and ran at a smart rate, through the woods, for about fifteen miles, and that night we slept on the Allegheny Mountain, without fire.

The next morning they divided the last of their provision which they had brought from Fort DuQuesne, and gave me an equal share, which was about two or three ounces of mouldy biscuit—this and a young Ground-Hog, about as large as a Rabbit, roasted, and also equally divided, was all the provision we had until we came to the Loyal-Hannan,[3] which was about fifty miles; and a great part of the way we came through exceeding rocky Laurel thickets, without any path. When we came to the west side of Laurel-Hill, they gave the scalp halloo, as usual, which is a long yell or halloo, for every scalp or prisoner they have in possession; the last of these scalp halloos were followed with quick and sudden shrill shouts of joy and triumph. On their performing this, we were answered by the firing of a number of guns on the Loyal-Hannan, one after another, quicker than one could count, by another party of Indians, who were encamped near where Ligonier now stands. As we advanced near this party, they increased with repeated shouts of joy and triumph; but I did not share with them in their excessive mirth. When we came to this camp, we found they had plenty of Turkeys and other meat there; and though I never before eat venison without bread or salt, yet as I was hungry, it relished very well. There we lay that night, and the next morning the whole of us marched on our way for

---

[2] The Juniata River.
[3] Another river, east of Fort Duquesne. At this crossing was Fort Ligonier, referred to later in the narrative.

Fort DuQuesne. The night after we joined another camp of Indians, with nearly the same ceremony, attended with great noise, and apparent joy among all, except one. The next morning we continued our march, and in the afternoon we came in full view of the fort, which stood on the point, near where Fort Pitt now stands. We then made a halt on the bank of the Allegheny, and repeated the scalp halloo, which was answered by the firing of all the firelocks in the hands of both Indians and French who were in and about the fort, in the aforesaid manner, and also the great guns, which were followed by the continued shouts and yells of the different savage tribes who were then collected there.

As I was at this time unacquainted with this mode of firing and yelling of the savages, I concluded that there were thousands of Indians there ready to receive General Braddock; but what added to my surprize, I saw numbers running toward me, stripped naked, excepting breech-clouts, and painted in the most hideous manner, of various colors, though the principal color was vermilion, or a bright red; yet there was annexed to this, black, brown, blue, etc. As they approached, they formed themselves into two long ranks, about two or three roods apart. I was told by an Indian that could speak English, that I must run betwixt these ranks, and that they would flog me all the way, as I ran, and if I ran quick, it would be so much the better, as they would quit when I got to the end of the ranks. There appeared to be a general rejoicing around me, yet, I could find nothing like joy in my breast; but I started to the race with all the resolution and vigor I was capable of exerting, and found that it was as I had been told, for I was flogged the whole way. When I had got near the end of the lines, I was struck with something that appeared to me to be a stick, or the handle of a tomahawk, which caused me to fall to the ground. On my recovering my senses, I endeavoured to renew my race; but as I arose, some one cast sand in my eyes, which blinded me so, that I could not see where to run. They continued beating me most intolerably, until I was at length insensible; but before I lost my senses, I remember my wishing them to strike the fatal blow, for I thought they intended killing me, but apprehended they were too long about it.

The first thing I remember was my being in the fort, amidst the French and Indians, and a French doctor standing by me, who had opened a vein in my left arm; after which the interpreter asked me how I did: I told him I felt much pain; the doctor then washed my wounds, and the bruised places of my body, with French brandy. As I felt faint, and the brandy smelt well, I asked for some inwardly, but the doctor told me, by the interpreter, that it did not suit my case.

When they found I could speak, a number of Indians came around me, and examined me, with threats of cruel death, if I did not tell the truth. The first question they asked me, was, how many men were there in the party that were coming from Pennsylvania, to join Braddock? I told them the truth, that there were three hundred. The next question was, were they well armed? I told them they were all well armed, (meaning the arm of flesh,) for they had only about thirty guns among the whole of them; which, if the Indians had known, they would certainly have gone and cut them all off; therefore, I could not in conscience let them know the defenceless situation of these road-cutters. I was then sent to the hospital, and carefully attended by the doctors, and recovered quicker than what I expected.

Some time after I was there, I was visited by the Delaware Indian already mentioned, who was at the taking of me, and could speak some English. Though he spoke but bad English, yet I found him to be a man of considerable understanding. I asked him if I had done any thing that had offended the Indians, which caused them to treat me so unmercifully? He said no, it was only an old custom the Indians had, and it was like how do you do; after that, he said, I would be well used. I asked him if I should be permitted to remain with the French? He said no—and told me, that, as soon as I recovered, I must not only go with the Indians, but must be made an Indian myself. I asked him what news from Braddock's army? He said, the Indians spied them every day, and he showed me by making marks on the ground with a stick, that Braddock's army was advancing in very close order, and that the Indians would surround them, take trees, and (as he expressed it,) *shoot um down all one pigeon.*

Shortly after this, on the 9th day of July, 1755, in the morning, I heard a great stir in the fort. As I could then walk with a staff in my hand, I went out of the door, which was just by the wall of the fort, and stood upon the wall and viewed the Indians in a huddle before the gate, where were barrels of powder, bullets, etc. and every one taking what suited; I saw the Indians also march off in rank, entire—likewise the French Canadians, and some regulars. After viewing the Indians and French in different positions, I computed them to be about four hundred, and wondered that they attempted to go out against Braddock with so small a party. I was then in high hopes that I would soon see them fly before the British troops, and that General Braddock would take the fort and rescue me.

I remained anxious to know the event of this day; and, in the afternoon, I again observed a great noise and commotion in the fort, and though at that time I could not understand French, yet I found that it was the voice of joy and triumph, and feared that they had received what I called bad news.

I had observed some of the old country soldiers speak Dutch: as I spoke Dutch, I went to one of them, and asked him, what was the news? He told me that a runner had just arrived, who said that Braddock would certainly be defeated; that the Indians and French had surrounded him, and were concealed behind trees and in gullies, and kept a constant fire upon the English, and that they saw the English falling in heaps, and if they did not take the river which was the only gap, and make their escape, there would not be one man left alive before sundown. Some time after this I heard a number of scalp halloos, and saw a company of Indians and French coming in. I observed they had a great many bloody scalps, grenadiers' caps, British canteens, bayonets, etc. with them. They brought the news that Braddock was defeated.[4] After that, another company came in, which appeared to be about one hundred, and chiefly Indians, and it seemed to me that almost every one of this company was carrying scalps; after this came another company with a number of waggon horses, and also a great many scalps. Those that were coming in, and those that had arrived, kept a constant firing of small arms, and also the great guns in the fort, which were accompanied with the most hideous shouts and yells from all quarters; so that it appeared to me as if the infernal regions had broken loose.

About sundown I beheld a small party coming in with about a dozen prisoners, stripped naked, with their hands tied behind their backs, and their faces and part of their bodies blacked—these prisoners they burned to death on the bank of Allegheny River opposite to the fort. I stood on the fort wall until I beheld them begin to burn one of these men; they had him tied to a stake, and kept touching him with firebrands, red-hot irons, etc. and he screaming in a most doleful manner, the Indians in the mean time yelling like infernal spirits. As this scene appeared too shocking for me to behold, I retired to my lodgings both sore and sorry.

When I came into my lodgings I saw Russel's Seven Sermons,[5] which they had brought from the field of battle, which a Frenchman made a present of to me. From the best information I could receive, there were only seven Indians and four French killed in this battle, and five hundred British lay dead in the field, besides what were killed in the river on their retreat.

The morning after the battle, I saw Braddock's artillery brought into the fort; the same day I also saw several Indians in British officers' dress, with sash, half-moon,[6] laced hats, etc. which the British then wore.

---

[4] Smith gave an accurate account of this battle, in which the British troops were surprised and dealt a crushing defeat. Braddock himself was mortally wounded and died on 13 July.

[5] This book of sermons by Robert Russel was first published in London around 1700 and many times in America thereafter.

[6] A half-moon is a semicircular gorget, a ceremonial metal plate derived from earlier armor and worn around the neck.

A few days after this the Indians demanded me, and I was obliged to go with them. I was not well able to march, but they took me in a canoe up the Allegheny river, to an Indian town, that was on the north side of the river, about forty miles above Fort DuQuesne. Here I remained about three weeks, and was then taken to an Indian town on the west branch of the Muskingum, about twenty miles above the forks, which was called Tulli-has, inhabited by Delawares, Caughnewagos and Mohicans. On our route betwixt the aforesaid towns, the country was chiefly black-oak and white-oak land, which appeared generally to be good wheat land, chiefly second and third rate, intermixed with some rich bottoms.

The day after my arrival at the aforesaid town, a number of Indians collected about me, and one of them began to pull the hair out of my head. He had some ashes on a piece of bark, in which he frequently dipped his fingers, in order to take the firmer hold, and so he went on, as if he had been plucking a turkey, until he had all the hair clean out of my head, ex-cept a small spot about three or four inches square on my crown; this they cut off with a pair of scissors, excepting three locks, which they dressed up in their own mode. Two of these they wrapped round with a narrow beaded garter made by themselves for that purpose, and the other they plaited at full length, and then stuck it full of silver brooches. After they bored my nose and ears, and fixed me off with ear-rings and nose jewels; then they ordered me to strip off my clothes and put on a breech-clout, which I did; they then painted my head, face, and body, in various colors. They put a large belt of wampum on my neck, and silver bands on my hands and right arm; and so an old chief led me out in the street, and gave the alarm hal-loo, *coo-wigh,* several times repeated quick; and on this, all that were in the town came running and stood round the old chief, who held me by the hand in the midst. As I at that time knew nothing of their mode of adop-tion, and had seen them put to death all they had taken, and as I never could find that they saved a man alive at Braddock's defeat, I made no doubt but they were about putting me to death in some cruel manner. The old chief holding me by the hand, made a long speech, very loud, and when he had done, he handed me to three young squaws, who led me by the hand down the bank, into the river, until the water was up to our middle. The squaw then made signs to me to plunge myself into the water, but I did not understand them; I thought that the result of the council was, that I should be drowned, and that these young ladies were to be the execu-tioners. They all three laid violent hold of me, and I for some time opposed them with all my might, which occasioned loud laughter by the multitude that were on the bank of the river. At length one of the squaws made out to speak a little English, (for I believe they began to be afraid of me) and said, *no hurt you;* on this I gave myself up to their ladyships, who were as good as their word; for though they plunged me under water, and washed and rubbed me severely, yet I could not say they hurt me much.

These young women then led me up to the council house, where some of the tribe were ready with new clothes for me. They gave me a new ruffled shirt, which I put on, also a pair of leggins done off with ribbons and beads, likewise a pair of mockasons, and garters dressed with beads, porcupine quills and red hair—also a tinsel laced cappo. They again painted my head and face with various colors, and tied a bunch of red feathers to one of these locks they had left on the crown of my head, which stood up five or six inches. They seated me on a bear skin, and gave me a pipe tomahawk, and polecat skin pouch, which had been skinned pocket fashion, and contained tobacco, killegenico, or dry sumach leaves, which they mix with their tobacco—also spunk, flint and steel. When I was thus seated, the Indians came in dressed and painted in their grandest manner. As they came in they took their seats, and for a considerable time there was a profound silence—every one was smoking—but not a word was spoken among them. At length one of the chiefs made a speech, which was delivered to me by an interpreter, and was as followeth: "My son, you are now flesh of our flesh, and bone of our bone. By the ceremony which was performed this day, every drop of white blood was washed out of your veins; you are taken into the Caughnewago nation, and initiated into a warlike tribe; you are adopted into a great family, and now received with great seriousness and solemnity in the room and place of a great man; after what has passed this day, you are now one of us by an old strong law and custom—My son, you have now nothing to fear, we are now under the same obligations to love, support, and defend you, that we are to defend one another; therefore, you are to consider yourself as one of our people." At this time I did not believe this fine speech, especially that of the white blood being washed out of me; but since that time I have found that there was much sincerity in said speech, for, from that day, I never knew them to make any distinction between me and themselves in any respect whatever until I left them. If they had plenty of cloathing, I had plenty; if we were scarce, we all shared one fate.

After this ceremony was over, I was introduced to my new kin, and told that I was to attend a feast that evening, which I did. And as the custom was, they gave me also a bowl and wooden spoon, which I carried with me to the place, where there was a number of large brass kettles full of boiled venison and green corn; every one advanced with his bowl and spoon, and had his share given him. After this, one of the chiefs made a short speech, and then we began to eat.

The name of one of the chiefs in this town was Tecanyaterighto, alias Pluggy,[7] and the other Asallecoa, alias Mohawk Solomon. As Pluggy and his party were to start the next day to war to the frontiers of Virginia, the next thing to be performed was the war dance, and their war songs. At their war dance they had both vocal and instrumental music. They had a short hollow gum, close in one end, with water in it, and parchment stretched over the open end thereof, which they beat with one stick, and made a sound nearly like a muffled drum—all those who were going on this expedition collected together and formed. An old Indian then began to sing, and timed the music by beating on this drum, as the ancients formerly timed their music by beating the tabor.[8] On this the warriors began to advance, or move forward in concert, like well disciplined troops would march to the fife and drum. Each warrior had a tomahawk, spear, or war-mallet in his hand, and they all moved regularly toward the east, or the way they intended to go to war. At length they all stretched their tomahawks towards the Potomack, and giving a hideous shout or yell, they whirled quick about, and danced in the same manner back. The next was the war song. In performing this, only one sung at a time, in a moving posture, with a tomahawk in his hand, while all the other warriors were engaged in calling aloud *he-uh, he-uh,* which they constantly repeated while the war song was going on. When the warrior that was singing had ended his song, he struck a war-post with his tomahawk, and with a loud voice told what warlike exploits he had done, and what he now intended to do, which were answered by the other warriors with loud shouts of applause. Some who had not before intended to go to the war, at this time were so animated by this performance, that they took up the tomahawk and sung the war song, which was answered with shouts of joy, as they were then initiated into the present marching company. The next morning this company all collected at one place, with their heads and faces painted with various colors, and packs upon their backs: they marched off all silent, except the commander, who, in the front, sung the travelling song, which began in this manner: *hoo caugh-tainte heegana.* Just as the rear passed the end of the town, they began to fire in their slow manner, from the front to the rear, which was accompanied with shouts and yells from all quarters.

    This evening I was invited to another sort of dance, which was a kind of promiscuous dance. The young men stood in one rank, and the young women in another, about one rod apart, facing each other. The one that

---

[7] Pluggy was later to become a famous Indian leader in battles with the colonists such as Dunmore's War in 1774, referred to later (see *Scoouwa* 33–34).
[8] A small drum, part of the fife and drum associated with Revolutionary troops.

raised the tune, or started the song, held a small gourd or dry shell of a squash, in his hand, which contained beads or small stones, which rattled. When he began to sing, he timed the tune with his rattle; both men and women danced and sung together, advancing towards each other, stooping until their heads would be touching together, and then ceased from dancing, with loud shouts, and retreated and formed again, and so repeated the same thing over and over, for three or four hours, without intermission. This exercise appeared to me at first, irrational and insipid; but I found that in singing their tunes, they used *ya ne no hoo wa ne,* etc. like our *fa sol la,* and though they have no such thing as jingling verse, yet they can intermix sentences with their notes, and say what they please to each other, and carry on the tune in concert. I found that this was a kind of wooing or courting dance, and as they advanced stooping with their heads together, they could say what they pleased in each other's ear, without disconcerting their rough music, and the others, or those near, not hear what they said.

Shortly after this I went out to hunt, in company with Mohawk Solomon, some of the Caughnewagos, and a Delaware Indian, that was married to a Caughnewago squaw. We travelled about south from this town, and the first night we killed nothing, but we had with us green corn, which we roasted and ate that night. The next day we encamped about twelve o'clock, and the hunters turned out to hunt, and I went down the run that we encamped on, in company with some squaws and boys to hunt plumbs, which we found in great plenty. On my return to camp I observed a large piece of fat meat: the Delaware Indian, that could talk some English, observed me looking earnestly at this meat, and asked me, *what meat you think that is?* I said I supposed it was bear meat; he laughed, and said, *ho, all one fool you, beal now elly pool,* and pointing to the other side of the camp, he said, *look at that skin, you think that beal skin?* I went and lifted the skin, which appeared like an ox hide: he then said, *what skin you think that?* I replied, that I thought it was a buffaloe hide; he laughed, and said, *you fool again, you know nothing, you think buffaloe that colo?* I acknowledged I did not know much about these things, and told him I never saw a buffaloe, and that I had not heard what color they were. He replied, *by and by you shall see gleat many buffaloe: he now go to gleat lick. That skin not buffaloe skin, that skin buck elk skin.* They went out with horses, and brought in the remainder of this buck-elk, which was the fattest creature I ever saw of the tallow kind.[9]

---

[9] That is, with animal fat suitable for making tallow, used for lamps and candles.

We remained at this camp about eight or ten days, and killed a number of deer. Though we had neither bread nor salt at this time, yet we had both roast and boiled meat in great plenty, and they were frequently inviting me to eat, when I had no appetite.

We then moved to the buffaloe lick, where we killed several buffaloe, and in their small brass kettles they made about half a bushel of salt. I suppose this lick was about thirty or forty miles from the aforesaid town, and somewhere between the Muskingum, Ohio, and Sciota.[10] About the lick was clear, open woods, and thin white-oak land, and at that time there were large roads leading to the lick, like waggon roads. We moved from this lick about six or seven miles, and encamped on a creek.

Though the Indians had given me a gun, I had not yet been admitted to go out from the camp to hunt. At this place Mohawk Solomon asked me to go out with him to hunt, which I readily agreed to. After some time we came upon some fresh buffaloe tracks. I had observed before this that the Indians were upon their guard, and afraid of an enemy; for, until now, they and the southern nations had been at war. As we were following the buffaloe tracks, Solomon seemed to be upon his guard, went very slow, and would frequently stand and listen, and appeared to be in suspense. We came to where the tracks were very plain in the sand, and I said, it is surely buffaloe tracks; he said, *hush, you know nothing, may be buffaloe tracks, may be Catawba.*[11] He went very cautious until we found some fresh buffaloe dung: he then smiled, and said, *Catawba cannot make so.* He then stopped and told me an odd story about the Catawbas. He said, that formerly the Catawbas came near one of their hunting camps, and at some distance from the camp lay in ambush; and in order to decoy them out, sent two or three Catawbas in the night, past their camp, with buffaloe hoofs fixed on their feet, so as to make artificial tracks. In the morning, those in the camp followed after these tracks, thinking they were buffaloe, until they were fired on by the Catawbas, and several of them killed; the others fled, collected a party and pursued the Catawbas; but they, in their subtlety, brought with them rattle-snake poison, which they had collected from the bladder that lieth at the root of the snakes' teeth; this they had corked up in a short piece of a cane stalk; they had also brought with them small cane or reed, about the size of a rye straw, which they made sharp at the end like a pen, and dipped them into this poison, and stuck them in the ground among the grass, along their own tracks, in such a position that they might stick into the legs of the pursuers, which answered the design;

---

[10] Three rivers in southern Ohio, the third now spelled Scioto.
[11] Native tribe of the Carolinas, a longtime foe of the Iroquois.

and as the Catawbas had runners behind to watch the motion of the pursuers, when they found that a number of them were lame, being artificially
snake bit, and that they were all turning back, the Catawbas turned upon
the pursuers, and defeated them, killed and scalped all those that were
lame. When Solomon had finished this story, and found that I understood
him, concluded by saying, *you don't know, Catawba velly bad Indian,
Catawba all one devil Catawba.*

Some time after this, I was told to take the dogs with me, and go down
the creek, perhaps I might kill a turkey; it being in the afternoon, I was also
told not to go far from the creek, and to come up the creek again to the
camp, and to take care not to get lost. When I had gone some distance
down the creek, I came upon fresh buffaloe tracks, and as I had a number
of dogs with me to stop the buffaloe, I concluded I would follow after and
kill one; and as the grass and weeds were rank, I could readily follow the
track. A little before sundown I despaired of coming up with them: I was
then thinking how I might get to camp before night: I concluded as the buffaloe had made several turns, if I took the track back to the creek, it would
be dark before I could get to camp; therefore I thought I would take a near
way through the hills, and strike the creek a little below the camp; but as
it was cloudy weather, and I a very young woodsman, I could find neither
creek or camp. When night came on I fired my gun several times, and hal-
looed, but could have no answer. The next morning early, the Indians were
out after me, and as I had with me ten or a dozen dogs, and the grass and
weeds rank, they could readily follow my track. When they came up with
me, they appeared to be in a very good humor. I asked Solomon if he
thought I was running away, he said, *no, no, you go too much clooked.* On
my return to camp they took my gun from me, and for this rash step I was
reduced to a bow and arrows, for near two years. We were out on this tour
for about six weeks.

This country is generally hilly, though intermixed with considerable
quantities of rich upland, and some good bottoms.

When we returned to town, Pluggy and his party had arrived, and
brought with them a considerable number of scalps and prisoners from
the south branch of the Potomack: they also brought with them an English Bible, which they gave to a Dutch woman who was a prisoner; but as
she could not read English, she made a present of it to me, which was very
acceptable.

I remained in this town until sometime in October, when my adopted
brother, called Tontileaugo, who had married a Wiandot squaw, took me
with him to Lake Erie. We proceeded up the west branch of Muskingum,
and for some distance up the river the land was hilly, but intermixed with
large bodies of tolerable rich upland, and excellent bottoms. We proceeded

on to the head waters of the west branch of Muskingum. On the head waters of this branch, and from thence to the waters of Canesadooharie,[12] there is a large body of rich, well lying land—the timber is ash, walnut, sugar-tree, buckeye, honey-locust, and cherry, intermixed with some oak, hickory, etc. This tour was at the time that the black haws were ripe, and we were seldom out of sight of them: they were common here both in the bottoms and upland.

On this route we had no horses with us, and when we started from the town, all the pack I carried was a pouch, containing my books, a little dried venison, and my blanket. I had then no gun, but Tontileaugo, who was a first rate hunter, carried a rifle gun, and every day killed deer, racoons, or bears. We left the meat, excepting a little for present use, and carried the skins with us until we encamped, and then stretched them with elm bark, in a frame made with poles stuck in the ground, and tied together with lynn or elm bark; and when the skins were dried by the fire, we packed them up, and carried them with us the next day.

As Tontileaugo could not speak English, I had to make use of all the Caughnewaga I had learned, even to talk very imperfectly with him; but I found I learned to talk Indian faster this way, than when I had those with me who could speak English.

As we proceeded down the Canesadooharie waters, our packs encreased by the skins that were daily killed, and became so very heavy that we could not march more than eight or ten miles per day. We came to Lake Erie about six miles west of the mouth of Canesadooharie. As the wind was very high the evening we came to the lake, I was surprised to hear the roaring of the water, and see the high waves that dashed against the shore, like the ocean. We encamped on a run near the lake; and as the wind fell that night, the next morning the lake was only in a moderate motion, and we marched on the sand along the side of the water, frequently resting ourselves, as we were heavy laden. I saw on the strand a number of large fish, that had been left in flat or hollow places; as the wind fell and the waves abated, they were left without water, or only a small quantity; and numbers of bald and grey eagles, etc. were along the shore devouring them.

Some time in the afternoon we came to a large camp of Wiandots, at the mouth of Canesadooharie, where Tontileaugo's wife was. Here we were kindly received: they gave us a kind of rough, brown potatoes, which grew spontaneously, and were called by the Caughnewagas *ohnenata*.

---

[12] The Black River, which flows into Lake Erie just west of Cleveland. Smith habitually commented on the quality of the land he saw in various parts of Ohio, information of interest to readers thinking of migrating to the area, which was still little known in 1799.

These potatoes peeled and dipped in racoons' fat, taste nearly like our sweet potatoes. They also gave us what they call *caneheanta,* which is a kind of homony, made of green corn, dried, and beans mixed together.

From the head waters of Canesadooharie to this place, the land is generally good; chiefly first or second rate, and, comparatively, little or no third rate. The only refuse is some swamps, that appear to be too wet for use, yet I apprehend that a number of them, if drained, would make excellent meadows. The timber is black oak, walnut, hickory, cherry, black-ash, white-ash, water-ash, buckeye, black-locust, honey-locust, sugar-tree, and elm: there is also some land, though, comparatively, but small, where the timber is chiefly white oak, or beech—this may be called third rate. In the bottoms, and also many places in the upland, there is a large quantity of wild apple, plumb, and red and black haw trees. It appeared to be well watered, and a plenty of meadow ground, intermixed with upland, but no large prairies or glades, that I saw or heard of. In this route, deer, bear, turkeys, and racoons, appeared plenty, but no buffaloe, and very little sign of elk.

We continued our camp at the mouth of Canesadooharie for some time, where we killed some deer, and a great many racoons; the racoons here were remarkably large and fat. At length we all embarked in a large birch bark canoe. This vessel was about four feet wide, and three feet deep, and about five and thirty feet long: and though it could carry a heavy burden, it was so artfully and curiously constructed, that four men could carry it several miles, or from one landing place to another, or from the waters of the Lake to the waters of the Ohio. We proceeded up Canesadooharie a few miles, and went on shore to hunt; but to my great surprise they carried the vessel that we all came in up the bank, and inverted it or turned the bottom up, and converted it into a dwelling house, and kindled a fire before us to warm ourselves by and cook. With our baggage and ourselves in this house we were very much crowded, yet our little house turned off the rain very well.

We kept moving and hunting up this river until we came to the falls; here we remained some weeks, and killed a number of deer, several bears, and a great many racoons. From the mouth of this river to the falls is about five and twenty miles. On our passage up I was not much out from the river, but what I saw was good land, and not hilly.

About the falls is thin chesnut land, which is almost the only chesnut timber I ever saw in this country.

While we remained here, I left my pouch with my books in camp, wrapt up in my blanket, and went out to hunt chesnuts. On my return to camp my books were missing. I inquired after them, and asked the Indians if they knew where they were; they told me that they supposed the puppies had carried them off. I did not believe them; but thought they were displeased at my poring over my books, and concluded that they had destroyed them, or put them out of my way.

After this I was again out after nuts, and on my return beheld a new erection, which were two white oak saplings, that were forked about twelve feet high, and stood about fifteen feet apart. They had cut these saplings at the forks, and laid a strong pole across, which appeared in the form of a gallows, and the posts they had shaved very smooth, and painted in places with vermilion. I could not conceive the use of this piece of work, and at length concluded it was a gallows. I thought that I had displeased them by reading my books, and that they were about putting me to death. The next morning I observed them bringing their skins all to this place, and hanging them over this pole, so as to preserve them from being injured by the weather. This removed my fears. They also buried their large canoe in the ground, which is the way they took to preserve this sort of a canoe in the winter season.

As we had at this time no horses, every one got a pack on his back, and we steered an east course about twelve miles and encamped. The next morning we proceeded on the same course about ten miles to a large creek that empties into Lake Erie, betwixt Canesadooharie and Cayahaga. Here they made their winter cabin in the following form. They cut logs about fifteen feet long, and laid these logs upon each other, and drove posts in the ground at each end to keep them together; the posts they tied together at the top with bark, and by this means raised a wall fifteen feet long, and about four feet high, and in the same manner they raised another wall opposite to this, at about twelve feet distance; then they drove forks in the ground in the centre of each end, and laid a strong pole from end to end on these forks; and from these walls to the pole, they set up poles instead of rafters, and on these they tied small poles in place of laths; and a cover was made of lynn bark,[13] which will run even in the winter season.

As every tree will not run, they examine the tree first, by trying it near the ground, and when they find it will do, they fell the tree and raise the bark with the tomahawk, near the top of the tree, about five or six inches broad, then put the tomahawk handle under this bark, and pull it along down to the butt of the tree; so that sometimes one piece of bark will be thirty feet long; this bark they cut at suitable lengths in order to cover the hut.

At the end of these walls they set up split timber, so that they had timber all around, excepting a door at each end. At the top, in place of a

---

[13] The linden tree.

chimney, they left an open place, and for bedding they laid down the aforesaid kind of bark, on which they spread bear skins. From end to end of this
hut along the middle there were fires, which the squaws made of dry split
wood, and the holes or open places that appeared, the squaws stopped
with moss, which they collected from old logs; and at the door they hung
a bear skin; and notwithstanding the winters are hard here, our lodging
was much better than what I expected.[14]

It was some time in December, when we finished this winter cabin; but
when we had got into this comparatively fine lodging, another difficulty
arose, we had nothing to eat. While I was travelling with Tontileaugo, as
was before mentioned, and had plenty of fat venison, bears meat and
racoons, I then thought it was hard living without bread or salt; but now
I began to conclude, that if I had anything that would banish pinching
hunger, and keep soul and body together, I would be content.

While the hunters were all out, exerting themselves to the utmost of
their ability, the squaws and boys (in which class I was,) were scattered out
in the bottoms, hunting red haws, black haws, and hickory nuts. As it was
too late in the year, we did not succeed in gathering haws; but we had tolerable success in scratching up hickory nuts from under a light snow,
which we carried with us lest the hunters should not succeed. After our return the hunters came in, who had killed only two small turkeys, which
were but little among eight hunters, and thirteen squaws, boys, and children; but they were divided with the greatest equity and justice—every
one got their equal share.

The next day the hunters turned out again, and killed one deer and
three bears.

One of the bears was very large and remarkably fat. The hunters carried in meat sufficient to give us all a hearty supper and breakfast.

The squaws and all that could carry, turned out to bring in meat—
every one had their share assigned them, and my load was among the least;
yet, not being accustomed to carrying in this way, I got exceeding weary,
and told them my load was too heavy, I must leave part of it and come
for it again. They made a halt, and only laughed at me, and took part
of my load and added it to a young squaw's, who had as much before as
I carried.

This kind of reproof had a greater tendency to excite me to exert myself in carrying without complaining, than if they had whipped me for lazi-
ness. After this the hunters held a council, and concluded that they must

---

[14]Smith described a somewhat smaller version of the longhouses customary among the
Iroquois.

have horses to carry their loads; and that they would go to war even in this
inclement season, in order to bring in horses.

Tontileaugo wished to be one of those who should go to war; but the
votes went against him; as he was one of our best hunters; it was thought
necessary to leave him at this winter camp to provide for the squaws and
children; it was agreed upon that Tontileaugo and three others should stay,
and hunt, and the other four go to war.

They then began to go through their common ceremony. They sung
their war songs, danced their war dances, etc. And when they were
equipped, they went off singing their marching song, and firing their guns.
Our camp appeared to be rejoicing; but I was grieved to think that some
innocent persons would be murdered not thinking of danger.

After the departure of these warriors we had hard times; and though
we were not altogether out of provisions, we were brought to short allowance. At length Tontileaugo had considerable success, and we had meat
brought into camp sufficient to last ten days. Tontileaugo then took me
with him in order to encamp some distance from this winter cabin, to try
his luck there. We carried no provision with us; he said he would leave
what was there for the squaws and children, and that we could shift for
ourselves. We steered about a south course up the waters of this creek, and
encamped about ten or twelve miles from the winter cabin. As it was
still cold weather and a crust upon the snow, which made a noise as we
walked and alarmed the deer, we could kill nothing, and consequently
went to sleep without supper. The only chance we had, under these circumstances, was to hunt bear holes; as the bears about Christmas search
out a winter lodging place, where they lie about three or four months without eating or drinking. This may appear to some incredible; but it is now
well known to be the case, by those who live in the remote western parts
of North America.

The next morning early we proceeded on, and when we found a tree
scratched by the bears climbing up, and the hole in the tree sufficiently
large for the reception of the bear, we then fell a sapling or small tree,
against or near the hole; and it was my business to climb up and drive out
the bear, while Tontileaugo stood ready with his gun and bow. We went
on in this manner until evening, without success; at length we found a
large elm scratched, and a hole in it about forty feet up; but no tree nigh,
suitable to lodge against the hole. Tontileaugo got a long pole and some
dry rotten wood, which he tied in bunches with bark; and as there was a
tree that grew near the elm, and extended up near the hole, but leaned the
wrong way, so that we could not lodge it to advantage; to remedy this inconvenience, he climbed up this tree and carried with him his rotten wood,
fire and pole. The rotten wood he tied to his belt, and to one end of the

pole he tied a hook, and a piece of rotten wood which he set fire to, as it would retain fire almost like spunk, and reached this hook from limb to limb as he went up; when he got up, with this pole he put dry wood on fire into the hole; after he put in the fire he heard the bear snuff, and he came speedily down, took his gun in his hand, and waited until the bear would come out; but it was some time before it appeared, and when it did appear, he attempted taking sight with his rifle; but it being then too dark to see the sights, he set it down by a tree, and instantly bent his bow, took hold of an arrow, and shot the bear a little behind the shoulder; I was preparing also to shoot an arrow, but he called to me to stop, there was no occasion; and with that the bear fell to the ground.

Being very hungry we kindled a fire, opened the bear, took out the liver, and wrapped some of the caul fat round, and put it on a wooden spit, which we stuck in the ground by the fire to roast; we then skinned the bear, got on our kettle, and had both roast and boiled, and also sauce to our meat, which appeared to me to be delicate fare. After I was fully satisfied I went to sleep; Tontileaugo awoke me, saying, come eat hearty, we have got meat plenty now.

The next morning we cut down a lynn tree, peeled bark and made a snug little shelter, facing the southeast, with a large log betwixt us and the north-west; we made a good fire before us, and scaffolded up our meat at one side. When we had finished our camp we went out to hunt, searched two trees for bears, but to no purpose. As the snow thawed a little in the afternoon, Tontileaugo killed a deer, which we carried with us to camp.

The next day we turned out to hunt, and near the camp we found a tree well scratched; but the hole was above forty feet high, and no tree that we could lodge against the hole; but finding that it was very hollow, we concluded that we would cut down the tree with our tomahawks, which kept us working a considerable part of the day. When the tree fell we ran up, Tontileaugo with his gun and bow, and I with my bow ready bent. Tontileaugo shot the bear through with his rifle, a little behind the shoulders; I also shot, but too far back; and not being then much accustomed to the business, my arrow penetrated only a few inches through the skin. Having killed an old she bear and three cubs, we hauled her on the snow to the camp, and only had time afterwards, to get wood, make a fire, cook, etc. before dark.

Early the next morning we went to business, searched several trees, but found no bears. On our way home we took three racoons out of a hollow elm, not far from the ground.

We remained here about two weeks, and in this time killed four bears, three deers, several turkeys, and a number of racoons. We packed as much meat as we could carry, and returned to our winter cabin. On our arrival, there was great joy, as they were all in a starving condition—the three hunters that we had left having killed but very little. All that could carry a pack, repaired to our camp to bring in meat.

Some time in February the four warriors returned, who had taken two scalps, and six horses from the frontiers of Pennsylvania. The hunters could then scatter out a considerable distance from the winter cabin, and encamp, kill meat and bring it in upon horses; so that we commonly after this had plenty of provision.

In this month we began to make sugar. As some of the elm bark will strip at this season, the squaws, after finding a tree that would do, cut it down, and with a crooked stick, broad and sharp at the end, took the bark off the tree, and of this bark made vessels in a curious manner, that would hold about two gallons each: they made above one hundred of these kinds of vessels. In the sugar-tree they cut a notch, sloping down, and at the end of the notch, stuck in a tomahawk; in the place where they stuck the tomahawk, they drove a long chip, in order to carry the water out from the tree, and under this they set their vessel, to receive it. As sugar-trees were plenty and large here, they seldom or never notched a tree that was not two or three feet over. They also made bark vessels for carrying the water, that would hold about four gallons each. They had two brass kettles, that held about fifteen gallons each, and other smaller kettles in which they boiled the water. But as they could not at all times boil away the water as fast as it was collected, they made vessels of bark, that would hold about one hundred gallons each, for retaining the water; and though the sugar-trees did not run every day, they had always a sufficient quantity of water to keep them boiling during the whole sugar season.

The way that we commonly used our sugar while encamped, was by putting it in bears fat until the fat was almost as sweet as the sugar itself, and in this we dipped our roasted venison. About this time some of the Indian lads and myself, were employed in making and attending traps for catching racoons, foxes, wild cats, etc.

As the racoon is a kind of water animal, that frequents the runs, or small water-courses, almost the whole night, we made our traps on the runs, by laying one small sapling on another, and driving in posts to keep them from rolling. The upper sapling we raised about eighteen inches, and set so, that on the racoons touching a string, or small piece of bark, the sapling would fall and kill it; and lest the racoon should pass by, we laid brush on both sides of the run, only leaving the channel open.

The fox traps we made nearly in the same manner, at the end of a hollow log, or opposite to a hole at the root of a tree, and put venison on a stick for bait; we had it so set that when the fox took hold of the meat, the trap fell. While the squaws were employed in making sugar, the boys and men were engaged in hunting and trapping.

About the latter end of March, we began to prepare for moving into town, in order to plant corn, the squaws were then frying the last of their bears fat, and making vessels to hold it; the vessels were made of deer skins, which were skinned by pulling the skin off the neck, without ripping. After they had taken off the hair, they gathered it in small plaits round the neck and with a string drew it together like a purse; in the centre a pin was put, below which they tied a string, and while it was wet they blew it up like a bladder, and let it remain in this manner until it was dry, when it appeared nearly in the shape of a sugar loaf, but more rounding at the lower end. One of these vessels would hold about four or five gallons; in these vessels it was they carried their bears oil.

When all things were ready, we moved back to the falls of Canesadooharie. In this route the land is chiefly first and second rate; but too much meadow ground, in proportion to the upland. The timber is white-ash, elm, black-oak, cherry, buckeye, sugar-tree, lynn, mulberry, beech, white-oak, hickory, wild apple-tree, red-haw, black haw, and spicewood bushes. There is in some places, spots of beech timber, which spots may be called third rate land. Buckeye, sugar-tree and spicewood, are common in the woods here. There is, in some places, large swamps too wet for any use.

On our arrival at the falls, (as we had brought with us on horse back, about two hundred weight of sugar, a large quantity of bears oil, skins, etc.) the canoe we had buried was not sufficient to carry all; therefore we were obliged to make another of elm bark. While we lay here, a young Wiandot found my books: on this they collected together; I was a little way from the camp, and saw the collection, but did not know what it meant. They called me by my Indian name, which was Scoouwa, repeatedly. I ran to see what was the matter; they showed me my books, and said they were glad they had been found, for they knew I was grieved at the loss of them, and that they now rejoiced with me because they were found. As I could then speak some Indian, especially Caughnewaga, (for both that and the Wiandot tongue were spoken in this camp,) I told them that I thanked them for the kindness they had always shown to me, and also for finding my books. They asked if the books were much damaged? I told them not much. They then showed me how they lay, which was in the best manner to turn off the water. In a deer skin pouch they lay all winter. The print was not much injured, though the binding was. This was the first time that I felt my heart warm toward the Indians. Though they had been exceedingly kind to me, I still before detested them, on account of the barbarity I beheld after Braddock's defeat. Neither had I ever before pretended kindness,

or expressed myself in a friendly manner; but I began now to excuse the
Indians on account of their want of information.

When we were ready to embark, Tontileaugo would not go to town,
but go up the river and take a hunt. He asked me if I choosed to go with
him? I told him I did. We then got some sugar, bears oil bottled up in bears
gut, and some dry venison, which we packed up, and went up Canesadooharie, about thirty miles, and encamped. At this time I did not know
either the day of the week, or the month; but I supposed it to be about the
first of April. We had considerable success in our business. We also found
some stray horses, or a horse, mare, and a young colt; and though they had
run in the woods all winter, they were in exceeding good order. There is
plenty of grass here all winter, under the snow, and horses accustomed to
the woods can work it out. These horses had run in the woods until they
were very wild.

Tontileaugo one night concluded that we must run them down. I told
him I thought we could not accomplish it. He said he had run down bears,
buffaloes and elks; and in the great plains, with only a small snow on the
ground, he had run down a deer; and he thought that in one whole day, he
could tire, or run down any four-footed animal except a wolf. I told him
that though a deer was the swiftest animal to run a short distance, yet it
would tire sooner than a horse. He said he would at all events try the experiment. He had heard the Wiandots say, that I could run well, and now
he would see whether I could or not. I told him that I never had run all day,
and of course was not accustomed to that way of running. I never had run
with the Wiandots, more than seven or eight miles at one time. He said
that was nothing, we must either catch these horses, or run all day.

In the morning early we left camp, and about sunrise we started after
them, stripped naked excepting breech-clouts and mockasons. About ten
o'clock I lost sight of both Tontileaugo and the horses, and did not see
them again until about three o'clock in the afternoon. As the horses run
all day, in about three or four miles square, at length they passed where I
was, and I fell in close after them. As I then had a long rest, I endeavoured
to keep ahead of Tontileaugo, and after some time I could hear him after
me calling *chakoh, chakoanaugh*, which signifies, pull away or do your
best. We pursued on, and after some time Tontileaugo passed me, and
about an hour before sundown, we despaired of catching these horses, and
returned to camp where we had left our clothes.

I reminded Tontileaugo of what I had told him; he replied he did not
know what horses could do. They are wonderful strong to run; but withal
we made them very tired. Tontileaugo then concluded, he would do as the
Indians did with wild horses, when out at war: which is to shoot them
through the neck under the mane, and above the bone, which will cause

them to fall and lie until they can halter them, and then they recover again. This he attempted to do; but as the mare was very wild, he could not get sufficiently nigh to shoot her in the proper place; however he shot, the ball passed too low, and killed her. As the horse and colt stayed at this place, we caught the horse and took him and the colt with us to camp.

We stayed at this camp about two weeks, and killed a number of bears, racoons, and some beavers. We made a canoe of elm bark, and Tontileaugo embarked in it. He arrived at the falls that night: whilst I, mounted on horseback, with a bear skin saddle, and bark stirrups, proceeded by land to the falls: I came there the next morning, and we carried our canoe and loading past the falls.

The river is very rapid for some distance above the falls, which are about twelve or fifteen feet nearly perpendicular. This river called Canesadooharie, interlocks with the West Branch of Muskingum, runs nearly a north course, and empties into the south side of Lake Erie, about eight miles east from Sandusky, or betwixt Sandusky and Cayahaga.

On this last route the land is nearly the same as that last described, only there is not so much swampy or wet ground.

We again proceeded toward the lake, I on horseback, and Tontileaugo by water. Here the land is generally good, but I found some difficulty in getting round swamps and ponds. When we came to the lake, I proceeded along the strand, and Tontileaugo near the shore, sometimes paddling, and sometimes polling his canoe along.

After some time the wind rose, and he went into the mouth of a small creek and encamped. Here we staid several days on account of high wind, which raised the lake in great billows. While we were here, Tontileaugo went out to hunt, and when he was gone, a Wiandot came to our camp; I gave him a shoulder of venison which I had by the fire, well roasted, and he received it gladly, told me he was hungry, and thanked me for my kindness. When Tontileaugo came home, I told him that a Wiandot had been at camp, and that I gave him a shoulder of venison: he said that was very well, and I suppose you gave him also sugar and bears oil, to eat with his venison. I told him I did not; as the sugar and bears oil was down in the canoe, I did not go for it. He replied, you have behaved just like a Dutchman.[15] Do you not know that when strangers come to our camp, we ought always to give them the best that we have. I acknowledged that I was wrong. He said that he could excuse this as I was but young; but I must learn to behave like a warrior, and do great things, and never be found in any such little actions.

---

[15] The Dutch he called Skoharehaugo, which took its derivation from a Dutch settlement called Skoharey. [Smith's note. Schoharie is in New York, just west of Albany.]

The lake being again calm,[16] we proceeded, and arrived safe at Suny-endeand, which was a Wiandot town, that lay upon a small creek which empties into the Little Lake below the mouth of Sandusky.

The town was about eighty rood above the mouth of the creek, on the south side of a large plain, on which timber grew, and nothing more but grass or nettles. In some places there were large flats, where nothing but grass grew, about three feet high when grown, and in other places nothing but nettles, very rank, where the soil is extremely rich and loose—here they planted corn. In this town there were also French traders, who purchased our skins and fur, and we all got new clothes, paint, tobacco, etc.

After I had got my new clothes, and my head done off like a red-headed wood-pecker, I, in company with a number of young Indians, went down to the corn field to see the squaws at work. When we came there, they asked me to take a hoe, which I did, and hoed for some time. The squaws applauded me as a good hand at the business; but when I returned to the town, the old men hearing of what I had done, chid me, and said that I was adopted in the place of a great man,[17] and must not hoe corn like a squaw. They never had occasion to reprove me for any thing like this again; as I never was extremely fond of work, I readily complied with their orders.

As the Indians on their return from their winter hunt, bring in with them large quantities of bears oil, sugar, dried venison, etc. at this time they have plenty, and do not spare eating or giving—thus they make away with their provision as quick as possible. They have no such thing as regular meals, breakfast, dinner, or supper; but if any one, even the town folks, would go to the same house several times in one day, he would be invited to eat of the best—and with them it is bad manners to refuse to eat when it is offered. If they will not eat, it is interpreted as a symptom of displeasure, or that the persons refusing to eat, were angry with those who invited them.

At this time homony, plentifully mixed with bears oil and sugar, or dried venison, bears oil and sugar, is what they offer to every one who comes in any time of the day; and so they go on until their sugar, bears oil and venison is all gone, and then they have to eat homony by itself, without bread, salt, or any thing else; yet, still they invite every one that comes in, to eat whilst they have any thing to give. It is thought a shame not to

---

[16] The lake, when calm, appears to be of a sky blue colour; though when lifted in a vessel, it is like other clear water. [Smith's note.]

[17] As in Isaac Jogues's narrative, Smith became aware of the custom of "requickening" and the individual whom he replaced when he was adopted.

invite people to eat, while they have any thing; but if they can, in truth, only say, we have got nothing to eat, this is accepted as an honorable apology. All the hunters and warriors continued in town about six weeks after we came in: they spent this time in painting, going from house to house, eating, smoking, and playing at a game resembling dice, or hustle-cap. They put a number of plumb-stones in a small bowl; one side of each stone is black, and the other white; they then shake or hustle the bowl, calling, *hits, hits, hits, honesey, honesey, rago, rago;* which signifies calling for white or black, or what they wish to turn up; they then turn the bowl, and count the whites and blacks. Some were beating their kind of drum, and singing; others were employed in playing on a sort of flute, made of hollow cane; and others playing on the jews-harp. Some part of this time was also taken up in attending the council house, where the chiefs, and as many others as chose, attended; and at night they were frequently employed in singing and dancing. Toward the last of this time, which was in June, 1756, they were all engaged in preparing to go to war against the frontiers of Virginia: when they were equipped, they went through their ceremonies, sung their war songs, etc. They all marched off, from fifteen to sixty years of age; and some boys, only twelve years old, were equipped with their bows and arrows, and went to war; so that none were left in town but squaws and children, except myself, one very old man, and another, about fifty years of age, who was lame.

The Indians were then in great hopes that they would drive all the Virginians over the lake, which is all the name they know for the sea. They had some cause for this hope, because, at this time, the Americans were altogether unacquainted with war of any kind, and consequently very unfit to stand their hand with such subtle enemies as the Indians were. The two old Indians asked me if I did not think that the Indians and French would subdue all America, except New England, which they said they had tried in old times. I told them I thought not: they said they had already drove them all out of the mountains, and had chiefly laid waste the great valley betwixt the North and South mountain, from Potomac to James River, which is a considerable part of the best land in Virginia, Maryland, and Pennsylvania, and that the white people appeared to them like fools; they could neither guard against surprize, run, or fight. These, they said, were their reasons for saying that they would subdue the whites. They asked me to offer my reasons for my opinion, and told me to speak my mind freely. I told them that the white people to the East were very numerous, like the trees, and though they appeared to them to be fools, as they were not acquainted with their way of war, yet they were not fools; therefore, after some time, they will learn your mode of war, and turn upon you, or at least defend themselves. I found that the old men themselves did not believe they

could conquer America, yet they were willing to propagate the idea, in order to encourage the young men to go to war.

When the warriors left this town, we had neither meat, sugar, or
bears oil left. All that we had then to live on was corn pounded into coarse
meal or small homony—this they boiled in water, which appeared like
well thickened soup, without salt or any thing else. For some time we had
plenty of this kind of homony; at length we were brought to very short allowance, and as the warriors did not return as soon as they expected, we
were in a starving condition, and but one gun in the town, and very little
amunition. The old lame Wiandot concluded that he would go a hunting
in a canoe, and take me with him, and try to kill deer in the water, as it
was then watering time. We went up Sandusky a few miles, then turned
up a creek and encamped. We had lights prepared, as we were to hunt
in the night, and also a piece of bark and some bushes set up in the canoe, in order to conceal ourselves from the deer. A little boy that was with
us held the light; I worked the canoe, and the old man, who had his
gun loaded with large shot, when he came near the deer, fired, and in this
manner killed three deer in part of one night. We went to our fire, ate
heartily, and in the morning returned to town, in order to relieve the hungry and distressed.

When we came to town, the children were crying bitterly on account
of pinching hunger. We delivered what we had taken, and though it was
but little among so many, it was divided according to the strictest rules
of justice. We immediately set out for another hunt, but before we returned
a part of the warriors had come in, and brought with them on horseback
a quantity of meat. These warriors had divided into different parties,
and all struck at different places in Augusta county. They brought in with
them a considerable number of scalps, prisoners, horses, and other plunder. One of the parties brought in with them one Arthur Campbell, that
is now Col. Campbell, who lives on Holston river, near the Royal-Oak.[18]
As the Wiandots, at Sunyendeand, and those at Detroit, were connected,
Mr. Campbell was taken to Detroit; but he remained some time with me
in this town; his company was very agreeable, and I was sorry when he left
me. During his stay at Sunyendeand he borrowed my Bible, and made
some pertinent remarks on what he had read. One passage where it is said,
"It is good for a man that he bear the yoke in his youth." He said we ought

---

[18] Campbell went on to a life very much like Smith's. He escaped from the Indians three
years later and returned to western Virginia, where the Holstun River is. He became involved in politics, in 1781 he led an attack against the Cherokee Indians, and he later
moved to Kentucky (*Scoouwa,* 64.)

to be resigned to the will of Providence, as we were now bearing the yoke in our youth. Mr. Campbell appeared to be then about 16 or 17 years of age.

There was a number of prisoners brought in by these parties, and when they were to run the gauntlet, I went and told them how they were to act. One John Savage was brought in, a middle aged man, or about forty years old. He was to run the gauntlet. I told him what he had to do; and after this I fell into one of the ranks with the Indians, shouting and yelling like them; and as they were not very severe on him, as he passed me, I hit him with a piece of a pumpkin—which pleased the Indians much, but hurt my feelings.

About the time that these warriors came in, the green corn was beginning to be of use, so that we had either green corn or venison, and sometimes both—which was, comparatively, high living. When we could have plenty of green corn, or roasting ears, the hunters became lazy, and spent their time, as already mentioned, in singing and dancing, etc. They appeared to be fulfilling the scriptures beyond those who profess to believe them, in that of taking no thought of tomorrow; and also living in love, peace, and friendship together, without disputes. In this respect, they shame those who profess Christianity.

In this manner we lived, until October; then the geese, swans, ducks, cranes, etc. came from the north, and alighted on this little Lake, without number, or innumerable. Sunyendeand is a remarkable place for fish in the spring, and fowl both in the fall and spring.

As our hunters were now tired with indolence, and fond of their own kind of exercise, they all turned out to fowling, and in this could scarce miss of success; so that we had now plenty of homony and the best of fowls; and sometimes, as a rarity, we had a little bread made of Indian corn meal, pounded in a homony-block, mixed with boiled beans, and baked in cakes under the ashes.

This with us was called good living, though not equal to our fat, roasted, and boiled venison, when we went to the woods in the fall; or bears meat and beaver in the winter; or sugar, bears oil, and dry venison in the spring.

Some time in October, another adopted brother, older than Tontileaugo, came to pay us a visit at Sunyendeand, and asked me to take a hunt with him on Cayahaga. As they always used me as a free man, and gave me the liberty of choosing, I told him that I was attached to Tontileaugo— had never seen him before, and therefore asked some time to consider of this. He told me that the party he was going with would not be along, or at the mouth of this little lake, in less than six days, and I could in this time be acquainted with him, and judge for myself. I consulted with Tontileaugo on this occasion, and he told me that our old brother Tecaughretanego, (which was his name) was a chief, and a better man than he was; and if I went with him I might expect to be well used, but he said I might do as I pleased; and if I staid he would use me as he had done. I told him that he had acted in every respect as a brother to me; yet I was much pleased with my old brother's conduct and conversation; and as he was going to a part of the country I had never been in, I wished to go with him—he said that he was perfectly willing.

I then went with Tecaughretanego to the mouth of the little lake, where he met with the company he intended going with, which was composed of Caughnewagas and Ottawas. Here I was introduced to a Caughnewaga sister, and others I had never before seen. My sister's name was Mary, which they pronounced *Maully*. I asked Tecaughretanego how it came that she had an English name; he said that he did not know that it was an English name; but it was the name the priest gave her when she was baptized, which he said was the name of the mother of Jesus. He said there were a great many of the Caughnewagas and Wiandots, that were a kind of half Roman Catholics;[19] but as for himself, he said, that the priest and him could not agree, as they held notions that contradicted both sense and reason, and had the assurance to tell him, that the book of God taught them these foolish absurdities; but he could not believe the great and good Spirit ever taught them any such nonsense; and therefore he concluded that the Indians' old religion was better than this new way of worshipping God.

The Ottawas have a very useful kind of tents which they carry with them, made of flags, plaited and stitched together in a very artful manner, so as to turn the rain or wind well—each mat is made fifteen feet long and about five feet broad. In order to erect this kind of tent, they cut a number of long strait poles, which they drive in the ground, in the form of a circle, leaning inward; then they spread the mats on these poles, beginning at the bottom and extending up, leaving only a hole in the top uncovered—and this hole answers the place of a chimney. They make fire of dry, split wood, in the middle, and spread down bark mats and skins for bedding, on which they sleep in a crooked posture, all round the fire, as the length of their beds will not admit of stretching themselves. In place of a door they lift up one end of a mat and creep in, and let the mat fall down behind them.

---

[19] Because French Jesuit missionaries such as Brébeuf and Jogues had been active among the Huron and at Caughnewaga since the seventeenth century, many of these Indians had converted. Most of Smith's Anglo-American readers, however, would have been hostile to Catholicism.

These tents are warm and dry, and tolerable clear of smoke. Their lumber they keep under birch-bark canoes, which they carry out and turn up for a shelter, where they keep every thing from the rain. Nothing is in the tents but themselves and their bedding.

This company had four birch canoes and four tents. We were kindly received, and they gave us plenty of homony, and wild fowl, boiled and roasted. As the geese, ducks, swans, etc. here are well grain-fed, they were remarkably fat, especially the green necked ducks. The wild fowl here feed upon a kind of wild rice that grows spontaneously in the shallow water, or wet places along the sides or in the corners of the lakes.

As the wind was high and we could not proceed on our voyage, we remained here several days, and killed abundance of wild fowl, and a number of racoons.

When a company of Indians are moving together on the lake, as it is at this time of the year often dangerous sailing, the old men hold a council; and when they agree to embark, every one is engaged immediately in making ready, without offering one word against the measure, though the lake may be boisterous and horrid. One morning, tho' the wind appeared to me to be as high as in days past, and the billows raging, yet the call was given *yohoh-yohoh*, which was quickly answered by all—*ooh-ooh* which signifies agreed. We were all instantly engaged in preparing to start, and had considerable difficulties in embarking.

As soon as we got into our canoes we fell to paddling with all our might, making out from the shore. Though these sort of canoes ride waves beyond what could be expected, yet the water several times dashed into them. When we got out about half a mile from shore, we hoisted sail, and as it was nearly a west wind, we then seemed to ride the waves with ease, and went on at a rapid rate. We then all laid down our paddles, excepting one that steered, and there was no water dashed into our canoes, until we came near the shore again. We sailed about sixty miles that day, and encamped some time before night.

The next day we again embarked and went on very well for some time; but the lake being boisterous, and the wind not fair, we were obliged to make to shore, which we accomplished with hard work and some difficulty in landing. The next morning a council was held by the old men.

As we had this day to pass by a long precipice of rocks, on the shore about nine miles, which rendered it impossible for us to land, though the wind was high and the lake rough; yet, as it was fair, we were all ordered to embark. We wrought ourselves out from the shore and hoisted sail, (what we used in place of sail cloth were our tent mats, which answered the place very well,) and went on for some time with a fair wind, until we were opposite to the precipice, and then it turned toward the shore, and we began to fear we should be cast upon the rocks. Two of the canoes were considerably farther out from the rocks, than the canoe I was in. Those who were farthest out in the lake did not let down their sails until they had passed the precipice; but as we were nearer the rock, we were obliged to lower our sails, and paddle with all our might. With much difficulty we cleared ourselves of the rock, and landed. As the other canoe had landed before us, there were immediately runners sent off to see if we were all safely landed.

This night the wind fell, and the next morning the lake was tolerably calm, and we embarked without difficulty, and paddled along near the shore, until we came to the mouth of Cayahaga,[20] which empties into Lake Erie on the south side, betwixt Canesadooharie and Presq'Isle.

We turned up Cayahaga and encamped—where we stayed and hunted for several days; and so we kept moving and hunting until we came to the forks of Cayahaga.

This is a very gentle river, and but few riffles, or swift running places, from the mouth to the forks. Deer here were tolerably plenty, large and fat; but bear and other game scarce. The upland is hilly, and principally second and third rate land. The timber chiefly black-oak, white-oak, hickory, dogwood, etc. The bottoms are rich and large, and the timber is walnut, locust, mulberry, sugar-tree, red-haw, black-haw, wild-appletrees, etc. The West Branch of this river interlocks with the East Branch of the Muskingum; and the East Branch with the Big Beaver creek, that empties into the Ohio about thirty miles below Pittsburgh.

From the forks of Cayahaga to the East Branch of Muskingum, there is a carrying place, where the Indians carry their canoes, etc. from the waters of Lake Erie, into the waters of the Ohio.

From the forks I went over with some hunters, to the East Branch of Muskingum, where they killed several deer, a number of beavers, and returned heavy laden, with skins and meat, which we carried on our backs, as we had no horses.

The land here is chiefly second and third rate, and the timber chiefly oak and hickory. A little above the forks, on the East Branch of Cayahaga, are considerable rapids, very rocky for some distance; but no perpendicular falls.

About the first of December, 1756, we were preparing for leaving the river: we buried our canoes, and as usual hung up our skins and every one had a pack to carry: the squaws also packed up their tents, which they carried in large rolls, that extended up above their heads; and though a great

---

[20] The Cuyahoga River, which flows into Lake Erie at Cleveland.

bulk, yet not heavy. We steered about a south east course, and could not march over ten miles per day. At night we lodged in our flag tents, which when erected, were nearly in the shape of a sugar loaf, and about fifteen feet diameter at the ground.

In this manner we proceeded about forty miles, and wintered in these tents, on the waters of Beaver creek, near a little lake or pond, which is about two miles long, and one broad, and a remarkable place for beaver.

It was received opinion among the Indians, that the geese turn to beavers, and the snakes to racoons; and though Tecaughretanego, who was a wise man, was not fully persuaded that this was true, yet he seemed in some measure to be carried away with this whimsical notion. He said that this pond had been always a plentiful place of beaver. Though he said he knew them to be frequently all killed, (as he thought,) yet the next winter they would be as plenty as ever. And as the beaver was an animal that did not travel by land, and there being no water communication to or from this pond—how could such a number of beavers get there year after year? But as this pond was also a considerable place for geese, when they came in the fall from the north, and alighted in this pond, they turned beavers, all but the feet, which remained nearly the same.

I said, that though there was no water communication, in, or out of this pond; yet it appeared that it was fed by springs, as it was always clear, and never stagnated: and as a very large spring rose about a mile below this pond, it was likely that this spring came from this pond. In the fall, when this spring is comparatively low, there would be air under ground sufficient for the beavers to breathe in, with their heads above water, for they cannot live long under water, and so they might have a subterraneous passage by water into this pond. Tecaughretanego granted that it might be so.

About the sides of this pond there grew great abundance of cranberries, which the Indians gathered up on the ice, when the pond was frozen over. These berries were about as large as rifle bullets—of a bright red colour—an agreeable sour, though rather too sour of themselves; but when mixed with sugar, had a very agreeable taste.

In conversation with Tecaughretanego, I happened to be talking of the beavers' catching fish. He asked me why I thought that the beaver caught fish? I told him that I had read of the beaver making dams for the conveniency of fishing. He laughed, and made game of me and my book. He said the man that wrote that book knew nothing about the beaver.[21] The beaver

---

[21] Beaver pelts were a very valuable commodity in colonial North America, and the beaver became the subject of much folklore. (See Sayre, *Les Sauvages Americains*, 218–47.)

never did eat flesh of any kind; but lived on the bark of trees, roots, and other vegetables.

In order to know certainly how this was, when we killed a beaver I carefully examined the intestines, but found no appearance of fish; I afterward made an experiment on a pet beaver which we had, and found that it would neither eat fish nor flesh; therefore I acknowledged that the book that I had read was wrong.

I asked him if the beaver was an amphibious animal, or if it could live under water? He said that the beaver was a kind of subterraneous water animal, that lives in or near the water, but they were no more amphibious than the ducks and geese were—which was constantly proven to be the case, as all the beavers that are caught in steel traps are drowned, provided the trap be heavy enough to keep them under water. As the beaver does not eat fish, I inquired of Tecaughretanego why the beaver made such large dams? He said they were of use to them in various respects—both for their safety and food. For their safety, as by raising the water over the mouths of their holes, or subterraneous lodging places, they could not be easily found; and as the beaver feeds chiefly on the bark of trees, by raising the water over the banks, they can cut down saplings for bark to feed upon without going out much upon the land: and when they are obliged to go out on land for this food, they frequently are caught by the wolves. As the beaver can run upon land but little faster than a water tortoise, and is no fighting animal, if they are any distance from the water, they become an easy prey to their enemies.

I asked Tecaughretanego, what was the use of the beaver's stones, or glands, to them; as the she beaver has two pair, which is commonly called the oil stones, and the bark stones? He said that as the beavers are the dumbest of all animals, and scarcely ever make any noise; and as they were working creatures, they made use of this smell in order to work in concert. If an old beaver was to come on the bank and rub his breech upon the ground, and raise a perfume, the others will collect from different places and go to work; this is also of use to them in travelling, that they may thereby search out and find their company. Cunning hunters finding this out, have made use of it against the beaver, in order to catch them. What is the bate which you see them make use of, but a compound of the oil and bark stones? By this perfume, which is only a false signal, they decoy them to the trap.[22]

---

[22] Beavers have special glands which secrete castoreum, an oily substance used to maintain their water-repellent fur. Colonists collected it as a perfume and medicament. When

Near this pond, beaver was the principal game. Before the water froze up, we caught a great many with wooden and steel traps: but after that, we hunted the beaver on the ice. Some places here the beavers build large houses to live in; and in other places they have subterraneous lodgings in the banks. Where they lodge in the ground, we have no chance of hunting them on the ice; but where they have houses, we go with malls and hand-spikes, and break all the hollow ice, to prevent them from getting their heads above the water under it. Then we break a hole in the house, and they make their escape into the water; but as they cannot live long under water, they are obliged to go to some of those broken places to breathe, and the Indians commonly put in their hands, catch them by the hind leg, haul them on the ice, and tomahawk them. Sometimes they shoot them in the head, when they raise it above the water. I asked the Indians if they were not afraid to catch the beavers with their hands? they said no: they were not much of a biting creature; yet if they would catch them by the fore foot they would bite.

I went out with Tecaughretanego, and some others a beaver hunting: but we did not succeed, and on our return we saw where several racoons had passed, while the snow was soft; tho' there was now a crust upon it, we all made a halt looking at the racoon tracks. As they saw a tree with a hole in it, they told me to go and see if they had gone in thereat; and if they had, to halloo, and they would come and take them out. When I went to that tree, I found they had gone past; but I saw another the way they had went, and proceeded to examine that, and found they had gone up it. I then began to halloo, but could have no answer.

As it began to snow and blow most violently, I returned and proceeded after my company, and for some time could see their tracks; but the old snow being about three inches deep, and a crust upon it, the present driving snow soon filled up the tracks. As I had only a bow, arrows, and toma-hawk with me, and no way to strike fire, I appeared to be in a dismal situation—and as the air was dark with snow, I had little more prospect of steering my course, than I would in the night. At length I came to a hollow tree, with a hole at one side that I could go in at. I went in, and found that it was a dry place, and the hollow about three feet diameter, and high enough for me to stand in. I found that there was also a considerable quantity of soft, dry rotten wood, around this hollow: I therefore concluded that I would lodge here, and that I would go to work, and stop up the door

---

trappers learned to use it as bait in metal traps, it increased the take of beavers and nearly led to the species' extinction.

of my house. I stripped off my blanket, (which was all the clothes that I had, excepting a breech-clout, leggins, and mockasons,) and with my toma-hawk, fell to chopping at the top of a fallen tree that lay near, and carried wood and set it up on end against the door, until I had it three or four feet thick, all round, excepting a hole I had left to creep in at. I had a block pre-pared that I could haul after me, to stop this hole: and before I went in I put in a number of small sticks, that I might more effectually stop it on the inside. When I went in, I took my tomahawk and cut down all the dry, rot-ten wood I could get, and beat it small. With it I made a bed like a goose-nest or hog-bed, and with the small sticks stopped every hole, until my house was almost dark. I stripped off my mockasons, and danced in the centre of my bed for about half an hour, in order to warm myself. In this time my feet and whole body were agreeably warmed. The snow, in the mean while, had stopped all the holes, so that my house was as dark as a dungeon; though I knew that it could not yet be dark out of doors. I then coiled myself up in my blanket, lay down in my little round bed, and had a tolerable nights lodging. When I awoke, all was dark—not the least glimmering of light to be seen. Immediately I recollected that I was not to expect light in this new habitation, as there was neither door nor window in it. As I could hear the storm raging, and did not suffer much cold, as I was then situated, I concluded I would stay in my nest until I was certain it was day. When I had reason to conclude that it surely was day, I arose and put on my mockasons, which I had laid under my head to keep from freezing. I then endeavored to find the door, and had to do all by the sense of feeling, which took me some time. At length I found the block, but it be-ing heavy, and a large quantity of snow having fallen on it, at the first at-tempt I did not move it. I then felt terrified—among all the hardships I had sustained, I never new before, what it was to be thus deprived of light. This, with the other circumstances attending it, appeared grievous. I went straightway to bed again, wrapped my blanket round me, and lay and mused awhile, and then prayed to Almighty God to direct and protect me, as he had done heretofore. I once again attempted to move away the block, which proved successful; it moved about nine inches. With this a consid-erable quantity of snow fell in from above, and I immediately received light; so that I found a very great snow had fallen, above what I had ever seen in one night. I then knew why I could not easily move the block, and I was so rejoiced at obtaining the light, that all my other difficulties seemed to vanish. I then turned into my cell, and returned God thanks for having once more received the light of Heaven. At length I belted my blanket about me, got my tomahawk, bow and arrows, and went out of my den.

I was now in tolerable high spirits, tho' the snow had fallen above three feet deep, in addition to what was on the ground before; and the only imperfect guide I had, in order to steer my course to camp, was the trees; as the moss generally grows on the north-west side of them, if they are straight. I proceeded on, wading through the snow, and about twelve o'clock (as it appeared afterward, from that time to night, for it was yet cloudy,) I came upon the creek that our camp was on, about half a mile below the camp; and when I came in sight of the camp, I found that there was great joy, by the shouts and yelling of the boys, etc.

When I arrived, they all came round me, and received me gladly; but at this time no questions were asked, and I was taken into a tent, where they gave me plenty of fat beaver meat, and then asked me to smoke. When I had done, Tecaughretanego desired me to walk out to a fire they had made. I went out, and they all collected round me, both men, women, and boys. Tecaughretanego asked me to give them a particular account of what had happened from the time they left me yesterday untill now. I told them the whole of the story, and they never interrupted me; but when I made a stop, the intervals were filled with loud acclamations of joy. As I could not, at this time, talk Ottawa or Jibewa well, (which is nearly the same,)[23] I delivered my story in Caughnewaga. As my sister Molly's husband was a Jibewa, and could understand Caughnewaga, he acted as interpreter, and delivered my story to the Jibewas and Ottawas, which they received with pleasure. When all this was done, Tecaughretanego made a speech to me in the following manner:

"*Brother,*

"You see we have prepared snow-shoes to go after you, and were almost ready to go when you appeared; yet, as you had not been accustomed to hardships in your country, to the east, we never expected to see you alive. Now, we are glad to see you in various respects; we are glad to see you on your own account; and we are glad to see the prospect of your filling the place of a great man, in whose room you were adopted. We do not blame you for what has happened, we blame ourselves; because, we did not think of this driving snow filling up the tracks, until after we came to camp.

"*Brother,*

"Your conduct on this occasion hath pleased us much: You have given us an evidence of your fortitude, skill and resolution; and we hope you will always go on to do great actions, as it is only great actions that can make a great man."

---

[23] The languages of the Ottawa and the Ojibwa or Chippewa Indians are both of the Algonquian linguistic group. By *Caughnewaga,* Smith refers to a Mohawk dialect of Iroquoian, which is in a different language group.

I told my brother Tecaughretanego, that I thanked them for their care of me, and for the kindness I always received. I told him that I always wished to do great actions, and hoped I would never do any thing to dishonor any of those with whom I was connected. I likewise told my Jibewa brother-in-law to tell his people that I also thanked them for their care and kindness.

The next morning some of the hunters went out on snow-shoes, killed several deer, and hauled some of them into camp upon the snow. They fixed their carrying strings, (which are broad in the middle, and small at each end,) in the fore feet and nose of the deer, and laid the broad part of it on their heads or about their shoulders, and pulled it along; and when it is moving, will not sink in the snow much deeper than a snow-shoe; and when taken with the grain of the hair, slips along very easy.

The snow-shoes are made like a hoop-net, and wrought with buckskin thongs. Each shoe is about two feet and an half long, and about eighteen inches broad before, and small behind, with cross-bars, in order to fix or tie them to the feet. After the snow had lay a few days, the Indians tomahawked the deer, by pursuing them in this manner.

About two weeks after this, there came a warm rain, and took away the chief part of the snow, and broke up the ice: then we engaged in making wooden traps to catch beavers, as we had but few steel traps. These traps are made nearly in the same manner as the racoon traps already described.

One day as I was looking after my traps, I got benighted, by beaver ponds intercepting my way to camp; and as I had neglected to take fire-works with me,[24] and the weather very cold, I could find no suitable lodging-place; therefore, the only expedient I could think of to keep myself from freezing, was exercise. I danced and halloo'd the whole night with all my might, and the next day came to camp. Though I suffered much more this time than the other night I lay out, yet the Indians were not so much concerned, as they thought I had fire-works with me; but when they knew how it was, they did not blame me. They said that old hunters were frequently involved in this place, as the beaver dams were one above another on every creek and run, so that it is hard to find a fording place. They applauded me for my fortitude, and said, as they had now plenty of beaver skins, they would purchase me a new gun at Detroit, as we were to go there the next spring; and then if I should chance to be lost in dark weather, I could make fire, kill provision, and return to camp when the sun shined. By being bewildered on the waters of Muskingum, I lost re-

---

[24] Materials for starting a fire, most likely flint and steel.

pute, and was reduced to the bow and arrow; and by lying out two nights here, I regained my credit.

After some time, the waters all froze again, and then, as formerly, we hunted beavers on the ice. Though beaver meat, without salt or bread, was the chief of our food this winter, yet we had always plenty, and I was well contented with my diet, as it appeared delicious fare, after the way we had lived the winter before.

Some time in February, we scaffolded up our fur and skins, and moved about ten miles, in quest of a sugar camp, or a suitable place to make sugar, and encamped in a large bottom on the head waters of Big Beaver creek. We had some difficulty in moving, as we had a blind Caughnewaga boy, about 15 years of age, to lead; and as this country is very brushy, we frequently had him to carry. We had also my Jibewa brother-in-law's father with us, who was thought by the Indians to be a great conjurer— his name was Manetohcoa; this old man was so decrepit, that we had to carry him this route upon a bier, and all our baggage to pack on our backs.

Shortly after we came to this place, the squaws began to make sugar. We had no large kettles with us this year, and they made the frost, in some measure, supply the place of fire, in making sugar. Their large bark vessels, for holding the stock water, they made broad and shallow; and as the weather is very cold here, it frequently freezes at night in sugar time; and the ice they break and cast out of the vessels. I asked them if they were not throwing away the sugar? they said, no; it was water they were casting away, sugar did not freeze, and there was scarcely any in that ice. They said I might try the experiment, and boil some of it, and see what I would get. I never did try it; but I observed, that after several times freezing, the water that remained in the vessel changed its colour, and became brown and very sweet.

About the time we were done making sugar the snow went off the ground; and one night a squaw raised an alarm. She said she saw two men with guns in their hands, upon the bank on the other side of the creek, spying our tents—they were supposed to be Johnston's Mohawks.[25] On this the squaws were ordered to slip quietly out, some distance into the bushes; and all who had either guns or bows were to squat in the bushes near the tents; and if the enemy rushed up, we were to give them the first fire, and let the squaws have an opportunity of escaping. I got down beside Tecaughretanego, and he whispered to me not to be afraid, for he would

---

[25] William Johnson (not Johnston) was the superintendent of Indian affairs for the British colonial government in New York. He was adopted by the Mohawk tribe and led Iroquois forces against the French during the Seven Years' War.

speak to the Mohawks, and as they spake the same tongue that we did, they would not hurt the Caughnewagas, or me; but they would kill all the Jibewas and Ottawas that they could, and take us along with them. This news pleased me well, and I heartily wished for the approach of the Mohawks.

Before we withdrew from the tents, they had carried Manetohcoa to the fire, and gave him his conjuring tools, which were dyed feathers, the bone of the shoulder blade of the wild cat, tobacco, etc. and while we were in the bushes, Manetohcoa was in a tent at the fire, conjuring away to the utmost of his ability. At length he called aloud for us all to come in, which was quickly obeyed. When we came in, he told us that after he had gone through the whole of his ceremony, and expected to see a number of Mohawks on the flat bone when it was warmed at the fire, the pictures of two wolves only appeared. He said, though there were no Mohawks about, we must not be angry with the squaw for giving a false alarm; as she had occasion to go out and happened to see the wolves, though it was moonlight; yet she got afraid, and she conceited it was Indians, with guns in their hands, so he said we might all go to sleep, for there was no danger—and accordingly we did.

The next morning we went to the place, and found wolf tracks, and where they had scratched with their feet like dogs; but there was no sign of mockason tracks. If there is any such thing as a wizzard, I think Manetohcoa was as likely to be one as any man, as he was a professed worshipper of the devil. But let him be a conjuror or not, I am persuaded that the Indians believed what he told them upon this occasion, as well as if it had come from an infallible oracle; or they would not, after such an alarm as this, go all to sleep in an unconcerned manner. This appeared to me the most like witchcraft, of any thing I beheld while I was with them. Though I scrutinized their proceedings in business of this kind, yet I generally found that their pretended witchcraft, was either art or mistaken notions, whereby they deceived themselves. Before a battle they spy the enemy's motions carefully, and when they find that they can have considerable advantage, and the greatest prospect of success, then the old men pretend to conjure, or to tell what the event will be, and this they do in a figurative manner, which will bear something of a different interpretation, which generally comes to pass nearly as they foretold; therefore the young warriors generally believed these old conjurers, which had a tendency to animate, and excite them to push on with vigor.

Some time in March, 1757, we began to move back to the forks of Cayahaga, which was about forty or fifty miles; and as we had no horses, we had all our baggage and several hundred weight of beaver skins, and some deer and bear skins—all to pack on our backs. The method we took to accomplish this, was by making short days' journies. In the morning we would move on with as much as we were able to carry, about five miles, and encamp; and then run back for more. We commonly made three such trips in the day. When we came to the great pond, we staid there one day to rest ourselves, and to kill ducks and geese.

While we remained here, I went in company with a young Caughnewaga, who was about sixteen or seventeen years of age, Chinnohete by name, in order to gather cranberries. As he was gathering berries at some distance from me, three Jibewa squaws crept up undiscovered, and made at him speedily, but he nimbly escaped, and came to me, apparently terrified. I asked him what he was afraid of? he replied did you not see those squaws? I told him I did, and they appeared to be in a very good humour. I asked him wherefore then he was afraid of them? He said the Jibewa squaws were very bad women, and had a very ugly custom among them. I asked him what that custom was? he said that when two or three of them could catch a young lad, that was betwixt a man and a boy, out by himself, if they could overpower him, they would strip him by force, in order to see whether he was coming on to be a man or not. He said that was what they intended when they crawled up, and ran so violently at him; but, said he, I am very glad that I so narrowly escaped. I then agreed with Chinnohete in condemning this as a bad custom, and an exceeding immodest action for young women to be guilty of.

From our sugar camp on the head waters of Big Beaver creek, to this place is not hilly, and some places the woods are tolerably clear: but in most places exceeding brushy. The land here is chiefly second and third rate. The timber on the upland is white-oak, black-oak, hickory, and chesnut; there is also in some places walnut upland, and plenty of good water. The bottoms here are generally large and good.

We again proceeded on from the pond to the forks of the Cayahaga, at the rate of about five miles per day.

The land on this route is not very hilly, it is well watered, and in many places ill timbered, generally brushy, and chiefly second and third rate land, intermixed with good bottoms.

When we came to the forks, we found that the skins we had scaffolded were all safe. Though this was a public place, and Indians frequently passing, and our skins hanging up in view, yet there was none stolen; and it is seldom that Indians do steal anything from one another; and they say they never did, until the white people came among them, and learned some of them to lie, cheat, and steal, but be that as it may, they never did curse or swear, until the whites learned them; some think their language will not admit of it, but I am not of that opinion; if I was so disposed, I could find language to curse or swear, in the Indian tongue.

I remember that Tecaughretanego, when something displeased him, said, God damn it. I asked him if he knew what he then said? he said he did; and mentioned one of their degrading expressions, which he supposed to be the meaning, or something like the meaning of what he had said. I told him that it did not bear the least resemblance to it; that what he said, was calling upon the Great Spirit to punish the object he was displeased with. He stood for some time amazed, and then said, if this be the meaning of these words, what sort of people are the whites? when the traders were among us, these words seemed to be intermixed with all their discourse. He told me to reconsider what I had said, for he thought I must be mistaken in my definition; if I was not mistaken, he said the traders applied these words not only wickedly, but oftentimes very foolishly and contrary to sense or reason. He said, he remembered once of a trader's accidentally breaking his gun-lock, and on that occasion calling out aloud, God damn it—surely, said he, the gun-lock was not an object worthy of punishment for Owaneeyo, or the Great Spirit: he also observed the traders often used this expression when they were in a good humor, and not displeased with any thing. I acknowledged that the traders used this expression very often, in a most irrational, inconsistent, and impious manner. Yet I still asserted that I had given the true meaning of these words. He replied, if so, the traders are as bad as Oonasahroona, or the under ground inhabitants, which is the name they give the devils; as they entertain a notion that their place of residence is under the earth.

We took up our birch-bark canoes, which we had buried, and found that they were not damaged by the winter; but they not being sufficient to carry all that we now had, we made a large chestnut bark canoe; as elm bark was not to be found at this place.

We all embarked, and had a very agreeable passage down the Cayahaga, and along the south side of lake Erie, until we passed the mouth of Sandusky; then the wind arose, and we put in at the mouth of the Miami of the lake, at Cedar Point, where we remained several days, and killed a number of turkeys, geese, ducks and swans. The wind being fair, and the lake not extremely rough, we again embarked, hoisted up sails, and arrived safe at the Wiandot town, nearly opposite to fort Detroit, on the north side of the river. Here we found a number of French traders, every one very willing to deal with us for our beaver.

We bought ourselves fine clothes, amunition, paint, tobacco, etc. and, according to promise, they purchased me a new gun: yet we had parted with only about one-third of our beaver. At length a trader came to town with French brandy: We purchased a keg of it, and held a council about who was to get drunk, and who was to keep sober. I was invited to get drunk, but I refused the proposal—then they said that I must be one of those who were to take care of the drunken people. I did not like this; but of the two evils I chose that which I was the least—and fell in with those who were to conceal the arms, and keep every dangerous weapon we could out of their way, and endeavor, if possible, to keep the drinking club from killing each other, which was a very hard task. Several times we hazarded our own lives, and got ourselves hurt, in preventing them from slaying each other. Before they had finished this keg, near one-third of the town was introduced to this drinking club; they could not pay their part, as they had already disposed of all their skins; but that made no odds, all were welcome to drink.

When they were done with this keg, they applied to the traders, and procured a kettle full of brandy at a time, which they divided out with a large wooden spoon, and so they went on, and never quit while they had a single beaver skin.

When the trader had got all our beaver, he moved off to the Ottawa town, about a mile above the Wiandot town.

When the brandy was gone, and the drinking club sober, they appeared much dejected. Some of them were crippled, others badly wounded, a number of their fine new shirts tore, and several blankets were burned: a number of squaws were also in this club, and neglected their corn planting.

We could now hear the effects of the brandy in the Ottawa town. They were singing and yelling in the most hideous manner, both night and day; but their frolic ended worse than ours; five Ottawas were killed, and a great many wounded.

After this a number of young Indians were getting their ears cut, and they urged me to have mine cut likewise; but they did not attempt to compel me, though they endeavoured to persuade me. The principal arguments they used were its being a very great ornament, and also the common fashion—the former I did not believe, and the latter I could not deny. The way they performed this operation was by cutting the fleshy part of the circle of the ear close to the gristle quite through. When this was done they wrapt rags round this fleshy part until it was entirely healed; they then hung lead to it and stretched it to a wonderful length: when it was sufficiently stretched, they wrapt the fleshy part round with brass wire, which formed it into a semicircle about four inches diameter.

Many of the young men were now exercising themselves in a game resembling foot ball;[26] though they commonly struck the ball with a crooked stick, made for that purpose; also a game something like this, wherein they used a wooden ball, about three inches diameter, and the instrument they

---

[26] This is actually a form of lacrosse, a game invented by the Iroquois.

moved it with was a strong staff, about five feet long, with a hoop net on the end of it, large enough to contain the ball. Before they begin the play, they lay off about half a mile distance in a clear plain, and the opposite parties all attend at the centre, where a disinterested person casts up the ball, then the opposite parties all contend for it. If any one gets it into his net, he runs with it the way he wishes it to go, and they all pursue him. If one of the opposite party overtakes the person with the ball, he gives the staff a stroke which causes the ball to fly out of the net; then they have another debate for it; and if the one that gets it can outrun all the opposite party, and can carry it quite out, or over the line at the end, the game is won: but this seldom happens. When any one is running away with the ball, and is likely to be overtaken, he commonly throws it, and with this instrument can cast fifty or sixty years. Sometimes when the ball is almost at the one end, matters will take a sudden turn, and the opposite party may quickly carry it out at the other end. Oftentimes they will work a long while back and forward before they can get the ball over the line, or win the game.

About the first of June, 1757, the warriors were preparing to go to war, in the Wiandot, Pottowatomy, and Ottawa towns; also a great many Jibewas came down from the upper lakes; and after singing their war songs, and going through their common ceremonies, they marched off against the frontiers of Virginia, Maryland, and Pennsylvania, in their usual manner, singing the travelling song, slow firing, etc.

On the north side of the river St. Laurence, opposite to Fort Detroit,[27] there is an island, which the Indians call the Long Island, and which they say is above one thousand miles long, and in some places above one hundred miles broad. They further say that the great river that comes down by Canesatauga, and that empties into the main branch of St. Laurence, above Montreal, originates from one source, with the St. Laurence, and forms this island.[28]

Opposite to Detroit, and below it, was originally a prairie, and laid off in lots about sixty roods broad, and a great length: each lot is divided into two fields, which they cultivate year about. The principal grain that the French raised in these fields was spring wheat and peas.

They built all their houses on the front of these lots on the river side; and as the banks of the river are very low, some of the houses are not above

---

[27] Fort Detroit had been established by the French in 1701. Smith referred to the St. Clair River as the St. Lawrence, since it is a continuation of the drainage of the Great Lakes.
[28] The Ottawa River flows into the St. Lawrence at Ganesetake (another Indian name with many spellings). Because the Ottawa led to Lake Nippissing and thence to a well-established canoe portage route into Lake Huron, Smith had the impression that this route was a continuous river, forming an island of all of southern Ontario.

three or four feet above the surface of the water; yet they are in no danger of being disturbed by freshes, as the river seldom rises above eighteen inches; because it is the communication, of the river St. Laurence, from one lake to another.

As dwelling-houses, barns, and stables are all built on the front of these lots; at a distance it appears like a continued row of houses in a town, on each side of the river for a long way. These villages, the town, the river, and the plains, being all in view at once, affords a most delightful prospect.

The inhabitants here chiefly drink the river water; and as it comes from the northward, it is very wholesome.

The land here is principally second rate, and comparatively speaking, a small part is first or third rate; though about four or five miles south of Detroit, there is a small portion that is worse than what I would call third rate, which produces abundance of hurtle berries.

There is plenty of good meadow ground here, and a great many marshes, that are overspread with water. The timber is elm, sugar-tree, black-ash, white-ash, abundance of water-ash, oak, hickory, and some walnut.

About the middle of June the Indians were almost all gone to war, from sixteen to sixty; yet Tecaughretanego remained in town with me. Though he had formerly, when they were at war with the southern nations, been a great warrior, and an eminent counsellor; and I think as clear and able a reasoner upon any subject that he had an opportunity of being acquainted with, as I ever knew; yet he had all along been against this war, and had strenuously opposed it in council. He said, if the English and French had a quarrel let them fight their own battles themselves; it is not our business to intermeddle therewith.

Before the warriors returned we were very scarce of provision: and though we did not commonly steal from one another; yet we stole during this time any thing that we could eat from the French, under the notion that it was just for us to do so; because they supported their soldiers; and our squaws, old men and children were suffering on the account of the war, as our hunters were all gone.

Some time in August the warriors returned, and brought in with them a great many scalps, prisoners, horses and plunder; and the common report among the young warriors, was, that they would intirely subdue Tulhasaga, that is the English, or it might be literally rendered the Morning Light inhabitants.

About the first of November a number of families were preparing to go on their winter hunt, and all agreed to cross the lake together. We encamped at the mouth of the river the first night, and a council was held, whether we should cross through by the three islands, or coast it round the lake. These islands lie in a line across the lake, and are just in sight of each other.[29] Some of the Wiandots or Ottawas frequently made their winter hunt on these islands. Though excepting wild fowl and fish, there is scarcely any game here but racoons which are amazingly plenty, and exceedingly large and fat; as they feed upon the wild rice, which grows in abundance in wet places round these islands. It is said that each hunter, in one winter, will catch one thousand racoons.

It is a received opinion among the Indians, that the snakes and racoons are transmutable; and that a great many of the snakes turn racoons every fall, and the racoons snakes every spring. This notion is founded on observations made on the snakes and racoons in this island.

As the racoons here lodge in the rocks, the trappers make their wooden traps at the mouth of the holes; and as they go daily to look at their traps, in the winter season, they commonly find them filled with racoons; but in the spring, or when the frost is out of the ground, they say, they then find their traps filled with large rattle snakes. And therefore conclude that the racoons are transformed. They also say that the reason why they are so remarkably plenty in the winter, is, every fall the snakes turn racoons again.

I told them that though I had never landed on any of these islands, yet from the numerous accounts I had received, I believed that both snakes and racoons were plenty there; but no doubt they all remained there both summer and winter, only the snakes were not to be seen in the latter; yet I did not believe that they were transmutable.

These islands are but seldom visited; because early in the spring and late in the fall it is dangerous sailing in their bark canoes; and in the summer they are so infested with various kinds of serpents, (but chiefly rattle snakes,) that it is dangerous landing.

I shall now quit this digression, and return to the result of the council at the mouth of the river. We concluded to coast it round the lake, and in two days came to the mouth of the Miami of the lake, and landed on cedar point, where we remained several days. Here we held a council, and concluded we would take a driving hunt in concert, and in partnership.

The river in this place is about a mile broad, and as it and the lake forms a kind of neck, which terminates in a point, all the hunters, (which were 53.) went up the river, and we scattered ourselves from the river to the lake. When we first began to move, we were not in sight of each other, but as we all raised the yell, we could move regularly together by the noise. At length we came in sight of each other, and appeared to be marching in

---

[29] The Bass Islands in western Lake Erie.

good order; before we came to the point, both the squaws and boys in the canoes were scattered up the river, and along the lake, to prevent the deer from making their escape by water. As we advanced near the point, the guns began to crack slowly; and after some time the firing was like a little engagement. The squaws and boys were busy tomahawking the deer in the water, and we shooting them down on the land: We killed in all about thirty deer; though a great many made their escape by water.

We had now great feasting and rejoicing, as we had plenty of homony, venison, and wild fowl. The geese at this time appeared to be preparing to move southward—It might be asked what is meant by the geese preparing to move? The Indians represent them as holding a great council at this time concerning the weather, in order to conclude upon a day, that they may all at or near one time leave the northern lakes, and wing their way to the southern bays. When matters are brought to a conclusion, and the time appointed that they are to take wing, then they say, a great number of expresses are sent off, in order to let the different tribes know the result of this council, that they may be all in readiness to move at the time appointed. As there is a great commotion among the geese at this time, it would appear from their actions, that such a council had been held. Certain it is, that they are led by instinct to act in concert, and to move off regularly after their leaders.

Here our company separated. The chief part of them went up the Miami river, that empties into Lake Erie, at cedar point, whilst we proceeded on our journey in company with Tecaughretanego, Tontileaugo, and two families of the Wiandots.

As cold weather was now approaching, we began to feel the doleful effects of extravagantly and foolishly spending the large quantity of beaver we had taken in our last winter's hunt. We were all nearly in the same circumstances—scarcely one had a shirt to his back; but each of us had an old blanket which we belted round us in the day, and slept in at night, with a deer or bear skin under us for our bed.

When we came to the falls of Sandusky, we buried our birch bark canoes as usual, at a large burying place for that purpose, a little below the falls. At this place the river falls about eight feet over a rock, but not perpendicular. With much difficulty we pushed up our wooden canoes, some of us went up the river, and the rest by land with the horses, until we came to the great meadows or prairies, that lie between Sandusky and Sciota.

When we came to this place, we met with some Ottawa hunters, and agreed with them to take, what they call a ring hunt, in partnership. We waited until we expected a rain was near falling to extinguish the fire, and then we kindled a large circle in the prairie. At this time, or before the bucks began to run, a great number of deer lay concealed in the grass in the day, and moved about in the night; but as the fire burned in toward the centre of the circle, the deer fled before the fire: the Indians were scattered also at some distance before the fire, and shot them down every opportunity, which was very frequent, especially as the circle became small. When we came to divide the deer, there were about ten to each hunter, which were all killed in a few hours. The rain did not come on that night to put out the out-side circle of the fire, and as the wind arose, it extended through the whole prairie, which was about fifty miles in length, and in some places nearly twenty in breadth. This put an end to our ring hunting this season, and was in other respects an injury to us in the hunting business; so that upon the whole, we received more harm than benefit by our rapid hunting frolic. We then moved from the north end of the glades, and encamped at the carrying place.

This place is in the plains, betwixt a creek that empties into the Sandusky, and one that runs into Sciota: and at the time of high water, or in the spring season, there is but about one half mile of portage, and that very level, and clear of rocks, timber or stones; so that with a little digging, there may be water carriage the whole way from Sciota to Lake Erie.

From the mouth of Sandusky to the falls, is chiefly first rate land, lying flat or level, intermixed with large bodies of clear meadows, where the grass is exceeding rank, and in many places three or four feet high. The timber is oak, hickory, walnut, cherry, black-ash, elm, sugar-tree, buckeye, locust and beech. In some places there is wet timber land—the timber in these places is chiefly water-ash, sycamore, or button-wood.

From the falls to the prairies, the land lies well to the sun, it is neither too flat nor too hilly—and chiefly first rate. The timber nearly the same as below the falls, excepting the water-ash—There is also here, some plats of beech land, that appears to be second rate, as it frequently produces spice-wood. The prairie appears to be a tolerable fertile soil, though in many places too wet for cultivation; yet I apprehend it would produce timber were it only kept from fire.

The Indians are of the opinion that the squirrels plant all the timber; as they bury a number of nuts for food, and only one at a place. When a squirrel is killed, the various kinds of nuts thus buried will grow.

I have observed that when these prairies have only escaped fire for one year, near where a single tree stood, there was a young growth of timber supposed to be planted by the squirrels; but when the prairies were again burned, all this young growth was immediately consumed; as the fire rages in the grass, to such a pitch, that numbers of racoons are thereby burned to death.

On the west side of the prairie, or betwixt that and Sciota, there is a large body of first rate land—the timber, walnut, locust, sugar-tree, buckeye, cherry, ash, elm, mulberry, plumb-trees, spice-wood, black-haw, red-haw, oak and hickory.

About the time that the bucks quit running, Tontileaugo, his wife and children, Tecaughretanego, his son Nungany and myself, left the Wiandot camps at the carrying place, and crossed the Sciota river at the south end of the glades, and proceeded on about a south-west course to a large creek called Ollentangy, which I believe interlocks with the waters of the Miami, and empties into Sciota on the west side thereof. From the south end of the prairie to Ollentangy, there is a large quantity of beech land, intermixed with first rate land. Here we made our winter hut, and had considerable success in hunting.

After some time, one of Tontileaugo's step-sons, (a lad about eight years of age,) offended him, and he gave the boy a moderate whipping, which much displeased his Wiandot wife. She acknowledged that the boy was guilty of a fault, but thought that he ought to have been ducked, which is their usual mode of chastisement. She said she could not bear to have her son whipped like a servant or slave—and she was do displeased that when Tontileaugo went out to hunt, she got her two horses, and all her effects, (as in this country the husband and wife have separate interests,) and moved back to the Wiandot camps that we had left.

When Tontileaugo returned, he was much disturbed on hearing of his wife's elopement, and said that he would never go after her, were it not that he was afraid that she would get bewildered, and that his children that she had taken with her might suffer. Tontileaugo went after his wife, and when they met they made up the quarrel, and he never returned; but left Tecaughretanego and his son, (a boy about ten years of age) and myself, who remained here in our hut all winter.

Tecaughretanego who had been a first rate warrior, statesman and hunter; and though he was now near sixty years of age, he was yet equal to the common run of hunters, but subject to the rheumatism, which deprived him of the use of his legs.

Shortly after Tontileaugo left us, Tecaughretanego became lame, and could scarcely walk out of our hut for two months. I had considerable success in hunting and trapping. Though Tecaughretanego endured much pain and misery, yet he bore it all with wonderful patience, and would often endeavor to entertain me with chearful conversation. Sometimes he would applaud me for my diligence, skill and activity—and at other times he would take great care in giving me instructions concerning the hunting and trapping business. He would also tell me that if I failed of success, we would suffer very much, as we were about forty miles from any one living, that we knew of; yet he would not intimate that he apprehended we were in any danger, but still supposed that I was fully adequate to the task.

Tontileaugo left us a little before Christmas, and from that until some time in February, we had always plenty of bear meat, venison, etc. During this time I killed much more than we could use, but having no horses to carry in what I killed, I left part of it in the woods. In February, there came a snow, with a crust, which made a great noise when walking on it, and frightened away the deer; and as bear and beaver were scarce here, we got entirely out of provision. After I had hunted two days without eating any thing, and had very short allowance for some days before, I returned late in the evening faint and weary. When I came into our hut, Tecaughretanego asked what success? I told him not any. He asked me if I was not very hungry? I replied that the keen appetite seemed to be in some measure removed, but I was both faint and weary. He commanded Nunganey, his little son, to bring me something to eat, and he brought me a kettle with some bones and broth—after eating a few mouthfuls, my appetite violently returned, and I thought the victuals had a most agreeable relish, though it was only fox and wild-cat bones, which lay about the camp, which the ravens and turkey-buzzards had picked—these Nunganey had collected and boiled, until the sinews that remained on the bones, would strip off. I speedily finished my allowance, such as it was, and when I had ended my *sweet* repast, Tecaughretanego asked me how I felt? I told him that I was much refreshed. He then handed me his pipe and pouch, and told me to take a smoke. I did so. He then said he had something of importance to tell me, if I was now composed and ready to hear it. I told him that I was ready to hear him. He said the reason why he deferred his speech till now, was because few men are in a right humor to hear good talk, when they are extremely hungry, as they are then generally fretful and discomposed; but as you appear now to enjoy calmness and serenity of mind, I will now communicate to you the thoughts of my heart, and those things that I know to be true.

"*Brother,*

"As you have lived with the white people, you have not had the same advantage of knowing that the great being above feeds his people, and gives them their meat in due season, as we Indians have, who are frequently out of provisions, and yet are wonderfully supplied, and that so frequently, that it is evidently the hand of the great Owaneeyo[30], that doth this: whereas the white people have commonly large stocks of tame cattle, that they can kill when they please, and also their barns and cribs filled with grain, and therefore have not the same opportunity of seeing and knowing that they are supported by the ruler of Heaven and Earth.

---

[30] This is the name of God in their tongue, and signifies the owner and ruler of all things. [Smith's note.]

"*Brother,*

"I know that you are now afraid that we will all perish with hunger, but you have no just reason to fear this.

"*Brother,*

"I have been young, but am now old—I have been frequently under the like circumstance that we now are, and that some time or other in almost every year of my life; yet, I have hitherto been supported, and my wants supplied in time of need.

"*Brother,*

"Owaneeyo sometimes suffers us to be in want, in order to teach us our dependance upon him, and to let us know that we are to love and serve him: and likewise to know the worth of the favors that we receive, and to make us more thankful.

"*Brother,*

"Be assured that you will be supplied with food, and that just in the right time; but you must continue diligent in the use of means—go to sleep, and rise early in the morning and go a hunting—be strong and exert yourself like a man, and the Great Spirit will direct your way."

The next morning I went out, and steered about an east course. I proceeded on slowly for about five miles, and saw deer frequently, but as the crust on the snow made a great noise, they were always running before I spied them, so that I could not get a shot. A violent appetite returned, and I became intolerably hungry—it was now that I concluded I would run off to Pennsylvania, my native country. As the snow was on the ground, and Indian hunters almost the whole of the way before me, I had but a poor prospect of making my escape, but my case appeared desperate. If I staid here, I thought I would perish with hunger, and if I met with Indians, they could but kill me.

I then proceeded on as fast as I could walk, and when I got about ten or twelve miles from our hut, I came upon fresh buffaloe tracks—I pursued after, and in a short time came in sight of them, as they were passing through a small glade—I ran with all my might, and headed them, where I lay in ambush, and killed a very large cow. I immediately kindled a fire and began to roast meat, but could not wait till it was done—I ate it almost raw. When hunger was abated, I began to be tenderly concerned for my old Indian brother, and the little boy I had left in a perishing condition. I made haste and packed up what meat I could carry, secured what I left from the wolves, and returned homeward.

I scarcely thought on the old man's speech while I was almost distracted with hunger, but on my return was much affected with it, reflected on myself for my hard-heartedness and ingratitude, in attempting to run off and leave the venerable old man and little boy to perish with hunger. I also considered how remarkably the old man's speech had been verified in our providentially obtaining a supply. I thought also of that part of his speech which treated of the fractious dispositions of hungry people, which was the only excuse I had for my base inhumanity, in attempting to leave them in the most deplorable situation.

As it was moonlight, I got home to our hut, and found the old man in his usual good humor. He thanked me for my exertion, and bid me sit down, as I must certainly be fatigued, and he commanded Nunganey to make haste and cook. I told him I would cook for him, and let the boy lay some meat on the coals for himself—which he did, but ate it almost raw, as I had done. I immediately hung on the kettle with some water, and cut the beef in thin slices, and put them in: when it had boiled awhile, I proposed taking it off the fire, but the old man replied, "let it be done enough." This he said in as patient and unconcerned a manner, as if he had not wanted a single meal. He commanded Nunganey to eat no more beef at that time, least he might hurt himself; but told him to sit down, and after some time he might sup some broth—this command he reluctantly obeyed.

When we were all refreshed, Tecaughretanego delivered a speech upon the necessity and pleasure of receiving the necessary supports of life with thankfulness, knowing that Owaneeyo is the great giver. Such speeches from an Indian, may be thought by those who are unacquainted with them, altogether incredible; but when we reflect on the Indian war, we may readily conclude that they are not an ignorant or stupid sort of people, or they would not have been such fatal enemies. When they came into our country they outwitted us—and when we sent armies into their country, they outgeneralled, and beat us with inferior force. Let us also take into consideration that Tecaughretanego, was no common person, but was, among the Indians, as Socrates in the ancient heathen world; and, it may be, equal to him—if not in wisdom and learning, yet, perhaps, in patience and fortitude. Notwithstanding Tecaughretanego's uncommon natural abilities, yet in the sequel of this history you will see the deficiency of the light of nature, unaided by revelation, in this truly great man.

The next morning Tecaughretanego desired me to go back and bring another load of buffaloe beef: As I proceeded to do so, about five miles from our hut I found a bear tree. As a sapling grew near the tree, and reached near the hole that the bear went in at, I got dry dozed or rotten wood, that would catch and hold fire almost as well as spunk. This wood I tied up in bunches, fixed them on my back, and then climbed up the sapling, and with a pole, I put them touched with fire, into the hole, and then came down and took my gun in my hand. After some time the bear came out, and I killed and skinned it, packed up a load of the meat, (after securing the remainder from the wolves,) and returned home before night.

On my return, my old brother and his son were much rejoiced at my success. After this we had plenty of provision.

We remained here until some time in April, 1758. At this time Tecaughretanego had recovered so, that he could walk about. We made a bark canoe, embarked, and went down Ollentangy some distance, but the water being low, we were in danger of splitting our canoe on the rocks: therefore Tecaughretanego concluded we would encamp on shore, and pray for rain.

When we encamped, Tecaughretanego made himself a sweat-house, which he did by sticking a number of hoops in the ground, each hoop forming a semi-circle—this he covered all round with blankets and skins; he then prepared hot stones, which he rolled into this hut, and then went into it himself, with a little kettle of water in his hand, mixed with a variety of herbs, which he had formerly cured, and had now with him in his pack—they afforded an odoriferous perfume. When he was in, he told me to pull down the blankets behind him, and cover all up close, which I did, and then he began to pour water upon the hot stones, and to sing aloud. He continued in this vehement hot place about fifteen minutes—all this he did in order to purify himself before he would address the Supreme Being. When he came out of his sweat-house, he began to burn tobacco and pray. He began each petition with *oh, ho, ho, ho,* which is a kind of aspiration, and signifies an ardent wish. I observed that all his petitions were only for immediate or present temporal blessings. He began his address by thanksgiving, in the following manner:

"Oh great being! I thank thee that I have obtained the use of my legs again—that I am now able to walk about and kill turkeys, etc. without feeling exquisite pain and misery: I know that thou art a hearer and a helper, and therefore I will call upon thee.

"*Oh, ho, ho, ho,*

"Grant that my knees and ankles may be right well, and that I may be able, not only to walk, but to run, and to jump logs, as I did last fall.

"*Oh, ho, ho, ho,*

"Grant that on this voyage we may frequently kill bears, as they may be crossing the Sciota and Sandusky.

"*Oh, ho, ho, ho,*

"Grant, that we may kill plenty of turkeys along the banks, to stew with our fat bear meat.

"*Oh, ho, ho, ho,*

"Grant that rain may come to raise the Ollentangy about two or three feet, that we may cross in safety down to Sciota, without danger of our canoe being wrecked on the rocks—and now, O great being! thou knowest how matters stand—thou knowest that I am a great lover of tobacco, and though I know not when I may get any more, I now make a present of the last I have unto thee, as a free burnt offering; therefore I expect thou wilt hear and grant these requests, and I, thy servant, will return thee thanks, and love thee for thy gifts."

During the whole of this scene I sat by Tecaughretanego, and as he went through it with the greatest solemnity, I was seriously affected with his prayers. I remained duly composed until he came to the burning of the tobacco, and as I knew that he was a great lover of it, and saw him cast the last of it into the fire, it excited in me a kind of merriment, and I insensibly smiled. Tecaughretanego observed me laughing, which displeased him, and occasioned him to address me in the following manner:

"*Brother,*

"I have somewhat to say to you, and I hope you will not be offended when I tell you of your faults. You know that when you were reading your books in town, I would not let the boys or any one disturb you; but now, when I was praying, I saw you laughing. I do not think you look upon praying as a foolish thing; I believe you pray yourself. But, perhaps you may think my mode, or manner of prayer foolish; if so, you ought in a friendly manner to instruct me, and not make sport of sacred things."

I acknowledged my error, and on this he handed me his pipe to smoke, in token of friendship and reconciliation; though at that time he had nothing to smoke, but red-willow bark. I told him something of the method of reconciliation with an offended God, as revealed in my Bible, which I had then in possession. He said that he liked my story better than that of the French priest, but he thought that he was now too old to begin to learn a new religion, therefore he should continue to worship God in the way he had been taught, and that if salvation or future happiness was to be had in his way of worship, he expected he would obtain it, and if it was inconsistent with the honor of the great spirit to accept of him in his own way of worship, he hoped that Owaneeyo would accept of him in the way I had mentioned, or in some other way, though he might now be ignorant of the channel through which favor or mercy might be conveyed. He said that he believed that Owaneeyo would hear and help every one that sincerely waited upon him.

Here we may see how far the light of nature could go; perhaps we see it here almost in its highest extent. Notwithstanding the just views that this great man entertained of Providence, yet we now see him (though he acknowledged his guilt) expecting to appease the Deity, and procure his favor, by burning a little tobacco. We may observe that all Heathen nations, as far as we can find out either by tradition or the light of Nature, agree with Revelation in this, that sacrifice is necessary, or that some kind of atonement is to be made, in order to remove guilt, and reconcile them to God. This, accompanied with numberless other witnesses, is sufficient evidence of the rationality and truth of the Scriptures.

A few days after Tecaughretanego had gone through his ceremonies, and finished his prayers, the rain came and raised the creek a sufficient height, so that we passed in safety down to Sciota, and proceeded up to the carrying place. Let us now describe the land on this route, from our winter hut, and down Ollentangy to the Sciota, and up the carrying place.

About our winter cabin is chiefly first and second rate land. A considerable way up Ollentangy on the southwest side thereof, or betwixt it and the Miami, there is a very large prairie, and from this prairie down Ollentangy to Sciota, is generally first rate land. The timber is walnut, sugar-tree, ash, buckeye, locust, wild-cherry, and spice-wood, intermixed with some oak and beech. From the mouth of Ollentangy on the east side of Sciota, up to the carrying place, there is a large body of first and second rate land, and tolerably well watered. The timber is ash, sugar-tree, walnut, locust, oak, and beech. Up near the carrying place, the land is a little hilly, but the soil good.

We proceeded from this place down Sandusky, and in our passage we killed four bears, and a number of turkeys. Tecaughretanego appeared now fully persuaded that all this came in answer to his prayers—and who can say with any degree of certainty that it was not so?

When we came to the little lake at the mouth of Sandusky we called at a Wiandot town that was then there, called Sunyendeand. Here we diverted ourselves several days, by catching rock-fish in a small creek, the name of which is also Sunyendeand, which signifies Rock-Fish. They fished in the night, with lights, and struck the fish with giggs or spears. The rock-fish here, when they begin first to run up the creek to spawn, are exceeding fat, and sufficient to fry themselves. The first night we scarcely caught fish enough for present use, for all that was in the town.

The next morning I met with a prisoner at this place, by the name of Thompson, who had been taken from Virginia: he told me if the Indians would only omit disturbing the fish for one night, he could catch more fish than the whole town could make use of. I told Mr. Thompson that if he was certain he could do this, that I would use my influence with the Indians, to let the fish alone for one night. I applied to the chiefs, who agreed to my proposal, and said they were anxious to see what the Great Knife (as they called the Virginian) could do. Mr. Thompson, with the assistance of some other prisoners, set to work, and made a hoop net of Elm bark; they then cut down a tree across the creek, and stuck in stakes at the lower side of it, to prevent the fish from passing up, leaving only a gap at the one

side of the creek—here he sat with his net, and when he felt the fish touch
the net he drew it up, and frequently would haul out two or three rock-fish
that would weigh about five or six pounds each. He continued at this until he had hauled out about a waggon load, and then left the gap open, in
order to let them pass up, for they could not go far, on account of the shallow water. Before day Mr. Thompson shut it up, to prevent them from
passing down, in order to let the Indians have some diversion in killing
them in day-light.

When the news of the fish came to town, the Indians all collected, and
with surprise beheld the large heap of fish, and applauded the ingenuity of
the Virginian. When they saw the number of them that were confined in
the water above the tree, the young Indians ran back to the town, and in a
short time returned with their spears, giggs, bows and arrows, etc. and
were the chief of that day engaged in killing rock-fish, insomuch that we
had more than we could use or preserve. As we had no salt, or any way to
keep them, they lay upon the banks, and after some time great numbers of
turkey-buzzards and eagles collected together and devoured them.

Shortly after this we left Sunyendeand, and in three days arrived at
Detroit, where we remained this summer.

Some time in May we heard that General Forbes, with seven thousand
men, was preparing to carry on a campaign against Fort DuQuesne, which
then stood near where Fort Pitt was afterward erected. Upon receiving
this news, a number of runners were sent off by the French commander at
Detroit, to urge the different tribes of Indian warriors to repair to Fort
DuQuesne.

Some time in July, 1758, the Ottawas, Jibewas, Potowatomies, and
Wiandots, rendezvoused at Detroit, and marched off to Fort DuQuesne, to
prepare for the encounter of General Forbes. The common report was,
that they would serve him as they did General Braddock, and obtain much
plunder. From this time, until fall, we had frequent accounts of Forbes's
army, by Indian runners that were sent out to watch their motion. They
spied them frequently from the mountains ever after they left Fort Loudon.
Notwithstanding their vigilence, Colonel Grant, with his Highlanders, stole
a march upon them, and in the night took possession of a hill about eighty
rood from Fort DuQuesne—this hill is on that account called Grant's hill
to this day. The French and Indians knew not that Grant and his men were
there until they beat the drum and played upon the bag-pipes, just at daylight. They then flew to arms, and the Indians ran up under covert of the
banks of Allegheny and Monongahela, for some distance, and then sallied
out from the banks of the rivers, and took possession of the hill above
Grant; and as he was on the point of it in sight of the fort, they immediately surrounded him, and as he had his Highlanders in ranks, and in very

close order, and the Indians scattered, and concealed behind trees, they defeated him with the loss only of a few warriors—most of the Highlanders were killed or taken prisoners.

After this defeat, the Indians held a council, but were divided in their opinions. Some said that general Forbes would now turn back, and go home the way that he came, as Dunbar had done when General Braddock was defeated: others supposed he would come on. The French urged the Indians to stay and see the event—but as it was hard for the Indians to be absent from their squaws and children, at this season of the year, a great many of them returned home to their hunting. After this, the remainder of the Indians, some French regulars, and a great number of Canadians, marched off in quest of General Forbes. They met his army near Fort Ligoneer, and attacked them, but were frustrated in their design. They said that Forbes's men were beginning to learn the art of war, and that there were a great number of American riflemen along with the red-coats, who scattered out, took trees, and were good marks-men; therefore they found they could not accomplish their design, and were obliged to retreat. When they returned from the battle to Fort DuQuesne, the Indians concluded that they would go to their hunting. The French endeavored to persuade them to stay and try another battle. The Indians said, if it was only the red-coats they had to do with, they could soon subdue them, but they could not withstand *Ashalecoa,* or the Great Knife, which was the name they gave the Virginians. They then returned home to their hunting, and the French evacuated the fort, which General Forbes came and took possession of without further opposition, late in the year 1758, and at this time began to build Fort Pitt.

When Tecaughretanego had heard the particulars of Grant's defeat, he said he could not well account for his contradictory and inconsistent conduct. He said as the art of war consists in ambushing and surprizing our enemies, and in preventing them from ambushing and surprizing us; Grant, in the first place, acted like a wise and experienced officer, in artfully approaching in the night without being discovered; but when he came to the place, and the Indians were lying asleep outside of the fort, between him and the Allegheny river, in place of slipping up quietly, and falling upon them with their broad swords, they beat the drums and played upon the bag-pipes. He said he could account for this inconsistent conduct no other way than by supposing that he had made too free with spirituous liquors during the night, and became intoxicated about day-light. But to return:

This year we hunted up Sandusky, and down Sciota, and took nearly the same route that we had done the last hunting season. We had considerable success, and returned to Detroit, some time in April, 1759.

Shortly after this, Tecaughretanego, his son Nungany and myself, went from Detroit, (in an elm bark canoe) to Caughnewaga, a very ancient Indian town, about nine miles above Montreal, where I remained until about the first of July. I then heard of a French ship at Montreal that had English prisoners on board, in order to carry them over sea, and exchange them. I went privately off from the Indians, and got also on board; but as general Wolfe had stopped the River St. Laurence, we were all sent to prison in Montreal, where we remained four months. Some time in November we were all sent off from this place to Crown Point, and exchanged.[31]

Early in the year 1760, I came home to Conococheague,[32] and found that my people could never ascertain whether I was killed or taken, until my return. They received me with great joy, but were surprized to see me so much like an Indian, both in my gait and gesture.

Upon enquiry, I found that my sweet-heart was married a few days before I arrived. My feelings I must leave on this occasion, for those of my readers to judge, who have felt the pangs of disappointed love, as it is impossible now for me to describe the emotion of soul I felt at that time.

Now there was peace with the Indians, which lasted until the year 1763. Some time in May, this year, I married, and about that time the Indians again commenced hostilities,[33] and were busily engaged in killing and scalping the frontier inhabitants in various parts of Pennsylvania. The whole Conococheague Valley, from the North to the South Mountain, had been almost entirely evacuated during Braddock's war. This state was then a Quaker government,[34] and at the first of this war the frontiers received no assistance from the state. As the people were now beginning to live at home again they thought it hard to be drove away a second time, and were determined, if possible, to make a stand; therefore they raised as much money by collections and subscriptions, as would pay a company of riflemen for several months. The subscribers met and elected a committee to manage the business. The committee appointed me captain of this com-

---

[31] A point of land jutting into Lake Champlain, in New York State. This exchange followed General Wolfe's victory over Montcalm in September, 1759, the climactic battle of the Seven Years' War.

[32] Now Mercersburg, Pennsylvania.

[33] This was the beginning of Pontiac's War. Pontiac was an Ottawa chief who led a coordinated rebellion of the tribes against the British colonists in 1763.

[34] Pennsylvania had begun as land granted to William Penn, a Quaker, and Quakers were powerful in the colonial government. Because of their pacifist doctrines, many refused to contribute to wartime taxes, which led to political conflicts with non-Quakers, such as Benjamin Franklin.

pany of rangers, and gave me the appointment of my own subalterns. I chose two of the most active young men that I could find, who had also been long in captivity with the Indians. As we enlisted our men, we dressed them uniformly in the Indian manner, with breech-clouts, leggins, mockasons, and green shrouds, which we wore in the same manner that the Indians do, and nearly as the Highlanders wear their plaids. In place of hats we wore red handkerchiefs, and painted our faces red and black, like Indian warriors. I taught them the Indian discipline, as I knew of no other at that time, which would answer the purpose much better than British. We succeeded beyond expectation in defending the frontiers, and were extolled by our employers. Near the conclusion of this expedition, I accepted of an ensign's commission in the regular service, under King George, in what was called the Pennsylvania line. Upon my resignation, my lieutenant succeeded me in command, the rest of the time they were to serve. In the fall (the same year,) I went on the Susquehannah campaign, against the Indians, under the command of General Armstrong. In this route we burnt the Delaware and Monsey towns, on the West Branch of the Susquehannah, and destroyed all their corn.

In the year 1764, I received a lieutenant's commission, and went out on General Bouquet's campaign against the Indians on the Muskingum. Here we brought them to terms, and promised to be at peace with them, upon condition that they would give up all our people that they had then in captivity among them. They then delivered unto us three hundred of the prisoners,[35] and said that they could not collect them all at this time, as it was now late in the year, and they were far scattered; but they promised that they would bring them all into Fort Pitt early next spring, and as security that they would do this, they delivered to us six of their chiefs, as hostages. Upon this we settled a cessation of arms for six months, and promised upon their fulfilling the aforesaid condition, to make with them a permanent peace.

A little below Fort Pitt the hostages all made their escape. Shortly after this the Indians stole horses, and killed some people on the frontiers. The king's proclamation was then circulating and set up in various public places, prohibiting any person from trading with the Indians, until further orders.

---

[35] Bouquet led a force against the Indians of Pontiac. This prisoner exchange is portrayed very powerfully in *Historical Account of Bouquet's Expedition against the Ohio Indians, in 1764,* by William Smith (not the same William Smith, Esq., whom James mentions as his brother-in-law at the start of the narrative, and who defends him when he is arrested later on). Many of these captives were reluctant to leave their Indian families.

Notwithstanding all this, about the first of March, 1765, a number of waggons loaded with Indian goods, and warlike stores, were sent from Philadelphia to Henry Pollens's, Conococheague, and from thence seventy pack-horses were loaded with these goods, in order to carry them to Fort Pitt. This alarmed the country, and Mr. William Duffield raised about fifty armed men, and met the pack-horses at the place where Mercersburg now stands. Mr. Duffield desired the employers to store up their goods, and not proceed until further orders. They made light of this, and went over the North Mountain, where they lodged in a small valley called the Great Cove. Mr. Duffield and his party followed after, and came to their lodging, and again urged them to store up their goods—He reasoned with them on the impropriety of their proceedings, and the great danger the frontier inhabitants would be exposed to, if the Indians should now get a supply: He said as it was well known that they had scarcely any amunition, and were almost naked, to supply them now, would be a kind of murder, and would be illegally trading at the expence of the blood and treasure of the frontiers. Notwithstanding his powerful reasoning, these traders made game of what he said, and would only answer him by ludicrous burlesque.

When I beheld this, and found that Mr. Duffield would not compel them to store up their goods, I collected ten of my old warriors, that I had formerly disciplined in the Indian way, went off privately, after night, and encamped in the woods. The next day, as usual, we blacked and painted, and waylaid them near Sidelong Hill. I scattered my men about forty rod along the side of the road, and ordered every two to take a tree, and about eight or ten rod between each couple, with orders to keep a reserve fire, one not to fire until his comrade had loaded his gun—by this means we kept up a constant, slow fire, upon them from front to rear. We then heard nothing of these traders' merriment or burlesque. When they saw their pack-horses falling close by them, they called out, *pray, gentlemen, what would you have us to do?* The reply was, *collect all your loads to the front, and unload them in one place; take your private property, and immediately retire.* When they were gone, we burnt what they left, which consisted of blankets, shirts, vermilion, lead, beads, wampum, tomahawks, scalping knives, etc.

The traders went back to Fort Loudon, and applied to the commanding officer there, and got a party of Highland soldiers, and went with them in quest of the robbers, as they called us, and without applying to a magistrate, or obtaining any civil authority, but barely upon suspicion, they took a number of creditable persons prisoners, (who were chiefly not any way concerned in this action,) and confined them in the guard-house in Fort Loudon. I then raised three hundred riflemen, marched to Fort Loudon, and encamped on a hill in sight of the fort. We were not long there, until we had more than double as many of the British troops prisoners in our camp, as they had of our people in the guard-house. Captain Grant, a Highland officer, who commanded Fort Loudon, then sent a flag of truce to our camp, where we settled a cartel, and gave them above two for one, which enabled us to redeem all our men from the guard-house, without further difficulty.

After this, Captain Grant kept a number of rifle guns, which the Highlanders had taken from the country people, and refused to give them up. As he was riding out one day, we took him prisoner, and detained him until he delivered up the arms; we also destroyed a large quantity of gunpowder that the traders had stored up, lest it might be conveyed privately to the Indians. The king's troops, and our party, had now got entirely out of the channel of the civil law, and many unjustifiable things were done by both parties. This convinced me more than ever I had been before, of the absolute necessity of the civil law, in order to govern mankind.

About this time, the following song was composed by Mr. George Campbell, (an Irish gentleman, who had been educated in Dublin,) and was frequently sung to the tune of the Black joke:

> Ye patriot souls, who love to sing,
> What serves your country and your king,
>   In wealth, peace and royal estate;
> Attention give, whilst I rehearse
> 5   A modern fact, in jingling verse,
> How party interest[36] strove what it cou'd
> To profit itself by public blood,
>   But justly met its merited fate.
>
> Let all those Indian traders claim,
> 10 Their just reward, inglorious fame,
>   For vile, base and treacherous ends.
> To Pollins, in the spring, they sent
> Much warlike stores, with an intent
> To carry them to our barbarous foes,
> 15 Expecting that no-body dare oppose
>   A present to their Indian friends.
>
> Astonish'd at the wild design,
> Frontier inhabitants combin'd,
>   With brave souls, to stop their career;

---

[36] Republican ideals of the time sought to suppress political parties or factions in favor of the national interest.

20   Although some men apostatiz'd,
     Who first the grand attempt advis'd,
     The bold frontiers they bravely stood,
     To act for their king and their country's good,
         In joint league, and strangers to fear.

25   On March the fifth, in sixty-five,
     The Indian presents did arrive,
         In long pomp and cavalcade,
     Near Sidelong Hill, where in disguise,
     Some patriots did their train surprize,
30   And quick as lightning tumbled their loads,
     And kindled them bonfires in the woods,
         And mostly burnt their whole brigade.

     At Loudon, when they heard the news,
     They scarcely knew which way to choose,
35   For blind rage and discontent;
     At length some soldiers they sent out,
     With guides for to conduct the route,
     And seized some men that were trav'ling there,
     And hurried them into Loudon where
40   They laid them fast with one consent.

     But men of resolution thought,
     Too much to see their neighbors caught,
         For no crime but false surmise;
     Forthwith they join'd a warlike band,
45   And march'd to Loudon out of hand,
     And kept the jailors pris'ners there,
     Until our friends enlarged were,
         Without fraud or any disguise.

     Let mankind censure or commend,
50   This rash performance in the end,
         Then both sides will find their account.
     'Tis true no law can justify,
     To burn our neighbor's property,
     But when this property is design'd,
55   To serve the enemies of mankind,
         It's high treason in the amount.

After this we kept up a guard of men on the frontiers, for several
months, to prevent supplies being sent to the Indians, until it was pro-

claimed that Sir William Johnson had made peace with them, and then we let the traders pass unmolested.

In the year 1766, I heard that Sir William Johnson, the king's agent for settling affairs with the Indians, had purchased from them all the land west of the Appalachian Mountains, that lay between the Ohio and the Cherokee River;[37] and as I knew by conversing with the Indians in their own tongue, that there was a large body of rich land there, I concluded I would take a tour westward, and explore that country.

I set out about the last of June, 1766, and went, in the first place, to Holstein River, and from thence I travelled westward in company with Joshua Horton, Uriah Stone, William Baker, and James Smith, who came from near Carlisle. There was only four white men of us, and a mulatto slave about eighteen years of age, that Mr. Horton had with him. We explored the country south of Kentucky, and there was no more sign of white men there then, than there is now west of the head waters of the Missouri. We also explored Cumberland and Tennessee Rivers, from Stone's[38] River down to the Ohio.

When we came to the mouth of Tennessee, my fellow travellers concluded that they would proceed on to the Illinois, and see some more of the land to the west: this I would not agree to. As I had already been longer from home than what I expected, I thought my wife would be distressed, and think I was killed by the Indians; therefore I concluded that I would return home. I sent my horse with my fellow travellers to the Illinois, as it was difficult to take a horse through the mountains. My comrades gave me the greatest part of the amunition they then had, which amounted only to half a pound of powder, and lead equivalent. Mr. Horton also lent me his mulatto boy, and I then set off through the wilderness, for Carolina.

About eight days after I left my company at the mouth of Tennessee, on my journey eastward, I got a cane stab in my foot which occasioned my leg to swell, and I suffered much pain. I was now in a doleful situation—far from any of the human species, excepting black Jamie, or the savages, and I knew not when I might meet with them—my case appeared desperate, and I thought something must be done. All the surgical instruments I had, was a knife, a mockason awl, and a pair of bullet moulds—with these I determined to draw the snag from my foot, if possible. I stuck the awl in

---

[37] Now the Tennessee River.

[38] Stone's river is a south branch of Cumberland, and empties into it above Nashville. We first gave it this name in our journal in May, 1767, after one of my fellow travellers, Mr. Uriah Stone, and I am told that it retains the same name unto this day. [Smith's note.]

the skin, and with the knife I cut the flesh away from around the cane, and
then I commanded the mulatto fellow to catch it with the bullet moulds,
and pull it out, which he did. When I saw it, it seemed a shocking thing to
be in any person's foot; it will therefore be supposed that I was very glad
to have it out. The black fellow attended upon me, and obeyed my directions faithfully. I ordered him to search for Indian medicine, and told him
to get me a quantity of bark from the root of a lynn tree, which I made him
beat on a stone, with a tomahawk, and boil it in a kettle, and with the ooze
I bathed my foot and leg—what remained when I had finished bathing, I
boiled to a jelly, and made poultices thereof. As I had no rags, I made use
of the green moss that grows upon logs, and wrapped it round with elm
bark: by this means, (simple as it may seem,) the swelling and inflamma-
tion in a great measure abated. As stormy weather appeared, I ordered
Jamie to make us a shelter, which he did by erecting forks and poles, and
covering them over with cane tops, like a fodder-house. It was but about
one hundred yards from a large buffaloe road. As we were almost out of
provision, I commanded Jamie to take my gun, and I went along as well as
I could, concealed myself near the road, and killed a buffaloe. When this
was done, we jirked[39] the lean, and fryed the tallow out of the fat meat,
which we kept to stew with our jirk as we needed it.

While I lay at this place, all the books I had to read, was a Psalm Book,
and Watts upon Prayer.[40] Whilst in this situation, I composed the following verses, which I then frequently sung.

> Six weeks I've in this desart been,
>   With one mulatto lad,
> Excepting this poor stupid slave,
>   No company I had.
>
> 5   In solitude I here remain,
>   A cripple very sore,
> No friend or neighbor to be found,
>   My case for to deplore.
>
> I'm far from home, far from the wife,
> 10   Which in my bosom lay,

---

[39] Jirk, is a name well known by the hunters, and frontier inhabitants, for meat cut in
small pieces and laid on a scaffold, over a slow fire, whereby it is roasted till it is thoroughly dry. [Smith's note.]

[40] Isaac Watts, an English clergyman and author of the most popular hymnal of the eighteenth century.

> Far from the children dear, which used
>   Around me for to play.
>
> This doleful circumstance cannot
>   My happiness prevent,
> 15 While peace of conscience I enjoy,
>   Great comfort and content.

I continued in this place until I could walk slowly, without crutches. As I now lay near a great buffaloe road, I was afraid the Indians might be passing that way, and discover my fire-place, therefore I moved off some distance, where I remained until I killed an elk. As my foot was yet sore, I concluded that I would stay here until it was healed, lest by travelling too soon, it might again be inflamed.

In a few weeks after, I proceeded on, and in October, I arrived in Carolina. I had now been eleven months in the wilderness, and during this time, I neither saw bread, money, women, or spirituous liquors; and three months of which I saw none of the human species, except Jamie.

When I came into the settlement, my clothes were almost worn out, and the boy had nothing on him that ever was spun. He had buck-skin leggins, mockasons, and breech-clout—a bear-skin dressed with the hair on, which he belted about him, and a racoon-skin cap. I had not travelled far, after I came in before I was strictly examined by the inhabitants. I told them the truth, and where I came from, etc. but my story appeared so strange to them, that they did not believe me. They said that they had never heard of any one coming through the mountains from the mouth of Tennessee, and if any one would undertake such a journey, surely no man would lend him his slave. They said that they thought that all I had told them were lies, and on suspicion they took me into custody, and set a guard over me.

While I was confined here, I met with a reputable old acquaintance, who voluntarily became my voucher, and also told me of a number of my acquaintances that now lived near this place, who had moved from Pennsylvania. On this being made public, I was liberated. I went to a magistrate, and obtained a pass, and one of my old acquaintances made me a present of a shirt. I then cast away my old rags, and all the clothes I now had was an old beaver hat, buck-skin leggins, mockasons, and a new shirt; also an old blanket, which I commonly carried on my back in good weather. Being thus equipped, I marched on with my white shirt loose, and Jamie with his bear-skin about him—myself appearing white, and Jamie very black, alarmed the dogs wherever we came, so that they barked violently. The people frequently came out, and asked me where we came from, etc. I told them the truth, but they for the most part suspected my story, and I generally had to show them my pass. In this way I came on to Fort Chissel,[41] where I left Jamie at Mr. Horton's Negro-quarter, according to promise. I went from thence to Mr. George Adams's, on Reed Creek, where I had lodged, and where I had left my clothes as I was going out from home. When I dressed myself in good clothes, and mounted on horseback, no man ever asked me for a pass; therefore I concluded that a horse thief, or even a robber, might pass without interruption, provided he was only well dressed, whereas the shabby villain would be immediately detected.

I returned home to Conococheague, in the fall 1767. When I arrived, I found that my wife and friends had despaired of ever seeing me again, as they had heard that I was killed by the Indians, and my horse brought into one of the Cherokee towns.

In the year 1769, the Indians again made incursions on the frontiers; yet the traders continued carrying goods and warlike stores to them. The frontiers took the alarm, and a number of persons collected, destroyed and plundered a quantity of their powder, lead, etc. in Bedford county. Shortly after this, some of these persons, with others, were apprehended and laid in irons in the guardhouse in Fort Bedford, on suspicion of being the perpetrators of this crime.

Though I did not altogether approve of the conduct of this new club of black-boys, yet I concluded that they should not lie in irons in the guardhouse, or remain in confinement, by arbitrary or military power. I resolved, therefore, if possible, to release them, if they even should be tried by the civil law afterward. I collected eighteen of my old black-boys, that I had seen tried in the Indian war, etc. I did not desire a large party, lest they should be too much alarmed at Bedford, and accordingly prepare for us. We marched along the public road in daylight, and made no secret of our design: We told those whom we met, that we were going to take Fort Bedford, which appeared to them a very unlikely story. Before this I made it known to one William Thompson a man whom I could trust, and who lived there: him I employed as a spy, and sent him along on horseback before, with orders to meet me at a certain place near Bedford, one hour before day. The next day a little before sun-set, we encamped near the crossings of Juniata, about fourteen miles from Bedford, and erected tents, as though we intended staying all night, and not a man in my company knew to the contrary, save myself. Knowing that they would hear this in Bedford, and wishing it to be the case, I thought to surprize them by stealing a march.

[41] Near Wytheville in western Virginia.

As the moon rose about eleven o'clock, I ordered my boys to march, and we went on at the rate of five miles an hour, until we met Thompson at the place appointed. He told us that the commanding officer had frequently heard of us by travellers, and had ordered thirty men upon guard. He said they knew our number, and only made game of the notion of eighteen men coming to rescue the prisoners, but they did not expect us until towards the middle of the day. I asked him if the gate was open? He said it was then shut, but he expected they would open it as usual, at daylight, as they apprehended no danger. I then moved my men privately up under the banks of Juniata, where we lay concealed about one hundred yards from the fort gate. I had ordered the men to keep a profound silence, until we got into it. I then sent off Thompson again, to spy. At daylight he returned, and told us that the gate was open, and three centinels were standing on the wall—that the guards were taking a morning dram, and the arms standing together in one place. I then concluded to rush into the fort, and told Thompson to run before me to the arms. We ran with all our might, and as it was a misty morning, the centinels scarcely saw us, until we were within the gate, and took possession of the arms. Just as we were entering, two of them discharged their guns, though I do not believe they aimed at us. We then raised a shout, which surprized the town, though some of them were well pleased with the news. We compelled a blacksmith to take the irons off the prisoners, and then we left the place. This, I believe, was the first British fort in America, that was taken by what they called American rebels.[42]

Some time after this, I took a journey westward, in order to survey some located land I had on and near the Youhogany. As I passed near Bedford, while I was walking and leading my horse, I was overtaken by some men on horseback, like travellers. One of them asked my name, and on telling it, they immediately pulled out their pistols, and presented them at me, calling upon me to deliver myself, or I was a dead man. I stepped back, presented my rifle, and told them to stand off. One of them snapped a pistol at me, and another was preparing to shoot, when I fired my piece—one of them also fired near the same time, and one of my fellow travellers fell. The assailants then rushed up, and as my gun was empty, they took and tied me. I charged them with killing my fellow traveller, and told them he was a man that I had accidently met with on the road, that had nothing to do with the public quarrel. They asserted that I had killed him. I told them that my gun blowed, or made a slow fire—that I had her from my face before she went off, or I would not have missed my mark; and from

---

[42] Smith represented this jailbreak as a harbinger of the Revolution to come.

the position my piece was in when it went off, it was not likely that my gun killed this man, yet I acknowledged I was not certain that it was not so. They then carried me to Bedford, laid me in irons in the guardhouse, summoned a jury of the opposite party, and held an inquest. The jury brought me in guilty of wilful murder. As they were afraid to keep me long in Bedford, for fear of a rescue, they sent me privately through the wilderness to Carlisle, where I was laid in heavy irons.

Shortly after I came here, we heard that a number of my old black-boys were coming to tear down the jail. I told the sheriff that I would not be rescued, as I knew that the indictment was wrong; therefore I wished to stand my trial. As I had found the black-boys to be always under good command, I expected I could prevail on them to return, and therefore wished to write to them—to this the sheriff readily agreed. I wrote a letter to them, with irons on my hands, which was immediately sent; but as they had heard that I was in irons, they would come on. When we heard they were near the town, I told the sheriff I would speak to them out of the window, and if the irons were off, I made no doubt but I could prevail on them to desist. The sheriff ordered them to be taken off, and just as they were taken off my hands, the black-boys came running up to the jail. I went to the window and called to them, and they gave attention. I told them, as my indictment was for wilful murder, to admit of being rescued, would appear dishonorable. I thanked them for their kind intentions, and told them the greatest favor they could confer upon me, would be to grant me this one request *to withdraw from the jail and return in peace;* to this they complied, and withdrew. While I was speaking, the irons were taken off my feet, and never again put on.

Before this party arrived at Conococheague, they met about three hundred more, on the way, coming to their assistance, and were resolved to take me out; they then turned, and all came together, to Carlisle. The reason they gave for coming again, was, because they thought that the government was so enraged at me, that I would not get a fair trial; but my friends and myself together, again prevailed on them to return in peace.

At this time the public papers were partly filled with these occurrences. The following is an extract from the Pennsylvania Gazette, No. 2132, Nov. 2d, 1769.

Conococheague, October 16th, 1769

Messrs. Hall & Sellers,
     Please to give the following narrative a place in your Gazette, and you will much oblige

Your humble servant,
William Smith

*Whereas, in this Gazette of September 28th, 1769, there
appeared an extract of a letter from Bedford, September 12th,
1769, relative to James Smith, as being apprehended on suspicion of being a black-boy, then killing his companion, etc. I
look upon myself as bound by all the obligations of truth, justice to character and to the world, to set the matter in a true
light; by which, I hope the impartial world will be enabled
to obtain a more just opinion of the present scheme of acting
in this end of the country, as also to form a true idea of the
truth, candor, and ingenuity of the author of the said extract,
in stating that matter in so partial a light. The state of the case,
(which can be made appear by undeniable evidence,) was this:
"James Smith, (who is styled the principal ring-leader of the
black-boys, by the said author,) together with his younger
brother and brother-in-law, were going out in order to survey
and improve their land on the waters of Youghoghany, and
as the time of their return was long, they took with them their
arms, and horses loaded with the necessaries of life; and as
one of Smith's brothers-in-law was an artist in surveying, he
had also with him the instruments for that business. Travelling
on the way, within about nine miles of Bedford, they overtook
and joined company with one Johnson and Moorhead, who
likewise had horses loaded, part of which loading was liquor,
and part seed wheat, their intentions being to make improve-
ments on their lands. When they arrived at the parting of the
road on this side Bedford, the company separated, one part
going through the town, in order to get a horse shod, were
apprehended, and put under confinement, but for what crime
they knew not, and treated in a manner utterly inconsistent
with the laws of their country, and the liberties of Englishmen—
Whilst the other part, viz. James Smith, Johnson and Moorhead, taking along the other road, were met by John Holmes,
Esq. to whom James Smith spoke in a friendly manner, but
received no answer. Mr. Holmes hasted, and gave an alarm
in Bedford, from whence a party of men were sent in pursuit
of them; but Smith and his companions not having the least
thought of any such measures being taken, (why should they?)
travelled slowly on. After they had gained the place where
the roads joined, they delayed until the other part of their company should come up. At this time a number of men came
riding, like men travelling; they asked Smith his name, which
he told them—on which they immediately assaulted him as*

*highway-men, and with presented pistols, commanded him
to surrender, or he was a dead man; upon which Smith stepped
back, asked them if they were highway-men, charging them at
the same time to stand off, when immediately, Robert George,
(one of the assailants,) snapped a pistol at Smith's head, and
that before Smith offered to shoot, (which said George himself acknowledged upon oath;) whereupon Smith presented
his gun at another of the assailants, who was preparing to
shoot him with his pistol. The said assailant having a hold
of Johnson by the arm, two shots were fired, one by Smith's
gun, the other from a pistol, so quick as just to be distinguish-
able, and Johnson fell. After which, Smith was taken and carried into Bedford, where John Holmes, Esq., the informer, held
an inquest on the corpse, one of the assailants being as an
evidence, (nor was there any other troubled about the matter,)
Smith was brought in guilty of wilful murder, and so committed
to prison. But a jealousy arising in the breasts of many, that
the inquest, either through inadvertency, ignorance or some
other default, was not so fair as it ought to be: William Deny,
coroner of the county, upon requisition made, thought proper
to re-examine the matter, and summoning a jury of unexcep-
tionable men, out of three townships—men whose candor,
probity, and honesty is unquestionable with all who are acquainted with them, and having raised the corpse, held an
inquest in a solemn manner, during three days. In the course
of their scrutiny they found Johnson's shirt blacked about the
bullet-hole, by the powder of the charge by which he was killed,
whereupon they examined into the distance Smith stood from
Johnson when he shot, and one of the assailants being admitted
to oath, swore to the respective spots of ground they both stood
on at that time, which the jury measured, and found to be
twenty-three feet, nearly; then, trying the experiment of shooting at the same shirt, both with and against the wind, and at
the same distance, found no effects, not the least stain from
the powder, on the shirt—And let any person that pleases, make
the experiment, and I will venture to affirm he shall find that
powder will not stain at half the distance above mentioned,
if shot out of a rifle gun, which Smith's was. Upon the whole,
the jury, after the most accurate examination and mature deliberation, brought in their verdict that some one of the assailants themselves must necessarily have been the perpetrators
of the murder."*

I have now represented the matter in its true and genuine
colors, and which I will abide by. I only beg liberty to make
a few remarks and reflections on the above mentioned extract.
The author says, "James Smith, with two others in company,
passed round the town, without touching," by which it is plain
he would insinuate, and make the public believe that Smith,
and that part of the company, had taken some bye road, which
is utterly false, for it was the king's high-way, and the straight-
est, that through Bedford being something to the one side; nor
would the other part of the company have gone through the
town, but for the reason already given. Again, the author says,
that "four men were sent in pursuit of Smith and his companions, who overtook them about five miles from Bedford, and
commanded them to surrender, on which Smith presented his
gun at one of the men, who was struggling with his companion,
fired it at him, and shot his companion through the back." Here
I would just remark again, the unfair and partial account given
of this matter by the author; not a word mentioned of George's
snapping his pistol before Smith offered to shoot, or of another
of the assailants actually firing his pistol, though he confessed
himself afterward, he had done so; not the least mention of
the company's baggage, which, to men in the least open to a
fair enquiry, would have been sufficient proof of the innocence
of their intentions. Must not an effusive blush overspread the
face of the partial representer of facts, when he finds the veil
he had thrown over truth thus pulled aside, and she exposed
to naked view? Suppose it should be granted that Smith shot
the man, (which is not, and I presume never can be proven
to be the case,) I would only ask, was he not on his own defence? Was he not publicly assaulted? Was he not charged, at
the peril of his life, to surrender, without knowing for what?
No warrant being shown him, or any declaration made of
their authority. And seeing these things are so, would any
judicious man, any person in the least acquainted with the
laws of the land, or morality, judge him guilty of wilful murder?
But I humbly presume, every one who has an opportunity of
seeing this, will by this time be convinced, that the proceedings against Smith were truly unlawful and tyranical, perhaps
unparalleled by any instance in a civilized nation; for to endeavor to kill a man in the apprehending of him, in order to
bring him to trial for a fact, and that too on a supposed one,
is undoubtedly beyond all bounds of law or government.

> *If the author of the extract thinks I have treated him unfair,*
> *or that I have advanced any thing he can controvert, let him*
> *come forward as a fair antagonist, and make his defence, and I*
> *will, if called upon, vindicate all that I have advanced against*
> *him or his abettors.*

William Smith

I remained in prison four months, and during this time I often thought of those that were confined in the time of the persecution, who declared their prison was converted into a palace. I now learned what this meant, as I never since, or before, experienced four months of equal happiness.

When the supreme court sat, I was severely prosecuted. At the commencement of my trial, the judges, in a very unjust and arbitrary manner, rejected several of my evidences; yet, as Robert George (one of those who was in the fray when I was taken) swore in court that he snapped a pistol at me before I shot, and a concurrence of corroborating circumstances, amounted to strong presumptive evidence, that it could not possibly be my gun that killed Johnson, the jury, without hesitation, brought in their verdict, NOT GUILTY. One of the judges then declared that not one of this jury should ever hold any office above a constable. Notwithstanding this proud, ill-natured declaration, some of these jurymen afterward filled honorable places, and I myself was elected the next year, and sat on the board[43] in Bedford county, and afterward I served in the board three years in Westmoreland county.

In the year 1774, another Indian war commenced,[44] though at this time the white people were the aggressors. The prospect of this terrified the frontier inhabitants, insomuch that the greater part on the Ohio waters, either fled over the mountains eastward, or collected into forts. As the state of Pennsylvania apprehended great danger, they at this time appointed me captain over what was then called the Pennsylvania line. As they knew I could raise men that would answer their purpose, they seemed to lay aside their former inveteracy.

In the year 1776, I was appointed a major in the Pennsylvania association. When American independence was declared, I was elected a member of the convention in Westmoreland county, state of Pennsylvania, and of the assembly as long as I proposed to serve.

---

[43] A board of commissioners was annually elected in Pennsylvania, to regulate taxes, and lay the county levy. [Smith's note.]

[44] Later known as Dunmore's War.

While I attended the assembly in Philadelphia, in the year 1777, I saw in the street, some of my old boys, on their way to the Jerseys, against the British, and they desired me to go with them—I petitioned the house for leave of absence, in order to head a scouting party, which was granted me. We marched into the Jerseys, and went before General Washington's army, way-laid the road at Rocky Hill, attacked about two hundred of the British, and with thirty-six men drove them out of the woods into a large open field. After this, we attacked a party that was guarding the officers baggage, and took the waggon and twenty-two Hessians;[45] and also re-took some of our continental soldiers which they had with them. In a few days we killed and took more of the British, than was of our party. At this time I took the camp fever,[46] and was carried in a stage waggon to Burlington, where I lay until I recovered. When I took sick, my companion, Major James M'Common, took command of the party, and had greater success than I had. If every officer and his party that lifted arms against the English, had fought with the same success that Major M'Common did, we would have made short work of the British war.

When I returned to Philadelphia, I applied to the assembly for leave to raise a battalion of riflemen, which they appeared very willing to grant, but said they could not do it, as the power of raising men and commissioning officers, were at that time committed to General Washington; therefore they advised me to apply to his excellency. The following is a true copy of a letter of recommendation which I received at this time, from the council of safety:

> *In Council of Safety,*[47]
> *Philadelphia, February 10th, 1777*
>
> Sir,
>
>   *Application has been made to us by James Smith, Esq., of Westmoreland, a gentleman well acquainted with the Indian customs, and their manners of carrying on war, for leave to raise a battalion of marks-men, expert in the use of rifles, and such as are acquainted with the Indian method of fighting, to be dressed entirely in their fashion, for the purpose of annoying and harrassing the enemy in their marches and encampments. We think two or three hundred men in that way, might be very useful. Should your excellency be of the same opinion, and*

---

[45] German soldiers from Hesse served as hired troops of the British in the war.
[46] Typhoid fever.
[47] These councils were created during the Revolution and had the power to investigate suspected British loyalists and seize their property.

*direct such a corps to be formed, we will take proper measures
for raising the men on the frontiers of this State, and follow
such other directions as your excellency shall give in this matter.*
    To his excellency General Washington.
    *The foregoing is a copy of a letter to his excellency
Gen. Washington, from the council of safety.*

                                        Jacob S. Howell,
                                        Secretary

    After this I received another letter of recommendation, which is as
follows:

*We, whose names are under written, do certify that James
Smith, (now of the county of Westmoreland), was taken prisoner by the Indians, in an expedition before General Braddock's
defeat, in the year 1755, and remained with them until the year
1760; and also that he served as ensign, in the year 1763, under
the pay of the province of Pennsylvania, and as lieutenant, in
the year 1764, and as captain, in the year 1774; and as a military officer, he has sustained a good character. And we do rec-
ommend him as a person well acquainted with the Indian's
method of fighting, and, in our humble opinion, exceedingly fit
for the command of a ranging or scouting party, which, we are
also humbly of opinion, he could, (if legally authorized,) soon
raise. Given under our hands at Philadelphia, this 13th day of
March, 1777.*

Thomas Paxton, capt.	*William Duffield, esq.*
David Robb, esq.	*John Piper, col.*
William M'Comb,	*William Pepper, lieut. col.*
James M'Clane, esq.	*John Proctor, col.*
Jonathan Hoge, esq.	*William Parker, capt.*
Robert Elliot,	*Joseph Armstrong, col.*
Robert Pebbles, lieut. col.	*Samuel Patton, capt.*
William Lyon, esq.	

    With these and some other letters of recommendation, which I have
not now in my possession, I went to his excellency, who lay at Morristown.
Though General Washington did not fall in with the scheme of white men
turning Indians, yet he proposed giving me a major's place in a battalion
of rifle-men already raised. I thanked the general for this proposal; but as
I entertained no high opinion of the colonel that I was to serve under, and
with him I had no prospect of getting my old boys again, I thought I would

be of more use in the cause we were then struggling to support, to remain with them as a militia officer, therefore I did not accept this offer.

In the year 1778, I received a colonel's commission, and after my return to Westmoreland, the Indians made an attack upon our frontiers. I then raised men and pursued them, and the second day we overtook and defeated them. We likewise took four scalps, and recovered the horses and plunder which they were carrying off. At the time of this attack, Captain John Hinkston pursued an Indian, both their guns being empty, and after the fray was over, he was missing. While we were enquiring about him, he came walking up, seemingly unconcerned, with a bloody scalp in his hand—he had pursued the Indian about a quarter of a mile, and tomahawked him.

Not long after this, I was called upon to command four hundred riflemen, on an expedition against the Indian town on French Creek. It was sometime in November, before I received orders from General M'Intosh, to march, and then we were poorly equipped, and scarce of provisions. We marched in three columns, forty rod from each other. There were also flankers on the outside of each column, that marched a-breast in the rear, in scattered order—and even in the columns, the men were one rod apart—and in the front, the volunteers marched a-breast, in the same manner of the flankers, scouring the woods. In case of an attack, the officers were immediately to order the men to face out and take trees—in this position the Indians could not avail themselves by surrounding us, or have an opportunity of shooting a man from either side of the tree. If attacked, the centre column was to reinforce whatever part appeared to require it most. When we encamped, our encampment formed a hollow square, including about thirty or forty acres—on the outside of the square, there were centinels placed, whose business it was to watch for the enemy, and see that neither horses nor bullocks went out. And when encamped, if any attacks were made by an enemy, each officer was immediately to order the men to face out and take trees, as before mentioned; and in this form they could not take the advantage by surrounding us, as they commonly had done when they fought the whites.

The following is a copy of general orders, given at this time, which I have found among my journals:

At Camp—
Opposite Fort Pitt,
November 29th, 1778
General Orders:
A copy thereof is to be given to each captain and subaltern,
and to be read to each company.

*You are to march in three columns, with flankers on the front
and rear, and to keep a profound silence, and not to fire a gun,
except at the enemy, without particular orders for that purpose;
and in case of an attack, let it be so ordered that every other
man only, is to shoot at once, excepting on extraordinary occasions. The one half of the men to keep a reserve fire, until their
comrades load; and let every one be particularly careful not to
fire at any time without a view of the enemy, and that not at too
great a distance. I earnestly urge the above caution, as I have
known very remarkable and grievous errors of this kind. You
are to encamp on the hollow square, except the volunteers,
who, according to their own request, are to encamp on the front
of the square. A sufficient number of centinels are to be kept
round the square, at proper distance. Every man is to be under
arms at the break of day, and to parade opposite to their fire-
places, facing out, and when the officers examine their arms,
and find them in good order, and give necessary directions, they
are to be dismissed, with orders to have their arms near them,
and be always in readiness.*

Given by
James Smith, Colonel

In this manner, we proceeded on, to French Creek, where we found
the Indian town evacuated. I then went on further than my orders called
for, in quest of Indians: but our provisions being nearly exhausted, we
were obliged to return. On our way back, we met with considerable difficulties on account of high waters and scarcity of provision; yet we never
lost one horse, excepting some that gave out.

After peace was made with the Indians, I met with some of them in
Pittsburg, and inquired of them in their own tongue, concerning this expedition—not letting them know I was there. They told me that they
watched the movements of this army ever after they had left Fort-Pitt, and
as they passed through the glades or barrens they had a full view of them
from the adjacent hills, and computed their number to be about one thousand. They said they also examined their camps, both before and after
they were gone, and found, they could not make an advantageous attack, and therefore moved off from their town and hunting ground before
we arrived.

In the year 1788, I settled in Bourbon county, Kentucky, seven miles
above Paris; and in the same year was elected a member of the convention,
that sat at Danville, to confer about a separation from the State of Virginia,
and from that year until the year 1799, I represented Bourbon county,

either in convention or as a member of the general assembly, except two years that I was left a few votes behind.

On the Manners and Customs of the Indians

The Indians are a slovenly people in their dress. They seldom ever wash their shirts, and in regard to cookery they are exceedingly filthy. When they kill a buffaloe they will sometimes lash the paunch of it round a sapling, and cast it into the kettle, boil it, and sup the broth: though they commonly shake it about in cold water, then boil and eat it. Notwithstanding all this, they are very polite in their own way, and they retain among them, the essentials of good manners; though they have few compliments, yet they are complaisant to one another, and when accompanied with good humour and discretion, they entertain strangers in the best manner their circumstances will admit. They use but few titles of honor. In the military line, the titles of great men are only captains or leaders of parties—In the civil line, the titles are only councillors, chiefs, or the old wise men. These titles are never made use of in addressing any of their great men. The language commonly made use of in addressing them is, Grandfather, Father, or Uncle. They have no such thing in use among them as Sir, Mr. Madam or Mistress—The common mode of address, is, my Friend, Brother, Cousin, or Mother, Sister, etc. They pay great respect to age; or to the aged Fathers and Mothers among them of every rank. No one can arrive at any place of honor, among them, but by merit. Either some exploit in war, must be performed before any one can be advanced in the military line, or become eminent for wisdom before they can obtain a seat in council. It would appear to the Indians a most ridiculous thing to see a man lead off a company of warriors, as an officer, who had himself never been in a battle in his life; even in case of merit, they are slow in advancing any one, until they arrive at or near middle age.

They invite every one that comes to their house, or camp to eat, while they have any thing to give; and it is accounted bad manners to refuse eating, when invited. They are very tenacious of their old mode of dressing and painting, and do not change their fashions as we do. They are very fond of tobacco, and the men almost all smoke it mixed with sumach leaves or red willow bark, pulverized; though they seldom use it any other way. They make use of the pipe also as a token of love and friendship.

In courtship they also differ from us. It is a common thing among them, for a young woman, if in love, to make suit to a young man; though the first address may be by the man; yet the other is the most common. The squaws are generally very immodest in their words and actions, and will often put the young men to the blush. The men commonly appear to be possessed of much more modesty than the women; yet I have been acquainted with some young squaws that appeared really modest: genuine it must be, as they were under very little restraint in the channel of education or custom.

When the Indians meet one another, instead of saying how do you do, they commonly salute in the following manner—you are my friend—the reply is, truly friend, I am your friend—or, cousin, you yet exist—the reply is, certainly I do. They have their children under tolerable command: seldom ever whip them, and their common mode of chastising is, by ducking them in cold water; therefore their children are more obedient in the winter season, than they are in the summer, though they are then not so often ducked. They are a peaceable people, and scarcely ever wrangle or scold, when sober; but they are very much addicted to drinking, and men and women will become basely intoxicated, if they can, by any means, procure or obtain spirituous liquor; and then they are commonly either extremely merry and kind, or very turbulent, ill-humoured and disorderly.

On Their Traditions and Religious Sentiments

As the family that I was adopted into was intermarried with the Wiandots and Ottawas, three tongues were commonly spoke, viz. Caughnewaga, or what the French call Iroque,[48] also the Wiandot and Ottawa; by this means I had an opportunity of learning these three tongues; and I found that these nations varied in their traditions and opinions concerning religion; and even numbers of the same nations differed widely in their religious sentiments. Their traditions are vague, whimsical, romantic, and many of them scarce worth relating: and not any of them reach back to the creation of the world. The Wiandots comes the nearest to this. They tell of a squaw that was found when an infant, in the water in a canoe made of bullrushes: this squaw became a great prophetess and did many wonderful things; she turned water into dry land, and at length made this continent, which was, at that time, only a very small island, and but a few Indians in it. Though they were then but few they had not sufficient room to hunt; therefore this squaw went to the water side, and prayed that this little island might be enlarged. The great being then heard her prayer, and sent

[48] Iroquois.

great numbers of Water Tortoises and Muskrats, which brought with them mud and other materials, for enlarging this island, and by this means, they say, it was encreased to the size that it now remains;[49] therefore they say, that the white people ought not to encroach upon them, or take their land from them, because their great grand mother made it. They say, that about this time the angels or heavenly inhabitants, as they call them, frequently visited them and talked with their forefathers; and gave directions how to pray, and how to appease the great being when he was offended. They told them they were to offer sacrifice, burn tobacco, buffaloe and deer bones; but they were not to burn bears or racoons bones in sacrifice.

The Ottawas say, that there are two great beings that rule and govern the universe, who are at war with each other; the one they call *Maneto,* and the other *Matchemaneto.*[50] They say that Maneto is all kindness and love, and that Matchemaneto is an evil spirit that delights in doing mischief; and some of them think, that they are equal in power, and therefore worship the evil spirit out of a principle of fear. Others doubt which of the two may be the most powerful, and therefore endeavour to keep in favour with both, by giving each of them some kind of worship. Others say that Maneto is the first great cause and therefore must be all-powerful and supreme, and ought to be adored and worshipped; whereas Matchemaneto ought to be rejected and dispised.

Those of the Ottawas that worship the evil spirit, pretend to be great conjurors. I think if there is any such thing now in the world as witchcraft, it is among these people. I have been told wonderful stories concerning their proceedings; but never was eye witness to any thing that appeared evidently supernatural.

Some of the Wiandots and Caughnewagas profess to be Roman Catholics; but even these retain many of the notions of their ancestors. Those of them who reject the Roman Catholic religion, hold that there is one great first cause, whom they call *Owaneeyo,* that rules and governs the universe, and takes care of all his creatures, rational and irrational, and gives them their food in due season, and hears the prayers of all those that call upon him; therefore it is but just and reasonable to pray, and offer sacrifice to this great being, and do those things that are pleasing in his sight; but they differ widely in what is pleasing or displeasing to this great being. Some

---

[49] This version of the "Earth-diver" creation story was common to Iroquoian peoples including the Wiandots and Caughnewagas. Among the Hurons, for example, the "squaw" is called Aataentsic.

[50] *Manitou* in the Algonquian languages signifies spirit.

hold that following nature or their own propensities is the way to happiness, and cannot be displeasing to the deity, because he delights in the happiness of his creatures, and does nothing in vain, but gave these dispositions with a design to lead to happiness, and therefore they ought to be followed. Others reject this opinion altogether, and say that following their own propensities in this manner, is neither the means of happiness nor the way to please the deity.

Tecaughretanego was of opinion that following nature in a limited sense was reasonable and right. He said that most of the irrational animals by following their natural propensities, were led to the greatest pitch of happiness that their natures and the world they lived in would admit of. He said that mankind and the rattle snakes had evil dispositions, that led them to injure themselves and others. He gave instances of this. He said he had a puppy that he did not intend to raise, and in order to try an experiment, he tyed this puppy on a pole and held it to a rattlesnake, which bit it several times; that he observed the snake shortly after rolling about apparently in great misery, so that it appeared to have poisoned itself as well as the puppy. The other instance he gave was concerning himself. He said that when he was a young man, he was very fond of the women, and at length got the venereal disease, so that by following this propensity, he was led to injure himself and others. He said our happiness depends on our using our reason, in order to suppress these evil dispositions; but when our propensities neither lead us to injure ourselves nor others, we might with safety endulge them, or even pursue them as the means of happiness.

The Indians generally, are of opinion that there are great numbers of inferior Deities, which they call *Carreyagaroona,* which signifies the Heavenly Inhabitants. These beings they suppose are employed as assistants, in managing the affairs of the universe, and in inspecting the actions of men; and that even the irrational animals are engaged in viewing their actions, and bearing intelligence to the Gods. The eagle, for this purpose, with her keen eye, is soaring about in the day, and the owl, with her nightly eye, perched on the trees around their camp in the night; therefore, when they observe the eagle or the owl near, they immediately offer sacrifice, or burn tobacco, that they may have a good report to carry to the Gods. They say that there are also great numbers of evil spirits, which they call *Onasahroona,* which signifies the Inhabitants of the Lower Region. These they say are employed in disturbing the world, and the good spirits are always going after them, and setting things to right, so that they are constantly working in opposition to each other. Some talk of a future state, but not with any certainty; at best their notions are vague and unsettled. Others deny a future state altogether, and say that after death they neither think or live.

As the Caughnewagas and the six nations[51] speak nearly the same language, their theology is also nearly alike. When I met with the Shawanees or Delawares, as I could not speak their tongue, I spoke Ottawa to them, and as it bore some resemblance to their language, we understood each other in some common affairs; but as I could only converse with them very imperfectly, I cannot from my own knowledge, with any certainty, give any account of their theological opinions.

On Their Police, or Civil Government

I have often heard of Indian kings, but never saw any. How any term used by the Indians in their own tongue, for the chief man of a nation, could be rendered King, I know not. The chief of a nation is neither a supreme ruler, monarch or potentate—He can neither make war or peace, leagues or treaties—He cannot impress soldiers, or dispose of magazines—He cannot adjourn, prorogue or dissolve a general assembly, nor can he refuse his assent to their conclusions, or in any manner controul them—With them there is no such thing as hereditary succession, title of nobility or royal blood, even talked of—The chief of a nation, even with the consent of his assembly, or council, cannot raise one shilling of tax off the citizens, but only receive what they please to give as free and voluntary donations—The chief of a nation has to hunt for his living, as any other citizen—How can they, with any propriety, be called kings? I apprehend that the white people were formerly so fond of the name of kings, and so ignorant of their power, that they concluded the chief man of a nation must be a king.

As they are illiterate, they consequently have no written code of laws. What they execute as laws, are either old customs, or the immediate result of new councils. Some of their ancient laws or customs are very pernicious, and disturb the public weal. Their vague law of marriage is a glaring instance of this, as the man and his wife are under no legal obligation to live together, if they are both willing to part. They have little form, or ceremony among them, in matrimony, but do like the Israelites of old—the man goes in unto the woman, and she becomes his wife. The years of puberty, and the age of consent, is about fourteen for the women, and eighteen for the men. Before I was taken by the Indians, I had often heard that in the ceremony of marriage, the man gave the woman a deer's leg, and she gave him a red ear of corn, signifying that she was to keep him in bread,

---

[51] The Iroquois were known as the Six Nations after the addition of the Tuscaroras in 1716.

and he was to keep her in meat. I inquired of them concerning the truth of this, and they said they knew nothing of it, further than that they had heard it was the ancient custom among some nations. Their frequent changing of partners prevents propagation, creates disturbances, and often occasions murder and bloodshed; though this is commonly committed under the pretence of being drunk. Their impunity to crimes committed when intoxicated with spirituous liquors, or their admitting one crime as an excuse for another, is a very unjust law or custom.

The extremes they run into in dividing the necessaries of life, are hurtful in the public weal; though their dividing meat when hunting, may answer a valuable purpose, as one family may have success one day, and the other the next; but their carrying this custom to the town, or to agriculture, is striking at the root of industry; as industrious persons ought to be rewarded, and the lazy suffer for their indolence.

They have scarcely any penal laws: the principal punishment is degrading: even murder is not punished by any formal law, only the friends of the murdered are at liberty to slay the murderer, if some atonement is not made. Their not annexing penalties to their laws, is perhaps not as great a crime, or as unjust and cruel, as the bloody penal laws of England, which we have so long shamefully practised, and which are in force in this state, until our penitentiary house is finished, which is now building, and then they are to be repealed.

Let us also take a view of the advantages attending Indian police: They are not oppressed or perplexed with expensive litigation—They are not injured by legal robbery—They have no splendid villains that make themselves grand and great upon other peoples labor—They have neither church or state erected as money-making machines.

On Their Discipline and Method of War

I have often heard the British officers call the Indians the undisciplined savages, which is a capital mistake—as they have all the essentials of discipline. They are under good command, and punctual in obeying orders: they can act in concert, and when their officers lay a plan and give orders, they will chearfully unite in putting all their directions into immediate execution; and by each man observing the motion or movement of his right hand companion, they can communicate the motion from right to left, and march a-breast in concert, and in scattered order, though the line may be more than a mile long, and continue, if occasion requires, for a considerable distance, without disorder or confusion. They can perform various necessary maneuvers, either slowly, or as fast as they can run: they can form a circle, or semi-circle: the circle they make use of, in order to sur-round their enemy, and the semi-circle, if the enemy has a river on one side of them. They can also form a large hollow square, face out and take trees: this they do, if their enemies are about surrounding them, to prevent be-ing shot from either side of the tree. When they go into battle, they are not loaded or encumbered with many clothes, as they commonly fight naked, save only breech-clout, leggins and mockasons. There is no such thing as corporeal punishment used, in order to bring them under such good disci-pline: degrading is the only chastisement, and they are so unanimous in this, that it effectually answers the purpose. Their officers plan, order and conduct matters until they are brought into action, and then each man is to fight as though he was to gain the battle himself. General orders are commonly given in time of battle, either to advance or retreat, and is done by a shout or yell, which is well understood, and then they retreat or ad-vance in concert. They are generally well equipped, and exceeding expert and active in the use of arms. Could it be supposed that undisciplined troops could defeat Generals Braddock, Grant, etc.? It may be said by some that the French were also engaged in this war: true, they were; yet I know it was the Indians that laid the plan, and with small assistance put it into execution. The Indians had no aid from the French, or any other power, when they besieged Fort Pitt, in the year 1763, and cut off the com-munication for a considerable time, between that post and Fort Loudon, and would have defeated Gen. Bouquet's army, (who were on the way to raise the siege,) had it not been for the assistance of the Virginia volunteers. They had no British troops with them when they defeated Colonel Craw-ford, near the Sandusky, in the time of the American war with Great Brit-ain; or when they defeated Colonel Loughrie, on the Ohio, near the Miami, on his way to meet General Clarke: this was also in the time of the British war. It was the Indians alone that defeated Colonel Todd, in Kentucky, near the Blue licks, in the year 1782; and Colonel Harmar, betwixt the Ohio and Lake Erie, in the year 1790, and General St. Clair, in the year 1791; and it is said that there were more of our men killed at this defeat, than there were in any one battle during our contest with Great Britain. They had no aid when they fought even the Virginia rifle-men almost a whole day, at the Great Kanhawa, in the year 1774; and when they found they could not prevail against the Virginians, they made a most artful re-treat. Notwithstanding they had the Ohio to cross, some continued firing, whilst others were crossing the river; in this manner they proceeded until they all got over, before the Virginians knew that they had retreated; and in this retreat, they carried off all their wounded. In most of the foregoing defeats, they fought with an inferior number, though in this, I believe it was not the case.

Nothing can be more unjustly represented, than the different accounts we have had of their number from time to time, both by their own computations and that of the British. While I was among them, I saw the account of the number that they in those parts gave to the French, and kept it by me. When they, in their own council-house, were taking an account of their number, with a piece of bark newly stripped, and a small stick, which answered the end of a slate and a pencil, I took an account of the different nations and tribes, which I added together, and found there were not half the number, which they had given the French; and though they were then their allies, and lived among them, it was not easy finding out the deception, as they were a wandering set, and some of them almost always in the woods hunting. I asked one of the chiefs what was their reason for making such different returns? He said it was for political reasons, in order to obtain greater presents from the French, by telling them they could not divide such and such quantities of goods among so many.

In the year of General Bouquet's last campaign, 1764, I saw the official return made by the British officers, of the number of Indians that were in arms against us that year, which amounted to thirty thousand. As I was then a lieutenant in the British service, I told them I was of opinion that there were not above one thousand in arms against us, as they were divided by Broadstreet's army being then at Lake Erie. The British officers hooted at me, and said they could not make England sensible of the difficulties they labored under in fighting them, as England expect that their troops could fight the undisciplined savages in America, five to one, as they did the East Indians, and therefore my report would not answer their purpose, as they could not give an honorable account of the war, but by augmenting their number. I am of opinion that from Braddock's war, until the present time, there never were more than three thousand Indians at any time, in arms against us, west of Fort Pitt, and frequently not half that number. According to the Indians' own accounts, during the whole of Braddock's war, or from 1755, till 1758, they killed or took fifty of our people, for one that they lost. In the war that commenced in the year 1763, they killed comparatively few of our people, and lost more of theirs, as the frontiers (especially the Virginians) had learned something of their method of war: yet, they in this war, according to their own accounts, (which I believe to be true,) killed or took ten of our people, for one they lost.

Let us now take a view of the blood and treasure that was spent in opposing, comparatively, a few Indian warriors, with only some assistance from the French, the first four years of the war. Additional to the amazing destruction and slaughter that the frontiers sustained, from James river to Susquehanna, and about thirty miles broad; the following campaigns were also carried on against the Indians: General Braddock's, in the year 1755;

Colonel Armstrong's against the Cattanyan town, on the Allegheny, 1757; General Forbes's, in 1758; General Stanwick's, in 1759; General Monkton's, in 1760; Colonel Bouquet's in 1761—and 1763, when he fought the battle of Brushy Run, and lost above one hundred men; but, by the assistance of Virginia volunteers, drove the Indians: Colonel Armstrong's, up the west branch of Susquehanna, in 1763; General Broadstreet's, up Lake Erie, in 1764; General Bouquet's, against the Indians at Muskingum, in 1764; Lord Dunmore's, in 1774; General M'Intosh's, in 1778: Colonel Crawford's, shortly after his; General Clarke's, in 1778–1780; Colonel Bowman's, in 1779; General Clarke's, in 1782—against the Wabash, in 1786; General Logan's, against the Shawanees, in 1786; General Wilkinson's, in ———; Colonel Harmar's, in 1790; and General St. Clair's, in 1791; which, in all, are twenty-two campaigns, besides smaller expeditions—such as the French Creek expedition, Colonels Edwards's, Loughrie's, etc. All these were exclusive of the number of men that were internally employed as scouting parties, and in erecting forts, guarding stations, etc. When we take the foregoing occurrences into consideration, may we not reasonably conclude, that they are the best disciplined troops in the known world? Is it not the best discipline that has the greatest tendency to annoy the enemy and save their own men? I apprehend that the Indian discipline is as well calculated to answer the purpose in the woods of America, as the British discipline in Flanders: and British discipline in the woods, is the way to have men slaughtered, with scarcely any chance of defending themselves.

Let us take a view of the benefits we have received, by what little we have learned of their art of war, which cost us dear, and the loss we have sustained for want of it, and then see if it will not be well worth our while to retain what we have, and also to endeavor to improve in this necessary branch of business. Though we have made considerable proficiency in this line, and in some respects out-do them, viz. as marksmen, and in cutting our rifles,[52] and keeping them in good order; yet, I apprehend, we are far behind in their maneuvers, or in being able to surprize, or to prevent a surprize. May we not conclude, that the progress we had made in their art of war, contributed considerably towards our success, in various respects, when contending with Great Britain for liberty? Had the British king attempted to enslave us before Braddock's war, in all probability he might readily have done it, because, except the New Englanders, who had formerly been engaged in war with the Indians, we were unacquainted with

---

[52] A rifle, unlike a musket, has a bore cut with a spiral groove that imparts a spin to the ball fired from it, increasing its accuracy.

any kind of war: but after fighting such a subtile and barbarous enemy as the Indians, we were not terrified at the approach of British red-coats. Was not Burgoyne's defeat[53] accomplished, in some measure, by the Indian mode of fighting? and did not General Morgan's rifle-men, and many others, fight with greater success, in consequence of what they had learned of their art of war? Kentucky would not have been settled at the time it was, had the Virginians been altogether ignorant of this method of war.

In Braddock's war, the frontiers were laid waste for above three hundred miles long, and generally about thirty broad, excepting some that were living in forts, and many hundreds, or perhaps thousands, killed or made captives, and horses, and all kinds of property carried off: but, in the next Indian war, though we had the same Indians to cope with, the frontiers almost all stood their ground, because they were by this time, in some measure, acquainted with their maneuvers; and the want of this in the first war, was the cause of the loss of many hundred of our citizens, and much treasure.

Though large volumes have been wrote on morality, yet it may be all summed up in saying, do as you would wish to be done by: so the Indians sum up the art of war in the following manner:

The business of the private warriors is to be under command, or punctually to obey orders—to learn to march a-breast in scattered order, so as to be in readiness to surround the enemy, or to prevent being surrounded—to be good marksmen, and active in the use of arms—to practice running—to learn to endure hunger or hardships with patience and fortitude—to tell the truth at all times to their officers, but more especially when sent out to spy the enemy.

Concerning Officers—They say that it would be absurd to appoint a man an officer whose skill and courage had never been tried—that all officers should be advanced only according to merit—that no one man should have the absolute command of an army—that a council of officers are to determine when, and how an attack is to be made—that it is the business of the officers to lay plans to take every advantage of the enemy—to ambush and surprize them, and to prevent being ambushed and surprized themselves—it is the duty of officers to prepare and deliver speeches to the men, in order to animate and encourage them; and on the march, to prevent the men, at any time, from getting into a huddle, because if the enemy should surround them in this position, they would be exposed to the

---

[53] General John Burgoyne, whose forces captured Jane McCrea, and who was soon after defeated at Saratoga, New York, in October 1777.

enemy's fire. It is likewise their business at all times to endeavor to annoy their enemy, and save their own men, and therefore ought never to bring on an attack without considerable advantage, or without what appeared to them the sure prospect of victory, and that with the loss of few men; and if at any time they should be mistaken in this, and are like to lose many men by gaining the victory, it is their duty to retreat, and wait for a better opportunity of defeating their enemy, without the danger of losing so many men. Their conduct proves that they act upon these principles; therefore it is, that from Braddock's war to the present time, they have seldom ever made an unsuccessful attack. The battle at the mouth of the Great Kanhawa[54] is the greatest instance of this; and even then, though the Indians killed about three for one they lost, yet they retreated. The loss of the Virginians in this action was seventy killed, and the same number wounded— The Indians lost twenty killed on the field, and eight, who died afterward, of their wounds. This was the greatest loss of men that I ever knew the Indians to sustain in any one battle. They will commonly retreat if their men are falling fast—they will not stand cutting like the Highlanders or other British troops: but this proceeds from a compliance with their rules of war, rather than cowardice. If they are surrounded they will fight while there is a man of them alive, rather than surrender. When Colonel John Armstrong surrounded the Kittaning town, on the Allegheny river, Captain Jacobs, a Delaware chief, with some warriors, took possession of a house, defended themselves for some time, and killed a number of our men. As Jacobs could speak English, our people called on him to surrender. He said that he and his men were warriors, and they would all fight while life remained. He was again told that they should be well used if they would only surrender; and if not, the house should be burnt down over their heads—Jacobs replied he could eat fire; and when the house was in a flame, he, and they that were with him, came out in a fighting position, and were all killed. As they are a sharp, active kind of people, and war is their principal study, in this they have arrived at considerable perfection. We may learn of the Indians what is useful and laudable, and at the same time lay aside their barbarous proceeding. It is much to be lamented, that some of our frontier rifle-men are too prone to imitate them in their inhumanity. During the British war, a considerable number of men from below Fort Pitt, crossed the Ohio, and marched into a town of friendly Indians, chiefly Delawares, who professed the Moravian religion. As the Indians apprehended no danger, they neither lifted arms nor fled. After these rifle-men were some time

---

[54] At Point Pleasant, West Virginia, in 1774. A key battle of Dunmore's War.

in the town, and the Indians altogether in their power, in cool blood, they massacred the whole town, without distinction of age or sex.[55] This was an act of barbarity beyond any thing I ever knew to be committed by the savages themselves.

Why have we not made greater proficiency in the Indian art of war? It is because we are too proud to imitate them, even though it should be a means of preserving the lives of many of our citizens? No! We are not above borrowing language from them, such as homony, pone, tomahawk, etc. which is of little or no use to us. I apprehend that the reasons why we have not improved more in this respect are as follows: no important acquisition is to be obtained but by attention and diligence; and as it is easier to learn to move and act in concert, in close order, in the open plain, than to act in concert in scattered order in the woods, so it is easier to learn our discipline than the Indian maneuvers. They train up their boys in the art of war from the time they are twelve or fourteen years of age; whereas, the principal chance our people had of learning, was by observing their maneuvers when in action against us. I have been long astonished that no one has written upon this important subject, as their art of war would not only be of use to us in case of another rupture with them; but were only part of our men taught this art, accompanied with our continental discipline, I think no European power, after trial, would venture to shew its head in the American woods.

If what I have wrote should meet the approbation of my countrymen, perhaps I may publish more upon this subject, in a future edition.

---

[55] This 1782 massacre destroyed the mission of Gnaddenhutten, founded by the German Moravian missionaries David Zeisberger and John Heckewelder.

A Legend of the American Revolution

JANE McCREA

During the American War of Independence, captivity narratives changed their ideological thrust. The enemy to which the Indians were equated was no longer the French Catholics but the British redcoats. And consistent with the ideals of the Revolution, captivity was figured less as a conversion or test of faith and more as a violation of the individual's rights of freedom and self-determination. Moreover, since Indian allies of the British were fighting only in limited areas, some narratives employed the devices of the genre but dispensed with the Indians altogether. For example, Ethan Allen, the Vermont patriot who organized a group of guerrilla fighters dubbed the Green Mountain Boys, published a book recounting in sensational terms his imprisonment in England and celebrating his own rugged primitivism over his captors' sophistication.

The tale of Jane McCrea and her redcoat fiancé, like that of Pocahontas and John Smith, combines love and war and arises out of contested and uncertain historical events. Although McCrea's story is not widely known today outside the upper Hudson Valley region where it took place, it was one of the most sensational real-life dramas of the Revolutionary period. General Horatio Gates as well as his commander George Washington used McCrea's murder for wartime propaganda, accusing British general John Burgoyne of paying Indians for the scalps of murdered civilians. Contemporary periodicals quickly picked up on the story, and it helped build support for and increase enlistment in the Revolutionary army. It inspired poetry and paintings by leading artists throughout the nineteenth century, and figured in histories by Washington Irving, Mercy Otis Warren, and many others. Joel Barlow, revolutionary poet and politician, included McCrea's story (changing her name to Lucinda) in *The Columbiad,* his epic poem for the new nation. He then commissioned a painting by John Vanderlyn, which is reproduced below. The painting, Barlow hoped, would capture his lines:

> She starts, with eyes upturn'd and fleeting breath,
> In their raised axes views her instant death,
> Spreads her white hands to heaven in frantic prayer,

Figure Three: John Vanderlyn, *Death of Jane McCrea* (ca. 1804) Oil on canvas. Courtesy of the Wadsworth Atheneum, Hartford. Purchased by the Wadsworth Atheneum.

Then runs to grasp their knees and crouches there.
Her hair, half lost along the shrubs she past,
Rolls in loose tangles round her lovely waist;
Her kerchief torn betrays the globes of snow
That heave responsive to her weight of woe.
Does all this eloquence suspend the knife?
Does no superior bribe contest her life?
There does: the scalps by British gold are paid;
A long-hair'd scalp adorns that heavenly head;
And comes the sacred spoil from friend or foe,
No marks distinguish and no man can know. (bk. 6, ll. 661–74)

Vanderlyn's work has since eclipsed these rhymes in importance, for the melodrama of young Jane's exposed bosom and luxuriant hair under assault from two muscular and swarthy Mohawks is much more provocative in visual form than in verse. Art critic Samuel Edgerton has studied ten other paintings and engravings of the murder and has demonstrated how these images developed a tradition independent of the written sources for the event.

Michel René Hilliard d'Auberteuil's *Mis MacRea* (corrected to *Miss McCrea* in translation) was published seven years after the title character's celebrated death and thus became the second literary portrayal of the murder and the events that led to it, (the first being a brief mention in Philip Freneau's 1778 poem "America Independent"). Although the title page says Philadelphia, the book was actually printed in Brussels, Belgium. In the polarized political climate of the 1780s such a book could not have appeared in Britain. In fact, loyalists had their own version of McCrea's death—according to some English and Canadian accounts, she was killed by a stray patriot bullet, not by Indians in the service of Burgoyne. France, on the other hand, was an ally of the United States, and radical French republicans like Hilliard d'Auberteuil were greatly inspired by American independence in their own hopes for a revolution in France. Thus, although it was published in French, the novel is very much a part of the patriotic and sentimental literature surrounding the American Revolution.

Today he is virtually unknown among early American writers, but Hilliard d'Auberteuil traveled through the Northeast in 1777 and 1778 and published a two-volume history of the American colony and nation, in which he mentioned the McCrea incident. He also wrote a book based on his earlier travels to the Island of St. Domingue (Hispaniola) and several other works. Hilliard d'Auberteuil's attacks on the abuses against African slaves in St. Domingue in his earlier writings were informed by the radical politics of the Enlightenment and caused him continual trouble with the

French authorities. *Miss McCrea* is also a strongly political work, as it combines the bare facts of the event with concerns about political loyalty, which were magnified by the Revolution, and about family. As a preface to the work states, "to embellish his subject, the author has added everything that could be allowed." He changed the name of Jane's lover from David Jones to Belton, and of her father, the Reverend James McCrea, who actually died in 1769, to Nathaniel, a fervent patriot and a central character in the story.

June Namias has written in her fine study of the Jane McCrea legend that it functioned as "a warning against the dangers of female autonomy and misdirected emotion" (140–41). In *Miss McCrea,* as in two better-known sentimental novels of the Early Republic, Susanna Rowson's *Charlotte Temple* and Hannah Webster Foster's *The Coquette,* a virtuous tragic heroine falls in love with a handsome yet dangerous man, disobeys parental advice, and suffers an untimely death. In *Miss McCrea,* however, the political meaning of the tale is much more overt. Her love leads her toward treason, for the pageantry of Belton and his uniformed troops convince her that the cause of the patriots is hopeless, and she persists in this belief even when threatened with punishment (as many loyalists were). Her father, Nathaniel, is perhaps too zealous in his support of the revolutionary cause—he abandons his daughter to join the war effort. Hilliard d'Auberteuil also introduces several supporting characters who have no basis in any of the fragmentary historical sources: Rachel Rideworld and Betsy, who serve as procuresses to set up Belton's rendezvous with Jane, reflect popular prejudice against the Jews and the Irish. Emilia Fairlove, as the girl whose virtue and chastity is already lost to the seducer, plays the dark double to Jane. Finally, Kiashuta appears as a favorable counterpart to Belton, although he is doomed to an honorable death, as many Indian chiefs were in literature of the period. Although the Indian captivity does not occur until the final scenes of the novel, the entire work is characteristic of how the captivity genre began to intersect with other concerns in popular literature in the late eighteenth century, particularly the issues of the independence of young women and the relationship between sexual and political virtue. Because the scholarly studies of this novel are few, the list of supplementary readings includes works on the captivity narrative during the Revolutionary period.

Source

Hilliard d'Auberteuil, Michel René. *Miss McCrea: A Novel of the American Revolution.* 1784. Trans. Eric LaGuardia. Gainesville: Scholars', 1958.

Supplementary Readings

Amelia, or the Faithless Briton: An Original American Novel. Boston: Spotswood, 1798.

Barlow, Joel. *The Columbiad.* Philadelphia: Conrad, 1809.

Foster, Hannah Webster. *The Coquette.* 1797. Rpt. New York: Oxford UP, 1986.

Freneau, Philip. *The Poems of Philip Freneau, Poet of the American Revolution.* Ed. Fred Lewis Pattee. Vol. 1. Princeton: University Library, 1902–1907. 271–82.

Irving, Washington. *The Life of George Washington.* 5 vols. New York: Putnam, 1855–59.

Leary, Lewis. Introduction. *Miss McCrea: A Novel of the American Revolution.* Gainesville: Scholars', 1958.

Namias, June. *White Captives: Gender and Ethnicity on the American Frontier.* Chapel Hill: U of North Carolina P, 1993. 117–44.

Rowson, Susanna. *Charlotte Temple.* 1791. Rpt. New York: Oxford UP, 1986.

Warren, Mercy Otis. *History of the Rise, Progress, and Termination of the American Revolution.* Boston: Manning, 1805.

MISS McCREA:
A NOVEL OF THE
AMERICAN REVOLUTION

Michel René
Hilliard d'Auberteuil

Publisher's Preface (1784)

We enjoy novels. We read them earnestly because in them we find sentiments similar to our own. When they portray truthfully the heart of a man,
his emotions, his pleasures, and his sorrows, we can not tear ourselves
away from such interesting reading. We think and act with characters who
are often imaginary; we share their hardships and their joys. Since no emotion, however delightful it may be, can be lasting without becoming difficult to endure, we devour each page of a novel. We hurry to the end without being able to interrupt ourselves, like a lover who does not prolong his
bliss by slackening the signs of his ardor but hastens to consummate it.

No topic is more moving to me than the story of *Miss McCrea*. It offers the reader a description of emotions that he himself has felt, together
with the hardships these may entail; we can observe many struggles in it,
of which war is the most dazzling and most horrible; and finally it presents descriptions of a rich new land that will long hold the interest of European nations.

The essence of this story is, unfortunately, too true; but the accessory
details are the author's. They reflect a vivid imagination which perceives
subjects in all the brilliance of their coloring long after they have ceased
to exist.

We deemed it wise to change the name of the English officer; to embellish his subject, the author has added everything that could be allowed.
By contrasting the fierceness of the Indians with the good qualities of their
leaders, and American innocence with European vices, he has displayed

the causes and the development of prejudice. History has given him his subject, but the way it is told is, without doubt, original.

The French language is not very poetic and lends itself poorly to verse. What in France is called a poem is often a work of patience rather than of genius. The difficulty of rhyming and the defects of meter and prosody hinder the expressiveness and beauty of figures of speech. In a French line too many useless words are inserted; in heroic couplets the second line often owes its existence merely to the necessity of rhyming it with the first. That is why Fenelon, although born a poet, wrote his *Telemaque* and Montesquieu his *Temple de Gnide* in prose. Nothing is more poetic than some of the passages of the *Nouvelle Heloise,* yet J. J. Rousseau rarely wrote in verse.

The author of *Miss McCrea,* not caring to have his work called a poem, will be pleased if readers prefer it to many works in verse.

I

I am setting out to tell of the misfortunes brought about by love. I write for innocent young girls who fear the consequences of such a natural yet dangerous inclination.

Manhattan Island, lying in the mouth of the famous Hudson River, bristled with fortifications, entrenchments, and batteries of cannon. This island, once so peaceful and happy, was now to the observer a regrettable scene of preparations for war and of the remains of its former prosperity. Forts were built in the middle of blooming orchards and alongside farmhouses. In the city of New York, lately so flourishing, valuable beaver pelts had been removed from the shops in order to make room for guns and military stores; and the counting-house had been converted into an army headquarters. English ships had cast anchor off Staten Island [in July, 1776]. After swarms of ferocious and well-disciplined German soldiers were debarked on Long Island, brutal and bloody crimes were committed there by them. General Washington had saved the remnants of his army by a prudent retreat over the piles of bodies on the battlefield. The blood of the soldiers, mingling with the flowing brooks, had reddened the edges of the sea.

Such are the horrors of civil war. From all corners of Europe friends and kin, accompanied by mercenary assassins, flocked to America to slaughter their own friends and kin. Neither the distance that separates the two continents nor the raging sea that fills man with dread and shows his weakness at every moment could appease their fury. Their general was William Howe. Already thirty thousand men had landed on the banks of the Hudson River, and after feeble resistance the terrified Americans retreated to Kingsbridge.[1] The citizens scurried to the countryside, carrying their most valuable belongings. Swooning women, supported by their husbands, were themselves holding the fruit of their wedlock. Everyone was fleeing, not knowing which way to run. The bloodthirsty Germans were on every street, and with an excess of wine to add to their barbarism they killed anyone who obstructed their way. They broke into homes, stores, and warehouses. They poured away torrents of rum and beer intended for the refreshment of the laboring men of this commercial city. The noise of the artillery; the cries of the women, children, and old folks; the shouts of the bargemen struggling to save themselves by going back up the river, added to the general desolation of the scene.

During this turmoil Miss Jane McCrea was alone in her father's house. With disheveled hair and hands raised to the sky, she voiced vain prayers to Him who hurls the thunderbolt and brings peace.

"Thou," she said, "who once suffered the banks of the Jordan to be bathed in Thy people's blood, restore us to happiness and peace. Spare our brothers who march under Washington's banner; they support Thy cause by supporting their country's, for one can not cease loving his country without failing in his duty toward Thy laws."[2]

Toward the end of the day, when the carnage of war could only be dimly seen, Jane heard the doors of the house burst open and soldiers clatter in with their weapons. Mustering her courage, the innocence of her heart giving her assurance, she dared to face her enemies.

Captain Belton, followed by several English grenadiers, presented himself to her. She saw in the light of the flickering torches that he was in the flower of youth, but this only made him seem more terrible. Disheveled blond hair covered the beauty of his brow; his fiery eyes seemed only to foretell death; blood covered his face; and his erect figure and stately manner only made him appear all the more formidable. Jane was not able to stifle a cry, but what was her surprise when all of a sudden she saw the look of fierceness that had frightened her change to one of kindness and gentleness, and heard a sweet and tender voice pronounce words of reassurance.

---

[1] The historical setting at the beginning of the American Revolution, with the names of the British generals and the itinerary of George Washington's retreat, is basically accurate, although the number of British troops is exaggerated.

[2] We must caution the reader that Americans are, in general, very pious and are accustomed to the language of the Holy Book, which they use in their conversation on every important occasion. Their wives and daughters are likewise nourished by the Scriptures, and on Sunday each family assembles to read from the Bible. The author has felt obliged to put as much verisimilitude in the utterances ascribed to them as in the descriptions of their customs. [Original publisher's note.]

"Whoever you are, do not be afraid. Without doubt you are the most beautiful girl in this land. We have not come to fight enemies such as you. We put our weapons down. If I dare to enter your house, it is only to give you protection; my companions and I are entirely at your command."

Jane was affected by this speech; her face, that of a sixteen-year-old, reddened with blushes. The emotion of love, which seizes every faculty as quickly as a flash of lightning, pierced her heart.

"What!" she said to him. "As an enemy of my country do you respect my sex and the weakness of my age? Are the English of Europe not as cruel as I have been told? But how about yourself? Are you not in need of assistance? That blood which I see flowing—"

Indeed, during the attack Belton had received a wide but hardly dangerous wound over his right eye. Since he had not wished to interrupt his military duties to have it dressed, he grew pale suddenly and collapsed from weakness. This was no longer a warrior who spread terror about him; this was a young man, wounded, sensitive, submissive, and worthy of compassion. His faintness was caused less by loss of blood than by the blow with which love had struck his heart. The shock precipitated by two contrary sensations had caused an emotion too acute for him to endure.

Jane drew near to him. The concern that she felt for him in this distressing situation swept away all other considerations. As she tried to revive him she believed herself merely charitable, but she was affectionate, too. After having washed Belton's wound with rum in which salt had been dissolved, she spread on it a few drops of fragrant and soothing sugar balm. In her eagerness she did not wait for the return of her servant to fetch the necessary bandages, but tore in pieces the kerchief that covered her fair bosom, which had been heaving violently for some moments.

Belton opened his eyes and saw her in this charming disarray. Her eyes met his, she became disconcerted, her hand trembled, she could not finish. He fell at her feet; respect, gratitude, and love overwhelmed all his senses. Jane raised him up and was supporting this dangerous enemy's head on her breast in order to bandage his wound, when Nathaniel McCrea, her father, entered the room.

This American, a rich and long-established trader in New York, had just begun all the necessary preparations to flee one hundred and twenty-five miles from the city to Manor County in the neighborhood of Albany, where he owned some prosperous farms on the banks of the Hudson. He had determined to abandon his home and all untransportable possessions to plunder rather than submit to the conqueror.

"Jane, what is this I see?" he cried. "Has not the horror which the soldiers of George III, instruments of our enslavement, should inspire been able to suppress in your heart the sentiment of mercy? Come to my arms, my daughter. Preserve this compassion, virtue's consort. But come; we must hurry to flee this ruthless one whom you have consented to assist. These vile agents of European tyranny are human only in outward appearance. You would like to nurse him back to health; but not only has he reduced your father and his friends to despair, he would, if he could, take away even your innocence and break your heart."

At these words Belton arose and colored. Haughtiness reappeared in his countenance.

"You are unarmed," he said to McCrea, "and I am your conqueror. Why trouble me with useless insults? However, you have a power over me which you could not have gained by force of arms, because you are the father of this lovely girl. Believe that I lament the fate that forces me to engage in war against you, but military honor does not allow me to cease to serve my sovereign. It is my duty to obey, and it does not behoove us to reason on the justice or vengeance of kings."

"So, then," replied Nathaniel with anger, "you renounce man's most precious rights, liberty and justice; and you want to make us slaves like you! Permit me—permit me to save my daughter, or take my life!"

Belton and Jane combined their efforts to calm the irritated old man and to lessen his desperation and anger. Belton beseeched him not to leave the house, not to hazard being detained in the countryside by raging soldiers who had been rendered uncontrollable by arrogance in victory and by a lust for spoils. He implored him to remain within his house until the disorder that accompanies every conquest was entirely abated. He told him that General Howe had prohibited the perpetration of violence or of harmful acts against inhabitants of the city who remained in their homes. Accordingly, he had afforded protection to all who requested it, personally dispatching detachments to search all homes that appeared deserted, and assuring himself, before they were given up to pillage, that no one remained inside.

"I do not object," he added, "to your desire to follow the example of the American Congress. Forget the name of enemy; I ceased to be one on seeing your daughter. But wait at least one day; one day more and you will be able to leave without running any risk. I myself will escort you, and all that belongs to you will be respected."

Nathaniel appeared to be inflexible at first, but his daughter was shedding tears. He trembled at the thought of seeing her pursued through the fields by fierce soldiers. He agreed to spend twenty-four more hours in these surroundings which added to his anguish by reminding him of happy days—days that would never return.

Belton remained with them a few moments longer. He was a man of intelligence, he had traveled, and he possessed to an eminent degree that false good breeding and dexterity of language which, lending itself to the concerns of others, only too often conceals a hard and deceitful heart. While listening to him, Miss McCrea became less sensible to the public calamity, and Nathaniel went so far as to express his regret that this amiable warrior, whom he found to be worthy of fighting the natural and hereditary enemies of Great Britain, had taken part in the most evil of causes. Belton replied that this was the effect of what the nobles of England called duty. Finally, night having already come, he took leave of father and daughter, and placed a sentinel outside the house.

This good man, Nathaniel, was unable to enjoy any rest; ideas of liberty, oppression, and natural rights occupied his thoughts. All the odious events that had taken place during the American war passed through his mind. He saw nothing but young girls cornered and trembling at the licentious conduct of an unrestrained grenadier, Indians armed with hatchets, and villages on fire. He prayed for consolation from the God of Jerusalem, the God of mercy who had delivered the Hebrews from the Egyptian captivity. He continually repeated passages from the Bible, the inexhaustible source of relief for the afflicted, where the eloquence of the soul is found on every page like a fountain that never runs dry.

Jane, innocent Jane, could not close her eyes or forget for one instant the image of Captain Belton. She remembered his gentle voice, his handsome features; she described to herself the dangers he must have experienced. She imagined she saw him triumph over an American regiment single-handed; she imagined she saw an enemy saber strike his forehead, and his arm plunge a sword into the ribs of the audacious rebel who had dared to wound him. She was in this languorous, weak, and rapturous state which follows a lengthy reverie, when the sound of bagpipes suddenly startled her.

The break of day brought to light the misfortunes of New York. In the streets one could see stripped bodies, homes that had been broken into, young girls tearing their hair and running, without knowing where, to hide their shame and their misery. The valleys resounded with the cries of shepherds as they tried to gather their vagabond flocks in the surrounding countryside.

Jane lent an attentive ear, but she could distinguish nothing clearly in the confusion of so many diverse noises, just as those who station themselves on an eminence above a large city to listen silently to the murmur of men working and bestirring themselves hear a din which they would not have noticed if they had remained active in the scene below.

Her confusion was augmented by a military band of English Guards and Hessian and Brunswick soldiers sounding reveille. The shores of Manhattan had never heard anything so flawless. The sounds of flute, clarinet,

French horn, and bassoon filled her with emotion. Presently they played a march that imitated the songs of Orpheus, and then a shepherd's dance. Thus does the man who is clever at deceiving himself with respect to his ferocity blend the tones of joy with the carnage and horror of war. Nathaniel's conscience murmured at this. "Alas," it said, "the people of God danced before the ark after exterminating the Philistines; and now the people of God, divided into opposing parties, strive to annihilate each other."

Jane, although still true to the principles that her father had instilled in her against the vices of Europe, was not able to restrain an admiration for its arts.

Belton appeared in the morning to pay a visit to Jane and her father. He seemed much more amiable; yet he had, altogether, a friendly and respectful air which nature alone had not given him and which Jane had never noticed in her own young countrymen. He told Nathaniel that the English army was about to set out on a march in order to attack Kingsbridge, the military post which Washington had proposed to defend to the death; and that General Howe would remain in the city only long enough to receive the oaths of allegiance of those who wished to again come under the authority of George III. Belton added that the army would pass by at noon, and promised them that before nightfall he would return to the city to help them cross the Hudson and look out for their safety. Nathaniel could not refuse him thanks. Jane's gratitude was filled with naive affection, which the young officer noticed with pleasure. Everything conspired to lead this obliging American astray.

It had not been more than an hour after the captain terminated his visit when the army began its march. In crossing the city the army had to pass before the house of McCrea. This worthy man had secluded himself with books likely to soothe the anguish of a Puritan philosopher. Jane could not refrain from stationing herself behind the blinds to watch the passing of the troops and her lover. She was immediately charmed by the splendor of the arms, the vivid and varied colors of the uniforms, the precision of the battalions, and the skill and promptitude of the leaders as they directed the movements of their men in a hundred different ways. Stalwart horses at the rear of each regiment pulled gun-metal cannon which glistened in the sun so that they seemed to be on fire. Banners, covered with rich armorials and military devices, indicated the road the soldiers must follow to victory or to death. At the head of each corps, marching bands regulated the pace of the great army. Jane noticed, among the German officers, the brave Kniphausen and the handsome Colonel von Donop, who was later killed in the attack on Fort Red Bank; and among the English she saw General Howe, always courageous but addicted to the pleasures of indulgence. How her heart fluttered when she saw Belton at the head of a company of English Guards. He was mounted upon a white horse adorned with braid and superbly harnessed. He possessed the dignity of Mars and the beauty of Apollo; the kerchief that covered his wound seemed to be Cupid's.

When he was scarcely within ten steps of the window where Jane was seated, he cast his eyes upward and gazed at the house. He saw a girl behind the blind and, certain that it was the beautiful Jane, immediately made a deep bow to her, and with so much nobility and grace that he would have succeeded in charming a girl much more accustomed to flattery. Belton was imitated by three other officers of the same company, which constrained Jane to withdraw, but with her face aflame and her eyes bathed with tears. It was at this moment that she became aware of the arrows that love had cast into her heart. She was through steeping herself in a melancholy poison; she was no longer afraid of love.

She convinced herself that it would not take long for an army so powerful to subdue the American troops, so poorly armed and even more poorly disciplined. Possibly, from that moment on, she began to wish it. At the very least she hoped that the Americans would be forced to sue for peace, so that her fondness for Belton would speedily be permitted expression. She could not conceal from herself how much her choice would offend Nathaniel when he discovered it, but the laws of the country did not allow her father to restrain her inclinations.

These ideas occupied her until nightfall. Meanwhile Belton had returned to the city to assist Nathaniel in his preparations for escape. When everything had been accomplished, and when the baggage, carried by their faithful servants, had been sent out on the route indicated by the captain, father and lover went up to Jane's room where she was waiting in silence.

"Come," Belton said to her. "Your happiness is a thousand times more important to me than my own. Outside the city you will find a boat ready to take you across the river, and horses waiting for you on the other side. What I am doing now, without guarding against the danger of appearing to have a liaison with the rebels, is very distressing since it is going to separate me from you for a long time, from you whom I adore. But I am well rewarded if I am able to contribute to your well-being and to prove to you how much I love you."

"You love me!" exclaimed Jane, abashed and bewildered, not knowing what she was saying. "But my father, I await his word—"

"He is here," answered Belton, pressing her hand that he had found in the darkness.

"Yes," said Nathaniel, "this generous enemy has been of service in helping to save all the things that will make living in retirement as comfortable as possible for you. I am charmed by his manner; he is worthy of having been born among us; and if he would agree to leave this horrible profession of war to live in our country, to renounce ambition and ostentation in order to seek happiness, I could not want you to have another man as husband."

Belton was unwilling to make any promise that would sever his connection with the service of George III. He remained true to that which he called his duty. Nathaniel, seeing that he was immovable, forbade his daughter to listen to him. The prohibition was useless—love had spoken.

While they conversed, and the various troubles that concerned them kept them engaged longer than was wise, the city took fire and became enveloped in flames. The west wind howled vehemently and abetted the plans of the arsonists. Some inhabitants, who had remained in the city under the pretext of surrendering to the conquerors and returning under the authority of the king, resolved to flee; they chose to burn their homes rather than let them become booty for the enemy.

Women cried, "Ground where we were born! We leave you forever rather than surrender our liberty." They ran through the streets carrying flaming torches and candles. The soldiers stopped one of the women. "What are you doing, mad woman?" asked an officer. She replied courageously, "I am setting the city afire!" Immediately they placed her in shackles, but they could not shake her firmness. "I saw my home burn," said another; "at least the tyrants will not have it. Now I will flee to the ocean and across the waves to find another homeland." Several women stabbed themselves at the very instant of capture.

The houses of New York, constructed entirely of wood, boarded with double layers of spruce, painted on the inside, and tarred on the outside and on the roof, ignited almost as soon as torches of resin and pitch were thrown on their roofs.

Belton and Nathaniel, taking Jane by the arms, tried to leave. The fire had already enveloped the stairs; eddies of flame, swirling up at them, threatened to choke father and daughter. Belton darted through the fire, broke down the burning doors, and made sure that they could get out. He rushed back upstairs, but he could not find Jane or the old trader. The old man's courage had been revived by the threat of danger to his daughter; after having wrapped her in something to lessen the impact of her fall, he seized her in his arms and hurled himself forward. He received no more than a bad bruise on the knee, and he did not notice it in such an exciting moment.

One section of the city was already burned out. Soldiers, scattered through the streets, instantly killed anyone they caught trying to revive the fire. Several arsonists were thrown into the flames that they themselves had kindled.

Jane, her father, and her lover left the city. Belton accompanied Jane to the other side of the river, where they parted most tenderly, promising to meet again, vowing to love each other forever, omitting nothing. Finally it was necessary to separate. Nathaniel and Jane, on horseback and preceded by their servants and their belongings, traveled all the rest of the night.

At daybreak they found themselves close to the famous falls that form the Hudson as the water cascades from the mountain tops. They crossed the gorge at West Point, studded with fortifications which have become, so to speak, the key to the western provinces of America. They came to Esopus, the village made memorable by the cruelties of the ferocious Vaughan. Everywhere they encountered bands of their countrymen who had traveled far to seek a refuge where they could await days of greater happiness.

Arriving at their home in Manor County, Nathaniel became so much more intensely distressed that nothing was able to comfort him. Jane, although continually occupied with thoughts of her love, was not able to restrain her tears when she thought of the misfortunes of her country. She shed them more abundantly when she thought of Belton and the dangers that he encountered every day. She was the first to inform herself of the news of the army and to read the newspapers that came from New York and Perth Amboy. She learned, before long, that the English had driven Washington's army from Kingsbridge, had forced the Americans to flee from Bergen to White Plains, and had seized the forts intended to prevent an entry into New Jersey.

Nathaniel was disconsolate. He gathered his neighbors together and addressed them, imploring the young men to take up arms. Jane, obliged to feel responsive to the public calamity, had difficulty in hiding her secret joy and her hope that she would soon see the colonies forced to surrender and sue for peace. It was the first time she had ever been compelled to pretend; her color and her eyes, moist with tears of love, were every moment near to betraying her.

II

While the minds of old McCrea and his daughter were troubled differently according to their interests and desires, a courier arrived. He brought from Albany the dispatches of Congress, and spread alarm and fear throughout the region. He stated that Washington had been deserted by

his army and that only two thousand men remained under his command;
that the English were threatening Philadelphia from no farther away than
twenty-five miles. He made public a proclamation from Congress asking
all men to take up arms and proceed promptly to defend the crossings of
the Delaware River, on the banks of which is situated the city of Philadelphia. Already its inhabitants, carrying their belongings, were withdrawing
into the interior of the country; and Congress had taken refuge in Baltimore, Maryland [in December, 1776].

"What we have in view," said this proclamation, "is to arouse the
citizens of Pennsylvania and of the adjacent states to a prompt and vigorous effort to oppose the army that at this moment threatens to seize our
principal city. A brief offer of resistance would be sufficient, since General
Lee is advancing with reinforcements. O, Philadelphia! Peaceful city, so
prosperous and happy, will you fall to the enemy? Will we rise to this opportunity to destroy their army, since it is now distant from the warships
which constitute their greatest power?"

With this message, Nathaniel in his warmth fancied himself repos-
sessed of his youthful vigor. He assembled the workmen and young men
of the region.

"My friends," he said to them, "although the winter of years has
whitened my hair, it has not frozen my courage. I shall march at your head
and lead you on the road of duty and honor. What! Shall mercenaries—
the refuse of Europe, bought for a few cents, our tyrants—triumph over
us? The English did well to hire German serfs to exterminate us. They do
not know what liberty is; ignorance gives them the boldness to fight us. Let
us show them what a man can do when he is driven by a love for the welfare of his country. Can you not hear the laments of your wives and daughters as they learn of the reverses suffered by our brothers in New Jersey?
Ah, each tear they shed is a command for you to set forth to protect them
to the last drop of your blood. See these trees that you planted! Will their
fruits be for the conqueror? And these children, the objects of your joy, did
God admit them to your love so that they may become enslaved? Do you
want to give them a heritage other than one of fetters?"

Immediately each man ran to fetch his rifle, and Nathaniel went to say
good-bye to his beloved Jane.

"I am leaving," he said to her. "I am going to join in the defense of the
country. I am old, but my blood can be useful to my country. I will take
the place of a younger man, and in this way preserve the generation of which
he will be the father. I have gathered three hundred of our young men; if I
can trust my presentiments and if all the leaders in the district have done
the same as I, nothing will be left to our tyrants but discipline and cruelty.
We will have courage and enough men; we shall vanquish them in good

season. Jane, promise me to renounce the mother country forever, never hereafter to use anything that has been produced or manufactured there, and not to contract an alliance with or marry anyone who desires to live as a subject of the king."

"Alas, father," Jane replied, "I would be false to such a vow. I am in love. I can not hide it from you any longer, and reason herself is in accord with my love. I love Belton. I find in him the model of virtues that you taught me to desire in the one who would be my husband. He is handsome, a sign of the candor of his heart; he seems to me to be like Joseph as he is described in the Holy Book; he combines courage with generosity, an enlightened mind with a kind heart. Ah, father, if you had seen him commanding his troops, you would have been convinced that the English are bound to triumph over us. Their music resembles the concert especially played by the cherubim for the God of war, and the precision of their battalions is comparable to that of the celestial army when it passed in review prior to conquering the arrogant demons. Give up, father, give up an unfortunate rebellion; hasten to withdraw from it before it becomes harder for us to accept the indignity of more shameful conditions. And of what importance is this myth of liberty and independence? Shall we not always be obliged to pay duties? Would it not be necessary for us to govern ourselves? What do we risk by leaving this troublesome problem to a powerful monarch who is willing to take the responsibility? Does he not offer us all that clemency can give: a pardon for our offense and protection as the price of our obedience? Remain quietly here with us in this comfortable retreat, and let time and necessity restore the peace."

"What do I hear, God of justice and liberty! Do you permit my daughter to desert our sacred cause!"

He was able to pronounce only these words. Tears ran down his cheeks, and soon a silent anguish took hold of his senses. But suddenly he arose, equipped himself with a saber and a rifle, and tearing himself from the arms of Jane, who tried in vain to restrain him, went to rejoin his young countrymen.

The men, having shortened their hair[3] and having gathered all the weapons they could find, were waiting only for McCrea to begin their journey. They were poorly clothed and in bare feet; a few sacks of flour and rice composed all their provisions; but they were brisk, jovial, and filled with fervor. They traveled seventy-five miles without rest. In all the towns through which they passed the citizens came out to offer them meat and fruit. Young girls—dressed in simple cotton or linen but as beautiful

---

[3] This style was adopted by many revolutionaries.

as virtue itself—carried gourds filled with rum and syrup, and promised to marry them if they returned victorious.

Jane, meanwhile remaining with her servants in her father's house, was thrown into deep distress. Her fears were divided constantly between her father and her lover. To add to this unhappiness, the rumor spread that she had become a Tory, that she was in love with an English officer, and that she kept up a correspondence with him. Those who were wont to call on her suddenly stopped their visits; she was shunned when she appeared in the village. Merchants and workmen refused to enter her house even for the most necessary errands. Travelers were advised not to go near the house, so that she was deprived of the sweet pleasure of having guests and showing her hospitality. She was the last to be informed of public news, and her servants did not dare to speak to anyone. During the time that she was thus forsaken, she suffered a severe but just punishment for infidelity to the duties of patriotism.

Washington's army grew larger every day. This skillful general, profiting by the first fervor of the warriors of the Republic who had sworn to consecrate their blood on the altar of liberty, had stormed the city of Trenton and surprised Princeton by clever maneuver. A great number of prisoners were taken in both battles. Finally, after forcing the English to abandon their positions and forgo for the year a siege of Philadelphia, and then rendering them inactive by enclosing them at New Brunswick, Washington made his encampment for the winter at Morristown. Fifteen days had been sufficient for this great man to strip clean the banks of the Delaware, put himself in control of New Jersey, and seize from the English the fruits of their victories.

Nathaniel made haste to inform his daughter of this by mail. Not knowing that the secret in her heart had become public, he burdened her with the responsibility of gathering the citizens of the district in his house to inform them of the happy events. However difficult this request appeared to Jane, however disagreeable it would be for her, she resolved to discharge it with a nobleness of spirit.

On receiving the invitation, everyone believed that she—as fickle women do everywhere—had changed her opinions with the circumstances. They rejoiced over it because they were fond of her. It had taken nothing less than a proclamation of Congress and a recognition of the seriousness of her shortcomings to force the people to despise so charming a Tory. When all the freeholders and people of note were in her presence, she said:

"Your sons and brothers have distinguished themselves by their bravery, and Washington has clad himself in glory. Read this letter from my father; he wants us to drink a toast together to the prosperity of the country. At my direction the fattest ox in the herd has been slaughtered; the best keg of strong beer has been opened; and added to that are fifty bottles of Madeira that have made the voyage from Europe four times, and ten flagons of old rum from Barbados. I feel very keenly the tears of joy and respect that the name of my father, a good and courageous old man, awakens in you now. I love him dearly, but you must excuse me if I do not adopt the general sentiment on public affairs. I have beheld Captain Belton, and he has shown me what to delight in. I have seen the English army, and it is clear to me what you should fear. Certainly we were happy under the authority of Great Britain, and it is doubtful that we shall enjoy such good fortune in our independence. Moreover, it is to be feared that a momentary success—which the enthusiasm of the Republic exaggerates, perhaps— would add to the anger of the king and delay a reconciliation, which is, believe me, our only hope."

Everyone gathered there was astonished to hear this girl, only seventeen, speak in such a manner. Several listeners thought as she did, but they did not dare to speak up for fear that they would be taken as Tories. They now applauded her speech; the effect thereof was such that the County Electors in the Assembly gave instructions to their representative in Congress to support any effort toward a reconciliation with the mother country.

Jane sought a way to inform her lover of the news. She had in her service a woman named Betsy, who had lived for a time among the Indians. This woman, born in Dublin, had been condemned by the courts of London to be transported to America for having been the accomplice in a crime. Her age, an enjoyment of life's amenities, and the example of proper morals seemed to have corrected her sinful tendencies. However, she retained a fancy for dangerous intrigue and a delight in talking of the luxury of Europe, which indicated how much she regretted being deprived of it. It was she whom Jane chose to be her confidante.

Betsy undertook to send a letter to Belton by an extremely artful Indian warrior who, under the pretext of trading furs, mingled with both the English and the Americans; he had been successively and under different circumstances a spy for each party. Belton received Jane's letter with transports of joy, and gave ten guineas and a flask of brandy to the messenger, who promised faithfully to carry back the reply.

The cunning Betsy attached a note of her own to Miss McCrea's letter. It was expressed in these terms:

"I do not know you, but you are a military man, and that is enough to show that you are gallant and generous. In me you will find a loyal friend; I can serve you well near my young mistress, who is already more than fond of you. I am not aware if you know how much wealth she has. Her father's holdings in Manor County, not to mention what could be saved of their property in New York, come to more than seven thousand pounds sterling in income. And she is an only daughter. I will pledge myself to bring about your marriage if you promise to give me two thousand guineas so that I may return to England, for I am vexed at having been exiled so long. I speak to her constantly of the delights of London and the difference between our amiable lords and the sober Americans, to whom each day is the same. Indeed, life is hardly worth living here, and I am anxious that this wretched rebellion should come to an end. For the accomplishment of this I rely on you and your companions; your forte is to conquer and to please."

Such zeal did not remain uncompensated. Belton entrusted to the Indian a small package for Betsy; it contained a piece of muslin from India, beautifully embroidered with gold, and the promise of two thousand guineas in case the marriage should take place. Thus everyone conspired for the ruin of the beautiful Jane.

She was on the verge of swooning with joy when she read Belton's letter; never had anyone employed with more art such vivid and passionate expressions. Jane, who in her heart seized only the phrases that served to betoken his love, was ashamed that the expressions of her love were less impassioned than those of her lover.

This correspondence lasted for some time, with the Indian constantly carrying letters and returning with replies. But before long Belton, like so many of his fellows, allowed himself to be diverted by dissoluteness. Not able to resist the impulse of vanity, he shared the confidence of his intrigue with one of his friends, who gossiped about it in the camp. Belton became guilty to the point of letting others read the letters which he had received and of provoking the roguish spirits of the young officers at the expense of the unfortunate Jane, whose letters combined moralizing sentences and Bible verses with the most tender language of love. Finally, bored with so much writing, he burdened his valet with answering all future letters.

Jane noticed that the letters she now received were no longer in the same handwriting. Filled with passionate sentiments, she sighed on not finding in these letters the unaffectedness and outpourings of the heart that are known only to those in love. She grew anxious; it seemed as if her heart cried out to Belton but his did not reply. She gave him signs of her uneasiness. In his next letter he explained that he had ceased to write in his own hand because the general had prohibited, under the most severe penalty, any correspondence with the rebels, and he was afraid to lay himself open to dangerous suspicions. This obstacle increased Jane's distress; she wanted to see her lover again, and she made this known to him. The image of her beauty aroused Belton's desires; iniquity took the place of love in him. He returned this note with the Indian messenger:

"Oh, Jane, you choose to make me the happiest of mortals, yet you fear that danger will hold me back! Even though the whole army opposes me, even though it would be necessary to choose between certain death—preceded by the pleasure of seeing you for a moment—and wealth and honor—gained away from you—I would not hesitate. I will slip away from camp; on Tuesday, disguised as an Indian, I will be at the appointed place."

It was at the home of a Jewess, in the mountains that separate New York from New Jersey. There in the center of a dense forest on the side of a hill, Rachel Rideworld, weary of moving in fashionable society where she had been known for her love affairs, had chosen her retreat. It was a peaceful, charming locale, worthy of a more virtuous owner. Three acres of land, covered with grass that flourished all year, served as a pasture for two cows and a dozen sheep which she tended herself. One acre sown with seed and an orchard of the same size furnished her with food. A well-cultivated garden adorned the circumference of her house, which was surrounded by a wooden fence. An old friend of Betsy's, Rachel was industrious and thrifty, but the influence of vices acquired in her girlhood could still overcome her at the age of fifty.

The night of the meeting having arrived, the two lovers set out from different directions. Galloping horses, hastened by their riders' impatience, brought them to Rachel's house at the same time. What an enviable delight it is to see someone you love after a year of separation! Jane was happy at this moment, and she longed for even more. Belton, feeling guilty, thought himself happy, but as he clasped her to his breast and kissed her he was not. His senses relished her voluptuousness, but his heart could not bear to find itself unworthy of sharing a pure and honest ardor. Jane sighed, her heart throbbed, her lips quivered, and her trembling knees refused to support her.

"Oh, Belton," she said, withdrawing from the embrace, "stand aside; my happiness is too keenly felt for my heart to be equal to it."

Belton feigned the same rapture, but he had only rash thoughts. He employed the most cunning arts to augment the turmoil of this bewildered girl. Under the pretext of giving her help in her weakness, he pushed her down on a bed of cornstalks covered with a mat of reeds; this natural couch had replaced the down quilts ornamented with silk and gold upon which Rachel had been loved in her earlier years. Jane faltered dumbfounded, unable to take a breath. She had believed that their meeting would be a moment uniting ecstasy and virtue, but after the audacity of Belton she could not mistake the danger to which she was exposed. The torch of justice does not bring a more vivid light to the eyes of a man than when he is caught in sin.

"Stop," she cried, raising herself with force. "How imprudent I have been, and how mistaken you are! I came with confidence, looking to you as my protector. I came to prove my love and to ask you how to endure it while awaiting the happy moment when we can be joined forever. Your sensual demands are stronger than the fear of making me the most unfortunate of maidens; you would make me unworthy of having you as a husband. My youthful friends, would I not be the object of your scorn! No, no, I will die a victim of love rather than sacrifice my honor."

Jane's firmness served to halt Belton's boldness. He stood abashed for some moments, so great is the influence of real virtue over disconcerted vice. But, little by little, Jane regained confidence in him. Unable to retain their severity for long or capable of withholding an expression of tenderness and regret, her eyes overflowed with tears. To seduce her he made use of all that he fancied of greatest persuasiveness, but he got only tears and a pledge to marry him as soon as circumstances would permit them to go to a church. At last they parted. Jane was crestfallen at the bold conduct of the man she believed most virtuous, and Belton was humiliated to have found a girl capable of doting upon her lover and of triumphing over a seducer. Jane's thoughts, however, did not serve to weaken her love; a rash person is easily excused in the heart of one who loves him.

Betsy kept up the longing in her young mistress with magnificent descriptions of the splendor that prevailed at the Court of England; the variety and grandeur of the daily spectacles at the London theaters; and the differences that separate the rich from the poor, the powerful from the weak, under the oppressive names of nobility and masses, and under the awe-inspiring influence of deference and contempt. These accounts inflamed Jane's imagination. She was eager to have Belton as a husband, to become a woman of society, and to ride in a gilt carriage through the great cities of Europe.

Meanwhile in the spring the English army had been forced to evacuate New Jersey, and Belton embarked for England without informing Jane of his departure. She shed a torrent of tears until she learned that he had departed for London. She wrote to him and painted in vivid language her love and anxiety.

Three months elapsed before she received a reply. Pale cheeks indicated the sadness in her heart. Old Nathaniel felt sorry for her. He was convinced of Belton's infidelity after learning that the officer had left for London, and he hoped that his absence and the lapse of time would abate an unfortunate sentiment. But he was mistaken; his daughter became more listless each day. Nothing could cheer her, but she appeared to be more composed when she was with Betsy. She no longer occupied herself with the spinning of wool or cotton, and she no longer assigned tasks to her servants. The garden that she was accustomed to cultivate with her own hands no longer produced fruits or flowers; and her bees, to which she had formerly given so much attention, died. One day when she spoke of her love to the scheming Betsy and told her for the hundredth time how Belton captured her heart in New York, she received a letter from the young officer.

"My dear Jane, I will be in America almost as soon as my letter. I can not live away from you, so I am returning under the banners of General Burgoyne to conquer your country and you in order to possess you forever. You are the most beautiful girl in the Western World and would reign over it if only you could be seen there! Beauty is queen in Europe. Look at yourself and judge the effect you would have on a heart as passionate as mine."

This letter, by giving her hope, caused her beauty to reappear with a new brilliance. Each day increased her charms. It was near the end of winter now, and she spent her days at the window watching from a distance the ice floes drifting on the Hudson River. She longed for spring to come and open the mouth of the St. Lawrence River, to thaw the ice that had accumulated in its descent from the mountains and encircled the shores of Canada.

III

When Miss Jane McCrea learned in May that Burgoyne's army was about to disembark in the roadstead at Quebec, she could not contain her happiness. Each day brought her more exciting news. The English retook Ticonderoga and Crown Point, and captured Fort Edward. Already a detachment from Montreal had arrived at Lake Ontario to besiege Fort Stanwix, while Burgoyne, after passing Lake Champlain and Lake George, advanced toward the plains of Saratoga conquering man and nature. Jane thrilled with pleasure each time she heard of progress made by the English armies.

One day when she was returning from a visit with General Schuyler's daughters, she heard a mockingbird's cry.[4] After imitating an Indian's yell and the sound of wind in the trees, it uttered a soft and languid plaint, distinctly pronouncing, "Poor Emilia" and "Ah, Belton." These words were

---

[4] The mockingbird, found in several provinces, is extremely curious. It is a bird which, uniting the talents of the nightingale and the parrot, imitates all the sounds and noises it hears. M. de Chastellux, of the French Academy, has spoken of it in great detail, having heard it himself. [Original publisher's note.]

repeated by the mountain echoes. Jane halted in astonishment. Thinking herself mistaken, she listened more attentively and heard the bird again pronounce the same words. She could have believed that this indiscreet witness of the sighs of love had overheard her plaint, but the name Emilia alarmed her. As she rode forward, she discovered a young soldier lying in the grass. His face was kind, but grief and misery seemed to have blighted his handsome features. At the noise of the horses he arose and started to flee into the forest, but a servant, a determined enemy of the English uniform, pursued him and made him prisoner. He was brought before Jane. She thought that his face was clouded by trouble that was not of his own making; however, she asked him why he was not with the army. The soldier replied that ill-usage by an officer had forced him to desert.

"Do you know Captain Belton of the English Guards," she asked him, "and can you give me any news of him?"

At the mention of Belton's name, the soldier fainted. When the servants went to assist him, they discovered that he was a girl. Jane, who had her carried to her father's house, wished to care for her. She put her to bed in her own room, and hastened to bring her everything that might restore her lost strength. After night had fallen and the women servants had retired, Jane endeavored to discover who this unfortunate young girl was. She wondered at—yet all the while feared to hear—the reason for her fainting spell at the mention of Belton.

"My name is Emilia Fairlove," the stranger said to her. "It would be useless to hide my misfortunes from you. They are such that they can not be alleviated or made worse. I was born in Yorkshire. My father, a clergyman, is revered in England, rather more for his learning than for his saintliness. He has never been able to give his children any other fortune than the talents that adorn his mind and the example of those noble qualities that assure peace of heart. Belton, the son of a baronet, was brought up at my father's house. In his childhood he loved me and I loved him, and we were content just to tell each other so. Age changed this inclination into a more dangerous passion. I expected only the best from it, for Belton, in the presence of my father, promised to marry me. His parents, although wealthy, were not unfeeling and did not oppose my hopes. They called me their daughter, and said that beauty, youth, and the fruits of a good education are worth more than a large dowry and a title of nobility. Until the age of seventeen I lived in the midst of great happiness, but Belton preferred the manners of London to those of Yorkshire. After he entered a regiment of Guards, I realized that he was not the same. There was more grace in his manner and less love in his heart. He was ordered to war, and as the appointed time for our marriage drew near, I awaited his return with impatience. I yearned to see him again.

"Alas, that I have been so foolish. He took advantage of my weakness and confidence to seduce and dishonor me; he shunned me and then abandoned me. I was ashamed of myself and unable to endure the looks of my father, who did not reproach me but whose face showed his sorrow. Because I was unable to persuade myself to detest the cruel one who betrayed me or to live away from him, I set out in this disguise in order to see him again. We met each other three days ago, and I believed that my tears would move him. He rebuffed my affections. Unable to cease the torrents of tears, afraid of being found out, sick, pining, and acutely conscious of the inconveniences that are the result of the weakness of our sex, I left the camp to hide in the woods. I was resolved to die there of sorrow and hunger. When your servants captured me, they revived my suffering by restoring my life."

During this account Jane blushed and wept. She could not hide from Emilia the distress in her heart. Together they spent a restless night. When morning came, Jane could not find the minister's daughter from Yorkshire. Emilia had recognized a rival; having too much pride to accept favors and too much love not to be jealous, she slipped away just before daybreak.

Jane thought constantly of this unfortunate girl's story. She could not believe Belton capable of falseness; however, she recalled with chagrin his rashness at Rachel's house and his promise to be true to her. Emilia's mishaps seemed only to have begun after Belton's voyage to London, and it was before this voyage that he had given Jane his pledge of eternal love. He was, consequently, a liar and a deceiver. But ought one put faith in the statements of a stranger? Betsy had no difficulty in persuading her mistress that Emilia was, perhaps, one of the stray women who follow armies and that she could have been sent to make Jane despise Captain Belton, whom her father and all her friends desired her to give up. She was occupied with these thoughts when the following letter was brought to her:

"I am no more than twenty-five miles from you, my adorable Jane; and it is on you that the assurance of my happiness depends. I have obtained permission from the general to marry you here at the camp. There would be great danger if I were to come to you, but there will be little if you will come to me. Prove to me that you want to be mine. All our women, who have followed their husbands in this conquest, wait for you with impatience; everyone, after seeing you, will blush for being less beautiful than you. Madame la Comtesse de ———, wife of the general of the Brunswick soldiers, is very amiable. She left everything to follow her husband. Give reason for this to be said of you, and add heroism to the other perfections that compel me to adore you. Already I can see you passing in triumph in the midst of our ranks, with the whole army paying respect to you. I will wait for you near our advanced posts. Our general, as gallant as he is brave, wants very much to accompany me on this occasion to pay you the respects of his camp.

"In six days at the most, General Clinton and his forces will join us; the American army, caught between two fires, will not be able to hold out. At this moment, Vaughan's division is advancing toward Esopus, and this week we will be before Albany."

Jane reread this letter with enthusiasm several times, and Betsy urged her not to delay her departure. She went to Nathaniel and said to him:

"My father, give me your blessing. I am going to leave you to marry the man I love. He is at the camp of those you call your enemies, but in a few days the banner of victory will bring us all together. Here is Belton's letter."

As he read it, he grew pale; he trembled with anger. He faced his daughter; but this father, so filled with compassion, was only able to speak these words, so much more affecting than threats or reproaches:

"Where do you go, cruel child! Who will close my eyelids at my death? A fatal presentiment tells me that I am never to see you again."

He fell into an armchair and raised his trembling hands. Tears coursed the creases of his cheeks; he was unable to speak. Jane, sobbing, turned to him, unable to leave; but the pitiless Betsy kept watch, and she tore her from her swooning father's arms. All was in readiness, and Betsy, followed by a valet whom she had employed in Belton's interest, set the horses into a gallop toward Burgoyne's army.

This general kept in his pay the ferocious Indians of the Mohawk Valley plus some other barbarous tribes of the Lake Ontario region. They were dispatched in advance of his army to serve as scouts. They pillaged homes, massacred men, women, children, and even old people. The Ministers of England added, so to speak, a new horror to the scourge of war, paying fifteen guineas for each murdered American's scalp. The officers of Burgoyne's army kept these Indians continually intoxicated in order to increase their ferocity and to encourage them to murder and commit atrocities. These simple people did not love cruelty for its own sake but for the reward offered by the Europeans. It is not, then, upon them that our horror for the crimes should fall but upon the nations that provoked them, nations that dare to call themselves civilized.

A party of these manhunters, who had received a double ration of brandy this day, surrounded Jane and those who accompanied her. The Indians stripped them completely naked, tied them to trees, and divided their clothes and baggage among themselves. Then they decided to scalp all the prisoners. Betsy, who knew several Indian phrases, explained to them in vain that she was not one of the rebels and that she and her mistress were going to General Burgoyne's camp to live there with their friends. This false confidante was the first to be massacred, and the other servants soon met the same fate. The opinions of the savages were divided concerning Jane. The most important among them, taken with her beauty, stared desirously at her charms.

Each of them had laid claim to her when Kiashuta, the most renowned of their chiefs, arrived from a hunt. He approached her and was touched by pity. Her anguish added to her beauty; her hair, long enough to serve as a veil for her modesty, made the whiteness of her skin appear lustrous. He questioned her.

"Oh," she replied to him, "you who scorn death and fear nothing, do not abandon me to the remains of your ancestors. I am so young, and I am not an enemy of George, the great king! Do you know Captain Belton of the English Guards?"

"Yes," said Kiashuta.

"Ah, well! It is he who reigns in my heart. I was going to camp to join him and break the calumet of wedlock [5] with him. He awaits me. Give me my liberty. Take up that letter which your comrades have wrested from my bosom, the words of which are etched in my memory, and if you doubt what I tell you, take it to him."

"No," he said, "I believe you are sincere. I have seen white women with silver eyes that shine like stars, but I have never seen one as beautiful as you. I will protect you, I promise you that. Yes, I pledge to take you to your lover or die."

Immediately he gathered the Indians together and said to them:

"This girl whom you see here is too beautiful to be sacrificed, and she is not made to be the wife or slave of any one of you. I do not consider myself worthy of her, yet I am as superior to you as are the spruce trees of the Appalachian Mountains to a blade of grass. My arm can knock down four of you at once. I can follow the great lake to the sea before the sun sets. Stop making her an object of dispute. I have pledged to conduct her safely to the English officer by whom she is beloved."

Their brutal natures made them indignant at this speech; in vain he tried to appease them. Each one felt that he deserved to have Jane, and each wished to lead her to his tent as a compensation for services rendered in the war. Cruelty became a mark of distinction as each told of his crimes and how many rebels he had massacred in carrying out the orders of the great king.

---

[5] A calumet is a peace pipe. Some reports of Native American marriage customs described the bride and groom grasping a stick during the ceremony, then breaking it and each keeping part.

Kiashuta had wanted to protect himself against hostile Indians; he had tried to get the Six Nations to pledge to maintain neutrality in the quarrel between the English colonies and their mother country. The Indians acknowledged that he was strong and skillful, but they reproached him for being too soft-hearted and for having too little desire to spill the blood of prisoners on the bones of his ancestors.

Now they began to grumble openly about him, whispers turned to shouts, and the confusion created a din. They all took up their weapons, and each one attempted to carry off Jane. Kiashuta placed himself before her; each blow of his club knocked down one of the bold savages. His muscular arms resembled those of Hercules in the fable. He felled all who dared advance; his desire to shield an innocent victim from death caused a great many of the raging men to lose their lives. During this terrible fight, which their shrieks, called war-whoops, made even more frightful, Jane regained courage; her blood revived in her veins on seeing that of her enemies spilled. She made an effort to release herself from the tree to which she was tied, and had about succeeded when one of the Indians, whom Kiashuta had spared by repulsing him with a single kick, got up in a rage and rushed at Jane with his hatchet raised. He struck her with it and said, "Die! May the passion which you prompted from Kiashuta turn to rage and revenge us for it!"

Brave Kiashuta found no more enemies, and those who had not taken part in the dispute exalted his name to the heavens with great cries of joy. He returned to the spot where he had left the beautiful American and saw that she was on her back, motionless and lifeless. The savage had scalped her and carried away her long locks, the finest ornament of her beauty. Kiashuta pursued him with the speed of a hound chasing a frightened rabbit, and by throwing his hatchet twenty feet he split open the warrior's chest and heart. After this revenge Kiashuta returned in sorrow to the fires[6] lit by his fierce companions. He lifted up and clasped Jane's body and turned to the Indians. He gave this speech with interruptions of sobs:

"My brothers, she is no more. A moment ago her beautiful eyes cast glowing rays as vivid as those of the noonday sun; her tears were as clear and sparkling as morning dew when it falls from young flowering trees. Nature had made her as a comfort to the world, a comfort that man's passion invariably desolates; and we have killed her. Yes, the Europeans have reason to call us barbarians and savages if one of her sighs could not stop the arm of the one who struck her. Weep, and let us lament for her."

---

[6] The Indians gather around a large fire to hold their councils. It is their signal of assembly. [Hilliard d'Auberteuil's note.]

The Indians were immediately affected. Quickly changing from one sentiment to another like all those whose reason is in its infancy, they began to cry and give a mournful concert of sorrow and regret.

Kiashuta had a tomb of earth raised for her. He set up his lance there with the body of the cruel one who committed the crime. He sprinkled the mound with milk and brandy, and covered it with leaves and flowers. When this pious duty, revered by all mortals, was accomplished, he ran to Burgoyne's camp shouting for Belton with loud cries.

The officer was at this moment in the general's tent. Kiashuta entered and presented him with Jane's tresses, saying, "Here is all that remains of your beloved. I was not able to protect her, and I come with regret to bring you a gift that is for you a command to die."

At these words each man was seized with horror and disbelief, and Belton burst forth in anguish.

"Do not distress yourself, my friend. Take courage," continued Kiashuta. "Here is my hatchet, the finest that ever served an Indian, and if you do not dare to kill yourself, my arm will not fail."

Immediately the officers surrounded the Indian and drew him away from Belton.

"What," continued Kiashuta, "do you not have the courage to follow to the grave the one who loved you so much, who sacrificed everything for you? Should so beautiful a victim leave this life without having someone to accompany her to the happy island?[7] I pledged to conduct her to her lover or to die. I promised it, and Kiashuta has never failed to keep his word. He shall not fail now."

He immediately plunged his hatchet into his side. The witnesses were astonished and horrified.

It was not for lack of courage that Belton did not follow his example. In this dreadful moment he realized the worth of all he had lost; the circumstances of Jane's death increased his agony and added to his despair. In Burgoyne's camp everyone would have thought him weak to commit suicide for a woman. He preferred to seek death in combat, and it was not long in presenting itself in a cruel guise.

The army was surrounded on all sides and, having no more bribes to give to the Indians, was deserted by them. These savages suddenly changed to the American side without being prompted. Dispersed in the woods, they attacked the English as they tried to leave the camp at Saratoga.

---

[7] The Indians believe that the world is composed of a great number of islands floating in a sea. Apparently they have borrowed from the Europeans their ideas of the after-life. [Hilliard d'Auberteuil's note.]

Belton, at the head of a detachment, was mortally wounded by a poisoned arrow. The unfortunate Emilia, who followed and adored him always, saw him fall and rushed to him to try to save his life. She sucked his wound, and together they died from the effects of a powerful and unknown poison.[8]

The death of Miss McCrea spread grief and consternation among the Americans. Horatio Gates, Burgoyne's vanquisher, wrote to him on the subject and reproached him for hiring the savages who massacred friends and enemies indiscriminately. The inept response of the Royalists was that a rebellion is not an ordinary war and that, therefore, there should be no means disallowed to force the rebels into submission.

---

[8] This event, recorded in all the English gazettes and in the *Courier de l'Europe,* provided M. Berquin with the subject of a very touching ballad. [Original publisher's note. No such work by an Arnauld Berquin is known, but this plot was adopted in other works of the period, such as *Amelia: Or, the Faithless Briton.*]

Two Captivity Poems

BY LUCY TERRY
AND JOHN ROLLIN RIDGE

These two short poems demonstrate the pervasiveness of the captivity drama in nineteenth-century America. Neither author was a captive of the Indians. In fact, one might sooner call them captives of Anglo-Americans. Yet both chose Indian captivity as a topic for their literary efforts, perhaps because the mainstream audience would accept it, even coming from an unrecognized author.

Lucy Terry, like Olaudah Equiano, survived the Middle Passage from Africa to America, where she became a slave to Ebeneezer Wells of Deerfield, Massachusetts. She did not publish an autobiography, however, and the poem below was only published years after her death, appearing in Josiah Holland's *History of Western Massachusetts* in 1855. It must have been preserved in local oral history, or in a now-lost manuscript copy, for at least 35 years. It is not known whether Terry wrote other poems that have been lost. Holland wrote that she "was noted for her wit and shrewdness" and called her "one of the most noteworthy characters in the history of Deerfield" (2:354). This small town in the Connecticut River valley was already famous for an attack upon it in 1704, during the Queen Anne's War, in which its minister John Williams, his family, and more than one hundred others were taken captive. Williams's subsequent *The Redeemed Captive Returning to Zion* was the first major captivity narrative by a New England Puritan male. Terry's poem, titled "Bars Fight" after an area near the town called the Bars, commemorates a later attack, during King George's War. Holland recounted that she moved to Vermont with her husband, a free black who had bought her freedom, and told of how she became involved in a land dispute and argued her own case in court before Judge Royal Tyler, a prominent jurist and playwright and author of *The Algerine Captive.*

John Rollin Ridge had a more established literary career, and there is much more to tell about him. A Cherokee Indian, he was born in 1827 in Georgia at the beginning of the controversy over the removal of the tribe to Oklahoma. Many resisted the confiscation of the tribe's ancestral lands, while others, including Ridge's father and grandfather, determined that the assaults of hostile local whites would not relent and removal was the best option. When they reached Oklahoma in 1839, the two elder Ridges, along with the notable newspaper editor Elias Boudinot, were murdered by members of the antiremoval party. John Rollin witnessed the crime and continued to suffer from this factional strife. In the late 1840s he killed a man, probably in self-defense, and was forced to flee west, joining Cherokees and others in the Gold Rush to California. He made a career as a journalist in San Francisco, often using his Indian moniker, Yellow Bird, and contributing many pieces that advocated for the rights of Indians through an assimilationist policy consistent with the ideology of progress so pervasive at the time. His most famous single work is the novel *Joaquin Murieta,* a swashbuckling western adventure tale based on the folk legends surrounding the Mexican outlaw and the violent revenge he took on Anglo-Americans who were invading California in the Gold Rush era.

"The Stolen White Girl" was published in 1868 in a volume of Ridge's poetry. It presents an Indian captivity from the point of view of the captor, a "half-breed" who might be a projection of Ridge himself, given that his mother was a white woman. The "girl of the 'pale face'" does not react as a stereotypical captive but shares a pastoral idyll with her new lover and expresses her love with the passionate "heaving bosom" so common in nineteenth-century fiction and poetry.

Sources

Holland, Josiah Gilbert. *History of Western Massachusetts.* Vol. 2. Springfield: Bowles, 1855. 360.

Ridge, John Rollin. *Poems.* San Francisco, 1868. Rpt. *The Heath Anthology of American Literature,* ed. Paul Lauter. 3rd ed. Vol. 1. Boston: Houghton, 1998. 1896–97.

Supplementary Readings

Mulford, Carla, and Pattie Cowell. "Lucy Terry, 1730–1821." *The Heath Anthology of American Literature.* 3rd ed. Ed. Paul Lauter. Vol. 1. Boston: Houghton, 1998: 675.

Yellow Bird [John Rollin Ridge]. *The Life and Adventure of Joaquin Murieta, The Celebrated California Bandit.* Norman: U of California P, 1955.

BARS FIGHT

Lucy Terry

August, 'twas the twenty-fifth,
Seventeen hundred forty-six;
The Indians did in ambush lay,
Some very valiant men to slay,
5 The names of whom I'll not leave out.
Samuel Allen like a hero fout,
And though he was so brave and bold,
His face no more shall we behold.
Eleazer Hawks was killed outright,
10 Before he had time to fight,
Before he did the Indians see,
Was shot and killed immediately.
Oliver Amsden he was slain,
Which caused his friends much grief and pain.
15 Simeon Amsden they found dead,
Not many rods distant from his head.
Adonijah Gillett, we do hear,
Did lose his life which was so dear.
John Sadler fled across the water,
20 And thus escaped the dreadful slaughter.
Eunice Allen see the Indians coming,
And hopes to save herself by running,
And had not her petticoats stopped her,
The awful creatures had not catched her,
25 Nor tommy hawked her on her head,
And left her on the ground for dead.
Young Samuel Allen, Oh lackaday!
Was taken and carried to Canada.

1855

THE STOLEN WHITE GIRL

John Rollin Ridge

The prairies are broad, and the woodlands are wide
And proud on his steed the wild half-breed may ride,
With the belt round his waist and the knife at his side.
And no white man may claim his beautiful bride.

5   Though he stole her away from the land of the whites,
Pursuit is in vain, for her bosom delights
In the love that she bears the dark-eyed, the proud,
Whose glance is like starlight beneath a night-cloud.

Far down in the depths of the forest they'll stray,
10 Where the shadows like night are lingering all day;
Where the flowers are springing up wild at their feet,
And the voices of birds in the branches are sweet.

Together they'll roam by the streamlets that run,
O'ershadowed at times then meeting the sun—
15 The streamlets that soften their varying tune,
As up the blue heavens calm wanders the moon!

The contrast between them is pleasing and rare;
Her sweet eye of blue, and her soft silken hair,
Her beautiful waist, and her bosom of white
20 That heaves to the touch with a sense of delight;

His form more majestic and darker his brow,
Where the sun has imparted its liveliest glow—
An eye that grows brighter with passion's true fire,
As he looks on his loved one with earnest desire.

25 Oh, never let Sorrow's cloud darken their fate,
The girl of the "pale face," her Indian mate!
But deep in the forest of shadows and flowers,
Let Happiness smile, as she wings their sweet hours.

1868

Two Popular Nineteenth-Century Tales

CHARLES EATON
AND GERTRUDE MORGAN

"The Indian Captive: As Related by a First Settler" appeared in the *Columbian Almanac* for the year 1838, published in Philadelphia by Joseph McDowell. Since 1639, when an almanac was the first book printed in the New England colony, it had been the most popular kind of book in American publishing, often the only one in a household besides the Bible. Almanacs were primarily calendars and included solar, lunar, tidal, astronomical, and religious information for each day of the year. In the original publication, "The Indian Captive" appears across from the calendar charts and on the same pages as a "conjecture of the weather" and the schedule for court sessions in Philadelphia. The story and a second captivity narrative about one David Morgan were entertainment for the almanac's readers and were likely to have been reread several times during the year.

The tale takes place on the Androscoggin River and on Mount Washington in northern Maine and New Hampshire. By the mid-nineteenth century, New England was no longer the scene of frequent warfare and captivity, as it had been from the 1670s to 1770s. The wilderness was now associated not with Indians and the danger of war and violence, but with the aestheticized danger of the sublime. The sublime associated emotional and artistic pleasure with the fear and awe felt by witnesses to Nature's power, and it is in search of this kind of fearful pleasure that the narrator attempts to climb Mount Washington, already famous as the highest peak

in the region. Nathaniel Hawthorne had dramatized the legends and hazards of Nature in his popular short stories "The Ambitious Guest," which
took place in the White Mountains, and "The Great Carbuncle," set in the
Maine wilderness. Thus although Charles Eaton's captivity began, as he
says, "About sixty years ago" in the era of colonial warfare in northern New
England, and the narrative's opening line sets it in "September 17—," the
story reflects the time it was published, 1838.

The true author of "The Indian Captive" is unknown, and the tale is
told with a brevity and generality that suggests a folk legend that had
evolved in oral traditions before it was set down in print. In this regard it
resembles the "Panther Captivity" of 1787, in which the narrator meets a
woman living alone in a cave, and she tells how her fiancé was killed by Indians and how she slew another assailant, then took up residence in the
slain man's retreat. Both stories seem to convey that, on a semiconscious
level, Anglo-Americans were searching for a way to merge their identity
with that of the Indians or at least for a symbolic reconciliation of the long
history of colonial warfare. "The Indian Captive" involves a series of merciful exchanges: Eaton's father, forced like Thomas Dustan to surrender
one member of his family in order to save the others, spares the life of the
injured Indian, who pledges to save the life of the captive Charles in return.
Charles then becomes the inseparable companion of his Indian protector. Finally, the narrator himself benefits from Charles's generosity, for he
would have perished on Mount Washington without the stranger's assistance. To his father as well as to the narrator, Charles appears to be an Indian, yet he speaks in an elevated style, suggesting that the wilderness has
made him not more savage, but more civilized.

Gertrude Morgan, or Life and Adventures among the Indians is an example of popular fiction from later in the century. Like "The Indian Captive," its author is unknown, for Morgan herself is surely a fictional per-
sona, notwithstanding the assurances offered by the editor in the opening
paragraph. In the years after the Civil War, publishers and readers were
still concentrated in the eastern states, but public fascination with the West
and with Indians continued to grow, as did the population west of the Mississippi. Morgan's narrative begins plausibly enough with her marriage
and her husband's departure for California as part of the Gold Rush, but
it soon takes on aspects of the sensational popular genre known as the
dime western. These "Cowboy and Indian" stories flourished in periodicals and cheaply printed books from the 1860s to the 1920s. The genre
was pioneered by publisher Erastus Beadle, whose company sold nearly
five million books between 1860 and 1865. He employed a staff of writers, some of whom could produce a thirty-five-thousand-word tale in less

than two days. The novels typically had dual titles separated by an "or" just as Morgan's did, and often included sensational illustrations, one of which appears on page 405.

As are modern pulp romance novels, dime westerns were written according to formulas, and as time passed authors relied on increasing levels of sensational violence, often against Indians, to maintain readers' interest. The same might be said to apply to the captivity narrative, however. The patterns of the initial attack, the threats of torture, and the sentimental scenes between captive mothers and children had all become formulaic by the mid-1800s. The propagandistic appeal against the French and British military foes gave way to overtly racist denunciations of Indian cruelty that served to justify the predatory tactics of the military against the Plains tribes. It became increasingly difficult to distinguish real captivities from fictional narratives, as even accounts by well-documented captives sometimes incorporated implausible tall tales or optimistic promotional appeals for western lands.

In blending the captivity narrative and dime western genres, the author of *Gertrude Morgan* creates an interesting hybrid. Female captives came to predominate in nineteenth-century narratives—the ideology of domestic, sentimental femininity further enhanced the sensational effect aroused in readers by a helpless victim of Indian violence. Yet the fainting, frail flower stereotype of passive femininity was not monolithic. Female heroines (and female authors) were also fairly common in dime novels—cowgirls whose skills at gunfighting and horsemanship matched those of their male costars. Gertrude has these cowgirl skills, but she also has skills of early captives such as Hans Staden and Cabeza de Vaca. Her feats of healing raise her status within the tribe, and she becomes a trusted friend of her captor, The Buffalo Horn. Fears of sexual aggression are expressed only toward The Yellow Face, an Afro-Indian mixed-blood who speaks in black dialect. Notwithstanding this racist caricature, the ending of the story reveals Gertrude's loyalty for the North in the Civil War as she flees across the battle lines to reach the Union army.

As with Charles Eaton in "The Indian Captive," Gertrude Morgan's captivity reconfigures her identity to the point where she barely recognizes her husband, even though he has experienced a similar captivity. Because these two stories come from the anonymous reams of popular literature in the nineteenth century and were probably composed by hack writers who had never been captives and knew little of Indian life, they do not describe a detailed process of adoption and initiation as James Smith did. However, the writers show the influence of the narratives of assimilated captives insofar as they express the popular fantasy of "playing Indian." This fantasy reveals Anglo-Americans' interest in Indian culture, yet also suggests their deeper prejudice of Anglo-Saxon cultural superiority. The very ease with which these characters perform the indigenous practices of hunting, healing, and woodcrafting implies that Anglo-Americans' cultural training equipped them to do all that Native Americans ever needed to do.

Sources

"The Indian Captive: As Related by a First Settler." *Columbian Almanac for 1838*. Philadelphia: McDowell, 1838. Rpt. *The Garland Library of Narratives of North American Indian Captivities*. Ed. Wilcomb Washburn. Vol. 52. New York: Garland, 1977–83. 13–21.

Gertrude Morgan: Or Life and Adventures among the Indians of the Far West. Philadelphia: Barclay, 1866. Rpt. *The Garland Library of Narratives of North American Indian Captivities*. Ed. Wilcomb Washburn. Vol. 79. New York: Garland, 1977–83.

Supplementary Readings

Armitage, Shelley. "Rawhide Heroines: The Evolution of the Cowgirl and the Myth of America." *The American Self: Myth, Ideology, and Popular Culture*. Ed. Sam B. Girgus. Albuquerque: U of New Mexico P, 1981. 166–81.

Hawthorne, Nathaniel. "The Ambitious Guest" and "The Great Carbuncle." *Hawthorne: Tales and Sketches*. New York: Library of America, 1996. 299–307, 435–49.

Kolodny, Annette. *The Land before Her: Fantasy and Experience of the American Frontiers, 1630–1860*. Chapel Hill: U of North Carolina P, 1984.

Panther, Abraham [pseudonym]. "The Panther Captivity." *Women's Indian Captivity Narratives*. Ed. Kathryn Zabelle Derounian-Stodola. New York: Penguin, 1998. 83–90.

Smith, Henry Nash. *Virgin Land: The American West as Symbol and Myth*. Cambridge: Harvard UP, 1950.

THE INDIAN CAPTIVE

As Related by a First Settler

In the month of September, 17—, my health having become considerably impaired, I was advised by my friends and the physician of the village to journey, as a means of improving it. Possessing naturally a disposition to become acquainted with the situation of the country, especially in my own state and neighbourhood, I readily acceded to the advice. But the next question which arose, was where should I travel—how far, and in what parts? It was agreed, finally, that I should go to the White Mountains. I accordingly prepared for my journey, and on the morning of 6th September, receiving from my friends their united wishes that I might have a pleasant season and return in improved health, I took my departure for the beautiful village of ———, situated on the banks of the Kenebec, in the state of Maine. The distance from my own residence to the mountains was mostly performed in carriages, with an occasional ride on horseback. On arriving at the hospitable mansion of Mr. ———, the dwelling nearest the mountains, I had, much to my satisfaction, become recruited and so much improved in strength as to feel almost like climbing the mountains at a breath. Singularly enough, as I thought, I happened there at a time when no other stranger was present—not a solitary being could be found to accompany me to the heights of Mount Washington, even so much as a humble guide. But I was now determined not to return without seeing the originally proposed end of my journey. To scale the heights before me, stranger and alone, was, to be sure, no desirable task, but my ambition led me to attempt it even at the hazard of losing my way and becoming exhausted. I started from my friend's at eight o'clock in the morning of a delightfully pleasant day, and before the sun had reached the middle of its daily course, I was well nigh at the summit of the mountain; yet, not without feeling that I could not endure such exertion with the freedom of one who had never been broken down by disease. It is needless to say that I amused myself with the grand prospect afforded and the wild scenery around, until it became necessary to return. I made, on my ascension, by the path, such marks and observations as I thought would enable me to find my way back without difficulty. But I was mistaken. The entire afternoon was consumed in fruitless endeavours to find the path which I had followed on going up. I was now weary and faint, and as the sun sunk beneath the western horizon, seemed to tell me in fearful language, that I should never look upon his countenance, nor feel his enlivening influences again! but there was no time to be lost—my life was in danger! I flew first to one extremity of the height which I had ascended and then to the other, little removed from derangement in viewing the awful horrors of my situation. Alas! night had came over me—a faint, fatigued and sick being, and almost unmanned by fear. But what was my suprise, mingled with joy, at this crisis, on seeing at a little distance from me, and coming toward me, a tall, but well proportioned man, with a musket in his hand, whom I took to be an Indian!

"Ah, young man," said he on coming up, "what has brought you to this lonely place at this hour of the night? Have you no guide, no protector, nor means of securing yourself to night from this cold damp air?"

"None!" said I, and I immediately informed him of my adventures and the reason of my being thus exposed.

"Rash and unfortunate youth!" said the stranger, "you deserve some punishment for thus voluntarily exposing yourself to danger and death! Have you no food with you?"

"Not one morsel!" I answered. "In my hurry and anxiety to reach the mountain this morning, I entirely forgot to take any with me!"

Putting his hand into his pocket he drew forth a small piece of broiled meat and a slice of bread.

"Here," said he, "eat this—it may afford you a little strength, and prevent you from becoming entirely exhausted; a singular freak this from a pale-face like you!" he added, and I thought he was about to leave me.

"For Heaven's sake, my dear sir!" I exclaimed, "would you leave me here in this chilling air, and on those cold and dreary mountains to perish, without a friend and alone?"

His keen black eyes were fixed full and steadily upon me, as if to read the inmost secrets of my heart, when he approached, and taking me by the hand—

"Hear me!" said he, sternly, "Will you swear?"

"What? by whom?" I replied earnestly.

"By him who sent me hither to save you! Swear that you will not, in my life time, reveal to any living being, the spot or dwelling to which I may lead you—and all shall be well."

I swore. He then requested me to follow him. In silence and with some difficulty, for I had become much exhausted, I obeyed. He led me a considerable distance to a part of the mountain where the footsteps of few if any but his own were ever marked; and on guiding me into a secret and curious cave, the old man (I had already observed that, from his appearance, he had numbered at least three score and ten,) looking at me with a smiling countenance, said—

"Here, young stranger, is the place that I call *my home;* sit down," said he, "on that smooth stone, and I will soon kindle a blaze—I have also some game in my pockets, which I have just had the fortune to seize, and that with a little roasting will please the palate and repair the system. You have been a rash youth," continued he, "but you are safe now; and as soon as you regain your strength, I will put you in a way, should you wish it, to find the foot of the mountain."

We had found it necessary before reaching the cave, to procure a torch, by which I was enabled to see my way well along the narrow, and in many places perilous path that we were obliged to travel. The old man soon built a good fire, and before one hour had elapsed, he had prepared a supper, which appeared to me, under the circumstances, more inviting even than the sumptuous viands of the rich; I never ate with a better relish.

In the meantime I could not banish the wonder and surprise excited by the fact, that an individual, possessing the faculties, both mental and physical, of my kind protector, should take up his abode in a place so cold and barren, and affording so few opportunities for a life of ease and happiness. I was exceedingly anxious, as was natural, to learn the history of one, whose whole character appeared so singular and strange. Could I dare solicit of him the desired information? I almost feared to ask it; but the hospitable board having been removed, and the old man seeming in a cheerful mood, I ventured to offer an intimation that a little conversation relative to his own history would to me be peculiarly interesting, and it had its effect. His eyes flashed, and he sat for some time in silence. At length, drawing his seat nearer to me, and with a look which seemed to say that none but himself should ever know his history, he observed—

"I am old, young stranger, as you see—ready to lie down in my grave. There are, it is true, many incidents connected with my life, which, if related, might perhaps amuse one of your age and capacity; but it grieves me to think of them! I will, however, if you are not too much fatigued," he continued, "tell you a short story."

I was of course anxious to hear what he might have to relate, knowing that if I could learn nothing of his own life, his knowledge of early events enabled him to give a narration of many rare and interesting occurrences, and I begged that he would proceed.

"About sixty years ago," the old man commenced, "there lived on the banks of the Androscoggin, in what is now called the town of Bethel, a man who was married and had two children, a son and daughter, and who obtained a livelihood by hunting and fishing. At that time, there were several tribes of Indians in the neighbourhood, and this friendly and peaceable family were not unfrequently disturbed by their near approach and nightly yells. They, however, managed by prudence and caution to live safely for several years, until at length one evening of a beautiful summer day, just as the sun was going down behind the trees, a hostile and wandering tribe of Indians approached the humble, but hitherto comparatively quiet dwelling of those lonely settlers. The mother and her little daughter of seven years were employed in the house, while the father and son, who was about ten years of age, were gathering wood at a short distance from his dwelling. The father, leaving his little boy busily engaged in picking sticks, went with his arms full of wood to the house, and had no sooner reached it, than he saw his hostile foes coming up, and standing almost directly between him and his son. He called to him, and thought at first to run to his protection, but saw on a moment's reflection that by endeavouring to save his life he would endanger his own (for already several arrows were pointed at him) and put it out of his power to protect his wife and daughter, who were alarmed almost to fainting in the house. The only alternative left him was to flee to his house and prepare to defend them and himself there. The Indians now gave a horrible yell, and attemped by every means in their power to enter; but the father was enabled to beat them back until his wife had loaded one or two muskets, which were immediately discharged upon them with good effect. The contest was continued for about half an hour, the wife loading and the husband firing the guns, when the Indians finding their attempts to enter the house fruitless, and that powder and balls were more fatal in their effect than their own weapons, they took their departure, such of them as were able, yelling most hideously. The night passed; but the fear of the Indians and the thought that their child might already be suffering the most cruel tortures prevented the parents, as may well be supposed, from receiving one moment's rest. The morning dawned, and six Indians were seen lying dead on the ground near the house. The brave hunter had not fought without carrying sorrow to the bosoms of his enemies; though he suffered the loss, as he believed, forever of his little Charles, whom the Indians he well knew would preserve only to torment. He ventured out and immediately saw at a short distance from the house, another Indian, who, from his appearance, he judged had been wounded. In his wrath he approached and would have despatched him at once, had not the Indian, in a most heart touching manner, begged to be spared, offering at the same time, as an inducement to the hunter to let him live, to prevent the life of his son being destroyed and return him safe to his parents. On his promising to do this, he was taken

into the house, and a little attention to his wounds enabled him to follow
his savage comrades.

"Years passed away, but no son came. The hunter now felt that he had
been deceived, and regretted that he had not despatched the savage at a
blow. Ten years had now already elapsed, and all hopes of ever seeing
Charles had long since been abandoned. The mother had made herself, in
appearance and feeling, old and almost helpless by grief and mourning,
and Ellenor, her daughter, was in the last stage of consumption, from the
same cause, and from seeing an affectionate mother sinking so rapidly. She
could remember her little brother, and how he looked before the savages
came and took him away. Her thoughts were ever upon him; and the following lines, composed and presented her by a friend, she was often heard
to sing with a pensive air, as she sat at her window in the evening twilight.

> O, blest were those hours when gay on the banks
>   Of the clear Androscoggin I played,
> With my own honest Charles, and when by the side
>   Of my mother, I kneeled, as she prayed!
> 5 Then sickness and sorrow, and cold discontent,
>   Were unknown to childhood so free;
> And death, with his arrows so awful and sure,
>   Possessed no dread terrors for me!
> But alas! those blest days are forever no more,
> 10   And mourning and sorrow now reign;
> The savage, in wrath, has invaded our home,
>   And dear Charles has been captured and slain;
> No more shall we sport on the banks of the stream,
>   Or walk, hand and hand, through the grove,
> 15 He has gone to the rest of those regions afar,
>   Where dwells naught save quiet and love!

"Ellenor died while yet in her seventeenth year, and was buried in a
spot selected by herself, near a large oak tree by the house; under whose
shades she used often to sport with her dear brother, and where, in the
summer hours, when deprived of his presence, she had frequently resorted
for contemplation and study.

"The parents were now left entirely alone, and few inducements to
make even life itself desirable. Their only daughter had died in autumn,
and a freezing and dreary winter was at hand.

"It was a severe cold night in the month of December, and the moon shone upon the snow bright and full almost as the sun itself, when two men were seen approaching the dwelling of this lonely settler. They walked up to the house and kindly asked admittance. Supposing them to be Indians belonging to some friendly tribe near by, who wished to warm and rest themselves, they were without hesitancy permitted to enter.

" 'Cold weather this, old man,' said the eldest of the two strangers, who was at once observed to be an Indian, addressing the hunter as they seated themselves by the fire.

" 'Yes' was the reply,— 'and have you far to walk this cold night?'

" 'I have come,' said the Indian, 'to fulfil my promise, made to you a long, long time since. You will recollect———'

" 'What! *my son!* and does he *live?*' asked the old man, with much emotion.

" 'He lives! behold him there, before you!'

"Without waiting for answer, the aged parent, recognizing, in the, till then, supposed Indian, *his own son* had embraced him, neither being able, so overwhelmed with joy were they, to utter a syllable; and the feeble mother, at witnessing so unexpected an event, had fainted and fallen on the floor. She soon, however, revived, and was permitted once more to clasp in her arms the son, whom she had long believed dead, and soon expected to meet in Heaven. It was a scene indeed, which can much better be imagined than described.

"You will judge what were the feelings of Charles on learning the death of his sister.

"But the cause of this long delay in the return of the Indian was now to be explained. It may now be done in few words.

"He overtook his party in a short time, after recovering from his wounds, and found them mourning and almost distracted with grief, for in their contest with the hunter they had lost their chief and several others of their most daring warriors; and they were just preparing to feed their revenge by torturing to death with every cruel means which their savage and blood thirsty hearts could invent, their captive boy. But happily he arrived in time to save him, though it had been utterly out of his power to return him to his parents before. They continued their march into the western wilderness, where they were finally forced to remain; on account of a war which soon broke out between their own and several hostile tribes of Indians, and lasted for nearly the whole time that had elapsed since they had left the banks of the Androscoggin.

"Charles had not forgotten his parents, though he had become habituated to the usages, customs and hardships of his savage comrades, and worn, indeed, the resemblance of an Indian. He now, with his preserver,

whom he would not permit to leave him, lived with his parents and supported them until worn out with age and sorrow, they both in the course
of two years were laid in the grave nearly at the same time.

"Charles Eaton, (for that was his name), had now but one friend in
the world—his Indian protecter and preserver. They lived and wandered
together for many years, obtaining their living, as they were taught to do,
in the wilderness, until at length the poor Indian was taken suddenly ill
and died, leaving Charles entirely friendless and without a home.

"Charles lived now, not because it was his own pleasure, but because
it was the will of Heaven that he should live. He for a time sought to make
himself happy in society; but the noisy and cold hearted world possessed
no charms for him. He sought the mountains, where he discovered a cave
in which he entered and at once declared it his home, while life remained.
He has thus far kept his word, and," said the old man, springing from his
seat with the activity of a boy, "*Charles Eaton* is the man who just saved
you, my young friend, from the awful pangs of death!"

I cannot describe my surprise on hearing this announcement, coming
upon me, as it did, so suddenly. I had in fact become so interested in the
old man's story that I had even forgotten the situation in which I was
placed.

We now sought rest from sleep, but little did I obtain. I however by
the morning found myself sufficiently recruited to venture to return to the
dwelling at the foot of the mountain and from thence home, which I did after first having been directed to the right path by my own *kind preserver*—
the INDIAN CAPTIVE!

GERTRUDE MORGAN:
OR
LIFE AND ADVENTURES
AMONG THE INDIANS
OF
THE FAR WEST

The experience of this accomplished lady, a native of New York City, during the past eleven years, nearly all of which time she has lived among the Indians of the Far West, by whom she was captured in 1855, is, perhaps, one of the most thrilling and romantic that has ever been given to the public. The narrative, the reliability of which is unquestionable, is written by Mrs. Morgan herself, and has just been put, by the fair authoress, into the hands of the editor, who, with the exception of here and there introducing an explanatory paragraph or sentence, has made no alteration whatever in it.

A full detailed account of my early history would, as far as the object of this narrative is concerned, be of no consequence to the general reader, and I shall, therefore, pass it with but a casual allusion.

Born of wealthy parents in New York City, I experienced, from the time of my birth up to my twentieth year, none of those ills, or vicissitudes, or trials, which fall to the lot of so many. My doting father and mother, who had no other child but myself, lavished upon me all that heart could wish for, and yet guided my inclinations and disposition so gently and skillfully in the right direction, that I escaped the result so generally brought about by parental indulgence, that of becoming a spoiled child. At the time of which I speak, however—my twentieth year—the cloudless, azure sky, that had hitherto smiled so brightly upon my life path, suddenly became obscured. My father, by an unfortunate speculation, failed in his business, lost all he had, and in a single day became a penniless man.

This fearful reverse of fortune so deeply affected my mother, that in a very short time after its occurrence, we were called on to follow her to the tomb, where, thank Heaven, worldly trouble at last terminates. My father never looked up from that day out, and in less than a year from the time that the green sods were placed on my mother's grave, I laid him beside her, whom he had so dearly loved. Of all the hosts of friends who had smiled upon me when surrounded by affluence, there was only one who then, in the moment of my adversity, stood with me and wept over my father's coffin, as the attendants lowered it gently in its dusty resting place: and this one friend was William Morgan, who had, for several years, been my father's confidential clerk.

For sometime previous, there had existed between us a mutual feeling of affection, which had continually increased in strength until this sorrowful day, on which we vowed to live only for each other. In about two weeks after my father's funeral, William obtained a situation, at a moderate salary, and we were, soon after, united in the holy bonds of wedlock. Although reduced to such humble circumstance, when compared to those in which I had passed the previous part of my life, yet I was very happy— happy as the day was long, in the love of my dear husband, whose unalloyed affection for me seemed to grow more and more intense.

We had been married about nine months, when the California Gold Fever reached such a height that thousands were emigrating to the new El Dorado, with brilliant expectations of untold wealth. For a long time William had resisted its influence; but at length he became so imbued with the idea of building up a speedy fortune, that he obtained my consent to his departure for the land of gold, concerning which, the papers were daily giving such dazzling accounts.

It did not occupy him more than a week to make the necessary preparations for his journey; and on the 7th of May, 1850, he bade me farewell, and started for the modern Ophir. Until the beginning of June I received letters from him nearly every day, each one dated farther and farther West, until at last he wrote me, that when I should get another letter he could not tell, as he was just about to plunge, with a party of companions, into the boundless, prairie wilderness that laid between him at Chouteau's Landing, or Station, and the Rocky Mountains. Chouteau's Station was about twelve or fifteen miles west of the Missouri, and close to the right bank of the Kansas river.

Once more before he reached California, I heard from him, and after that I got no word for many long months: in fact I had begun to have misgivings whether or no he was alive, when I received an epistle, crumpled and stained with travel, but oh, how welcome, informing me that he was not only still living, but in capital health and spirits, and making money rapidly. In it he stated that his realizations had already nearly equalled his utmost hopes, and, as an earnest of this, informed me in what manner to dispose, to the best advantage, of nearly five hundred dollars in gold dust, which would arrive some three or four weeks later. The next message I got, he was doing an extensive and lucrative business in Sacramento. This time he sent word also to his brother James, in Philadelphia, to come out and join him the next summer. He had now been absent four years, and did not expect to return, even on a visit, for some three years yet.

This seemed a long, long time to be separated from my dear husband, and, as I perused his letter over and over again, a new idea sprang to life within me: why could I not go to him? True, there were dangers to be faced, hardships to be encountered, and obstacles to be surmounted in the execution of such an intention, but I feared them not, and, ere I closed the letter, my resolution was fixed.

The next day I went on to Philadelphia and had an interview with my brother-in-law, James, who, upon learning my intentions, endeavored to dissuade me from such an hazardous undertaking, but in vain. Upon finding my determination unalterable, he consented that I should accompany him the following May (1855), at which time we accordingly started to join William.

In due season we arrived in St. Louis, where we were detained a few days waiting for the arrival of some six or eight adventurers who were to fill up our little company to its full number of forty, including, beside myself, two other females, one of whom, like me, was going out for the purpose of joining her husband in California. When thirty-eight of the party had arrived, it was unanimously agreed to wait no longer for the other two, but to push forward immediately.

This being decided, we were soon steaming up the mighty highway of the West, and after a voyage of about four hundred miles, we reached, without accident, Chouteau's Landing. Here we rested two days for the purpose of completing all our arrangements before committing ourselves to the wilderness.

At dawn of the day on which we commenced our journey we were aroused, and, after taking breakfast, we struck off into the deep forests that belt the Kansas river. During our progress through these forests we often came upon cultivated farms and clearings, many of which belonged to Indians. We were guided by one of these Indian farmers for thirty or forty miles until we emerged upon the prairies. The latter came in view just at sunset of the third day, and of all the scenes or scenery that I ever beheld, that which then burst upon my view was the grandest I ever contemplated.

From our feet the ocean of grass swept far, far away Westward, in beautiful, swelling billows of verdure, that, moving gently to and fro in the evening breezes, and, being gilded with the deep rays of the descending sun, looked like moulten gold and emerald. Rooted to the spot in which I stood, I gazed in admiration until the sun sank out of sight among the distant grassy waves, and a melancholy, bluish mist rose over the boundless prairie, like an almost intangible vail. And even then, as the starry host overhead came glistening into the firmament, I continued my wrapt contemplation until aroused by James, who, with a joke and a laugh, passed my arm through his and led me away to our tent for supper.

We resumed our journey the next morning about seven or eight o'clock, all the time between that hour and daylight being consumed in grazing the animals we had with us, and obtaining our own breakfast. Halting an hour or two at noon for rest and refreshment, we again set forward and camped before sunset on the banks of a romantic stream. We soon reached the dangerous locality of hostile Indians, and thenceforward our little party was subjected to almost military regularity and discipline. Every night the horses and mules and oxen were driven in and picketed, and our wagons so arranged as to afford us a shelter or barricade, from behind which we could repel any attack that might be made upon us.

Three or four of the party in turn were also detailed each night to perform the duty of sentinels, and thus prevent us from being surprised. At first we journied along the regular Santa Fe Trail, but learning that the savages were likely to be more numerous and troublesome than usual in this direction, our leader, who had crossed the plains in 1842 with Captain (now General) John C. Fremont, determined to turn aside, reach, and advance over the former route of that indefatigable officer.

Up to the third week in June we met with nothing calculated to discourage us, but about this time a circumstance occurred that threw a gloom over our little party and inaugurated a series of mishaps and disasters which subsequently took place.

Two men, relatives of each other, went a little distance up the banks of the Vermillion river for a hunt or excursion. They remained away but a short time, and on their return resumed a quarrel that had sprung up between them just after setting out. Awhile before we took up our afternoon march they became so incensed that blows were exchanged.

In an instant more each drew his knife, and clenched in mortal combat with his adversary. Oh, what a horrible sight was it to see those stalwart, powerful men reeling, stumbling and wrestling about, each endeavoring to gain the advantage. How it curdled the blood to see their deadly weapons cutting and slashing each other's flesh, and now and then plunged with strange, shuddering quiver deeply into one another's body. It was impossible, without much peril, to interfere with the combatants, and so the contest continued until both men, cut, hacked and stabbed literally to pieces, fell dying to the turf which was already crimsoned with their blood.

And even now it required the united strength of several men to tear them from their deadly embrace.

The one who was most badly injured died within a few minutes, and his livid features were distorted with a scowl of agony and rage, with a curse on his lips, his soul was ushered into the presence of that Being whose law he had so broken. The survivor lingered until sunset, and then died with words of contrition and sorrow upon his tongue, crying to be forgiven for the fearful deed he had committed.

The next morning we buried the two dead foes side by side in a wild ravine, through which dashed a small but turbulent stream. To prevent the wolves from tearing out their bodies and devouring them, a huge red sandstone boulder, of which numbers were lying around, was rolled upon their graves, and on it was rudely graved their names and the date of their deaths.

This sad duty performed we once more moved on our way, but not in our usual good spirits. A deep gloom settled upon us all, and more than one predicted "bad luck" throughout the rest our journey. I never was, nor can I say that I am now, a believer in "luck," either good or bad, but a singular fatality, that attended our steps from that day forth, seemed to bear out the superstitious predictions made on the occasion. Our oxen died suddenly, as did also several of our horses, three or four of our wagons broke down, and finally, after being mended again and again, had to be abandoned with nearly all their contents.

By the time we were about to leave our course along the left or Northern bank of the Little Blue, we found ourselves in the most deplorable condition. Still we pushed onward, fervently hoping the while for some propitious change of fortune, and we had nearly reached the Platte or Nebraska river, when we met a party of four hunters or trappers, who brought us the startling intelligence that a large war party of Pawnee Indians were in the neighborhood. After a hurried and immediate consultation it was resolved that, as it would be impossible for us to advance with any hope of success, we should forthwith return in company with our new companions, who were bound for St. Louis. We, therefore, retraced our steps until we reached our last night's camp, situated on the margin of the Little Blue.

Here we remained until the next morning, when we were in motion by seven o'clock, but had only travelled about two miles, when we were thrown into a terrible excitement by the shout of "Indians! Indians!" I can scarcely describe my feelings, as, after listening to the blood-curdling stories of the trappers, who had joined us the preceding afternoon, I now heard that wild cry of alarm. My eager eyes ranged up and down the luxuriant valley, through which the stream ran, and then over and along the verdant slopes of the hills. Not seeing any living thing, with the exception of a few antelopes that were bounding along in the distance, I was beginning to congratulate myself that the alarm was a false one. But I had scarcely arrived at this partial and too hasty conclusion, when, over the crest of a ridge, about three-quarters of a mile distant, I beheld a party of savages, stripped to the waist, and mounted on fleet horses, dash into sight.

As they discovered us, they uttered a deafening yell, and halted, apparently to reconnoitre our position and strength. A moment more, and several other companies of our dusky foes, galloping over the hill-tops, joined their companions, when they all proceeded to hold a council of war. But while I was gazing, horror-struck, upon the enemy, the gleaming of whose guns and spears chilled my blood, I felt myself lifted quickly from the ground, and was carried to one of the wagons in which I was hurriedly placed for shelter during the coming battle. It was my brother-in-law, James, and one of the four hunters who had thus cared for my safety.

"Be calm, Gertrude," said the former, in a low, anxious tone, "be calm, and do not attempt to get out until I come to you. I think we can beat them off yet."

With these words the speaker turned away to assist in the general defense. The wagons had been quickly arranged, so as to afford our party a barricade, from behind which they might defend themselves to the best advantage.

The expected attack was not long delayed, for the savages, having soon decided upon their plan, came dashing down upon us with the most deafening yells and whoops. But our men stood nobly to their work, and a volley from their deadly rifles emptied several saddles and caused the foe to retreat. There is no doubt also that had the Indians, notwithstanding their vast superiority in numbers been armed with only their regular weapons— bows and spears—they would have been speedily and effectually repulsed; but nearly half of them carrying rifles, they were enabled before withdrawing, to return our fire, and with such effect, that two of our force fell dead on the spot, while fully six or eight were more or less wounded.

I have often read glowing accounts of parties of three, four, or half a dozen white men defeating fifty and even a hundred savages at once, but never took into consideration the fact—generally omitted also by the authors—that the savages were without fire arms, while the whites carried both guns and pistols. Experience has taught me, however, that a long Missouri rifle, in the hands of an Indian warrior, makes him entirely the equal, nay, oftentimes his superior.

The Indians now divided into three companies, and while two of these prepared for a second charge upon us, the third passed out of view behind a wooded ridge, doubtless intending to make a circuit and come in upon our rear. In this emergency, our leader determined to cross the stream at our side, and reach if possible, a position on the opposite bank where we could better offer battle than in our present exposed situation. At a given signal, therefore, the wagons, of which we had three left, suddenly wheeled, and started at full speed into the water. Before the Indians recovered from their astonishment at this bold and unexpected maneuver, two of the wagons gained the other bank in safety, but the third, in which I was, had no more than reached the middle of the stream, when the savages, galloping within range, fired upon the mules by which it was drawn. Both animals sank down into the water, struggling in their death agonies, and the wagon of course became stationary. Several times subsequently my friends, headed by James, attempted, with the most desperate valor, to save me, but were each time repulsed by the foe, and found themselves obliged at last to retreat close into the position that they had selected for their final stand.

As had been suspected, the third party, that had disappeared over the wooded ridge, reappeared some distance down the valley, and were doubtless much surprised as they came dashing up on the other side of the stream, to find that we had changed our position. Our stratagem amounted not to much, however, for while the strongest party crossed the river to attack my friends, the other captured the wagon in which I was, and, dragging it ashore, after cutting the traces of the dead mules, commenced the work of overhauling its contents.

Of course, of these latter, I being the most prominent, was the first seized, and was violently jerked out upon the ground by a tall, powerful fellow, who instantly drew his tomahawk, and was about to finish my earthly career, when he was interrupted by a companion, who succeeded in persuading him to give me up to him. Regardless, however, of my own fate, I kept my gaze fixed anxiously upon the combatants on the other side. Volley succeeded volley; first from one and then the other of the contending parties, but those of the whites grew fewer and fewer, until at last only two men were left alive, who, seeing the utter hopelessness of their situation, surrendered to their foes. The latter, however, instead of showing them the mercy always due to a valiant but conquered foe, instantly tomahawked and scalped them.

As I beheld the fearful finale of the horrid butchery, I sank groaning to the earth. Of all the company, men and women, that had set forth in such high hope from St. Louis, I was the only living person left, and how long I might be spared I did not know.

Our wagons and their contents were a rich booty for the savages, who were so well pleased with their success, that they resolved to return without delay to their towns, some three or four days' journey to the southwest of the Big Blue. Before setting out, however, they dragged all the bodies of their victims to a deep ravine among the hills and threw them down into it, and, after holding a council concerning the wagons, resolved to burn two of them and load the remaining one with what plunder they could. The corpses of their own slain were all buried in a beautiful spot on the north bank of the river. The pains they thus took to conceal their diabolical work were induced from the fear they entertained, that some future white travellers, discovering the bodies of their murdered countrymen, might carry information thereof to the forts, and cause a detachment of soldiers to be sent out to avenge their deaths. And of the military power of the government all the Indians have a wholesome dread.

After they had completed, as far as they were able, the concealment of their butchery, the Pawnees set forward, as I have already said, for their village, three or four days' journey to the Southwest. My captor, or rather he to whom my captor had given me, forced me to mount a half wild horse and ride beside him. This, thanks to the fact that I was a good horsewoman, I accomplished without having my neck broken by the restiveness of the vicious animal I rode.

At the moment that I had seen the last of our party fall before their dusky murderers, I resolved to force my captors to take my life also; but, strange as it may seem, a hope at that very instant sprang up in my breast that I might some day or other again see my husband. I resolved, therefore, to live if possible, and ever afterward, even when my trials and tribulations thickened darkest about me, this hope, with its concomitant feelings, grew more and more intense.

On the evening of the third day we reached the Pawnee village, situated on a large stream of water, that I subsequently learned was an affluent of the Republican Fork of the Kansas river. The spot where the lodges were pitched was chosen with that taste for romantic scenery so inherent in the Indian breast. According to some custom or ceremony my captors did not enter the village that night, but remained out on a bluff on the river bank until morning; when all the village was aroused by runners to prepare for their reception. All being in readiness, the chief of the returned war party gave the required signal, and his braves moved forward to meet their friends who were awaiting them in a body. The scene that followed beggared all description, even the dogs joining in the noisy welcome. All were elated with the valuable prize that had been taken and the number of paleface scalps that dangled at the belts of the victorious warriors.

I, being the only prisoner, soon became the centre of all observation, especially with the women, who universally bestowed on me nothing but the most malignant scowls. As I was, however, the captive of the second chief in the nation their demonstration reached no farther than this. To the lodge of this chieftain, whose euphonious name was The Buffalo Horn, I was soon taken, or, more properly speaking, driven by two of his wives into whose charge he had given me. These termagents, after shaking their fists in my face and brandishing knives over me, to intimidate me what my fate would be should I attempt to escape from my new quarters, left me and went out to join in the festivities that were proceeding. Up to this time my pride had forbidden the exhibition of any grief or fear on account of the perilous situation in which I was placed, but now that I found myself alone, and yet in the midst of relentless blood-thirsty enemies, I gave full vent to my feelings in a flood of tears. I compared my present condition with what it had been but a few years before, and oh! what cruel, terrible changes had been wrought upon me during the intervening years of sorrow.

While in the midst of these sad contemplations, I was suddenly startled by the report of a gun, which was followed by the screaming and crying of women and children, and a trampling of many feet. These sounds also came nearer and nearer to the lodge in which I was, and, a minute or so later, the body of a man was borne carefully into the lodge and deposited upon a rude pallet of skins. At a glance I recognised him as my captor, The Buffalo Horn. The unfortunate chief laid writhing in great agony for full a quarter of an hour before the doctors, or "Medicine Men," made their appearance. The latter had been thus detained in attiring themselves in their Medicine dresses, an indispensable operation to their success. The chieftain's wound, which I afterward learned was caused by the accidental discharge of his own piece, was directly through the right lung, and, of course, apparently fatal. Yet, nothing daunted, the Indian doctors set themselves to work, and, strange to say, succeeded for two or three days in keeping their patient up. But about this time a change for the worse took place and The Buffalo Horn began to sink with alarming rapidity.

At this juncture an idea struck me that perhaps his life might be saved in the same manner as was that of an American General, who, during a battle in the Mexican war, received a wound of the same nature.[1] To several of the chief's friends, who could understand English, I therefore, immediately communicated my thoughts, which were by them made known without delay to The Buffalo Horn himself. The latter ordered that I should be allowed to make the attempt. Until this moment what I had read concerning the manners, customs and disposition of the Indians never once crossed my mind, but it all occurred to me now, and I trembled at the

---

[1] Mrs. Morgan doubtless refers to the case of General James Shields, who, during an action, was struck by a copper ball, that entered his breast, and, passing straight through his body, came out at his back; so that "daylight shone through him." After being given up by all his own army surgeons, his life was preserved by the skill of a native physician.—Ed. [Note in original.]

thought of the danger into which my temerity and pity had led me. But to withdraw at this crisis was to seal my doom with certainty, for the superstitious and revengeful "Medicine Men," whose medicines had been pronounced "no good," would then, without doubt, accuse me of causing the death of the chief. So, without further delay, I began my hazardous task, I am free to confess I did so with much trepidation.

Among several articles which my enemies had left in my possession was a white, India silk handkerchief, which had been presented to me by a sea captain years before. After making all the preparations I deemed necessary, I took this handkerchief, and, wrapping it in a peculiar manner about a thin willow wand, from which the bark had been stripped, I insinuated it into the wound, and gently and gradually worked it completely through. Upon drawing it forth there came with it a mass of coagulated blood, and at this moment, to use a common expression, "daylight shone through the wounded man's body." Immediately after this I applied the preparations I had made ready, and, before another day passed, I had the supreme satisfaction of seeing my dusky patient much easier. From this time out he steadily improved, until at last he was perfectly recovered, and became as hale and hearty as any of his braves.

The effect upon my ignorant and superstitious captors was marvellous. They now looked upon me as a being specially favored by the Great Spirit, and in short, to use their own expressive language, "Great Medicine." A portion of the lodge of The Buffalo Horn was devoted to my exclusive use; no one, not even that chieftain himself, ever intruding upon my privacy, which I maintained as much as lay in my power, leaving my rude apartment as little as possible.

In this way the summer months glided away one after another. Autumn also passed, and winter came, with its gloomy skies and fierce storms, ere I beheld the first opportunity of escape. The hope of being able to effect the latter had lived within my breast ever since I had been first spared by my strange friends. But now, as I heard the howling of the tempests that swept mercilessly over prairie and forest, and saw the blinding drifts of snow whirled furiously along the plains, and heard the cries of famishing wild beasts, I perceived that any attempt at flight would be death in its most terrible form. I, therefore, prepared to pass the dreary season as well as I could, resolving to escape during the next summer.

I often wept unconsciously as my previous life hurried before my eyes like a panorama. Each scene was distinctly brought into view, and the bright and those of bygone years, so bright, so beautiful, contrasted strangely, painfully with the dark and repulsive ones of the present. From this mental contemplation my mind would go groping blindly into the future, would reach forth into the time yet to come. My dear husband, ignorant of my captivity, would write, as usual, and his letters would be sent to the Dead Letter Office, from where it would go back a long, long journey, to tell him that I was not to be found. Weeks, months, perhaps years, would pass away, and then giving up all hope of ever seeing me again, he would mourn for me as dead, and then—but, beyond this point I could not, dared not think.

Wearily the winter dragged away, and the spring began to appear. The snows became lighter, the skies brighter, and the streams deeper. The winds, also, became more genial, and the trees and shrubs began to put forth their buds, and the birds to chirp and warble; while the grass and flowers, which, throughout the winter had been protected in the gorges and dingles of the hills, began, as it were, to flow gently, timidly out from their hiding places, in numberless streams, that, soon uniting, would cover the prairies with a sea of fragrant beauty.

When the spring had fully set in, my captors commenced to make preparations for their incursions into the plains, which they made every season when the whites were travelling to Santa Fe, Oregon, or Central California. Some little time elapsed ere these preparations were completed, and then the band of warriors, headed by my patron, The Buffalo Horn, departed upon their marauding journey. I endeavored to obtain leave to accompany the expedition with the expectation of being enabled at some time to escape, but was steadily refused, and finally obliged to retire to my lodge.

This was a sad and bitter disappointment to me, and for a few days I was much depressed, but my hopes soon began to revive again; why, I could not tell, for my chances of getting away from my vigilant friends, if I may use that term, seemed to grow less every day. Yet hope I did, and with a strength and bouyancy that astonished even myself.

During the last week in June there were but a few warriors left in the village, the rest being all absent in the expedition to which I have already referred. Among those that remained was a third chief of the tribe, who, however, was not an Indian, but a mulatto slave that had escaped from Missouri or Arkansas, and managed to make his way to the haunts of the savages. Among these latter he had, by reason of his prowess and daring, raised himself thus, and it is likely that, but for the event I am about to relate, he would have finally gained the position of first chief. This occurrence happened on the thirtieth day or rather night of June, and for awhile produced the wildest excitement in the village.

On the night in question, a messenger came to my lodge, and said that The Yellow Face—the fugitive's name among the Indians—was very sick, and wanted to see me immediately. Of late I had noticed The Yellow Face casting upon me leering glances and looks, that made me tremble, and now

I felt a chill come over me as I heard his ominous message. But I feared to disobey, and, accordingly, with the utmost trepidation, I repaired to his lodge, where I found him reclining upon a rude but comfortable couch of skins and robes. For some moments he did not take any notice of my entrance, nor in fact until I spoke. This roused him, or more properly seemed to, for that he was acting a part I now felt fully convinced, and, as he fixed upon me his black, basilisk eyes, he said:

"The Yellow Face is very sick, and has sent for the White Medicine, because her medicine is good."

The look that accompanied these words only enhanced my fears, and I was unable to utter a single word in reply, so occupied was my mind with thoughts of how I might best escape from my dangerous companion. After a moment or so of silence, The Yellow Face rose and stepped toward me, saying, in his own natural voice and language:

"Don't be afeard, Missus, I'ze not agwine to hurt you. Yah! yah! I jes want you to come and be my wife; now won't you?"

With these words the ignorant and sensual brute sprang between me and the entrance of the lodge, and then, drawing a huge scalping-knife, grinned a mocking smile, as coming toward me again, he said, in low, chuckling tones:

"Look yere, Missus, you'd better not make no noise now, else you's a dead woman, dat's all!"

The diabolical intention of the villain was instantly revealed, or rather about to be consummated, for its revelation had been cotemporary with my entrance into the lodge. Yet what availed my puny strength in the grasp of such a giant, or what aid would my shrieks bring me? None whatever for the Indians were too used to hearing the outcries of the women when beaten by the men. All this rushed through my mind, and guided my ensuing action, which was not a moment too soon, for, just as I sprang to the opposite side of the lodge, my foe was in the very act of clasping me in his foul embrace.

"God of mercy, save me!" I breathed in almost a whisper, as I bit my tongue and lips in an agony of fear and suspense, and kept my wildly staring eyes fixed upon the mulatto.

The latter, enraged that I had thus escaped him, scowled fiercely upon me, and, with a bitter oath, made a fresh attempt to grasp me. But again I managed to elude him, and bounded close to a frame of willow boughs on which were hung his shield and trappings, and against which leaned his spear and bow. With demon-like rage the monster, on finding himself thus foiled twice, leaped toward me, with an agility that precluded escape.

At this critical moment, however, and just as I gave myself up for lost, a thought struck me like an electric flash, and almost involuntarily I seized

Figure Four: "The following instant the spear head was plunged up to the pole directly in the heart of my lecherous foe, who, with a deep groan, sank dead at my feet."

the keen-pointed spear that stood within my reach, and presented it at the breast of my antagonist. Both of our motions were so sudden and equally timed, that the following instant the spear head was plunged up to the pole directly in the heart of my lecherous foe, who, with a deep groan, sank dead at my feet.

Never, never shall I forget, nor shall I ever be able truly to describe, the feelings that seized me as I looked down upon the silent and now harmless giant, whose herculian arms could, a moment previous, have crushed my life out with a single effort. For an instant a pang of sorrow wrung my heart, and then followed that peculiar sensation, or self-conviction, of having shed the blood of a fellow being. As though fascinated, I continued to gaze down upon my dead foe, the handle of the avenging spear in my hand and the blade in his bosom. From this fearful reverie I was at last suddenly aroused by a wild scream, and, starting back, I beheld the dead man's favorite squaw rush into the hut and cast herself wildly down upon the corpse.

I waited no longer; the spell of horror was broken, and, uttering a stifled shriek, I bounded from the lodge, and, with flying steps gained my own, where I shut myself up, expecting every instant to be dragged forth and torn to pieces by the infuriated friends of the deceased.

I thought my hour had come when about ten minutes later a crowd commenced yellow and hooting and screaming outside my retreat. My eyes were closed, and, bowed to earth, I commended my soul to its maker.

Minute followed minute, however, and hour succeeded hour, and yet, though the clamor seemed to increase, no one ventured to enter the lodge in which I sat trembling and despairing. Matters continued thus until the next morning, when, about two hours after sunrise, the savages who were collected around my wigwam, suddenly, and with a loud shouting, started away to some other point, and silence reigned profoundly for sometime after. Then came a scarcely audible murmur of human voices at a distance, which sound gradually increased in volume until I became convinced that the savages were returning. They had been, as I subsequently learned, summoned away to meet the war party of The Buffalo Horn, who had come back at that juncture from his marauding expedition in the plains.

I knew the revengeful dispositions of my wild companions, and I was moreover aware of the celebrity of the Chief whom, in defence of what was far dearer to me than life, I had, God knew, unintentionally slain. And, in this connection, I deem it only justice to the Indians, to say, that in their primitive state, far removed from the frontier, the crime of ravishing captive women, so common and hellish a vice among civilized nations, is entirely unknown. This statement may dissipate the romance many writers have imparted to their stories of the Indians and beautiful white captive maidens, but it is nevertheless a fact. An American savage will mercilessly butcher white women, but a wild and chivalrous honor deters him from ravishing or scalping them.

It must have been noon when at last my anxiety was somewhat relieved by a crier or runner of The Buffalo Horn, who announced to me that that chieftain wished to see me. The name and order of my friend seemed instantly to revive my spirit, and, strangely enough, I immediately began to hope. I was soon in the presence of The Buffalo Horn, who questioned me concerning the tragedy, in the manner rather of an old practitioner of law, than that of an untutored savage. I stated the whole matter simply and truthfully from beginning to end, confident that there was no other or better cause I could pursue.

How the doom that I had so fully expected would meet me, was ever turned aside, I never learned, but the following morning The Buffalo Horn told me that the friends of the deceased were satisfied, and that I was, therefore, in no further danger. Upon hearing this I fell upon my knees, and thanked my Heavenly Father that even far away in the wilderness, and in the midst of barbarous enemies, He had not forgotten me, but had thus far mercifully preserved me, and brought me safely through all dangers and tribulations. Oh, what a holy unction to the soul is the confidence of the humblest Christian, in the goodness and mercy of God. It is a well of pure water in the desert, and the shadow of a great rock in a dry and barren land.

My mind had no sooner became freed from the terrible suspense which had hung over me than I immediately began to devise new plans for my escape. It was a strange, wild idea that had taken possession of me, was this idea of escape, and it is certain that had I been fully informed of the fearful perils attending the attempt, I should never have had the courage or temerity to put it in execution. But, at the time, I thought to myself that all I had to do was to steal away from the village, get safely out of sight of my foes, and then ride along until I fell in with some caravan or other crossing the plains to California.

My long wished and prayed for opportunity at length presented itself, and, one morning, just after sunrise, with a few necessary articles secured about my person, I mounted a splendid horse belonging to a noted warrior, and, giving him the whip, dashed away from the village with lightning speed. What emotions took possession of me as I swept over the swelling prairie, or through a woodland glade, it would be impossible for me even faintly to describe. I felt free, and yet it seemed as though an invisible arm was continually stretching forth to seize and drag me back into captivity.

The astonished groups of squaws and children through whom I rode, gazed at me in mute wonderment, as I flew onward, and never seemed to be aware of my intentions till I had cleared the last row of lodges, when at once comprehending all, they raised a terrible clamor, which, being borne on the wind to my ears, told me what I might now expect.

Desperation lent calmness, and, with a firm, steady hand, I guided my horse in the best directions, and kept the while a sharp look out in front, behind, and on either side of me for any outlying or pursuing parties of my dusky captors. Thank Heaven, none appeared, and I was beginning to congratulate myself that all was going well, when I dashed into a piece of woodland which, though open at first, immediately began to get thicker and more difficult. The long branches and limbs of the trees, as the wind imparted motion to them, seemed to reach down and snatch at me as I stooped close to my animal's neck to avoid or escape them.

Twenty minutes thus riding at speed through a forest is an extremely dangerous undertaking, for the horseman may in a twinkling be swept from the saddle, and left bleeding, perhaps killed, in his own track. I was fortunate, however, and with many hard brushes and several narrow misses of the leafy arms that continually grasped at me, I at length emerged into a stretch of open plain, and once more sat easily on my flying steed.

For several hours I rode forward, hoping every instant to see wagons, and white men who would, of course, rescue and protect me. But my eyes were strained in vain. I beheld no sign of human or even animal life in any direction. All was grand; all was beautiful; all was silent. Beneath me was the prairie with its lakes and rivers of fragrant, beautiful flowers, and its rich, green grass. Miles away behind me I could just catch glimpses of the forest that bordered the streams in that direction. Miles away before me I beheld the same undulating lakes and rivers of fragrant flowers and rich, green grass, while overhead was, what cannot be more aptly termed, the prairie sky. There is a peculiarity in this prairie sky, entirely cloudless as it often is, from the zenith to the horizon, and lit up by the full blaze of the summer sun. The bright, dark blue of the firmamental dome seems toned down somewhat by the whiteness, a barely perceptible vail or film, which makes the beholder think of spirit, fills his mind involuntarily with ideas of the soul, ideas of God.

Thus I mused even in the midst of danger, not knowing at what moment my pursuers might come in sight, and as I continued riding along at a slower pace in this grand, wild solitude, my thoughts gradually turned upon my husband. How long I remained in this abstracted mood I know not, but I was awakened at last from the delicious reverie by the sudden stopping of my horse.

In an instant I recovered myself, and scanned the horizon in all directions, but saw no foe. My steed, feeling himself to be his own master, had halted to rest himself, and drink of a little stream of water, that was here so narrow, that it was completely hidden beneath the long, rank grass of the plain through which it meandered. The action of the animal immediately reminded me of my own necessities, and, dismounting, I proceeded to prepare a meal.

Imagine my despair, however, on finding that the bundle in which I had wrapped up my scanty supply was gone. It must have been swept from my back, to which it had been secured or lashed by a strong pair of thongs, during my perilous ride through the forest some hours previous. At first I gave myself up for lost; for I knew I could obtain no food in the wilderness, and, as I had not yet met with the white travellers I had expected to fall in with, I instantly went to the other extreme, and decided that I never would.

However, after taking a deep draught from the welcome stream, and bathing my face and aching head in its cool waters, I felt much better, and praying to my Heavenly Father to guide me safely, I once more mounted my steed, and set forward at a venture. Just before sunset I espied at a distance a clump of bushes, and riding up to it, I tied my horse, and threw myself down upon the grass to stretch and rest my cramped and tired limbs.

As I did so, my eyes were attracted by the glitter of something in the grass at the edge of the clump. Upon reaching forth my hand to take it, I perceived it to be a small pocket compass. I did not, however, touch it, for at that instant, I discovered another fact, one which made my heart cease beating with horror. The compass rested among the bones of a human skeleton, which, having been scarcely covered with earth when buried, had become in the course of time thus partially exposed to view. It was now almost hidden, at least to a careless traveller, by the rank grass and flowers of the prairie.

Shuddering throughout my whole being, I started up, seized the bridle of my steed, and was just in the act of mounting, and speeding away from the fearful spot, when a thought restrained me. The compass was an article of the highest value in this vast wilderness; I had none. By its guidance I might reach friends; how, I could not tell; but the disturbed idea floated through my mind, like a flitting will-o'-the-wisp, that compasses led people in the right direction, guided them wherever they wished to go. This to me was rescue, it was life, it was safety; and, despite the chill of horror that crept over me at the thought of taking the coveted prize from amongst the mouldering bones of an unfortunate human being, who thus lay dreamlessly reposing in his shallow, prairie grave, I resolved to take it.

Quickly turning, therefore, I stepped back a pace or two, stooped down, and, with great drops of perspiration falling from my brow, I seized the compass, thrust it in the folds of the Indian blanket, which was wrapped about me, vaulted to the back of my horse, and dashed away like one guilty of a sacrilegious act.

The sun finally went down below the horizon, the twilight deepened into gloom, the stars, one after another, twinkling forth in the sky, night stole gradually over the prairie, and I was still a lost wanderer. Alone on the prairie! How much is contained in that little sentence. So terrible were the feelings that oppressed me, as I continued riding hither and thither, that I wished myself back a hundred times with my wild and savage captors, the Pawnees. I had tasted no food since daylight, and I began also to suffer extremely with thirst. But there was no help, no food, no water! It seemed as though I was doomed to die of starvation.

Exhausted and despairing, I at length dismounted from my nearly worn out animal and threw myself down upon the grass and fragrant flowers to sleep. And sleep I did, soundly enough, until perhaps midnight, when I was suddenly aroused by a loud clap of thunder. In an instant my eyes were opened, but fear prevented me from rising, for immediately over my head, and glaring directly at me, were a pair of huge eyeballs, and a hot, heavy breath came upon my face. I gave myself up for lost; a wild beast had found me, and I was about to be devoured. Judge of my delighted surprise, however, when, a moment later the horrid monster gave a whinny of pleasure at finding himself successful in awakening me. It was the noble animal which had borne me so faithfully during the day. Affrighted by the approaching storm he had come thus to me for protection and companionship. I immediately arose and remained awake throughout the night, gently carressing him, and cowering behind him from the tempest which raged with fearful violence until daybreak.

Famishing, wet and despairing as I was, I felt ready, as I gazed through the falling rain over the prairie, to put an end to my miserable life. But once more came that same old thought—I might yet see my husband—and immediately all ideas of self-destruction were banished. But whither should I turn? I knew no path nor direction in which to travel.

In this dilemma I resolved to mount my dripping steed, and, leaving him to his own instinct, allow him to carry me wherever he chose. No sooner was my resolution made than it was put into execution, and, a few minutes later, the sagacious animal, with the bridle lying loosely upon his neck, was cantering toward the Northwest. By this time my hunger had become so intense, that I gnawed ravenously at the raw-hide whip I carried, hoping thus to partially allay the fierceness of my appetite.

One fact struck me particularly, which was, that my horse swerved neither to right or left, but kept steadily on in the direction he had first taken. His speed also seemed to increase, as he progressed. A thrill of joy passed through me, as, calling to mind all I had ever read concerning the sagacity of horses, I became confident that the one I rode was bearing me to friends and rescue. Though ready to fall to the earth with debility, the cheering thought buoyed me up, and I continually swept the horizon in front with anxious eyes, expecting every instance to catch sight of some friendly camp of whites.

Late in the afternoon it seemed to me as though the more noticeable spots, past which I had been riding for the last two hours, had a familiar look. Yet on I went, entirely unsuspecting, until, just as I rose over a ridge of the prairie, I came in full view of the identical Pawnee village from which I had, with so much peril, escaped. With my crooked, devious travelling I had only gone a distance away from it in a whole day and part of a night that my horse accomplished in half the time, and going at a much slower pace. My heart sank within me at the sight, and I felt ready now to curse the sagacity of my steed, or rather my own stupidity, in supposing that when I left him to his own instinct he would bear me to a white camp instead of back to his master's lodge.

However, a crisis was before me, and my desperate condition forced me to put a bold face upon the matter. So, without hesitation, I galloped straight into the village, through groups of my dusky captors, who, to my utter astonishment, received me with marks of joy and respect. My astonishment was immediately followed by pleasure, as, by this manifestation, it became evident to me that the savages looked upon my journey as "Medicine," or "a great mystery." When on the day previous I had ridden forth into the wilderness, it was thought my intention was to escape; but when the Indians saw me, as they supposed, thus voluntarily returning, it was "Medicine."

A terrible load was thus removed from off my mind, and, with a lightened heart, I dashed up to my own lodge, turned my horse loose, and entered the humble, and I must confess, at the moment, very welcome abode.

My escape had been so narrow that I could not summon nerve enough during the remainder of the summer to attempt another one, and, of course, it would have been sheer madness for me to brave the rigors of the wilderness in winter. So, Fortune, that fickle goddess, compelled me to remain a helpless captive until the following summer, when I once more made an effort to gain my freedom, or, more properly speaking, to reach some party of whites journeying to California. This getting to California, that I might rejoin my husband, was the only thought which had continual possession of my mind. As I sat alone in my rude wigwam, it was before me, as I slept at night it haunted me in dreams, and I could never banish it. It became a monomania. Often and often I almost repeated to myself those beautiful, beautiful lines:

> No! the heart that has truly lov'd never forgets,
> But as truly loves on to the close,
> As the sunflower turns on her God when he sets
> The same look which she turned when he rose.

Before making this last attempt for liberty, I took every precaution so as to insure my success, and, so far as effecting my release from my present captors was concerned, my fortune was all that I could have desired. But the fate of the fish, that leaped from the frying pan into the fire, was an exact parallel with my own, for; after travelling eastwardly for several days, I fell in with a small party of Kaskaskia Indians, who, though not exactly capturing me, as the term is usually accepted, for they were just then on friendly terms with the whites, would not suffer me to proceed in the direction I wished, but forced me to go along with them to their village. This was built, or rather pitched, upon the north bank of the Kansas river, one hundred and fifty or two hundred miles Southwest of Fort Leavenworth.

It was not long before I discovered that my fame, as "The Great White Medicine," had reached my new captors, and, on apparently assenting to remain always with the Kaskaskias, I was treated by them with as much respect, I may say reverence, as I had been by the Pawnees. Still, however, the village being in such close proximity to the border, the savages kept so strict a watch upon all my movements, that I found it utterly impossible to make any successful endeavor to escape. Several times indeed, I had every preparation made, but was each time baffled by some unexpected circumstance or other. On the last occasion it seemed as though Fate had sternly set her face against my ever regaining my freedom.

At the time of which I speak I had been a prisoner among the Kaskaskias two years. During the latter portion of these two years I had, as I fully believed, induced my captors to place the fullest confidence in my intentions of remaining with them during the rest of my life. It was not long after this that I determined to start for Fort Leavenworth, where, could I only succeed in reaching it, I would be safe. Since my first effort to escape from the Pawnees I had gained a vast amount of information which it was necessary that I should possess to make success certain, or at least to make it as nearly attainable as human events could be. How far I succeeded the sequal will show.

On the day I finally resolved to start for the Fort, I arranged the most minute particulars of my future programme with the utmost precision. The weather favored my design. Rain had been falling heavily all day, which had the effect of keeping the Indians close in their lodges. To make assurance doubly sure, however, I deferred setting forth on my perilous journey until nightfall. My hopes increased as the day wore away without any abatement of the storm, and I felt certain of success as, at midnight, I stole stealthily to where the horses were coralled, selected the best one, mounted him, and rode softly, slowly away until I got at a safe distance from the town. Then, with a fervently breathed prayer to that God, who watches the mighty, solemn wilderness with equal care as he does the bustling metropolis, I dashed swiftly forward into the pitchy gloom. On I sped for Fort Leavenworth.

Soon after I had set out, it began to thunder heavily, and lighten frequently and very vividly. Indeed, so terrific did the scene at length become, that I was forcibly reminded by it of the plague sent upon the ancient Egyptians. From the zenith, the livid glare would burst forth, and leap instantly and in all directions to the horizon, while almost at the same moment, the bellowing thunder would come booming and rattling down from heaven, and go rumbling away over the prairie, only to be immediately followed by still more vivid flashes, and still louder thunder claps.

Oh! how strange did my situation at this moment seem, when I compared it to that which I had occupied in the earlier part of my life. I, who was then a delicate, puny girl, shrinking from airs too chilly, or sunshine too warm; I, who then trembled at the slightest peril, was now dashing fearlessly through a fearful tempest, over a mighty prairie, with the blazing bolts of Heaven falling at my very feet, the wind howling in my ears, and torrents of rain drenching me through and through. Yet, I was not cast down, for my trust was in God, and I knew that if it was His holy will to bring me safely through, nothing could prevail against me.

With this comforting assurance, I pushed on during the dreary night, until just before I supposed the dawn to be at hand, when, coming to a stretch of timber, I resolved to halt and give my good steed, as well as myself, some rest.

As the sun came up, the storm began to break away, and, by the time the former had been shining two hours, the sky was, with the exception of here and there a fleecy bank, entirely clear of clouds. After making a frugal meal from some dried meat and parched corn, I again hastened forward, confident that my trail from the Indian village had been entirely obliterated by the heavy rain which had fallen. Consulting the precious compass, mentioned in a former page, and which I had preserved with religious care, I found that I was travelling in the proper direction. Full of joy, I became light of heart, and I fear light of head also, for I patted my steed lovingly on the neck, and addressed him in the most endearing terms, promising him another rest at a stream which I knew to be only a short distance ahead, from the line of trees within sight, growing on its margin.

Nearly a mile to the northward of where I was, I perceived a large band of buffaloes, that, with furious bellowings, was rushing headlong in the same direction as myself. This convinced me of two things, one of which at least was far from agreeable. The first was that these buffaloes, or correctly speaking, bisons, were crossing the stream beyond, and the second was that being so far out of their usual range, they must have been pursued by Indians. This latter fact rendered me uneasy, for I knew of no tribe in this section of country save the Kaskaskias, and should I unfortunately fall in with any party of the latter I feared that Fortune might not furnish me as good a plea as she had on the occasion of my flight from the Pawnee village. But there was no time to waste in calculations now. It was forward, forward with all speed to Fort Leavenworth, and forward did I go.

I reached the bank of the creek which I had seen, with the intention of resting awhile on this side, and then fording it, continue my journey till sunset. My feelings, however, may be imagined when, instead of a crystal, pearly stream, I found a muddy, rushing torrent, roaring angrily, and bearing fiercely along on its bosom, huge quantities of drift wood and trees, besides many an unfortunate bison. These last had been swept down by the tremendous force of the current, and were struggling frightfully, endeavoring to climb up on each other's backs, and hooking each other's eyes out. Many also had been dashed against the opposite shore, where they now stood panting, unable to climb the steep, slippery bank, and half submerged in mud and water. The scene was appalling, and I shrank back as did also my horse.

But at this instant, and even while I was debating what I should do, I chanced to cast my eyes back over the route in which I had come, and there, not far off, I beheld a sight still more appalling than the rushing river; a score of naked savages, mounted on half wild horses. As they noticed that I saw them, they set up a fearful yelling, and galloped faster than ever to overtake me.

Instantly my determination was fixed, and, with a wild and involuntary shriek, I dashed my noble, high-mettled steed straight into the foaming torrent. A moment, and then the angry waves were lashing about me, and causing my horse to snort with terror. Yet on he kept, guided by my hand, until we had neared the opposite shore, when all at once a fearful whoop resounded from the bank behind, followed instantly by a ringing of rifles, and a whistling of bullets around us. But neither of us, strange to say, was struck, although an unfortunate bison beside us sank dead at the fire.

We were close to the other bank, which, as I have said, was lined for some distance down with half exhausted bisons, which, however, as they saw us approaching, prepared to give us battle, fearful that we were going to push them from their foothold.

"Great God!" I gasped, as I saw this new danger, "even the wild beasts are against me!"

The words had scarcely left my lips before the noble steed, that had carried me so faithfully, was forced directly against the horns of a huge bull, who, with a bellow of rage, and a last effort at self-preservation, gored him, and actually tossed him, with me still on his back, several feet into the air. All I remember after that was pitching upward and forward, striking heavily on the bank, and scrambling to a level spot out of danger of rolling back into the river. When consciousness returned I found myself lying at the foot of a tree, and my hands tied securely behind me with a long thong, which in turn was fastened around the trunk of a tree.

I saw in a moment that they were a roving band of Indians, who having recognized and captured me, intended to carry me back to their village, from which I had escaped.

I will not dwell upon the rough treatment I received at the hands of these savages, who, had I been a common prisoner, instead of "The Great Medicine," would have soon tomahawked me; neither is it necessary that I should minutely record the events of my subsequent life among them.

Suffice it to say, that in the latter part of 1861 an agent from Albert Pike, a man well known among the Indians, arrived at the village, and held several conferences with the principal men of the tribe, the result of which was, that nearly all the warriors prepared themselves to follow their chief to battle. Obtaining an interview with this man, I related my story to him, and begged of him to intercede with my captors. This he promised to do, expressing at the same time great commiseration with me in my misfortunes. From him I learned for the first time that a bloody war was being waged between the North and South. I could not bring myself to believe it, and yet the preparations going forward indicated something unusual. All I could do was to wait and see how matters would turn out.

Before the agent left, it was agreed between him and the Indians, that I should be allowed to accompany them until reaching Arkansas, when I should be set free. I named Fort Leavenworth to him, but he peremptorily refused to allow me to go thither, why I did not realize at the time, but it has since become clear to me. I was also too thankful for the privilege already granted, to complain of any seeming inconvenience.

From that time forward I looked anxiously every day for the departure of the warriors, who were to march at a given signal into Arkansas, to join an Indian army there under the command of General Pike. This signal was not given until the beginning of February. There was, however, no delay after that, and accordingly we soon found ourselves in Pike's camp, where were already congregated a large number of Indians—some four or five thousand—gathered from many different tribes along the frontiers.

It was during my stay in the rebel camp, that I fully learned the nature of the contest that was going on, from a sick Union prisoner, whom I tended.

I could see that it was not intended that I should escape, as a guard was placed at the opening of my tent, both night and day.

I resolved to escape, if possible, at the first opportunity. I was informed that a battle was about to take place between the Union and a portion of the Southern army. At last the time for action came. It was the night before the battle. Who could say, what the next day would bring forth?

As I lay in the tent assigned me by the General, I thought I heard a sound, as if some one was talking, yes, I was not mistaken; it was two guards, one of whom was placed there to guard me, the other had come to relieve the first, I could hear every word they said.

"You know the captain said we must watch her well, cause you know she might give us the slip," said one of the men.

"Yes, yes," said the other, "but we can just slip over to Jim Carsons, and get a little of his whiskey, the 'gal's' sound asleep 'fore this."

"Don't talk so loud," said the first, "she might wake up and hear you."

"Well, here goes," said the second.

I then heard their footsteps, as they silently left my tent.

As I lay thus the thought entered my mind, that escape was possible. I might try; if they did catch me, they would only bring me back, and guard me more securely. Why not try it? My mind was made up instantly.

I quietly arose and softly wended my way to the opening in the tent. I felt the fresh air as it was gently wafted upon my fevered cheeks and brow. "Oh for liberty once again!" I looked upon both sides of me, all was as silent as the grave. I advanced a few steps, and then stopped. I trembled in every limb. I could not move. I stood there like a marble statue. I stood thus for a few moments before I could regain my composure enough to go forward. I had taken but a few steps, when I heard the guards returning. I crouched behind some bushes which grew near the place where I then stood. Having reached the tent, one of them looked in, saying at the same time, "he supposed the 'gal' was all right."

"Never fear for that," said the other.

They then separated, one going toward his own tent, and the other having stationed himself in front of mine.

I dared hardly breathe, the guard lay within eight feet of where I was. None can describe my feelings on that occasion.

The guard would frequently drink of whiskey, which he had in his canteen. This frequent pulling at the canteen (as the soldiers say) soon made him drunk.

As soon as I was sure that he was too drunk to create any alarm, I quickly arose from my painful position, and turned in the direction of the Union encampment, which I reached two hours before sunrise.

I was taken before the General in command, to whom I told a portion of my story. After he had heard it, he informed me that I was very welcome, as I brought him news of the Confederates, and that I might be of some use on the morrow.

I was shown a tent in which to sleep. I laid down, and was soon fast asleep. I awoke in the morning to hear the firing of cannon, and the cries of the wounded.

The battle had now began in earnest; it lasted three days. On the second, as I was standing among the wounded in the rear, I beheld a Confederate, who had apparently been leading his company, running and fighting his way through the companies in advance of him, reached the Union army, his clothing perfectly riddled by bullets, having also (as I learned afterward) received several serious wounds.

I saw them lift this man off of the ground on which he had fallen, and bring him toward the sick and wounded. Yes, even toward the tent near which I then stood.

"Who is he?" I exclaimed.

"We don't know, marm," said one of the men who had brought him. "We heard the Rebs say that he was a traitor."

"Traitor! who calls me a traitor?" exclaimed the wounded man. No one answering, he said "No, thank God! The man who fights for that glorious ensign of American Independence, is no traitor. I repeat it, is no traitor."

The exertion had been too much for him; he fainted in the arms of a soldier, who was holding him.

As he was speaking, it seemed to me that I had seen that man before. Where had I seen that face? It seemed strangely familiar to me, but I could not place it.

They laid him on the couch that I had occupied before he came. As they did so, one of the soldiers turning to me said, "Madame, we leave this wounded, perhaps dying, man in your charge."

They then left me, perhaps never to return again. I watched by the side of this wounded soldier's bed for five long weary hours. At last he opened his eyes and gazed upon me in a wild manner. He had a burning fever; he talked of fighting Indians and digging for gold. At last his eyes were closed; he slept, and in his dream I heard him talk of a wife whom he had not seen for years.

One day as I watched, as usual by his bedside, I heard him utter the name of Gertrude; I turned toward him, and his lips again uttered the name of Gertrude. What could this mean? I uttered my thoughts aloud, which awoke him, he looked at me in that same strange manner.

"Those eyes! Where had I seen them before? They were my husband's. Thank God! I knew him now."

I told my story to the Doctor, who informed me, that if I valued the life of my husband, I must keep out of the tent, as any sudden excitement would kill him.

Thus for two weeks I waited. Oh, how long they seemed; it was almost as if two years instead of weeks had passed.

At last I was permitted to see him, and converse with him.

I will pass over the joy of both, after having been separated so long. After I had told my story, (which the reader already knows,) he related his, which I will give in his own words. He began as follows:

"After I left Chouteau's Station, I fell in with some hunters, and learning that they were going in the same direction as I, we joined company.

"I will pass over the many dangers encountered, and hardships endured by us, (as it would fill a whole volume;) suffice it to say that we reached the gold regions; and after having lived there nearly six years, (not having heard from you all this time, except that you had been taken captive, I had long since mourned you as dead,) I started for home, (having amassed a fair fortune.) I had come about half the distance, between Chouteau's Station and the Missouri river, when I was captured by a band of Indians. I supposed immediately, that my captors were a roving band of Kaskaskias, whom I had thus accidentally fallen in with, and who, having captured me, intended to carry me to their village. The event proved the correctness of the supposition.

"I need not dwell upon the rough usage I met with at the hands of the savages. Suffice it to say, that in a few days we reached the village.

"The day arrived for me to be burned at the stake, but an All-seeing Providence prevented it. A terrible storm arose, carrying off every thing in its course. The stake to which I was to have been burned was uprooted and carried away by the wind; the lightning flashed, the thunder roared, and the rain came down in torrents. The storm lasted three hours.

"The Indians, being of a very superstitious nature, thought that it was an interposition of their Great Spirit, or God, and from that time I was treated in the best possible manner, for white man to be treated by the uncivilized Indians. They looked upon me as a wonderful personage, though, at the same time, I was guarded in the strictest manner.

"I lived among these savages for almost five years. I joined in their sports until I became quite an adept. One day, as I with several others was hunting near the village, a runner came in, out of breath, from whom we learned (I had learned to speak the Indian tongue) that a war had broken out between the North and South, and that the tribe to which they belonged was offered very enticing inducements to join the Southerners.

"I will pass over the excitement which prevailed among those belonging to the tribe; it having been decided that they should join the Confederates, I asked the privilege of going with them, which was granted.

"In due time we arrived at the confederate encampment, where I was selected as a lieutenant of an infantry company. With seeming gladness I accepted the commission, resolving at the same time never to fight against the Old Flag.

"During the first day's engagement, I was too sick to join my company, but on the second, the captain being killed in the first engagement, the command, of course, devolved upon me—therefore I was obliged to comply.

"As I was apparently leading my company, I turned and fought my way to the Union Army, where I am, thank God, this day."

I will pass over the events which occurred during our stay in the Union Army. Suffice it to say, that after procuring a pass for New York, we reached that city in due time.

And now that my narrative is finished, dear reader, I would say to you, may you never encounter the dangers or endure the hardships of Gertrude Morgan.

THE END

A Captive Indian

GERONIMO

I f one mentioned the term *American Indian captivity* to an uninformed
person on the street, the words might be understood to refer to an Indian
or Indians being held captive, not to the captivity of a white person among
Indians. And indeed the Indian captivity narrative genre, with its pervasive
racial perspective, needs to be turned inside out. During the same period
when hundreds of Anglo-American settlers were captured and held as prisoners by American Indians, many thousands of Indians were captured, imprisoned, or relocated by colonial and U.S. military forces. The removal of
the Cherokee from their southeastern homelands to Oklahoma "Indian
Territory" in the 1830s is only the most infamous of many such forced re-
locations, and it did arouse some political opposition from sympathetic
whites. Popular captivity narratives, particularly during the nineteenth century, did the ideological work of justifying such removals by branding Indians with a collective responsibility for the capture of white women.

The capture and relocation of Native Americans has been less recognized. In the twentieth century, official U.S. government policy toward Indians included sending children to boarding schools far from home where
they were prohibited from speaking their native languages. Even today,
when native cultures are better recognized, many native people leave reser-
vations to seek jobs in large cities. This process of assimilation, forced or
voluntary, might be seen as a version of the initiation rites endured by
James Smith and others. The process can be examined in an extreme form
in the story of Ishi, a Yahi Indian of northern California who in 1911 was
taken from his hunter-gatherer life and spent his last five years as a kind of
living exhibit in a San Francisco museum.

Yet even during times of shrill racist diatribes against American Indians, the violent resistance of a few heroic Indian leaders aroused great

admiration from the American public. Black Hawk of the Sauk, Osceola of the Seminole, Joseph of the Nez Percé, and Geronimo of the Apache all became popular heroes after they were defeated and captured. Their courage inspired Americans' romantic identification with the underdog, while their final fate emblematized the figure of the "vanishing Indian" and the official policy of destroying or assimilating Native American peoples.

Geronimo was born in 1829 in what is today southeastern Arizona, the homeland of the Chiricahua band of the Apache, which he called "Bedonkohe" in his narrative. The opening chapter of his autobiography tells the origin story of his tribe, and although the Apache were a mobile, raiding people, Geronimo recalls no conflicts with colonists before he reached maturity and became a warrior. Before 1853 this area was part of Mexico, and Part 2 of *Geronimo's Story*, which immediately precedes the chapters included here (chaps. 13–17, 19, and 21–23) is titled "The Mexicans" and recounts a series of battles beginning with the massacre at Kaskiyeh. The effect is to cast the Mexican army as a different class of enemy from the Americans or "white men" introduced in chapter 13. After all, many readers would remember the war fought against Mexico in which the Apache homelands became territories of the United States. In 1875 U.S. troops began trying to force the Chiricahuas onto a reservation at San Carlos, Arizona. After the betrayal of the band led by chief Mangus-Colorado (recounted in chap. 14), Geronimo had good reason to be suspicious of the whites' promises, and he preferred to stay at Fort Bowie, near Apache Pass (described in chap. 15). So he and an ally, Victoria, leader of another Apache band, fled from this captivity, first in 1876 and again in 1881 (misdated as 1883 in chap. 16). The army's General George Crook was sent out to recapture Geronimo, and in a meeting at Cañon de los Embudos in March 1886 he thought he had accomplished his mission. But as Geronimo explained (at the beginning of chap. 17), he did not trust in these promises either. His band continued to run from the U.S. Army, now commanded by General Nelson Miles, until September 4, when he surrendered and his captivity began.

Geronimo and his small band of Apaches were sent by train to Florida, from where their captors could be confident they would not escape again. After eight years there and in Alabama, they were moved again, to Fort Sill, Oklahoma. In 1904 Stephen Melvil Barrett, superintendent of schools in Lawton, Oklahoma, met Geronimo and conceived the project of taking down his life story. Since few Indians could write English, such "as told to" texts were the typical way in which Indian personal narratives reached print. Black Hawk's autobiography of 1832 was perhaps the first book of this type, and scholars Arnold Krupat and David Brumble have examined the peculiar features and problems such bicultural documents pose for readers. Geronimo, like Black Hawk, did not speak English. Geronimo's nephew, Asa Daklugie, translated for Barrett, who paid both of them for their work. Although the story of a courageous Indian chief was sure to find a market, Barrett was apprehensive about censorship by the Army, which, of course, still held Geronimo as a captive at Fort Sill. At first the fort commander denied Barrett permission to do the book; only the intervention of President Roosevelt cleared the way for the project. Barrett then included footnotes disclaiming responsibility for the text's criticism of Crook and other military personnel, and Geronimo sprinkled the text with references to his relationship to the president, from whom he requested freedom and the return of his tribe's Arizona lands. (All footnotes in the selection that follows are from Barrett's original edition.) Geronimo died in 1909, nearly eighty years old and still a captive at Fort Sill.

Source

Geronimo. *Geronimo's Story of His Life.* 1906. Ed. S. M. Barrett. Williamstown: Corner House, 1973.

Supplementary Readings

Brumble, H. David, III. *American Indian Autobiography.* Berkeley: U of California P, 1988.

Kroeber, Theodora. *Ishi in Two Worlds: A Biography of the Last Wild Indian in North America.* Berkeley: U of California P, 1961.

Krupat, Arnold. *Ethnocriticism: Ethnography, History, Literature.* Berkeley: U of California P, 1992.

———, ed. *Native American Autobiography: An Anthology.* Madison: U of Wisconsin P, 1994.

FROM *GERONIMO'S STORY OF HIS LIFE*

S. M. Barrett

XIII
Coming of the White Men

About the time of the massacre of "Kaskiyeh" (1858) we heard that some white men were measuring land to the south of us. In company with a number of other warriors I went to visit them. We could not understand them very well, for we had no interpreter, but we made a treaty with them by shaking hands and promising to be brothers. Then we made our camp near their camp, and they came to trade with us. We gave them buckskin, blankets, and ponies in exchange for shirts and provisions. We also brought them game, for which they gave us some money. We did not know the value of this money, but we kept it and later learned from the Navajo Indians that it was very valuable.

Every day they measured land with curious instruments and put down marks which we could not understand. They were good men, and we were sorry when they had gone on into the west. They were not soldiers. These were the first white men I ever saw.

About ten years later some more white men came. These were all warriors. They made their camp on the Gila River south of Hot Springs. At first they were friendly and we did not dislike them, but they were not as good as those who came first.

After about a year some trouble arose between them and the Indians, and I took the warpath as a warrior, not as a chief.[1] I had not been wronged, but some of my people had been, and I fought with my tribe; for the soldiers and not the Indians were at fault.

---

[1] As a tribe they would fight under their tribal chief, Mangus-Colorado. If several tribes had been called out, the war chief, Geronimo, would have commanded.

Not long after this some of the officers of the United States troops invited our leaders to hold a conference at Apache Pass (Fort Bowie). Just
before noon the Indians were shown into a tent and told that they would
be given something to eat. When in the tent they were[2] attacked by soldiers. Our chief, Mangus-Colorado, and several other warriors, by cutting through the tent, escaped; but most of the warriors were killed or
captured. Among the Bedonkohe Apaches killed at this time were Sanza,
Kladetahe, Niyokahe, and Gopi. After this treachery the Indians went
back to the mountains and left the fort entirely alone. I do not think that
the agent had anything to do with planning this, for he had always treated
us well. I believe it was entirely planned by the soldiers.

From[3] the very first the soldiers sent out to our western country, and
the officers in charge of them, did not hesitate to wrong the Indians. They
never explained to the Government when an Indian was wronged, but always reported the misdeeds of the Indians. Much that was done by mean
white men was reported at Washington as the deeds of my people.

The Indians always tried to live peaceably with the white soldiers and
settlers. One day during the time that the soldiers were stationed at Apache
Pass I made a treaty with the post. This was done by shaking hands and
promising to be brothers. Cochise and Mangus-Colorado did likewise. I
do not know the name of the officer in command, but this was the first regiment that ever came to Apache Pass. This treaty was made about a year
before we were attacked in a tent, as above related. In a few days after the
attack at Apache Pass we organized in the mountains and returned to fight
the soldiers. There were two tribes—the Bedonkohe and the Chokonen
Apaches, both commanded by Cochise. After a few days' skirmishing we
attacked a freight train that was coming in with supplies for the Fort. We
killed some of the men and captured the others. These prisoners our chief
offered to trade for the Indians whom the soldiers had captured at the
massacre in the tent. This the officers refused, so we killed our prisoners,

---

[2] Regarding this attack, Mr. L. C. Hughes, editor of *The Star,* Tucson, Arizona, to whom
I was referred by General Miles, writes as follows:
  "It appears that Cochise and his tribe had been on the warpath for some time and
he with a number of subordinate chiefs was brought into the military camp at Bowie under the promise that a treaty of peace was to be held, when they were taken into a large
tent where handcuffs were put upon them. Cochise, seeing this, cut his way through the
tent and fled to the mountains; and in less than six hours had surrounded the camp with
from three to five hundred warriors; but the soldiers refused to make fight."
[3] This sweeping statement is more general than we are willing to concede, yet it may be
more nearly true than our own accounts. [Barrett's note.]

Figure Five: Geronimo in a watermelon patch at Fort Sill. At the left is his sixth wife, Zi-yah. (*Courtesy of the U.S. Army Museum, Fort Sill, Oklahoma*)

disbanded, and went into hiding in the mountains. Of those who took part in this affair I am the only one now living.

In a few days troops were sent out to search for us, but as we were disbanded, it was, of course, impossible for them to locate any hostile camp. During the time they were searching for us many of our warriors (who were thought by the soldiers to be peaceable Indians) talked to the officers and men, advising them where they might find the camp they sought, and while they searched we watched them from our hiding places and laughed at their failures.

After this trouble all of the Indians agreed not to be friendly with the white men any more. There was no general engagement, but a long struggle followed. Sometimes we attacked the white men—sometimes they attacked us. First a few Indians would be killed and then a few soldiers. I think the killing was about equal on each side. The number killed in these troubles did not amount to much, but this treachery on the part of the soldiers had angered the Indians and revived memories of other wrongs, so that we never again trusted the United States troops.

XIV
Greatest of Wrongs

Perhaps the greatest wrong ever done to the Indians was the treatment received by our tribe from the United States troops about 1863. The chief of our tribe, Mangus-Colorado, went to make a treaty of peace for our people with the white settlement at Apache Tejo, New Mexico. It had been reported to us that the white men in this settlement were more friendly and more reliable than those in Arizona, that they would live up to their treaties and would not wrong the Indians.

Mangus-Colorado, with three other warriors, went to Apache Tejo and held a council with these citizens and soldiers. They told him that if he would come with his tribe and live near them, they would issue to him, from the Government, blankets, flour, provisions, beef, and all manner of supplies. Our chief promised to return to Apache Tejo within two weeks. When he came back to our settlement he assembled the whole tribe in council. I did not believe that the people at Apache Tejo would do as they said and therefore I opposed the plan, but it was decided that with part of the tribe Mangus-Colorado should return to Apache Tejo and receive an issue of rations and supplies. If they were as represented, and if these white men would keep the treaty faithfully, the remainder of the tribe would join him and we would make our permanent home at Apache Tejo. I was to remain in charge of that portion of the tribe which stayed in Arizona. We gave almost all of our arms and ammunition to the party going to Apache Tejo, so that in case there should be treachery they would be prepared for any surprise. Mangus-Colorado and about half of our people went to New Mexico, happy that now they had found white men who would be kind to them, and with whom they could live in peace and plenty.

No word ever came to us from them. From other sources, however, we heard that they had been treacherously[4] captured and slain. In this dilemma we did not know just exactly what to do, but fearing that the troops who had captured them would attack us, we retreated into the mountains near Apache Pass.

During the weeks that followed the departure of our people we had been in suspense, and failing to provide more supplies, had exhausted all of our store of provisions. This was another reason for moving camp. On this retreat, while passing through the mountains, we discovered four men with a herd of cattle. Two of the men were in front in a buggy and two were behind on horseback. We killed all four, but did not scalp them; they were not warriors. We drove the cattle back into the mountains, made a camp, and began to kill the cattle and pack the meat.

Before we had finished this work we were surprised and attacked by United States troops, who killed in all seven Indians—one warrior, three women, and three children. The Government troops were mounted and so were we, but we were poorly armed, having given most of our weapons to the division of our tribe that had gone to Apache Tejo, so we fought mainly with spears, bows, and arrows. At first I had a spear, a bow, and a few arrows; but in a short time my spear and all my arrows were gone. Once I was surrounded, but by dodging from side to side of my horse as he ran I escaped. It was necessary during this fight for many of the warriors to leave their horses and escape on foot. But my horse was trained to come at call, and as soon as I reached a safe place, if not too closely pursued, I would call him to me.[5] During this fight we scattered in all directions and two days later reassembled at our appointed place of rendezvous, about fifty miles from the scene of this battle.

About ten days later the same United States troops attacked our new camp at sunrise. The fight lasted all day, but our arrows and spears were all gone before ten o'clock, and for the remainder of the day we had only rocks and clubs with which to fight. We could do little damage with these weapons, and at night we moved our camp about four miles back into the mountains where it would be hard for the cavalry to follow us. The next day our scouts, who had been left behind to observe the movements of the soldiers, returned, saying that the troops had gone back toward San Carlos Reservation.

---

[4] General Miles telegraphed from Whipple Barracks, Arizona, Sept. 24, 1886, relative to the surrender of the Apaches. Among other things he said: "Mangus-Colorado had years ago been foully murdered after he had surrendered."

[5] Geronimo often calls his horses to him in Fort Sill Reservation. He gives only one shrill note and they run to him at full speed.

A few days after this we were again attacked by another company of United States troops. Just before this fight we had been joined by a band of Chokonen Indians under Cochise, who took command of both divisions. We were repulsed, and decided to disband.

After we had disbanded our tribe the Bedonkohe Apaches reassembled near their old camp vainly waiting for the return of Mangus-Colorado and our kinsmen. No tidings came save that they had all been treacherously slain.[6] Then a council was held, and as it was believed that Mangus-Colorado was dead, I was elected Tribal Chief.

For a long time we had no trouble with anyone. It was more than a year after I had been made Tribal Chief that United States troops surprised and attacked our camp. They killed seven children, five women, and four warriors, captured all our supplies, blankets, horses, and clothing, and destroyed our tepees. We had nothing left; winter was beginning, and it was the coldest winter I ever knew. After the soldiers withdrew I took three warriors and trailed them. Their trail led back toward San Carlos.

XV
Removals

While returning from trailing the Government troops we saw two men, a Mexican and a white man, and shot them off their horses. With these two horses we returned and moved our camp. My people were suffering much

---

[6] Regarding the killing of Mangus-Colorado, L. C. Hughes of the Tucson, Ariz., *Star*, writes as follows: "It was early in the year '63, when General West and his troops were camped near Membras, that he sent Jack Swilling, a scout, to bring in Mangus, who had been on the warpath ever since the time of the incident with Cochise at Bowie. The old chief was always for peace, and gladly accepted the proffer; when he appeared at the camp General West ordered him put into the guard-house, in which there was only a small opening in the rear and but one small window. As the old chief entered he said: 'This is my end. I shall never again hunt over the mountains and through the valleys of my people.' He felt that he was to be assassinated. The guards were given orders to shoot him if he attempted to escape. He lay down and tried to sleep, but during the night, someone threw a large stone which struck him in the breast. He sprang up and in his delirium the guards thought he was attempting escape and several of them shot him; this was the end of Mangus.

"His head was severed from his body by a surgeon, and the brain taken out and weighed. The head measured larger than that of Daniel Webster, and the brain was of corresponding weight. The skull was sent to Washington, and is now on exhibition at the Smithsonian Institution."

and it was deemed advisable to go where we could get more provisions.
Game was scarce in our range then, and since I had been Tribal Chief I had
not asked for rations from the Government, nor did I care to do so, but we
did not wish to starve.

We had heard that Chief Victoria of the Chihenne (*Oje Caliente*)
Apaches was holding a council with the white men near Hot Springs in
New Mexico, and that he had plenty of provisions. We had always been
on friendly terms with this tribe, and Victoria was especially kind to my
people. With the help of the two horses we had captured, to carry our sick
with us, we went to Hot Springs. We easily found Victoria and his band,
and they gave us supplies for the winter. We stayed with them for about a
year, and during this stay we had perfect peace. We had not the least
trouble with Mexicans, white men, or Indians. When we had stayed as
long as we should, and had again accumulated some supplies, we decided
to leave Victoria's band. When I told him that we were going to leave he
said that we should have a feast and dance before we separated.

The festivities were held about two miles above Hot Springs, and
lasted for four days. There were about four hundred Indians at this celebration. I do not think we ever spent a more pleasant time than upon this
occasion. No one ever treated our tribe more kindly than Victoria and his
band. We are still proud to say that he and his people were our friends.

When I went to Apache Pass (Fort Bowie) I found General Howard[7]
in command, and made a treaty with him. This treaty lasted until long
after General Howard had left our country. He always kept his word with
us and treated us as brothers. We never had so good a friend among the
United States officers as General Howard. We could have lived forever at
peace with him. If there is any pure, honest white man in the United States
army, that man is General Howard. All the Indians respect him, and even
to this day frequently talk of the happy times when General Howard was
in command of our Post. After he went away he placed an agent at Apache
Pass who issued to us from the Government clothing, rations, and supplies, as General Howard directed. When beef was issued to the Indians I
got twelve steers for my tribe, and Cochise got twelve steers for his tribe.
Rations were issued about once a month, but if we ran out we only had to
ask and we were supplied. Now, as prisoners of war in this Reservation,
we do not get such good rations.[8]

---

[7] General O. O. Howard was not in command, but had been sent by President Grant, in
1872, to make peace with the Apache Indians. The general wrote me from Burlington,
Vt., under date of June 12, 1906, that he remembered the treaty, and that he also remembered with much satisfaction subsequently meeting Geronimo.—ED. [Barrett's note.]
[8] They do not receive full rations now [1906], as they did then.

Out on the prairie away from Apache Pass a man kept a store and saloon. Some time after General Howard went away a band of outlawed Indians killed this man, and took away many of the supplies from his store. On the very next day after this some Indians at the Post were drunk on *tiswin*, which they had made from corn. They fought among themselves and four of them were killed. There had been quarrels and feuds among them for some time, and after this trouble we deemed it impossible to keep the different bands together in peace. Therefore we separated, each leader taking his own band. Some of them went to San Carlos and some to Old Mexico, but I took my tribe back to Hot Springs and rejoined Victoria's band.

XVI
In Prison and on the Warpath

Soon after we arrived in New Mexico two companies of scouts were sent from San Carlos. When they came to Hot Springs they sent word for me and Victoria to come to town. The messengers did not say what they wanted with us, but as they seemed friendly we thought they wanted a council, and rode in to meet the officers. As soon as we arrived in town soldiers met us, disarmed us, and took us both to headquarters, where we were tried by court-martial. They asked us only a few questions and then Victoria was released and I was sentenced to the guardhouse. Scouts conducted me to the guardhouse and put me in chains. When I asked them why they did this they said it was because I had left Apache Pass.

I do not think that I ever belonged to those soldiers at Apache Pass, or that I should have asked them where I might go. Our bands could no longer live in peace[9] together, and so we had quietly withdrawn, expecting to live with Victoria's band, where we thought we would not be molested. They also sentenced seven other Apaches to chains in the guardhouse.

I do not know why this was done, for these Indians had simply followed me from Apache Pass to Hot Springs. If it was wrong (and I do not think it was wrong) for us to go to Hot Springs, I alone was to blame. They asked the soldiers in charge why they were imprisoned and chained, but received no answer.

---

[9]Victoria, chief of the Hot Spring Apaches, met his death in opposing the forcible removal of his band to a reservation, because having previously tried and failed he felt it impossible for separate bands of Apaches to live at peace under such arrangement.

I was kept a prisoner for four months, during which time I was transferred to San Carlos. Then I think I had another trial, although I was not present. In fact I do not know that I had another trial, but I was told that I had, and at any rate I was released.

After this we had no more trouble with the soldiers, but I never felt at ease any longer at the Post. We were allowed to live above San Carlos at a place now called Geronimo. A man whom the Indians called "Nick Golee" was agent at this place. All went well here for a period of two years, but we were not satisfied.

In the summer of 1883 a rumor was current that the officers were again planning to imprison our leaders. This rumor served to revive the memory of all our past wrongs—the massacre in the tent at Apache Pass, the fate of Mangus-Colorado, and my own unjust imprisonment, which might easily have been death to me. Just at this time we were told that the officers wanted us to come up the river above Geronimo to a fort (Fort Thomas) to hold a council with them. We did not believe that any good could come of this conference, or that there was any need of it; so we held a council ourselves, and fearing treachery, decided to leave the reservation. We thought it more manly to die on the warpath than to be killed in prison.

There were in all about 250 Indians, chiefly the Bedonkohe and Nedni Apaches, led by myself and Whoa. We went through Apache Pass and just west of there had a fight with the United States troops. In this battle we killed three soldiers and lost none.

We went on toward Old Mexico, but on the second day after this United States soldiers overtook us about three o'clock in the afternoon and we fought until dark. The ground where we were attacked was very rough, which was to our advantage, for the troops were compelled to dismount in order to fight us. I do not know how many soldiers we killed, but we lost only one warrior and three children. We had plenty of guns and ammunition at this time. Many of the guns and much ammunition we had accumulated while living in the reservation, and the remainder we had obtained from the White Mountain Apaches when we left the reservation.

Troops did not follow us any longer, so we went south almost to Casa Grande and camped in the Sierra de Sahuaripa Mountains. We ranged in the mountains of Old Mexico for about a year, then returned to San Carlos, taking with us a herd of cattle and horses.

Soon after we arrived at San Carlos the officer in charge, General Crook, took the horses and cattle away from us. I told him that these were not white men's cattle, but belonged to us, for we had taken them from the Mexicans during our wars. I also told him that we did not intend to kill these animals, but that we wished to keep them and raise stock on our range. He would not listen to me, but took the stock. I went up near Fort Apache and General Crook ordered officers, soldiers, and scouts to see that I was arrested; if I offered resistance they were instructed to kill me.

This information was brought to me by the Indians. When I learned of this proposed action I left for Old Mexico, and about four hundred Indians went with me. They were the Bedonkohe, Chokonen, and Nedni Apaches. At this time Whoa was dead, and Naiche was the only chief with me. We went south into Sonora and camped in the mountains. Troops followed us, but did not attack us until we were camped in the mountains west of Casa Grande. Here we were attacked by Government Indian scouts. One boy was killed and nearly all of our women and children were captured.[10]

After this battle we went south of Casa Grande and made a camp, but within a few days this camp was attacked by Mexican soldiers. We skirmished with them all day, killing a few Mexicans, but sustaining no loss ourselves.

That night we went east into the foothills of the Sierra Madre Mountains and made another camp. Mexican troops trailed us, and after a few days attacked our camp again. This time the Mexicans had a very large army, and we avoided a general engagement. It is senseless to fight when you cannot hope to win.

That night we held a council of war; our scouts had reported bands of United States and Mexican troops at many points in the mountains. We estimated that about two thousand soldiers were ranging these mountains seeking to capture us.

General Crook had come down into Mexico with the United States troops. They were camped in the Sierra de Antunez Mountains. Scouts told me that General Crook wished to see me and I went to his camp. When I arrived General Crook said to me, "Why did you leave the reservation?" I said: "You told me that I might live in the reservation the same as white people lived. One year I raised a crop of corn, and gathered and stored it, and the next year I put in a crop of oats, and when the crop was almost ready to harvest, you told your soldiers to put me in prison, and if I resisted to kill me. If I had been let alone I would now have been in good circumstances, but instead of that you and the Mexicans are hunting me with soldiers." He said: "I never gave any such orders; the troops at Fort Apache, who spread this report, knew that it was untrue." Then I agreed to go back with him to San Carlos.

---

[10] Geronimo's whole family, excepting his eldest son, a warrior, was captured.

It was hard for me to believe him at that time. Now I know that what he said was untrue,[11] and I firmly believe that he did issue the orders for me to be put in prison, or to be killed in case I offered resistance.

XVII
The Final Struggle

We started with all our tribe to go with General Crook back to the United States, but I feared treachery and decided to remain in Mexico. We were not under any guard at this time. The United States troops marched in front and the Indians followed, and when we became suspicious, we turned back. I do not know how far the United States army went after myself, and some warriors turned back before we were missed, and I do not care.

I have suffered much from such unjust orders as those of General Crook. Such acts have caused much distress to my people. I think that General Crook's death[12] was sent by the Almighty as a punishment for the many evil deeds he committed.

Soon General Miles was made commander of all the western posts, and troops trailed us continually. They were led by Captain Lawton, who had good scouts. The Mexican[13] soldiers also became more active and more numerous. We had skirmishes almost every day, and so we finally decided to break up into small bands. With six men and four women I made for the range of mountains near Hot Springs, New Mexico. We passed many cattle ranches, but had no trouble with the cowboys. We killed cattle to eat whenever we were in need of food, but we frequently suffered greatly for water. At one time we had no water for two days and nights and our horses almost died from thirst. We ranged in the mountains of New Mexico for some time, then thinking that perhaps the troops had left Mexico, we returned. On our return through Old Mexico we attacked every Mexican found, even if for no other reason than to kill. We believed they had asked the United States troops to come down to Mexico to fight us.

South of Casa Grande, near a place called by the Indians Gosoda, there was a road leading out from the town. There was much freighting

---

[11] Geronimo's exact words, for which the Editor [Barrett] disclaims any responsibility.
[12] These are the exact words of Geronimo. The Editor [Barrett] is not responsible for this criticism of General Crook.
[13] Governor Torres of Sonora had agreed to cooperate with our troops in exterminating or capturing this tribe.

carried on by the Mexicans over this road. Where the road ran through a mountain pass we stayed in hiding, and whenever Mexican freighters passed we killed them, took what supplies we wanted, and destroyed the remainder. We were reckless of our lives, because we felt that every man's hand was against us. If we returned to the reservation we would be put in prison and killed; if we stayed in Mexico they would continue to send soldiers to fight us; so we gave no quarter to anyone and asked no favors.

After some time we left Gosoda and soon were reunited with our tribe in the Sierra de Antunez Mountains.

Contrary to our expectations the United States soldiers had not left the mountains in Mexico, and were soon trailing us and skirmishing with us almost every day. Four or five times they surprised our camp. One time they surprised us about nine o'clock in the morning, and captured all our horses[14] (nineteen in number) and secured our store of dried meats. We also lost three Indians in this encounter. About the middle of the afternoon of the same day we attacked them from the rear as they were passing through a prairie—killed one soldier, but lost none ourselves. In this skirmish we recovered all our horses except three that belonged to me. The three horses that we did not recover were the best riding horses we had.

Soon after this we made a treaty with the Mexican troops. They told us that the United States troops were the real cause of these wars, and agreed not to fight any more with us provided we would return to the United States. This we agreed to do, and resumed our march, expecting to try to make a treaty with the United States soldiers and return to Arizona. There seemed to be no other course to pursue.

Soon after this scouts from Captain Lawton's troops told us that he wished to make a treaty with us; but I knew that General Miles was the chief of the American troops, and I decided to treat with him.

We continued to move our camp northward, and the American troops also moved northward,[15] keeping at no great distance from us, but not attacking us.

I sent my brother Porico (White Horse) with Mr. George Wratton on to Fort Bowie to see General Miles, and to tell him that we wished to return to Arizona; but before these messengers returned I met two Indian scouts—Kayitah, a Chokonen Apache, and Marteen, a Nedni Apache. They were serving as scouts for Captain Lawton's troops. They told me that General Miles had come and had sent them to ask me to meet him. So I went to the camp of the United States troops to meet General Miles.

---

[14] Captain Lawton reports officially the same engagement, but makes no mention of the recapture (by the Apaches) of the horses.

[15] See note 14.

When I arrived at their camp I went directly to General Miles and told him how I had been wronged, and that I wanted to return to the United States with my people, as we wished to see our families, who had been captured[16] and taken away from us.

General Miles said to me: "The President of the United States has sent me to speak to you. He has heard of your trouble with the white men, and says that if you will agree to a few words of treaty we need have no more trouble. Geronimo, if you will agree to a few words of treaty all will be satisfactorily arranged."

So General Miles told me how we could be brothers to each other. We raised our hands to heaven and said that the treaty was not to be broken. We took an oath not to do any wrong to each other or to scheme against each other.

Then he talked with me for a long time and told me what he would do for me in the future if I would agree to the treaty. I did not greatly believe General Miles, but because the President of the United States had sent me word I agreed to make the treaty, and to keep it. Then I asked General Miles what the treaty would be. General Miles said to me: "I will take you under Government protection; I will build you a house; I will fence you much land; I will give you cattle, horses, mules, and farming implements. You will be furnished with men to work the farm, for you yourself will not have to work. In the fall I will send you blankets and clothing so that you will not suffer from cold in the winter time.

"There is plenty of timber, water, and grass in the land to which I will send you. You will live with your tribe and with your family. If you agree to this treaty you shall see your family within five days."

I said to General Miles: "All the officers that have been in charge of the Indians have talked that way, and it sounds like a story to me; I hardly believe you."

He said: "This time it is the truth."

I said: "General Miles, I do not know the laws of the white man, nor of this new country where you are to send me, and I might break their laws."

He said: "While I live you will not be arrested."

Then I agreed to make the treaty. (Since I have been a prisoner of war I have been arrested and placed in the guardhouse twice for drinking whisky.)

We stood between his troopers and my warriors. We placed a large stone on the blanket before us. Our treaty was made by this stone, and it was to last until the stone should crumble to dust; so we made the treaty, and bound each other with an oath.

---

[16] See page 431.

I do not believe that I have ever violated that treaty; but General Miles[17] never fulfilled his promises.

When we had made the treaty General Miles said to me: "My brother, you have in your mind how you are going to kill men, and other thoughts of war; I want you to put that out of your mind, and change your thoughts to peace."

Then I agreed and gave up my arms. I said: "I will quit the warpath and live at peace hereafter."

Then General Miles swept a spot of ground clear with his hand, and said: "Your past deeds shall be wiped out like this and you will start a new life." . . .

XIX
A Prisoner of War

When I had given up to the Government they put me on the Southern Pacific Railroad and took me to San Antonio, Texas, and held me to be tried by their laws.

In forty days they took me from there to Fort Pickens (Pensacola), Florida. Here they put me to sawing up large logs. There were several other Apache warriors with me, and all of us had to work every day. For nearly two years we were kept at hard labor in this place and we did not see our families until May, 1887. This treatment was in direct violation of our treaty made at Skeleton Cañon.

After this we were sent with our families to Vermont, Alabama, where we stayed five years and worked for the Government. We had no property, and I looked in vain for General Miles to send me to that land of which he had spoken; I longed in vain for the implements, house, and stock that General Miles had promised me.

During this time one of my warriors, Fun, killed himself and his wife. Another one shot his wife and then shot himself. He fell dead, but the woman recovered and is still living.

We were not healthy in this place, for the climate disagreed with us. So many of our people died that I consented to let one of my wives go to the Mescalero Agency in New Mexico to live. This separation is according to our custom equivalent to what the white people call divorce, and so she

---

[17]The criticisms of General Miles in the foregoing chapter are from Geronimo, not from the Editor [Barrett].

married again soon after she got to Mescalero. She also kept our two small children, which she had a right to do. The children, Lenna and Robbie, are still living at Mescalero, New Mexico. Lenna is married. I kept one wife, but she is dead now and I have only our daughter Eva with me. Since my separation from Lenna's mother I have never had more than one wife at a time. Since the death of Eva's mother I married another woman (December, 1905) but we could not live happily and separated. She went home to her people—that is an Apache divorce.

Then,[18] as now, Mr. George Wratton superintended the Indians. He has always had trouble with the Indians, because he has mistreated them. One day an Indian, while drunk, stabbed Mr. Wratton with a little knife. The officer in charge took the part of Mr. Wratton and the Indian was sent to prison.

When[19] we first came to Fort Sill, Captain Scott was in charge, and he had houses built for us by the Government. We were also given, from the Government, cattle, hogs, turkeys and chickens. The Indians did not do much good with the hogs, because they did not understand how to care for them, and not many Indians even at the present time keep hogs. We did better with the turkeys and chickens, but with these we did not have as good luck as white men do. With the cattle we have done very well, indeed, and we like to raise them. We have a few horses also, and have had no bad luck with them.

In the matter of selling[20] our stock and grain there has been much misunderstanding. The Indians understood that the cattle were to be sold and the money given to them, but instead part of the money is given to the Indians and part of it is placed in what the officers call the "Apache Fund." We have had five different officers in charge of the Indians here and they have all ruled very much alike—not consulting the Apaches or even explaining to them. It may be that the Government ordered the officers in charge to put this cattle money into an Apache fund, for once I complained and told Lieutenant Purington[21] that I intended to report to the Govern-

---

[18] These are not the words of the Editor [Barrett], but of Geronimo.

[19] They were in Alabama from May, 1888, to October, 1894.

[20] The Indians are not allowed to sell the cattle themselves. When cattle are ready for market they are sold by the officer in charge, part of the money paid to the Indians who owned them and part of it placed in a general (Apache) fund. The supplies, farming implements, etc., for the Apaches are paid for from this fund.

[21] The criticism of Lieutenant Purington is from Geronimo. The Editor [Barrett] disclaims any responsibility for it, as in all cases where individuals are criticized by the old warrior.

ment that he had taken some of my part of the cattle money and put it into the Apache Fund, he said he did not care if I did tell.

Several years ago the issue of clothing ceased. This, too, may have been by the order of the Government, but the Apaches do not understand it.

If there is an Apache Fund, it should some day be turned over to the Indians, or at least they should have an account of it, for it is their earnings.

When General Miles last visited Fort Sill I asked to be relieved from labor on account of my age. I also remembered what General Miles had promised me in the treaty and told him of it. He said I need not work any more except when I wished to, and since that time I have not been detailed to do any work. I have worked a great deal, however, since then, for, although I am old, I like to work[22] and help my people as much as I am able. . . .

XXI
At the World's Fair

When I was at first asked to attend the St. Louis World's Fair I did not wish to go. Later, when I was told that I would receive good attention and protection, and that the President of the United States said that it would be all right, I consented. I was kept by parties in charge of the Indian Department, who had obtained permission from the President. I stayed in this place for six months. I sold my photographs for twenty-five cents, and was allowed to keep ten cents of this for myself. I also wrote my name for ten, fifteen, or twenty-five cents, as the case might be, and kept all of that money. I often made as much as two dollars a day, and when I returned I had plenty of money—more than I had ever owned before.

Many people in St. Louis invited me to come to their homes, but my keeper always refused.

Every Sunday the President of the Fair sent for me to go to a wild west show. I took part in the roping contests before the audience. There were many other Indian tribes there, and strange people of whom I had never heard.

---

[22] Geronimo helped make hay and care for the cattle, but did not receive orders from the Superintendent of the Indians.

When people first came to the World's Fair they did nothing but parade up and down the streets. When they got tired of this they would visit the shows. There were many strange things in these shows. The Government sent guards with me when I went, and I was not allowed to go anywhere without them.

In one of the shows some strange men[23] with red caps had some peculiar swords, and they seemed to want to fight. Finally their manager told them they might fight each other. They tried to hit each other over the head with these swords, and I expected both to be wounded or perhaps killed, but neither one was harmed. They would be hard people to kill in a hand-to-hand fight.

In another show there was a strange-looking Negro. The manager tied his hands fast, then tied him to a chair. He was securely tied, for I looked myself, and I did not think it was possible for him to get away. Then the manager told him to get loose.

He twisted in his chair for a moment, and then stood up; the ropes were still tied, but he was free. I do not understand how this was done. It was certainly a miraculous power, because no man could have released himself by his own efforts.

In another place a man was on a platform speaking to the audience; they set a basket by the side of the platform and covered it with red calico; then a woman came and got into the basket, and a man covered the basket again with the calico; then the man who was speaking to the audience took a long sword and ran it through the basket, each way, and then down through the cloth cover. I heard the sword cut through the woman's body, and the manager himself said she was dead; but when the cloth was lifted from the basket she stepped out, smiled, and walked off the stage. I would like to know how she was so quickly healed, and why the wounds did not kill her.

I have never considered bears very intelligent, except in their wild habits, but I had never before seen a white bear. In one of the shows a man had a white bear that was as intelligent as a man. He would do whatever he was told—carry a log on his shoulder, just as a man would; then, when he was told, would put it down again. He did many other things, and seemed to know exactly what his keeper said to him. I am sure that no grizzly bear could be trained to do these things.

One time the guards took me into a little house[24] that had four windows. When we were seated the little house started to move along the

[23] Turks.
[24] Ferris wheel.

ground. Then the guards called my attention to some curious things they had in their pockets. Finally they told me to look out, and when I did so I was scared, for our little house had gone high up in the air, and the people down in the Fair Grounds looked no larger than ants. The men laughed at me for being scared; then they gave me a glass to look through (I often had such glasses which I took from dead officers after battles in Mexico and elsewhere), and I could see rivers, lakes and mountains. But I had never been so high in the air, and I tried to look into the sky. There were no stars, and I could not look at the sun through this glass because the brightness hurt my eyes. Finally I put the glass down, and as they were all laughing at me, I too, began to laugh. Then they said, "Get out!" and when I looked we were on the street again. After we were safe on the land I watched many of these little houses going up and coming down, but I cannot understand how they travel. They are very curious little houses.

One day we went into another show, and as soon as we were in, it changed into night. It was real night, for I could feel the damp air; soon it began to thunder, and the lightnings flashed; it was real lightning, too, for it struck just above our heads. I dodged and wanted to run away, but I could not tell which way to go in order to get out. The guards motioned me to keep still, and so I stayed. In front of us were some strange little people who came out on the platform; then I looked up again and the clouds were all gone, and I could see the stars shining. The little people on the platform did not seem in earnest about anything they did; so I only laughed at them. All the people around where we sat seemed to be laughing at me.

We went into another place and the manager took us into a little room that was made like a cage; then everything around us seemed to be moving; soon the air looked blue, then there were black clouds moving with the wind. Pretty soon it was clear outside; then we saw a few thin white clouds; then the clouds grew thicker, and it rained and hailed with thunder and lightning. Then the thunder retreated and a rainbow appeared in the distance; then it became dark, the moon rose and thousands of stars came out. Soon the sun came up, and we got out of the little room. This was a good show, but it was so strange and unnatural that I was glad to be on the streets again.

We went into one place where they made glassware. I had always thought that these things were made by hand, but they are not. The man had a curious little instrument, and whenever he would blow through this into a little blaze the glass would take any shape he wanted it to. I am not sure, but I think that if I had this kind of an instrument I could make whatever I wished. There seems to be a charm about it. But I suppose it is very difficult to get these little instruments, or other people would have them. The people in this show were so anxious to buy the things the man made that they kept him so busy he could not sit down all day long. I bought many curious things in there and brought them home with me.

At the end of one of the streets some people were getting into a clumsy canoe, upon a kind of shelf, and sliding down into the water.[25] They seemed to enjoy it, but it looked too fierce for me. If one of these canoes had gone out of its path the people would have been sure to get hurt or killed.

There were some little brown people[26] at the Fair that United States troops captured recently on some islands far away from here.

They did not wear much clothing, and I think that they should not have been allowed to come to the Fair. But they themselves did not seem to know any better. They had some little brass plates, and they tried to play music with these, but I did not think it was music—it was only a rattle. However, they danced to this noise and seemed to think they were giving a fine show.

I do not know how true the report was, but I heard that the President sent them to the Fair so that they could learn some manners, and when they went home teach their people how to dress and how to behave.

I am glad I went to the Fair. I saw many interesting things and learned much of the white people. They are a very kind and peaceful people. During all the time I was at the Fair no one tried to harm me in any way. Had this been among the Mexicans I am sure I should have been compelled to defend myself often.

I wish all my people could have attended the Fair.[27]

XXII
Religion

In our primitive worship only our relations to Usen and the members of our tribe were considered as appertaining to our religious responsibilities. As to the future state, the teachings of our tribe were not specific, that is, we had no definite idea of our relations and surroundings in after life.

---

[25] Shooting the chute.

[26] Iggorrotes from the Philippines.

[27] Geronimo was also taken to both the Omaha and the Buffalo Expositions, but during that period of his life he was sullen and took no interest in things. The St. Louis Exposition was held after he had adopted the Christian religion and had begun to try to understand our civilization.

We believed that there is a life after this one, but no one ever told me as to what part of man lived after death. I have seen many men die; I have seen many human bodies decayed, but I have never seen that part which is called the spirit; I do not know what it is; nor have I yet been able to understand that part of the Christian religion.

We held that the discharge of one's duty would make his future life more pleasant, but whether that future life was worse than this life or better, we did not know, and no one was able to tell us. We hoped that in the future life family and tribal relations would be resumed. In a way we believed this, but we did not know it.

Once when living in San Carlos Reservation an Indian told me that while lying unconscious on the battlefield he had actually been dead, and had passed into the spirit land.

First he came to a mulberry tree growing out from a cave in the ground. Before this cave a guard was stationed, but when he approached without fear the guard let him pass. He descended into the cave, and a little way back the path widened and terminated in a perpendicular rock many hundreds of feet wide and equal in height. There was not much light, but by peering directly beneath him he discovered a pile of sand reaching from the depths below to within twenty feet of the top of the rock where he stood. Holding to a bush, he swung off from the edge of the rock and dropped onto the sand, sliding rapidly down its steep side into the darkness. He landed in a narrow passage running due westward through a cañon which gradually grew lighter and lighter until he could see as well as if it had been daylight; but there was no sun. Finally he came to a section of this passage that was wider for a short distance, and then closing abruptly continued in a narrow path; just where this section narrowed two huge serpents were coiled, and rearing their heads, hissed at him as he approached, but he showed no fear, and as soon as he came close to them they withdrew quietly and let him pass. At the next place, where the passage opened into a wider section, were two grizzly bears prepared to attack him, but when he approached and spoke to them they stood aside and he passed unharmed. He continued to follow the narrow passage, and the third time it widened and two mountain lions crouched in the way, but when he had approached them without fear and had spoken to them they also withdrew. He again entered the narrow passage. For some time he followed this, emerging into a fourth section beyond which he could see nothing: the further walls of this section were clashing together at regular intervals with tremendous sounds, but when he approached them they stood apart until he had passed. After this he seemed to be in a forest, and following the natural draws, which led westward, soon came into a green valley where there were many Indians camped and plenty of game. He said that he saw and recognized many whom he had known in this life, and that he was sorry when he was brought back to consciousness.

I told him if I knew this to be true I would not want to live another day, but by some means, if by my own hands, I would die in order to enjoy these pleasures. I myself have lain unconscious on the battlefield, and while in that condition have had some strange thoughts or experiences; but they are very dim and I cannot recall them well enough to relate them. Many Indians believed this warrior, and I cannot say that he did not tell the truth. I wish I knew that what he said is beyond question true. But perhaps it is as well that we are not certain.

Since my life as a prisoner has begun I have heard the teachings of the white man's religion, and in many respects believe it to be better than the religion of my fathers. However, I have always prayed, and I believe that the Almighty has always protected me.

Believing that in a wise way it is good to go to church, and that associating with Christians would improve my character, I have adopted the Christian religion.[28] I believe that the church has helped me much during the short time I have been a member. I am not ashamed to be a Christian, and I am glad to know that the President of the United States is a Christian, for without the help of the Almighty I do not think he could rightly judge in ruling so many people. I have advised all of my people who are not Christians, to study that religion, because it seems to me the best religion in enabling one to live right.

XXIII
Hopes for the Future

I am thankful that the President of the United States has given me permission to tell my story. I hope that he and those in authority under him will read my story and judge whether my people have been rightly treated.

There is a great question between the Apaches and the Government. For twenty years we have been held prisoners of war under a treaty which was made with General Miles, on the part of the United States Government, and myself as the representative of the Apaches. That treaty has not at all times been properly observed by the Government, although at the present time it is being more nearly fulfilled on their part than heretofore.

---

[28] Geronimo joined the Dutch Reformed Church and was baptized in the summer of 1903. He attends the services regularly at the Apache Mission, Ft. Sill Military Reservation.

In the treaty with General Miles we agreed to go to a place outside of Arizona and learn to live as the white people do. I think that my people are now capable of living in accordance with the laws of the United States, and we would, of course, like to have the liberty to return to that land which is ours by divine right. We are reduced in numbers, and having learned how to cultivate the soil would not require so much ground as was formerly necessary. We do not ask all of the land which the Almighty gave us in the beginning, but that we may have sufficient lands there to cultivate. What we do not need we are glad for the white men to cultivate.

We are now held on Comanche and Kiowa lands, which are not suited to our needs—these lands and this climate are suited to the Indians who originally inhabited this country, of course, but our people are decreasing in numbers here, and will continue to decrease unless they are allowed to return to their native land. Such a result is inevitable.

There is no climate or soil which, to my mind, is equal to that of Arizona. We could have plenty of good cultivating land, plenty of grass, plenty of timber and plenty of minerals in that land which the Almighty created for the Apaches. It is my land, my home, my fathers' land, to which I now ask to be allowed to return. I want to spend my last days there, and be buried among those mountains. If this could be I might die in peace, feeling that my people, placed in their native homes, would increase in numbers, rather than diminish as at present, and that our name would not become extinct.

I know that if my people were placed in that mountainous region lying around the headwaters of the Gila River they would live in peace and act according to the will of the President. They would be prosperous and happy in tilling the soil and learning the civilization of the white men, whom they now respect. Could I but see this accomplished, I think I could forget all the wrongs that I have ever received, and die a contented and happy old man. But we can do nothing in this matter ourselves—we must wait until those in authority choose to act. If this cannot be done during my lifetime—if I must die in bondage—I hope that the remnant of the Apache tribe may, when I am gone, be granted the one privilege which they request—to return to Arizona.

Annotated List of Earlier Captivity Anthologies

Calloway, Colin G., ed. *North Country Captives: Selected Narratives of Indian Captivity from Vermont and New Hampshire*. Hanover: UP of New England, 1992.

Derounian-Stodola, Kathryn Zabelle, ed. *Women's Indian Captivity Narratives*. New York: Penguin, 1998.

Drake, Samuel, ed. *Indian Captivities, or Life in the Wigwam*. Boston: 1839. [Fifteen subsequent editions, some with different titles, including *Indian Atrocity!*]

Drimmer, Frederick, ed. *Scalps and Tomahawks*. 1961. [Rpt. Dover, 1985, with the title *Captured by Indians: Fifteen Firsthand Accounts, 1750–1870*. Most captives are male, and texts are heavily abridged.]

Frost, John, ed. *Heroic Women of the West*. 1854. [Retells thirty-four stories of female pioneers and captives, with an emphasis on violent "Amazons'" revenge against their captors.]

Indian Anecdotes and Barbarities: Being a Description of Their Customs and Deeds of Cruelty, with an Account of the Captivity, Sufferings, and Heroic Conduct of Many Who Have Fallen into Their Hands, Or Who Have Defended Themselves from Savage Vengeance; All Illustrating General Traits of Indian Character. 1837.

Kephart, Horace, ed. *Captives among the Indians*. 1915. [Includes John Smith, the Jesuit missionary Bressani, Mary Rowlandson, and Massy Harbeson.]

Kestler, Frances Roe, ed. *The Indian Captivity Narrative: A Woman's View*. New York: Garland, 1990. [Abridged excerpts with scholarly commentary.]

Levernier, James, and Hennig Cohen, eds. *The Indians and Their Captives*. Westport: Greenwood, 1977. [Short excerpts from a wide range of captivity texts, including novels, plays, poems, and histories, with interesting commentary.]

Loudon, Archibald, ed. *A Selection of Some of the More Interesting Narratives of Outrages Committed by the Indians in Their Wars with the White People.* Carlisle, 1808. [Includes James Smith's narrative and the Manheim Anthology, which was first published in 1793 and frequently thereafter, and was included within other anthologies, such as Drake's, Loudon's, and VanDerBeets', and James Smith's narrative.]

Metcalf, Samuel L., ed. *A Collection of Some of the Most Interesting Narratives of Indian Warfare.* 1821.

Peckham, Howard Henry, ed. *Captured by Indians: True Tales of Pioneer Survivors.* New Brunswick: Rutgers UP, 1954. [Like Frost's work, this is a popular history and retelling of captives' stories, not a collection of the original narratives.]

Vail, R. W. G., ed. *The Voice of Old Frontier.* 1949. New York: Octagon, 1970. [A bibliography.]

VanDerBeets, Richard, ed. *Held Captive by Indians.* U of Tennessee P, 1973, 1994.

Vaughan, Alden T., and Edward W. Clark, eds. *Puritans among the Indians: Accounts of Captivity and Redemption.* Cambridge: Belknap-Harvard UP, 1981. [The core of the New England tradition, including Rowlandson, Dustan, Swarton, and Gyles. Excellent bibliography.]

Washburn, Wilcomb, ed. *Garland Library of Narratives of North American Indian Captivities.* 112 volumes. New York: Garland, 1977–83. [The definitive collection of the genre, although available only in a few research libraries. Volume 112 is a bibliography edited by Alden T. Vaughan.]

Withers, Alexander Scott, ed. *Chronicles of Border Warfare.* (1831).

Works Cited

Alexie, Sherman. *First Indian on the Moon*. Brooklyn: Hanging Loose P, 1993.

Anderson, Terry. *Den of Lions*. New York: Ballantine, 1994.

Arber, Edward, ed. *Travels and Works of Captain John Smith, President of Virginia and Admiral of New England (1608–1631)*. 1910. 2 vols. New York: Franklin, 1967.

Axtell, James. *The European and the Indian: Essays in the Ethnohistory of Colonial America*. New York: Oxford UP, 1981.

Baepler, Paul, ed. *White Slaves, African Masters*. Chicago: U of Chicago P, 1999.

Barbour, Philip, ed. *The Complete Works of Captain John Smith (1580–1631)*. 3 vols. Chapel Hill: Institute for Early American History and Culture/ U of North Carolina P, 1986.

Biocca, Etienne. *Yanoama: The Narrative of a White Girl Kidnapped by Amazonian Indians*. New York: Dutton, 1970.

Bleecker, Ann Eliza. *History of Maria Kittle*. Hartford: 1797.

Black Hawk. *Black Hawk: An Autobiography*. Ed. J. B. Patterson. Trans. Antoine LeClair. 1833. Ed. Donald Jackson. Urbana: U of Illinois P, 1955.

Bradford, William. *Of Plymouth Plantation, 1620–1647*. New York: Modern Library, 1981.

Burnham, Michelle. *Capitivy and Sentiment: Cultural Exchange in American Literature, 1682–1861*. Hanover: UP of New England, 1997.

Cabeza de Vaca, Alvar Nuñez. *Castaways*. Trans. Frances M. López-Morillas. Berkeley: U of California P, 1993.

Castiglia, Christopher. *Bound and Determined: Captivity, Culture-Crossing, and White Womanhood from Mary Rowlandson to Patty Hearst*. Chicago: U of Chicago P, 1996.

Cervantes, Miguel de. *Don Quixote.* Trans. J. M. Cohen. Harmondsworth, UK: Penguin, 1950.

Colden, Cadwallader. *The History of the Five Indian Nations Depending on the Province of New York in America.* 1747. Ithaca: Cornell UP, 1964.

Coleman, Emma Lewis. *New England Captives Carried to Canada between 1677 and 1760 during the French and Indian Wars.* 2 vols. Portland: Southworth, 1925.

Crèvecoeur, J. Hector St. John de. Letters from an American Farmer *and* Sketches of Eighteenth-Century America. Ed. Albert E. Stone. Harmondsworth: Penguin, 1981.

Deloria, Philip. *Playing Indian.* New Haven: Yale UP, 1998.

Dennis, Matthew. *Cultivating a Landscape of Peace: Iroquois-European Encounters in Seventeenth-Century America.* Ithaca: Cornell UP, 1993.

Derounian-Stodola, Kathryn Zabelle, ed. *Women's Indian Captivity Narratives.* New York: Penguin, 1998.

Derounian-Stodola, Kathryn Zabelle, and James Levernier. *The Indian Captivity Narrative, 1550-1900.* New York: Twayne, 1993.

Donner, Florinda. *Shabono: A True Adventure in the Remote and Magical Heart of the South American Jungle.* New York: Delacorte, 1982.

Drinnon, Richard. *White Savage: The Case of John Dunn Hunter.* New York: Schocken, 1972.

Erdrich, Louise. *Jacklight.* New York: Holt, 1984.

Fiedler, Leslie. *The Return of the Vanishing American.* New York: Stein, 1968.

Foss, John D. *A Journal of the Captivity and Sufferings of John Foss, Several Years a Prisoner in Algiers.* Newburyport, 1789.

Franchot, Jenny. *Roads to Rome: The Antebellum Protestant Encounter with Catholicism.* Berkeley: U of California P, 1994.

Franklin, Benjamin. *The Papers of Benjamin Franklin.* 34 vols. Ed. Leonard W. Labaree. New Haven: Yale UP, 1959–99.

Franklin, H. Bruce. *Prison Literature in America: The Victim as Criminal and Artist.* New York: Oxford UP, 1989.

Frederick, Bonnie. "Reading the Warning: The Reader as the Image of the Captive Woman." *Chasqui: Revista de literatura latinoamericana* 18: 2 (1989) 3–11.

Gyles, John. *Memoirs of Odd Adventures, Strange Deliverances, etc. in the Captivity of John Gyles, Esq.* 1736. Vaughan and Clark 91–132.

Hanson, Elizabeth. "God's Mercy Surmounting Man's Cruelty." 1728. Vaughan and Clark 227–46.

Hartman, James D. *Providence Tales and the Birth of American Literature*. Baltimore: Johns Hopkins UP, 1999.

Heard, J. Norman. *White into Red: A Study of the Assimilation of White Persons Captured by Indians*. Metuchen: Scarecrow, 1973.

Henry, Alexander. *Travels in Canada and the Indian Territories between the Years 1760 and 1776, By Alexander Henry, Fur Trader*. Ed. James Bain. Toronto: Morang, 1901.

Hunter, John Dunn. *Memoirs of a Captivity among the Indians of North America*. London: 1824. Ed. Richard Drinnon. New York: Schocken, 1973.

Jacobs, Harriet A. *Incidents in the Life of a Slave Girl*. 1861. Ed. Jean Fagan Yellin. Cambridge: Harvard UP, 1987.

Jacquin, Philippe. *Les Indiens blancs: Français et Indiens en Amerique du Nord, XVIième–XVIIIième*. Paris: Payot, 1987.

Jewitt, John. *Narrative of the Adventures and Sufferings of John R. Jewitt, Only Survivor of the Crew of the Ship* Boston, *During a Captivity of Nearly 3 Years among the Savages of Nootka Sound: With an Account of the Manners, Mode of Living, and Religious Opinions of the Natives*. Ithaca: 1851. Ed. Hilary Stewart. Vancouver: Douglas, 1987.

Knight, Francis. *A Relation of Seven Yeares Slaverie under the Turkes of Argeire, Suffered by an English Captive Merchant . . . Wherunto Is Added a Second Booke Conteining a Description of Argeire. . . .* London: Cotes, 1640.

Kolodny, Annette. *The Land before Her: Fantasy and Experience of the American Frontiers, 1630–1860*. Chapel Hill: U of North Carolina P, 1984.

Lafitau, Joseph-François. *Customs of the American Indians Compared with the Customs of Primitive Times*. 1724. Trans. and ed. William Fenton and Elizabeth Moore. Toronto: Champlain Soc., 1974.

Lahontan, Louis de lom d'Arce. *New Voyages to North America*. London: 1703. Ed. Reuben Gold Thwaites. Chicago: McClurg, 1905.

Lewis, James R. "'Mind-Forged Manacles': Anti-Catholic Convent Narratives in the Context of the American Captivity Tale Tradition." *Mid-America* 72:3 (1990): 149–67.

Mahmoody, Betty, with William Hoffer. *Not without My Daughter*. New York: St. Martin's, 1987.

Mather, Cotton. *Magnalia Christi Americana: Or, The Ecclesiastical History of New England.* 1702. 2 vols. Rpt. New York: Russell, 1967.

Melville, Herman. *Typee.* 1846. New York: Oxford UP, 1996.

Mott, Frank Luther. *Golden Multitudes: The Story of Best Sellers in the United States.* New York: Macmillan, 1947.

Namias, June. *White Captives: Gender and Ethnicity on the American Frontier.* Chapel Hill: U of North Carolina P, 1993.

Okeley, William. *Eben-ezer: Or, A Small Monument of Great Mercy, Appearing in the Miraculous Deliverance of William Okeley, William Adams, John Anthony, John Jephs, John ——— Carpenter, From the Miserable Slavery of Algiers . . .* London: 1684.

Pearce, Roy Harvey. "The Significances of the Captivity Narrative." *American Literature* 19 (1947): 1–20

Phelps, Thomas. *True Account of the Captivity and Sufferings of Thomas Phelps, at Machaness in Barbary, And of His Strange Escape in Company of Edmund Baxter and Others . . .* London: Hills, 1685.

Pratt, Mary Louise. "Fieldwork in Common Places." *Writing Culture: The Poetics and Politics of Ethnography.* Ed. James Clifford and George E. Marcus. Berkeley: U of California P, 1986. 27–50.

Radisson, Pierre-Esprit. *Voyages of Peter Esprit Radisson, Being an Account of His Travels and Experience among the North American Indians from 1652 to 1684.* Boston: Prince Soc., 1885.

Richard, Samuel. *Clarissa, or, the History of a Young Lady.* 1748. 8 vols. New York: AMS, 1990.

Riley, James. *An Authentic Narrative of the Loss of the American Brig Commerce.* Hartford: Andrus, 1831.

Sagard-Théodat, Gabriel. *The Long Journey to the Country of the Hurons.* 1632. Trans. H. H. Langton. Toronto: Champlain Soc., 1939.

Salisbury, Neal. "Squanto: Last of the Patuxets." *Struggle and Survival in Colonial America.* Ed. Gary B. Nash and David G. Sweet. Berkeley: U of California P, 1981. 228–46.

———, ed. *The Sovereignty and Goodness of God, Together with the Faithfulness of His Promises Displayed, Being A Narrative of the Captivity and Restoration of Mrs. Mary Rowlandson, and Related Documents.* Boston: Bedford, 1997.

Sayre, Gordon M. *"Les Sauvages Américains": Representations of Native Americans in French and English Colonial Literature.* Chapel Hill: U of North Carolina P, 1997.

Seaver, James. *A Narrative of the Life of Mrs. Mary Jemison.* 1824. Ed. June Namias. Norman: U of Oklahoma P, 1992.

Slotkin, Richard. *Regeneration through Violence: The Mythology of the American Frontier, 1600–1860.* Middletown: Wesleyan UP, 1973.

Slotkin, Richard, and James K. Folsom. *So Dreadfull a Judgment: Puritan Responses to King Philip's War, 1675–1676.* Middletown: Wesleyan UP, 1978.

Smith, John. *The Complete Works of Captain John Smith (1580–1631).* Ed. Philip Barbour. 3 vols. Chapel Hill: Inst. for Early American History and Culture/U of North Carolina P, 1986.

[Smith, William, and Thomas Hutchins.] *Historical Account of Bouquet's Expedition against the Ohio Indians in 1764.* Philadelphia: 1765. Cincinnati: Clarke, 1868.

Stowe, Harriet Beecher. *Uncle Tom's Cabin.* 1852. New York: Bantam, 1981.

Swanton, John R. "Notes on the Mental Assimilation of Races." *Journal of the Washington Academy of Sciences* 16 (1926): 493–502.

Tanner, John. *Narrative of the Captivity and Adventures of John Tanner (U.S. Interpreter at the Saut de Ste. Marie) during Thirty Years Residence among the Indians in the Interior of America.* Ed. Edwin James. 1830. Minneapolis: Ross, 1956.

Thwaites, Reuben Gold, ed. *The Jesuit Relations and Allied Documents: Travels and Explorations of the Jesuit Missionaries in New France, 1610–1791.* 73 vols. Cleveland: Burrows, 1896–1901.

Tyler, Royall. *The Algerine Captive.* 1797. New Haven: College and University P, 1970.

Ulrich, Laurel Thatcher. *Good Wives: Image and Reality in the Lives of Women in Northern New England, 1650–1750.* New York: Oxford UP, 1980.

VanDerBeets, Richard. "The Indian Captivity Narrative as Ritual." *American Literature* 43 (1972): 548–62.

———, ed. *Held Captive by Indians.* Knoxville: U of Tennessee P, 1973.

Vaughan, Alden T., and Edward W. Clark, eds. *Puritans among the Indians: Accounts of Captivity and Redemption, 1676–1724.* Cambridge: Belknap-Harvard UP, 1981.

Vaughan, Alden T., and Daniel Richter. "Crossing the Cultural Divide." *Proceedings of the American Antiquarian Society* 90 (1980): 15–80.

White, Richard. *The Middle Ground: Indians, Empires, and Republics in the Great Lakes Region, 1650–1815.* New York: Cambridge UP, 1991.

Williams, John. "The Redeemed Captive Returning to Zion." Vaughn and Clark 165–226.

Zafar, Rafia. "Capturing the Captivity: African Americans among the Puritans." *MELUS* 17:2 (1991–92): 19–35.

Credits